AF527863

Developments in Indian Philosophy from Eighteenth Century Onwards: Classical and Western

Publications in PHISPC–Conssavy Series

HISTORY OF SCIENCE, PHILOSOPHY AND CULTURE IN INDIAN CIVILIZATION

***General Editor & Project Director:* D.P. Chattopadhyaya**

Conceptual Volumes

*	Part 1	Science, Philosophy and Culture: Multi-disciplinary Explorations	D.P. Chattopadhyaya & Ravinder Kumar (ed.)
*	Part 2	Science, Philosophy and Culture: Multi-disciplinary Explorations	D.P. Chattopadhyaya & Ravinder Kumar (ed.)

Volume I The Dawn and Development of Indian Civilization

*	Part 1	The Dawn of Indian Civilization (up to *c.* 600 BC)	G.C. Pande (ed.)
*	Part 2	Life, Thought and Culture in India (from *c.* 600 BC to *c.* AD 300)	G.C. Pande (ed.)
*	Part 3	India's Interaction with Southeast Asia	G.C. Pande (ed.)
†	Part 4	A Golden Chain of Civilizations: Indic, Iranic, Semitic and Hellenic (upto c. 600 BC)	G.C. Pande (ed.)
†	Part 5	A Golden Chain of Civilizations: Indic, Iranic, Semitic and Hellenic from c. 600 BC to c. AD 600	G.C. Pande (ed.)
†	Part 6	Purāṇas, History and Itihāsa	Vidya Niwas Misra & N.S.S. Raman (ed.)

Volume II Life, Thought and Culture in India (AD 300–1100)

*	Part 1	Life, Thought and Culture in India (AD 300–1000)	K. Satchidananda Murty (ed.)
*	Part 2	Advaita Vedānta	R. Balasubramanian (ed.)
*	Part 3	Theistic Vedānta	R. Balasubramanian (ed.)
*	Part 4	Origin and Development of the Vaiśeṣika System	Anantalal Thakur
†	Part 5	A Social History of India in the First Millennium AD	B.D. Chattopadhyaya (ed.)
*	Part 6	Pūrvamīmāṁsā from an Interdisciplinary Point of View	K.T. Pandurangi (ed.)

Volume III Development of Philosophy, Science and Technology in India and Neighbouring Civilizations

*	Part 1	History of Indian Science, Technology and Culture (AD 1000–1800)	A. Rahman (ed.)
*	Part 2	India's Interaction with China, Central and West Asia	A. Rahman (ed.)
*	Part 3	Development of Nyāya Philosophy and its Social Context	Sibajiban Bhattacharyya (ed.)
*	Part 4	Philosophical Concepts Relevant to Sciences in Indian Tradition	Pranab Kumar Sen (ed.)
*	Part 5	Philosophical Concepts Relevant to Sciences in Indian Tradition	Pranab Kumar Sen (ed.)
*	Part 6	India and China: Twenty Centuries of Civilizational Interaction and Vibrations	Tan Chung & Geng Yinzeng
†	Part 7	The Trading World of the Indian Ocean, AD 1500–1800	Om Prakash (ed.)

Volume IV Fundamental Indian Ideas of Physics, Chemistry, Life Sciences and Medicine

*	Part 1	Chemistry and Chemical Techniques in India	B.V. Subbarayappa (ed.)
*	Part 2	Medicine and Life Sciences in India	B.V. Subbarayappa (ed.)
*	Part 3	Indian Perspectives on the Physical World	B.V. Subbarayappa (ed.)
†	Part 4	History of Indian Astronomy and Mathematics	B.V. Subbarayappa (ed.)

Volume V Agriculture in India

†	Parts 1 & 2	A History of Agriculture in India	Lallanji Gopal & V.C. Srivastava (ed.)

Volume VI Culture, Language, Literature and Arts

†	Part 1	Aesthetic Theories and Forms in Indian Tradition	S.S. Barlingay, Kapila Vatsyayan and D.P. Chattopadhyaya (ed.)
†	Part 2	Architecture in India	M.A. Dhaky (ed.)
*	Part 3	Indian Art: Forms, Concerns and Development in Historical Perspective	B.N. Goswamy (ed.)
†	Part 4	Language, Grammar and Linguistics in Indian Tradition	V.N. Jha (ed.)
‡	Parts 5–10	PHISPC in Regional Languages and Literatures	(Under Plan)

Volume VII The Rise of New Polity and Life in Villages and Towns

*	Part 1	The State and Society in Medieval India	J.S. Grewal (ed.)
*	Part 2	Religious Movements and Institutions in Medieval India	J.S. Grewal (ed.)
†	Parts 3, 4 & 5	Religious Systems of India	S.R. Saha, N.S.S. Raman, M. Rafique and Others (ed.)

Volume VIII Economic History of India

†	Part 1	Economic History of India from Thirteenth to Seventeenth Century	Irfan Habib (ed.)
†	Part 2	Economic History of India from Eighteenth to Twentieth Century	B.B. Chaudhuri
*	Part 3	Economic History of India from Eighteenth to Twentieth Century	B.B. Chaudhuri (ed.)

Volume IX Colonial Period

*	Part 1	Medicine in India: Modern Period	O.P. Jaggi
†	Part 2	Women in India: Ancient and Medieval Period	Bhuvan Chandel (ed.)
*	Part 3	Women of India: Colonial and Post-colonial Periods	Bharati Ray (ed.)

Volume X Towards Independence

*	Part 1	Development of Indian Philosophy from Eighteenth Century Onwards	Daya Krishna
†	Part 2	Colonial Development, Education and Social Awareness up to 2000	S. Gopal, Ravinder Kumar & S. Bhattacharya (ed.)
*	Part 3	Historical Perspectives of Warfare in India: Some *Morale* and *Material* Determinants	S.N. Prasad (ed.)
†	Part 4	Cultural Foundations of Mathematics: The Nature of Mathematical Proof and the Transmission of the Infinitesimal Calculus from India to Europe in the 16th c. CE	C.K. Raju

* Already Published

† In the Process of Publication

‡ Under Plan

. . . continued at the back of this volume

History of Science, Philosophy and Culture in Indian Civilization

General Editor D.P. Chattopadhyaya

Volume X Part I

Developments in Indian Philosophy from Eighteenth Century Onwards: Classical and Western

DAYA KRISHNA

Project of History of Indian Science, Philosophy and Culture

CENTRE FOR STUDIES IN CIVILIZATIONS

Publication of this Volume and much of the research it represents has been made possible by continuing grants with full financial assistance from the Department of Secondary Education and Higher Education Ministry of Human Resource Development, Government of India, which has supported multidisciplinary exploration of the Project of History of Indian Science, Philosophy and Culture.

First published in 2002
Reprinted 2006
by Professor Bhuvan Chandel, Member Secretary, CSC
for the Project of History of Indian Science, Philosophy and Culture
36 Tughlakabad Institutional Area, New Delhi 110062

Distributed by
Motilal Banarsidass
Bungalow Road, Jawahar Nagar
Delhi 110 007

ISBN: 81-87586-08-7

Typeset in Nalandabaskar

Typeset by PHISPC, New Delhi 110062
Printed at Pauls Press, New Delhi 110020

Centre for Studies in Civilizations

Governing Board

In Memoriam

FRANCINE ELLISON KRISHNA

(December 22, 1931–February 8, 1999)

Contents

SECTION THREE

SECTION FOUR

Table of Transliteration

अ	a	आ	ā	इ	i	ई	ī		
उ	u	ऊ	ū	ऋ	ṛ	ॠ	ṝ		
ऌ	ḷ	ए	e	ऐ	ai	ओ	o		
औ	au	अं	aṁ	अः	aḥ				
क्	k	ख्	kh	ग्	g	घ्	gh	ङ्	ṅ
च्	c	छ्	ch	ज्	j	झ्	jh	ञ्	ñ
ट्	ṭ	ठ्	ṭh	ड्	ḍ	ढ्	ḍh	ण	ṇ
त्	t	थ्	th	द्	d	ध्	dh	न्	n
प्	p	फ्	ph	ब्	b	भ्	bh	म्	m
य्	y	र्	r	ल्	l	व्	v		
श्	ś	ष्	ṣ	स्	s	ह्	h		
ळ्	ḻ	क्ष्	kṣ	त्र्	tr	ज्ञ्	jñ		

General Introduction

I

It is understandable that man, shaped by Nature, would like to know Nature. The human ways of knowing Nature are evidently diverse, theoretical and practical, scientific and technological, artistic and spiritual. This diversity has, on scrutiny, been found to be neither exhaustive nor exclusive. The complexity of physical nature, life-world and, particularly, human mind is so enormous that it is futile to follow a single method for comprehending all the aspects of the world in which we are situated.

One need not feel bewildered by the variety and complexity of the worldly phenomena. After all, both from traditional wisdom and our daily experience, we know that our own nature is not quite alien to the structure of the world. Positively speaking, the elements and forces that are out there in the world are also present in our body-mind complex, enabling us to adjust ourselves to our environment. Not only the natural conditions but also the social conditions of life have instructive similarities between them. This is not to underrate in any way the difference between the human ways of life all over the world. It is partly due to the variation in climatic conditions and partly due to the distinctness of production-related tradition, history and culture.

Three broad approaches are discernible in the works on historiography of civilization, comprising science and technology, art and architecture, social sciences and institutions. Firstly, some writers are primarily interested in discovering the general laws which govern all civilizations spread over different continents. They tend to underplay what they call the noisy local events of the external world and peculiarities of different languages, literatures and histories. Their accent is on the unity of Nature, the unity of science and the unity of mankind. The second group of writers, unlike the generalists or transcendentalists, attach primary importance to the distinctiveness of every culture. To these writers human freedom and creativity are extremely important and basic in character. Social institutions and the cultural articulations of human consciousness, they argue, are bound to be expressive of the concerned people's consciousness. By implication they tend to reject concepts like archetypal consciousness, universal mind and providential history. There is a third group of writers who offer a composite picture of civilizations, drawing elements both from their local as well as common characteristics. Every culture has its local roots and peculiarities. At the same time, it is pointed out that due to demographic migration and immigration over the centuries an element of compositness emerges almost in every culture. When due to a natural calamity or political exigencies people move from one part of the world to another, they carry with them, among other things, their language, cultural inheritance and their ways of living.

In the light of the above facts, it is not at all surprising that comparative anthropologists and philologists are intrigued by the striking similarity between different language families and the rites, rituals and myths of different peoples. Speculative philosophers of history, heavily relying on the findings of epigraphy, ethnography, archaeology and theology, try to show in very general terms that the particulars and universals of culture are 'essentially' or 'secretly' interrelated. The spiritual aspects of culture like dance and music, beliefs pertaining to life, death and duties, on analysis, are found to be mediated by the material forms of life like weather forecasting, food production, urbanization and invention of script. The transition from the oral culture to the written one was made possible because of the mastery of symbols and rules of measurement. Speech precedes grammar, poetry prosody. All these show how the 'matters' and 'forms' of life are so subtly interwoven.

II

The PHISPC publications on History of Science, Philosophy and Culture in Indian Civilization, in spite of its unitary look, do recognize the differences between the areas of material civilization and those of ideational culture. It is not a work of a single author. Nor is it being executed by a group of thinkers and writers who are methodologically uniform or ideologically identical in their commitments. In conceiving the Project we have interacted with, and been influenced by, the writings and views of many Indian and non-Indian thinkers.

The attempted unity of this Project lies in its aim and inspiration. We have in India many scholarly works written by Indians on different aspects of our civilization and culture. Right from the pre-Christian era to our own time, India has drawn the attention of various countries of Asia, Europe and Africa. Some of these writings are objective and informative and many others are based on insufficient information and hearsay, and therefore not quite reliable, but they have their own value. Quality and view-points keep on changing not only because of the adequacy and inadequacy of evidence but also, and perhaps more so, because of the bias and prejudice, religious and political conviction, of the writers.

Besides, it is to be remembered that history, like Nature, is not an open book to be read alike by all. The past is mainly enclosed and only partially disclosed. History is, therefore, partly objective or 'real' and largely a matter of construction. This is one of the reasons why some historians themselves think that it is a form of literature or art. However, it does not mean that historical construction is 'anarchic' and arbitrary. Certainly, imagination plays an important role in it.

But its character is basically dependent upon the *questions* which the historian raises and wants to understand or answer in terms of the ideas and actions of human beings in the past ages. In a way, history, somewhat like the natural sciences, is engaged in answering questions and in exploring relationships of cause and effect between events and developments across time. While in the natural sciences, the scientist poses questions about nature in the form of hypotheses, expecting to elicit authoritative answers to such questions, the historian studies the past, partly for the sake of understanding it for its own sake and partly also for the light which the past throws upon the present, and the possibilities which it opens up for moulding the future. But the difference between the two approaches must not be lost sight of. The scientist is primarily interested in discovering laws and framing theories, in terms of which different events and processes can be connected and anticipated. His interest in the conditions or circumstances attending the concerned events is secondary. Therefore, scientific laws turn out to be basically abstract and easily expressible in terms of mathematical language. In contrast, the historian's main interest centres round the *specific* events, human ideas and actions, not *general* laws. So, the historian, unlike the scientist, is obliged to pay primary attention to the circumstances of the events he wants to study. Consequently, history, like most other humanistic disciplines, is concrete and particularist. This is not to deny the obvious truth that historical events and processes consisting of human ideas and actions show some trend or other and weave some pattern or other. If these trends and patterns were not there at all in history, the study of history as a branch of knowledge would not have been profitable or instructive. But one must recognize that historical trends and patterns, unlike scientific laws and theories, are not general or purported to be universal in their scope.

III

The aim of this Project is to discover the main aspects of Indian culture and present them in an interrelated way. Since our culture has influenced, and has been influenced by, the neighbouring cultures of West Asia, Central Asia, East Asia and South-East Asia, attempts have been made here to trace and study these influences in their mutuality. It is well known that during the last three centuries, European presence, both political and cultural, in India has been very widespread. In many volumes of the Project considerable attention has been paid to Europe and, through Europe, to other parts of the world. For the purpose of a comprehensive cultural study of India, the existing political boundaries of the

South Asia of today are more of a hindrance than help. Cultures, like languages, often transcend the bounds of changing political territories.

If the inconstant political geography is not a reliable help to the understanding of the layered structure and spread of culture, a somewhat comparable problem is encountered in the area of historical periodization. Periodization or segmenting time is a very tricky affair. When exactly one period ends and another begins is not precisely ascertainable. The periods of history designated as ancient, medieval and modern are purely conventional and merely heuristic in character. The varying scopes of history, local, national and continental or universal, somewhat like the periods of history, are unavoidably fuzzy and shifting. Amidst all these difficulties, the volume-wise details have been planned and worked out by the editors in consultation with the Project Director and the General Editor. I believe that the editors of different volumes have also profited from the reactions and suggestions of the contributors of individual chapters in planning the volumes.

Another aspect of Indian history which the volume editors and contributors of the Project have carefully dealt with is the distinction and relation between civilization and culture. The material conditions which substantially shaped Indian civilization have been discussed in detail. From agriculture and industry to metallurgy and technology, from physics and chemical practices to the life sciences and different systems of medicines—all the branches of knowledge and skill which directly affect human life—form the heart of this Project. Since the periods covered by the PHISPC are extensive—prehistory, proto-history, early history, medieval history and modern history of India—we do not claim to have gone into all the relevant material conditions of human life. We had to be selective. Therefore, one should not be surprised if one finds that only some material aspects of Indian civilization have received our pointed attention, while the rest have been dealt with in principle or only alluded to.

One of the main aims of the Project has been to spell out the first principles of the philosophy of different schools, both pro-Vedic and anti-Vedic. The basic ideas of Buddhism, Jainism and Islam have been given their due importance. The special position accorded to philosophy is to be understood partly in terms of its proclaimed unifying character and partly it is to be explained in terms of the fact that different philosophical systems represent alternative world-views, cultural perspectives, their conflict and mutual assimilation.

Most of the volume editors and at their instance the concerned contributors have followed a middle path between the extremes of narrativism and theoreticism. The underlying idea has been this: If in the process of working out a comprehensive Project like this every contributor attempts to narrate all those interesting things that he has in the back of his mind, the enterprise is likely to prove unmanageable. If, on the other hand, particular details are consciously forced into a fixed mould or pre-supposed theoretical structure, the details lose their particularity and interesting character. Therefore, depending on the nature of the problem of discourse, most of the writers have tried to reconcile in their presentation, the specificity of narrativism and the generality of theoretical orientation. This is a conscious editorial decision. Because, in the absence of a theory, however inarticulate it may be, the factual details tend to fall apart. Spiritual network or theoretical orientation makes historical details not only meaningful but also interesting and enjoyable.

Another editorial decision which deserves spelling out is the necessity or avoidability of duplication of the same theme in different volumes or even in the same volume. Certainly, this Project is not an assortment of several volumes. Nor is any volume intended to be a miscellany. This Project has been designed with a definite end in view and has a structure of its own. The character of the structure has admittedly been influenced by the variety of the themes accommodated within it. Again it must be understood that the complexity of structure is rooted in the aimed integrality of the Project itself.

IV

Long and in-depth editorial discussion has led us to several unanimous conclusions. Firstly, our Project is going to be *unique,* unrivalled and discursive in its attempt to integrate different forms of science, technology, philosophy and culture. Its comprehensive scope, continuous character and accent on culture distinguish it from the works of such Indian authors as P.C. Ray, B.N. Seal, Binoy Kumar Sarkar and S.N. Sen and also from such Euro-American writers as Lynn Thorndike, George Sarton and Joseph Needham. Indeed, it would be no exaggeration to suggest that it is for the first time that an endeavour of so comprehensive a character, in its exploration of the social, philosophical and cultural characteristics of a distinctive world civilization—that of India—has been attempted in the domain of scholarship.

Secondly, we try to show the linkages between different branches of learning as different modes of experience in an *organic* manner and without resorting to a kind of reductionism, materialistic or spiritualistic. The internal dialectics of organicism without reductionism allows fuzziness, discontinuity and discreteness within limits.

Thirdly, positively speaking, different modes of human experience—scientific, artistic, etc. have their own individuality, not necessarily autonomy. Since all these modes are modification and articulation of *human* experience, these are bound to have between them some finely graded commonness. At the same time, it has been recognized that reflection on different areas of experience and investigation brings to light new insights and findings. Growth of knowledge requires humans, in general, and scholars, in particular, to identify the distinctness of different branches of learning.

Fourthly, to follow simultaneously the twin principles of: (a) individuality of human experience as a whole, and (b) individuality of diverse disciplines, are not at all an easy task. Overlap of themes and duplication of the terms of discourse become unavoidable at times. For example, in the context of *Dharmaśāstra,* the writer is bound to discuss the concept of value. The same concept also figures in economic discourse and also occurs in a discussion on fine arts. The conscious editorial decision has been that, while duplication should be kept to its minimum, for the sake of intended clarity of the themes under discussion, their reiteration must not be avoided at high intellectual cost.

Fifthly, the scholars working on the Project are drawn from widely different disciplines. They have brought to our notice an important fact that has clear relevance to our work. Many of our contemporary disciplines like economics and sociology did not exist, at least not in their present form, just two centuries ago or so. For example, before the middle of nineteenth century, sociology as a distinct branch of knowledge was unknown. The term is said to have been coined first by the French philosopher Auguste Comte in 1838s. Obviously, this does not mean that the issues discussed in sociology were not there. Similarly, Adam Smith's (1723–90) famous work *The Wealth of Nations* is often referred to as the first authoritative statement of the principles of (what we now call) economics. Interestingly enough, the author was equally interested in ethics and jurisprudence. It is clear from history that the nature and scope of different disciplines undergo change, at times very radically, over time. For example, in India by *arthaśāastra* does not mean the science of economics as understood today. Besides the principles of economics the *arthaśāstra* of ancient India discusses at length those of governance, diplomacy and military science.

Sixthly, this brings us to the next editorial policy followed in the Project. We have tried to remain very conscious of what may be called indeterminacy or inexactness of translation. When a word or expression of one language is translated into another, some loss of meaning or exactitude seems to be unavoidable. This is true not only in the bilingual relations like Sanskrit-English and Sanskrit-Arabic, but also in those of Hindi-Tamil and Hindi-Bengali. In recognition of the importance of language-bound and context-relative character of meaning we have soli-cited from many learned scholars, contributions, written in vernacular languages. In order to minimize the miseffect of semantic inexactitude we have solicited translational help of that type of bilingual scholars who know both English and the concerned vernacular language, Hindi, Tamil, Telegu, Bengali or Marathi.

Seventhly and finally, perhaps the place of technology as a branch of knowledge in the composite universe of science and art merits some elucidation. Technology has been conceived in very many ways, e.g. as autonomous, as 'standing reserve', as liberating or enlargemental, and alienative or estrangemental force. The studies undertaken by the Project show that, in spite of its much emphasized mechanical and alienative characteristics, technology embodies a very useful mode of knowledge that is peculiar to man. The Greek root words of technology are *techne* (art) and *logos* (science). This is the basic justification of recognizing technology as closely related to both epistemology, the discipline of valid knowledge, and axiology, the discipline of freedom and values. It is in this context that we are reminded of the definition of man as *homo technikos.* In

Sanskrit, the word closest to *techne* is *kalā* which means any practical art, any mechanical or fine art. In the Indian tradition, in *Śaivatantra*, for example, among the arts (*kalā*) are counted dance, drama, music, architecture, metallurgy, knowledge of dictionary, encyclopaedia and prosody. The closeness of the relation between arts and sciences, technology and other forms of knowledge are evident from these examples and was known to the ancient people. The human quest for knowledge involves the use of both head and hand. Without mind, the body is a corpse and the disembodied mind is a bare abstraction. Even for our appreciation of what is beautiful and the creation of what is valuable, we are required to exercise both our intellectual competence and physical capacity. In a manner of speaking, one might rightly affirm that our psychosomatic structure is a functional connector between what we are and what we could be, between the physical and the beyond. To suppose that there is a clear-cut distinction between the physical world and the psychosomatic one amounts to denial of the possible emergence of higher logico-mathematical, musical and other capacities. The very availability of aesthetic experience and creation proves that the supposed distinction is somehow overcome by what may be called the bodily self or embodied mind.

V

The ways of classification of arts and sciences are neither universal nor permanent. In the Indian tradition, in the *Ṛgveda*, for example, *vidyās* (or sciences) are said to be four in number: (i) *Trayī*, the triple Veda; (ii) *Ānvīkṣikī*, logic and metaphysics; (iii) *Daṇḍa-nīti*, science of governance; (iv) *Vārtta*, practical arts such as agriculture, commerce, medicine, etc. Manu speaks of a fifth *vidyā*, viz. *Ātma-vidyā*, knowledge of self or of spiritual truth. According to many others, *vidyā* has fourteen divisions, viz. the four Vedas, the six *Vedāngas*, the *Purāṇas*, the *Mīmāṁsā*, *Nyāya*, and *Dharma* or law. At times, the four *Upa-vedas* are also recognized by some as *vidyā*. *Kalās* are said to be 33 or even 64.

In the classical tradition of India, the word *śāstra* has at times been used as synonym of *vidyā*. *Vidyā* denotes instrument of teaching, manual or compendium of rules, religious or scientific treatise. The word *śāstra* is usually found after the word referring to the subject of the book, e.g. *Dharma-śāstra*, *Artha-śāstra*, *Alaṁkara-śāstra* and *Mokṣa-śāstra*. Two other words which have been frequently used to denote different branches of knowledge are *jñāna* and *vijñāna*. While *jñāna* means knowing, knowledge, especially the higher form of it; *vijñāna* stands for the act of distinguishing or discerning, understanding, comprehending and recognizing. It means worldly or profane knowledge as distinguished from *jñāna*, knowledge of the divine.

It must be said here that the division of knowledge is partly conventional and partly administrative or practical. It keeps on changing from culture to culture, from age to age. It is difficult to claim that the distinction between *jñāna* and *vijñāna* or that between science and art is universal. It is true that even before the advent of modern age, both in the East and the West, two basic aspects of sciences started gaining recognition. One is the *specialized character* of what we call scientific knowledge. The other is the concept of *trained skill* which was brought close to scientific knowledge. In the medieval Europe, the expression 'the seven liberal sciences' has so often been used simultaneously with 'the seven liberal arts', meaning thereby, the group of studies by the *Trivium* (Grammar, Logic and Rhetoric) and *Quadrivium* (Arithmetic, Music, Geometry and Astronomy).

It may be observed here, as has already been alluded to earlier, that the division between different branches of knowledge, between theory and practice, was not pushed to an extreme extent in the early ages. *Praxis*, for example, was recognized as the prime *techne*. The Greek word, *technologia* stood for systematic treatment, for example, of Grammar. *Praxis* is not the mere application of *theoria*, unified vision or integral outlook, but it also stands for the active impetus and base of knowledge. In India, one often uses the terms *Prayukti-vidyā* and *Prayodyogika-vidyā* to emphasize the practical or applicative character of knowledge. *Prayoga* or application is both the test and base of knowledge. Doing is the best way of knowing and learning.

That one and the same word may mean different 'things' or concepts in different cultures and thus create confusion has already been stated before. Two such words which in the context of this Project under discussion deserve special mention are *dharma* and *itihāsa.* Ordinarily, *dharma* in Sanskrit-rooted languages is taken to be conceptual equivalent of the English word *religion.* But, while the meaning of religion is primarily theological, that of *dharma* seems to be manifold. Literally, *dharma* stands for that which is established or that which holds people steadfastly together. Its other meanings are law, rule, usage, practice, custom, ordinance and statute. Spiritual or moral merit, virtue, righteousness and good works are also denoted by it. Further, *dharma* stands for natural qualities like burning (of fire), liquidity (of water) and fragility (of glass). Thus one finds that meanings of *dharma* are of many types—legal, social, moral, religious or spiritual, and even ontological or physical. All these meanings of *dharma* have received due attention of the writers in the relevant contexts of different volumes.

This Project, being primarily historical as it is, has naturally paid serious attention to the different concepts of history—epic-mythic, artistic-narrative, scientific-causal, theoretical and ideological. Perhaps the point that must be mentioned first about history is that it is not a correct translation of the Sanskrit word *itihāsa.* Etymologically, it means what really happened (*iti-ha-āsa*). But, as we know, in the Indian tradition *purāṇa* (legend, myth, tale, etc.), *gāthā* (ballad), *itivṛtta* (description of past occurrence, event, etc.), *ākhyāyikā* (short narrative) and *vaṃśa-carita* (genealogy) have been consciously accorded a very important place. Things started changing with the passage of time and particularly after the effective presence of Islamic culture in India. Islamic historians, because of their own cultural moorings and the influence of the Semitic and Graeco-Roman cultures on them, were more particular about their facts, figures and dates than their Indian predecessors. Their aim to bring history close to statecraft, social conditions and the lives and teachings of the religious leaders imparted a mundane character to this branch of learning. The Europeans whose political appearance on the Indian scene became quite perceptible only towards the end of the eighteenth century brought in with them their own view of historiography in their cultural baggage. The impact of the Newtonian Revolution in the field of history was very faithfully worked out, among others, by David Hume (1711–76) in *History of Great Britain from the Invasion of Julius Caesar to the Revolution of 1688* (6 Vol. 1754–62) and Edward Gibbon (1737–94) in *The History of the Decline and Fall of the Roman Empire* (6 Vol., 1776–88). Their emphasis on the principles of causality, datability and continuity/linearity of historical events introduced the spirit of scientific revolution in European historiography. The introduction of English education in India and the exposure of the elites of the country to it largely account for the decline of the traditional concept of *itihāsa* and the rise of the post-Newtonian scientific historiography. Gradually, Indian writers of our own history and cultural heritage started using more and more European concepts and categories. This is not to suggest that the impact of the European historiography on Indian historians was entirely negative. On the contrary, it imparted an analytical and critical temper which motivated many Indian historians of the nineteenth century to try to discover and represent our heritage in a new way.

VI

The principles which have been followed for organizing the subjects of different volumes under this Project may be stated in this way. We have kept in view the main structures which are discernible in the decomposible composition of the world. The first structure may be described as physical and chemical. The second structure consists, broadly speaking, of biology, psychology and epistemology. The highest and the most abstract structure nests many substructures within it, for example, logic, mathematics and musical notes. It is well known that the substructures within each structure are interactive, i.e. not isolable. The more important point to be noted in this connection is that the basic three structures of the world, viz., (a) physico-chemical, (b) bio-psychological, and (c) logico-mathematical are all simultaneously open to upward and downward causation. In other words, while the physico-chemical structure can causally influence the bio-psychological one and the latter can causally influence the most abstract logico-mathematical, the reverse process of causation is also operative in the world. In spite of its relative abstractness and durability, the logico-mathematical world has its downward causal impact on our bio-psychological and epistemological processes and products. And the latter can also bring about change in the structures of the physical world and its chemical composition. Applied physics and bio-technology make the last point abundantly clear.

Many philosophers, life-scientists, and social scientists highlight the point that nature loves hierarchies. Herbert Simon, the economist and the management scientist, speaks of four steps of partial ordering of our world, namely; (i) chemical substances, (ii) living organisms, tissues and organs, (iii) genes, chromosomes and DNA, and (iv) human beings, the social organizations, programmes and information process. All these views are in accord with the anti-reductionist character of our Project. Many biologists defend this approach by pointing out that certain characteristics of biological phenomena and process like unpredictability, randomness, uniqueness, magnitude of stochastic perturbations, complexity and emergence cannot be reduced without recource to physical laws.

The main subjects dealt with in different volumes of the Project are connected not only conceptually and synchronically but also historically or diachronically. For pressing practical reasons, however, we did not aim at presenting the prehistorical, proto-historical and historical past of India in a continuous or chronological manner. Besides, it has been shown in the presentation of the PHISPC that the process of history is non-linear. And this process is to be understood in terms of human praxis and an absence of general laws in history. Another point which deserves special mention is that the editorial advisors have taken a conscious decision not to make this historical Project primarily political. We felt that this area of history has always been receiving extensive attention. Therefore, the customary discussion of dynastic rule and succession will not be found in a prominent way in this series. Instead, as said before, most of the available space has been given to social, scientific, philosophical and other cultural aspects of Indian civilization.

Having stated this, it must be admitted that our departure from conventional style of writing Indian history is not total. We have followed an inarticulate framework of time in organizing and presenting the results of our studies. The first volume, together with its parts, deals with the prehistorical period to AD 300. The next two volumes, together with their parts, deal with, among other things, the development of social and political institutions and philosophical and scientific ideas from AD 300 to the beginning of the eleventh century AD. The next period with which this Project is concerned spans from the twelfth century to the early part of the eighteenth century. The last three centuries constitute the fourth period covered by this Project. But, as said before, the definition of all these periods by their very nature are inexact and merely indicative.

Two other points must be mentioned before I conclude this General Introduction to the series. The history of some of the subjects like religion, language and literature, philosophy, science and technology cannot for obvious reason be squeezed within the cramped space of the periodic moulds. Attempts to do so result in thematic distortion. Therefore, the reader will often see the overflow of some ideas from one period to another. I have already drawn attention to this tricky and fuzzy and also the misleading aspects of the periodization of history, if pressed beyond a point.

Secondly, strictly speaking, history knows no end. Every age rewrites its history. Every generation, beset with new issues, problems and questions, looks back to its history and reinterprets and renews its past. This shows why history is not only contemporaneous but also futural. Human life actually knows no separative wall between its past, present and future. Its cognitive enterprises, moral endeavours and practical activities are informed of the past, oriented by the present and addressed to the future. This process persists, consciously or unconsciously, wittingly or unwittingly. In the narrative of this Project, we have tried to represent this complex and fascinating story of Indian civilization.

General Editor
Centre for Studies in Civilizations
New Delhi

D.P. CHATTOPADHYAYA

Introduction

History, as a cognitive enterprise, seems to be amongst the strangest of endeavours undertaken by man for it claims to know the past, that is, something which does not presently exist. But, how can that which is 'not', be understood? For, to understand that, it would be to endow it with some sort of 'being'. The anomaly and paradox inherent in this attempt to know and understand the past has generally been ignored, as it raises questions about the very foundations of the enterprise in which historians are engaged. For the 'past' that one tries to know was at one time existent and hence cannot be regarded as a 'pure nothing'. If it were so, it would not have left any evidence of itself. 'Non-being' does not produce effects or leave any evidence from which it can be constructed as the 'cause' of that which is in the present and on the basis of which we try to understand what was. Thus, the cognitive justification for the enterprise named history is said to lie in the relation between the present and the past and the linkages that can be established between the two.

But even if this is accepted, the question remains of how one who claims to be a historian 'validates' this linkage between the present and the past, as the past, that is no more and can never be there, in principle shall never be 'present' to verify the linkage that is postulated. Normally, the hypotheses that one forms to explain or understand what is in the present are supposed to lead to further consequences which can be observed or met with in the future, which would be the 'present' at that time, and thus establish, to some extent at least, the plausible truths of the hypotheses that were formed. This is, to a large extent, the established method in most of the cognitive enterprises of man. But as far as history is concerned, the situation seems to be just the reverse. Here the evidence which is supposed to be in the present, validates or corroborates or establishes the truth of the hypothesis which is postulated about the past without any further attempt at finding whether the hypothesis so postulated is itself valid or not. In fact, the terms 'hypothesis', 'postulation', 'validation', 'corroboration' are seldom used in the cognitive enterprise known as 'history'. Rather, the whole thing about the past is presented as if it were 'really' so, and that the historian has somehow got access to it and 'knows' it as if he himself had been a star witness to the events he is writing about and that his veracity is itself the guarantee of the truth of what he is writing about.

There is bound to be also the objection that we are assuming a momentary, evanescent view of reality which is Heraclitean or Buddhist in character. But this is just not true. There are things which endure and which survive the passage of time without any serious damage being done to what they essentially are. The Aśokan pillar which we find today existed when it was constructed on Aśoka's orders, even though subsequently it may have been damaged or the inscription on it dimmed or defaced to some extent. Thus it can legitimately be said to provide incontrovertible evidence in the present of something that occurred thousands of years ago as is also the case with many other things present today on the basis of which the historian tries to know about the past. Further, the use of memory in the self-conscious attempts at preservation and transmission, with exact fidelity, is also evident in what is preserved. This was so with the oral transmission of the Vedic *mantras* and the dialogues of the Buddha and the Mahāvīra, to give but some examples from the oral traditions of India, as is also the case in respect of the sacred texts in other traditions. The invention of writing added another dimension to the preservation and transmission of the 'evidence' establishing the truth of the so-called hypothesis about the past namely that it is present here in the 'present'.

However, the 'decision' to preserve, perpetuate and transmit, in as unadulterated a form as possible, is itself a decision of someone or some institution. It is based on certain reasons and implies that certain things among others were considered 'worthy' of preservation, perpetuation and transmission. Thus, the decision-makers of the past determined in a selective, substantive sense what should constitute the basis through which the past itself would be known and the 'real', the veridical 'truth' about it, be determined. This is a strange situation where one's access to the truth itself is edited, censored from the beginning and, strangely, the historian, willingly or unwillingly, conspires by selecting what was to be preserved for posterity. However, all that was selected to be preserved has not been preserved. That which has been lost far outnumbers that which has survived even the most self-conscious attempts at its preservation. This may have been the result of deliberate destruction on the part of those who did not want that what was preserved be available to succeeding generations. Besides this, there were also accidents which no one can help and which destroyed things that the earlier generations had tried to preserve and perpetuate with such perseverance and care. Thus, the basis on which the historian constructs his knowledge of the past is subject not only to the deliberate decisions of those who decided what was to be preserved or destroyed, but also to the vagaries of time or accident or chance. It is, of course, true that 'chance' also preserves things that were never intended to be preserved in the sense in which the so-called sacred texts and other *śāstric* works are generally sought to be preserved.

But, then, what is this knowledge of the past that the historian claims to know or to have discovered and about which he writes with such authority, and the truth of which he wants others to believe without any shadow of doubt or disbelief. The past, in other words, is what the historian has "created". It is his/her creation and he/she does not let the reader have the least suspicion that it is so. Rather, one is lulled into thinking that what one is reading about is the 'real' past, the past as it actually occurred, the past to which the historian has a special access and which he/she is sharing with the reader. In fact, most of the 'past' is irretrievably lost and is, in a fundamental sense, meant to be lost. But the past which the historian creates is not fully a function of the evidence that is available for one reason or another but is usually built on the basis of a half conscious selection by the historian in respect of the available evidence itself. It is this fact which is generally never made known to the reader and, many a time, the historian himself is not aware of it. It is, of course, true that the notion of 'evidence' is itself a function of relevant knowledge in other domains, and as this knowledge changes over a period of time, what is to be counted as evidence also changes. The historian, of course, is not responsible for this change in the character of what is to be counted as evidence, but he/she is certainly responsible for the act of selection that generally operates in connection with what is to be counted as evidence in the context of the relevant knowledge that is obtained in his/her own time. Many a time, it is assumed that the evidence which has not been taken into account will not substantially affect the picture being built. In fact, in many other disciplines statistical evidence is compiled on the basis of selection, but there it is generally methodologically ensured that new data will not substantially affect the conclusion by adopting the simple device of including further instances of the evidence to see whether or not they affect the result in any substantial sense. The historian, unfortunately, does not do this, and even where it is difficult for him to do so for any reason, his reader does not know that he has not been able to use the relevant evidence in his construction even though it was available when he was building his picture.

There exists also the startling fact that while in most of the social sciences the relevant data can be statistically treated in terms of the investigation that is being carried on, such cannot be the case with regard to history. What history studies is almost a unique phenomenon and to the extent that it is repeatable and is seen as an instance of some "universal", it ceases to be the subject of historical investigation. There are, of course, historians who have tried to turn their study into something which may be nearer to what is considered a science and have even gone so far as to change the very title of their discipline from 'history' to something such as 'Cliometrics'. In fact, many of the historians of today try to distance their discipline from what is usually called the humanities to have this included instead in what is termed the social sciences. At the other extreme are those who can be regarded as philosophers of history and those who try to see historical events in terms of some general pattern in which individual events are subsumed under or seen as mere illustrations of something higher or nobler or of some principles that are more abstract and universal. The so-called Christian view of history, the Marxist and the Hegelian views, and the views embodied in the writings of Sri Aurobindo and Teilhard de Chardin, may be said to represent this trend. But then, these are even more selective in their approach and hardly care for the counter evidence which abounds in plenty, as it would refute their theory if it were seriously taken into consideration. In fact, their theories are not subject to refutation in principle as the evidence, whatever it is, is bound to fit, in an *a priori* manner, with those theories.

This paradoxical character of the 'evidence' on the basis of which the historian builds his picture has seldom been seriously considered. How and why is it that this type of evidence permits 'constructions' of alternative pictures—'pictures' from among which it is difficult to decide as to which is the valid construction given the evidence on which it is built. Perhaps it is the differences in the principles of interpretation employed by different historians which give rise to these alternative constructions. But if it is so, then the principles themselves, on the basis of which the historian has built his construction, should be clearly articulated; as without knowing what they are, the reader will be left in the dark regarding how the whole thing has been built up in one way rather than in another. The principles of interpretation may require a justification which is seldom found in the writings of historians, nor is it ever stated as to why the principles employed are 'better' or more 'suitable' to the evidence concerned than are others which could perhaps also be employed to build different pictures.

The situation gets even more complicated if the distinction between 'manifest' and 'latent' meanings with respect to the evidence is taken seriously, for then, the interpretation that is in accordance with the manifest content of the evidence, may be seen to be unreal or illusory, as the so-called real meaning is hidden by it and can be revealed only if the 'manifest' is ignored or not seriously taken into account. Not only this, but also, as the source of most of the evidence on which the historians build their pictures is based on what human beings have written or said, the problem of "intentionality" enters in a serious way to affect the interpretation that one chooses to make.

It is true that there has been strong criticism regarding the bringing in of intentionality in respect of interpretation in literature. The debate about the 'intentionalist fallacy' is well known, and the autonomy of the text has been repeatedly emphasised to underline the independence of the text from its author. On the other hand, most of the interpretation of evidence in the legal context has necessarily to take into account the intentions of the agent, as otherwise, there would remain no difference between murder and manslaughter. The texts of the historian may be said to lie somewhere between the pure literary text which may be treated as autonomous, and legal evidence, where intentionality is the heart of the matter, so that intentionality of agents and authors can never be completely ignored in a historical construction built on the basis of evidence. But, as everyone knows, it is almost impossible to get at intentionality correctly, and one can never be sure if what one has assumed about it is really correct.

The essential ambiguity in the evidence, an ambiguity intrinsic and unavoidable, renders the historian's construction always suspect unless he/she makes a determined effort to lay his/her cards on the table to make the reader aware of all that has gone into the making of the construction. This, of course, is a difficult demand to fulfil, and even when attempted, is bound to fall short of what is 'objectively' necessary in the situation. Not only this, it is bound also to affect the readability of the historian's construction, as no 'narrative' can be written if one tries to fully expose the machinery behind the construction of the narrative. The reader is bound to be bored by whatever is written even if it be true that what is so written becomes more scientific in character.

The conflict between being objective, scientific, veridical on the one hand, and something interesting, readable, imaginatively gripping on the other, is thus always present. So is the 'know-all' impression which the historian inevitably tries to create in the reader's mind about what he is writing, as any element of doubt or tentativeness would affect adversely the reader's interest in what he has constructed.

II

An objection is bound to occur that most of the considerations we have been urging against the 'honest' practice of the historian's craft are irrelevant not only because they are akin to the usual arguments which philosophical skepticism puts forth against the possibility of any knowledge whatsoever, but because any enterprise is always carried on within the limitations imposed by the subject matter on the one hand and the feasible means on the other. The historian practises his craft within the limitations imposed by these two factors and, ultimately, history is what the historian does.

This all may be regarded as a fair refutation of what we have been saying but what we have urged has arisen not out of generalised, abstract philosophical considerations with which we are all too familiar, but from a direct 'living' encounter with the problems as they have arisen in our attempt to write about developments in classical Indian thought from the eighteenth century onwards, a task which I accepted in almost complete ignorance of what it might entail if I was to do it with even some honesty to myself and to the task I had undertaken. I am no historian and, in fact, never was one. My own training was in the field of philosophy, being primarily concerned with 'thinking' about things in general. As for history, I generally felt that it was totally irrelevant to the vital cognitive concerns of man. How could it ever matter that someone did something at some time in the past? The activity of 'thinking' was always exercised on a problem that had a non-temporal dimension, and that was the real heart of the matter. If Plato thought more than two and a half millennia ago, the time when he thought about things was irrelevant: what really mattered was the content of his thought, and this *was*, and *is* and *will be* relevant for ever. Thus, to undertake an exercise which had an essential temporal dimension to it was something new, at least as far as I was concerned.

The problems that I encountered therefore, in this exercise were a matter of 'discovery' and hence posed challenges in the strictly cognitive sense of the term which I had not thought of before. But whatever the historians may feel about the issues I have raised, I, at least, feel that they are genuine enough to be articulated and shared with others, particularly for the reason that they have 'shaped' the format of this work.

The first 'discovery' that I made was that one could not understand what was happening in the various domains of classical Indian thought from the eighteenth century onwards without becoming aware of what had gone on before. This going 'backwards' to understand the period I had been given to write about had literally no boundary. Thinking in India shows such a remarkable continuity that the temporal divisions one usually makes prove to be utterly irrelevant. There certainly are landmarks in its history, but they have little to do with the socio-political history of this civilisation. This provided the necessity and the justification for a chapter dealing with the earlier history of these thought currents so that what happened from the eighteenth century onwards might make some sense to the reader. But the real problems emerged while dealing with 'material' from the eighteenth century onwards. What was this material? What did it consist in? Did we have a complete roster of it? And if we had it, how could it all be handled, understood and made sense of in the context of the task that we had set for ourselves?

The search for material written during this period concerning the intellectual disciplines in which we were primarily interested was made possible due to two major bibliographical sources—the first by Karl H. Potter and the second by Thangaswami Sarma. The former comprises Volume I of the *Encyclopedia of Indian Philosophies*, which contains the most comprehensive bibliographical source material for the subject available in English. The bibliography volume had run into the second edition when we started our work, and hence this became the major source for the collection of reference material along with the dating given in it. However, in the last stages of the work, the third edition of the bibliography was published, and needed to be examined to rule out any substantial changes in the dating, or in the material, which we had not taken into account. A comparative study of the two editions led to the review article, 'Potter's bibliography' published in the *Journal of the Indian Council of Philosophical Research*.[1] The review article led to a comment by Prof. Karl H. Potter himself, resulting subsequently in a reply by myself.[2] Basically, however, no substantial changes were occasioned by the modifications in the third edition of the bibliography.

Thangaswami Sarma's work is little known in the scholarly world as it is in Sanskrit and has received no great publicity or even reviews in reputed journals.[3] Yet, in many ways, it is superior to Potter's work, as it gives not only brief summaries of the contents of the works cited but also the interrelationships between them in terms of the schools and sub-schools that proliferated around some seminal works in the field that was being dealt with. Also, it gives some biographical information about the authors of the works, including information about their teachers or gurus, which is of vital importance in the Indian tradition. However, Thangaswami Sarma's work covered only Nyāya, Vaiśeṣika and Advaita Vedānta when we started our work and dealt only with works in Sanskrit, caring little for the secondary material with respect of these or the translations that had been made into various languages of the world. The bibliographical volume on Mīmāṁsā by Thangaswami Sarma was published later and, thus, was available to us only in the final stages of the completion of our work.

The two major sources of our bibliographical information, however, related only to the field of philosophy and provided no information regarding either the literature on Alaṁkāra Śāstra or that which dealt with the political, social and legal thought of India. Luckily for us the *Dharma Koṣa* volumes edited by Paṇḍit Laxman Shastri Joshi provided a fairly comprehensive introduction to the material on the subject even though it was not primarily meant to be a bibliographical source of information on it.[4] The volumes dealing with *rājnīti*, *saṁskāra* and *vyavahāra* provided ample information which could be used for bibliographical purposes also. As for material on Alaṁkāra śāstra, there was hardly any information regarding the works written from the eighteenth century onwards even though fairly adequate information was available about the major works written up to Paṇḍitarāja Jagannātha in the first quarter of the seventeenth century. Later we stumbled upon a work in Hindi by A.K. Srivastava which provided detailed information regarding the authors who had written on this subject in recent times.[5] We had been given information about this work by Professor Radhavallabha Tripathi, Professor of Sanskrit, Sagar University, and we are grateful to him. Later still we had the good fortune of getting the manuscript of a monograph on the post-Jagannātha period of Alaṁkāra Śāstra by Professor Siva Kumar Swamy, Sanskrit Department, Bangalore University, which gave a more comprehensive account of the developments in this field from the eighteenth century onwards.[6]

The bibliographical material collected from these sources is given in the appendices to this volume as evidence of the extent of the material that should provide the basis for the 'construction' of any reasonable and legitimate picture of intellectual developments during the period in the fields we are concerned with. But as would be evident to any reader of this volume, this was an impossible task not only for us, it would have been impossible for anyone else who might have undertaken to do this work. The texts have generally been written in the technical language of Navya Nyāya, which is scarcely intelligible except to a few specialists in the discipline. Unfortunately, their number is sharply declining, and even those who have specialised in the field we find that they are conversant with only a few well known texts which they probably learnt from their teachers. There is also the added problem that in the absence of any qualitative assessment of the works mentioned, there is hardly any substantive ground for choosing between them except on the basis of some vague hunch that some might be more important than others as they have been written by a well known person held in high esteem in the tradition or because they deal with a subject that is important in itself.

A preliminary attempt, therefore, was made to find which traditional thinkers during this period were considered to be of outstanding importance by living scholars within the field; and the result thereof is given in the appendix, particularly highlighting those whose names occurred in the lists provided by different scholars independent of each other. But most of these belong to the period after the middle of the nineteenth century, and hardly any one belongs to the earlier period covered by us. However, even among these, if we take only the most common names from the list provided to us by scholars from different regions, there is hardly a single one on whom intensive work has been done or on whose work monographs have been written. Basically, it is a *terra incognita* which no one seems to have explored up to now.

Besides these obvious difficulties there were others which, in our opinion, were even more fundamental. Our initial survey of developments in various fields of knowledge before the eighteenth century had revealed that their centre was around certain key controversies which had occurred earlier and were carried into the period that we were concerned with. The whole material thus had to be seen from the perspective of these debates and discussions. Unless there was a clear awareness of the stage that the controversy had reached before the dawn of the eighteenth century, subsequent developments in the debate could not be properly understood or assessed. This, however, was not the perspective from which the scholars viewed their own disciplines. Thus, the questions that we asked them appeared both new and inconvenient, as they had to reorganise their whole knowledge in the context of the way in which we were trying to look at material which was familiar to them but which they had not seen from this perspective. Scholars are generally as conservative in their intellectual habits and ways of looking at things as are most of us, and thus it was not easy to find persons who had both the ability and the willingness to look at familiar texts in a new way. Luckily, we did find some outstanding scholars who were willing not only to look at the material from the new perspective that we had suggested, but also to answer our unending queries regarding what they wrote. The names of Professor Prahlada Char, Kutumba Shastri and Thangaswami Sarma stand out in this connection, but there were others like Paṇḍit Kishornath Jha and Dr Achyutanand Das who also helped us.

Besides the new perspective of discussion and debate around the central issues which had emerged earlier and which were carried on incessantly during this period, there was the even more difficult problem of what may be called sensitivity to philosophical novelty in the points that were being made by a particular thinker and the promise or potential they had for significant departures in philosophical thought seen in the way it had developed until then. This was obstructed by an almost axiomatic belief shared by everybody whom we approached that, fundamentally, there was nothing new in the writings of this period and that, at best, there was only what is called *pariṣkāra* in the tradition, which we may render as refinement or a more exact and subtler reformulation of what had already been said. This was the view commonly shared by traditional and modern scholars alike, and we had great difficulty in getting over this prejudice of those who 'knew' the material in the original better than we could ever hope to do. But once we became self-consciously aware of the fact that this widely-shared opinion had only a superficial basis in the situation as it really obtained, we repeatedly found what, in our opinion, were genuinely new insights which had a great deal of philosophical relevance even in the context of what is called modern thought in relation to these subjects. A careful reader will become aware of this fact if he or she compares our 'construction' with the texts in the appendices prepared by scholars who were profoundly acquainted with the material they were writing about. Perhaps this is nowhere more evident than in our chapter on Sāṁkhya, which is almost completely based on the volume on the same subject in the *Encyclopedia of Indian Philosophies* edited by Gerald Larson and Ramasamkara Bhattacharya. The volume contains summaries of the works of almost all the writers of that period, and our own 'construction' is based on what different scholars have written about them in the volume. The most outstanding of these summaries are given by Kalidasa Bhattacharya, who himself happened to be one of the most eminent philosophers of his time in the country. Yet, as far as we were concerned, we found that even he had missed the philosophical significance of many of the points that he was writing about, which were raised in the works that he was summarising for the volume. As for others, the less said the better. Professor Larson himself, one of the most outstanding authorities on Sāṁkhya in the world today and the chief editor of the volume concerned, has not said anything about the developments that took place during the period covered in the volume. Basically, this seems to result from a firmly-held, unconscious view that all these systems of thought belong to the past and that there can only be exegetical work now with regard to them.

Surprisingly, the situation seems no different in respect of the philosophical writings in India during the last hundred years under the impact of the new system of education introduced by the British. Here there was no need to postulate that nothing new could be said on the issues that were being written about. But, somehow, the same attitude seems to have persisted, and the general feeling is that nothing significant or new has been said by any one who has written on these subjects in the English language. An exception is grudgingly made in the case of one or two philosophers, but no one has used their thinking as a point of departure for his own or subjected it to the critical attention that it deserved. Perhaps this is due to another unconscious attitude amongst the English-educated persons in this country: that the sources of real knowledge are all in the

West and that nothing new can ever be discovered by any non-western thinker except accidentally. The two attitudes combine to create an intellectual atmosphere in which all cognitive enterprises seem to be carried on in this country. They seem to ensure that, however innovative and significant may be the departures by any one, in the context of thought in the past or in the present and deriving from the tradition of the West, they would not be seen as such by colleagues, who would ignore it altogether even if their attention were drawn to it.

There is, thus, a double "innovation" in our 'construction' of the developments in both Sanskritic and non-Sanskritic traditions of Indian thought from the eighteenth century onwards in that we have continuously focussed upon the novelty and the innovativeness of thinking in these fields. Also, as our construction of the picture itself is based on what others have said or written about them, we have continually pointed to the need for a more careful examination of the original material in the light of what we have said about it or 'discovered' in it. Not only this, the new lines of investigation and research that are needed have also been pointed out so that any one who is interested in and concerned with the developments that took place during this period may pursue them on his own to find whether what we have said is correct or not and/or discover something different from what we have been able to do with our limited capacities.

To focus attention on the extremely limited nature of the material on the basis of which we have built our picture of developments from the eighteenth century onwards, and the tentativeness of even this construction because of various limiting factors mentioned above, we have explicitly added a separate chapter wherein we have tried to point out in detail the work that remains to be done. We hope that this will provide an incentive to future researchers in this area to test our construction and conclusions on the basis of new data. They may, we hope, arrive at new insights of their own and compare them critically with those which we have discovered.

III

An enterprise of this size can obviously not be carried on by a single person. It needs the cooperation of many scholars with different specialisations, hence the format of the volumes in this project consists of various chapters written by different scholars at the request of the editor. We have departed from this format in a fundamental manner as it was difficult to build a coherent and consistent picture if the usual procedure were to be followed in the preparation of the volume, except perhaps through the introduction, which the editor may have written for the volume concerned. But the introduction can never take the place of the multifarious chapters that constitute the main body of the book. We decided to take upon ourselves the entire responsibility for presenting the full picture as we saw it ourselves. But as no one can satisfactorily render the material relating to so many disciplines, we also had to request specialists to give us their pictures of developments in their areas. But there was a radical difference between the approach we adopted and the approach of the editors of most of the other volumes in the project. We not only indicated to the specialists what we wanted them to do with the material but constantly interrogated them with respect to what they wrote about it. This resulted in a continuous give-and-take, a clarification, modification and amendation of what they had written in the first instance. Our continuous questioning and raising of objections made the scholars look at the material again and also search for additional information regarding it as it became clear during the process that things were not as clear-cut as they had assumed when they had sent us their first drafts. The developments in Nyāya, and specially the controversy regarding *saṁsargatā* and *prakāratā*, are a classic example of this. Professor Prahlada Char is a rare scholar who never lost his patience in spite of our repeated questioning of the material that he sent to us in this connection. In fact, the questioning resulted in a joint exploration of the issues, in which others began to take part, and ultimately we discovered that there was a real difference of opinion between reputed scholars. Thus, though we talk of Nyāya, Mīmāṁsā, Vedānta, Sāṁkhya, etc., basically there seem to be only Naiyāyikas, Mīmāṁsakas, Vedāntins or Sāṁkhyans who have their individual, personal ideas about what these so-called schools of Indian philosophy consisted in. There is, no doubt, a fair amount of agreement regarding certain things and also a distinctive approach to the problems that scholars raise and the manner in which they deal with them. But the seeming unanimity and overlapping of views hides important differences which cannot be resolved by reference to any particular text, as the so-called standard texts themselves differ substantially on many issues.

The truth of the matter is that the 'systems' of Indian philosophy are themselves a 'construct' out of innumerable texts that are supposed to articulate their positions, and as these have changed over a period of time and have been written by individual thinkers who had something to say of their own regarding the tenets of the system, they have undergone substantive modifications over time, some of which are openly acknowledged, such as the intrusion of personal God or Īśvara into Nyāya and Mīmāṁsā, while others remain unacknowledged. A close look at developments in various fields of thought from the eighteenth century onwards reveals that thinkers with independent personalities have tried to approach traditional formulations creatively and to make original contributions of their own. Many a time things have been added, or modifications made, which are generally treated as *pariṣkāra* only. But this characterisation is basically self-deceptive, as it often undermines the traditional formulation or takes it in a new and unexpected direction.

The same appears to be true of those who have written in the English language after the coming of the British and have obviously been influenced by the western traditions of philosophising to which they were exposed by their education. This was internationalised so deeply that much of the thinking in

India may be seen as a branching-off and an important development of the western philosophical tradition in a new intellectual and cultural setting. It has not, of course, been seen in this way. There has been much talk of 'Commonwealth' literature but little of new developments in western thought that occurred after its transplantation into Commonwealth countries. Nor has any continuity or development been seen in the successive thinkers of this period, or in their interaction with traditional learning in the areas they were writing about. This aspect, though highlighted, wherever it struck us could not be examined in detail. A lot, thus, remains to be done, and we have focussed attention on this for the benefit of those who may be concerned with exploring it further.

It is difficult to imagine how a work of this magnitude could ever have taken its present shape without the scholarly contributions of Professors Prahalada Char and Kutumba Shastri, Sri Thangaswami Sarma, Shri Kishornath Jha, Shri K.T. Pandurangi and others. All of them have continuously given guidance without which the volume was not possible. Professor Prahlada Char's articles on Kroḍapatra and on the developments in Nyāya from the eighteenth century onwards form an important part of this volume. Professor Kutumba Shastri has written on the arguments given by Pt. Anantakrisna Shastri in his *Ṣatbhūṣaṇī and Advaitatattva Sudhā* wherein has been refuted the criticism of *Vedāntadeśika* in his *Ṣaṭdūṣaṇī* and of Jayatīrtha in his *Nyāya Sudhā*, respectively. Pt. Thangaswami Sarma wrote for us a basic paper on developments in Mīmāṁsā from the eighteenth century onwards and Pt. Kishornath Jha wrote, at our request, a long piece on the contribution of Bachcha Jha to developments in Nyāya in the early twentieth century. The said paper gave rise to a long debate seeking clarification regarding the concepts of *saṁsargatā* and *prakāratā* and the respective positions of Jagdīśa and Gadādhara on these. Later, Dr Acyutanand Das joined the controversy with his own contribution. The triangular discussion between these scholars gave us 'outsiders' a surprisingly intimate view of the internal tensions in the understanding of Nyāya among those who are regarded as 'specialists' on the subject. I must confess, though, that I find myself still undecided about the issue in spite of the repeated attempts of Professor Prahlada Char to clarify it and satisfy my doubts regarding their views concerning this. Similarly, very few scholars really understand the Kroḍapatras, and even those who do have hardly taken note of all the Kroḍapatras that are available. My response to Professor Prahlada Char's excellent but difficult piece on the Kroḍapatras evoked an angry response from Professor N.S. Dravid while Professor V.N. Jha, who had seen it earlier in manuscript form, simply said that I did not understand the 'Nyāya position' at all.[7] I, of course, have yet to be convinced but, ultimately, it is not a question of what the Nyāya position is but whether, however it may be formulated, it is adequate and can be sustained against objections that are philosophically relevant and important. Also, the question is not one of who is right or wrong, but how the thinking itself becomes clarified through the process of incessant questioning, that raises new possibilities for thinking on the subject which were not seen before.

The debate between the Advaitin and the non-Advaitin, as exemplified in the work of Pt. Anantakrishna Shastri, revealed another facet of the same issue. Most scholars identify themselves with one or the other sampradāya and hence can seldom see the importance of the points being made independently of the context in which they are advanced.

As for the other participants in this long debate, we could find hardly anybody to undertake the difficult task of scrutinising closely the texts for the arguments and counter-arguments given in them.

Regarding the other schools of Indian philosophy, we had the good fortune of getting a piece from Pt. Thangaswami Sarma on developments in Mīmāṁsā from the eighteenth century onwards, which provided us with the main basis for our reconstruction of contributions made to Mīmāṁsā during this period. The volume on Sāṁkhya in the *Encyclopedia of Indian Philosophies*, as pointed out earlier, provided us with the basis for our own construction which, however, departs substantially from it and breathes a different spirit. But we were surprised to learn that even Professor Ramashankar Bhattacharya, one of the editors of the volume, did not quite agree with the way Sāṁkhya was presented in it. There were many others who seemed to have a different idea of Sāṁkhya, giving some support to our view that each scholar has his/her own version of the particular school of Indian philosophy in which he/she has specialised, and that the so-called general picture is only the one that is repeated in textbooks on the subject. But this hardly affected the picture of developments in Sāṁkhya from the eighteenth century onwards, as none of the scholars seems to have been interested in that period or in what was happening amongst Sāṁkhyan thinkers then.

Apart from the contributions of the scholars whose names we have mentioned (see appendices), we have had the good fortune of getting information/ assistance at the right time from diverse sources convincing us that there were 'transcendental forces' helping us in our work on the project even though it appears irrational to believe in them. The monograph of Siva Kumar Swamy on developments in Alaṁkāra Śāstra thus arrived just when we had despaired of finding any material on the subject relating to the period we were covering. Only a little earlier we had been told by Professor Radhavallabh Tripathi of Sagar University about a book in Hindi on the subject which with great difficulty we subsequently procured from the author himself. Similarly, our attention was drawn to the lectures of Pt. Omkaranath Thakur by Dr Mukund Lath, who had learnt of them during a visit to Banaras. We discovered that the lectures were in Gujarati, and it was only when Jyotsna Milan, a well-known writer and a personal friend, agreed to translate them that we became aware of their relevance to the work that we were engaged in. We could multiply the instances further. It was only in response to a chance remark in a letter, for example, that Professor Navjivan Rastogi, the well-known scholar on Kashmir Śaivism, brought to our attention the work of Sankara Chaitanya Bharati, who had discussed Abhinava-gupta's position and refuted it from the Advaitic point of view.

The story of this book would not be complete without mention of the Bangalore seminar on "Creative development of Indian philosophy during the nineteenth and twentieth centuries", which was organised by Professors K.T. Pandurangi and Prahlada Char in August 1995 with such meticulous precision. Almost all the papers that were presented there, both in English and in Sanskrit, helped us in carrying our work further in a way which would have been inconceivable in their absence. These papers have since been bound and made available by the Indian Council of Philosophical Research. The very titles of the papers would be sufficient to give an idea of the wide range of topics covered therein. Besides general reviews of works in the fields of Nyāya, Pūrvamīmāṁsā and Dvaita Vedānta, there were several papers on important individual works and commentaries written in the period by well known Paṇḍits such as Abhyankar Vasudeva Shastri, Vijayendratirtha, Ramanuja Tatacharya, Satyapramodatirtha, Uttamurvira Raghavacharya, and several others. As for the participants in the seminar, these included some of the most outstanding Paṇḍits in the field who were available in the country: Shri R. Thangaswami Sarma, Dr V.N. Jha, Dr U.N. Shaulhag, Shri Ramanuja Tatacharya, Dr Ujjvala Pannse, Dr S. Revthi, Shri P.S. Sheshgiri Rao, to name but a few of them.

A research project of this nature requires continuous information and access to reference material of all kinds and, luckily for us, Dr S.C. Biswas, one of the foremost librarians of the country, was always there to help us in this regard. As has been that of others who helped to get us photocopies of material scattered in different libraries all over the world. The help that Professor R.S. Bhatnagar extended in connection with the part of the work dealing with modern philosophy was of a radically different kind, as it practically meant reading through the Presidential Addresses to the Indian Philosophical Conference which had, again, by a strange coincidence, been brought together and published by Professor S.C. Dube of Jabalpur University just as our work was being finalised. Professor Bhatnagar not merely accepted our request to make a brief summary of each Presidential Address published in the four volumes, but did the job so thoroughly that just by reading the summary one could feel the strength of the insights presented in the original address, before one turned to that for more details and clarification. This difficult job was undertaken by Professor Bhatnagar who is a rare person, in not only performing this task for us but doing it with a love, affection, concern and commitment which he alone can combine in his personality.

No scholar, howsoever eminent, can by himself accomplish a work of this kind. One needs a lot of what can only be called scholarly infrastructural support without which little can be really achieved. Dr Rashmi Patni, Dr Francine Krishna and Shri D.D. Mathur too stand out in this connection for having provided scholarly support. Rashmi has been associated with this project since its beginning six years ago. Her commitment and dedication to the spirit of this project has been truly amazing. In fact, few persons, would have been able to devote so much of their time, energy and patience to considering the multifarious and unsuspected directions in which the project unfolded over all these years. Perhaps it is her interest in history, for she is a professional historian, being an Associate Professor in the Department of History in the University of Rajasthan, that has sustained her involvement in this work over so long a period.

Francine has been associated with almost everything I wrote and in scrutinising each line and word that was written, she pointed out with meticulous care ambiguities and inadequacies in the formulations so that they could be rewritten with greater clarity and simplicity. She ensured that nothing was missing, not even the bibliographical references that I always find hard to take care of.

Shri D.D. Mathur has assisted me for so long now that it is difficult to say what I would have done if he had not been there. The enormous correspondence that the work has entailed has been taken care of by him, and he alone has kept the record of correspondence with scholars scattered all over the country. In the last stages of the work, Rachana Sharma also helped in editing this volume.

Finally, Dr Mukund Lath has continually stood behind us and helped us with all the work that we have done during this period. Apart from his generous devotion of time his amazing interest in almost all fields of learning combined with a knowledge of the Sanskrit language made him a perennial source for information and clarification on any issue in the wide range of disciplines that we have covered in this volume. His help and advice has always been invaluable, and perhaps there is not a single page of this volume which has not benefited from what he has said directly or indirectly.

Long work on a project of this kind inevitably throws up directions which sometimes are only tangentially related to it. Much has been written during this period which may be considered as having arisen from our concerns in this volume. The volume entitled *Prolegomena to Any Future Historiography of Cultures and Civilisations* was directly concerned with the writing of this volume and has already been published under the auspicies of the Project. Other publications such as *Indian Philosophy: A New Approach* and *Problematic and Conceptual Structure of Classical Indian Thought about Man, Society and Polity* have also arisen partly as a result of our involvement in the project. So also the numerous articles which have been written in response to the questions which have arisen during work on the project. Besides these, there still remain a very large number of questions that demand answers but which we have not been able to attend to for one reason or another. Many of the more important ones are mentioned in the chapter devoted to this subject, and it is hoped that others will take up the endeavour from where we have left it. We wish them luck and hope that they will have learnt something from the achievements and deficiencies of this volume, which attempted the writing of a new type of history. How professional historians will respond to this effort is difficult to say. But new departures are generally not welcome and intellectuals, as a class, happen to be as 'conservative' as anyone else. Perhaps I was 'saved' from the usual traditions of history writing as I was never trained as a historian and, even in the field of philosophy, I have been an 'outsider' as I have not belonged to any 'school', whether modern or traditional. I have been, if anything, a 'thinker' at large for whom the activity of 'thinking' has always been more important than the products of that activity, and hence, have always questioned the obvious, so easily accepted by most. My encounter with 'history', or rather, the practice of historical writing, fortunately or unfortunately, is of the same character evident in the other subjects/topics on which I have written. Let the reader or the student, unencumbered with the 'prejudices' of the past, judge for himself/herself whether or not the departure from the traditional way of writing history has been successful.

NOTES AND REFERENCES

1. Krishna, Daya. 1996. Potter's New Bibliography of Indian Philosophy: One Step Forward and Three Steps Backwards. *Journal of Indian Council of Philosophical Research*, XIII(3) (May–August): 162–68.
2. Potter, Karl H. 1997. Reply to Daya Krishna's Review of Bibliography of Indian Philosophies. *JICPR*, XV(1) (Sept.–Dec.): 120–22, and Daya Krishna. Potter's Clarification—Does It Change the Situation. in the same issue of the *JICPR*, XV(1): (Sept.–Dec): 123–125.
3. (i) Sarma, R. Thangaswami. 1980. *A Bibliographical Survey of Advaita Vedānta*, University of Madras.
   (ii) ——— 1985. *Darśanamañjarī, Annals of Oriental Research*, University of Madras.
   (iii) ——— 1998. *Mīmāṁsāmañjarī*, Delhi, ICPR, 1998.
4. Joshi, Laxman Shastri, ed., *Dharmakośa.*
5. Srivastava, A.K. 1990. *Adhunika Sanskrit Kavyashastra*, Delhi.
6. Swamy, Siva Kumar, 1998. *Alaṁkāraśāstra in the Post-Jagannātha Period*, Unpublished Monograph.
7. For this discussion see D. Prahlada Char, On the Kroḍapatras: A Brief Discussion of Some of the Issues Contained in This New Genre of Philosophical Writing in India, *JICPR*, XIV(3) (May–August 1997): 99–119, on which I published my comments: Have the Neo-Naiyāyikas been leading us up the garden path?, along with the comments of V.N. Jha, in *JICPR*, XV(3) (May–August 1998), 121–141. Professor Prahlada Char's reply to my comment is contained in the same issue of *JICPR*, p. 141.

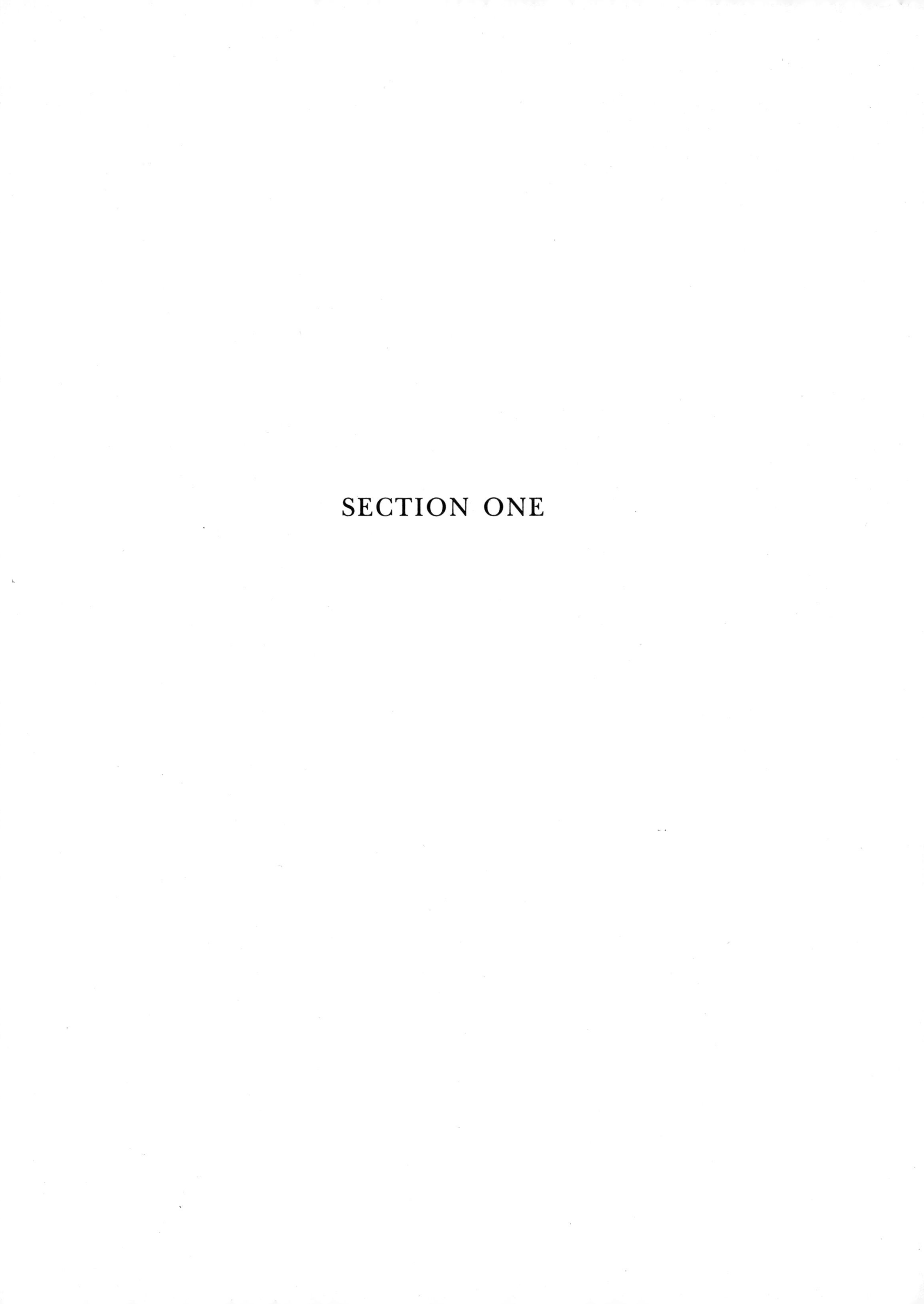

SECTION ONE

CHAPTER 1

Background to Developments in Traditional Indian Thought from Eighteenth Century Onwards

The eighteenth century constitutes no significant break in the intellectual history of India, especially in the development of traditions of philosophising which were prevalent before it and which had had a continuous growth at least from the time of Śamkara. If any break can be perceived in this continuity it came around A.D. 1200 when Nālanda was destroyed by Bakhtiyar Khilji, resulting in the disappearance of Buddhists from the philosophical scene in India. The disappearance of Buddhism is usually ascribed to Śaṁkara, even though it is well known that Udayana, who came a few centuries later, boasted that had he not been there to save the existence of God from the attacks of the Buddhists, HE would perhaps not have been there. Yet even Udayana's boast was premature as the Buddhists continued to flourish until A.D. 1200 and the last Buddhist thinker in India mentioned in Potter's bibliography in his *Encyclopedia of Indian Philosophies* is dated at A.D. 1250.

It is not quite clear why the destruction of Nālandā, the international intellectual centre of the Buddhists should have resulted in the disappearance of Buddhism from India, particularly when all the non-Buddhist schools continued to flourish even in regions which were politically dominated by Muslim rulers. Yet, though there is some evidence of the shifting of Buddhist intellectual activity to Tibet and other places outside India, there is little doubt that it ceased to be a living presence on the Indian philosophical scene. As a result, the Buddhist arguments and positions which had dominated the philosophical scene in India at least from B.C. 200 onwards, were almost totally forgotten. If one remembers the number and quality of Buddhist thinkers during this fourteen hundred year period, one is surprised at how scholar after scholar who has written on the history of Indian philosophy has failed to place Buddhism at the centre of his presentation. Instead Buddhism has been treated mainly in the context of its opposition to the so-called orthodox schools of Indian philosophy, which are placed centre stage.

However, with the disappearance of Buddhism in A.D. 1200, the stage was set for another intense debate. This consisted in interaction and the development of those schools of Indian philosophy which self-consciously prided themselves on being within the Vedic tradition, that was somehow regarded as 'orthodox'. Surprisingly, thinkers of the other great Śramaṇa tradition which, in a certain sense, was even older than Buddhism, seem to have never been taken seriously by any of the great traditions of philosophising in India, including that of the Buddhists. Though Jainism produced great thinkers, and from Kunda-Kunda (A.D. 200) onwards, there was no dearth of outstanding Jaina philosophers, they did not make the impact which they should have made considering both the quantity and the quality of the philosophical work they produced. Potter's bibliography lists ninety-two Jaina thinkers until A.D. 1250, which is a large number, only less than that of the Buddhists during this period. With the Buddhist's disappearance from the scene in A.D. 1250, the Jainas seemed to have gained momentum between A.D. 1250 and 1750, when there were about seventy-six thinkers, an average of fifteen thinkers per century, while in the earlier period covering about eleven hundred years the average was around eight.

The eighteenth century is seen as providing a significant dividing line for the development of philosophical enterprise in India. This division can be traced mainly to political reasons, as Aurangzeb's death in A.D. 1707 is supposed to have led to the decline of the Mughal rule, just as the consolidation of this rule under Akbar is said to have inaugurated the glorious period of the Mughals.. But as far as philosophical traditions were concerned, there seems to have been no influence at all traceable either to the Mughals or the earlier Turkish and Afghan rulers in this country. If one reads the philosophical texts produced from A.D. 1200 onwards, or even from A.D. 1000 onwards, when Mahmud Ghazni invaded northern India, one would hardly be aware of the great political changes that were taking place in northern India during this period. The philosophical dividing line, then, has to be seen in a different way from the political dividing lines which until now have dominated the writing of Indian history and its periodization into ancient, medieval and modern.

The development of the philosophical schools in India took a significant turn somewhere around the middle of the tenth century, when Vācaspati Miśra I both summarised and reinterpreted the important philosophical traditions of India centering around Nyāya, Sāṁkhya and Vedānta, and when Udayana (fl. A.D. 984) gave a decidedly theistic turn to Nyāya thought and raised new epistemological issues in the history of that school. Oddly enough, though Vācaspati Miśra I also wrote on Mīmāṁsā and the Yoga Sūtras, his work does not seem to have made any significant contribution to the development of these schools. This is the period which also saw the advent of Yāmunācārya (fl. A.D. 1080), the first great non-Advaitic ācārya who self-consciously argued for the *khilji* of the *āgamic* texts along with those of the Vedas and tried to establish their coordinate authority in the orthodox tradition. His *Āgama-prāmāṇya* is a classic expression of this new attempt to establish the orthodoxy of the non-Vedic tradition in Indian culture, though he still excluded the Buddhists and the Jainas from its purview. Besides Yāmunācārya, it is in this period that Abhinavagupta (fl. 1014) from Kashmir, propounded a new theory of pure consciousness. He saw this as being essentially active rather than purely inactive and passive as had generally been understood both in Sāṁkhya and in Advaita Vedānta. He also brought aesthetic considerations into ontology, which is indeed a rare feature in Indian philosophical thought. The foundations of Śaiva Siddhānta in the South had earlier been laid by Śrīkaṇṭha in A.D. 850,[1] and it seems to have come into its own in the early thirteenth century with Meyakānta Tevar (fl. 1221).

Other traditions of philosophising centred more on a renewed search for what has been called "transgressive sacrality", that is, an attempt to sacralize all those tabooed aspects of life which are normally looked at askance and are condemned by puritans of all sects. This finds expression in the many varieties of Tantra during this period, a development which penetrated not only almost all schools of Indian spirituality but also Buddhism and Jainism, which have been renunciatory traditions *par excellence* in India from very ancient times. The transgressive sacrality embodied in Tāntric practices turns its attention once again to the body and its diverse functions and tries to change the very attitude towards the body, which was either negative in the earlier spiritual traditions or had ignored this to a great extent. The same outlook seems to have prevailed regarding the life of feelings, which had previously been either rejected or ignored in favour of knowledge or of a life of action primarily centred on the notion of *dharma*.

This is also the time of Rāmānujācārya (fl. A.D. 1120), the founder of the Viśiṣṭādvaita school, the first self-conscious non-Advaitic school of interpretation of the Upaniṣads, the *Brahma Sūtra* and the *Gītā*. This school initiated an unending polemic against Śaṁkara's Advaitic position propounded in the early eighth century. The polemic against the Advaitins acquired increasing importance as the Advaitic view became the focus of sustained criticism by all the non-Advaitic schools of Vedāntic interpretation. While Yāmunācārya in A.D. 1080 had argued for the equal authority of the āgamic texts, Rāmānuja and other non-Advaitic ācāryas appear to have accepted the basic authority of the texts in the Vedic tradition and tried to give them an interpretation which was different from that of Śaṁkara. The tradition of non-Advaitic ācāryas, though initiated with Yāmunācārya, that is, in A.D. 1080, really gained its momentum with the appearance of Rāmānuja. Nimabārka, who appears in A.D. 1250, that is, about 130 years after Rāmānuja, seems to have made no noticeable impact on either the religious or the philosophical scene of India. On the other hand, Madhva, who appears forty years after Nimbārka and 160 years after Rāmānuja, made a decisive impact on the philosophical scene as he stood squarely against the notion of Advaita and argued for a radical difference not only between self and God, but also between the self and other selves and between self and nature. He, thus self-consciously stood in complete opposition to Śaṁkara's position in this respect. The last of the great ācāryas, Vallabha (1525), came more than four hundred years after

Rāmānuja and almost 250 years after Madhva. Earlier, in 1014, Abhinavagupta in northern Kashmir had formulated a radically different notion of consciousness, treating its active aspect as an integral part of its very nature. But though he made a decisive impact on the theory of literature, he seems to have had little impact on the philosophical scene of India. He is not even counted among the non-Advaitic Vedāntins as he did not write on the *Brahma Sūtras* or the Upaniṣads, though, surprisingly, he did write a commentary on the *Gītā*, but even that has hardly been noticed in the tradition. It was primarily Madhva and his disciples, along with those belonging to the Rāmānuja school, who entered into an active discussion with the followers of Śaṁkara, resulting in an unending debate between the Advaitin and the non-Advaitin.

Besides the rise of the Advaitic and non-Advaitic schools of philosophy and the debate between them, the AD second millennium also witnessed developments in Nyāya after Udayana which gradually become so striking that they are characterised by all philosophical observers of the scene as something radically different are hence named "Navya Nyāya", a trend which crystallises in Gaṅgeśa (1350). Having assumed a distinctive direction which remained unchanged until modern times. In fact, Udayana calls himself an "*ādhunika*", thus self-consciously contrasting his thought with that of the older Naiyāyikas, including Jayanta, whom he calls "*prācīna*". This has generally not been noticed, but if it were taken seriously, it would require a further distinction to be made not merely between the older or prācīna Nyāya and Navya Nyāya but also between the ādhunika Nyāya of Udayana and the Navya Nyāya which occurs after Gaṅgeśa in the fourteenth century. From Gaṅgeśa to Gadādhara, that is, from A.D. 1350–1650, in a period of three hundred years, we have about sixty-nine thinkers who were totally devoted to carrying this development in new directions so that it not only became successively refined and differentiated but also assumed an analytic power of such magnitude that all other disciplines adopted it for their own purposes. We have, thus an intellectual renaissance in which any cognitive discipline claiming a śāstric status reformulated itself in the light of this new sophisticated technology of precise intellectual discourse almost in the same way as developments in modern logic have affected many areas of philosophical discourse in contemporary times. A still better analogy would be the adoption of mathematical techniques in modern knowledge which aspires to a śāstric, scientific status.

Besides this, there is fair evidence of increasing specialisation in the treatment of philosophical issues. This appears to be most evident in the independent monographs on *vyutpattivāda, śaktivāda, sādṛśyavāda, muktivāda,* etc. written by Gadādhara himself. He has even written an independent text on Mīmāṁsā entitled, *Vidhi Svarūpa Vicāra.* This tendency to deal with important topics in a self-contained manner is so prominent that even his well-known commentary on the work of Raghunātha Śiromaṇi is viewed as important contribution to such topics as *viṣayatāvāda, prāmāṇyavāda, pratibandhakatāvāda,* and *avayava prakaraṇa,* edited and published independently of the original text of which they formed a part. The emergence of a new genre of philosophical writing called the *Kroḍapatras* also attests to this tendency. The first *Kroḍapatra*, according to Potter's bibliography, was supposed to have been written in 1660 by Dinakara,[2] though the fashion did not appear to have caught on until later. This new style of philosophical writing became more frequent as people started elaborating on specific topics, presumably for their students, though their works seem to have become well known also among scholars of the subject.

Earlier, different traditions on the interpretation of the basic texts of both Advaita Vedānta and Mīmāṁsā had developed. According to Thangaswami Sarma, there were separate traditions of commentaries on the *Tattva Cintāmaṇi*, such as: (i) the *Ālok* tradition, in which at least thirty-one works are mentioned;[3] or (ii) the *Dīdhiti* tradition, started by Raghunātha Śiromaṇi (1530), with thirty-two thinkers, including the famous Gadādhara (iii) and also an independent minor tradition of Rucidutta (1510), whose work on the *Tattva Cintāmaṇi* has at least eight commentaries. There are other traditions of understanding the *Tattva Cintāmaṇi*, such as the *Māthurī paramparā* deriving from Mathurānātha (1650), which comprises eight commentaries. Another major tradition relates to the understanding of the *Dīdhiti* tradition and its subdivisions itself. This consists of Jagadīśa's twenty-one works on it. The other tradition of understanding the *Dīdhiti* is that of Bhavānanda (1600),[4] which has six works within it.

Similarly, in the *Advaita paramparā* there is the well-known distinction from Śaṁkara's even disciples, Padmapāda and Sureśvara. Also well-known is the tradition of Vācaspati Miśra I which, at a superficial level seems different from that of Padmapāda and Sureśvara. Yet, while the developments in Advaita Vedānta which have taken place after A.D. 1000 seem primarily to be a response to the criticisms of the non-Advaitic schools of Vedānta, the developments in Nyāya appear to have been more internally determined, particularly in logic and epistemology.

The denial of the reality of difference by the Advaitin thinkers posed a fundamental challenge which the Nyāya thinkers took seriously and responded to, particularly as they were interested in maintaining the plurality and the reality of the world. Śaṁkara Miśra I (1430) remained perhaps the most famous example of this response. His *Bheda Ratnam* seems to have disturbed the Advaitic thinkers considerably, as Madhusūdana Sarasvatī (1570) felt the need to reply to it in his *Advaita Ratna Rakṣānant*. Earlier, as Malla Nārāyaṇācārya (1490) and Nṛsiṁhaśarma (1555) had tried to reply to this attack in their works, *Abheda Ratnam* and *Bheda Dhikkāra*, respectively. It is interesting to note that Madhusūdana Sarasvatī (1570) also felt it necessary to reply to the work of Śaṁkara Miśra in his *Advaita Ratna Rakṣānant*, even though two well-known stalwarts of the Advaita school had already controverted the argument. It is clear that according to Madhusūdana Sarasvatī, the defence of the Advaita position was not satisfactory. The controversy continued, and the Naiyāyikas do not seem to have been overawed by the arguments of Madhusūdana Sarasvatī in spite of his eminence and fame, as borne out by the fact that Viśvanātha Nyāya-siddhānta Pañcānana wrote his *Bheda Siddhi* around A.D. 1640, seventy years after the work of Madhusūdana

Sarasvatī. The debate was continued by Rakhaldas Nyayaratna Bhattacharya (1890), who wrote *Advaita Vāda Khaṇḍana,* and by Panchanana Bhattacharya (1906), who wrote the *Dvaitokti Ratna Mālā.* It is interesting to note that even as late as the end of the nineteenth century and the beginning of the twentieth century we had scholars arguing in Sanskrit against the position of Advaita Vedānta, trying to defend the reality of difference.

The text book picture of the history of Indian philosophy is thus doubly wrong, as the Advaita position continues to be challenged not only by all the non-Advaitic schools of Vedānta but also by the Nyāya School. The situation fluctuates from century to century, but it is fairly clear that the usual picture presented of the total victory of the Advaitin position in the field of Indian philosophy as we approach modern times is highly mistaken. In fact the period from A.D. 1550–1750 sees eighty-seven Advaitin thinkers against eighty-eight non-Advaitin thinkers belonging to the Vedānta schools, and eighty-nine Naiyāyikas who may be assumed to subscribe to non-Advaitin positions. It is true that non-Advaitic Vedāntins include all those who belong to the schools of Madhva, Rāmānuja, Nimbārka and Vallabha and have important differences among themselves, but they are united in rejecting the Advaitic denial of the reality of difference.

The plea for the admission of the reality of difference arises, however, from different motivations amongst the non-Advaitic Vedāntins, on the one hand, and the Naiyāyikas on the other. The non-Advaitic Vedāntin is primarily interested in maintaining the difference between the self and the Lord so that he may preserve the ultimate reality of *bhakti* as a meaningful relationship and thus accept it as a *paramapuruṣārtha* over and above *mokṣa,* or even as a denial of mokṣa. On the other hand, the Naiyāyika is interested in maintaining the difference as he wants to safeguard the plurality and reality of the objects in the world. That is one reason why Gadādhara refuses to accept the definition of *abheda* as the absence of *bheda* or *bhedābhāva,* as *bheda* or difference is the sort of thing which, in the Nyāya framework, can never be absent. It is, to use the Nyāya terminology, a *kevalānvayī.* But Gadādhara did not ask himself how something that is always present can ever be known, as generally knowing, at least at the level of self-consciousness, can only occur when something is sometimes present and sometimes absent in one's experience. That, of course, would imply that neither *kevalānvayī* or *kevalvyatirekī* can ever be known as the one is supposed to be always present while the second is supposed to be always absent. One may, of course, logically postulate them as "possibilities", but one would not be able to find any instance of their exemplification because of the very condition in which knowledge as a self-conscious phenomenon occurs.

Difference is continuously experienced, but then one has to assume that there is not just difference but rather differences, where each particular difference is qualified by the objects in the context of which it is apprehended. The difference of a chair from a table would then be seen as being different from the difference of a chair from, say, a wall. In fact, as difference is a symmetrical relation, to use the terminology of Western logic, it would occur between any two objects which are apprehended through an act of self-consciousness. But if Nyāya analysis is to be believed, then the difference between A and B or, say, between a chair and a table would not be the same as, that between the table and the chair. In other words, though a difference between X and Y necessarily means that there is also a difference between Y and X, it also means that the difference between X and Y is not the same as the one between Y and X. Thus, difference would become some sort of a universal, every specific instance of which would be conditioned and differentiated by the specific *upādhis* under which it would appear.

The situation becomes even more complicated if we remember that the relation of *tādātmya,* as understood in Advaita Vedānta, or even that of *svarūpa sambandha,* is not one of complete identity as is generally accepted in the western tradition formulated by Aristotle in the famous law of identity, exemplified in the statement "A is A". For Nyāya, and perhaps even for Advaita Vedānta, such a statement would be not only inadmissible but also meaningless, as according to them knowledge must give us something new which was not known before. Thus, the Naiyāyika will not accept a statement like "*Ghaṭo Ghaṭaḥ*", as it does not say anything new about the *ghaṭa,* or the pot, which is supposed to be already known as the statement is being made about it. On the other hand, "*nīlo ghaṭaḥ*" is an admissible statement, for it gives us some new information about the *ghaṭa,* telling us that it is blue.

But if this is the common position of both the Advaitin and the Naiyāyika, then we must ask where exactly do they differ in their understanding of the notion of difference. Perhaps a clue may be found in the Advaitins contention that the assertion of difference is the result of a foundational ignorance which obstacle, when removed, clears the way for the apprehension of the non-difference in the two entities which were supposed to be different. This is perhaps the reason why their position is characterised in terms of a negation, that is, *Advaita,* which may be taken as being close to what the Naiyāyikas mean by *abheda.* Further, the way they tried to interpret the three-fold assertion of identity in the well-known three *mahāvākyas* of the Upaniṣad is also similar.

Such an interpretation of the Advaitin position would not really differentiate between what it holds to be the genuine understanding of the notion of '*abheda*' and the way as it is understood by the Naiyayika. In fact, as '*abheda*' is accepted by Gadādhara, it would be interesting to know how his understanding of *abheda* is different from the understanding of the Advaitin. What is required, therefore, is a clear understanding of the notions of identity and difference and of the way they have been understood in different schools of Indian philosophy. Till this is done, we may accept the fact that it was around the notion of 'difference' or '*bheda*' that the great controversy raged between the Advaitins and the non-Advaitic Vedāntins, and between the Advaitins and the Naiyāyikas. It would also be interesting in this regard to examine the way in which the reality of difference was understood by different schools of non-Advaitic Vedānta, by the Mīmāṁsaka and the Sāṁkhyans. Generally, it is the difference between the theories of error as elaborated in various schools of Indian philosophy that has engaged the attention of historians and not their understanding of the notion of difference. But perhaps it is the latter that should be seen as being the heart of the controversy between the Advaitins and the non-Advaitins and all those who do not subscribe to the authority of the *Brahma-Sūtra,* the Upaniṣad, the *Gītā* and the *Śrīmad Bhāgvat.*

The situation, however, is further complicated by the fact that many non-Advaitic schools of Indian philosophy such as Sāṁkhya and Nyāya hold that in the state of liberation there is no awareness of differences. As far as Nyāya is concerned, there is supposed to be no consciousness at all in the state of liberation, while in the case of Sāṁkhya, there is supposed to be a de-identification between the *buddhi* and the *puruṣa* in the state of *kaivalya.* As the *buddhi* is supposed to be the source of discrimination, there can be no awareness in the *puruṣa* of its absolute difference from *prakṛti.* While both positions are very close to that held by Advaita Vedānta, Udayana maintains that the Nyāya concept of liberation is superior to that of Advaita Vedānta which asserts the existence of consciousness in the state of liberation, and as consciousness cannot but be awareness of something, some duality and difference inevitably remains.[5] On the other hand, no one has raised the question as to whether, in the state of *kaivalya,* there is any awareness of *prakṛti* and of its absolute difference from the *puruṣa.* In case it cannot have any such awareness, then how can it be different from Advaitic realisation, which is supposed to be of a similar character? The central issue, of course, is whether one can conceive of consciousness without its being consciousness of something or other. Yet, as both Advaita Vedānta and Īśvara Kṛṣṇa, the author of the *Sāṁkhya Kārikā,*[5] seemed to opt for the view that consciousness in its pure state is devoid of all intentionality, their position with regard to consciousness in the state of liberation cannot be considered to be different. As for Nyāya, its denial of consciousness to *ātman* in the state of liberation seems to be due to the fact that it appears to regard consciousness as an emergent property which arises when certain conditions obtain, a position very close to that of Cārvāka. Though this is the general reason attributed for Nyāya's denial of consciousness in the state of liberation, it does not form a part of Udayana's own formulation, on the basis of which he regards Advaita Vedānta's position regarding liberation as just below that of the Naiyāyika.

Further, even in some schools of non-Advaitic Vedānta a type of ultimate realisation in *bhakti* is postulated, which is known as *sāyujya,* that is, complete identification with the Lord where the reality of "difference" is only provisionally accepted for purposes of *līlā.*

The situation created by the nature of consciousness in the ultimate state of liberation, or rather when it is established in its pure state, seems to have no ontological consequences as almost all thinkers except the Advaitins do not seem to believe that differences in this regard have any consequences for the reality of the world. The world does not become unreal for the Naiyāyika, nor does *prakṛti* become unreal for the Sāṁkhya thinker. Similarly, for the non-Advaitic Vedāntins, it is the *līlā* which is real, and the postulation of the *sāyujya* ideal is mainly a theoretical postulation without any ontological implications. It is only the Advaitin who draw the radical conclusion regarding the "unreality", of the world from his postulation of an undifferentiated consciousness as the ultimate state in terms of which liberation or *mokṣa* is to be conceived. This, perhaps, is also the reason why opponents of Advaita Vedānta tried to argue for the reality of "difference" while the Advaitins insist on denying it. All concerned seemed to have agreed at least on the negative point that the usual life in the world, even when it was conceived of as the pursuit of ideal values, including *dharma*, could not be conceived of in terms of liberation or *mokṣa*, which was supposed to be the ultimate *puruṣārtha* for all humankind. The difference in the conception of what ultimately the state of *mokṣa* consisted in becomes, then, relatively insignificant when compared with their agreement about this foundational perspective with regard to human life which reduces it to an utter nullity. Even the concept of *līlā* makes a mockery of the seriousness of human pursuits, including all the genuine *dharma saṁkaṭa* or moral dilemmas in which one becomes necessarily involved in human life. Also, as it is only in *asaṁprajñāt samādhi* that consciousness is supposed to lose or transcend all differentiated awareness, the differences in the conceptions of the state of liberation are, for all practical purposes, basically only marginal in character. The same seems to be the case so far as the debate around the possibility of *jīvana mukti* is concerned, that is, whether one can attain complete liberation while being alive or whether one has to give up the body in order to attain the final state of liberation.

Yet, just as Buddhism by its insistent denial of the reality of substances, universals, wholes and unities, had provided a continuous challenge to all philosophical schools in India during the first 1500 years of philosophising in this country, so also it may be said that Advaita Vedānta, with its persistent denial of the reality of all "difference", provided a continuous challenge to all schools of Indian philosophy in the second millennium A.D.

While developments in Indian philosophy that occurred in the first and second millenniums A.D. may be seen in terms of this framework, there can be little doubt that many other developments arose from an internal necessity as thinkers sorted out various inconsistencies or removed the weaknesses and incompleteness in the systems. The direction of development was thus determined both internally and externally, in each school of classical Indian philosophy in any particular period in its history. In addition, tension provided by the larger socio-political context which generally functioned as a facilitating or obstructing environment for the pursuit of these philosophical concerns, which had achieved a relatively autonomous intellectual life of their own cannot be disregarded.

This may be apparent in terms of changes in socio-political structures that often led to the migration of scholars from one area to another due to the emergence of new centres of power and patronage as well as the desire to seek more congenial environments for philosophic pursuits. The emergence of regional, national and even international centres of learning need to be investigated and their history traced during these two thousand years of India's intellectual life. Moreover, as the philosophical development of the various schools of Indian philosophy were closely linked, at least in certain cases, to religious and spiritual sects, understanding their linkage to the history and location of their particular sect will be rewarding. This seems to have taken place particularly in the case of various schools of Vedānta. In the second millennium A.D. were already established the well-known *maṭhas,* of Śaṁkara in the four corners of India, though not much is known of their history before a certain period. Though Śaṁkara had come from Kerala in the extreme south-west of India, but he is not associated with that region in any pre-eminent manner. The Advaita school of philosophy which he founded does not seem to have any special place where it was pursued, though it may be assumed that the four centres founded by him must have continued this tradition to the extent that they functioned effectively. Their very location in the so-called four corners of India must have assured a pan-Indian identity for his thought which would have had institutional support of the strongest kind. However, this hypothesis, even though it has a strong presumption in its favour, is hardly backed by the fact that Advaita Vedānta does not show any significant spread or growth for centuries after Śaṁkara and seems to come into its own only after the disappearance of Buddhism in A.D. 1200 after the destruction of Nālandā. There seems *prima facie* evidence that the more active institutions of Advaitic thinking were located in the south rather than in the east, west or north. Neither Puri nor Dwaraka ever became known for contribution to Advaita.

In the south, each of the great Vedāntic ācāryas of the non-Advaitic persuasion from Yāmunācārya onwards, established a separate institution for the propagation of the unique interpretation of philosophy founded in the Upaniṣads and the *Brahma Sūtras.* Śaṁkara had proclaimed these texts as the source of true "orthodox" philosophy in the Vedic tradition and, along with the *Gītā*, these came to be mistakenly known as the "*prasthānatrayī*", that is, the foundational sources of all philosophy in India. The myth of the "*prasthānatrayī*" is evident not only in that there were no sources of authority for the non-Vedāntic schools of philosophy in India, but that many of the non-Advaitic founders of the Vedāntic schools did not comment on all of them to establish that their views were in accordance with these three basic texts of 'orthodox' philosophising. It was hardly noticed by many that even Śaṁkara rejected the claim of the *Gītā* to be considered as an *Upaniṣad* and gave it only the status of an important *smṛti* text and not a *śruti* proper. Strangely, hardly anyone seems to have noticed that the claims for the *Gītā* to be considered not only as an *Upaniṣad* but also as a text that propounds the essential doctrine of the *Upaniṣads,* was also a competing claim to that made by the *Brahma Sūtras.* The relation between the *Brahma Sūtras* and the *Gītā* with respect to the classical Upaniṣadic texts has seldom been the subject of investigation. Nor has it been seen as to how the two attempt to give a unified picture of Upaniṣadic thought, and what aspects are emphasised by each in this enterprise. It would be interesting to find those aspects of Upaniṣadic thought which have been ignored or underplayed by both the *Brahma Sūtras* and the *Gītā* and to highlight them in order to find what aspects seemed unacceptable or unpalatable to the authors of these works. The myth of the *prasthānatrayī* has been perpetuated not only by ignoring the fact that none of the non-Vedāntic schools accepts the authority of these texts as well as the fact that there are important non-Advaitic thinkers who do not comment on all of them. Moreover, many of them accept the equal and even over-riding authority of texts such as the *Śrīmad Bhāgvat,* thus completely subverting the notion that the foundational texts were the only three mentioned in the list.

The establishment of institutions of non-Advaitic Vedānta in the south implied that the debate between the Advaitin and the non-Advaitin was confined primarily to this region of India, specially as Rāmānuja in his *Śrībhāṣya* had started the tradition of controverting the Advaita position in detail after expounding it in his well-known *Pūrvapakṣa.* Similarly, the strong defence of five radical differences by Madhva, between god and soul, soul and soul, soul and nature, god and nature and perhaps between one natural object and another, in his *Aṇubhāṣya* and other works, provided the dynamic motif for the debate between the Advaitins, who denied all difference, and the followers of Madhva, who had to assert the reality of difference at all levels. The arguments of Rāmānuja were carried further by Vedāntadeśika (1330), whose *Ṣaḍdūṣaṇī* was one of the strongest attacks on the Advaita position.

Madhva's challenge to Advaita, on the other hand, was perpetuated by Jayatīrtha (1370) in his six-volume work, the *Nyāya Sudhā,* which treats encyclopaedically all the important philosophical issues of his time, and by Vyāsatīrtha II (1535), who in his *Nyāyāmṛta* launched an attack on the Advaita position which became doubly famous because of Madhusūdana Sarasvatī's point-by-point reply to it in his *Advaitasiddhi.*

Mainly confined to the south, these debates were primarily motivated by sectarian commitments. As far as I know, no comparative study of the arguments and counter-arguments in the debate has been made from a purely philosophical point of view by one affiliated to any *saṁpradāya.* It would be interesting, for example, to compare the arguments given by Vedantadeśika, on the one hand, and Jayatīrtha and Vyasatīrtha II on the other, against the Advaitic position.

As against these *sāmpradāyika* controversies, the attack by Nyāya thinkers on the Advaitic position seems to have been motivated purely by philosophical considerations as the Naiyāyikas did not have a *saṁpradāya* or an *ācārya* in the same sense as did the non-Advaitic Vedāntins, as this school of philosophy was not associated with any *sādhanā* for the realisation of the *nīḥśreyasa* or *apavarga,* though this had certainly been talked about in the *Nyāya Sūtras* as also by Udayana and Gaṅgeśa. The attack on the Advaita position by Śaṁkara Miśra (1430) in his *Bhedaratna* was thus a purer philosophical critique than that of Vedāntadeśika, Jayatīrtha and Vyāsatīrtha II coming, as was to be expected, from outside the southern zone where the Vedāntic schools flourished. Śaṁkara Miśra came from eastern India, where Nyāya had flourished in Bengal and Bihar for a long time. However, as far as we know, no one has made a comparative study of the arguments given in the *Advaita Siddhi* and those that Vyāsatīrtha II advanced in his *Nyāyāmṛta* or the ones given in *Advaitaratna Rakṣaṇam* and those given by Śaṁkara Miśra in his *Bhedaratnam.* Śaṁkara Miśra's arguments were replied to by Madhusūdana Sarasvatī in his *Advaitaratna Rakṣaṇam.* It is strange that Madhusūdana Sarasvatī, who was so philosophically sensitive to arguments made against the Advaita position by earlier thinkers, did not take into account Vedāntadeśika's work, *Ṣaḍdūṣaṇī.* It is also not clear whether the work of Śaṁkara Miśra was used by thinkers of the Rāmānuja and the *Madhva sampradāya* in their polemics against Advaita, or, for that matter, what were the exact differences between the arguments given by Śaṁkara Miśra on the one hand and Vedāntadeśika and Vyāsatīrtha II on the other. However, what is interesting in this controversy between the Naiyāyikas and the Advaitins is that the Naiyāyikas who took part in it were concentrated in the region of Bihar and Bengal, where they enjoyed a long established and unchallenged supremacy.

Mithila and Bengal had already started specialising in Nyāya, at least from the time of Gaṅgeśa. In fact, if the surname Miśra in Vācaspati I's name connotes any regional association, then Mithila may be regarded as having become a centre of learning as early as the tenth century. The status of Bengal and Bihar has to be looked at in particular to learn why the region of Mithila and Bengal became such a powerful centre for the study of Nyāya. All in all, one needs to have an idea not only of the shifting centres of political patronage in India but also in the shifting centres of religion and culture to discover the reason for the clustering of centres of philosophical activity in different parts of the country.

Western India had seen a strong concentration of Jaina thinkers almost from the tenth century, possibly due to the influence of the Gurjar Pratiharas and/or the Solankis. The last of the great thinkers, Yaśovijaya (A.D. 1679) hailed from here but, interestingly, he shows strong influences in his work of both Advaita Vedānta and Nyāya as well as the *Gītā.* The *Vallabha sampradāya* also flourished in Gujarat and Maharashtra and it would be interesting to find whether philosophers belonging to this school were also primarily located in this region.

By contrast, it appears that there were no distinctly recognisable centres in the north. Ujjain and Kannauj must have disappeared much earlier. In any case, while they were great centres of the literary arts in general, they were never strong centres of philosophy, even though Bāṇabhaṭṭa (seventh century A.D.) in his *Harṣacarita* has given descriptions of philosophers belonging to various schools who were located there. Kashmir, which had emerged as an intellectual and philosophical centre in the ninth century, had ceased to be important after 1200.

The philosophical scene after 1200, then was concentrated in the south, east and west, having left northern India, where Islamic rule had firmly entrenched itself and from where, by and large, traditional intellectuals had withdrawn to seek patronage elsewhere. Benaras, of course, continued to be the sole exception, and it retained its all-India character as a pan-Indian authority in intellectual matters, drawing scholars from all over the country. The story of the survival of Benaras as a powerful intellectual centre in an environment which was politically uncongenial has not been written, and it would offer an extremely interesting history of how an intellectual centre survived in a hostile environment for more than a millennium, as clear evidence exists of its overriding intellectual pre-eminence even in the time of Śaṁkara.

Along with this, there occurred the rise of literature in the non-Sanskritic languages of India, which themselves had a long history starting from the time of the Buddha and the Mahāvīra. Pālī, Prākṛit and Apabhraṁśa gradually crystallised into what are now known as the regional languages of India. Tamil, of course, is the oldest of these, and has perhaps had the earliest grammar after the one formulated by Pāṇini for the Sanskrit language. The history of the successive formulations of the grammars of Prākṛt and the various Apabhraṁśa languages, and of the literatures written in them, is an interesting story in itself but, from the philosophical point of view, perhaps the more important point is that except for the Tamil language, no important philosophical work seems to have been written in any of them. The literature of the non-Sanskritic languages of India was generally either confined to translations or to a reworking of stories and themes already dealt with in the writings in Sanskrit, or else concentrated on devotional themes relating to the major gods or goddesses of epic mythology such as Rāma, Kṛṣṇa, Śiva and Śakti. Oddly enough, while Sanskrit literature in general and philosophical literature in particular does not seem to reflect the changing socio-political situation in the country, literature in the non-Sanskritic languages definitely does so. Perhaps for such a reflection in the Sanskrit literature, one would have to go to the Smṛti and Vyavahāra texts, which deal with questions of law and thus have inevitably to deal with changes occurring in society and polity as they directly affect the settling of legal disputes between those who seek justice from the courts.

The relations between such languages of the south as Telugu, Kannada and Malayalam, which emerged later, and Tamil has not been the subject of much investigation, nor has been the relation between these other languages and the cultures of the people who spoke them. The term 'south', though generally used from ancient times, should be treated in a more differentiated manner as there is a distinct difference between the Tamil region, which has a long history of language and culture from Graeco-Christian times, and other regions which are today known as Andhra, Karnataka and Kerala. There are reasons to think that there was a distinct difference between the relation of Tamil to Sanskrit and the relation of the other languages of the south to Sanskrit. Tamil, being an older language with a rich literary culture of its own, had an ambiguous relationship with Sanskrit, which was the pan-Indian language of intellectual and cultural discourse at least from the time of Pāṇini Kātyāyana, the first commentator on Pāṇini's work and also his critic, seems to have been from the south and perhaps symbolises this relationship, which had some sort of an in-built tension in it. However, the story of this relationship has, as far as I know, seldom been apparent except in recent times, when orthodox lovers of Tamil have tried to purge it of all Sanskritic mixtures and have claimed for their language and culture a pre-Aryan or a non-Aryan purity, bringing the suppressed or subterranean hostility into the open. Some indirect evidence of an ambivalent relationship between Tamil and Sanskrit in earlier times also exists particularly in the development of a mixed language consisting of Tamil and a variety of Sanskrit termed "Maṇipravāla", in which some significant literature is said to have been produced. A related development is that of what has come to be called the "Ubhaya Vedānta", that is, Vedānta in both Sanskrit and Tamil, the great exemplar of which is said to have been Vedāntadeśika himself, who wrote in both languages.

Besides these instances, attention has recently been drawn to the work of Maṇvāla (thirteenth century) and Lokācārya Pillai, who are said to have interpreted the well-known works of the Ālvārs, specially the work of Nammālvār. These presented an opposition to the traditional four Vedas of the Sanskritic tradition, and contrasted the religion of the Sanskritic Vedas with that of the Tamil Veda, emphasising that while the former conceived of man in terms of *varṇa* and *dharma* (consisting in the performance of Vedic rituals, the supremacy of Brahmins, etc.), the Tamil Veda rejected this and conceived of man in terms of his inner impulses and relationship with Lord Viśṇu. This interpretation of the vedas did not accept the *varṇa* division and the social hierarchy implicit in it or the supremacy of Brahmins, both of which were so central to the orthodox religious tradition deriving from the Vedas.

That the developments well-known in *bhakti* took place in the Tamil region or that the *Śrīmad Bhāgvata* was composed in the south are a commonplace of the north. *Bhakti* was brought to north by Ramānanda. It has recently been argued by Wilhelm Hardy that the intense emotional *bhakti* which thrives on separation, arose and grew in the south and was later transported to other parts of India.[6] He has called it '*virahabhakti*'. However, emotion became a passion only in Bengal, where Chaitanya took it to its climax and his disciples, Jīva and Rūpa Gosvāmī, developed its philosophical aspects and gave it the intellectual grounding it had lacked. It is of course true that all the great non-Advaitic *ācāryas* had given some sort of intellectual formulation and foundation to the pursuit of *bhakti* as a path of realisation, but the relations between their formulations and those of the Chaitanya school do not seem to have been investigated. Even Śaṁkara, the great Advaitic ācārya belonging to the early part of the eighth century, who composed hymns possessing great intensity of feeling and emotion in praise of various gods and goddesses does not seem to have given it a place alongside, let alone above *jñāna* in his system. That *Bhagvad Gītā*, itself was commented upon by Saṁkara is noteworthy as his is supposed to be, at least in parts, a foundational text devoted to the pursuit of the path of *bhakti* as a means to ultimate realisation.

Just as there is a fundamental difference between the Tamil region and all the other regions in peninsula of India, Kerala too is significantly distinct. Being cut off from the rest of southern India by the Western Ghats, this geographical barrier has given Kerala a cultural distinctiveness and a development in relative isolation from the rest of the south. Similarly, one should distinguish between the region now known as Karnataka, which comprises Mysore, and other neighbouring areas which were once the centre of the Vijayanagar Empire lasting as late as A.D. 1565 and where, even after the collapse of this empire, the Naiyāyikas ruled for quite some time. The region known today as Andhra is, by contrast, more in contact with central and western India than the other regions of the south.

In spite of these differences among the four regions comprising southern India, its history has a distinctive character because of certain features which differentiate it from large parts of northern and central India. This unique character was shaped by various factors which have not been paid sufficient attention until now. One among these is the prolonged rule of various dynasties which shared a common cultural and traditional ethos dating back to the earliest period of the recorded history of the sub-continent.

The character of Islam in southern India has been significantly different from that in the north. This was perhaps due to the fact that the Muslims who came to the south by sea were primarily traders while those who came to northern India were military adventurers from north-west Asia. Islamic rule in the south was also more accommodating towards the culture of that region. That Aurangzeb, when he planned to conquer the south, wanted to get a *fatwa* for his attack as, in his view, it was almost a *jihad* against the unbelievers is evidence of this. The *fatwa* was refused, but the fact that he made this charge against the Muslim rulers of the south speaks volumes for the differences in the style and the spirit of governance that determined life in the two regions. An interesting divergence and even some sort of hostility in the way the ruling Muslim elite of north India perceived the Muslims in the south must have existed. Most of the rulers in north India traced their descent from the great ruling houses of central and west Asia, and it is well-known that, in innumerable paintings Akbar and Jahangir showed themselves as descendants of Timur, the legendary figure from that region who had conquered the "world" of those times. On the other hand, Andre Wink recalls in his well-known book *Al Hind*, that the Muslims of south India considered themselves to be 'purer' than those of the north. Further as Hindu kingdoms in the south had ruled continuously for a long time and many of them, as in the case of the Vijayanagar Empire, self-consciously thought of themselves as carrying on the great cultural and intellectual traditions which derived from Vedic times, this ensured that a substantial pursuit of traditional learning went on in this region. Sayaṇa and Madhva are well known example, as is Vidyāraṇya, but there must have been many others whose stories are not so well known. The history of the renaissance of traditional learning under the Vijayanagar Empire his yet to be written. The sixteenth century was also a significant period for the region now known as Kerala, where there were important astronomical pursuits, as has recently been reported in some scientific journals. There were developments in mathematics and in non-Pāṇinian grammar also which have not yet been studied and evaluated in detail.

The connections of southern India from the earliest times with the other countries of south and south-east Asia were strengthened during the rule of the Cholas (872–1279) and were extended from Ceylon to Indonesia, which must have added another dimension to the consciousness of traditional Indian civilisation in the south as distinct from the way it developed in the north during this period.

However, there are evidence of contact even of the Harappan civilisation with the south, particularly Mysore, as the gold found at Harappan sites appears to have come from the gold mines of Mysore. If this was so, the contact must have been through the coastal route rather than the land route which would have been extremely difficult to traverse in those times. The relations between the Harappans and the Dravidians are a matter of conjecture, but it is significant that from Mauryan times onwards, southern scholarship has been an evidence in the intellectual traditions of India, and the route to Sri Lanka was known to lie through this region. Kātyāyana, the first known critic of Pāṇini, is said to have been from the south, as we have noted earlier. Also Aśoka had sent his son and daughter to preach Buddhism in Sri Lanka. Jaina monks went to the south in large numbers during the period of prolonged famine, and the area around Śravaṇabelagolā was a great centre of Digambara life and thought.

It is surprising that in the east the region known as Orissa today, in spite of its proximity to Bengal, did not have an intellectual centre of any repute though it witnessed great creativity in art and architecture. Similarly, Assam in the extreme eastern part of India did not show any signs of development as an intellectual centre even though it remained independent of Islamic rule and self-consciously boasted about it, as is evidenced by the unique historical documents called *buranjis.*

It appears, therefore, that there was little correlation between artistic, architectural and intellectual creativity in different regions of India, and though the nature of political rule exercised in a particular region played a part in the fostering of traditional intellectual pursuits, this was only one factor among several and had a varying significance depending on the nature of the ruler and on the strength of the intellectual traditions and institutions in the region. The exact nature of the rule at the local level in Bengal and Bihar during the period of Muslim domination is yet to be examined. However, Hindu *zamindars* might have ensured a long flourishing of the Nyāya tradition in this region.

The seventeenth century as noted by several studies was also a period of relative peace and prosperity in large parts of India. Silver and gold poured into India because of the favourable balance of trade in this period is an evidence contrary to the contention of Irfan Habib, which had earlier been uncritically accepted. In any case Bengal, and parts of Bihar, were prosperous regions of the Mughal Empire, and it is well established that this region continued to send regular sums to Delhi even during the early part of the eighteenth century when the relatively weak central power was on the verge of total impotence due to the rising Maratha power and the independence shown by both Muslim and Hindu regional rulers.

The drastic break with the past came in A.D. 1000, when Islamic invasions in the north starting with that of Mahmud Ghaznavi, who repeatedly attacked north India and not only destroyed the famous temple of Somnath in Gujarat but also punished unorthodox followers of Islam in Multan who had allowed the continuance of a sun temple there. Yet, though Al-Baruni said that many of the scholars had fled from north India, it appears that Kashmir remained untouched, as not only apparent from the presence of Abhinavgupta but also because Kashmir Śaivism flourished during this period. The south, on the other hand, did not seem to have been affected very much by the invasions of the north, as the first great *ācārya*, Yāmuna, appeared there in A.D. 1010 and Rāmānuja in A.D. 1120. However, the consolidation of Islamic rule in north India started only around 1192, when Mahmud of Ghur defeated Prithviraj Chauhan. This was almost two hundred years after the invasion of Mahmud Ghaznavi, during which period south India had seen such outstanding dynasties as that of the Cholas, whereas the Gang empire had flourished in Orissa. During this period the rule of the Pals and the Sens in Bengal is recorded. Of the two hundred years in northern and western India, that is, between the invasion of Ghaznavi and that of Mahmud of Ghur, it was in 1279 that Rajendra III, the last king of the Chola dynasty, ceased to reign, and in 1250, that the Sun Temple of Konark was built. Thus, it is only at the end of the thirteenth century, when the Khilji dynasty took over at Delhi, that we can think of the establishment of a firm Islamic rule in India. However, the Khiljis ruled only for thirty years, from 1290 to 1320, and Allauddin Khilji, almost the last Khilji, ruled for only twenty-one years. It was in 1313, just three years before his death, that he marched down to Devagiri in the south and established his suzerainty over the Kakatiyas of Warangal, the Hoysals of Dvarasaumaras and much of the Coromandel coastal region. This so-called suzerainty must have been "notional": it did not last for long since he could have had no time to enforce it. And though his rule in north and central India is supposed to have extended up to Bihar and Tirhut, the situation was difficult because of the repeated Mongol invasions. A firm administration and a cultural presence in an alien civilisation surely requires a longer time interval and a larger time spread than the brief period of 20 years, for which the Khiljis ruled some parts of this country. The Tughlaks who came after them also ruled only for 68 years, and that too mostly in the north. It seems, *prima facie*, that undue importance has been given to these rules around Delhi by Indian historiographers because of Mughal rule which occurred later in history. This is the familiar phenomenon of "retrospective illusions" imposed by the historiography of Indian civilisation, which we also notice in the history of Indian philosophy in the first millennium A.D., where what happened in the second millennium has been read into the earlier material resulting in a topsy-turvy picture of Indian philosophy during that period which highlights minor movements in philosophy and marginalises major trends.[7]

The Sultanate of Madurai's rule from 1334 to 1337 indicates a long and interesting period of Islamic rule in the extreme south while from 1338 there was a separate Sultanate of Bengal. Nevertheless, it is during this very period, that is, from around 1350 onwards, that Mithila and Bengal became great centres of the development of Nyāya with Gaṅgeśa (1350). Around the same time, in 1346, is laid the foundation of the Vijayanagar Empire, while in 1347 Bahman Shah established the Bahmani Sultanate in Central India. In 1370, Vijayanagar conquered the Sultanate of Madurai and, in 1361, Firozeshah Tughlaq invaded Orissa.

The fourteenth century, thus, is perhaps one of the most interesting interregnums in the second millennium A.D. when the political situation is extremely fluid in almost all parts of India. Dynasties succeed dynasties in the north. Independent sultanates begin to rule in Bengal and Madurai. The Vijayanagar Empire came into being, Firozeshah Tughlaq invades Orissa, while Timur devastated Delhi in 1398. In the middle of the century occured the establishment of the Bahmani Kingdom in Central India. The beginning of the fifteenth century saw the establishment of a separate Sultanate of Gujarat, while the Vijayanagar Empire extended itself to the east coast during 1406–1422 and a new dynasty is established by Kapila in Orissa in 1436, which ruled for forty-one years.

The second millennium A.D. witnessed a marked difference between its first and second halves, a difference which has not been noted in the histories of this period, particularly as it relates to the intellectual and cultural creativity of India. There appears to be a distinct difference between that part of India which lies to the north of the Narmada and the part which lies to the south. These southern Kingdoms generally characterised rule which had a cultural continuity with the past and provided a congenial atmosphere for the development of knowledge, art, culture and spirituality deriving from the first millennium A.D. and going back even earlier to the period of the Upaniṣads, the Mahāvīra and the Buddha. The only significant difference was the disappearance of the Buddhists from the intellectual scene after the destruction of Nālandā. However, the Jainas continued to flourish, and as did the pursuits of knowledge, art and culture. Northern India on the other hand was the scene of political instability after the invasion of Ghazni as also of an intermittent but continuous rule by various Islamic dynasties centred around Delhi which, in their different ways, brought a radically new religion to the Indian sub-continent. At the same time, it opened north India to developments that were taking place in the Arab world in the fields of medicine, mathematics, astronomy and other sciences. The period from the tenth to the thirteenth century was extremely rich and creative in diverse fields of knowledge in the Arab world, particularly in the translation of Greek knowledge into Arabic and its subsequent transformation in the hands of the Arabic masters. Moreover, the influence of neo-Platonism, of Plato and of Aristotle, provided a rich background for the contact that was taking place in India in the political realm and thereby secondarily creating an opportunity for such an interchange in diverse fields of knowledge. Developments in art, particularly in architecture, are to be noticed as almost all the Islamic rulers in Delhi are known to have constructed buildings in Delhi and the neighbouring areas, though there is nothing earlier than the Qutub Minar built by Qutubuddin Aibak in 1206 (and evidence is still to be found in Sind and in Ghazni mosques and other buildings built by Muslims who were settled there much earlier).

As for painting, it is well known that Humayun had brought two great masters with him who provided a powerful impetus to Indian painting at the court of Akbar. A rough indication of the interaction in the field of scientific knowledge between the Arab and Persian world and the Delhi-based north Indian world is found in Rahman's Bibliography, which lists works in Arabic, Persian and Sanskrit from the eighth century to the eighteenth in such diverse fields as mathematics, medicine and astronomy. The different dynasties of Islamic rule in the north had, however, come from different parts of West Asia at different times. They must have brought with them memories of the arts and the sciences that flourished there. The scholars and savants who accompanied them would normally have belonged to those disciplines which flourished in West Asia. The history of the developments in West Asian Islam and the developments in science and art and technology which occurred there, are therefore, relevant variables for understanding what exactly was happening in north India during this period. It is noticeable, for example, that a world of difference exists between what the Calipha had written in his famous letter to the representative of Islam in Sind some time in the ninth century and what later conquerors such as Mohammad Ghazni or Ghur felt about the same issue. This implies that a tremendous change had occurred in what Islam stood for in West Asia, the causes of which have not been sufficiently investigated. Besides this, there were parallel movements in the expansion of Islam in this very period both towards the west, right up to Spain and certain East European countries; towards the north in Central Asia, as well as in the south towards North Africa. The expansion in the east was only a small part of what was happening in West Asia and this itself must have been the cause of radical transformations in the nature of Islam during this period.

However, what is most relevant for our purpose is the effect these changes had on the nature of successive periods of Islamic rule in India as well as the opportunities provided thereby for interaction with Arab learning and Persian arts during this period. The differences in the Islamic rule of the north which was marked by relative periods of expansion and contraction during the first five hundred years in existence from the centre in Delhi and the character of Islamic rule in south India particularly starting from the establishment of the Bahmani kingdom in 1347 has already been commented upon. The Bahmani kingdom which is supposed to have ended in 1527, was followed by the successor states of Ahmadnagar, Bijapur, Golkonda, and so on, which defeated the Vijayanagar Empire in 1556. In the last days of his reign, Akbar had moved towards the south, but though he is supposed to have had some initial successes against Ahmadnagar, they do not seem to have been decisive, unlike his conquest of Khandesh, which thereafter came permanently under Mughal rule. The character of the Bahmani kingdom along with that of the successor states needs to be examined and compared with that of the states in north India. Historians need to explore also the character of the Islamic states in the south. Parallels could be drawn with the Hindu kingdoms of Rajasthan, which not only resisted the Islamic rule centred in Delhi and Agra but also kept their relative autonomy and independence during this period. Apart from examining from this perspective, their composition, their places of origin and the character of their rule have the character of any resistance to their rule is also relevant. It is well known, for example, that Shivaji's initial resistance was against the Bijapur ruler and only secondarily to Mughal rule. Were there any other Shivajis in Bijapur, Golkonda and Ahmadnagar after the disappearance of the Vijayanagar Empire? The Nayaks were the successors to the Vijayanagar Empire in the extreme south, but the extent of their kingdom and the character of their rule have to be ascertained.

Moving to the east, we find that the whole of Orissa was under the Gangs from 1077 to 1435. But it was later on under the non-Gang rulers that the Sun Temple in Konark (1250) was built. As far as Orissa was concerned, Islamic rule came with the Mughals while Bengal and Bihar came under Islamic rule (non-Mughals) much earlier in 1338.

Thus, the first half of the second millennium A.D. can be divided into two major periods: one, extending to around 1300, that is, up to the time when substantial parts of eastern India were under non-Muslim rule; and two, that starting with the establishment of Islamic rule in various parts of India at different times in the latter part of the second millennium A.D., starting somewhere around 1500. The establishment of a consolidated Mughal rule in almost the whole of northern, central and western India around 1560, and later extending deep into the south by 1707, at the death of Aurangzeb, was punctuated partly by the rise of the Marathas and also that of the Sikhs and the Jats on the other. The period from 1707 onwards has to be further divided into the period of Maratha and Sikh supremacy, and later, somewhere from the end of the eighteenth century, to the beginning and consolidation of British rule.

Intellectual activity in the second millennium A.D., then, seems to have been primarily centred in southern and eastern India, areas which were further divided into regions where the great debate between the Advaitins and the non-Advaitins took place in south India while those in which the developments in Nyāya occurred were concentrated in parts of Bihar and Bengal. There was another difference in the two regions where specialisation occurred in the field of philosophy, as the philosophical debate around Advaita is closely related to religious and spiritual differences amongst the followers of these different schools of Vedāntic philosophy, while the developments in Nyāya were motivated purely by logical and epistemological considerations, having nothing to do with any spiritual pursuit.

It is, of course, true that Bengal and Bihar also gave rise to the intense emotional *bhakti* of Jayadeva and Caitanya, which led to the philosophical formulations of Jīva Gosvāmī, Rūpa Gosvāmī and others. The intellectual element, however, appears to be weak in the philosophical formulations of the Caitanya school, while it is substantially present in the reflections of the south Indian *ācāryas* and their followers, necessitated perhaps by the intense polemics which continued between them over centuries. The philosophical writings of the Chaitanya school do not appear to have given rise to any tradition of philosophical controversy, presumably because the works in that tradition were not written in refutation of any *pūrvapakṣa* propounded by other thinkers. On the other hand, it would be interesting to discover the differences in the treatment of *bhakti* and the philosophical reflection on it in the works of the southern masters and their disciples; one would like to know the differences in this regard between their treatment of the subject and that of the Bengal school which derived its inspiration from Chaitanya, who himself did not write any philosophical text.

Another neglected aspect of the southern masters of non-Advaita Vedānta starting from Yāmuna onwards exists in that there has not been any serious exploration or study of the differences and debates among the non-Advaitic schools themselves.

The second millennium may be divided into the following periods taking into consideration the political and cultural changes that occurred in India directly or indirectly affecting the intellectual life of the country:

1. From 1000 to 1200.
2. From 1200 to 1560.
3. From 1560 to 1720.
4. From 1720 to 1857.
5. From 1857 to 1947.
6. From 1947 onwards.

An interesting overview of these periods is provided by Potter's *Bibliography* so that a period-wise analysis reveals significant developments in the movements of traditional schools of philosophy.

Accepting provisionally this division of the second millennium, which is primarily based on the changing political situation, during the period 1000–1200 numerically there exist Buddhist thinkers, 43 Jaina thinkers, 6 Advaitins, 8 Mīmāṁsakas, 11 Sāṁkhyans, 4 Viśiṣṭādvaita thinkers, 3 Yoga thinkers, 11 Kashmir Śaiva thinkers, 6 philosophers of Śaiva Siddhānta, 2 Vaiśeṣika thinkers, and 11 Naiyāyikas, and only one thinker in the philosophy of Grammar. Thus, it is noticeable that during this period Jainism suddenly begins to acquire a pre-eminence not present before, as during the whole of the first millennium A.D. it had only 38 thinkers, while in the two hundred years from 1000 to 1200 there are 43. The Advaitins still lag behind almost every school including the Buddhists, who now disappear from the scene. The interesting emergence of the tradition of Kashmir Śaivism, which indicates the powerful presence of Kashmir in the extreme north of India is witnessed. There is also now the perceptible dominance of Nyāya and Sāṁkhya, though they are less prominent than both the Jainas and the Buddhists.

If we take the period from 1200 to 1500, the Jainas continue to predominate, with 56 thinkers being mentioned in Potter's Bibliography; the Advaitins, with only 30 thinkers, are obviously not a significant presence as one would have normally expected. The Nyāya thinkers number as many as the Advaitins. However, if we include those who appear to have made a common contribution to both Nyāya and Vaiśeṣika, the Naiyāyikas outnumber the Advaitins. Visiṣṭādvaita, a philosophy which was a recent entrant in the earlier period, now converts philosophers to its camp, with 11 persons in its fold. Kashmir Śaivism seems to have totally disappeared, perhaps due to the changing political situation in Kashmir. The Buddhists are represented by one lonely straggler who seems to have survived the destruction of Nālandā in 1200. Similarly, the presence of Mīmāṁsā and Sāṁkhya during this period is modest as compared to other schools.

From 1500 to 1700 the clear dominance of Nyāya, with 97 exponents, is followed by Advaita Vedānta thinkers, forming a close second. However, one of the interesting things about this period is the growing popularity of Mīmāṁsā, the number of thinkers in which almost equals the Jainas which school now registers a decline. There is the significant rise of Śuddhādvaita, the school founded by Vallabhācārya, and the noticeable presence of non-Advaitic Vedānta, particularly Dvaita.

The period from 1700 to 1900 is marked by a continued dominance of Nyāya and Advaita Vedānta on the Indian philosophical scene. There is a decline in the number of Jaina thinkers in this period. On the other hand, a slight increase in those who have worked on Sāṁkhya, while the interest in Mīmāṁsā appears to have declined as compared to the earlier period. Surprisingly, this period has fewer thinkers belonging to the Madhva and the Vallabha Schools as against the distinct increase in thinkers belonging to the Visiṣṭādvaita school.

From 1900 onwards, the pre-eminent position of the Nyāya and Advaita Vedānta thinkers continues, and significantly, the Naiyāyikas still dominate. At the same time, the Jainas have improved their position while the Viśiṣṭādvaitins have maintained their lead over Madhva and the Vallabha Vedānta philosophers, though the latter have improved their position.

This brief survey of the relative strengths of various schools of Indian philosophy reveals many interesting facts while posing questions which need to be explored further. For instance, what was the situation regarding the availability of paper in India from the thirteenth century onwards as this has a bearing on the production of manuscripts. Paper technology is said to have been brought to India by the Arabs. Similarly, how did the introduction of printing in India sometime in the late eighteenth century, as also the establishment of educational institutions, affect the production of books. Various institutions of education, both Sanskrit and non-Sanskrit, were established by the British from the nineteenth century onwards. Similarly, the establishment of societies, such as the Royal Asiatic Society, for the discovery and publication of manuscripts in the classical languages of India, may have had a substantial effect on the production of books during this period. It is extremely likely that the new educational system encouraged the production of a large number of books which were purely introductory in character, meant for students. It is true that even earlier such texts were written, which were meant for an easy understanding of the subject for novices. The usual description in Sanskrit for these texts is *bālānām sukhbodhāya.* But it is obvious that these must have been increasingly available in large numbers because of the creation of numerous institutions by the British as well as the facility of printing during this period.

Besides the new climate created by the availability of printing in the country, the setting up of educational institutions by the British and the interest generated in the intellectual and cultural achievements of India due to the emergence of interest in the history of past civilisations in the West, the developments in this period were affected by the rise of:

1. The successor states to the Mughal Empire in the eighteenth century.
2. The gradual political and military penetration by the British in different parts of India and the consolidation of their rule from 1750 to 1857.
3. The division of India into 'princely' and British states of different sizes; the power of patronage for traditional knowledge and culture being exercised by the princely states.
4. The unification of British and princely India under a unitary federal government after the transfer of power in 1947, along with the partition into India and Pakistan, including what is now Bangladesh.

As the successor states to the Mughal Empire were ruled by both Hindus and Muslims in different parts of India, they naturally tended to foster the kind of learning to which they were accustomed. Thus Arabic, Persian and later Urdu were fostered by the Muslim rulers, while Sanskrit and other languages were fostered in areas ruled by the Hindus. The British brought new institutions of western learning to the places where their political domination had been consolidated over a period of time, and hence Western learning penetrated different regions depending on when British rule was consolidated there. The emergence of princely states repeats the story of differential patronage of diverse kinds of traditional learning as had occurred earlier during the period of the emergence of successor states to the Mughal Empire. The only difference was that the British actively encouraged the introduction of the western type of education and set the standard by means of model institutions created by them in British India.

The story of the intellectual developments in India during this period, thus, has four different but overlapping parts: the first relates to that which had continued uninterrupted from earlier times, but later got increasingly affected by the new institutions which the British created in that part of India which was ruled directly by them. The second consists in the continuation and development of classical traditional knowledge in various fields in those princely states where it was valued and patronised. The third would examine developments in the study of traditional knowledge which were centred primarily outside India and were known as "Indology". These influenced both directly and indirectly the study in these fields carried on in India. The fourth part of this story would be about those Indians who were primarily educated in British institutions in India and who were fairly grounded in western traditions of knowledge in various fields and possessed the facility to read and write in English. Many of these persons had some sort of interest in India's ancient traditions of learning but had little knowledge, if any, of the classical articulation or discussion of those subjects, both because of insufficient knowledge of the language in which the original texts were written, and also because they were untrained to grasp these in the way that was traditionally formulated. Also, the perspective they brought to bear on whatever little they knew of the tradition was primarily structured by their Western knowledge of the subject in which they generally had a fairly good grounding.

The prelude to the gradual penetration and eventual consolidation of British rule in India, though studied in fair detail, has not been seen as a tumultuous interregnum in the intellectual life of the country where different intellectual traditions attempted to respond to and cope with the situation created by the decline and disintegration of Mughal rule and by the rise of various regional powers, both Hindu and non-Hindu, in different parts of the country. The responses of Muslims and non-Muslims to this developing situation were, of course, different, as the Muslim intellectuals viewed this as a period of decline while the Hindus in general saw it as a relaxation from the rigidities of the Islamic imposition on the freedom of their religious practices, particularly during the last part of Aurangzeb's rule. The response of the Muslim intellectuals to this situation was basically to search for ways to ensure preservation of their identity in a situation where they no longer had a monopoly of political power. This, by and large, resulted in their going back to the *Quran* and the Hadis and becoming more orthodox. The establishment of various schools of Islamic orthodoxy and learning, such as the Firangi Mahal, the Deoband and Nadwa, are evidence of this. Before the establishment of these schools, centres of Islamic studies in Delhi had some relation to the Delhi College, established by the British as a centre of both traditional and modern learning, catering to the needs of the Muslim community. One does not have any exact information regarding the extent of the teaching and development of classical Arabic and Persian learning as it had developed in west Asia, particularly in its non-theological forms. It would be interesting to know, for example, whether classical Persian or Arabic philosophy, astronomy, mathematics, medicine, etc., were actually taught in these institutions from the time of the Sultanate onwards. It will be equally interesting to learn whether there were substantial differences in this regard between the north and the south. It seems clear that even if there were such traditions of non-theological Arabic learning in India, they ceased to be actively pursued in the context of the preservation of Islamic identity by the Muslims consequent upon the decline of their political authority in the country. Moreover, it seems that these institutions of secular learning did not have as strengthened tradition as the corresponding non-Islamic traditions and institutions of Sanskrit learning in India had. Therefore non-Islamic traditions and institutions of Sanskrit learning continued even when Islamic rule existed in large parts of the country. In fact, the continuity of India's intellectual traditions in the second millennium A.D. is truly remarkable if one remembers the political climate in which these flourished. This proves that the institutions of maintenance, transmission and development of the intellectual life in India were strong and yet sufficiently dispersed so that they could yet be substantially affected by the political climate of the times. On the other hand, it indicates the commitment to the free life of the intellect, which in Islam had come under the sustained attack of the orthodox Ulema to such an extent that even the spiritual pursuits of the Sufis were not only under constant supervision but under persistent attack from those who considered themselves to be the real inheritors of Islam as embodied in the life and sayings of the Prophet. By contrast in almost all traditions of Indian intellectual life, the spiritual personality has always been granted a higher status than either the intellectual or the one who propounded legal precepts or, as they were known in the Indian tradition, *dharma* and *vyavahāraśāstra.*

The period from the eighteenth century onwards is thus one of continuity along with change, as all of the traditional pursuits continued under the new dispersed systems of patronage. This occurred almost throughout the whole of India after the decline of the central authority of Mughal rule in Delhi and the slow consolidation of British rule, which started first around the cities of Calcutta, Madras and Bombay. This reduced the autonomy of many of the erstwhile states ruled by Hindu and Muslim princes. However, they continued to exercise sufficient internal power, particularly in relation to the patronage that they could extend to artists and to men of learning. There arose, in the period of transition and during the final British consolidation of political power, new centres of cultural, artistic and intellectual interests where even small states attained fame because of the support given by their rulers to these pursuits in their territory. Many of the new schools of painting which have now become internationally known for their achievements and the development of the new styles of music associated with the *gharānās* fostered by these princes are or ought to be more widely known than they have generally been until now. Besides the new creative innovations in art centred around these places, there were also centres where Sanskrit, Arabic and Persian learning was encouraged and pursued during this period. Generally Muslim rulers encouraged Urdu, Persian and Arabic learning, whereas Hindu rulers encouraged traditional Sanskritic learning.

The coming of the British and their scholarly interest in the ancient Indian civilisation led to a new kind of activity towards which a large number of traditional scholars were drawn. This was the search for manuscripts in all domains of knowledge, their preservation and cataloguing, and the publication of definitive editions of works with all the paraphernalia of western scholarship, which itself had developed in Europe earlier in the context of the editing of their own Greek and Latin texts. Moreover, as the western world wanted access to the traditional knowledge of India, the presentation of these texts in English translation was undertaken by a large number of English scholars who thought that in this way the western world would come to know and appreciate the achievements of Indian civilisation and not consider it as inferior as Macaulay had done. Thus, a large part of the activity of the best traditional scholars in India was devoted not to developing traditional thought further, but rather to its preservation, collection, publication and translation. This resulted in an archival attitude among some towards the past knowledge of the civilisation, which was treated as something finished and final, only to be researched into, interpreted and written about; as something which was dead and gone, no longer living and with no future of its own. Thus, the advancement of learning was seen as belonging only to the knowledge that had been imported from the West and taught in the English language. The dynamics of growth and development of the knowledge from the West lay elsewhere, and as it was both the preserve and the vision of the other, one could hardly view oneself as playing any significant role in its growth and development.

This was not a "renaissance" as it has generally been labelled until now, but a counter-renaissance as it developed in the Indian mind, with regard to both India's traditional heritage in the field of knowledge and the new knowledge which was imported from the West. Indians, it was felt, could not do anything on their own to help it grow in new directions nor could they be active participants in the collective enterprise of knowledge which belonged to no single civilisation or people or to those who were located in any particular space or time. The far-reaching consequences of this are writ large on the intellectual scene of India in the last three centuries. What is surprising is that in spite of the deep inculcation of this attitude by all the forces and institutions during this period, innovative pursuits in the field of knowledge did not completely disappear.

Intellectual activity within the framework of traditional schools of Indian philosophy continued unabated and even took some interesting directions, as will be evident in the surveys which will occur in the course of this work. Along with this, there was also a healthy growth of interest in the diverse philosophical traditions of the West and attempts at making creative contributions to that tradition. The two traditions, then, intermingled and interacted in the personalities of some outstanding thinkers whom India produced during this period, whose thoughts we will examine later on.

NOTES

1. Potter, Karl H. 1983. Bibliography. *Encyclopedia of India Philosophies*, Delhi: Motilal Banarsidass. 1: 193.
2. *Ibid.* 429.
3. Sarma, Thangaswami. 1985. *Darśanamañjarī*, Madras, 52–53.
4. Udayana. 1940. *Ātmatattvaviveka.* Varanasi: Chowkhamba Prakashana.
5. Daya Krishna. Is Iśvarakṛṣṇa's Sāṁkhya-Kārikā Really Sāmkhyan. *Philosophy—East and West*, July 1968.

6. Hardy, Wilhelm. 1995. The Ācāryarahasyam and Its Wider Implications. In *Representing Hinduism*, ed. Vasudha Dalmia and H. Von Stietencron, 40–41. New Delhi, London; Sage Publications.
7. See, for example, Vedānta in the First Millennium A.D., A Retrospective Illusion imposed by historiography of India.

CHAPTER 2

The Search for Sources of Renewal and Strength in Times of Crisis

The period from the eighteenth century onwards was one of crisis in polity and society for both the Muslims and the Hindus. The Mughal Empire gradually dis-integrated after the death of Aurangzeb in 1707 leaving in its wake 'times of trouble' that lasted till 1857 when the British finally consolidated their hold over India. However, as the situation was not the same in all parts of India and, there was a distinct difference particularly between the North and the South. The Vijayanagar Empire fell only in 1565 and even after its demise the Naiks who are supposed to have ruled over considerable parts of the region formerly occupied by the Vijaynagar Empire. As the British consolidated their rule in different parts of the country at different times, this too, led to a lack of uniformity in the crisis.

In 'times of trouble' one tends to look to the past to discover reasons for one's present situation as well as for guidance and inspiration from earlier ideal constructs for meeting the challenge. The Muslims turned back to the Koran and the *Hadis* and, to a number of leaders who attempted in diverse ways to meet the challenge and to find a way out. The Hindus, of course, had the Vedas to turn to but, unlike the Muslims they did not have any one text to which they could unambiguously turn for guidance and inspiration. There were not only a number of other texts accepted in the tradition as authoritative besides the Vedas, such as the *Bhagvadgītā*, the *Śrīmad Bhāgvat,* but also no one exactly knew what to include and what to exclude in the Vedic corpus itself. The authority of the four Saṁhitās, of course, formed the indisputable hard core of the Vedic corpus but whether the Brāhmaṇas, the Āraṇyakas and the *Upaniṣads* were to be included in this corpus or not was uncertain. Moreover, as the *Upaniṣads* themselves form a large number, it has never been clear as to which of them are to be included or excluded from the Vedic Canon even if they are accepted as belonging to the Vedic corpus. This problem was present from the beginning as is clearly shown by the division between the Mīmāṁsakas and the Vedāntins. The authority of the

Mīmāṁsāsūtras and that of the *Brahmasūtras* are opposed to each other and though many have tried to reconcile the differences between them, there has generally been no consensus about how the problem raised by these two different traditions should be resolved.

These considerations are important in understanding the diverse responses of various groups in different parts of the country in either selecting certain parts of the Vedic corpus or some other recognised authoritative text of the tradition to meet the challenge posed by the contemporary crisis in Indian polity and society.

The earliest response seems to have occurred in Bengal where the British consolidated their position very early and is associated with the name of Ram Mohan Roy (1772–1833) and the Brahma Samaj. The Brahma Samaj chose the *Upaniṣads* as its primary text for deriving inspiration and guidance and under Devendranath Tagore turned away even from these texts to rely on personal spiritual experiences. As against this, Swami Dayanand Saraswati (1824–1883) in the North turned to the Vedic Saṁhitās alone rejecting the Brāhmaṇas, Āraṇyakas and the *Upaniṣads* and, especially, the later Paurāṇic texts which had become such an integral part of Hinduism. In the West, in Gujarat, the Svāmīnārāyaṇa Saṁpradāya founded by Svāmīnārāyaṇa (1781–1830) in the early part of the nineteenth century accepted, unlike Ram Mohan and Dayanand, not only the authority of the Vedas but also that of the *Śrīmad Bhāgvat*, the *Bhagvadgītā* and even the *Yājñavalkya Smṛti*. His inclusion of *Yājñavalkya Smṛti* is surprising while, his exclusion of the *Upaniṣads* seems strange unless it be assumed that he included them in the *Brahmasūtras* whose basic authority he seems to have accepted. However, he seems to belong more to the older Bhakti traditions than to the type of movements that occurred in Bengal, north India and even Maharastra where the Prarthana Samaj was established (1867) on the lines of the Brahma Samaj by Bhandarkar and Atmaram Pandurang. The Svāmīnārāyaṇa movement in Gujarat should not be confused with the movement associated with Nārāyaṇa Guru in Kerala which appears to be a far more radical movement than the one that occurred in Gujarat.

The attempt to seek inspiration from the Vedas does not seem to have ceased with Dayanand Saraswati as his radical rejection not only of all the other accepted texts in the tradition but also of the *Upaniṣads* aroused a counter attempt to rehabilitate the older orthodox interpretation of the Vedas, which perhaps, also sought to come to terms with the newly-emerging awareness of the scientific challenge from the West. Madhusudana Ojha's work on the Vedas is perhaps the clearest indication of this. However, it is so obscure that even the attempts of his disciple, Paṇḍit Motilal Shastri and of Surjandas Swami do not appear to have made clear what exactly his contention was? Karpatriji's commentary on the Vedas may also be taken as a response to Dayanand's interpretation.

A different kind of interpretation was made by Kapali Shastri and Shri Anirwanji who wrote under the inspiration of Sri Aurobindo's interpretation of the Vedas. The latter's *Veda Mīmāṁsā* is in Bengali while the former's work is in

Sanskrit. Sri Aurobindo wrote his *Secret of Vedas* in English and also wrote *Hymns to the Mystic Fire* on the *mantras*. These do not seem to be in the strictly Sanskritic tradition and appear to be attempts at an understanding of the Vedas independent of the tradition. Sri Aurobindo, however, has written on Dayanand and spoken with appreciation of him.

Attempts at understanding the Vedas occur from the earliest times, particularly in the works known as *Nighaṇṭu* and *Nirukta* ascribed to Yāska. The exact history of Vedic interpretation is, however, not really known even though the *Śrauta Sūtras* and the *Mīmāṁsā sūtras* along with the works deriving from these two basic sources are supposed to elucidate the ritual part of the Vedas and the problem arising from a correct interpretation of those parts of the Brāhmaṇas which deal with them. There, however, seems that no detailed Bhāṣya on each of the Vedic Saṁhitās exists as is usually found on most of the foundational texts of the Indian tradition. Even the texts known as the *Upaniṣads* do not seem to have had detailed commentaries on them before Śaṁkara in the early part of the eighth century A.D. As far as the Brāhmaṇas and the Āraṇyakas are concerned one hardly knows of any detailed commentary on them. The earliest commentaries that we hear of are those of Uvaṭa, Skandasvāmin, Nārāyaṇa and Udgītha belonging to A.D. seventh century, who residing in Vallabhī, collectively seem to have written a *Bhāṣya* on the *Ṛgveda*. As for the *Bhāṣya* on the *Saṁhitā*, the earliest that we know of is *Ṛigvarthadīpikā* of Venkaṭa Mādhava written in the tenth century. After this, we seem to have a commentary on the *Sāmaveda* by Bharata Svāmin in the thirteenth century in the Hoysala kingdom in the South. The most well-known attempt at writing a comprehensive commentary on the Vedic *Saṁhitās, Brāhmaṇas* and *Āraṇyakas* occurred in the Vijayanagar kingdom under the leadership of Sāyaṇa Mādhava, even though it is not clear as to whether all the Brāhmaṇas and Āraṇyakas were also commented upon during this period. Sāyaṇa's commentary is one of the most well-known before the modern period but no one seems to have noticed the radical position of the great commentator with respect to the very notion of *mantra* which is so central to the whole of the Vedic Saṁhitās. In his introduction to the *Ṛgveda Bhāṣya*, Sāyaṇa asserts that a *mantra* is what the *ṛtvik* takes to be a *maṅtra*. This reminds one of the ultramodern behaviouristic position such as is exemplified, for example, in psychology when it is said that intelligence is what the intelligence tests measure. Unlike the behavioural psychologists however, Sāyaṇa does not offer his definition without examining all other possible definitions that were given in the tradition of what was a *maṅtra*. He examines each and all of them and finds them to be suffering from either an *ativyāptidoṣa* or an *avyāptidoṣa*, that is, if the definition were accepted, then either it will apply to those cases which are obviously not mantras at all or exclude some which everyone accepted as a mantra.

An interesting parallel exists between the modern attempts to return to Vedic roots and those of Sāyaṇa Mādhava in the fifteenth century; both deriving from a self-conscious attempt to revive and preserve the tradition endangered by events in the contemporary situation. The Vijayanagar Empire was consciously aware of the danger posed to the classical traditions of India from the establishment of Islamic rule in large parts of northern and central India, as also making deep inroads even into the south. The return to Vedic roots in nineteenth-century India also seems to be a self-conscious response to the inroads and challenges that western civilization embodied not only in the actual presence of the British empire in large parts of India but also in the critique they offered of the past traditions of this country in their totality. There was, however, a significant difference between the two situations, in that the European scholars offered not only a critical evaluation of the whole of India's past but also presented a picture of it in terms of their own perspective based on new methods of philological and comparative research backed by a study of the historical past which had never been done in earlier times. The new interpretations of the Vedas thus either completely ignored or bypassed the whole ritualistic aspect of the Vedic *yajña* and tried to give a symbolic and mystical interpretation of the mantra portions, while ignoring the Brāhmaṇas almost completely and even the conflicting evidence from the *Upaniṣads* which classify the Vedas in what they call *aparāvidyā* or, from the *Gītā* which openly criticises them for their undue emphasis on the ritual aspects.

However, there appears to be a difference between interpretations which exclusively emphasize the symbolic and mystical aspects of the Vedas, such as, by Sri Aurobindo and his followers, Kapali Shastri and Sri Anirvanaji or other interpretations providing evidence of modern scientific knowledge in the Vedas which according to them, were a reservoir of all knowledge. The interpretations of Paṇḍit Madhusudana Ojha and Paṇḍit Motilal Shastri appear to illustrate this second aspect, though a reference to modern knowledge occurs even in Dayanand Saraswati's introduction to his commentary on the *Ṛgveda*. The latter in fact, tried to combine both modern and ancient systems of knowledge through the establishment of Anglo-Vedic institutions of learning sponsored by the Arya Samaj which he had founded. The attempt to find all modern scientific knowledge in the Vedas has continued with extravagant claims, generally founded on arbitrary exegetical interpretations and ignoring the fact that 'scientific' knowledge is not static in its formulations and that it can easily give up any of the so-called 'accepted' truths, if the evidence against them is overwhelming—a position which the orthodox interpretations of the Vedas can never accept.

It may be remembered in this connection that the 'modern' attempt to find 'scientific' knowledge in the Vedas goes not only against its mystical interpretation but also against the whole tradition of the Vedic interpretation of the Mīmāṁsakas or the Vedāntins who held that the *śruti* had no authoritative status in respect of the empirical realm. The Mīmāṁsakas had developed a whole theory of *arthavāda* to ward off the literal interpretation of the descriptive statements in the *śruti* and Śaṁkara had clearly stated that even if a hundred *śrutis* were to declare fire to be cold, no one would believe it, implying thereby that the *śruti* could not be accepted as a *pramāṇa* as far as empirical matters of fact were concerned. What, however, appears to be even more surprising is the fact that the first school of interpreters do not seem to be concerned with the rival interpretation, sufficiently to show how it is inadequate and has to be rejected. This is strange as most of these interpretations have occurred during the last hundred years or so. A comparative study of their contributions and their awareness of each other's work is still to be made. But it appears that they generally ignore each other's work and follow a hermeneutically sealed system of interpretation which does not provide for any criterion by which their own interpretation could possibly be rejected or refuted.

It is not only that they do not seem to take into account the conflicting interpretations of their own contemporaries but, surprisingly, they do not seem to deal seriously with the counter-evidence that is to be found in the *Brāhmaṇa* texts or in the long tradition of Vedic exegetics. To give but one example, not only Dayanạnd but also almost everybody else ignores the overwhelming evidence for animal sacrifice in the Vedic *yajña* which is found in the *Brāhmaṇa* texts, necessitating the long discussion in the tradition about the justification of *hiṁsā* in the context of the Vedic ritual. There is nothing 'mystical' or esoteric about the animal sacrifice, as the text itself shows an awareness of the conflict involved in the ritual killing.

The following passage from the *Aitereya Brāhmaṇa* will confirm the self-awareness of the conflict in an eminent manner:

paśurvai nīyamānaḥ sa mṛtyuṁ prāpaśyatsa
devānnānvakāmayataituṁ, taṁ devā abruvannehi
svargaṁ vai tvā lokaṁ gamiṣyāma iti, sa
tathetyabravīttasya vai me yuṣmākamekaḥ
purastādaitviti, tatheti tasyāgniḥ.
purastādaitso'gnimanupracyavat iti ... anvenaṁ
mātā manyatāmanu pitā'nu bhrātā sagarbhyo'nu sakhā
sayūthya iti, janitraivenaṁ
tatsamanumatamālabhante iti.
(*Aitareya Brāhmaṇa*, 6th khaṇḍa of 6th adhyāya; pp.163–64, part 1, of the Ananda Ashram edn.)

As it was being led, the (sacrificial) animal saw death around it. He did not want to go to the gods. The gods asked him to come to them (saying), 'come we will lead you to heaven'. The animal agreed, saying, 'let one of you walk before me'. Agni walked before it and it followed Agni. ...Let its mother (allow the animal to go); let its father and its brother, born of the same mother (allow him), let its friend, who is from the same herd (allow him). It is to be taken with the permission of those related to it by birth.

saiṣā svargyāhutiryadagnyāhutiryadi ha vā
apyabrāhmaṇokto yadi duruktokto yajate'tha
haiṣāhutirgacchatyeva devānna pāmpanā saṁsṛjyate iti.
(*Aitareya Brāhmaṇa*, Ananda Ashram edn., 3, 5)

The offering of *agni* to *agni* is a heavenly offering (*āhuti*). Even though it may be made without relying on the utterance of a Brāhmaṇa (meaning, as Sāyaṇa says, both a Brāhmaṇa priest and a Brāhmaṇa text), or be made with an utterance not rightly formed, yet it surely reaches out to the gods; it remains untouched by sin.

There are many other such instances but the modern interpreters of the Veda do not seem to have had the *niḥsaṅga buddhi* or 'unattached intellect' in this matter. Perhaps, they were less interested in understanding the Vedic texts as objectively as possible rather than in reviving the contemporary Indian consciousness by re-establishing its connection with those primeval roots which had nourished the tradition for millennia. Yet, this 'interested' search has sometimes brought to attention those aspects of the *mantra* portion which had not been paid attention to in the tradition for a long time.

Kapali Shastri, for example, utilises his vast knowledge of *tantra* to unfold the possible hidden meanings in the hymn to Varuṇa wherein he is enjoined to help one in untying the three knots which bind the soul and keep it in bondage. These, according to him, are the bonds of mind, life and body, each binding the soul in its own way. There are many other such insights abounding in the works of these writers but one always wonders how much of this is really contained in the mantras themselves.

The search for the hidden secret in the works considered to be sacred in a particular tradition has been widespread and, if one were to compare, say, the secret of the Veda, as interpreted by Sri Aurobindo, Kapali Shastri and Sri Anirvana with the one that is found with respect to the Torah, the Bible and the Koran, one might begin to appreciate both the arbitrariness and the inevitability of the approach. The search for the secret meaning of the Torah in the Jewish tradition is well known. So also are the mystical interpretations of the Song of Solomon in the Bible. Even the Koran has had its mystical interpreters and the *Nur-e-Mohammadi* has been postulated as being coeval with the creation of the world and eternally co-present with it. Similarly, there is no dearth of persons who try to find all present empirical knowledge in their sacred books as well as indications of the past and future history of mankind. Perhaps, the very notion of the 'sacredness' of a text implies all this.

What are the historical circumstances in the context of which attempts at such interpretations are situated? Even in India, the interpretation of the Vedas had languished for a long time after the *Nighaṇṭu* and the *Nirukta* as both the Mīmaṁsakas and the Vedāntins had hardly paid any attention to the mantra portion of the Vedic texts. It is only in the seventh century that we seem to have a revival of interest in the interpretation of the *Ṛgveda*, an attempt that seems to have gained momentum from the tenth century onwards.

But, though a number of interpretations of the Vedas exist from the middle of the nineteenth century onwards, the main source of inspiration were the *Upaniṣads* and the *Gītā*, particularly among those who knew little Sanskrit and did not know much of the pure Sanskritic traditions deriving from the earliest times.

If the Hindus turned to the Vedas and *Upaniṣads* to derive strength and inspiration in these times of crisis, the Muslims turned to the Koran and the *Hadis* which are the two perennial sources of their faith. There was, however, an interesting difference between the two as while the Hindus, in general, tempted to reach out towards an inward, mystical, trans-rational, universal element in their tradition, the Muslims turned to the observance of extreme behavioural norms prescribed in the *Shariyat* and embodied in the *Hadis* which is mainly concerned with describing the life and behaviour of Muhammad, the sole final authority in their religion. The inward mystical aspect of Islam developed by the various Sufi sects, was not only played down but looked at unfavourably by the new thinkers of the Muslim community as in their opinion it allowed greater latitude and laxity in personal behaviour which was felt by them to be harmful to the preservation of Muslim identity at a time when they had been deprived of political power and even of the favours of the new rulers who considered them as mainly responsible for the revolt of 1857. Shah Waliyullah's (1702–1762) name stands out in this connection and his son Abdul Aziz (early nineteenth century) played an important role in galvanizing the Muslim community. An attempt was made at purifying the Muslim practices of all that seemed to them to have been borrowed from the Indian environment in which Islam had lived for long. The movement in India is supposed to have been greatly influenced by the Wahabi movement of Abdul Wahab in South Arabia.

The more extreme wing of the movement is represented by a Syed Ahmad of Rai Bareilly (1786–1831) who took the idea of *Jihad* seriously. He ws uncertain however as to whether such religious battles could be launched from a place ruled by writers of the Book, that is, who share belief in the Old Testament as do the Muslims along with the Jews and Christians. He, therefore, ultimately went to Afghanistan where he collected followers and attacked the Sikhs at the frontiers of India. After an initial victory he with his followers was trapped and killed in some narrow passage among the hills in the north-west frontiers. Syed Ahmad Barelawi of Bareilly who seems to have been against the Wahabi movement espoused the cause validating many of the current practices such as the worship of the *pīrs* which were widely prevalent among Indian Muslims.

An interesting aspect of these movements is highlighted by the formation of such groups as *Ahl-i-Hadis*[1] and *Ahl-i-Quran*[2] which give primacy to one or the other for the regeneration of the Muslim community in India. Amongst the controversies between the two groups one related to the omnipotent power of the god Allah. It was asked by members of one group whether Allah could create another Muhammad, which is a very difficult question to answer in the context of Islam. In an interesting anecdote, it is said Ghalib, the famous poet was asked the question and replied that whatever world God may create there would always be a Muhammad in it, thus cleverly avoiding to give a straight answer of either yes or no, in the context of the Islamic faith.

Ultimately, these theological issues were replaced by the demands and exigencies of acquiring a modern western education imparted through an English medium which alone could provide avenues for employment in those times. Sir Syed Ahmad is strongly associated with this type of movement and a fairly large number of Anglo-Arabic institutions of learning were formed on the same pattern as the Anglo-Vedic ones instituted under the auspices of the Arya Samaj.

There, however, remained a significant difference between the two. The power of the orthodox Mullahs who could issue a *fatwa* on any matter of behaviour or practice or writing by a Muslim increasingly ensured that departures from 'orthodoxy' had dangerous personal and social consequences. Besides this, the status of an institution such as that of Deoband amongst the Muslims resulted in ensuring 'orthodoxy' in the interpretation of the Islamic faith and acquired an authority and prestige which was hardly matched by any institution devoted to Vedic learning or the practice of behaviour prescribed in the *Dharmaśāstras*. This ensured 'orthodoxy' in the interpretation of the Islamic faith and its imposition on the behaviours and practices of Muslims as any transgression was met with social disapproval and punishment by the custodians of the faith. There were, undoubtedly, long-drawn serious debates between the orthodox pandits well versed in the *Smṛti* literature and the *Dharmaśāstras* and the social reformers about such matters as widow remarriage, the practice of Satī, the education of women, the age of marriage, etc., but they never acquired the same status as among the Muslim community. These issues continue to be of central concern even today amongst the Muslims.

Another fact which deserves to be noticed about the developments in the Muslim community during this period is that, the division between the Sunni and the Shia is well known, from the very beginning of Islam, little attention has been paid to the proliferation of sects within the Shia community particularly those that have occurred in India. The Ismaili sect among the Shias appeared very early in the history of Islam but the fact that Ismailis came to India and seem to have got further divided into various sub-sects in the Indian environment has not attracted much attention. Many of these Ismaili sub-sects show a fair affinity with Hindu believers and practices and there exists not only an inter-mixture of Hindu and Muslim practices, but also an emergence of families where even close relatives seem to have subscribed to these two diametrically opposite faiths. The emergence of a sect that treated Muhammad as an *avatāra* a claim substantiated by the work *Daśāvatāra* remains the strongest evidence of this as does the recent empirical study on the living communities which belies the Hindu-Muslim division by Dominique Khan and Shaila Mayaram. Some of the other sects have been known by the name of Bohra (Khojas ?) and the followers of the Agha Khan, but the history of the formation of these sects and their differential response to the changes that were taking place in the social and political sphere during this period, has hardly been studied.

In fact, most of the studies have concentrated heavily on the movements around Delhi and Western U.P. and have ignored the response of other Muslim communities spread all over India during those times with the exception of Bengal.

Surprisingly, this is also the period of the great florescence of Urdu literature just as Islamic scholars were trying to seek reassurance from the *Quran* and *Hadis* while giving up the mystical dimensions of Islam that had flourished amongst some of the Sufi sects in India. The period of Mir to Ghalib extending from the beginning of the eighteenth century to the middle of the nineteenth century is one of the richest period in the history of Urdu literature when poetic creativity reached its greatest heights. The stature of Mir and Ghalib is unquestionable and the latter is considered by many to be one of the greatest poets produced in any language of the world. In fact, it was not only literature that flourished during this period but also music and dance when many new *rāgas* were supposed to be created in the court of Mohammad Shah by Sadarang and his brother. Similarly, the Kathak style of dancing which is the most distinctive gift of the north to the repertoire of dance styles of India is supposed to be a creation of Lucknow which had become a rival centre to Delhi from 1748 onwards, particularly after 1819, when East India Company made Oudh independent of the Mughal court at Delhi.

Thus, there seems to have been radically, different responses by the religious and the artistic elites of the Muslim world of the north to the challenge posed by the decline of the Mughal empire at the beginning of the eighteenth century. In fact, with the rise of new centres of patronage and power, the artists and the writers found a new freedom in the sense that they did not have to look up to only one central court or patronage or to model themselves on the standards set by it, if they were located elsewhere. The story of the rise of these centres has not yet been written, though the various schools of painting and music are associated with the names of such states, which were generally not very large in size. The little state of Rampur, for example, attracted not only a number of outstanding musicians, but also a large number of Arabic and Persian scholars who lived close to each other in a locality which, because of this, came to be known as the Madarasa-Mohalla. Elsewhere we have Hindu and Muslim rulers vying for poets, artists and scholars to grace their courts and thus make them famous all around the country. This was, for example, the period when the little state of Jaipur, a new planned city, also became known as second Kashi because of the quantity and quality of Sanskrit scholars it had attracted to itself.

The popular religious movements, on the other hand, showed little awareness of the vast changes occurring in the political realm and the problems they were posing for the educated elite of both the Hindu and Muslim communities. These popular religious movements showed a greater continuity with the past movements as they were primarily confined to those sections of the community who were less formally educated. Thus, the movements of Svāmī Nārāyaṇa sect in Gujarat and Nārāyaṇa Guru in Kerala continued the tradition of the earlier saint poets of India and practically conveyed the same teaching as they had done in the past.

One may, therefore, perhaps make a distinction between the response of those who were more self conscious about the changes in political sphere, than the large mass of people who responded to problems only as they affected them at the personal level. The story of man, however, is mostly given voice by those who apprehend at the self conscious level and articulate this in terms of concepts.

NOTES

1. Metcalfe, Barbara Holy. *Islamic Revival in British India: Deoband, 1860–1900.* Princeton. 13, 72, 141, 143.
2. *Ibid.*, 289, 295, 322.

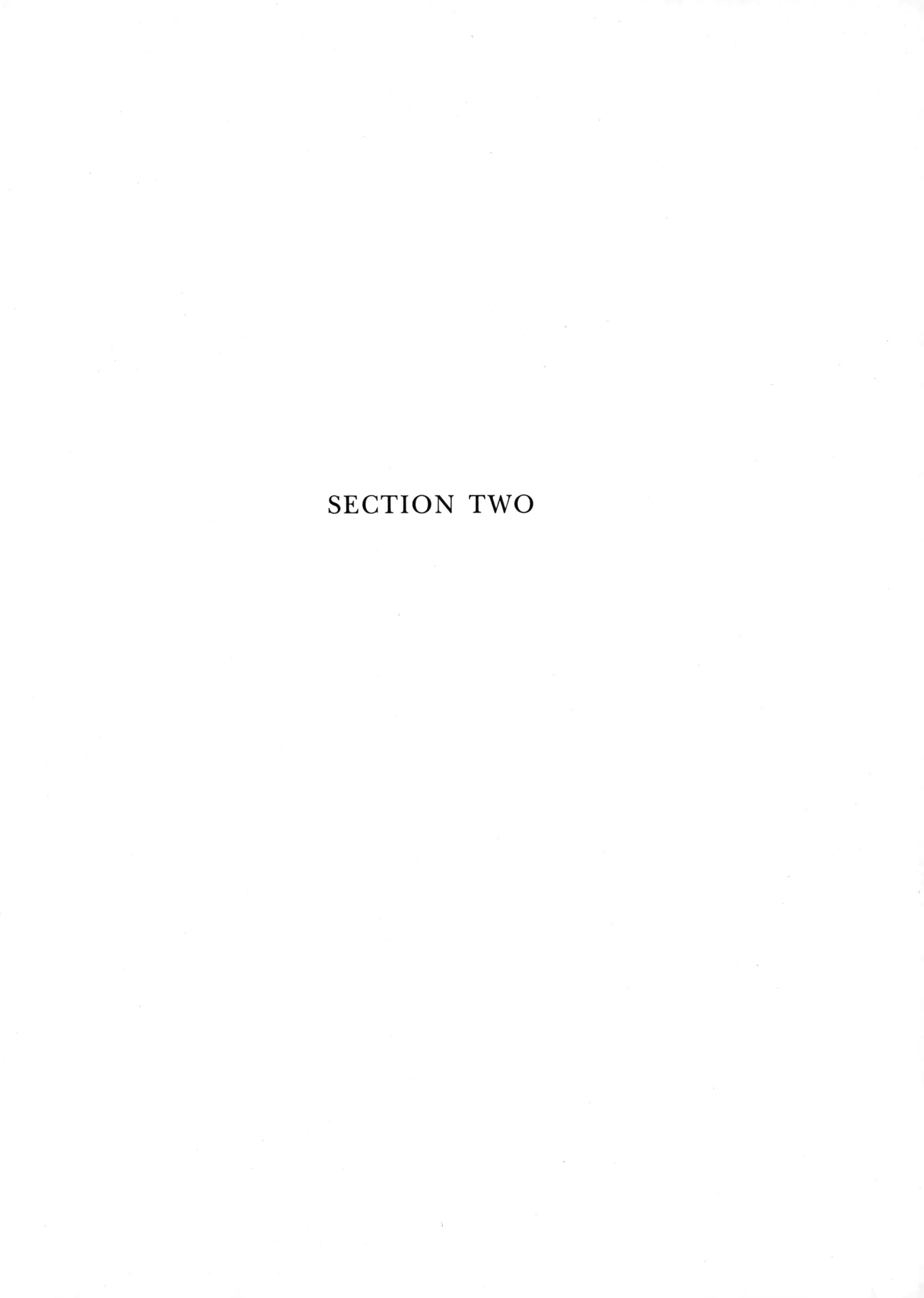

SECTION TWO

CHAPTER 3

Some New Perspectives in Looking at the Classical Traditions of Indian Philosophising in Indian Terms

Writings in Indian philosophy in the English language usually ignore the earlier Sanskrit works on the subject and start their survey of the philo sophical scene in India as if nothing similar had been attempted before. The only exceptions sometimes made are by some authors who refer to the *Sarvadarśana Saṁgraha* of Madhva belonging to the fourteenth century. However, even when they refer to it, they do not try to place their own writings on the various schools of Indian philosophy within its context. Similarly, there is no reason to show why they depart from the scheme which the author of *Ṣaḍdarśana Saṁgraha* had adopted. Fewer still show any awareness of the *Ṣaḍdarśana Samuccaya* which Haribhadra Sūri wrote in the middle of the eighth century. But, while it is acknowledged that, these two works have dealt with the various schools of Indian philosophy known in their times yet little attention is paid to the differences between them.

The general impression thus created is that there has hardly been any self-reflection in Sanskrit philosophical writing on the various trends and schools which had developed in the Indian philosophical tradition over two thousand years of its written history. Yet, this is not a fact and, at least, about thirty works are known to have been written right from the beginning of the eighth century upto the middle of the twentieth century:

1. *Sarvadarśana Siddhānta Saṁgraha* by Śaṁkara (710 A.D.)
2. *Sarvavedānta Siddhānta Sārasaṁgraha* by Śaṁkara (710 A.D.)
3. *Ṣaḍdarśana Samuccaaya* by Haribhadra Sūri (750 A.D.)
4. *Ṣaḍdarśana Samuccya* by Rājaśekhara Sūri (900 A.D.)
5. *Sarvasiddhānta Praveśaka* by unknown Jaina monk (1150 A.D.)
6. *Vivekavilāśa* by Jinadatta Sūri (1220 A.D.)
7. *Sarvadarśana Saṁgraha* by Vidyāraṇya or Sāyaṇa Madhva or Bharatīrtha (1350 A.D.)

8. *Sarvadarśana Saṁgraha* by Chennambhaṭṭa (1390 A.D.) traditionally attributed to Madhava Cf. under Vidyāraṇya.
9. *Ṣaḍdarśananirṇaya* by Merutuṅga Sūri (1395 A.D.)
10. *Sarvadarśaṇa Kaumudī* of Madhava Sarasvatī ·(1515 A.D.)
11. *Siddhānta-sāraviveka* by Vijayindra Bhikṣu (1560 A.D.)
12. *Prasthānabheda* of Madhusūdana Sarasvatī (1570 A.D.)
13. *Sarvasiddhānta Saṁrgraha* Commentary on Śaṁkara's *Sarvasiddhāntasaṁgraha* by Govinda Śeṣa (1590 A.D.)
14. *Sarvavedānta Sārasaṁgraha* by Sadāśiva (1720 A.D.) (*Advaita*)
15. *Sarvavedānta Siddhānta* by *Upaniṣad* Brahmayogin (1740 A.D.)
16. *Sarvasiddhānta Sāravivecana* of Vijayindra Tīrtha (1850 A.D.)
17. *Sarvajñāna Mañjarī* by Nandakumara Datta (1857 A.D.)
18. *Sarvavedāntasvarasārtha Pradīpikā* by Appaya Dikshita (1890 A.D.) (Anubhavādvaita)
19. *Darśanodaya* by Srinivasacharya Lakshmipuram (1905 A.D.)
20. Introduction to *Sarvadarśana Saṁgraha* edited by Vasudeva Shastri Abhyankar (1929 A.D.)
21. *Sarvadarśana Kaumudī* by Damodara Mahapatra (1971 A.D.) (Sāṁkhya)
22. *Tattvasaṁgraha* by Śāntarakṣita.

Authors Whose Dates are Unknown

Sarvamatasaṅgraha of T. Ganpati Shastri
Sarvamatasaṅgrahavilāsa of Ramasubramanyacharya
Mānameyarahasya Ślokavārttikasaṁgraha (1925 A.D.)
Śrauta Saṁgraha (1927 A.D.)
Dvādaśadarśanasopānāvali of Śrīpada Śāstri
Svamatasiddhāntarahasyasāra by Trilocana Shivacharya
Sarvmataśikṣā by Keshavacharya (son of Sūra Sūri). ed. 1886 A.D.
Darśanasarvasva by Śankara Chaitanya Bharati (1949 A.D.)
Sarvadarśana Śiromaṇi by Rāmānujācārya
Sarvamatasaṁgraha by Rāghavānanda
Sarvasiddhāntasaṁgraha by Bodhanidhi

The history of works of survey in philosophy starts sometime at the beginning of eighth century with two works in Sanskrit which are generally ascribed to Śaṁkara even though most of the scholars are highly doubtful about this ascription. In fact, the title of one of these raises serious doubts as to whether Śaṁkara could have written this as it appears to deal with all schools of Vedānta when these could hardly have existed in his times. As for the other work which is also ascribed to him, it is supposed to deal with all the schools of Indian philosophy. It would be interesting to find out what are the schools referred to and the doctrines discussed therein.

A close analysis of the list reveals that thirteen works occur earlier than the eighteenth century and twelve occur after that period. (These include at least four works whose dates are unknown but which have been edited and published during this period.)

Another interesting division in the surveys is between those which deal exclusively with schools of Vedānta and those which seem to deal with all the schools of philosophy known to the author. This division continues right up to modern times. If we divide the survey works between those which deal only with the Vedānta and its various schools, we find that there are four such works comprising the following:

1. *Sarvavedānta Siddhānta*
2. *Sarvavedānta Sārasaṁgraha* by Sadāśiva (A.D. 1720) (*Advaita*)
3. *Sarvavedānta Siddhānta* by Upaniṣadbrahmayogin (A.D. 1740)
4. *Sarvavedāntasvarasārtha Pradīpikā* by Appaya Dikshita (A.D. 1890) (Anubhavādvaita).

One of the significant features of the pre-eighteenth century works is that five of them have been written by well-known Jaina thinkers thus revealing that the interest of Jainas in all the other schools of philosophy was motivated not for the sake of criticism but for understanding and presenting their viewpoint as objectively as possible. There seems also an interesting indication that some of these surveys have been specifically written from the viewpoint of some special school of philosophy such as Sāṁkhya and Śaiva Siddhānta. The Jainas seem to have lost active interest in other schools of philosophy after the fourteenth century as we only have one work by a Jaina thinker. This conjecture is based on his father's name which has been given as Sūra Sūri and this work was partly edited according to Potter, by Gottingin in A.D. 1886. The cluster of Jaina thinkers who wrote such survey works occur mostly at the beginning of A.D. second millennium when there seems to have been a sudden spurt in Jaina writings.

The last known work in this genre published in A.D. 1971 by Shri Damodara Mahapatra is entitled, *Sarvadarśana Kaumudī*. Earlier, in the twentieth century, Vasudeva Shastri Abhyankar had, in his introduction to *Sarvadarśana Śaṁgraha* of Madhva, given a new classification of Indian philosophical schools which, though quite novel, has not attracted the attention of scholars. In fact, just a few years before he wrote his introduction, the well-known scholar, Rama Subramanyashastri had written a work entitled, *Sarvamata Saṁgraha* which again has hardly been discussed by any one.

In his introduction to *Sarvadarśana Saṁgraha* published in 1924, Vasudeva Shastri Abhayankar attempts a new classification of the Indian philosophical schools based on the importance they give to *śruti* and *tarka*, respectively. His contention is that knowledge of the ultimate cannot be gained either by *pratyakṣa* or by *anumāna* if it is without any attributes or without any relation as these could not provide any ground or basis for knowing it. The only way it could even become an object of possible awareness is through the third pramāṇa which has been called *śabda*. However, in case one admits that the ultimate reality possesses any property or relations then obviously that could provide some grounds for its knowledge. The basic difference, then, would lie between those who consider the ultimate reality to be without any attributes or relationship and others who do not agree with this. On the other hand, this difference itself could be a function of the fact that one considers the ultimate reality to be "knowable" by reasoning. As the learned Shastri puts it—the Indian schools of philosophy are divisible into those which give primacy to *śruti* and those which give primacy to *tarka.* The word *tarka* is used here in the general sense of reasoning and not the technical one in which it is used in the Nyāya system. The Shastri further divides the *tarka-pradhāna* schools into *āstika* and *nāstika,* that is, those which believe in the reality of God and those which do not. Under the former he includes Sāṁkhya, Yoga, Nyāya and Vaiśeṣika, while under the latter he mentions Bauddha, Jaina, Kapālika and Cāravāka thought. Besides these classifications, Shastri also introduces another term to describe those who ostensibly refer to the *śruti* but really do not believe in it. These he calls *pracchanna tārkika* and by it he primarily means the non-Advaitic Vedāntins such as Rāmānuja and Madhva. He, however, does not seem to be aware of the implications of his own insight that if one holds that the ultimate reality has both attributes and relations, then reasoning or *tarka* will obviously play a different role than if one denies that it has attributes and relations. The non-Advaitic Vedāntins employ both *śruti* and *tarka* as for them, the ultimate reality has both attributes and relations while the Advaitin who does not believe this can use reasoning only in the negative sense, that is, to refute the opponents' position and to dispute the counter or alternative interpretation of the *śruti* passages offered by the non-Advaitin Vedāntins in support of their view. However, the distinction between *tārkika* and *pracchanna tārkika* is important because while the latter has to give credence to *śruti* and thus make his reason subservient to the text accepted as authoritative, the *tārkika* schools need not do so.

The distinction between *āstika* and *nāstika* amongst the *tārkikas* or those who accept reason as competent to discover ultimate reality and determine its nature seems to be hastily drawn. For Sāṁkhya and Vaiśeṣika obviously have no special place for Īśvara and even Nyāya introduces it at a very late stage. Also, Shastri does not take into account those who have used reason to demolish reason, such as Nāgārjuna or Śrī Harṣa. Similarly, the pure Śrauta philosophy, that is, Mīmāṁsā, is strangely almost atheistic or *nirīśvarvādī,* while the other predominantly Śrauta philosophy, that is, Advaita Vedānta, which uses reason only negatively, is also atheistic in the sense that it does not believe in the reality of Īśvara except for the purposes of *vyavahāra,* that is, in the same sense as the world which also is real in that perspective. Still, it is interesting to note that Shastri is concerned with the problem of the relative position of *śruti* and *tarka* in India's philosophical traditions and introduces a new category of philosophers who were, according to him, '*pracchanna tārkika*'. By the term *pracchanna tārkika* he seems to refer to those philosophers who give the appearance of being wedded to argumentation and reasoning but are not really so as they feel themselves bound by the authority and views of the *śruti,* or rather what they regard as the *śruti.*

In fact, the whole debate between the relative place of reason and revelation in various schools of Indian philosophy has to be discussed once again in the light of what Shastri and Halbfass have said in this connection. Not only this, if we remember that the authority of the *śruti,* even amongst those who explicitly subscribe to it is confined only to those matters which cannot be known by perception and inference, and hence does not extend to any statements about the empirical world which can be known by the other *pramāṇas,* then one would realise how little scope is given for the authority of the *śruti* to operate in. The famous statement of Śaṁkara that even if a hundred *śrutis* were to declare that fire is cold, no one would believe it, is evidence of this, even though it has been underplayed by most people who have quoted it.[1] Halbfass is the latest example of such an 'underplaying' as, even though he quotes it, he does not examine its implications for the issue he is writing about.

There is another aspect of this notion which Shastri introduced but did not explore. This relates to the raising of the issue as to why one has to be a *pracchanna tārkika* or why has one to 'hide' one's real belief, either in the *śruti* or in reason and to give an appearance to the contrary. This can only be explained by a socio-cultural situation where an open rejection of the *śruti* was considered inadvisable for it led to undesirable consequences for one self. Thus, the verbal acceptance of the *śruti* as a *pramāṇa* on the part of many Indian schools of philosophy would only show that they were living in a socio-cultural climate where such an adherence would make them acceptable to the prevalent orthodoxy. This may even account, at least to some extent, for the change towards the advocacy of God or *Īśvara* in many schools of Indian philosophy in later periods of their development. This, as everyone knows, seems to have occurred both in the case of Nyāya and Sāṁkhya, sometime around A.D. 1000. On the other hand, the use of the *śruti* by the non-Advaitic Vedāntins to establish their position may be seen as part of the attempt to reconcile the āgamic and the Vedic traditions and to give the former a legitimacy in order to be acceptable in the socio-cultural context. Efforts from the time of Yāmuna or Rāmānuja onwards to establish the ultimate metaphysical reality of *Īśvara* may be seen in this regard between Udayana on the one hand and Rāmānuja on the other. Udayana, who had also earlier played a decisive role in establishing the ontological reality of *Īśvara* in the Nyāya tradition, may himself be regarded as *pracchanna advaitic* if one takes the concluding part of his *Ātmatattva Viveka* seriously.

Shastri's introduction of this new category of understanding the philosophical traditions of India, however, opens the possibility of another category similar to this which may be called '*pracchanna śrauta*'. Of course, this category has not been mentioned by the learned Shastri in his new picture of India's philosophical traditions but it may reasonably be regarded as implicit in it. This category would refer to all those who do try to argue and behave as if reason was their primary concern but, in reality, were only interested in saving the truth of the *śruti* as they saw it. Perhaps, all the schools of Vedānta may be placed in this category as they were hardly concerned with the whole of the *śruti* but with only one part of it, that is, the *Upaniṣads.* The only real ·believers in the *śruti* then would be the Mīmāṁsakas who are prepared to accept inconsistencies in the *śruti* in case the *śruti* itself explicitly declares unambiguously that it says so. The Mīmāṁsā, of course, is not interested in the *Upaniṣads* and perhaps does not genuinely regard it as part of the *śruti.* It also confines the authority of the *śruti* to the *vidhi vākya* only and treats the rest as an adjunct to it. But if one compares the strategies that the various ācāryas in the Vedānta tradition adopt to reconcile conflicting passages in the *Upaniṣads* and force on them the interpretation that they prefer, with those adopted by the Mīmāṁsakas, one would realise how much closer the latter are to accepting the authority of the *śruti* in the matter of the *vidhi vākyas* than the Vedāntins are with respect to the interpretation of the utterances relating to the Brahmana in the *Upaniṣads.*

But whatever may be one's view regarding these matters, there can be little doubt that the Shastri has opened a new way of looking at India's philosophical traditions where the problem of reason and faith is placed at the very centre of viewing these traditions as they developed over time.

Another survey of the various schools of Indian philosophy was made earlier, in the middle of the nineteenth century by Vijayendratirtha. He classified these not on the basis of *śruti* and *tarka* as Vasudeva Shastri Abhyankar has done but on the basis of their being *vaidika or avaidika.* The distinction, of course is old, but the novelty of Vijayendratirtha consists in the fact that he introduces a new category consisting of those, who according to him, are both *vaidika* and *avaidika.* Under this category he includes Sāṁkhya, Yoga, Nyāya, Vaiśeṣika, Kumārila and Vyākaraṇa schools while under the category of *vaidika,* he includes Śaṁkara, Yādavaprakāśa, Bhāskara, Rāmānuja, Śrīkaṇṭha and Madhva. However, the basis of this distinction is based on whether one accepts both the *Karmakāṇḍa* and the *Jñānakāṇḍa* of the Vedas or accepts only the former and not the latter. In case one accepts the *Karmakāṇḍa* portion only and rejects the *Jñānakāṇḍa* one is regarded as both *vaidika* and *avaidika.* But while one may accept such a description of the Mīmāṁsakas, it is difficult to understand how this could be true of the Sāṁkhya, Yoga, Nyāya, Vaiśeṣika and Vyākaraṇa as stated by him. Also, it is not quite clear in what sense the various schools of Vedānta may be said to accept the *Karmakāṇḍa* portion of the Vedas, particularly in the sense the Mīmāṁsakas accepts them. It is interesting to note that Vijayendratirtha does not use the word Mīmāṁsā but indicates the school by use of Kumārila's name thus identifying it, not with the author of the Mīmāṁsā Sūtras but with Kumārila who is a very late Mīmāṁsā thinker. It is also not clear how he can include the Prabhākara school of Mīmāṁsā in his classification as Prabhākara belongs to that part of Mīmāṁsā tradition which is supposed to be completely opposed to Kumārila. Amongst the *avaidika* schools, his inclusion of the Pāśupatas is interesting, as normally they are not mentioned amongst the non-*vaidika* schools which are generally confined to the Buddhists, the Jainas and the Cārvākas. Similarly, amongst the pure thinkers of the Vedic schools, that is the Vedāntins, he includes, besides the well-known names, those of Yādavaprakāśa, Bhāskara, Śrīkaṇṭha.

While this middle-nineteenth century work written by Vijayendratirtha still describes India's philosophical traditions in terms of *vaidika-avaidika,* Vasudeva Shastri Abhyankar writing in the first quarter of the twentieth century moves away from the traditional way of looking at various schools of Indian philosophy and classifies them in a new way. The necessity for modifying the traditional dichotomy between *vaidika* and *advaika* had been felt by Vijayendratirtha and he introduced a third category, *vaidika-avaidika,* that is, containing both the elements in it. This hybrid category seems to have been forced on him by a reflection on such schools as the Nyāya, the Vaiśeṣika, the Sāṁkhya and Yoga which are usually placed by most modern writers on Indian philosophy in the *vaidika* category. Surprisingly, Vijayendratirtha, though a thinker in the pure Sanskritic tradition, is clearly aware of the difficulties in placing these schools in the *vaidika* category whereas the modern writers on Indian philosophy seem to be completely unaware of the difficulties which arise if these schools are considered as belonging to the Vedic tradition in the same sense as the Mīmāṁsā and the Vedānta are generally supposed to be. The twentieth century thinker Vasudeva Shastri Abhyankar goes a step forward and completely leaves the traditional classification aside. He attempts a new way of looking at India's philosophical traditions, thus showing, at least indirectly, an influence of the contemporary way of looking at philosophy deriving perhaps from his acquaintance with the way the Western writers on philosophy tended to define it. It was, therefore, a case of a pure Sanskritic scholar who responded to the challenges posed by the western way of seeing at India's philosophical traditions in a new perspective, unlike those who were writing in English. These writer continued to maintain the division between the so-called *āstika* and *nāstika* traditions of philosophising and enumerated the so-called six orthodox schools of Indian philosophy along with the three unorthodox schools in the accepted way of looking at Indian philosophy today, being taught to students worldwide through texts written in the English language.

Thinkers in the pure Sanskritic tradition however to continue look at the traditional classification in a new way. Thus Sankara Chaitanya Bharati, a well-known Advaita Vedāntin, writing sometime in 1948 reformulates the central philosophical problem and tries to articulate the differences between major schools of Indian philosophy around that.

In his work entitled, *Darśana Sarvasva* published in 1948 he formulates the issue in terms of the relation between *jñāna* and *jñeya,* that is knowledge and its object. Thus a new response to his philosophical heritage is made by a so-called traditional philosopher writing in Sanskrit rather than the 'modern' philosopher.

Sankara Chaitanya Bharati not only distances himself from the *vaidika*-non-*vaidika* or the *āstika-nastika* classification which had been almost axiomatically accepted by everybody earlier, displays, a clear awareness of the philosophical schoool of Kashmir Śaivism associated with the name of Abhinavagupta and underlines its close similarity to the Advaitic tradition in India's philosophising. In fact, he shows a remarkable awareness of how the *mādhyamika-śūnyavāda* and the *vijñānavāda* positions of the Buddhists are closely related with that of Advaita Vedānta and tries to distinguish between the two viewpoints, taking care to refute the subtle differences by extremely subtle argumentation. Interestingly, he describes the Kashmir Śaiva position of Abhinavagupta as *Svātantryavāda*, a totally new term to the Indian tradition and tries to articulate the differences between it and the hard core Advaita position and defends the latter against the former.

There is, thus, a rich diversity in the way writers in the Indian philosophical tradition have tried to look at the same at different points of times in its history. A close study reveals the changes that took place on the philosophical scene of India as also the perspective from which thinkers belonging to different schools were trying to view these and judge them from their own point of view. It may be interesting to find whether any of these works tried to present the position of different schools from their own point of view and not judged them from the point of view of the position that one held one self. In fact, there has been a tradition prevailing amongst classical Indian philosophers to write on different schools of Indian philosophy expounding their doctrines from their own point of view. For example, Vācaspati Miśra I not only expounded the doctrines of Nyāya, Advaita Vedānta and Sāṁkhya in his well-known works but also gave a new interpretation to each of them in such a decisive way that these schools did not remain the same after he wrote on them. However no comparative study has been made to find whether the presentation of these schools by these thinkers marks also a departure in their interpretation, as it did in the case of Vācaspati Miśra I. An understanding of India's diverse philosophical traditions from an "Indian" point of view, developed by its own thinkers and not by "outsiders" to it, as almost all of those who write on it at the present time, is possible by a study of these works of survey.

NOTES

1. Halbfass, Wilhelm. 1992. *Tradition and Reflection: Explorations in Indian Thought.* Delhi: Satguru Publications.

CHAPTER 4

Developments in Mīmāṁsā from Eighteenth Century Onwards:

A Reconstruction Based on the Construction by Thangaswami Sarma Entitled, "Development of the Literature Pertaining to Mīmāṁsā System of Philosophy"

I

The Mīmāṁsā texts are divided into the *sūtra granthas*, the *adhikaraṇa granthas* and the *prakaraṇa granthas*. The *sūtra granthas* consist of the *sūtra* texts themselves and the commentaries on the *sūtras*. Two major traditions of commentary are generally identified: the first deriving from Kumārila Bhaṭṭa whose work comprises of the *Śloka vārtika*, the *Tantra Vārtika* and the *Tripiṭikā*, while the other begins with Prabhākara (A.D. 700) who is the author of *Bṛhatī* and *Laghvī* on Śabara's *Mīmāṁsā sūtra bhāṣya*. The prominent commentators in the Bhāṭṭa tradition are Vācaspati Miśra I (A.D. 960), Pārthasārthi Miśra (A.D. 1075) and Appaya Dīkṣita I (A.D. 1585) whereas in the Prābhākara tradition there are Śalikanātha Miśra (A.D. 825), Bhavanātha Miśra (A.D. 1050), Nandīśvara (A.D. 1280), and Rāmānujācārya (A.D. 1750).

The *adhikaraṇa* texts include the *Śastradīpikā* of Pārathasārthi Miśra, the *Nyāyamālā Vistāra* of Vidyāraṇya (A.D. 1350), *Prābhākaravijaya* of Nandīśvara and *Nayaviveka* of Bhavanātha.

It is held that the works on Mīmāṁsā had declined with the Vijayanagar empire, particularly as the performance of the complicated *yajñas* themselves declined in the culture. This might have been an indirect consequence of the spread of Islamic rule in the country. However, as a hard-core intellectual component existed in Mīmāṁsā, it is not quite clear why works on it declined as this did not occur in Nyāya or Sāṁkhya. A number of expository works known as *prakarana granthas* however were written, many of which not only have new doctrines to propound. But also continue to explain the older doctrines in a clearer manner.

From the latter part of the sixteenth to the twentieth century, a number of *prakaraṇa granthas* were written. These can roughly be divided into three periods: A.D. 1550–1750, A.D. 1750–1850, and A.D. 1850–1950.

About twelve original works and fourteen explanatory works were written during A.D. 1550–1750; thirty-four original works and fourteen explanatory works from A.D. 1750–1850; and about eleven original works and fifteen explanatory texts from 1850–1950. A large part of these texts are unpublished. Besides these, we also find some *Vṛttigranthas.* The Mīmāṁsā texts do not generally discuss *pramāṇa-prameya* as do the Nyāya texts. Yet there is some discussion of it in certain texts.

Some of the more important of *prakaraṇa* texts have been written by Āpadeva (A.D. 1610), Khaṇḍadeva (A.D. 1640), Laugākṣī Bhāskara (A.D. 1660), Kṛṣṇa Yajvan (A.D. 1730) and Vanceśvara Yajvan (A.D. 1830), who have authored the *Mīmāṁsā Nyāya Prakāśa, Bhāṭṭadīpikā, Bhāṭṭa Rahasyam Artha Saṃgraha, Mīmāṁsā Paribhāṣā* and *Bhāṭṭacintāmaṇi,* respectively. The *Mīmāṁsā Nyāya Prakāśa* contains a detailed, lucid exposition of most of the issues central to Mīmāṁsā, supported by examples. Though it seems to follow the already accepted principles and does not try to say anything new, it is still one of the best *prakaraṇa granthas* available. Similarly, the *Mīmāṁsā Paribhāṣa,* a source of precise information regarding the definition of technical terms used in Mīmāṁsā shows that a need was felt for such a work.

Two important thinkers of the seventeenth century: Āpadeva and Khaṇḍadeva form the subject of studies from the eighteenth century onwards. The contribution of Āpadeva II is discussed in a work by Chinnaswamī Shastri (1910) and also by Vasudeva Shastri Abhyankar (1929). The first work on Khaṇḍadeva is by Śambhu Bhaṭṭa (1695), followed by one by Vañceśvara Yajvan (1830) and another by Rama Subramanyama Shastri (1927). In *Bhāṭṭacintāmaṇi* which is a commentary on *Bhāṭṭadīpikā,* Vañceśvara Yajvan criticised the foundation of the new *adhikaraṇas* by Khaṇḍadeva and tried to re-establish the old forms of classification of subjects on the basis of earlier texts in the tradition. One of the important thinkers after Āpadeva and Khaṇḍadeva is Kṛṣṇa Yajvan, whose work has been discussed and commented on by Gopāla Bhaṭṭa Śāstri almost immediately after it was composed in 1750. Further survey of Kṛṣṇa Yajvans work by Nityananda in A.D. 1915 and by Nathurama Sarma in 1906 also exist. Thus we have three works on Kṛṣṇa Yajvan between 1750–1915. His work, *Mīmāṁsā Paribhāṣā* appears to have been modelled on the well-known *Vedāntaparibhāṣā* in the Vedānta tradition which, according to Karl Potter, is a sophisticated culmination of the long tradition of Vedāntic thinking in India.[1]

From 1800 to recent times one does not see any specific development in Mīmāṁsā, though short works have been written explaining Mīmāṁsā doctrines. These are basically concerned with the old Mīmāṁsā rather than with the new writings which had come into being under the impact of Navya Nyāya.

Thus a total of about twenty-one important published works occur during this period which are primarily an explication of the following works :

1. *Śabara Bhāṣya.*
2. *Śāstra Dīpikā.*

3. *Mīmāṁsā Nyāya Prakāśa.*
4. *Bhāṭṭadīpikā.*
5. *Bhāṭṭa Rahasya.*
6. *Artha Saṃgraha.*
7. *Mīmāṁsā Paribhāṣā.*

If one looks at the commentaries, one finds that *Nyāya Prakāśa* has been commented upon four times, the *Artha Saṁgraha six* times, the *Bhāṭṭa Rahasya* thrice, apart from frequent commentaries on the *Śāstra Dīpikā* and *Mīmāṁsā Paribhāṣā*. Amongst some new works which try to discuss matters a little differently, the following may be mentioned:

Tattva Siddhānta Ratnāvalī by Jina Swami Shastri (1870–1950). (This is supposed to be one of the best books on Mīmāṁsā published during this period.)
Bhāṭṭasāra by Krisna Tatacharya (1875).
Bhāvabodhinī by Vidyasankara Bharati (1933).
Mānmeyodaya Śloka Vārtikam by Shrinivasacharya (1900 onwards). (This book discusses the issues relating to *pramāṇa* not only in Mīmāṁsā but also in other schools of Indian philosophy.)
Mīmāṁsā Nyāyamañjarī by Pattabhiram Shastri: (Twentieth century).

II

The main issues with which Mīmāṁsā seems to have been concerned right from the beginning are: the *Apauruṣeyatva* of the Veda; the *Svataḥ Prāmāṇya* of the Veda; and issues regarding the foundational basis of linguistic meaning *śabdasvarūpam*; issues regarding the self as being both an agent of action and the enjoyer of the fruits of that action; *ātmansvarūpam*, the determination of the exact meaning of those Vedic sentences which concern the Vedic ritual or the Vedic sacrifices—*vākyasvarūpam*; the determination of the exact nature of *dharma* and *adharma*, particularly as it relates to action; and finally the eternity of the relation between the word and its meaning (*śabdārtha sambandha*).

Bhāṭṭa Rahasyam by Khandadeva is in which the issue of linguistic meaning, which has played such an important role in the history of Indian philosophy, is raised. The work criticizes the views of other schools on this subject, particularly those of the grammarians who try to find the roots of meanings in the basic roots from which all words arise. It also criticizes the Nyāya view which attempts to find the primary meaning not in the roots of words but in the meaning of the word which is arrived at through an analysis of forms which comprise the most basic unit of a word in a language. It tries to compare this position with that of Mīmāṁsā in which an attempt is made to discover the basis of linguistic meaning in *bhāvanā*. Khaṇḍadeva strives in this connection to go beyond the earlier Mīmāṁsā in an analysis of what this *bhāvanā* consists in. The work is a refinement of the earlier presentations on the subject from the Mīmāṁsā point of view.

Khaṇḍadeva, thus is primarily concerned with the issue of linguistic meaning which again seems to be enmeshed in the specificities of the Sanskrit language while at the same time it touches the universal problem of meaning involved in all linguistic communications.

Whether linguistic communication should be treated primarily in the context of influencing others or even oneself, to do something or, better still, to bring about a change in some situation or merely to inform for the sake of information without this information being in any way related either to the changes in one's behaviour and/or feelings or even the cognitive perspective that one may have are further complications of the issue. It is of course difficult to say how the latter can ever be completely dissociated from the pure information that linguistic communication is supposed to provide to someone else. In this context, one of the primary problems is whether linguistic communication is seen as addressing someone else or establishing a relationship with the other from whom, in turn, one would require a complementary communication so that the relation may become a two-way affair. What exactly should be the nature of this complementary communication so that the circuit may, at least, be temporarily completed? The situation, in fact, is even more complicated as linguistic communication may be a one-to-one, a one-to-many, and sometimes even a many-to-one interaction. However, many of these issues have obviously not been addressed in the classical analysis of linguistic communication either in Mīmāṁsā or in any other school of Indian philosophy.

The following issues in linguistic meaning appear to have been discussed in this tradition:

1. The understanding of sentence meaning was an issue of whether meaning in a sentence was a result of the meaning of its constituent words or whether it was something over and above the meaning of the individual words that comprised the sentence. The problem was whether the meaning of the sentence was merely a summation of the individual words it consisted of or whether it was something new which emerged from the total meaning of the words but which could not be individually reduced to them. This is the well-known problem of the relation between the parts and the whole as well as what has usually been called the problem of "organic unities".
2. The other issue relates to the non-linguistic dimension of a human being which seems to be determined by the idea of "what ought-to-be" in contrast to all other types of beings who appear to be determined only by what there "is". The usual term for this in the Indian tradition is "*dharma*" which distinguishes man from all other beings.

One of the important issues emerging from the theory of conduct and the norms governing it relates to "*ekavākyatā*" in the texts of the tradition dealing with *dharma* and consisting of diverse injunctions for the regulation of conduct contained therein. The same issue also arises in those texts which are considered as primarily cognitive in character and are supposed to deal with the nature of reality. Thus whether the text deals with *dharma* or *tattva,* the problem always consists in interpreting it in such a way that the apparently inconsistent statements in it are given a consistent or coherent meaning. The Mīmāṁsā rules of interpretation try to perform this task in relation to the diverse and often conflicting injunctions regarding what is to be done. Similarly, the Vedāntic tradition tries to do the same with the Upaniṣadic texts which have sometimes differing and contradictory statements regarding the nature of reality. However, both school restrict their enterprise of finding non-contradiction between statements which occur in with matters that cannot be known either by perception or by reasoning. The search for such a unitary coherence of meaning between apparently conflicting statements was later on extended to the *āgamic* texts belonging to the so-called Vedic tradition such as the *Purāṇas,* the *Gītā* and the *Śrīmad Bhāgvat.* They generally excluded the Bauddha and the Jaina *āgamic* texts from such an enterprise, as these not only belonged to the non-Vedic tradition, but were explicitly self-proclaimed as anti-Vedic in character.

It was only after the late eighteenth century with the appearance of Ram Mohan Roy that this kind of enterprise was extended not only to include both Buddhism and Jainism, but also other religious tradition such as Christianity, Islam and Judaism, resulting in what has come to be described as the essential unity of all religions. Inspite of all these extensions, it never was extended to include those statements in either the *śruti* or the *āgamic* texts, or even the revealed texts of other religions which concerned empirical matters of fact and hence whose truth could be established by the normal processes of perception and influence. This essential limitation of what has been called *śabda pramāṇa* has scarcely been noticed or properly exercised as it leads to a radical demarcation between what has generally been called the *dṛṣṭa* and the *adṛṣṭa* in the tradition, thus severely restricting the authority of the *śruti* or the *āgamic* texts to that alone which could not, in principle, be ever known by human reasoning or empirical experience.

The presupposition of total coherence, of course, applied in a sense to all descriptive statements about reality, for any sign of incoherence may be an indication that either what is real has not been grasped in its totality or in its true nature, or that the incoherence is apparent in nature and can be resolved only if a further analysis of the statements were to be undertaken. Even in the domain of the empirical sciences there is a continuous attempt to unify all knowledge that is accepted as true, though this always remains an ideal as knowledge in different fields is always growing and the inter-relationship between knowledge in different fields is not easy to achieve in any unified manner.

The situation with respect to texts that are considered to be revealed, as having a foundational authority, is of course different as they always claim a completeness and finality. The notion of *ekavākyatā* here is axiomatically assumed, for otherwise it would basically contradict the completeness and infallibility of statements about reality. The Mīmāṁsā has however, explored the notion of *ekavākyatā* in respect to injunctive statements, an attempt which does not seem to have been seriously made in any other tradition of philosophizing. It does so as it sees the *śruti* texts as primarily concerned with injunctions or imperatives, and not with descriptions of reality, that is, such is the case or such is not the case. The problem of the coherence of all imperatives, is thus, open for philosophical consideration and though it has only been raised in connection with the injunctive statements in the Vedic canon, the issue is a far larger one and relates to the coherence of norms as well as to the specific injunctions following from them.

It is not clear whether the Mīmāṁsā school has addressed itself adequately to the issue. Every injunction to be carried out presupposes not only the freedom of the agent for whom the injunction is meant but also something about the nature of the relevant reality in which the action has to be performed. The reality in the human context consists of inert materials and objects as well as living beings, including some who are themselves agents and for whom also the injunction is meant by virtue of the fact that they are agents and thus able to carry out an injunctive command. On the other hand, those injunctions that are more specific and limited are meant for only certain types of agents who are in some particular situations or have some qualities distinguishing them from others.

Not only do we have the problem of the coherence of all injunctive statements, but there is also the problem of the coherence of all actions done by a human being, just as there is the co-ordination problem of the unity and coherence of reality which is presumably the subject of all descriptive statements. Do all actions form part of a totality just as all facts are supposed to be a part of a totality which we usually call reality? If so, what shall be the relation of a part to the whole in the context of action? In fact, the situation is even more complicated in the case of action as the unity, totality and coherence which we are seeking in the realm of action would have to belong not only to the actions of one agent alone but to all the agents together, including even those who are no more, having ceased to be and those who have not yet come into being and are still to appear in the future. The unity of a plurality of specificities which are different from each other as well as those which were there in the past and those which will occur in the future along with those which are in the present, arises in the case of facts also. But the situation in the realm of action is radically different as actions are supposed to emanate from an agent considered to be free and this freedom of agency tends to render essentially problematic the search for coherence, particularly with respect to those agents who are in the present or who are still to be there in the future. The Mīmāṁsā thinkers seem to have neglected this aspect of the question, though they have thought a great deal about the part and the whole in the case of actions, and the difference between primary and secondary actions. The primary, thus, consists only of that part of the action which is directly done for the achievement of the purpose for which the action is undertaken, while secondary actions consist of all those actions which are incidental to the former, and in which there can be a great deal of variation due to many factors including those of space, time and information available to one while undertaking the action. This, it should be remembered, is not the same distinction as the one which obtains between 'instrumental' and 'intrinsic' actions, though it certainly has some similarity to it. The distinction between *kṛtārtha* and *puruṣārtha*, that is, actions undertaken for the sake of performing a particular sacrifice and those that are done for the realization of a human purpose or end, points in this direction. Yet, the concept of a *puruṣārtha* raises the question as to whether any action, whatsoever, can ultimately be conceived of as a *puruṣārtha* in itself.

The notion of *dharma* or what "ought-to-be-done" and its relation to what "ought-to-be the case", leads Mīmāṁsāka thought in another direction. The distinction arises from the fact that an action is done to bring about a situation which is supposed to be "good". Further, the performance of such an action brings about a quality both in the action, and the situation of the agent who performs the action. Normally, this three-fold distinction has not been seen in reflection on human action in the context of the performance of *dharma*. But, one may make a distinction between the quality that arises in the action, particularly in a valuational context and call it "right" while the quality that arises in the agent by doing this action may be called "moral goodness". On the other hand, the quality that belongs to the situation as and when it is brought about by the "right action" may simply be called "good". This property, however, will have to be distinguished from the property that belongs to the same situation when it is desired to be brought about and hence given a different name, though generally such a distinction has not been made in the thought about the moral action. This is concerned with the question of the attribution of the property which arises when such an 'ought' is either fulfilled or violated. Such a property can only belong to the agent, that is, the *ātman* or the self and has been called *pāpa* and *puṇya*, that is, merit or demerit in the system.

The other question that arises in this context is how one can have such a knowledge, for both perception and inference can only give one the knowledge of what is the case. Perception, obviously, tells us only what "is" and as inference is based on perceptions, it cannot give us any other kind of knowledge except that which relates to what is the case. There is, of course, the question whether one can become perceptually aware of what is not there. But even if there are negative facts it will be difficult to accept that such a perceptual apprehension will arise apart from any expectation regarding what was supposed to be there or what one was looking for or wanting or desiring to be there. Without the notions of expectancy in terms of past experience or those of wanting and desiring, the notion of a negative apprehension of perceptual facts does not seem to make sense. But in case one accepts that both memory and desire lead to anticipations in experience, one may perhaps understand how the notion of "what is not there but should have been" or "should be" comes into being and how it gives rise to what one should do so that what one wants to happen may actually take place. The journey from "should" to "ought" is perhaps not very difficult, though many moral thinkers have considered it to be so. Yet, there is little doubt that the move from the "should" to the "ought" involves a move from subjectivity to objectivity and from particularity to universality in the sense that though the "should" would perhaps be meaningful for a particular case or individual, the "ought" generally can never be confined to the particular and the individual alone.

Besides the issues of unity, totality and coherence of action, there are the problems of knowledge and validity regarding the "ought-to-be" and the "ought-to-do", both of which are at the heart of human action. The apprehension that something "ought-to-be" involves the consciousness that something is not the case and thus involves an apprehension of "negativity" as a necessary element. The apprehension of negativity may arise either from memory or from desire. The apprehension of negativity which arises from memory is based on the fact that something which was formerly the case does not now obtain. On the other hand, the one deriving from desire sees it in terms of a future that might obtain if one made the necessary effort and which one would like, if it were to be there. The "felt demand" to use the phrase of K.C. Bhattacharya, that something which "is not there", "ought to be there" results in the awareness of the "ought" which, when self consciously reflected upon, gives rise to the genuine notion of "ought" cut off from all relation to individual memory and desire. This is analogous to what happens in the case of "knowledge" when self-conscious reflection on perceptual experience gives rise to the demand of rationality, that if something is really there and is known to be so although only by oneself, it should be the same for everybody else. Reason in the cognitive domain performs the same function as it does in the practical domain, converting that which was privately apprehended into something public, and objective thus making it shareable with all other human beings who have the same cognitive, connative and affective structure projecting a common world in which and through which they live.

But while there may be some continuity between the perceptual and the rational or the particular and the universal in both the domains of knowledge and action, self-conscious philosophical reflection finds a radical break between the transition from the subjective to the objective, and from the particular to the universal both in the realms of knowledge and action.

Mīmāṁsā, thus, from the very beginning, argues that the knowledge of *dharma* cannot be derived either from perception or inference, a position that is very close to the modern one which argues that "ought" cannot be derived from "is", or that to derive an "ought" conclusion, one must have within the premises, at least one premise, which already contains an "ought" within it. The modern discussion on the subject did not raise the question as to how this premise containing the ought was arrived at. Or, in other words, how the knowledge of ought arises at all if it is not derived from either perception or inference. The Mīmāṁsaka's answer to this question was that it is derived from the Veda or the *śruti* which was a source of the foundational "ought" given by no human or divine authority. Translated into modern language, the Mīmāṁsaka's contention seems to be that if "ought" cannot be derived from "is", then one has to postulate an ultimate "ought" or what Kelsan called a "grund norm" from which all other "oughts" and norms are derived. The idea can perhaps be better understood if we take the analogy of a constitution which provides the foundation for everything else, which derives its validity from it. The constitutions, however, though foundational and ultimate in a sense, nevertheless are human creations and are known to have originated in time; they also generally provide for amendments through a process which they themselves allow for. Thus they are contingent in a double sense in that they could have been otherwise than they are and that they can be different from what they are today. Also, there was a time when they were not there. The Mīmāṁsāka tries to remedy all these contingencies by postulating a timeless, eternal, non-human, foundational "ought" from which all other oughts are derived. This is generally named as the Veda or the *śruti.* Interestingly, it also formulates not only the non-human origin of this foundational "ought" but also its independence from any superhuman or divine authority. These foundational "oughts" are not formulated by any gods, as their autonomy will be essentially compromised if it were accepted that they were the result of some divine command. For, if they were to be accepted as having been given by Divine Will, then one would have to logically admit that the command could have been different and that the authority which has given the command was ultimately superior to the command itself. The doctrine of *apauruṣeyatva,* or the non-origination of the Veda by any human or divine authority, should be understood in some such way. This also necessitates the postulation of the doctrine of the eternity of sound, for if sounds have an origin, and if this ultimate "ought" has to be embodied in a language which involves a dimension of morality or *dharma* in it, then one would not to be able to accept the eternity of *dharma* or morality as it is essentially embodied in that which itself is not eternal.

The Mīmāṁsakas therefore, formulates the doctrine of the *nityatva* or the eternity of *śabda,* that is, the Word or the sound, besides the doctrine of *apauruṣeyatva.* It is not quite clear whether the Mīmāṁsā explores the question of the unity of this primordial eternal "ought" as formulated or embodied in language, or whether it discusses the question of the manifestation of sound in relation to a prior unmanifest stage as Bhartṛhari seems to have done in his *Vākyapadīya.* Nor it is clear whether the Mīmāṁsaka or even Bhartṛhari distinguish between sound and language. Pure sound as everybody knows, is explored in music which has little to do with what is usually called language.

The relation between *svara* and *śabda* is still to be explored and though the musical traditions of India have formulated a tradition of a primordial, foundational, undifferentiated sound in the notion of *nāda brahman,* it is not quite clear what its relation to the notion of *śabda brahman,* which Bhartṛhari is supposed to have formulated in his *Vākyapadīya,* is. *Śabda* can perhaps never be divorced from meaning. On the other hand, it seems strange to talk of *artha* or meaning in the case of *nāda* or even *svara.* The Mīmāṁsaka does not seem to have considered these issues as he appears to have got stuck in the specificity of the primordial texts known as the Veda and the injunctive commands contained therein. The *Mīmāṁsā Sūtras,* from which the Mīmāṁsā tradition of philosophizing is supposed to have originated, ensured this as they were concerned being only tangentially and fitfully concerned with the larger issues. Primarily, the specific injunctions regarding the various *yajñas* contained in the Vedic texts are what they were mainly occupied with especially in reconciling the apparent inconsistencies found with respect to them. The later commentators and thinkers in the Mīmāṁsā tradition did address themselves to various issues but could never free themselves of the limitations arising from the foundational perspective in which the *sūtras* were composed. Yet, there has perhaps never been such sustained thinking on the nature of the injunctive imperative in any other philosophical tradition as that which occurred in India in the Mīmāṁsā school of thought.

That the "ought" has to embody itself in a language created a crucial issue for the Mīmāṁsā thinkers. This resulted in the attempt to discover what that element of language was which contained this injunctive force for anyone who heard the language. Unfortunately, they made no clear distinction between an imperative sentence and a sentence containing an "ought", even though they seem to have distinguished between different kinds of *vidhi vākyas*, that is, sentences containing injunctions and the different ways in which language achieves or ensures this. Also, the relations between the primacy of the injunctive function in language with all the other functions that a language is supposed to perform and the diverse ways in which it simultaneously fulfills those functions appears to have been discussed in detail. In fact, the mapping of the *vidhi vākyas* and the relation of the *vidhyārtha* and all other *arthas* in the Mīmāṁsā tradition needs to be investigated so that a clear picture of Mīmāṁsā thought in this regard may be grasped.

Interestingly, Mīmāṁsā's focus on the injunctive implications of language and various modalities through which language performs its injunctive function arose from the fact that it had to construe the injunctive import of the Veda in the context of the various *yajñas* that it prescribes, and as no human or divine authority was supposed to have given these injunctions, its meaning could only be understood through an intensive reflection on the language in which they were embodied. The Vedic injunctions themselves appear, however, to be ambiguous in that they were not like the Ten Commandments which clearly spelt out in terms of "Thou shalt not" what was commanded not to be done. The usual form of the Vedic injunction was preceded by the phrase "One desirous of", epitomized in the word, "*kāma*" in the well-known injunction "*Svargakāmo yajet*", thus implying that one who was desirous of heaven should perform this sacrifice; but such an expression appears to be conditional on one's desiring heaven or desiring something else as without that precondition one would not perform the prescribed *yajña* which was meant to fulfill the desire if it was performed according to the ritual described in the Vedas. The distinction between the categorical and the hypothetical imperative, thus, seems to have never been clearly drawn. It is of course true that in some of the later discussions on the subject, it was emphasized that one "ought" to desire the "desiring" of the heaven as it was not an optional matter for the term "*svarga*" or heaven connoted that which was ultimately desirable for a human being. However, such a construction seems obviously forced, as there seems to be no grammatical difference between *svarga* and other things which are also desired such as *vṛṣṭi*, or rain, or a *putra*, that is, a son, which also are mentioned in the Vedas themselves and for which appropriate *yajñas* are prescribed.

There is, of course, the *agnihotra* which is prescribed unconditionally and which has to be performed daily. Yet, though it is not done for the sake of a specific fruit that one desires, still in case one does not perform it, it is said that some untoward evil consequences may ensue and hence in order to ward them off, one has to perform it regularly. It is interesting, in this connection, to note that the Ten Commandments of the Old Testament are primarily negative in character and it is not made quite clear as to what reward one will achieve if one observes them except that one will not incur the sin which one is supposed to get by violating them. This has some analogy with the logic of the daily *agnihotra* which, however is a positive and not a negative injunction. All in all, the Vedic injunctions are far more positive in character than their biblical counterparts and breathe a different atmosphere than those found in the Judeo-Christian tradition.

A philosophically important consequence of this was the sustained attention to the notion of an injunction or *vidhi* which became a subject of specialized study in Mīmāṁsā. Perhaps the first outstanding work in this regard was that of Maṇḍana Miśra in A.D. seventh century whose "*Vidhi Viveka*", inaugurates a discussion on how to clearly distinguish and demarcate those elements in a sentence which primarily lend it an injunctive force and thus determine the direction of action on the part of one who listens to it or reads it.

Vācaspati Miśra I in the A.D. tenth century wrote on the *Vidhiviveka* in a work entitled, *Nyāyakaṇikā*. However, one of the most controversial works in this regard appears to have been written by Appaya Dīkṣita I sometime in the sixteenth century. Appaya Dīkṣita I was associated with the Vijayanagar empire and though primarily an Advaita thinker, he wrote on many subjects including Mīmāṁsā. His work, *Vidhirasāyana*, gave rise to a long series of important commentaries written both in refutation of, and in support of what he had said. Besides these, there were also plain expository works on what he had written in the *Vidhirasayana*. The works which tried to controvert what he had written are *Vidhitrayaparitrāṇa* by Veṇkaṭādhvarin (1637), *Vidhidarpaṇa* and *Vidhi-viveka* by Kolluri Nārāyaṇa Śāstrin (1680), *Vidhirasāyanadūṣaṇam* by Śaṁkara Bhaṭṭa (1593), *Vidhibhūṣaṇam* by Veṇkaṭanārāyaṇa (1740) and *Vidhicamatkāracandrikā* by Nārāyaṇācārya. These works were written in criticism of the contentions in *Vidhirasāyana* by Appaya Dīkṣita I. There was also a series of works in support of Appaya Dīkṣita I, for example, *Durūha Sikṣā* written around A.D. 1650 by Appaya Dīkṣita III, *Vidhirasāyanabhūṣaṇam* (1650) A.D. by Gopāla Bhaṭṭa, *Phalasāṁkarya-khaṇḍanam* (1650) by Anantadeva, *Vidhiratnāvalī* (1750) by Śrīnivāsadāsa (D.U.). Besides these, there are a number of works which were mainly expository:

Mīmāṁsākaustubha and *Bhaṭṭadīpikā* by Khaṇḍadeva and *Mayūkham ṭīkā* by Somanātha Dikṣita (1640).

One of the important issues discussed in the above works particularly, *Phalasāṁkaryakhaṇḍanam* relates to whether the fruits or results of one's action can affect the results of another action. In other words, what are the interrelationships between actions? And, do actions have to be conceived of in an isolated monadic manner where each has its own consequences totally unaffected by other actions or where the consequences of one action are continuously affected and modified by those of other actions? This seems to be an important issue though perhaps it has not been as focally discussed as it should have been, particularly in the context of the theory of *karma,* which has played such an important part in Indian thinking about action.

The theory of *karma* usually conceives of action in terms of its consequences on the self, but as the actions are many and varied in nature, one does not know how exactly this cumulative effect occurs in respect of the agent or the doer of the action. Also, we have pointed out earlier that an action has at least three or four major dimensions and hence its consequences must be seen in all these separate, though related, dimensions. But, then, the question would arise what is the relation between the different consequences of an action in all these dimensions, and whether these different consequences affect one another in some intimate and integral way? We have called these qualities which an action produces as "moral goodness" or "*pāpa* and *puṇya*", or merit and demerit, when it relates to the self or the agent whose *saṁkalpa* or *will* has brought it into being. On the other hand, the action itself has the quality of "rightness" in it, if it is intended to produce a situation which is good, whose "goodness" is different from the goodness of the situation which is actually brought about by the action when it is done. But, whatever be the names that we may give to the qualities or the properties that an action may have in all these different dimensions, the question remains regarding the relationship between these, as the well-known discussion about the "rightness" and "goodness" in the works of Moore and Ross[2] on the subject have attested that the two properties may be and are independent of each other. Thus, an action may be right without the situation that it intends to bring about being necessarily good and, as everyone knows the actual situation produced by an action may be valuationally different even when the intended consequences were good. As for the effect on the self or agent one generally assumes that if the intention was good, then the quality that arises in the agent, may be called "moral goodness", but it would be strange if the actual situation produced by the action were to be valuationally different from what the person had intended, then it would not affect the consciousness of the person who had done the action. This may be regarded as "retrospective effect" of the action or rather of the consequences of one's action on oneself and thus the whole question of "retrospective effects" will be opened up which perhaps has never been seriously considered in the literature on *dharma* or the one that deals with moral issues either in India or in the West.

But the possibility that the consequences of an action may have retrospective effects on the agent also raises the question whether this retrospective effect, modifying the self in some manner, influences future actions and thus has a "prospective" effect also. This simultaneous backward-and-forward movement in the consequences of action generates a circular continum in such a way as to influence what future actions will be, thus ensuring consequences not only in the external situation which it was supposed to change or bring about but also future actions which the agent may do.

The whole problem of *phalasāṁkarya,* thus, seems to be far more complicated than appears at first sight and if we bring in the question of consequences of the action of different human agents on one another, then the problem of *phalasāṁkarya* will assume a dimension which may prove both baffling and troublesome for the theory of *karma.* In fact, no society perhaps can be conceived without postulating some such sort of mutual interaction where the consequences of the action of each person on others and the consequences of their action on him or her, as the case may be, is inevitably felt.

Thus, the great debate on the issue of *phalasāṁkarya* started by Appaya Dikṣita I would be seen in the light of these questions and a close analysis should be made of his arguments and issues raised therein. But this is a task for the future for, as far as we know, no such work has been done uptil now. Closer attention to the debate may also lead to an exploration of whether such an issue was raised by Mīmāṁsā thinkers earlier or not. It is unlikely that such an important point had been completely missed by them. Unless the whole discussion viewed on *Mīmāṁsā* is seen from this perspective, little can be said with any certainty at the present stage of our knowledge in respect of the issues mentioned above.

III

DEVELOPMENT OF THE LITERATURE PERTAINING TO MĪMĀṀSĀ SYSTEM OF PHILOSOPHY

(From A.D. sixteenth century to A.D. twentieth century)

Thangaswamy Sarma

The system of Mīmāṁsā maintains that: (i) the Vedas are *apauruṣeya* (not the composition of any particular individual or any person); (ii) the *Vedas* are self-sustained and authoritative by themselves; (iii) (a) all the Vedic utterances are meaningful because the words contained therein convey their respective and sequential meaning owing to their innate capacity, (b) all the Vedic utterances are meaningful because the words contained therein convey their overall meaning after adjusting themselves into a sequential order because of their intrinsic capacity; (iv) the *ātman* (individual self) is both agent and enjoyer; (v) among the Vedic statements—(a) some belonging to *Karma Kāṇḍa* section enjoin a person to perform certain actions that will make him accrue merits, and (b) some other belonging to *Karma Kāṇḍa* section prohibit a persoṅ from doing certain actions—if done, will make him accrue demerits, and; (vi) the Vedic statements along with their import have eternal validity (reality). This system of Mīmāṁsā is found to possess a continuous flow of literature—that is, similar to any other system and it has developed itself from unknown times. Just as it is found in other systems, even so in Mīmāṁsā, we come across innumerable books of highly significant and terse style.

Works of the Mīmāṁsā system may broadly be divided into three groups as *sūtra* (aphoristic) works, *adhikaraṇa* (analytical) works, and *prakaraṇa granthas* (systematic monographs). The works of the *sūtra* group include: (i) *sūtra,* (ii) commentaries such as *śabarabhāṣya, vārttikas,* commentaries and sub-commentaries on *vārtikas* and the works of Vācaspatimiśra, Pārthasārathimiśra, Appayadīkṣita and others—these belong to *Bhāṭṭa* school of Mīmāṁsā. Similarly, works belonging to Prabhākara school of Mīmāṁsā also find a place in the *sūtra* group of works, *viz. Śabarabhāṣya, Bṛhatī, Ṛjuvimalā, Nayaviveka, Prabhākara-vijaya, Prakaraṇapañcikā* and others, as well as the works of Prabhākara, Śālikanātha, Nandīśvara, Bhavanātha, Rāmānujācārya and others. So, with regard to the *sūtra* group, the two principal varieties are (i) *Bhāṭṭa* school: beginning with the works of Kumārilabhaṭṭa, continued with those of Pārthasārathimiśra, and ending with those of Appayadīkṣita; (ii) the Prābhākara school : beginning with the works of Prabhākara and Śālikanātha, those of Nandīśvara and Bhavanātha, and ending with the works of Rāmānujācārya.

The works of *adhikaraṇa* group include *Śāstradīpikā, Nyāyamālā, Vistāra,* etc.

The works of *prakaraṇa* group include mainly the small works of *Vāda* (dialectics) and expository types—which analyse and substantiate the Mīmāṁsā tenets enshrined in the source-books (i.e. belonging to the first two groups). The *prakaraṇa granthas* include: *Bhāṭṭadīpikā, Bhāṭṭacintāmaṇi, Bhāṭṭa Kaustubha, Bhāṭṭarahasya, Mīmāṁsā-Nyāya-paribhāṣā.* Even the *Nyāyamālā* is a *prakaraṇa grantha.* However, the works other than the *Nyāyamālā* have been written between sixteenth and twentieth centuries.

According to chronological sequence these works may be assigned to three periods: (i) A.D. 1550 to 1750, (ii) A.D. 1750 to 1850, (iii) A.D. 1850 to 1950. To the first period belong 12 original works and 19 commentaries. In the middle period 34 original works and 14 commentaries were written. To the modern period belong 11 original works and 15 commentaries. Sixty of the above works are yet not published and are only available in manuscripts in different oriental/ university manuscript libraries (in India) and ancient libraries (in India and abroad). The *Vṛtti* works of the Mīmāṁsā literature, namely *sūtra* (aphoristic), *bhāṣya* (commentarial), *vārtika* (brief exposition) are found in plenty. A few works discuss the specific topics (*adhikaraṇas*) and are in the form of commentary or brief exposition. Some other works deal with the system of Mīmāṁsā explaining *paribhāṣā* (technical terms) or *lakṣaṇa-pariṣkāra* (interpretation of definitions).

Being Vedic exegesis, the Mīmāṁsā system does not insist on the discussion of the *pramāṇa* (means of valid knowledge), and *prameya* (objects of valid knowledge), though such a discussion is the main *forte* of the Nyāya-Vaiśeṣika system. However, there are a few works relating to these areas as well in Mīmāṁsā literature. Such works belong to the category of *prakaraṇa* works. In the past centuries (fifteenth to nineteenth), the growth/development of works in the *Bhāṭṭa* system has outnumbered that in the *Prabhākara* system. In these centuries, a number of commentaries on the *Śāstradīpikā* have been written, and these exceed the commentaries on the *Bhāṭṭadīpikā.* The number of commentaries on the *Bhāṭṭarahasya* is fairly limited. However, all the works above mentioned only explain the original texts and no innovative ideas are found in them. Yet, there also exist works which explain certain principles explicitly, without quoting the relevant sections from the original source-books. In a few contexts, these works refute the views of earlier writers, or may even substantiate the earlier writers' contentions. Among the very important and note worthy compositions are: *Bhāṭṭakaustubha, Bhāṭṭadīpikā, Bhāṭṭarahasya, Śāstramālā, Mānameyodaya, Mīmāṁsā-Nyāya-prakāśa, Aṅgatva-nirukti, Arthasaṁgraha, Mīmāṁsā-paribhāṣā, Bhāṭṭa-cintāmaṇi, Adhvara-mīmāṁsā, Kutuhalavṛtti, Mīmāṁsā-maṇḍanam,* etc.

The *Bhāṭṭakaustubha*

This work covers the *Mīmāṁsā-sūtras* from the "*arthavāda-pāda*" to the end of the "*Balābalādhikaraṇa*" (from MS I. ii. 1 to MS.III. iii.37). It is a Navya-Mīmāṁsaka work, for it explains the *Mīmāṁsā-sūtras* almost following the Navya-Nyāya style, and it also deals with the main theme of *śābdabodha* (exegetical purport of Vedic statements). In a way, it is an elaborate commentary of the Pūrva-Mīmāṁsā system promulgated by Jaimini, and it contains discussions on very abstruse topics of the select *adhyāyas* of *Mīmāṁsā-sūtras.* However, it discusses in detail, the main contents of the 12 *adhyāyas* of the *Mīmāṁsā-sūtras.* The *Bhāṭṭakaustubha* is a unique treatise of elaborate analysis. All categories and principles of the Mīmāṁsā system find a place in this commentary, and hence, there is no need to consult other works for an exposition of the essential doctrines of this system. The views of earlier writer of this system are well analysed in this work. The contents of the terse text, *Bhāṭṭadīpikā* are also clearly explained in this commentary. Hence, one can say that the *Bhāṭṭadīpikā* is a summary, and the *Bhāṭṭakaustubha* is an elaborate gloss thereon.

The *Bhāttadīpikā*

This commentary on the *Mīmāṁsā-sūtras* covers almost the entire range of the original work, i.e. from the second *pāda* of the first *adhyāya* to the end of the twelfth *adhyāya.* This commentary follows the Navya-Nyāya style and mainly deals with an exposition of the essential topics. The important *Mīmāṁsā-nyāyas* (subtle explanatory techniques of the system) are also analysed in this work. The logical arguments of objections and the proper reply to them are also found herein. The main viewpoints of the *Bhāṭṭa* school of Mīmāṁsā are explained. The technical terms of Mīmāṁsā are dealt with in detail. The general principles, as explained in: (i) the *Mīmāṁsā-sūtras,* (ii) the *Bhāṣya* thereon, (iii) *Vārttika,* (iv) *Śāstradīpikā,* (v) *Nyāya-ratnākara,* (vi) *Vidhirasāyana,* etc., are given elaborate treatment in this commentary. Any views which are contradictory have been refuted but, the treatment of the topic *śabda-prayoga* [interpretative usage of Vedic proposition] is somewhat brief. Though the Navya-Nyāya style is adopted, this commentary belongs to Navya-Mīmāṁsā type of texts, for it refutes the views of the ancient masterpieces of the system, namely. *Tautātitamatatilaka, Śāstradīpikā, Nyāyasudhā,* etc.

A few commentaries on the *Bhāṭṭadīpikā,* are: *Prabhāvalī* of Śaṁbhūbhaṭṭa, *Bhāṭṭacandrodaya* of Bhāskarācārya, *Bhāṭṭa-cintāmaṇi* of Vanceśvarayajvan, and *Bhāṭṭakalpataru* of Ramasubrahmanya Shastri. There is also a very brief gloss by name *Bhāṭṭanayodyota* which has not yet been printed. Lakshmana Paṇḍita, grandfather of Lakshmidhara (a commentator on the *Saundaryalaharī*), has written a commentary (on the *Bhāṭṭadīpikā*) which seems to be a refutation of the views of the *Prabhāvalī.* This is mentioned in the commentary on the *Saundarayalaharī* by Lakshmidhara.

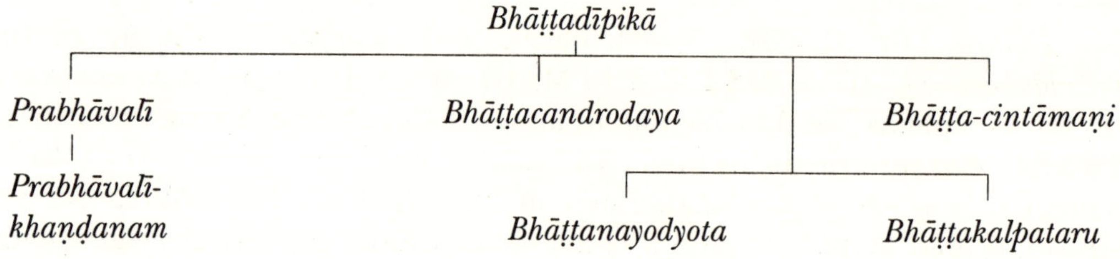

The *Bhāṭṭarahasya*

This Mīmāṁsā treatise explains *śābdabodha* (exposition of Vedic statements) and refutes the views of the alien systems. The view of Vaiyākaraṇas (grammarians), i.e. "meaning of verbal root is all-important in any proposition", and the view of the Naiyāyikas (followers of the Indian system of logic), i.e. exposition or derivation of the meaning of a statement is mainly based on the meaning of words in the nominative case(first declensional case) are refuted: and the proposition of the Mīmāṁsakas based on *bhāvanā* (interpretative exposition for *śābda-bodha*) is established on a firm pedestal. This work establishes the association of *bhāvanā* (in derivation) with regard to both verbs and noun-formations of verbal roots (namely *tiṅantas* and *kṛdantas*). It incorporates the following topics: *dharma* and *adharma* (the two principal objectives of the Mīmāṁsā systems), the import of *tiṅ* (*vidhitiṅ*), i.e. essential purport of commands, the true import of statements concerning do's and don'ts, the meaning of *dhātu* and *lakāras,* the objective import of accusative termination and the essential meaning of case endings of instrumental and other cases, etc. The work also refutes the views of other systems. By comparison, this work is quite unique in composition being based on the Navya-Nyāya style. Khaṇḍadeva the author of the above three works has refuted certain views of earlier writers—such as those asserted by: the author of the *Mīmāṁsābhāṣya* and the *Mīmāṁsāvārttika*; by Pārthasārathimiśra, and ending with Appaya Dīkṣita. In a few places he reiterates the views of ancient masters. However, in refuting the views of Śaṅkarabhaṭṭa—author of *Śāstradīpikā, Prakāśa, Bālaprakāśa,* and the *Vidhirasāyanadūṣaṇa,* etc. Khaṇḍadeva is found to be too involved, he does not refer to Śaṅkarabhaṭṭa by name (while criticising his views) but uses the words "*kaiścit*" (meaning—the views held by "some"). The reason for this may have been that Śaṅkarabhaṭṭa was the brother's son of Viśveśvara Bhaṭṭa who is the teacher of Khaṇḍadeva.

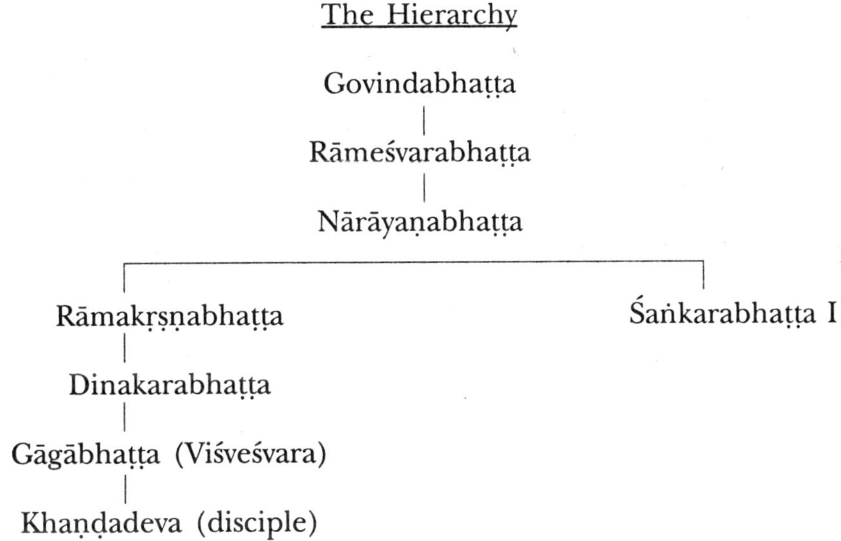

Development of the System
based on the exposition of main doctrines

The development (in exposition) is found to be more relevant with regard to: (i) elucidation of the meaning of the *sūtras* of the *Mīmāṁsā-sūtras,* (ii) discussion on *śābda-bodha* (the derivation of the meaning of Vedic texts), and (iii) refutation of the views of the opponents.

A. Discussion on Vākyārtha-bodha (Deducing or understanding the Meaning of the Vedic Statement/Sentence)

The meaning of a statement/sentence consists in: (i) a combination of the meaning of the words contained in it, or (ii) the meaning of the one chief/

principal word, with the meaning of the other words being subordinate (to that of the main word), or (iii) the status of the meaningful construction of the words constituting the statement/sentence. The cognition/understanding of the meaning of the statement/sentence is variously termed as: (i) *vākyārtha-bodha,* (ii) *anvaya-bodha* (understanding the purport through valid construction), and (iii) *śābda-bodha* (cognition of the purport through sound and sense-words and their meaning). The valid cognition (*pramā*) of *śābda-bodha* is produced by meaningful words and hence beyond the purview of *pratyakṣa* (perceptual cognition), and *anumiti* (inferential cognition), for *śabda* (verbal testimony) is a separate *pramāṇa* (means of valid knowledge). Those who accept two *pramāṇas* namely *pratyakṣa* and *anumāna* have to accommodate *śābda-bodha* within inference itself. In the case of inferential cognition, everywhere it essentially needs the presence of knowledge of pervasion and consistent observation of the application of *vyāpti* (pervasion). With regard to the knowledge of verbal testimony, even without the knowledge of pervasion, one arrives at *śābda-bodha* through the instruments of knowledge of *ākāṅkṣā* (expectancy), etc.; and hence *śābda-bodha* cannot be included under *anumiti* (inferential cognition). The person who wants to ascertain the presence of fire on the mountain, has no other resort than to seek the help of inferential cognition. Hence, such a desire to establish something necessitates the aid of *anumāna* (inference). However, *śābda-bodha* occurs even without the desire, when there is the presence of knowledge of ascertainment. Therefore, both inference and verbal testimony differ from each other; and no *śabda,* indeed, is a separate *pramāṇa* (means of valid knowledge).

Śābda-bodha (knowledge of verbal, scriptural testimony), though accepted by many systems of Indian philosophy, is found to be of three categories, namely as accepted by (i) Naiyāyikas (logicians), (ii) Vaiyākaraṇas (grammarians), and (iii) Mīmāṁsakas (Vedic exponents).

According to the Naiyāyikas, *śābda-bodha* consists in the primary significance of words ending in *prathamā vibhakti* (nominative case): for example, in the statement, "Caitra brings a pot", knowledge of the purport is gained as "Caitra is the agent favourable to the action of bringing the object, pot". This kind of arriving at the verbal cognition (interpretation) is pointed out by Vācaspati Miśra while explaining the aphorism, "*vidhirvidhāyakaḥ*" (a command enjoining the fulfilment of an action) (*Nyāyasūtra,* 2.1.64). Action (*kṛti*) is the prime signification of *ākhyātā* (nouns, etc.), and it is construed through *bhāvanā*; even *saṅkhyā* (numbers/counting) goes in consonance with the meaning of *ākhyātā* (nouns)—in this way, it has been explained in the first chapter of the *Nyāya-kusumāñjali.* In the *Śabda* chapter of the *Tattvacintāmaṇi* the derivation of *śābda-bodha* is further explained as: the words constituting a compound word give the meaning - even without the power of unifying factor between words—(i) through the construing of smaller words found in the compound-word, and (ii) through establishing the purport by the innate suggestive capacity of *upasargas* (grammatical prefixes), and (iii) through the discussion of the senses of verbal roots, etc. Jagadīśa Bhaṭṭācārya has explained, in his *Śabdaśaktiprakāśikā* all the necessary components needed for arriving at *śābda-bodha*, namely, meaning of nouns, verbs and compound words. The meaning of suffixes are discussed in the *Vyutpattivāda* and the meaning of stems, in the *Śaktivāda*. To get the correct *śābda-bodha*, the meanings of *avyayas* (indeclinables) such as *na, ca, yadi*, etc. are expatiated in the *Triṁśacchlokī*. Thus there are quite a few important works of Nyāya system on "*śābda-bodha*".

With regard to Vaiyākaraṇas (grammarian school of philosophy), it is held that the *ākhyāta* (nominal verb/verbal noun) tends to indicate mainly an action that is completed and so is existent for example "*bhāva-pradhānam-ākhyātam*". *Bhāva* stands for the meaning of the root, and *pradhāna* connotes the noun (that has an adjective). To explain: in the case of a statement, "Caitra brings a pot" the main purport (*śābda-bodha*) arrived at is "the action of bringing the pot (object) by Caitra (the agent)". The development of the analysis of *śābda-bodha* in the Vaiyākaraṇa (grammarian) tradition can be gauged from (i) the quotations of earlier works (ascribed to Kātyāyana and others, and not extant now) as found in the *Vākyapadīya* of Bhartṛhari, (ii) the brief indications made by the *Vākyapadīya*, (iii) slightly elaborated in the works like the *Śabda-kaustubha*, the *Vaiyākaraṇa-bhūṣaṇa-sāra* and the *Laghu-mañjūṣā*, etc.

The view of the Mīmāṁsaka is altogether different from that of both the Naiyāyikas and the Vaiyākaraṇas where the purport of a Vedic statement (*śābda-bodha*) is concerned. For, the Mīmāṁsaka holds that the purport consists in the *bhāvanā* (main action) suggested by the meaning of the *ākhyāta* (nominal verb). Here the *śābda-bodha* (understanding of the main purport of a statement) is derived as "Caitra brings a pot" portrays the action taking place now, of bringing one pot (object), as carried out by Caitra, the agent. In another example, "Devadatta cooks the (raw) rice", the Naiyāyikas derives the *śābda-bodha* (the main import of the statement), conveying: "raw rice" is the object of action, Devadatta is the agent (locus) of the action that is favourable to the cooking (of rice): in other words Devadatta is the agent of the cooking of rice. The Vaiyākaraṇa holds the *śābda-bodha* here as : the cooking has the object in 'raw rice", the agent of action being Devadatta.

However, the Mīmāṁsaka does not accept both these views : he points out the defect in these as follows : (i) *kārakas* (syntax based on verbs and declensions/nouns) go in unison with verbs alone—this is a main rule; hence even in the case of the meaning of first (nominative) case ending of a noun, it is proper to construe the verb with the noun in the first case (*abhihita-kāraka*). As the Naiyāyika does not adhere to the above rule in his derivation (interpretation), therefore, this is the lacuna in respect of the Naiyāyika. Universally the meaning of the suffix is primary: the meaning of the *prakṛti* (stem) qualifies it (the sense of the suffix). This is the rule of interpretation of the sentence—purport; but, if one transgresses the rule, by abandoning the meaning of the suffix which comes in juxtaposition with the verb, it is a lacuna; and this lacuna is found in the explanation of *śābda-bodha* by Vaiyākaraṇa. But the Mīmāṁsakas accept the derivation of *śābda-bodha* (knowing the import of Vedic statements) through the understanding of the meaning of *ākhyāta* (nominal verb/verbal noun) indicating the importance of *bhāvanā* (the fulfilment of an action) as the prime substantive idea. Therefore, the *bhāvanā* in the case of "Caitra cooks the raw-rice" implies the action of cooking presently with (i) the object being raw-rice, and (ii) the agent/ doer being Caitra. The *śābda-bodha* is understood in this way only whether it be Vedic or secular statements in contexts like *bhāva-ākhyāta* (the noun in the context of existent proposition), *vidhipratyaya* (suffix intended to convey order, and *nañvākya* (prohibitory statements).

The above *prakriyā* (derivation/interpretation) of the knowledge of *śābda-bodha* has been discussed mainly in (i) the *Tattvabindu* (of Vācaspati) that stresses the main basis of *śābda-bodha,* (ii) *Bhāvanāviveka* (of Maṇḍanamiśra) that proclaims the importance of *bhāvanā,* and (iii) the *Vidhiviveka* discussing the import of *vidhi* (essential injunctions). But, the discussion on *śābda-bodha* was just made in passing in the works that described the meaning of *adhikaraṇa* (main sectional topics of Mīmāṁsā), i.e. in the *Śāstradīpikā,* the commentary thereon namely *Śāstramālā* and in the *Bhāṭṭa-cintāmaṇi* etc.—which were written in twelfth century and later on. However, in the *Bhāṭṭa-cintāmaṇi,* in the first *pāda,* namely *Tarka-pāda,* six *pramāṇas* (means of valid knowledge) are discussed: herein, in a brief commentary through *sūci-kaṭhā-nyāya* (maxim of dealing with a few illustrations when a number of topics have to be analysed), a few topics of *śabda-khaṇḍa* (chapter on *śabda,* knowledge of verbal/scriptual testimony) are delineated. It may be added that the *Bhaṭṭa-cintāmaṇi* deals exclusively with the meaning of the *sūtras* of the Jaimini, and was written by Viśveśa-bhaṭṭa alias Gāgābhaṭṭa, preceptor of Khaṇḍadeva. Thus, the description of the meaning of verbs, noun (*ākhyāta*), *lakāras* (tense and moods), stems, noun-declensions, compounds words the main implied import of *samāsa* (compounds), and *nañ* (negative suffix), etc. are set forth. Based on *Bhāṭṭa-cintāmaṇi* alone, the main interpretation/derivation of the *śābda-bodha* is carried out even in the *Bhaṭṭarahasya.*

B. Definition of "Dharma"

The definition of *dharma* in the systems of Indian philosophy is the context of a vast spectrum of meanings. Thus, the Buddhists view *dharma* as *vāsanā* (a mental impression) belonging to *jñāna* (knowledge), but not produced from *jñāna.* The Jainas refer to *dharma* as *pudgala,* (i) that takes the shape as *deha* (body) etc., (ii) produced by *puṇya-viśeṣa* (special merit) and (iii) of the form of *paramāṇu-s* (minute particles). The Saṅkhyās call *dharma* as *Vṛtti-Viśeṣa* (special mode) of *antaḥ karaṇa* (internal organ/mind) produced from the rituals like *yāga* (sacrifice), etc. The Naiyāyikas (Indian logicians) hold *dharma* to be a special virtue of *ātman* (individual soul) generated by the performance of prescribed acts, and call it *adṛṣṭa* (unseen effect). Also one set of the followers of Mīmāṁsā call *dharma* as "*apūrva*" (which was not earlier, i.e. it is an effect or one that is generated). The followers of *Āgamas* call *dharma* worship of *pratīkas* or caitya (icons in temples).

The Bhāgavats point out *dharma* as the realization of the *ātman* through the practice of meditation (yoga). The Paurāṇikas (Torch-bearers of *Purāṇa* tradition) call *dharma* the main practice of spiritual righteous discipline (*ācāra*). The Vaiśeṣikas contend : that from which one attains the great progress and final beatitude is *dharma*. A few others opine that there is no *dharma* greater than *satyam* (truth). When there are so many different viewpoints about *dharma*, Sage Jaimini puts it in a nutshell as "*Codanā-lakṣaṇo artho dharmaḥ*" i.e. *dharma* consists in the meaning of Vedic utterances that enjoin a person as "do this" or "refrain from this". In the view of Navya-Mīmāṁsakas, namely Khaṇḍadeva and others, *dharma* is conducive of *iṣṭasādhana* (fulfilling one's desire) which is within the purview of the knowledge produced from the Vedic passages alone: whereas *adharma* is that which produces *aniṣṭa* (that which is not liked by a person) found within the range of the knowledge from the Vedic text alone. Therefore, *dharma* consists in *vidhīyamāna* (that which is enjoined as to be carried out),—(i) being different from *apūrva*, (ii) which is conducive of achieving the fruit—final beatitude through *adṛṣṭa* (unseen effect) that is completely bereft of any connection with *aniṣṭa* (not desired at all). Such a kind of definition for *dharma* has been accepted by the author of the *Mīmāṁsā-Nyāya-prakāśa, Kṛṣṇayajvan, Laugākṣī-Bhāskara* and others.

C. Discussion in the Import of "Liṅ" (in Vedic texts)

In the Vedic passages the meaning of the words (verbs) used in *Liṅ* (injunctions/prohibitions) is taken for interpretation/discussion; for these texts, in a way bring to light certain actions that are conducive to fulfil one's desire or to achieve certain aims/goals. Different systems of Indian philosophy (*dārśanikāḥ*) hold altogether different contentions with regard to the import of the verb used in *Liṅ* (potential mood).

The Nyāya system holds: *vidhi* or command is the specific import of the verbs used with suffixes of (i) *liṅ*, (ii) *loṭ*, and (iii) *tavya* (must). This has three aspects, first as being the means for fulfilling one's desire, second the urgent need to complete the task (one has to carry out the work without fail), and third it has no connection whatsoever with anything that is most harmful. In all the three aspects, the verbs used in *liṅ*, etc. convey their meaning fully, for they are inseparable from the import of the relationship existing between *viśeṣaṇa* (adjective) and *viśeṣya* (substantive). Because of the interpretational capacity intrinsic to them, those verbs produce three kinds of meaning simultaneously. Such knowledge intended by these suffixes of the verbs induces earnest activity on the part of the agent, and so these usages of the verbs are called *pravartanā* (directing or enjoining). Hence inducement is the main import of the suffixes, *liṅ*, etc.

The Vaiyākaraṇas (grammarians) hold that inducement or enjoining is there for the sake of achieving or fulfilling one's desire. It amounts to being the means (*upāya*). They contend that the meaning of *vidhi* is "inducement" (*pravartanā*), i.e. nothing but the means to attain one's aim/intention. In the *Vidhiviveka* of Maṇḍanācārya, the meaning of *vidhi* is set forth as *pravartanā*, in the explanation of *puṁso naiṣṭābhyupāyatvāt.* Pārthasārathimiśra, in his *Vidhinirṇaya* also, states that *vidhi* stands for *pravartanā*, that is, the means for achieving one's intention. In the *Nyāyasudhā*, the section with the commentary on *Arthavāda-adhikaraṇa-siddhānta-vārttika* sets forth that *vidhyartha* (meaning of *vidhi*) implies an *alaukikī* (extraordinary) act of the person who has the initiative, and the *vidhi* is the cause of an inducement to the agent. A particular viewpoint of a distinct group is also arrived at, namely *vidhyartha* (the import of *vidhi*) represents the intention of "encouraging one to fulfill one's desire"—as a corollary to all earlier views on *vidhyartha.* To corroborate such a distinct view, we are also ready to include "desire" as part and parcel of the meaning of suffixes like *liṅ*, etc. in Vedic texts. If "desire" is held to possess the locus in *ātman* alone and not having a locus in an insentient object, then one should accept the validity of *Īśvara* (God) as propounded and established in the *Upaniṣads* and also derive *vidhyartha* (import of *vidhi*) as forming part of the Lord's will. Or it is also to be accepted that an *alaukikī dharma* is *vidhyartha* (import of *vidhi*): (i) referred to by the words (verbs) with "*liṅ*" terminations etc., and (ii) found in those suffixes to make a person interested/involved. But *vidhyartha* (import of *vidhi*) does not provide the basis for the means, to attain one's desire fulfilled.

D. Reference to Bhāvanā

According to one prevalent view *bhāvanā* (intentional motivation)—as expressed by the word of nominal subject (noun) as found beyond the reach/range of the meaning of *dhātu* (verbal root)—is also derived, referring to the import of a statement (*śābda bodha*). To explain : When the question is put—"what does he do", the reply given is : "he cooks", herein, the *samānādhikaraṇya* (grammatical coordination) is quite well known between the terms, *karoti* (does) and *pacati* (cooks). The intentional purport of the term *karoti* in conjunction with that of the term *pacati*, through the coordinate relation between them, conveys the *bhāvanā* (intention in fulfilling a task) of the former, to enjoin the latter as well. Now, if it is asked whether the *bhāvanā* belongs to the verb of noun, the reply would be: the *bhāvanā* does belong to *ākhyāta* (noun) and not to *dhātu* (verb), because the verbal roots like *pac* etc. have multifarious senses and this is not the case with regard to *ākhyāta* (noun); hence the conclusion : *bhāvanā* is spoken of with regard to *ākhyāta* (noun) only.

E. The View of Khaṇḍadeva

In his works, *Bhāṭṭdīpikā*, and *Bhāṭṭarahasya*, etc., Khaṇḍadeva, a Navya-Mīmāṁsaka has in detail dealt with the meanings of *lakāras* (the suffixes of tenses and moods), *dhātus* (verbs), *suppratyayas* (suffixes added to grammatical compound words), and *nañ-pratyaya* (negative particles), etc. These have not been explained in the earlier works of Mīmāṁsā system. Especially the meanings of *liṅ-lakāra* and *sup-vibhakti pratyayas* are construed to imply *bhāvanā* (over-all action). Even *paramparā-sambandha* (relation through hierarchy) has been derived to mainly portray the *śābda-bodha* (chief import of the sentence).

F. Meaning of Verbs

With regard to meanings of *dhātus* (verbal roots), the Mīmāṁsā system upholds the pristine importance to their orientation to action—*sarvo vyāpāraḥ dhātvarthaḥ* after refuting the viewpoints of Vaiyākaraṇas (grammarians) and Naiyāyikas (logicians).

G. Navya-Mīmāṁsaka View

According to the Navya Mīmāṁsaka (latter-day adherents of Mīmāṁsā), *karmatva* (being an object), *kartṛtva* (being an agent/subject), *karaṇatva* (to be an instrument), etc.—all these form a unified *upadhi* (adjunct) to the chief action. Since the *dharma*—that is exclusive of *jāti* (genre) and *akhaṇḍopādhi* (undivided/unified adjunct)—alone is worth explanation (definition), having abandoned the view of *anirvacanīyatvam akhaṇḍatvam* (that which is impartite can never be described/declined as such and such), the definition of *akhaṇḍatva* (being impartite/ever being a whole) as, (i) being different from the *samavāya* (inherence) relation, and (ii) being different from the relation of an object to its own essential nature. Therefore, for the Navya Mīmāṁsakas who are fond of accommodating the principle of *akhaṇḍatva* (indivisibleness/wholeness/impartiteness), similar to *pratyayatva* (being suffix) etc., even *karmatva* (to be an object), *kartṛtva* (agency) etc. fall within the range of *akhaṇḍa* (impartite). So the meanings of *dhātus* such as *pākatva* (cooking) etc., in unison with their general purport, convey mainly the unified *dharma.* The meanings of declensional suffixes indicating *karmatva* (being an object, etc.) have to be construed with *bhavana* (the main enjoined action), (i) through *paramparā-sambandha* (step-by-step under-standing), i.e. through the meaning of their own verbal roots and being an instrument thereof, and (ii) not by the direct relation of self-identity—the latter being the Naiyāyika's view. The existence of *bhāvanā* is established in the case of the meaning of words ending in *kṛt-pratyaya* and *ṇamul pratyaya,* etc. The distinction of *bhāvanā* even in regard to the meaning of the *Kṛt*-suffixes which are found as subsequent part of *ākhyātas,* explains the meaning of the qualifying words (*viśeṣaṇa*) of a verb (*Kriyā*). the main import of *dvitīyāvibhakti* (accusative case suffix) is established through the discussion on the *vārttika* (a principle found in the sub-commentary)—*tato-na atrāpi dṛśyate.*

H. Authority of dharma in the Bhāṭṭdīpikā

It is finally established in the *Bhāṭṭdīpikā*, while dealing with the authority of *smṛti* and *ācāra* in expounding *dṛṣṭārtha* (seen effects), that the *smṛti* and *ācāra* which relate to *adṛṣṭārtha* (unseen effect) are to be regarded as superior in authority. Such a superiority in regard to the authority of *smṛti* and *ācāra* is even quite tenable in the sciences of Āyurveda, Sāmudrika, Vāstuvidyā, Ethics (Nītiśāstra), Śālihotra, Elephant-taming, Cookery, etc. *Śyenayāga* is accepted as *dharma* because it has been laid down in the Vedas, but people of modern research hold it to be *adharma* on the ground that its effect being destructive in character and hence *pratyavāya* (a type of crime).

I. The Main Doctrine - vidhi

The system of Mīmāṁsā holds *vidhi* (Enjoined Action) alone as the supreme treasure and as the most favoured doctrine. Therefore, through the foremost aphorism, "*vidhinātveka-vākyatvāt* ..." (because of being construed as a single proposition/statement along with *vidhi*), *arthavāda* (supplementary or secondary statement in the form of praise/eulogy), *mantra* (hymn), *nāmadheya* (nomenclature), *smṛti* (traditional scripture), *sadācāra* (righteous custom of elders), *ātmatuṣṭi* (self-satisfaction), etc. go in union with *vidhi* and, thus, they gain authority. Never are the Vedic texts held to be sensible or tenable without any connection with *vidhi-vākya* (an injunction/prohibition). Further, it is told that *vidhitva* (to be a *vidhi*—a command, law, rule) consists in: (i) "inducing a person to proceed with an act, after reminding him of a fact that he has not known earlier", (ii) making one to understand an object/principle that is purposeful/useful, (iii) the main purport of a statement that is supplemented by *arthavāda, mantra, nāmadheya,* etc. that render a person more enthusiastic in carrying out the main act (*vidhi*), (iv) producing the right knowledge of *dharmas* such as the form of the means to achieve a goal that is desired by a person (in the view of Navya Mīmāṁsaka), and (v) *dharma* as the prime import of the words with the '*Liṅ*' suffix etc.—as intended to be carried out—as enjoined in the statement with the application of the *Liṅ* suffix, etc. The meaning of *vidhi* is *śābda-bhāvanā* (main performance of action through verbal testimony)—in accordance with the Bhāṭṭa school of Mīmāṁsā. For the Prabhākaras the meaning of *vidhi* implies *Kāryam* (the action should be done). The Navya Mīmāṁsakas set forth the main import of *vidhi* as meaningful *bhāvanā* as construed with the *śabda-bhāvanā* (the essential order of *śabda*).

The inner classification of *vidhi* has been established in the commentary on the *Mīmāṁsāsūtra* 2.2.16 (in the *Siddhānta-sūtra* sub-commentary of *Ādhāra-Agnihotra adhikaraṇa*)—as numbering eight; and the following explanations are given in the *mantrādhikarṇa sūtra* of the *Mīmāṁsāsūtras*, 1.2.42: (i) *atyantam aprāpte vidhiḥ*: The injunction is when its fruit cannot be obtained by any other means; (ii) *Pākṣika sati niyamaḥ*: It is called *niyama* when the enjoined action of a *vākya* is optional; (iii) *Tatra anyatra ca parisaṇkhyā*: When the action intended to be carried out as feasible in one case at once, and similar to it for further instances as well. The illustrations (instance) for these technical aspects of *vidhi, niyama* and *parisaṅkhyā* have also been described. In the *Vidhirasāyana,* popularly referred to as a work of Appayya/dīkṣita, many discussions of the above-cited views are found; namely the defects like *avyāpti* (non-pervasion), etc. in the definitions of *vidhi* are pointed out first; but later on, the reply for the objections are indicated; the discussion on the important topics of the twelfth *adhyāya* (of the *Mīmāṁsāsūtras*) is made with profuse illustrations along with clear-cut definitions for some technical terms; the explanations of the *vārttika* are analysed, pointing out objections and clarifications thereon with examples. An self-commentary on the *Vidhirasāyana* is also extant. However, subsequently many criticisms and appreciations (on the *Vidhirasāyana*) by later writers on Mīmāṁsā have appeared. Among them a few works may be cited, namely the *Durūhaśikṣā*, the *Vidhibhūṣaṇa*, the *Vidhiratnāvalī*, the *Vidhidūṣaṇa*, the *Vidhītrayaparitrāṇa*, the *Vidhiviveka*, the *Vidhi-camatkāracandrikā*, the *Vidhidarpaṇa*, the *Mīmāṁsā-Vidhi-bhūṣaṇa*, etc.—while some of these have been printed, the others are in manuscript form. Even though a few criticisms against the *Vidhirasāyana* are found scattered in the *Mīmāṁsā Kaustubha*, *Bhāṭṭdīpikā* and *Bhaṭṭarahasya*, there is not available any independent work that refutes the *Vidhirasāyana* altogether. However, there has been some development in the discussion on *vidhi* and its classifications:

Vidhirasāyana

REFUTATION		APPRECIATION
1. *Vidhitrayaparitrāṇa* (1590–1660 A.D.)	1. *Mīmāṁsā Kaustubha* (1575–1665)	1. *Durūhaśikṣā* (1650)
2. *Vidhidarpaṇam* (1670–1750)	2. *Bhāṭṭadīpikā* (1575–1665)	2. *Vidhirasāyana-bhūṣaṇam* (1700)
3. *Vidhiviveka* (1670–1750)	3. *Bhāṭṭarahasyam* (1575–1650)	3. *Phalasāṁkarya Khaṇḍanam* (1715)
4. *Vidhirasāyanadūṣaṇam* (1650–1750)	4. *Mayūkhamālika* (1640)	4. *Vidhiratnāvalī* (1750)
5. *Vidhibhūṣaṇam* (1711)		
6. *Mīmāṁsāvidhibhūsanam* (1700)		
7. *Vidhicamatkāra Candrikā*		

J. Explanation of somena yajeta

According to the ancient Mīmāṁsā writers the explanation of *somena yajeta* is dependent on *matyartha-lakṣaṇa,* i.e. first of all, one has to procure *soma,* and then, it is enjoined on the agent to perform the *soma* sacrifice. This explanation was intended by them, out of fear of *Vākyabheda* (a contingency of using two sentences). However, Navya Mīmāṁsakas who accept the aspect of *paramparā-sambandha* (hierarchical relationship) in understanding the import of words (*śābda-bodha*), do not accept *matyartha-lakṣaṇa* (the secondary significance through *matyartha*) for the term *soma* with regard to the Vedic text *somena yajeta*; but they accept the meaning of *soma* through *bhāvanā* as construed with *karaṇatva* (being instrumental). They say: it cannot be said that many instruments could not be construed at a time, for it is tenable to have different kinds of instruments at a time, and it won't be possible to have any instruments of similar nature (same genre). As a means to achieve the fruit of sacrifice, *bhāvanā* (action) is a *karaṇa* (main instrument); but the *soma* plant is an instrument of the fruit namely. *yāga* (sacrifice) itself; thus there is *paramparā-sambandha* (hierarchical relation). So, *soma* is the *itikartavya* (procurable means), and hence, it is construed with *yāga* (sacrifice); ultimately, *matyartha-lakṣaṇa* is not at all applicable—according to the conclusion of the *Bhāṭṭadīpikā.*

K. Another Navya Mīmāṁsaka View

To say: a person is a brahmin only if he/she is born of brahmin couple alone, is not an inviolable condition for, through other criteria, even Sage Viśvāmitra among others are held to be brahmins, thus, the Navya Mīmāṁsakas contend.

L. The Bhāṭṭacintāmaṇi of Vāñceśvara Yajvan

The commentary on the *Bhāṭṭadīpikā,* namely the *Bhāṭṭacintāmaṇi* was composed by Vañceśvara Yajvan of south India. This commentary is of immense use as it explains vividly certain abstract topics contained in the original text. In many places, the commentary refutes the view of the original text as the latter sets forth a *Navya Adhikaraṇa - racanāprakāra* (i.e. a new method of classification of *adhikaraṇa*). This commentary follows the pattern and style of the *Bhāṣya, Vaṛttika* and the *Śāstradīpikā* with regard to the enumeration of *adhikaraṇas* (major sub-divisions) of the *Mīmāmśasūtras*; for example, this is clear in *Ākṛtyadhikaraṇa,* 1.3.10; *udbhid-adhikaraṇa,* 11.4.2; *vājapey-adhikaraṇa,* 1.4.6, etc. In the *vyākaraṇādhikaraṇa* even the regional language is accepted as authoritative.

After the period of Sāyaṇa Madhvācārya, very scholarly works of *Mīmāṁsā-Śāstra* are not available either as *Śūtragranthas* or *Adhikaraṇagranthas.* Similarly, after the period of Khaṇḍadeva, people became less interested in rituals like *yāga* (sacrifice), etc. Therefore, the traditional hierarchy of learning and teaching got eclipsed midway with regard to; (i) the works of *sūtra, bhāṣya, vārttika* etc. and (ii) later-day innovative treaties. In such a situation when the urge to learn and teach the Mīmāṁsā system or to acquire sound scholarship in the *Mīmāṁsāśāstra* surfaced, it was required to be fulfilled through easy means and within a short period. Great scholars, therefore, attempted to prepare simple manuals of Mīmāṁsā that pointed out the essential tenets (from the source-books), similar to the existence of such simple works in the Nyāya and Vaiśeṣika systems. As those works belonged to a particular thematic approach, they are known as *Prakaraṇa-granthas* being comprehensive with a concise rendering of the facts. A few works of this style are: Āpadeva's *Mīmāṁsā-Nyāya-prakāśa,* Kṛṣṇayajvan's *Mīmāṁsāparibhāṣā,* and Bhāskarabhaṭṭa's *Arthasaṁgraha,* etc.

The *Mīmāṁsā-nyāya-prakāśā* (A.D. 1700)

This work has been prepared to highlight the nyāya's (special themes) used in the tenets of Mīmāṁsā (on Vedic analysis and secular applications of those texts) mainly for the benefit of the lay readers who do not know the doctrines of Mīmāṁsā. Even though there are occasional cross-references, the work is easy to follow. Many definitions and illustrations are explained here in a lucid manner, for example: (i) the two kinds of *bhāvanā,* (ii) the subdivisions of *vidhi, mantras,* etc. in the Veda, (iii) authoritative passages of the vedas, (iv) the different types and aspects of *dharma,* (v) different kinds of *vidhi,* (vi) the different means of valid knowledge which refer to *dharma* as *aṅga* (subordinate), (vii) *smṛtyācāras* (customary adhering to *smṛti* digests), (viii) *pramāṇas* which deal with *krama,* (ix) *arthavāda* (laudatory subdivisions), (x) *apūrva-prameyas,* etc. For readers who want to learn and understand specific topics of *smṛti* and Mīmāṁsā, this work ably analyses these, especially, the subtle and intricate aspects so that it can be compared to the *Jaiminīya Nyāyamālā.*

The *Mīmāṁsāparibhāṣā* (A.D. 1700 1760)

Kṛṣṇa Yajvan's *Mīmāṁsaparibhāṣā* is a detailed text that explains the technical terms through a word-to-word interpretation, along with simple definitions and illustrations. There are no *śāstra carcā* (detailed discussions of the doctrines of the system) nor any innovatory approach to the principal teachings of Mīmāṁsā. So it is similar to the *Tarkasaṁgraha* of the Nyāya system.

In the recent period from the eighteenth to the twentieth century no development or growth in the study of Mīmāṁsā has occured. However, numerous short tracts of Mīmāṁsā and a few commentaries have been written in this period. These mainly deal with the ancient Mīmāṁsā tradition. Some among these are printed, while others have not been published at all.

A. Unpublished Commentaries

1. Campakanātha's C. on the *Śāstradīpikā* A.D. 1710, etc.

B. Printed Commentaries

1. Vāñceśvaradikṣita's C. *Bhāṭṭacintāmaṇi* on *Bhāṭṭadīpikā,* 1798–1832.
2. Vaidyanathashastri's C. on *Śābarabhāṣya* (up to Tarkapāda), 1850–1950.
3. V.S. Abhyankar's C. *Prabhā* on *Mīmāṁsānyāyaprakāśa* (MNP), 1880–1950.
4. Madan Mohan Sarma's C. on MNP, 1900–2000.
5. Cinnasvāmi Sastri's C. *Sāravivecanī* on MNP, twentieth century.
6. Uttamur Viraraghavacharya's C. *Suddhasvāda* on MNP, twentieth century.
7. Rāmeśvara Śivayogī's C. on *Arthasaṁgraha,* 1839.
8. Krisnanatha Panchanana's C. on *Arthasaṁgraha,* 1898.
9. Tatacharya's C. *Tantraprakāśikā* on *Arthasaṁgraha,* 1890–1945.
10. Jivananda Vidyasagara's C. on *Arthasaṁgraha,* 1900.
11. Pattabhiramashastri's C. *Arthadīpikā* on *Arthasaṁgraha,* twentieth century.
12. Pramathanatha Tarkabhusana's C. *Amalā* on *Arthasaṁgraha,* twentieth century.
13. Sudarshanacharya's C. on *Śāstradīpikā,* 1970.
14. Peri Suryanarayana Shastri's C. *Bhāvaprakāśikā* on *Bhāṭṭarahasya.*
15. Subrahmanya Shastri's C. *Viṣamagranthībhedinī on Bhāṭṭarahasya,* 1900–1992.
16. D.T. Tatacharya's C. *Pariṣkāra* on the *Mīmāṁsā Paribhāṣā,* 1922.

A few small manuals of Mīmāṁsā based on ancient source-books have been brought out in this period. Of course, these do not profess any novel approach. Among them, some unprinted texts are:

1. The *Tantravilāsa* of Lakṣmaṇa Paṇḍita, eighteenth century
   A brief treatise on the contents of six *Adhikaraṇas* of the *Mīmāṁsā-sūtras* (beginning with *Guṇakāmādhikaraṇa*).
2. The *Piṣṭa-paśu-nirṇaya* of Vaidyanātha Pāyeśuṇḍe (1710–1800)
   This unpublished work deals with the use of *piṣṭa-paśu* (an image prepared out of rice-flour in the form of animal/goat) during *yāga* (sacrifice) pointing out ways and means to continue Vedic rituals and practices even in the present century when *ahiṁsā* (non-violence) is strongly advocated by people and governments alike.
3. The *Aruṇādhikaraṇasāriṇī Vivaraṇī* of Śrīnivāsācarya - 1770
   This *Prakaraṇagrantha* explains in the style of Navya Nyāya, the "*Arunādhikaraṇa*" with regard to text, "*Aruṇayā piṅgākṣyā ekahāyanyā gavā somaṁ krīṇati*". When there arises the objection whether "*aruṇā*" is to be

taken as *guṇamātravācī* (only with the import of quality) or *guṇaviśiṣṭavācī* (meaning construed along with quality), it is explained on the confirmed view found in the *Śrībhāṣya* (or Rāmānuja) as found in the *Ānandamayādhikaraṇa* text.

4. The *Mīmāṁsā-sūtra-dīpikā* of Yallabhaṭṭa (Ella-bhaṭṭa) - 1900
   This is a small *vṛtti* (glossarial commentary) on the *Mīmāṁsā-sūtras* and not yet printed.
5. The *Matyarthalakṣaṇavicāra* of Bhaskaracharya and Svami Shastri - nineteenth century.
   A dialectical tract explaining the *lakṣaṇa* (secondary significance) of *matyartha* in the Vedic statement like *Paśunā Yajeta* - whether here one has to explain *paśunā* as *paśumalā* or just *paśunā* (i.e. through that which possesses *paśutva*, beasthood, or just that which is *pasu*—an animal). This unprinted tract follows the pattern of a dialogue between Svami Shastri and Bhaskaracharya, the former posing an argument and the latter giving a reply.
6. The *Tantranītilaharī* of Ramanujacharya - 1850
   This unprinted *vṛtti* (succinct commentary) on the *Mīmāṁsā-sūtras* follows both the Bhāṭṭa and Prabhākara schools of Mīmāṁsā. The author the *Śāstridīpikā* and the *Mīmāṁsā-Nyāya-viveka.*

A Few Printed Works on Mīmāṁsā of Modern Period

1. The *Tantra-Siddhānta-Ratnāvalī* of Chinnasvami Shastri 1870–1950
   A very good printed *prakaraṇa* (monograph) work, this *Ratnāvalī* provides an easy digest of important doctrines of Mīmāṁsā, even for beginners and general readers of philosophy.
2. The *Bhāṭṭasāra* of Krishna Tatacharya 1875.
   This period tract puts, in a nutshell, the essential teachings of the *Mīmāṁsā-sūtras* summarising the contents of each *pāda* of the twelve *adhyāyas* of the *Mīmāṁsā-sūtras.*
3. The (*Mīmāṁsā-sūtra*) *Bhāvabodhinī* of Vidya-Sankara Bharati, a chief pontiff of Karavīra-Śaṅkarapīṭha (Formerly known as Narahari Shastri) 1937
   A very useful printed work for the students of Mīmāṁsā, this *vṛtti* tract is a simple but unique glossarial commentary explaining, (i) each word found in a *sūtra* (aphorism), and (ii) the general purport of all *adhikaraṇas* (major sections) one after another.
4. The *Mānameyodaya-śloka-vārttika* of Srinivasacharya twentieth century
   An *anuṣṭubh* (*śloka*) type composition, this *Mānameyodaya* not only explains the principles of *pramāṇas* and *prameyas* but also the principal doctrines of the major systems of Indian philosophy.
5. The *Mīmāṁsā-Nyāya-mañjarī* of Pattabhirama Shastri 20th century
   The *Mīmāṁsā nyāyas* (special themes) and the purport of the important

adhikaraṇas of the *Mīmāṁsā-sūtras* are dealt with briefly in this printed *prakaraṇagrantha* (monograph).

NOTES

1. Potter, Karl H. 1977. *Encyclopedia of Indian Philosophies*, Vol. III, Delhi: Motilal Banarsidas.
2. Moore, G.E. 1903. *Principia Ethica.* Cambridge: Cambridge University Press; Ross, David. 1967. *The Right and the Good.* Oxford Clarendon Press.

CHAPTER 5

Developments in Sāṁkhya and Yoga from Eighteenth Century Onwards

A Reconstruction from the Volume on Sāṁkhya edited by G. Larson and Ramasankara Bhattacharya in the *Encyclopedia of Indian Philosophies* of Karl H. Potter, Vol. I.

The Sāṁkhya tradition of philosophising has a unique history of its own, different from that of other schools of Indian philosophy in that there seems to be no foundational text constraining the development of this thought. With other schools of philosophy basic foundational *sūtra* texts from which they proceed, exist and these are considered as authoritative for all those who regard themselves as belonging to that tradition. The very fact that the *Sāṁkhya sūtras* came to be written much later and do not occupy a unique and prestigious place in the history of the development of Sāṁkhyan thought, is a significant fact distinguishing Sāṁkhya from all other schools of Indian philosophy. The *Ṣaṣṭītantra,* which is supposed to be the earliest systematic text of Sāṁkhyan thought in India, never occupied the same place, specially as the *Sāṁkhyakārikā* replaced it soon after in the corpus of Sāṁkhyan writings and even though the *Sāṁkhyakārikā* continued to occupy an important place in Sāṁkhyan literature, it never had that overriding authority which was at least verbally accorded to the basic *sūtras* in other schools of Indian philosophy. This is further illustrated by the fact that in the volume on Sāṁkhya in the *Encyclopedia of Indian Philosophies,* Gerald Larson has divided the development of Sāṁkhya after the composition of the *Kārika* into what he has called the *Karika-Kaumudī-Sāṁkhya,* the *Samāsa Sāṁkhya* and the *Sūtra Sāṁkhya,* thus indicating that the *Sāṁkhyatattvakaumudī,* the *Tattvasamāsa* and the *Sāṁkhyasūtras* played as important a part in the development of Sāṁkhyan thought as the *Sāṁkhyakārikā.* The *Sāṁkhyatattvakaumudī* is supposed to have been written by Vācaspati Miśra I in A.D. 850 while the *Tattvasamāsa* and the *Sāṁkhyasūtras* were probably written sometime in A.D. fourteenth and fifteenth century, respectively. It is true that, according to many scholars, much of the material in the *Sāṁkhyasūtras* is quite old but at least in its present form, most authorities on the subject consider it to be a very late work, generally assigned to some time in the fifteenth century.

Thus, developments in Sāṁkhyan thought from the eighteenth century onwards can only be understood in the context of its earlier development from the *Sāṁkhyakārikā* onwards. The important phases in this development occurred with the *Yuktidīpikā*, the *Sāṁkhyatattvakaumudī* and the *Sāṁkhyapravacanabhāṣya*. The author of the first is unknown, but those of the two later works are Vācaspati Miśra I and Vijñānabhikṣu (A.D. 1515), respectively.

There appear to have been eight commentaries on the *Sāṁkhyakārikā* (A.D. 350–450) of which five are supposed to be very similar in their contents, with only marginal differences among them. These are: *Suvarṇasaptati* (A.D. 500) (translated by Parmārtha into Chinese), Gauḍapāda's *Bhāṣya* (A.D. 500–600), the *Māṭharavṛtti* (A.D. 800 or later), the *Sāṁkhyasaptativṛtti* (A.D. 500–600) and the *Sāṁkhyavṛtti* (A.D. 500–600). However, the remaining three, that is, the *Jayamaṅgalā* (700 or later), the *Yuktidīpikā* (A.D. 600–700) and the *Sāṁkhyatattvakaumudī* (A.D. 850–975) are supposed to not only show significant differences between each other but also to suggest some radical departures from the *Sāṁkhyakārikā*. The authors of the first two are not known but, as far as the last work is concerned, its author is the famous Vācaspati Miśra I who wrote well-known works both on Nyāya and Advaita Vedānta.

Sāṁkhyan thought on the *padārthas* in the *Yuktidīpikā* departs from that expressed in the *Sāṁkhyakārikā*. It apparently has a greater affinity with the *Ṣaṣṭītantra* which is earlier than the *Sāṁkhyakārikā*, though it shows remarkable differences from it. Moreover, apart from the radical departures, its use of the term *padārtha* seems very idiosyncratic, especially if one remembers that the term *padārtha* had a fairly determinate meaning in the *Vaiśeṣika Sūtras* authored much earlier than the writings of the *Yuktidīpikā*. It is of course true that the *Nyāya Sūtras* have referred to the basic enumeration of the topics in *Sūtra* 1.1.1 as the *padārthas* and that in later literature they are usually designated as such, even though they belong to a completely different type than those mentioned in the *Vaiśeṣika Sūtras*. However, the designation of the fifty "categories" mentioned by the *Yuktidīpikā*[1] as *padārthas* seems strange as they are neither epistemological nor ontological, nor logical. Perhaps the mapping of the world in terms of what the author of the *Yuktidīpikā* regards as *rūpa, pravṛtti* and *phala* may help us to understand why he calls them *padārthas*.[2] Under the category of *rūpa* it puts what are usually called *tattvas* in Sāṁkhyan thought which are termed *dravyas* in Vaiśeṣika terminology. Under the generalised category of *pravṛtti*, figure perhaps the dynamic processes or functions which belong to these *tattvas*. But then to be logical one would have to ascribe a specific function or *pravṛtti* to each of the *tattvas* except perhaps to the *puruṣa*. This *pravṛtti* is divided into that which is in the right direction (*hitakāmaprayojana*) and that which is not (*ahitkāmaprayojana*) and the result is what is called *phala* or the consequence which itself in turn is divided into that which is perceptible or manifest (*dṛṣṭa*) and that which is imperceptible or unmanifest (*adṛṣṭa*). However, both the *pravṛtti* and the *phala* should be further divided into *sātvika, rājasika* and *tāmasika* even though this does not seem to have been done in the text concerned. Basically in the Sāṁkhyan perspective, everything would have to have these threefold dimensions and hence even those *tattvas* which are given under *rūpa* would have to be distinguished in terms of these three basic types.

The world of the *Yuktidīpikā*, however, is not exhausted by this classification as it has yet another type of classification which cuts across this. Thus classification of the *tattvas* is further made into *ādhibhautika, ādhyātmika* and *adhidaivika*. The world of the non-living included in the *ādhibhautika* realm consists of the five primary elements, that is, earth, water, fire, air and ether and the five subtle elements that are the *tanmātras* which are associated with these. It comprises not only of material things, but includes also all living beings, such as plants and animals. The categorisation sharply excludes human beings from all other living and non-living beings included in the *ādhibhautika* realm. Human beings are said to belong only to the *ādhyātmika* realm. The *ādhidaivika* realm, of course, comprises divine beings who are radically different from all these other types of beings, belonging to a class by themselves.

Thus, the *Yuktidīpikā,* as pointed out above, does not distinguish between the living and the non-living as it includes animals, birds and insects along with plants in the *ādhibhautika* realm and assigns the *ādhyātmika* realm exclusively to humans. This, it should be pointed out, is a strange classification as it denies the continuity between the living world and the human world which generally is a postulate of all Indian thinking. However, a distinction is always maintained in that the human realm is supposed to be the only realm where new action can originate so that even the so-called *ādhidaivika* realm is where one only enjoys the fruits of the actions done at the human level. The realm of the living or where the life principle operates has been linked in the *Yuktidīpikā*, classification to the realm of the vital airs which have been divided, as usual, into five. There is also an attempt at a distinction between forms of reproduction in these realms. This operates, however, only in the *ādhidaivika* realm as in both the human, that is the *ādhyātmika* realm, and the realm of living beings who are included in the *ādhibhautika* realm, the mode of reproduction is the same.

The whole paraphernalia of classifications in the *Yuktidīpikā* seems to be basically against the spirit of Sāṁkhya which had made a radical distinction between consciousness and primordial materiality. Everything else was supposed to be a modification of the primordial materiality being induced by a fundamental confusion because of the reflection of consciousness in *buddhi* and the changes that this introduces in the primal materiality itself. However, as the *buddhi* itself is supposed to be the first stage in the manifestation of the unmanifest *prakṛti*, the confusion could not have started there. Also, while the doctrine of the five gross elements and the five subtle elements seems to make some sense in terms of the principle of materiality, the movement from *ahaṁkāra, buddhi, mana* and the five *jñānendriyas* and the five *karmendriyas* does not make sense, unless it be assumed that all that is object has to have a subjective counterpart. Similarly, the principle of life, which the *jñānendriyas* and the *karmendriyas* directly presuppose is not mentioned separately any where. This, of course, is based on the assumption that we may postulate the independent existence of *mana, buddhi* and *ahaṁkāra* without any necessary relation to the *jñānendriya* and the *karmendriya* and their objects, that is, the *pañcamahābhūtas* and the *tanmātras*. On the other hand, if they are regarded as necessarily presupposing the *jñānendriyas* and the *karmendriyas*, then one would have to postulate an independent principle of life which would sustain this relationship. Similarly, one would have to bring in the notion of *pravṛtti* in relation to the *karmendriyas, jñānendriyas* and perhaps even *mana, buddhi* and *ahaṁkāra*. All in all, it seems that Sāṁkhyan thought which is developed in the *Yuktidīpikā* takes a turn which is different from that of the *Sāṁkhyakārikā*.

The most important Sāṁkhyan thinking after the *Yuktidīpikā* appears to be embodied in the *Sāṁkhyatattvakaumudī* of Vācaspati Miśra I and the Sāṁkhyapravacanābhāṣya by Vijñānabhikṣu. Amongst these, the *Sāṁkhyatattva Kaumudī* does not say anything new and is considered to be important only because a number of sub-commentaries were later written on it and also because it is one of the most used works on Sāṁkhya by scholars. The work of Vijñānabhikṣu, on the other hand, is important as it tries to see Sāṁkhya in the wider perspective of other systems, primarily Vedānta and tries to synthesize the two in his own manner. There are hardly any important thinkers after Vijñānabhikṣu until we enter the eighteenth century.

Sāṁkhyan thought after Vijñānabhikṣu whose work itself is a commentary on the *Sāṁkhyasūtras* which are supposed to be a more expanded version of what was written in the *Tattva Samāsa*, takes a different turn, particularly with the writers in the nineteenth century. Most of the work of these thinkers is in the form of commentaries on either the works in the Kārikā tradition, such as the *Tattvakaumudī* or the *Sāṁkhyakārikā* itself or on those in the tradition of the *Sāṁkhyasūtras* such as the *Sāṁkhyasūtravṛtti* of Aniruddha or the *Sāṁkhyapravacanabhāṣya* of Vijñānabhikṣu. The *Tattvasamāsa* which is said to be an earlier and shorter version of the *Sāṁkhyasūtras* also has some commentators. The exact distribution of the Sāṁkhyan thinkers who have written on these different texts is roughly as follows :

Starting from the latter part of the sixteenth to the twentieth century, a number of *Prakaraṇa granthas* have been written. These can be divided into three periods: A.D. 1550–1750; A.D. 1750–1850 and A.D. 1850–1950.

About twelve original works and fourteen explanatory works were written during the first period (1550–1750). In the middle period (1750–1850) we have thirty-four original works and fourteen explanatory works. In the modern period (1850–1950) we have about eleven original works and fifteen explanatory texts. Amongst these a large part of the texts are unpublished. Besides these, we also find some *Vṛtti granthas*. The Mīmāṁsā texts do not generally discuss *pramāṇa-prameya* as do the Nyāya texts but some discussion of it does exist in certain texts.

Larson's volume lists about 33 thinkers from A.D. 1700 to 1976 out of whom a substantially larger number occurs in the twentieth century. There are several reasons for this including the fact that almost everything written on Sāṁkhya in Sanskrit, even if it be an elementary text book, has been included by the editors in their search for comprehensiveness and in their anxiety not to miss anything written or published during this period. The entries themselves are evidence of this. For example, from Naraharinatha (no.58) to Shri Rama Pandey (no.65) for eight thinkers belonging to the latest phase of Sāṁkhya in the twentieth century, only short descriptions are given and no analysis of their works has been undertaken. A number of other entries in the *Encyclopaedia* are similarly treated and even where there are summaries of some works, important contributions made by them are hardly highlighted. Surprisingly, one of the editors, Larson who has written a very long and scholarly introduction to the volume, has not cared to indicate the significant developments which occurred in Sāṁkhyan thought over such a long period of time or to indicate the importance of the Sāṁkhyan works composed from A.D. 1700 onwards. Moreover, most of the summaries do not highlight the importance of the particular contribution by the author or indicated why his work should have been included in the volume. The sole exception to this is Kalidasa Bhattacharya who has not only made excellent summaries of the thinkers he has dealt with, but has also tried to highlight their contribution and make a critical assessment of what they have said. However, no attempt is made in the *Encyclopedia* to give any overall assessment of these developments as they have taken place or to attempt to give a unified picture of the whole volume for the information and guidance of the serious student of the subject. Surprisingly, while the volume has two editors, that is, Larson and Rama Shankar Bhattacharya, the Introduction has been written only by the former without any indication whether the other editor agrees with all that has been said in it or not.

A critical study of the volume suggests that the most important contributions made during the period covered were by :

1. Pramathanatha Tarkabhusana
2. Panchanana Tarkaratna
3. Rameshachandra Tarkatirtha
4. Hariharananda Aranya

Besides these, it appears that Mudumba Narsimha Shastri (no.39) is perhaps the first important thinker in this period followed by Bhārati Yati (No.44), the summary of whose works has been given by Rama Shankar Bhattacharya and E. Solomon, respectively.

The work of M.N. Shastri has not yet been published, but according to Rama Shankar Bhattacharya, who has summarised its contents, Sastri "has shown remarkable originality in explaining some of the expressions of the *Sāṁkhyakārika*", (p.451). However, he has not highlighted the "original" points which the author is supposed to have made in the *Sāṁkhyataruvasanta* which he has summarised. Some interesting points in the summary are as follows: first, the distinction between two types of *puruṣārtha,* those that relate to ends that are *dṛṣṭa* and the others that are, what he calls, *ānuśrāvika* (p.451). The *Yuktidīpikā* had already distinguished between *dṛṣṭa* and *adṛṣṭa phala* and the distinction between *dṛṣṭa* and *adṛṣṭa* is well known in the tradition since the time of the *Mīmāṁsā Sūtras* and perhaps even earlier. Its extension to the theory of the *puruṣārthas* seems, however, new. The notion of *vṛttisārūpya* too appears to have been used creatively to explain the natural and spontaneous identification of consciousness with its *vṛttis*. The use of some of the concepts that occur in the *Yoga Sūtras* (1.4) is a striking feature of this work. For example, the distinction between the three kinds of *pariṇāma*, that is, *dharmapariṇāma, lakṣaṇapariṇāma* and *avasthāpariṇāma*, which are talked about in the *Yoga Sūtra* (3.13). The distinction between *dharma* and *lakṣaṇa* is interesting as the former is supposed to refer to essential properties while the latter is concerned with characteristics that are regarded as temporal in character but the distinction between these two and *avasthā* is not clear. From all this, it is apparent that Mudumba Narasimha Shastri's work is sufficiently important and deserves to be edited and published so that it can be studied more carefully for the interesting formulations that it might contain.

The work of Bharati Yati (1889), consists of a commentary on the *Sāṁkhyatattvakaumudī* of Vācaspati Miśra I. It is interesting as it explicitly makes use of Mīmāṁsā principles of interpretation and evinces a tendency to bring in Vedic authority in the discussion of Sāṁkhya, a tendency which is found in many other thinkers of this period as well. However, surprisingly he seems to have made a statement at the very beginning of his work which, if correctly stated by E.A. Solomon's summary of the work in the Larson volume on Sāṁkhya (*Encyclopedia of Indian Philosophies*, edited by Karl Potter), undermines in a serious way, the whole enterprise of Sāṁkhya as it has been generally understood. The statement by E.A. Solomon reads, "Frustration being of the nature of *rajas*, which is eternal, cannot be completely destroyed, but it can certainly be subdued and hence the relevance of this science".[3] It appears from the statement that it is an attempt to answer the objection by the *pūrvapakṣin* that, if *rajas* is eternal and if it is the cause of the three-fold suffering, then how can the suffering be ever destroyed? The answer that the teaching of Sāṁkhya is still relevant because it helps in subduing suffering, even though it cannot be completely done away with, forgets that Sāṁkhya is talking of the *ātyantikaduḥkhanivṛtti*, that is, the cessation of the very possibility of suffering ever occurring again, and not of its temporary cessation which is promised by the commentator.

A striking fact which emerges from this survey of contributors to the development of Sāṁkhyan thought during this period is that many of the Udāsīna sect also wrote on Sāṁkhya, indicating that this philosophical system was actively pursued by certain *sādhus* in India. Besides as mentioned earlier, a contribution from Krishnavallabhacharya of the Svāmī Nārāyaṇa sect has also written on Sāṁkhya during this period (1926). There is also included a thinker who is said to be a follower of Dayanand Sarasvati. Another important work by Kunjavihari Tarkasiddhanta seems to be a *Vādagrantha* as he has argued against the opponents of Sāṁkhya, a very rare type of writing in this school of philosophy.

The transformation in the milieu of even traditional scholars after the establishment of the new institutions of learning by the British in India is a noticeable phenomenon among sāṁkhyan scholars of this period. While it is true that the institutions of classical learning were formally separate from those of western learning, some interaction occurred between the two, particularly among those who were proficient not only in western learning derived through a knowledge of English, but also possessed some knowledge and interest in the classical knowledge of India through the Sanskrit language. This occurred primarily in Bengal and in many places in the South where an active interest in traditional fields of knowledge among western-trained scholars existed. Some indirect influence of this interaction may be found in the works of pure Sanskritists who have written on traditional subjects during this period. Thus, there is a radical distinction between the scholarly works produced in Sanskrit by traditional scholars during the eighteenth and the first part of the nineteenth century and those which were produced later. Pramathanatha Tarkabhūsana's (1865–1941), work on Sāṁkhya, for example, shows some traces of this in his sub-commentary on Aniruddha's *Vṛtti* (A.D. 1400–1500) on the *Sāṁkhyasūtras.* His interest in dating Aniruddha's work and in finding whether this came earlier than that of Vijñānabhikṣu and Vedāntin Mahādeva who also wrote commentaries, can be attributed to the new interest which western learning brought to the study of Indian texts in determining their chronological order. Similarly, he seems not only interested in explicating what Aniruddha is supposed to have said but also in studying the Sāṁkhyan arguments, the counter-arguments of the Buddhists, as well as the alternative interpretations of the texts that were made by others, and what could still be said to be potentially implicit in these. Pramathanatha's understanding of the well-known three-fold constituents of *prakṛti* in the Sāṁkhyan tradition, that is, *sattva, rajas* and *tamasa* is interesting. He regards these not as qualities but as being substantive in character, that is, as *dravya* rather than *guṇa* and argues that they are regarded as properties only in the context of their functioning or the liberation or bondage of the *puruṣa. Prakṛti,* therefore, is nothing over and above these three constituents and should not be considered as their receptacle or substratum. He does not ask as to how one might understand the notion of a three-fold substance or what exactly would be the inter-relation of these in case they are regarded as independent substances or whether it is the nature of a substance to be capable of being independent of others, both in terms of its existence and conceivability. In fact, the exact meaning and status of these three constituents, whether they are assumed as qualities or substances has perhaps never been adequately clarified. Similarly, he develops interesting arguments against both the Buddhists and the Advaitins. To the Advaitins who consider that *avidyā* is the cause of bondage, he suggests that ignorance necessarily postulates the reality of something of which one is ignorant and of which one will possibly have knowledge that will lead to the destruction of that ignorance. However, in case *avidyā* has to be understood as absolute negation, that is, whose object is totally non-existent then by itself it cannot be the cause of anything because that which is an absolute nothing can not cause anything to come into being.

On the other hand, if *avidyā* itself is regarded as positive, then not only the knowledge will have to be regarded as "real" but its object would also have to be given an ultimate reality inferior only to Brahman as it can be sublated by the knowledge of Brahman. However, as the knowledge of Brahman itself is sublated or obscured by *avidyā,* it will have to be regarded as almost co-ordinate with Brahman in the context of avidya's being regarded as ontologically "real" since it is causally effective in bringing into being the whole world of *prapañca* which Brahman is unable to do.

Pramathanatha has also elaborated some of Aniruddha's arguments against Buddhism, especially with regard to its doctrine of "momentariness" which follows from its criterion of reality, *arthakriyākārittva* or causal efficacity. If the Buddhist argument that the criterion of reality is supposed to be that only that can be regarded as "real" which has causal efficacity is accepted then that which is real can never exist without being causally effective, that is, without producing an effect and as the effect itself is also supposed to be "real", it will also in its turn give rise to another effect and so on *ad infinitum.* That which is real, then, can only be regarded as lasting for a moment for if it is real, it would already have given rise to its effect thus proving itself to be real, a situation which will continue indefinitely, giving rise to the necessity of each real lasting only for a moment and, by definition, not being able to remain any longer. Pramathanatha's objection to this view seems two-fold :

1. How can that be called a cause which has already ceased to be? That which does not exist cannot be a cause?
2. If mere antecedence were to entitle anything to be called a 'cause' then anything which precedes will be entitled to that description and we will not be able to distinguish between those antecedents which are the real cause from those which are not.

Pramathanatha's concern with the chronological issues on the one hand and his independent elaboration of Aniruddha's arguments against the Advaitins and the Buddhists on the other are evidence of a new freedom which even traditional philosophers had felt because of the development of a new ethos in the intellectual world of India in the second half of the nineteenth century. This impression is also strengthened by the fact that many of these scholars were not only conversant with almost all schools of Indian philosophy but had written independent works on them.

Krisnanatha Nyayapanchanana who wrote a sub-commentary on Sāṁkhya in A.D. 1902 was, for example, known more as a Naiyāyika than as a Sāṁkhyan, a fact evidenced by the title of *Nyāyapañcānana* which was awarded to him and which became a part of his name. He wrote on Vācaspati Miśra I's *Tattvakaumdī* which is itself a commentary on the *Sāṁkhyakārikā.* His work is entitled *Āvaraṇavāriṇī.* Interestingly, he starts with the sense of frustration or unhappiness which self-consciousness feels to be alien to itself and on this he builds an elucidation and construction of the Sāṁkhyan position, a strategy which Vācaspati Miśra himself had employed. Strangely, however, Vācaspati Miśra I had introduced a discussion in his *Tattvakaumudī* regarding the slaughter of animals in the Vedic *yajña* and its conflict with the general injunction in the Veda against inflicting injury on any living being. The discussion, though common in Indian literature, is odd in the context of Sāṁkhya as a Sāṁkhyan neither believes in the Vedas nor in Vedic ritual sacrifices for the attainment of worldly and non-worldly ends. The discussion is interesting as it leads to the issue as to whether the demerit incurred by the killing during the sacrifice outweighs the merit which accrues because of doing the *yajña* and whether this outweighing cancels the demerit altogether or whether the effects of the demerit continue and one has to suffer its consequences later in one's life or even after that. The issue is theoretically important as it concerns the relation between the merit and demerit earned by one's good and evil actions and whether the consequences of the two affect each other or are totally independent and hence have no influence on each other. This problem has been raised in the context of *phalsāṁkarya* by Mīmāṁsā and has been extensively discussed by thinkers following Appaya Dīkṣita, who had raised the issue focally in his work entitled, *Vidhi Rasāyana* on the subject. The Mīmāṁsaka thinkers, however formulate a principle which, at least in this specific context, seems to take care of the problem posed by it. The principle is, "if a discourse starts with a general prohibition but if in the same discourse the prohibition is explicitly suspended (and even the opposite course of action recommended) for certain specific cases, the suspension of the prohibition stands justified because the specific cases are of stronger import". The principle is perhaps meant to state that, in case an exception is itself mentioned under the rules then it cannot be construed as contrary to the general rule as the rule itself provides explicitly for the exception to it. However, it seems that Vācaspati Miśra I has tried to suggest that this may be permitted only if the exception is not clearly contrary to the rule itself. But it does not seem to be so in the case of the injunction regarding the killing of animals during the sacrifice. Vācaspati's point is not clear. The issue might possibly be formulated in a clearer manner if one remembers the principle of organic unities that Moore had argued for in his well-known book, *Principia Ethica,* in which his contention was that the value of the whole is not the sum of the value of the parts but independent of it. Moore, it is true, was not thinking so much in terms of wholes or unities formed out of a plurality of actions where one might be a means to something else or form a complementary part of the totality of the action. On the other hand, if it be argued that each action has an intrinsic value or disvalue which is not affected by its becoming a means to some other end or by its becoming part of a larger action, then the issue of the relation between the demerit incurred by the killing of animals and the merit earned by performing the ritual sacrifice would have to be understood differently. Also one of the interesting points incidentally made by Krishnanatha is that if one confines oneself to the hedonistic calculus of satisfaction and dissatisfaction alone, one would have to ask whether the total satisfaction outweighs the dissatisfaction incurred by the killing. But if the question is posed in terms of incurring merit or demerit, it will then not be so easy to mitigate or to wipe away the sin which was incurred by doing the wrong act. In fact, the problem is a wider one which has never been focally discussed as, for example, the same issue might arise in the context of *tapas* and *prāyaścitta* by doing which one is supposed to mitigate or wipe out the effects of the evil deeds one has committed, as one would then admit that an action can counteract the effects of another action and affect the calculus of merit and demerit just as much as the calculus of satisfaction and dissatisfaction or pain and pleasure is supposed to do. In fact, the situation is even more complicated as there may be pleasures and satisfaction which presuppose pain or dissatisfaction as their necessary precondition or even as their constituent part. Similarly, an action which is undesirable in itself may be a constituent part or a necessary means for the performance of that which is right or good. The whole notion of *dharma saṁkaṭa* involves these and it is strange that neither the Mīmāṁsakas nor any one else has seriously thought about it in the tradition.

In a discussion of intrinsic and extrinsic validity of awareness, Krishnanātha Nyayapanchanaṇa has formulated a criterion of intrinsic validity of awareness which perhaps comes closest to the notion of analytic truth in western philosophy. The principle as formulated by Kalidasa Bhattacharya is as follows:

> "An awareness is intrinsically valid only if the very factors which make us take it as an awareness also guarantee its validity, that is, when for its validation or for the awareness of its validity, other factors or other confirming awarenesses are not required".[4]

The example which he gives is that of hearing a sentence from the *śruti,* but that obviously is wrong as its validity will only be for that person who believes in the *śruti* and even he will have to interpret its meaning and see whether it coheres with other statements of the *śruti.*

Another interesting issue which appears to have been raised by Krishnanath Nyayapanchanana is the dual characteristic of the awareness of both word and sentence meaning as, on the one hand, it refers to some external state of affairs which may be supposed to be its referential meaning, and on the other, it also creates a difference in the psychic state of the mind which has an effect, sometimes even a radical and profound one, on experiencing consciousness. The latter has been generally neglected in the western discussions on the subject, but it is of great importance, particularly in the case of those sounds, words and sentences which are supposed to be "revelatory" and whose apprehension has a transformative effect on consciousness irrespective of what they are supposed to refer to. It may be noted that this difference is not the same as the one between sense and reference brought to the attention of the philosophical world by Frege in the western tradition. The concept of the *śruti* and the *śabda pramāṇa* become even more intelligible if they are seen in this light.

In his discussion of the distinction between the manifest and the unmanifest *prakṛti,* that is the *vyakta* and the *avyakta,* Krisnanatha Nyayapanchanana points out that this distinction, if seriously taken, will be in conflict with the theory of *Satkāryavāda* which Śāmkhya is also supposed to hold. The theory of *Satkāryavāda* states that the effect is already pre-existent in the cause and, if so, whatever is manifest should already be there in the unmanifest state and that, hence, the distinction between the manifest and the unmanifest cannot be from the view point of the "content" of either. There can, thus, be no real destruction just as there can be no real origination if one accepts the theory of *Satkāryavāda*. However, the more fundamental question as to how there can be a distinction between the manifest and the unmanifest at the ontological level has not been tackled. For, firstly, the notion of the manifest involves the "appearing" to consciousness and, secondly, it involves the reality of time. Interestingly, Sāṁkhya does not seem to accept space and time amongst the twenty-four *tattvas*. Besides this, Krisnanatha also seems to treat *sattva, rajas* and *tamas* as inferential qualities which are theoretically postulated to account for the empirical facts of agreeableness (*prīti*), disagreeableness (*aprīti*), apathy and lack of all interest altogether as denoted by the term *viṣāda*.

There is an interesting discussion regarding the reality of the inference of consciousness, that is, whether it should be inferred from the experience of the knowing consciousness or the enjoying consciousness (*bhoktṛabhāva*). It is surprising, however, that no one thought of the possibility of inferring it from the fact of volitional action (*krtṛttva*).

The role of the subtle body consisting of the *buddhi, ahaṁkāra, manas* and the five subtle elements was thought by Krishnanatha Panchanana to be a matter of inference from the facts of pain, pleasure and confusion. However, the terms subtle and gross and the distinction between them in philosophical discussion and analysis are not only relative terms, but it may be said that there can be no such thing as gross or subtle in itself. Moreover, if one accepts the distinction one would have to apply it throughout so that the subtle body would then need to have subtle *jñānendriyas* and *karmendriya* as well along with the gross. Interestingly, the Tantra accepted a subtle body as a counterpart of the gross body which we are generally not aware of.

Panchanana Tarkaratna

An interesting question as to what exactly is meant by *āgam ekam*, a statement found in the *Śvetāśvatara Upaniṣad*, is raised by Panchanana Tarkaratna. This is supposed to be the basis of the claim that Sāṁkhya is supported by the *śruti*. The philosophically interesting part of the discussion in which Tarakaratna appears to support Vācaspati Miśra I against Vijñānabhikṣu relates to the question of whether *prakrti* or what may have incorrectly been translated as primal materiality is both unborn, that is, beginningless and eternal and one. The philosophical issue with respect to the first relates to whether that which is beginningless is also endless, while with respect to the claim of oneness is raised the question, "One in what sense?" The first was countered by the Advaitin's assertion that though *avidyā*, or primal ignorance, is beginningless, it does have an end while the second raises two issues, specifically in the Sāṁkhya context as to how *prakṛti* can be called one when the system also accepts *puruṣa* as a co-eternal entity along with it. Secondly, as it holds *prakṛti* itself to be constituted of *sattva, rajasa* and *tamasa* how can it be regarded as one. The discussion about the one recalls the different interpretations given to the famous foundational sentence on which all schools of Vedānta are supposed to be based, that is, "*ekamevādvitīyam neha, nānāsti kiñcan*". Interestingly, Panchanana Tarakaratna gives two alternatives regarding the notion of oneness: that without a second, as the only one of its kind, or as being that which is a constituent of everything else but which has no constituents within itself. *Prakṛti* can certainly be considered as one in the first sense, but it will be difficult to understand it as being one in the second sense, if it is essentially understood as being constituted of *sattva, rajas* and *tamas* which are *prima facie* plural in character. This also goes counter to the supposed contention of Vācaspati Miśra who had suggested that *sattva, rajas* and *tamas* are entities which are inferred on the basis of the actual experience of agreeableness, disagreeableness and a lack of any interest or emotion, as was discussed by Krishnanatha in his work.

Panchanana Tarakaratna begin an interesting discussion on Mīmāṁsā,[5] particularly in connection with the issue as to whether ritual slaughter in the *yajña* as enjoined in the Vedas produces any demerit for the person concerned. In fact, an aspect not raised earlier is who should earn the demerit of the action concerned—the person who actually kills the animal or the *yajamāna* on whose behalf the *yajña* is being done?

There is yet another valuable debate available deriving from the Sāṁkhya theory of causation as to how anything can really appear or disappear. The point though discussed by earlier writers also, is given an added dimension by Panchanana Tarakaratna who seems to make a new point regarding this. It is suggested by him that disappearance can only mean that it becomes latent as there is no such thing as destruction. It is argued that the further latency of this latency can only mean its final disappearance in the *primal prakṛti* itself where everything is supposed to be non-manifest, that is *avyakta*. Thus, *abhāva* is treated as a lapse into latency and not as having any independent character of its own. But, then this notion of becoming latent itself would need an explanation as also the fact that while the notion of *avyakta* is accepted in the Sāṁkhyan tradition, normally it is applied only to *prakṛti* while all the other *tattvas* are treated only as *vyakta* and not as *avyakta*. In case the notion is extended with respect to all entities, Sāṁkhya will have to explain as to why and how this transition takes place in each of the so called *tattvas*. The problem becomes even more complicated as Sāṁkhya does not accept space and time as *tattvas*, a point that Panchanana Tarkaratna has emphasised in his discussion of Sāṁkhyan metaphysics. But if this is so, how can it maintain the distinction of manifest and unmanifest or becoming latent, which was given to explain what is known as *abhāva* in other systems?

Interestingly, neither Vācaspati Miśra I or Panchanana Tarakaratna tries to suggest that the *tattvas* of all other systems can be reduced to the *tattvas* of

Sāṁkhya and hence need not be considered as independent substantial entities besides those that are enumerated in the Sāṁkhya system. Not only this, the problem of the relationship between the different *tattvas* enumerated in the Sāṁkhya system does not appear to have been attended to, nor is their relation to the primeval *prakṛti* discussed.

Panchanana Tarkaratna also makes the point that, considering the fact that the intellect or *buddhi* in Sāṁkhya is an unconscious or material principle, knowledge cannot be considered as its function. However, the modification of *buddhi* as it is illuminated by the light of consciousness and which, therefore, attains the state of knowledge, is to be distinguished from those states of *buddhi* that are not so illuminated. The idea of the mode of intellect or *buddhi* needs to be further explained as there can be no mode other than that of the *sāttvika*, the *rājasika* or the *tāmasika* in the Sāṁkhyan system. Further, it is not clear as to what the relationship is between *buddhi, manas*, the *tanmātras* and the *mahābhūtas*, on the one hand, and the *karmendriyas* and the *jñānendriyas*, on the other. Writers on Sāṁkhya as all the others who write on Indian philosophy are more concerned with explaining what the text says rather than in formulating questions and problems of their own and in discovering whether the text has significant answers to them.

Besides the relation of the intellect with the object of sense perception, Sāṁkhya emphasises the relation of the intellect to consciousness through egoity. When the intellect relates with the object of sense perception it takes the form of the object and asserts it in the judgemental form that it is such and such while in the relation of the intellect to consciousness through egoity the whole is appropriated by the sense of the "I" which then apprehends the object as relevant to it in the context of desire and action. In the second stage, it also identifies with it in a deeper sense as now the 'ego' itself is seen as 'coloured' or 'determined' by the object which is believed to exist in 'such and such a way'. The term *pratyakṣa* is used in Sāṁkhya in two senses, the first sense obviously relates to the usual contact of the senses with the object concerned. The second sense of the term, however, brings the intellect into the picture and uses the term to denote the conjunction of the intellect with this contact of the senses with the object. It is not clear, however, that the second is the same as "introspection" or whether it is being maintained that the first cannot be called perception at the human level unless the second contact also takes place. In fact, there seems to be another problem with regard to this issue, as according to Sāṁkhya no knowledge can occur unless it is illuminated by the light of consciousness which is totally outside the system and which occurs, only because of a confusion. If, on the other hand, as was earlier said in the context of intellect or *buddhi*, a modality of it can occur without having knowledge as it was not being illuminated by consciousness, then Sāṁkhya will have to account for the reasons as to why this illumination or contact with consciousness occurs at certain times and not at others.

Regarding the Sāṁkhyan theory of *Satkāryavāda* Panchanana Tarkaratna suggests that if the theory is accepted, the distinction between the *pāramārthika, vyāvhārika* and *pratibhāsika* levels of reality will become untenable. Not only this, one will have to accept that everything including *manas, buddhi* and *ahaṁkāra* are already there in *prakṛti* in an unmanifest form. Also, as in the Sāṁkhyan system, *prakṛti* is supposed to be constantly changing, the distinction between the real and the unreal cannot be based on the ground of permanence and change. However, it is not clear as to how the doctrine of *satkāryavāda* will help in explaining erroneous cognition or deal with the problem of the ontological status of an illusory object or a dreamt object.

Another issue that Panchanana Tarkaratna raises in the context of the statement given by Vācaspati Miśra I is that if *rajas* is the principle of all motion it must be the cause of motion not only in *sattva* and *tamas* but also in itself. This raises the further problem of its being the cause of its own motion. But while Panchanana Tarkaratna draws our attention to the problem, he does not give any satisfactory solution to it.

In the context of the argument that the same object produces satisfaction, dissatisfaction and confusion in different persons due to the dominance of the *sāttvika, rājasika* and *tāmasika* elements in them and not due to any differences in the objects own qualities, Panchanana Tarkaratna makes a significant contribution. He says that if it were so, why should it not be true with respect to other qualities such as colour or taste, etc.? However, what is not considered is that the object is also made up of the *rājasika, tāmasika* and *sāttvika* qualities and, according to the Sāṁkhyan position, these qualities can only dominate alternatively and not solely all the time. Also unclear is how Sāṁkhya differenciate between qualities such as colour, taste, shape, size, etc., and those which are known as *sāttvika, rājasika, tāmasika.* Perhaps the latter qualities may be regarded as second under qualities which arise on the basis of the first order qualities, mentioned earlier. This will be analogous to Locke's primary and secondary qualities, though the distinction between them is made in a different context and at a different level. Most of the qualities that we have considered as first order qualities in the Sāṁkhya system are regarded as "secondary qualities" in Locke's system. However, as the *sāttvika, rājasika* and *tāmasika* qualities seen to be valuational in character, they may be regarded as third level or tertiary qualities from those which Locke has called "secondary qualities" in his system. In any case, this is the direction that Sāṁkhyan thought did not take but, at least, Pancānana Tarkaratna has pointed out the way by raising questions regarding the relation of qualities such as *sāttvika, rājasika* and *tāmasika* to other qualities such as colour, etc. which are accepted in the Sāṁkhyan system.

Regarding the non-composite character of consciousness, it is argued that consciousness cannot be characterised in terms of any entity or quality including that of *sattva, rajas* and *tamas.* However, Tarkaratna does not discuss what exactly it would mean to say that consciousness is composite in character or whether consciousness is affected in any sense whatsoever because of its identification with *prakṛti* and the resulting confusion. In fact, if the confusion were not to affect the consciousness, it would not be confusion at all, for *prakṛti* being totally inert cannot be affected by confusion.

In giving reasons for the postulation of twenty-five *tattvas* in Sāṁkhya, Panchanana begins by saying that experience is the primal fact from which all reflection begins and as it does so, it immediately has to make a distinction between consciousness and the object and the relation between them. But then, does this relation belong to consciousness or to the object or to something else. At this point a new consideration is introduced that the analysis should be such that it should permit the possibility of liberation. However, this is not clear as the issue of liberation has not yet arisen.

Another question that arises in this context is why does one have to postulate the senses, the mind, the intellect and egoity in order to understand this relationship of consciousness to the object. However, Tarkaratna does not seem to directly discuss the philosophical problems raised by such a relation and does not point to the distinction between the relations that obtains: (i) between objects, (ii) and those which obtain between objects and consciousness, (or) or between one consciousness and another.

Regarding rationality and objectivity in willing as compared to rationality and objectivity in cognition with which it is usually associated, Tarkaratna suggests that objectivity in willing is the awareness of what I ought to do and the rationality in willing is to be determined by this awareness. On the other hand, he argues that rational discerning leads to belief which gives rise to the idea of the rational objectivity which operates both in knowing and willing. Strangely, however, he thinks that rational objectivity in knowledge comes from the awareness of what ought-to-be rather than "what it is". It is not quite clear as to what are his grounds for drawing the distinction between what ought-to-be and what is the case.

Further he provides an interpretation of the term *aiśvarya*, supernormal powers, which is different from the way it is generally understood. If Kalidas Bhattacharya's summary is to be believed, Panchanana Tarkaratna interprets the term *aiśvarya* to mean a "form of willing" whose rational objectivity consists in the "awareness of attaining the maximum in life". This, however, does not seem to distinguish between the "form" of willing and the awareness of attaining the *maximum* in the field in respect of which the willing is being done. Also, it is not clear how such an understanding of the term is related to the idea of "supernormal powers" with which the term is usually associated, unless one assumes that if the modality of willing completely matches the "maximum" that is desired to be attained than one is bound to attain the "maximum" through the fact of this perfect "matching" between the will and the object of willing.

Another important point that he makes is that *rajas* has to be present in every state as there can be no motion without it and thus *sāttvika* and *tāmsika* must be taken as the positive and negative directions of that movement. Interestingly, one consequence of this is that *tamas* cannot be treated as the mere absence of that which is positive, but rather as something which is positively evil in itself. This, if taken seriously, will undermine the general understanding of *tamas* as inertia or passivity.

Vācaspati Miśra and Rameschandra Tarkatirtha

One of the surprising things ascribed to Vācaspati Miśra is the distinction between the *parā* and *aparā* with respect to non-attachment and the contention that the *para*, non-attachment, is disinterestedness even in the direct intuition of the difference of consciousness and materiality (Larson, p.541). Another point made by him relates to the contention that when one wakes from dreamless sleep, one passes through all the Sāṁkhya stages in reverse order, a point that is generally not made in the texts. However, he seems to have listed this on the basis of the passages in the *Upaniṣads* and the *Purāṇas.*[6]

He also discusses the types of contentment as well as the content of contentment and the notion of *tuṣṭiparyāya.* However, it is not clear as to what is exactly meant by contentment and whether there is any difference between the contentment that comes from following the path that increases the awareness of 'otherness' in consciousness or from a correct understanding of materiality at any level.

It appears that Vācaspati Miśra I has equated the positions of Sarvāstivāda Buddhism, Advaita Vedānta and *Yoga sūtra* of Patañjali with the following: (i) the world is not caused; (ii) it is a transformation of consciousness; (iii) God changes the ultimate substances into the world.[7] It is doubtful whether the ascription of these positions to the schools mentioned above is correct.

There seems to have been a problem as to how to understand the word "*Saṁyoga*". *Saṁyoga* has been understood, on the one hand, as "*yogyatā*" on the part of both consciousness and *prakṛti* to be related to each other and, on the other, of the actual contact caused by the prenatal disposition complex (*adṛṣṭa*) of the worldly person (*jīva*)".[8]

One of the commentators of the *Tattvakaumudī*, Rameshchandra Tarkatirtha (1881) had included an independent monograph on the subject entitled *Sāṁkhyatattvavilāsīya,* written by his teacher Raghunātha Tarkavāgīśa. Besides this, he displayed a modern trend in writing by writing a biography of Vācaspati Miśra I by listing the available Sanskrit works on Sāṁkhya. He also gives a number of couplets in the *Sāṁkhyakārikā* which are mentioned by the different commentators. He is perhaps the first to mention the Chinese interpretations and the number of couplets mentioned therein.

Rameschandra in examining how the sense of egoity or ahaṅkāra arises starts with the Sāṁkhyan formulation that it is the reflection of pure consciousness in the *buddhi* that leads to the conditioning of the awareness as an awareness of the 'I'. However, if it is so, then the sense of egoity or what is mentioned as *ahaṁkāra* should occur in Sāṁkhya after *buddhi* and not before it. Also, the specificiality of the 'I' in the *buddhi,* both in a general form and in its specific form, as belonging to the individual, will have to be distinguished and there will have to be a generalised egoity as well as specific egoities. While Sāṁkhya has not elobrated on this, possibly the postulate of the plurality of the *puruṣa* might help to solve this problem. The sense of 'I-ness' appearing consequent to the reflection of consciousness in the *buddhi* will then merely be a function of the specificity of the *puruṣa* in the plural world of *puruṣas* and not be purely the result of the fact of its being reflected in a radically alien medium, that is, the *buddhi*. The further specification of this egoity or sense of 'I-ness' is also a problem because of the differentially determinant nature of all the other adjuncts with which the *buddhi* is associated including, of course, the *buddhi* itself. But, if this is accepted, then each particular *Jīva*, to use a term from a different philosophical system, would have to have its "own" differentiated specific *manas* along with the *jñānendriyas* and *karmendriyas* and all the constitutents of the so-called individual in the Sāṁkhyan system. There would still remain the problem of the general sense of I-ness or egoity or *ahaṁkāra* whose very notion could not be formulated in the system as there is no reflection in the unitary, primordial *prakṛti* which perhaps provide the grounds for it. But all those questions arise from Rameshchandra's view as to how the sense of egoity or *ahamkāra* arises in the Sāṁkhyan system. It is not clear how other commentators on *Tattvakaumudī* have dealt with this issue, or how they differ from the position taken by Rameshchandra on it.

Another issue debated by Rameshchandra is that of the relation between the subtle elements and the gross elements and whether the subtle elements (*tanmātras*) have a form of their own. In case they do not have a form of their own, and are only a necessary part in the chain that relates the gross elements to the mind through the senses, what function then do they perform in the system? Are they only transmitting agents for the conveying of the gross elements to the mind so that the mind can more easily grasp the gross elements in a manner that is suited to its own nature. But even this would involve some sort of a transformation in the material received from the gross elements. On the other hand, if these subtle elements are supposed to have a form of their own then how does this "form" interact with the form of the gross elements before transmitting it to the mind. Also it is unclear as to whether Sāṁkhya would distinguish between 'subtle' and 'gross' at the level of the senses, the mind and the intellect as it does at the level of the gross elements. In fact, the distinction between the *sāttvika*, the *rājasika* and the *tāmasika* cuts across the distinction between the gross and the subtle, and what exactly is the relation between the two is unanswered. In case the subtle elements are regarded as not having a form, it will be difficult to distinguish one subtle element from another one of the same type. Neither Vācaspati Miśra I nor Rameshchandra Tarkatirtha seem to have addressed this problem.

The issue of the reflection of consciousness in the *buddhi* as giving rise to the awareness of the 'I', it is carried further in the discussion of consciousness and self-consciousness and the distinction between them. The discussion is further complicated by roles played by the mind, the *buddhi* and the *ahaṁkāra*, both separately and collectively, resulting in the awareness of consciousness as reflected at this level.

Rameshachandra Tarkatirtha also discusses the notion of "*svalakṣaṇa sāmānya*" which is a strange amalgam of the notion of *svalakṣaṇa* as given by the Buddhists and the notion of *sāmānya* as given by the Naiyāyikas. The idea is that both the specific particular and the universal, of which it is an instance, are apprehended simultaneously, as without this, no *vyāpti* would occur as it requires the simultaneous apprehension of the particular and the universal for it to take place. One has to apprehend not only the universal fireness which is related to smokeness but also the particular specific fire and smoke which are instances of this. Thus, one simultaneously infers both the fireness which is a universal and the specific instance of fire which, though unperceived, is the particular instance to it. For the Buddhists, the *sāmānya* is a *vikalpa* which is superimposed on the particular, while for the Naiyāyika the two are interfused. However, as to whether we can apprehend the *sāmānya* without necessarily apprehending the *svalakṣaṇa* in which it is instanciated as is the case with the *svalakṣaṇa*, which cannot be apprehended without simultaneously apprehending the *sāmānya* involved in it, is a problem raised here. It may be noted that for the Buddhists the *svalakṣaṇa* is a matter of inference or at least should be so, even though it may be directly apprehended in some extraordinary state of consciousness.

What exactly is meant by the *prakṛti* in Sāṁkhya or what do any of its specific formations for example, *Jaḍa*, unconscious or material denote. Rameshchandra Tarkatirtha makes it clear that these terms merely mean that it is other than consciousness and not that they are illumined by something else (Larson, p.510), as in Sāṁkhya awareness whether of the *puruṣa* or of anything else is itself the result of the reflection of *puruṣa* in the *buddhi.* Perhaps this is better illustrated when it said that the otherness to consciousness is something different from materiality as not only a living being but also creation of consciousness and acts of consciousness can be objects of someone else's consciousness and hence function as 'other' to it.

In distinguishing the Sāṁkhya concept of *guṇa* from the Vaiśeṣika concept, he suggests that *guṇa* is essentially for the purposes of some other and hence has primarily a teleological function. This, however, seems hardly tenable as one would then have to accept that the *tamas* and the *rajas* also have a purpose which obviously would be opposite to *sattva,* and their purpose would become independent of that for whom these purposes are exercised.

Why does consciousness have to be postulated as a separate principle? The intrinsic dynamism of *sattva, rajas, tamas* leading to perpetual change needs no explanation as it is intrinsic to them, while the heterogeneous changes leading to *ahaṁkāra,* etc., do need the postulation of consciousness as there is a teleological element in them which cannot be understood in terms of the dynamic nature of the three *guṇas* themselves.

Another reason according to Rameshchandra Tarkatirtha is that all experience is accompanied by an attitude of satisfaction or dissatisfaction towards the object experienced and this can only be outside the experience and hence some principle like consciousness has to be postulated. An interesting distinction is drawn by him between the "witness-consciousness" and the "knower- consciousness", that is, the *sākṣin* and the *dṛṣṭā* in that the former is only aware of the processes of consciousness through, of course, the usual processes of reflection, while in the latter, the objects of these processes are also included in the awareness. It may be noted that normally one does not distinguish between the *sākṣin* and the *dṛṣṭā*, yet the author seems to make a distinction between them, though he uses the term *dṛṣṭṛ* instead of *dṛṣṭā*.[9]

The need for postulating *buddhi* is given in detail[10] by Rameshchandra Tarkatirtha as also why it has to be distinguished from both mind and *ahaṁkāra* which are very similar to it and the sense capacities which are dissimilar to it. The need for the mind is as perception in many cases does not occur even where there is contact between the senses and the object when one is not attending to it. But then the mind should be identified with the faculty of attention or given the function of attending which generally is not done either in Nyāya or in Sāṁkhya. On the other hand, the need for postulating the *buddhi*, as distinct from mind and egoity is due to the phenomenon of dreamless sleep. However, it is not explained as to why the postulation of *ahaṁkāra* or egoity cannot perform this function. Also, the function of thinking and ratiocinative discrimination has been completely ignored in the discussion. Many other issues such as the lack of contact between the senses and the object in dreams is not paid any attention to, nor it is considered necessary to explain why other *tattvas*, besides the usual three, do not need to be postulated to account for experience, or to account for, say, imagination or memory. The field of action is totally left out of any consideration, particularly as action can never make sense at the level of perception alone.[11]

There is a strange notion in Iśvarakṛṣṇa's *Sāṁkhyakārikā* of *prakṛtilaya* or of a final absorption in primal materiality which has also been called liberation. Īśvarakṛṣṇa appears to have attributed this attainment to the practice of non-attachment, while Vācaspati Miśra I in his commentary seems to have said that the mere practice of non-attachment without the accompanying consciousness of one's total difference from all objects would not lead to *prakṛtilaya* or this kind of liberation. Rameshchandra Tarkatirtha suggests that the non-attachment which is accompanied by the awareness of consciousness of total separation would alone lead to liberation in the sense of *kaivalya*. It is not quite clear whether this is the exact contention, but in case the notion of *prakṛtilaya* is introduced by Iśvarakṛṣṇa, one would then have to explore the argument to see how it is different from the notion of *kaivalya* in the system.

Harihariananda Aranya

As a practicing Sāṁkhyan, Hariharananda Aranya has explicated the Sāṁkhya and Yoga doctrines more from an experiential point of view rather than as objects of philosophical reflection. In his discussion of consciousness he makes a distinction between a change in consciousness that occurs because of a change in the object of consciousness and a change that occurs even when the object of consciousness has remained the same. The latter he has called *lākṣaṇika,* while the former is called *aupādānika.* Oddly enough, he has not raised the question as to whether the latter affects our apprehension of the object in any way, for many a time a change in our consciousness affects the way we apprehend things.

Hariharananda Aranya also makes a distinction between awareness and consciousness as he argues that all stimulations after reaching of the intellect are transformed into awareness, while consciousness remains unaffected by these stimulations.[12] He also raises the issue of the plurality of consciouness.

Explaining. the term '*avyakta*' as it is applied to *prakṛti,* in a different way from that which is usually accepted in Sāṁkhyan philosophy in this context, he says that *prakṛti* is called '*avyakta'* because it is not an object of awareness to the liberated *puruṣa* and not because it is unmanifest as is usually held by the Sāṁkhyans. Hence, according to him, the descriptions of *prakṛti* as *vyakta* and *avyakta* are only in relation to the unliberated and the liberated *puruṣa* and have nothing to do with its own state. He calls this state *avyakta* also as "*tamas*" which is incomprehensible as no state of *prakṛti* can be purely described in terms of only one of its *guṇas,* least of all, in terms of *tamas.*

Sattva, rajas and *tamas* are described by him according to his own understanding as *prakāśa,* (capacity for expression), *kriyā* and *sthiti* and suggests that when these three achieve a state of equilibrium they dissolve into *prakṛti.* Here it may be noted that *sthiti* is understood as the capacity for remaining in a latent state and is identified with *tamas*; but that the concepts of latency and non-latency cannot be applied if *avyakta* is defined in relation to the situation that alone obtains in relation to the liberated *puruṣa* is not considered by him. Also, it is not clear what exactly would be the difference between unconsciousness and liberation if the notion of *avyakta* is understood in the manner proposed by him.

The phenomenal world as understood by Hariharanand is a result of the interaction between primordial materiality, or *prakṛti* and the absolute illuminator consciousness or *puruṣa.* The former is called *sthiti* and the latter *prakāśa.* The third that is *kriyā* stands for the relation between the two and is supposed to possess the character of constant change and transitoriness. However, this formulation is opposed to the earlier formulation where the concepts of *sthiti* and *tamas* were defined differently.[13]

Hariharanand Aranya formulates the relationship between *mana, buddhi* and *ahaṁkāra* in an interesting way and sees them in a unitary manner as constituting the internal organ or the *antaḥkaraṇa* with three different aspects also related to what he has called *prakāśa, kriyā* and *sthiti* and also to *sattva, rajas* and *tamas.* The function of the *buddhi* is *prakāśa* and it is essentially *sāttvika* in character. *Ahaṁkāra* or egoity is seen as the dynamic aspect of *buddhi,* or self, through which a self is related to the not-self and is associated with *kriyā* or *rajas,* while mind or *tamas* is supposed to be that aspect by which the self gets attached to the object. But the relation between the *antaḥkaraṇa* and the self does not seem to be clear. Also, while one may understand how the self can be related to the object without attachment, it is difficult to see how the self can be related to the other without illumining it in some sense or other.

However, there is another meaning of *prakāśa* given by Hariharanand Aranya which treats it as the capacity for expression. If so, this will be the free activity of consciousness resulting in its objectification, but then through what does the self express itself? In spite of these difficulties, it is clear that Hariharanand Aranya is trying to creatively rethink the Sāṁkhyan concepts and understand them in a new manner. The attempt to see *mana, buddhi* and *ahaṃkāra* as integrally related to each other results in an interesting formulation, suggesting that transformation in any one of them will not affect the conscious or *puruṣas.* He tries to answer the objection as to whether if such a plurality of *puruṣas* is admitted, would each limit the other as all of them are considered to be infinite. His reply to the objection is that it is irrelevant as consciousness is not spatial in nature and hence the idea of one limiting the other does not arise.[14] He may also have taken recourse to the notion that the Sāṁkhyan *puruṣa* is not supposed to be omnipotent or even omniscient and hence even the possible limitation of each by the other cannot be conceived. He, of course, does not raise the issue as to how one would distinguish between one *puruṣa* and another in case the notion of plurality is to be strictly maintained. If there is to be real plurality, then there has also to be a real difference. Would the *puruṣas* be like Leibnitzian monads with the difference that all of them are equally clear and distinct in their consciousness? He also does not seem to raise the question as to whether one consciousness is aware of another, or even if it is aware of itself would it necessarily result in the transformation of the remaining as well. However, as all the three that is *mana, buddhi* and *ahaṁkāra,* have been defined in a very simplistic manner, it is not clear what a change in them would mean; for any change will mean the abolition of their function and consequently of themselves also.

The concept of *ahaṁkāra* is treated as *asmitā* or the I-consciousness by Hariharanand Aranya and he suggests that the I-consciousness has two kinds of transformations, one which he calls *vidyāpariṇāma* and the other which he calls *avidyāpariṇāma.* The first, according to him, is *sāttvika,* while the second seems to arise more because of confusion or identification with anything other than itself. He also makes a distinction between a radical transformation which he calls *jātyantarpariṇāma* and the other as a change of state without any change in the type or the species to which one belongs (*avasthāpariṇama*). It appears that the *vidyāpariṇāma* is a change in *smitā* of the latter kind (*avasthāpariṇāma*)as here the distinction between the 'I' and the other obtains while the *avidyāpariṇāma* is of the former kind (*jātyantarapariṇāma*) as there the I-consciousness undergoes a radical transformation and begins to conceive of itself as the other which is entirely opposed to it. This may not be correct representation of his position as what he means by the statement is not quite clear (see p.584). However, it is an interesting formulation that the I-consciousness itself gives rise to cognitive consciousness which itself is of many kinds depending on its relationship to the 'other' of which it is conscious.

The operations of awareness which are ascribed to *antaḥkaraṇa*, that is, *mana*, *buddhi* and *ahaṁkāra* are divided into those of *śakti* and *avasthā*. The first are dynamic activities like thinking, etc. Similarly, the *antaḥkaraṇa* is supposed to have two kinds of properties: *pratyayas* which include both cognition and conations and *saṁskāras* that is latent dispositions.[15] (The use of the term *pratyaya* for conation seems very odd.) It is also not clear as to what the difference between *śakti* and *pratyaya* is on the one hand, and *avasthā* and *saṁskāra*, on the other. Perhaps *śakti* may be understood as the activity of the internal organ and *pratyaya* as the result of that activity. Similarly, *avasthā* may seen as giving rise to *saṁskāra*. However, the summary given does not clarify these issues.

Hariharanand Aranya gives a detailed analysis of the activity of cognition which, surprisingly, has been given as *prakhyā*. These activities are *pramāṇa, smṛti, pravṛttivijñāna* (cognition of activities), *vikalpa* (conceptual constructions) and *viparyaya*.[16] Similarly, *pravṛtti* has five subdivisions : *saṁkalpa, kalpanā, kṛti, vikalpanā* (doubt and hesitation) and *viparyasta* (futile effort).

Hariharanand Aranya makes a radical distinction in the understanding of *śabda* as a *pramāṇa* as he confines it to the spoken word only and that too by an *āpta puruṣa,* which of course, *is* not the Śāṁkhya *puruṣa*. He explicitly excludes anything written as being the basis of *śabda pramāṇa*.

The notion of *vikalpa* or what has been translated as conceptual construction is divided into *vastuvikalpa, kriyāvikalpa* and *abhāvavikalpa*. The last is interesting as here objects are supposed to exist because there are words for them, while in the first, an object is regarded as more or different from what it actually is. In the second, the agency is supposed to be wrongly attributed. Perhaps the notion could be widened and treated differently. However, Hariharanand Aranya has not taken into consideration the fact that any *vikalpa* can lead to genuine activity on the part of one because of the mistaken *vikalpa* which one considers to be true.

A detailed analysis of the five *pravṛttis*[17] is given by Aranya in which the notion of *saṁkalpa* or intentionality has been defined as the application of I-consciousness in conscious activities. While discussing the *avasthā vṛtti*,[18] which he identifies with satisfaction, frustration and confusion, he gives a new and interesting analysis of confusion as arising from excessive satisfaction and frustration.

Hariharanand Aranya uses a new word for love of life called *abhiniveśa* and defines it as dread in general and not only fear of death. He also regards *rāga*, *dveṣa* and the *abhiniveśa* as static operations relating to *kṛti*. He treats *jāgrat*, *svapna* and *suṣupti* as states of the body and equates them with *sattva*, *rajas* and *tamas* in his analysis of them. A new state which has not generally been paid attention to called *utsvapna* is introduced by him. This has been translated as nightmare and relates these four states to the active states of the body and the mind.[19]

He also discusses the notion of *vyvasāya* or determination which operates in consciousness and distinguishes *sadvyavasāya* (direct perception), *anuvyavasāya* (reflection) and *paridṛṣṭa vyavasāya* (undistinguished activity that causes mutation in sleep).

An interesting reason is put forth as to why the ultimate material cause of the object cannot be grasped in the same way as the external object itself is grasped through the knowing and acting capacities of the subject and the object.[20] He ascribes three characteristics to all objects in terms of their knowability (*bodhyatva*), their mutability (*kriyātva*) and inertness (or *jāḍya*). Perhaps it would have been better if *kriyātva* could have been translated as the capacity to be transformed or changed by human activity and inertness as resistance to both knowability and transformability.

In the Sāṁkhyan Tradition, Hariharanand Aranya gives yet another distinction between the subtle elements and the gross elements. He treats the former as having only generic properties with no differentiation within them which the gross elements are supposed to possess and hence the former do not give rise to frustration, satisfaction, etc.[21] He raises the question as to what might be the cause of the subtle elements and answers that it might be something akin to mind. In this connection, he postulates the notion of an objective mind or the *virāṭa puruṣa* to whose waking and sleeping states he ascribes the manifestation and dissolution of the universe. He also gives an argument as to why the cause of subtle elements can only be akin to something internal. The argument is based on the assumption that external qualities such as colour, sound, etc., do not belong to the subtle elements and hence as they cannot be external in nature, they must be internal. This however goes against the notion of *satkāryavāda* for, in case the gross elements are the result of subtle elements, they must possess the same properties though in a subtle form. It is obvious that Hariharanand Aranya is building his own version of the Sāṁkhya system, regardless of whether in this process he is violating some of the fundamental tenets of the system. In fact, the theory of cosmic creation and dissolution as given by him seems to have nothing to do with classical Sāṁkhya. It is an attempt to synthesize the usual non-Sāṁkhyan versions found in the *Purāṇas* and even some portion of the Vedas and to integrate them into the Sāṁkhya system. But the attempt does not seem to be very successful.

Rama Shankara Bhattacharya who co-edited the *Encyclopedia of Philosophy*, Volume IV on Sāṁkhya with Larson has himself written a commentary on Vijñānabhikṣu's interpretation of the *Sāṁkhya Sūtras* contained in his work, *Sāṁkhyapravacana Bhāṣya*. However, he sharply differs from Vijñānabhikṣu's interpretation of the *Sāṁkhya Sūtras* and has given substantive reasons of his own for doing so. Besides this, he has also changed the sequence of the *sūtras* in order to make their meaning and discussion more coherent.

Thus, it is apparant that there has been fresh thinking on many of the issues in the Śāṁkhya system from the eighteenth century onwards. In fact, if we take both the quantity and the quality of the work produced in this period, it would seem that there was some sort of renaissance among traditional scholars, who thought and wrote during this period. Some of these were Saṅyāsins belonging to the Udāsīn sect. Others, like Hariharananda Aranya established *āśramas* devoted to the practice of *Sāṁkhya sādhanā*, even though he himself has written new theoretical treatises on both Sāṁkhya and yoga which are well known to those who are interested in the subject.

The observations that we have presented in these pages are based primarily on the summaries given in the Larsen volume and they serve to give a glimpse of the new insights that are found in the works of all the thinkers so far discussed. However, it should be noted that only the summaries written by Kalidas Bhattacharya highlight the new directions in the philosophic points made by these writers and one would have to examine more closely the original material to find what other innovations and novelties are contained therein.

Except perhaps the work of Hariharananda Aranya, all the rest are commentaries either on the *Tattvakaumudī* or the *Sāṁkhya Pravacana Bhāṣya*, a mode of writing which generally is treated as being merely expository in nature, providing little room for innovative thought or creative departures on the part of the commentator. However, in practice, this is not true of most commentaries. Philosophical thinking in India has developed through the medium of commentaries which have diverse names such as *bhāṣya, vṛtti, vārttika, ṭīkā*, etc. and modern students of the subject are misled by this form of presentation. It is seldom noticed that this was merely a form of writing which the culture had developed to give a sense of both continuity and change as once an outstanding *bhāṣya* or *vārttika* or *ṭīkā* was written by anybody, it provided a new point of departure in thought for subsequent thinkers who wrote their own commentaries on it in order to highlight its originality and develop their own new insights in the context of what it had said. If one takes the developments in Sāṁkhyan thought during this period seriously, one would be amazed to find how the pervading picture of philosophical developments during this period is not only fundamentally misrepresented, but also that the usual presentation of Sāṁkhyan philosophy in the text books is generally far from the faithful presentation which it claims to be. The same is the case with other schools of thought as we shall see later during the subsequent chapters on *Nyāya, Vedānta* and *Alaṁkāra Śāstra* etc.

YOGA

Sāṁkhya is usually associated with Yoga and the two are treated together in most presentations of Indian philosophy, just as are Nyāya and Vaiśeṣika. But this treatment does not do justice to the individuality of these systems, nor to the radical differences between them. However, unlike Vaiśeṣika the case with the

Yoga system is totally different as it is not a theoretical cognitive enterprise at all, nor is it concerned with the usual problems of *uddeśa, lakṣaṇa* and *parīkṣā* with which Indian theoretical thought is supposed to be concerned. It is a transcendental praxis or, to use an Indian term, a *prayoga śāstra,* that is, a *śāstra* which is concerned essentially with practice aiming at the achievement of something outside itself and not just a theoretical, cognitive enterprise resulting in the conceptual understanding of something as is usually the case in the *śāstras* which are not essentially concerned with any particular praxis.

The *Yoga Sūtras* of Patañjali, in fact, proclaim themselves as a '*sāsana grantha*', that is, a treatise which deals with injunctions or rules or commands to be observed. Thus, it is not concerned with any discussion regarding what the *tattvas* are or what knowledge is and whose property it is and whether it is *nitya* or *anitya,* or what exactly the meaning of *śruti* is and whether it should be interpreted as primarily concerned with the performance of *yajñas* or with the knowledge of Brahman. The main interest for Yoga lies elsewhere, that is, in delineating the step by step means for the attainment of a particular state of consciousness which it calls '*samādhi*'. The developments in Yoga, therefore, have primarily been in the domain of praxis and almost all schools of spiritual seeking have had their own 'yogas' as a practical applied counterpart of what they seek to realize as the ultimate goal of human endeavour.

Developments in the thinking about yoga and the practices related to it have continued is, from the eighteenth century onwards. But most of them have occurred in non-Sanskritic contexts and perhaps the most significant of them all is Sri Aurobindo's integral yoga which he has theoretically propounded in his book entitled, *The Synthesis of Yoga,* the practical counterpart of which has been experimented upon at the Sri Aurobindo Ashrama in Pondicherry and Auroville, the Yoga township created after Sri Aurobindo's death. There are other movements and developments in the later half of the twentieth century, mainly under western influence and the demand generated by western seekers of yoga which have been associated with the names of such persons as Mahesh Yogi, Rajanish and others. But these shall be discussed later when the developments in traditional Indian thought under the western impact in the nineteenth century and thereafter are examined.

NOTES

1. Larson, G.E. and Bhattacharya, R.S. eds. 1987. *Encyclopedia of Indian Philosophies,* Delhi: Motilal Banarsidass, IV: 56–57.
2. *Ibid.,* 64–65.
3. Solomon, E.A. Summary of *Tattvakaumudīvyākhyā* by Sri Bharati Yati in *Encyclopedia of Indian Philosophies.* op. cit. p. 407.
4. Bhattacharya, Kalidasa. Summary of Āvaraṇavāriṇī on Tattvakaumudī in *Encyclopedia of Indian Philosophies.* op. cit. p. 492.
5. Bhattacharya, Kalidasa. Summary of Mīmāṁsā on Tattvakaumudī in *Encyclopedia of Indian Philosophies.* op. cit. pp. 523–24.

6. *Ibid.* p. 541.
7. *Ibid.* p. 543.
8. *Ibid.* p.543.
9. Bhattacharya, Kalidasa. Summary of Guṇamayī on Tattvakaumudī in *Encyclopedia of Indian Philosophies.* op. cit. p. 572.
10. *Ibid.*, pp. 572–73.
11. The translation of Saṁkalpa on p. 573, *Ibid.*, as intentionality appears to be highly questionable.
12. Bhattacharya, Shankar. Summary of Sāṁkhyatattvāloka in *Encyclopedia of Indian Philosophies.* op. cit. p. 582.
13. *Ibid.*, p. 583.
14. *Ibid.*, p. 582.
15. *Ibid.*, p. 584.
16. *Ibid.*, p. 584.
17. *Ibid.*, p. 586.
18. *Ibid.*, p. 586.
19. *Ibid.*, p. 587.
20. *Ibid.*, p. 588.
21. *Ibid.*, p. 588.

CHAPTER 6

Developments in Nyāya from Eighteenth Century Onwards

A Reconstruction Based on the Constructions by D. Prahlada Char

The philosophical traditions of India which had already crystallized in different regions continued to develop without being affected in any substantial way by the vast political changes that were occurring such as the Mughal collapse after the death of Aurangzeb in A.D. 1707, or the collapse of the Marathas in A.D. 1818, leading to the total British supremacy in A.D. 1857. After Raghunātha Śiromaṇi (A.D. 1530) the Mithila-Bengal region had already seen the emergence of several great Naiyāyika thinkers among whom the most outstanding persons occurred within a short period of about forty years Jagdīśa (1620 A.D.), Mathurānātha (1650 A.D.) and Gadādhara (1660 A.D.)

The details of the developments that took place in Navya Nyāya thought from Raghunātha Śiromaṇi to Gadādhara have not been studied; yet the direction of the development is quite clear as already in Raghunātha Śiromaṇi's work, we find a specialized discussion of such topics as *ākhyāta, sāmānyanirukti,* etc. The developments in Navya Nyāya too seem to have had an immanent character determined more by the internal logic of the mode of analysis accepted and the ideal of philosophical precision attempted by the system than by any other considerations including those which generally arose from criticism by other schools as seems to have been the case with the developments in the Advaitic and non-Advaitic traditions of Vedānta.

The primary motive force for the developments in Nyāya seem to have occurred because of their basic acceptance that all knowledge is relational in character and that it was mediated through language which not only embodied it essentially but whose articulation or embodiment determined it in such a unique way as to destroy the distinction between what, in recent western philosophical thought, has been described in terms of 'sense' and 'reference'. Normally, we tend to think that linguistically different sentences may convey the same fact whose facticity remains unaffected by the different formulations that it may have in the same language or in different languages. The Naiyāyika does not seem to accept this position and hence has not accepted the difference between sense and reference on the one hand and sentence and proposition on the other. This resulted in a situation where each different sentential formulation resulted in the postulation of a different meaning which then had to be analytically grasped by formulating it as a relational piece of knowledge where something was characterized by the way the sentence itself was formulated or constructed.

Normally, a sentence is supposed to have a subject and a predicate and the predicate is supposed to characterize the subject in a certain way but in an analytical framework in which different sentences may convey the same fact, the relation is embedded in a situation which is independent of the way it is known or the way this knowledge is formulated in language, and hence the distinction between substance and the attribute at the ontological level is supposed to provide the ground for the distinction between the subject and the predicate both at the epistemological and the linguistic level. In fact, even though the subject and the predicate at the linguistic level may apparently be different, they are not supposed to be so at the epistemological level if they refer to the same fact at the semantic level. The Naiyāyika does not seem to have accepted this position and hence the relational analysis of the "knowledge situation" that he attempted was determined by the linguistic formulation itself.

Also, it does not seem to have made a radical distinction between a sentence which predicates some property of an object and sentences which describe a relation between two objects; the predication was as much a relation for the Naiyāyika as, say, contact or conjunction. And, thus, the primary terms of the relationship were designated in terms of that which was characterized, that is, the *anuyogī* and that which characterized it or the *pratiyogī*. This appears to be very much like the traditional Aristotelian analysis of all sentences in terms of subject, predicate and the copula where everything that was said of the subject was treated as a 'predicate' and the predication was seen in terms of a timeless relation denoted by the timeless 'is' of the copula, characterizing the subject. However, the Nyāya analysis does not seem to have taken the term which the idealists appear to have imposed on the Aristotelian analysis by treating everything as a predicate and making 'reality' with a capital 'R' as the subject of all predicates denoted by a mere term such as 'it' or 'X' stripped of all predicates or as capable of taking any predicate whatsoever. The Nyāya analyst never seems to have wrestled with the problem as to how to distinguish between a sentence such as 'The jar is blue' and 'It is a jar'.

However, the Navya Nyāya analysis distinguishes among the predicates on the basis of the relation by which they were supposed to be related to the subject. The general term for relation was *sambandha* and these were distinguished as *samvāya, samyoga, svarūpa, tādātmya, vṛttitva, sāmānādhikaraṇya,* etc. But as the predicate could be related to the subject by any of these relations, it became necessary, in order to avoid confusion, to specify the relation through which (to use the technical Nyāya terms) the '*pratiyogī*' was related to the subject, that is, the *anuyogī*. Also, in order to clearly and unambiguously specify as to what was related to what by which relation, a new technical concept was evolved which was to indicate the scope and the limit of the relationships operating in the analysis as a number of different relations could simultaneously be mentioned in a sentence. This was called *avacchedaka* and performed almost an analogous function in the Navya Nyāya analysis to what in modern logic is called the 'scope of a quantifier'. It is surprising that the Navya Nyāya analysis did not develop the notion of a quantifier which plays such a crucial role in Aristotelian and modern logic. Perhaps it did not do so as it developed an analogous notion of *vyāpya* and *vyāpaka* which perhaps played the same role in its analysis. Also perhaps it did not develop the pure notions of quantification as it seemed to have been too tied to specific empirical examples and did not develop in a clear cut form the notion of a purely formal logic.

Due to its acceptance of the notion of a universal as almost inextricably involved in everything that was perceived or talked about the thrust of the Navya Nyāya analysis took another direction. Thus, one did not merely have universals relating to objects, that were perceived for example, a cow but also of such a notion as, for example, the subject and the predicate or, to use the Nyāya terms, *anuyogī* and *pratiyogī*. In fact, as everything can also be treated as a property and as every property must also have a universal, an *anuyogī* will have in it the property of *anuyogitā*, which itself will have a corresponding universal, *anuyogitātva*. The same will also hold for *pratiyogī* which will have the property of *pratiyogitā* which will have a universal, *pratiyogitātva*. However, this universal will have to be related to the property which itself, in its own turn, will have to be related to that of which it is the property. In the examples given above, *anuyogitātva* and *pratiyogitātva* will, thus, have to be related to *anuyogitā* and *pratiyogitā*, respectively, which in their own turn, will have to be related to *anuyogī* and *pratiyogī* and these relations will have to be specified in terms of one or the other relations mentioned above. However, a mere mention of the relation without a mention of the scope of the relation or the *avacchedaka* or the limitor, as it is generally called, would be inconceivable as it might possibly lead to confusion. The Naiyāyika therefore has not only to specify the relation but also to qualify it with the relevant *avacchedaka* required for precision as also unambiguity of the statement concerned. But to make matters even more difficult for the ordinary student of Navya Nyāya, the *avacchedaka* itself has to have a property and a universal known as *avacchedakatā* and *avacchedakatātva* which will have to be related in the same way as the others. As sentences can be more complex having multiple subjects and predicates, one needs to indicate which is the primary subject and the primary predicate and which are secondary in character. Therefore there is the need to indicate what the Naiyāyika calls the '*mukhya viśeṣyatā*' and the '*mukhya prakāratā*'. However, as the subsidiary subjects and predicates will be subjects and predicates in their own turn, one can imagine the complications that a complex sentence can introduce for a Navya Nyāya analyst.

A radically new dimension was introduced by the new relation *viṣayatā* and *viṣayitā* which bypassed all other relations as it made each and all of them as objects to a cognition which then is treated as a subject in relation to it. *Viṣayatā*, it is contended, is itself another name for knowledge or *jñāna* in general which is supposed to consist of *viśeṣyatā*, *prakāratā* and *saṁsargatā jñāna* according to Nyāya. In case this is correct, *viśeṣyatā* will just be another name for the complex property constituted by the analysis of 'knowledge' at the level of self-consciousness and its translation as 'knownness' would be incorrect. However, in case this is so, there is little point in coining a special term for the complex property constituted by *viśeṣyatā*, *prakāratā* and *saṁsargatā*, particularly when it is systematically misleading in character as it tends to denote an 'additional' property which just is not there. But, if the situation is understood in this way, what happens to the notion of *viṣayitā* which is the correlate term of *viṣayatā*, as unless *viṣayatā*, were to be treated as a separate, specific property, there would be little point in talking about that to which it is related as an 'object'. Would we then, have to treat *viṣayatā* as an emergent property of knowledge or *jñāna* in the Nyāya sense, when by itself it becomes an object to another cognition in what is called *anuvyavasāya* or self-reflective introspection. In case this is so, and if we accept the possibility of an indefinite number of *anuvyavasāya*, then we would have a series of cognitions where each would have the characteristics of *viṣayatā* and *viṣayitā* in relation to each other except perhaps the first one from where the whole chain had started as this would only have *viṣayatā* in it and never *viṣayitā*. It is not quite clear if the *viṣayitā* can itself be treated as *viṣayatā* in a cognition that becomes self-conscious of itself, a phenomenon denoted by the term *anuvyavasāya* in the Indian tradition.

But if we accept that *viṣayatā* is an emergent property in a cognition (consisting of *viśeṣyatā*, *prakāratā* and *saṁsargatā*) when it becomes an object of introspective reflection called *anuvyavsāya*, then what exactly will be the notion of *viṣayitā* and to what entity it will be supposed to belong. The problem arises as *viṣayitā* is supposed to be the co-relate relational term of *viṣayatā* and these together form a new relational complex where *viṣayatā* belongs to the first level cognitional whole which occurs at the *savikalpa* level. Whether *viṣayitā* and *viṣayatā* will themselves be related by the relation of *anuyogitā*, *pratiyogitā* and *Saṁsargatā* is unclear. For, according to the Navya Nyāya mode of analysis all knowledge above the *nirvikalpak* level is bound to have these three as necessary constituents of itself. On the other hand if *viṣayitā* is supposed to belong to the subject or the self in a self conscious reflective consciousness, then if this "self" or subject were itself to become the object of another self-conscious reflection or *anuvyavasāya*, then would it have the property *viṣayatā* in it?

An objection which may be formulated is that *viṣayitā* does not and cannot belong to any one single object of cognition such as self or subject. It belongs to the complex relationship of the *viṣayitā* and *viṣayatā* with some *saṁsargatā* relation between them if they are to become "objects" of the fact that while *viṣayatā* belongs properly to a differentiated complex of cognition at the level of reflective introspection, the *viṣayitā* is as its *anuyogī* in the Navya Nyāya framework of analysis. And though this new complex of *viṣayitā* and *viṣayatā* along with some relation between them has again to be treated as a complex object of some other, higher level, cognition, *viṣayitā* in it will have to "belong" or be a property of something "other" than that to which *viṣayatā* in this cognition is said to belong. The problem would occur at every level and, as far as we know, has not been seriously considered in the Nyāya uptil now. The problem, it may be noted, does not occur at the first level of *savikalpaka jñāna* as there it is quite clear to what the *viśeṣyatā* belongs which, at this level, may be said to be the analogue of what is called *viṣayitā* at other levels.

Regarding the discussion on whether *viṣayatā* should be treated as a separate independent *padārtha*, Harirama Tarkalamkara, for example, seems to argue that unless *viṣayatā* was accepted as a separate independent *padārtha*, one would not be able to distinguish between one piece of knowledge and another.[1] In fact, seems to distinguish not only between the *viṣayatā* that belongs to *nirvikalpaka pratyakṣa* from the one which belongs to *savikalpaka pratyakṣa* but also that which belongs to *viśeṣyatā* as he seems to contend that the *viṣayatā* which belongs to *viśeṣyatā* cannot be understood in terms of *prakāratā* which characterizes it.[2] Such a postulation, however, will make the situation even more complicated as not only *prakāratā* will have to have its own *viṣayatā* but the *viṣayatā* that belongs to the unity formed in *savikalpaka* knowledge by *viśeṣyatā*, *prakāratā* and *saṁsargatā* will have to have its separate *viṣayatā* distinct from the *viṣayatās* which *viśeṣyatā* and *prakāratā* would have.

In fact the problem seems to have arisen because of the acceptance of *abhāva* as a separate *padārtha* sometime around A.D. 1000. The discussion about *padārthas*, *abhāva* have been added to the list already enumerated by Kaṇāda in his *Vaiśeṣikasūtras*. Some of the innovations of Udayana seem to confirm this and this perhaps explains why he self-consciously proclaims himself to be an "*ādhunika Naiyāyika*" as opposed to Jayanta Bhaṭṭa whom he explicitly calls as belonging to the 'older school (*jaran*)'. However, the clearest indication of the decision to add a totally new *padārtha*, that is, *abhāva* to the earlier six mentioned by Kaṇāda seems to have been taken by Śivāditya who entitles his work specifically as '*Saptapadārthī*'. Potter gives his date around A.D. 1150, but some date him earlier than this. But, whatever the differences and dispute about the dating of Śivāditya, there can be no doubt that after him *abhāva* was regularly accepted as an independent *padārtha* having the same ontological status as the other six *padārthas* of Kaṇāda in the Vaiśeṣika system.

The consequences of this acceptance of *abhāva* as an independent *padārtha* were far-reaching as the whole Nyāya tradition began to concentrate on the new type of entities and relations generated by the acceptance of *abhāva* as a *padārtha*. The new mode of analysis introduced by Udayana and carried forward by Gaṅgeśa led to a proliferation of new relational entities which demanded to be given the status of *padārthas* in their own right even though it was not clear as to under which of the seven categories they were to be placed. It has been suggested by

Professor V.N. Jha in his introduction to Harirama Tarkalankar's *Viṣayatāvāda* that Raghunātha Śiromaṇi's reformulation of the number of *padārthas* was done in the context of this discussion.[3] However, unless further substantiated this suggestion, though interesting, needs to be judged in the light of the fact that Raghunātha not only argues for the acceptance of such new *padārthas* as *viṣayatā* but rejected many of the older *padārthas* on some ground of his own.

Besides, though the terms used are both psychological and epistemological, it is not clear whether the distinction is also linguistic, that is, whether it relates to what is called the subject and predicate in a sentence as cognition for the Nyāya analysis is determined by the *śābdabodha* or the way it is embodied in a linguistic formulation.

The Nyāya analysis of *śābdabodha* does not appear to distinguish between the speaker and the hearer or the one who writes and the one who reads, for if one does so, then one will have to accept the possibility of a non-linguistic cognition which articulates itself through language and may possibly fail to do so. It is, of course, true that the listener or the reader has nothing else but the sentential formulation through which to construe the cognition conveyed but even he can legitimately ask if this was the real meaning which was sought to be conveyed by the other and at least the speaker or the writer can always correct and reformulate what he has said or written as it did not convey what he wanted to say through the linguistic formulation. There are well-known cases where the corrections in what is written or even said are made by others and accepted by the writer or the speaker as conveying more adequately what one intended to convey. The case of Pound's correction of Eliot's '*Wasteland*' is well known but every author encounters the situation when his manuscript is copy edited by someone else. It is not quite clear how the traditional Nyāya formulations will take care of these situations.

Further, the Nyāya discussions on the subject seem to be prominently confined to the specificities of the Sanskrit language, even though most of the Nyāya thinkers, even in classical times, must have known that there were languages other than Sanskrit and that there were even translations from one language to the other. It is unbelievable, for example, that the Naiyāyikās would not have known of the translation of the *Gāthā Saptati* from Prākrit into Sanskrit done as early as the first centuries of the first millennium A.D. Yet, the problem of translation does not seem to have troubled the Naiyāyikās nor the related question of how two different linguistic formulations could convey the same meaning when the *śābdabodha*, in the two cases, according to the Nyāya analysis was, and could not but be different. In fact, the very criterion of meaningfulness, at least of cognitive meaningfulness, with respect to which questions of truth and falsity may be meaningfully raised, demands that what has been said in a particular linguistic formulation can be said through some other linguistic formulation in any language. The issue was raised in the context of the Vedic utterances which, it was claimed, could be said in no other way except in the manner that they were formulated by the Vedic seers at the very beginning of the philosophical tradition of India. Yāska refers to this view of Kautsa in his *Nirukta*.

It has been suggested that we must distinguish between cognitive meaning denoting truth and falsity in the ordinary sense of the used words and meaning which is primarily non-cognitive, as in the case of a poetic utterance which normally is difficult to translate. Most attempts at conveying what has been said in a word arrangement is different from the original tending either to say something more or something different from what was conveyed by the original sequence in which the words were arranged. But, even if one grants this, one will have to make a distinction between different kinds of non-cognitive meanings, as many of them can easily be conveyed in other ways which are different from the original sequence of words through which it was conveyed. Imperatives, interrogatives, requests, etc. may be considered as example of such non-cognitive meanings. On the other hand if meaning is conveyed primarily through the feelings, emotions, sentiments and attitudes that are aroused, it may be difficult to convey the same meaning through a different sequence of words than the one found in the original formulation. But whatever the difficulties, the emphasis on nontranslatability suggests a shift from cognitive to non-cognitive domains and even amongst non-cognitive domains, to those which are conveyed more through affective and attitudinal states than those which are not affected by them to any substantial degree.

It is, of course, true that Quine, in his well-known discussion of translatability has not taken this dimension into account and has confined his discussion purely to considerations of truth in the ordinary sense of the word and argued that the criterion of translatability as the preservation of truth in all senses of the word, if taken seriously, may make translatability impossible in principle. But, if truth is bound up so closely to any one specific linguistic formulation then it will not only become absolutely atomized but also monadic in character in the sense that the truth related to one linguistic formulation would have nothing to do with the truth related to another linguistic formulation, even though the two may be regarded as referring to the same state of affairs. Perhaps the criterion of *salva veritate* on which Quine relied will have to be given up in order to understand the notion of translatability and the objection which the *Nirukta* raised with respect to the Vedic utterances should be taken more seriously. One is, of course, not quite clear about the exact position of navya Nyāya on translatability of sentences into the same language or into different languages while preserving the meaning of the sentence concerned.

Mohanty's contention that Gaṅgeśa's definition of *pramā*, that is, valid knowledge combines both the epistemological and ontological part where *prakāratā* refers to the epistemological one. This does not take into account how such an understanding of Gaṅgeśa's definition, or even the notion of truth in general can be possibly accommodated within the theory of *śābdabodha* that the Naiyāyika accepts. Also, it is not quite clear as to what is the relation between meaning and truth in Navya Nyāya for while their doctrine of *Pramā* or valid knowledge seems to have an essential reference to the notion of referential or semantic truth, their denial, or at least apparent denial, of any identity of meaning between sentences with different *anuyogīs* and *pratiyogīs* such as, say "Dasharatha is the father of Rama" and "Rama is the son of Dasharatha" seems to suggest otherwise. Normally, one would say that both the sentences refer to the same fact which makes them true. But in case, the Navya Nyāya analyst accepts this as the ground of their being true, then why should he hesitate to accept that both of them are saying the same thing or, in other words, they are different ways of saying the same thing. Perhaps, the Navya Nyāya analyst is concerned with sentential meaning which is integrally bound with the way the sentence is formed and thus neglects the questions of meaning which remain independent of the specific sentential formulation or even of the particular language in which it has been embodied. Therefore, it is not able to distinguish between psychological meaning and epistemological meaning which is at the root of the difference between 'sense' and 'reference' in the western philosophical tradition. When exactly this identification with psychological meaning occurred and what exactly its consequences were for the developments in Nyāya thought later are interesting questions.

In any case, it is fairly clear that by the latter half of the seventeenth century, the attention of the Nyāya thinkers had shifted to considerations other than those which related to the 'notion' of truth. In fact, as analysis of the *Vādagranthas* which began to be produced during this period and continued later into the eighteenth and even nineteenth century shows that most of them were concerned with issues of epistemology, language and meaning. In fact, a rough analysis of the *Vādagranthas* as given in Thangaswami Sarma's *Darśana Mañjarī* reveals that there are sixty which deal with epistemological issues, twenty-five that deal with language and meaning, fourteen with metaphysical and onto-logical themes, eight with issues relating to logic and five which treat moral and ethical issues.[4]

A cursory analysis of topics discussed under these various heads reveals the type of issues that engage the attention of Nyāya thinkers during this period. Some of the topics mentioned seem strangely 'modern' to the contemporary student of the subject. For example, issues concerning the distinction between universals and pseudo-universals and the formulation of criteria to determine what is a pseudo-universal. The technical terms for these are *jāti* and *jāti-bādhaka.* Though the issue was raised by Udayana earlier, it is not clear how the discussion developed after him and how the criteria offered by him were added to, modified or rejected by other thinkers. Another issue concerned knowledge of those entities which are ever present in experience as well as those which are for ever absent as knowledge proceeds by noting both absence and presence or similarities and differences. Where the possibility of these does not obtain how can knowledge occur? The issues relating to knowledge also extend to the problems relating to its definition. The notion of predication and properties, the definition of perception, the possible simultaneity of different cognitions; repeated observation as the ground for inference, the Occham's razor or the principle of postulating the least number of entities in order to account for experience, etc. Many of these concerns are reflected in the discussion about language and its relation to meaning and many others are added to the discourse in the discussion regarding this important issue. There are, for example, discussions not only about the power of language to convey meaning and the criteria for determining whether meaning has been correctly grasped or not, but also a scrutiny of the relation between the unity of meaning and the diversity of the different words in a sentence whose separate meaning when combined together convey the unitary meaning.

The discussion seems to have had a long history starting from sometime in A.D. eighth century as the two rival views in this connection, *abhihitānvayavāda* and *anvitābhidhānavāda* are usually ascribed to Kumārila and Prabhākara, respectively. It is not clear however, as to what role these different views played in the interpretation of the Vedic injunctions, as presumably, that was the crucial issue for the Mīmāṁsakas and both Kumārila and Prabhākara are regarded primarily as Mīmāṁsakas and only secondarily as philosophers concerned with linguistic meaning. But, even though this is generally said in the tradition there seems to have been an earlier discussion of the issue in Bhartṛhari's *Vākya Padīya.*

The issue seems to have been concerned with what exactly is the unit of meaning in language. In other words, shall one consider word as the primary unit of meaning or the sentence as the primary unit, which alone conveys a full-fledged, complete meaning without which words cannot be said to have any meaning by themselves. A word when uttered or written is usually held to be incomplete and seen as requiring something else to complete or fulfill what is felt as incomplete. Not only this, the succeeding word may be seen as helping in the fulfillment of the demand which the earlier word makes for the realization of it's—still to be completed—meaning, or may be seen as completely irrelevant to it and thus frustrating the desired goal of the achievement of completed meaning. These two aspects are complimentary to each other and have thus been named as *ākāṅkṣā* and *yogyatā*, respectively in the tradition. The earlier word or set of words may be said to have an *ākāṅkṣā*, while the words that succeed may be said to have *yogyatā* or the 'fittingness' to fulfill the desired *ākāṅkṣā* of the earlier word or words, as may be the case. This process is supposed to go on till the *ākāṅkṣā* is realized and the completed meaning is actualized in what we call a sentence. But, as the terms *ākāṅkṣā* and *yogyatā* themselves imply, each word or set of words opens a limited domain of meanings in the context of which alone its incomplete meaning can be fulfilled, just as the succeeding word or words have also to belong to this domain in order to complete the meaning. Each word, therefore, simultaneously opens and closes the realm of possibilities in the world of meaning and this it could not do if it did not have any meaning at all. The words, therefore, must have some meaning, however incomplete it may be, as neither the notion of *ākāṅkṣā*, nor of *yogyatā* would make any sense if they had no meaning at all. An 'incomplete' meaning is not the total absence of meaning and, thus, words would have to be granted some meaning, however incomplete it may be. But, if words are granted a meaning, as the protagonists of the *abhihitānvayavāda* or the word theory of meaning contend, then one will have to assume some relation between words so that the completed meaning may emerge in the sentence. The terms *ākāṅṣkā* and *yogyatā* refer indirectly to this relationship between words but do not specify in what this relationship consists.

The discussion assumes a new form in the context of Nyāya analysis of knowledge, and its linguistic expression. In Nyāya, all knowledge, at least at the *savikalpaka* level has a differentiated character which is expressed simultaneously in both thought and language. The judgemental form that knowledge always takes is that 'this is this' or "this is such and such"—a fact which is expressed in the Nyāya analysis by saying that all knowledge has *viśeṣyatā*, *prakāratā* and *saṁsargatā* in it. Thus, the knowledge is an assertion or a denial of some *prakāratā* in something which therefore is considered to have *viśeṣyatā* in it. The usual English equivalents for these are 'qualifier' and 'qualificandum', and *saṁsargatā* is supposed to be the relation between the two. In the usual Aristotelian mode of analysis, the relation is conveyed by the assertion or the denial of whether the predicate belongs to the subject or not, and in case the actual situation obtains, the assertion or the denial is held to be true. The Nyāya analysis however is different in that it tries to specify the diverse possible relationships between what it considers as having *viśeṣyatā*, *prakāratā* in knowledge and as, according to it, the two are always relative, that which is considered to have *viśeṣyatā* or *prakāratā* in one context may itself be considered to have *prakāratā* or *viśeṣyatā*, respectively in another context.

Thus, normally, one would not have expected any dispute regarding the presence or importance of *saṁsargatā* and *prakāratā* in conveying the content for meaning of any knowledge as it is bound to have both of these besides, of course, the *viśeṣyatā*, according to the Nyāya mode of analysis. But, in philosophy the so called 'normal' thing seldom prevails and we have the strange spectacle of a long debate between the so-called *saṁsargatāvāda* versus the *prakāratāvāda* view of meaning associated with Jagdīśa and Gadādhara, respectively.

The debate seems to have been engendered by the peculiarities of the Sanskrit language as well as the question whether, in a specific context, it would be more economical to assume that the meaning was fully conveyed by *prakāratā* alone if one could dispense with the postulation of *saṁsargatā* in that situation. However, in the event of such a possibility ever occurring it does not appear that it would adversely affect the Nyāya contention that *viśeṣyatā*, *prakāratā* and *saṁsargatā* were necessary constituents of any knowledge at the *savikalpaka* level and that even at the *nirvikalpaka* level, they would have to be assumed to be there though, of course, completely amalgamated and hence undifferentiated from each other.

As the dispute and discussion centered around specific examples and questions of what was the ultimate unit of meaning it appears that the problem remained unsolved. Earlier discussions centering around *abhihitānvayavāda* and *anvitābhidhānavāda* seems to have assumed that either the word or the sentence was the unit of meaning. But, as words are composed of letters and the letters themselves are ultimately composed of phonemes or what may be called the ultimate units which are arrived at by the analysis of language. These may be called atomic units out of which the successive combinations are made. The question then is whether these ultimate units of language are to be considered also as the ultimate units of meaning. As everything else, including the so-called words are made out of them, the same problem of meaning will arise in respect of the units and combinations at each level which had earlier arisen in connection with the so-called word and sentence theories of meaning. Also what of the relations between these ultimate units and of those that occur between the smaller and larger units at each level. One could perhaps, with some justification, transpose the whole vocabulary relating to atoms, molecules, etc. to the linguistic realm and even break the ultimate atoms of language into the numerous different types of forces which particle physics has discovered in the heart of the atom which was once supposed to be unbreakable.

There is some foundation for this idea which appears wierd if we recall the notion of *dhātu* present in the analysis of the Sanskrit language and the idea of *śabda śakti* or the force, energy or power that resides in words. That this direction is not usual in an analysis of linguistic meaning in the Indian tradition, is no reason why such hints and ideas that exist therein may not be developed further, taking a clue from the developments that have taken place in physics and chemistry in recent times.

Indian thinking on the subject however particularly in the Nyāya tradition, asked whether the *vibhakti* which is such an integral part of the Sanskrit language should be regarded as having a distinct meaning of its own independent of the word to which it is applied. It also queried the fate of the word's independent meaning, in case it is regarded as having one, when it, at least manifestly, disappears, according to the rules of the Sanskrit language in *sandhi* and *samāsa.* In case it is regarded as having an independent meaning, it obviously cannot be credited with that meaning when it is absent, and yet the meaning of the complex expression formed due to the rules of *sandhi* and *samāsa* have, at least in most cases, the same meaning. If this is accepted, then the function that was being performed by the *vibhakti* for the declension in the conveying of the meaning, would have to be performed by something other than itself as it has ceased to do so due to its absence in the new complex formed by *sandhi* or *samāsa.* The situation may be illustrated by a simple example. Take the expression '*Nīlaḥ Ghaṭaḥ*'. The expression will be regarded as consisting of four words *nīla* + *su* and *ghaṭa* + *su,* if *vibhakti* is also regarded as a word, that is, an expression having a meaning of its own. Yet, if someone holds, as Gadādhara seems to do, that the two case-affixes added to the words *nīla* and *ghata* are 'meaningless' because they are only there for the sake of grammatical correctness then, really speaking, there will be only two words and not four and the unity of meaning will have to be conveyed by some unstated relation between the two which, according to Nyāya, is conveyed by *samabhivyāhāra,* that is the 'togetherness' or the joint occurrence of the two words in close proximity to each other. This is what is meant by saying that the unity of meaning is conveyed by *saṁsargatā* in a sentence.

On the other hand, one may hold, as Jagadīśa does that while the affix (*vibhakti*) in the *ghaṭa* is there only for the sake of grammatical reasons and not for performing any function, the one in the word *nīla* is performing a distinctive function by its presence as it connotes a relation of identity or 'non-difference', that is *abheda* between *nīla* and *ghaṭa.* Thus, as the *abheda saṁbandha* is being conveyed in the expression by a '*pada*', that is, the *vibhakti* concerned, the view held by Jagadīśa in this context will have to be described as *prakāratāvāda* instead of *saṁsargatāvāda.* However, if one accepts the *vibhakti* as independently conveying the relation of *abheda,* then one would have to face the problem as to how this meaning is related to the meaning of the word *nīla* on the one hand and that of *ghaṭa* on the other.

Jagdīśa describes these relations in terms of *pratiyogitātva* and *āśryatva,* respectively. But, in case this is so then, as these relations are not explicitly stated, they will have to be conveyed not by any *padārtha,* but only by *samabhivyāhāra* and, if so, one would have to be a *saṁsargatāvādin* to that content.

The situation does not seem to be so clear cut as jagadīśa himself, in his *Śabdaśakti Prakāśikā,* seems to give a different analysis of the expression, *nīlam utpalam* which, when combined, becomes *nīlotpalam* by the rules of *saṅdhi* in the Sanskrit language. Following the earlier analysis of the expression, *nīlaḥ ghaṭaḥ,* he seems to maintain that the *abheda sambandha* is conveyed by the *vibhakti* in the word *nīla* in the expression *nīlam utpalam,* even though the occurrence of the same in the word '*utpala*' is there only for grammatical purposes and has no independent meaning of its own. However, in the compound word, that is *nīlotpalam* formed out of the two expressions, the *abheda saṁbandha* is conveyed directly, that is, by the conjoint togetherness or '*saṁsargatā*' of the two expressions *nīla* and *utpala* which amount to holding the doctrine of *saṁsargatāvāda* in the context of understanding the meaning of the compound expression.

The point perhaps seems to be that the *vibhakti* whenever it occurs between two or more words itself divides them and hence stands in the way of their *saṁsargatā* which, however, in that situation would have to be regarded as occurring between the words and the *vibhakti* on the one hand and the *vibhakti* and the second word on the other. This, however, could only increase the number of *saṁsargatās* required to convey the meaning. Also, it would result in a radical difference in the analysis of the unity of meaning between expressions where the words are divided by *vibhakti* between them and those which are not so divided. Jagdīśa seems to be aware of the second problem and wants to hold a theory about the unity of meaning which does not differentiate between the two kinds of expressions, that is, the compound and the non-compound. He says, for example, that "*samāsavigrahayostulyārthakatva—hānyāpatteh*".[5] But it does not appear to have given any satisfactory solution to the problem, not seeing that no such solution can ever be given if one is prepared to accept *prakāratā* as performing the function of *saṁsargatā* in any linguistic situation whatsoever.

The Nyāya tradition itself is divided on the issue from the beginning. Gaṅgeśa, for example, is supposed to subscribe to the *saṁsargatā* view while Ragunātha opts for the *prakāratā* view. Gaṅgeśa also seems to have taken a strong position regarding the meaninglessness of '*ākhyāta*' or the verbal suffix and he states that *gaurava* is not always a defect. In his *Tattvacintāmaṇi*, Gaṅgeśa states '*ākhyātasya nirarthakatvam*' and '*phalamukham ca gauravam na doṣaḥ*'.[6]

Another aspect of this issue is that the *saṁsargatā* relation, though always there, is never supposed to be directly stated. In fact, it is said that according to Nyāya, it can not be stated in principle as any attempt to state it will turn the relation into something else. Mohanty, for example, says, "The relational component in knowledge always remains unmentioned. Conversely, if a relation finds mention, it ceases to be a relational component in knowledge".[7] He, however, seems to think that *saṁsargatā* is not a relation between words that gives rise to the unity of meaning but refers to actual relations themselves which may be of different kinds such as *saṁyoga, samavāya,* etc. In the example he has given (*parvato vahnimān*) he writes for instance, the unmentioned relational component is '*saṁyoga*'. But in the knowledge, 'The hill has *saṁyoga* with fire', '*Saṁyoga*' no more functions as a relational component but has got metamorphosed into a qualificandum and/or a qualifier. The relational component now refers to the unmentioned relation of *samavāya.*

However, if *saṁsargatā* is taken to mean: (i) the relation between words without assuming which no unity of meaning can be conceived of and which is only revealed by *samabhivyāhāra,* and (ii) also the *specific* relations which obtain between the objects mentioned in the sentence, then we would have two different kinds of *saṁsargatā* which, as far as I know, have not been distinguished. In the first sense, saṁsargatā can never be "mentioned" or "stated" in principle as, to use a Wittgensteinian phrase, it can only be "shown" and not itself mentioned or stated, while, in the second sense, the specific relation can always be stated, but it ceases to be a 'relation' when so stated or function as a relation which now would have to be assumed to be performed in some other way. The Nyāya analyst is always mentioning the relations but, if Mohanty is to be believed, they cease to function as relations when they are explicitly mentioned in the analysis.

Yet another problem which remained unnoticed by the Naiyayikas was that if two expressions have the same grammatical form they sould have the same analysis in respect of the way they are said to achieve their *vākyārtha* or completed meaning. For example, if the expression '*nīlaḥ ghaṭaḥ*' is analysed in one way, then '*rājñaḥ puruṣaḥ*' cannot or ought not to be analysed in another way. But, if it is analysed in the same way, then we will have to admit an *abheda saṁbandha* between the two which of course is absurd. Thus, even though the grammatical form is the same, the meaning conveyed by it, whether we consider the first *vibhakti* as conveying a meaning or being their just for grammatical reasons, cannot result in understanding the relation between '*rājñaḥ*' and '*puruṣaḥ*' in the same way as we do between '*nīla*' and '*ghaṭa*' in the expression *nīlaḥ ghaṭaḥ*.

As usual, however, the Nyāya thinker seems to be more concerned with the specific examples that create the problem, rather than with the generalized issue itself. Nor does he show any awareness of how the specific counter instance should lead to a reformulation of the theory. But, such an abstraction can perhaps be made out of the specific discussions that took place after Jagdīśa and *Gadādhara* regarding this issue in the eighteenth century and later.

Amongst the important Nyāya thinkers after Jagdīśa and Gadādhara, who tried in diverse ways, to support the contentions of these two in respect of the *saṁsargatā—prakāratā* debate in the tradition are: Gokulanātha Upādhyāya who flourished around A.D. 1720 and was regarded by P.B. Anantacharya, who edited his work for publication, as being even greater in some respects than such earlier masters as Jagdīśa and Gadādhara. His work is entitled *Padavākyaratnākara* and carries the debate further, supporting the views of Jagadīśa as against those of Gadādhara. However, he seems to treat Jagadīśa as *prakāratāvādin* and argues in his defence against Gadādhara whom he considers as supporting the *saṁsargatā* view. Surprisingly, Bachcha Jha of the late nineteenth and early twentieth century, regarded as one of the greatest Naiyāyikas this century has produced, appears to consider Jagadīśa as a *saṁsargatāvādin* and Gadādhdara as a *prakāratāvādin*. Bachcha Jha mentioned this in his *Gūḍhārthatattvāloka** a work which ostensibly is a commentary on the well-known work by Gadādhara entitled, *Vyutpattivādaḥ*. However, there does not seem to be much unanimity among scholars regarding the ascription of *saṁsargatāvāda* or *prakāratāvāda* exclusively to either Jagadīśa or Gadādhara as the difference between them appears to relate to the interpretation of particular instances, rather than in taking a position on the total unity of meaning which is conveyed by a sentence. Thus, in understanding the unity of meaning when the constituent words of a sentence happen to be ostensibly *different*, all Naiyāyikas are supposed to subscribe to the same position, that is, *abhihitānvayavāda* which necessarily involves the *saṁsargatā* view regarding the question as to how the unity of meaning is achieved in spite of the apparent diversity of the different meanings conveyed by different words. But this, though true, does not explain the detailed controversy over an apparently trivial matter which, though relating to specific instances, yet exercised some of the subtlest minds in the Navya Nyāya tradition. Perhaps, the continued concern hides the fact that *saṁsargatā* itself may be of different kinds and the controversy might have flourished because of lack of recognition of this fact.

The problem of different kinds of *saṁsargatā* should have been obvious if the Navya Nyāya thinkers had considered that the problem of unity of meaning does not apply to a single sentence only, but extends to the sequence of sen-

---

* *Vyutpattivāda* of Gadādhara Bhaṭṭācārya with *Gūḍhārthatattvāloka* by Sri Dharmadatta Jha, (Bachcha Jha) edited by Pt. Krityānanda Jha, Chaukhamba Amarabharati Prakashan, Varanasi, 1976.

tences occurring one after the other. Thus, if we forget the so-called plurality of words and focus attention on the plurality of sentences, then we would see that the problem is larger and deeper than the narrow context of *pada* and *vākya* in the context of which alone it seems to have been considered in the tradition. The tradition, of course, is not unaware of the problem as it had raised the question of *eka vākyatā*, meaning thereby the unity of meaning of the whole text, or even the whole discourse, or even the whole tradition in its totality. Yet, it is also true that the issue in this form did not engage the attention of any of the thinkers in the Navya Nyāya tradition, or even those outside it. The work of Bhartṛhari entitled *Vākyapadīyaḥ*, perhaps tried to show this direction in its distinction of different levels of meaning as *parā*, *paśyantī*,, *madhyamā* and *vaikharī*, the last referring to the ordinary level of spoken or written speech. But, though Bhartṛhari is supposed to have lived sometime in the fifth–sixth century, his work does not seem to have been the point of reference of the discussion between *abhihitānvayavāda* and *anvitābhidhānavāda* as far as we know.

The relation between different words and different sentences to generate unity of meaning is paralleled in the relation between the *viśeṣya* and the *prakāra* which, according to Nyāya, characterizes all knowledge at the *savikalpaka* level. Unfortunately, the problem has generally been considered only at the simplest level without taking into consideration the complex sentences which have clauses and subclauses within them where it is generally not clear what is the *viśeṣya* and the *prakāra*, as there seem to be, at least *prima facie*, many *viśeṣya* and *prakāra* occurring within the sentence itself. The Navya Nyāya analysis of *mukhya viśeṣyatā*, however does not answer the question of how one would determine what is *mukhya* and what is *gauṇa*, or what is primary and what is secondary. In the unity of meaning conveyed by a plurality of sentences, the distinction between *mukhya* and *gauṇa viśeṣyatā* does not reveal any awareness of the problem at all. Would it, for example, be necessary to postulate some over-arching *mukhya viśeṣayatā* in order to achieve this unity of meaning, and shall we have a hierarchy of these *mukhya viśeṣyatās* culminating in some final mukhya *viśeṣyatā* in the context of which everything else would function as *prakāratā*. The idealistic tradition of philosophical thought in the West has sometimes posited the ultimate reality as the only 'true' *viśeṣya* and all the rest as merely being a *prakāra* in relation to it.

But if one accepts the notion of an ultimate *mukhya viśeṣya* to which everything else is a *prakāra*, then the question will arise whether we have to distinguish between these different *prakāratās* and treat some as *mukhya* and the others as *gauṇa*. Also what relation exists between these *prakāratās* and the ultimate *viśeṣya* which they are supposed to qualify or characterize. The Advaitic position is well known that every qualification or characterization according, is only an *upādhi* or superimposition on that which by definition can never be characterized in any way whatsoever. This is the case even with the ultimate characterization in terms of *sat*, *cit* and *ānanda*, as in the Advaitic thinking even these would have to be treated as not really characterizing the Brahmana, but as some sort of superimposition on it because of the finite and imperfect nature of the human consciousness that tries to characterize it in some way or other even though it knows that it can never be characterized at all. The *viśeṣyatāvādin* might possibly hold such a position, but it is not clear whether such a position can be ascribed to it.

All such attempts to understand the unity of meaning ignore the facts of hidden 'incoherence' and contradictions that occur in any complex discourse and which destroy the unity of meaning at its very foundations. Thus, the unity apprehended will only be an apparent unity whose 'illusoriness' is realized only when one discovers the underlying incoherence or the contradictions which had escaped one's notice as well as of generations of thinkers spanning centuries and sometimes even millennia of human thought.

Earlier grammarians had attempted to deal with the unity of meaning through their doctrine of *sphoṭa,* but there seems little evidence of the navya-naiyāyikas showing much awareness of this discussion or of how the notion of *saṁsargatā* which they later postulate to account for the unity of meaning differs from the earlier attempt. Similarly, there appears to be hardly any discussion regarding the relationship between the notions of *samabhivyāhāra, ākāṅkṣā* (in the technical sense) and *saṁsargatā* which, many a time, are used in almost identical senses but some times also differently.

What of the unity of a multiplicity of distinguishable elements which has been discussed in the notions of *avayava* and *avayavī* in the Indian philosophical tradition? There seems hardly any attempt to bring the linguistic-cum-epistemological issues and meta-physical issues involved in the discussion together into one single focus and to see how the discussion in one field illuminates the discussion in the other. A parallel exists in the discussion of the difference between the reality of *bheda* and *abheda* between the Advaitins and the non-Advaitins similar to this debate on the identity of meaning apprehended through the multiplicity of meaning in linguistic cognition. If all these diverse discussions which have occurred in different contexts are interrelated they may illuminate one another. The notion of unity can also be further analysed into the different kinds of unities that are found in experience at all levels, particularly those, which have been referred to as organic unities in the western tradition.

Was it necessary to postulate *saṁsargatā* if the same function could be performed by *prakāratā* which, in any case, was always present in any *savikalpaka* cognition? Also the postulation of as few *saṁsargatās* as possible would reduce the unnecessary postulation of relationships where it could be easily avoided. There seems to have been a long history of such discussion in other contexts also, where some appear to have argued that there was no need for postulating an additional property or relationship if *prakārtā* could do the job. For example, this occurs in Harirama Tarkalankara's (or Tarkavagisha) work entitled, *Viṣayatāvāda,*[8] where it is contended that there was no necessity of postulating a separate property called '*vidheyatā*' when it could easily be understood in terms of *prakāratā.*[9] The problem of avoiding the defect of *gaurava* seems to have played an important role in the *prakāratā/saṁsargatā* debate and Bachcha Jha, in fact, has given this main argument as to why one view should be preferred to another. The postulation of *svarūpa saṁbandha* or what is usually called, 'self-linking' relation was supposed to do the same job in avoiding infinite regress which seems to have been necessitated by postulating relations which would relate the existing relations to the terms concerned. However, as pointed out earlier, even such an eminent authority as Gaṅgeśa appears to have argued that *gaurava* was not always a defect and that *lāghava* was not always a virtue. But we do not know whether he or any one else ever formulated the criteria on the basis of which one could judge whether *gaurava* was a defect or not. In any case, Bachcha Jha is supposed to have pointed out that if one accepts the *prakāratā* view one will have to accept 4320 *prakāratās* while if one opts for the *saṁsargatā* view then one would have to accept only 1440 *saṁsargatās*.

Partly, the problem is created by the nature of the Sanskrit language, wherein meaning is conveyed by the specific declension which a word necessarily has, as without it, it would have no meaning. But this language also permits the formation of compounds usually called *samāsa* where the particular declension disappears, so that whether the newly-formed compound has to be understood in terms of the previous declension or seen as arising afresh from the new conjunction that has been formed because of the formation of a *samāsa* is the issue. If the latter view is adopted, then it is the relational view of meaning, or what has been called *saṁsargatā* in the tradition. On the other hand, if the emphasis is on the declension or the *vibhakti*, then the contention is that meaning primarily arises from this declension, and not the so-called relationship or *saṁsargatā* which the *samāsa* generates. This may explain why Giridhara Upādhyāya, a student of Gokulnāth Upādhyāya, gave his work, the title *Vibhaktyartha Nirṇaya*, in A.D. 1720.

Giridhara Upādhyāya also seems to have disputed Gadādhara's view propounded in his *Vyutpattivādaḥ* in the context of the understanding that the *abhāva* which is referred to by a *pratiyogitā* need not have a non-occurrence exacting relation which is called *Vṛtti aniyāmaka* as a necessary deliminator or *avacchedaka*. Gadādhara seems to have held that acceptance of such a limiter would unnecessarily multiply the entities which need to be postulated. Giridhara Upādhyāya points out that if a relation is not *vṛttiniyāmaka*, it means the cognition of a thing as residing in a locus, where such relations can never arise. If even such relations are the limits of *abhāva*, *pratiyogitā*, *avacchedakatā*, then such absences will have to be considered as universally present, since such absences are without any opposition. Therefore, he holds that a non-occurrence exacting relation cannot be considered as a limitor of an *abhāvapratiyogitā*.

Another dimension is added to the issue by the fact that the Naiyāyika wants to have a uniform analysis of all types of sentences including those which may assert existence or deny it in any sense of the term, or, in their language, assert the *abhāva*, or non-existence of something.[10] The mode of analysis of such sentences is always in terms of *anuyogī*, *pratiyogī* and the *saṁbandha* between them. Thus, there inevitably, arises the question of what the *pratiyogī* would be in a sentence which asserts non-existence and what the relationship of this *pratiyogī* would be in a sentence which asserts non-existence and what the relationship of this *pratiyogī* is, the existence of which is being denied or the non-existence of which is being asserted. Quine, in his well-known essay entitled, "On What There Is" has dealt with this problem and questioned the so-called necessity of postulating in some sense the reality of that which one denies in order that the denial may be significant. Moreover, as one may deny the existence of more than one object, one would have to deal with the conjoint absence of more than one object and with the mutual relations which would simultaneously be held between them. Not only this, the relations between all the possible *pratiyogins* and that in which their absences are supposed to reside or, to use the Nyāya terminology, the locus in which they are absent, would have to be specified. One may further make a distinction between the absences of those objects which are present somewhere else or which were earlier present and are now absent and those which by their very nature are incapable of ever existing. The Nyāya theoreticians do not appear to have made such a distinction even though they have talked of such things as *vandhyāputra* or a barren woman's son and a *khapuṣpa* or a sky flower. Similarly, no distinction is made between that which is logically impossible and that which is only empirically so. But they have the notion of *atyantābhāva* which, however, is different from the notion of a logical impossibility. Yet, though all these considerations can become relevant in the context of the Nyāya mode of analysis, the direction that their thought has taken is somewhat different. This was determined by the specificities of the Sanskrit language in the sense that the examples they take assume the structure and grammar of that language as a kind of given constant, which limits exclusively the horizon of their thought. Whether such problems have arisen in the context of other languages which also have declension as a necessary part of their grammar, and where the same type of conjunctions occur as they do in the Sanskrit language because of the rules of *sandhi* and *samāsa* could be explored.

In fact specific philosophical problems arise because of the particular nature of the rules which pertain to that language alone and others arise from the nature of language as such in the context of the various functions which any language, *qua* language, has to perform. Much of the recent philosophical discussion in the British-speaking world appears, for example, to arise from the specificities of the English language and the way in which certain words are used in it. The work of Ryle and Austin and the later Wittgenstein may be mentioned in this regard. In the case of Wittgenstein, it is not quite clear whether his later work was written primarily in English or was translated from German as was the case with *Tractatus.* In case it was first written in German, in would then follow that the problems he was pointing out arose not primarily from the peculiar usages of those words in the English language, but from those prevalent in the German language. It is, of course, true that some works such as *Philosophical Investigations* and *Culture and Value* posthumously published were originally written in German and later translated into English. However, the original text of the notes taken and published by his students at Cambridge later on, could only have been in

English as the question of translating from German did not arise. Is there any radical difference between these two types of works introduced by the nature of the language in which the primary thinking was being done? However, such an investigation has yet not been undertaken, even though the situation parallels the case of those writers who write with equal facility in more than one language and whose case has been specifically investigated by George Steiner in his work entitled, *Extra-territorial.*

Thus, the Navya-Naiyāyikas may be distinguished by the fact that they are primarily dealing with problems created by the specificities of the Sanskrit language relating to declension and those concerning conjunction or combination due to *sandhi* and *samāsa,* as well as problems primarily arising from sentences asserting the reality of absence or *abhāva.* Often, these two different sorts of problems may arise in the same context.

Kṛṣṇa Bhaṭṭa Arde who lived around A.D. 1800, for example, deals with the issue created not only by the joint absence of two such objects as *ghaṭa* and *paṭa,* but also of *ghaṭatva* in the same locus, presumably because *ghaṭatva* is considered to be as much a *padārtha* as *ghaṭa* and *paṭa* by the Naiyāyika.

In the context of an earlier discussion by Gadādhara on the same issue, it is seen that from the eighteenth century onwards the problems discussed have a continuity with those dealt with earlier being refined by the raising of new objections and by attempts to meet these satisfactorily. In this exercise, the commentator is sometimes led towards a kind of explanation which makes the earlier text on which he is commenting appear inconsistent. When such a situation arises, he has also to make an attempt to show that the inconsistency is only apparent and that it could be met with by a subtler understanding of the issues involved. But, as the philosophical issues are deeply enmeshed in the specificities of the examples and the particular context of the discussion, it is not easy for a modern reader to appreciate this. To make these debates relevant to the ongoing philosophical concerns of the present times a knowledge of the nature of the controversies in which these thinkers were engaged and a philosophically sensitive approach to the wider relevance of the arguments and the issue involved is required.

Among the Navya Naiyāyika thinkers Raghunātha Parvate Śāstrī, (A.D. 1850) deals with the same issue in a new light. According to him, the conjoint absence of any two things such as *ghaṭa* and *paṭa* in the same locus would also have to take into account their conjointness (here two-ness of *ubhayatva*) as being limited by the specific property of the two objects (in this case, *ghaṭatva* and *paṭatva*), for unless this is done, it can easily be found not only elsewhere, but even in the same locus as there is nothing to prevent any other two things being present there. Raghunātha Parvate Śāstrī has not exactly presented the objection in such a manner, but his remarks suggest the possibility of such an objection. There is nothing in the assertion of the conjoint absence of two objects such as *ghaṭa* and *paṭa* in the same locus to suggest that there cannot be any other two objects together in the same locus.

There is another subtle consideration introduced by Raghunāth Parvate Śāstrī which perhaps had escaped the attention of earlier Naiyāyikas. It relates to the question as to whether in the statement of the conjoint absence of *ghaṭa* and *paṭa* in the same locus, it is the *ubhayatva* which is to be regarded as the *avacchedaka* of the *ghaṭatva* and *paṭatva*, or the *avacchedakatā* should be regarded as residing in the *ghaṭatva* and *paṭatva* which then are treated as the 'limitor' of *ubhayatva.* The point is obviously a subtle one, but unless the divergent consequences that flow from assuming the *avacchedakatā* in these two different ways are spelt out and their philosophical importance specified, it is difficult to say whether the new subtlety introduced by Parvate Śāstrin is of any substantive significance. That Paṇḍit Raghunātha Parvate Śāstrī is from Maharashtra provides evidence of the spread of Navya Nyāya outside Bengal and some parts of the south.

The issues relating to *saṁsargatā* and *prakāratā* on the one hand and those concerning the understanding of absence, that is, *abhāva*, specially in the context of the definition of *vyāpti* which is the ground of valid inference continue to exercise the minds of the Navya-Naiyāyikas in the twentieth century of whom Dharmadatta, or as he is more popularly known Bachcha Jha, is, by common consent, the most outstanding. He has commented, for example on the *Vyutpattivādaḥ* of Gadādhara taking part in the ongoing controversy concerning the *saṁsargatā* versus *prakāratā* debate on which Gokulnātha Upādhyāya and his disciple Giridhara Upādhyāya had earlier written. Similarly, in his commentary on the *Siddhāntalakṣaṇa* of Jagadīśa, he has discussed and refined the depletion of *vyāpti* as given earlier by Gaṅgeśa and successively modified by Raghunātha Śiromaṇi and Jagadīśa in their discussion on the subject.

Gaṅgeśa's objection to all the definitions of *vyāpti* that were given before his time was that they relied on something being sometimes absent and sometimes present and hence could not apply to anything which was always present or always absent. In order to avoid such a situation, Gaṅgeśa seem to have adopted the strategy of combining the property which was always present with something that was sometimes present and sometimes absent, treating them together as a conjoint property, so that it could now be treated in a unified manner allowing both its presence and absence as one element of its integral property was sometimes absent and sometimes present. This ingenious solution to the problem is called *vyādhikaraṇa dharmāvacchinnābhāva.* It led to a lot of discussion amongst later Nayiyāyikas including some who occur in the period of the eighteenth century onwards.

Bachcha Jha names all his commentaries, *Gūḍhārthatattvāloka* implying thereby that he is bringing to light hidden meanings involved in earlier discussions on the subject that had not been clearly formulated. Unlike earlier commentators, however, he does not elucidate or explicate every point made in the original but concentrates only on those points in the discussion which, according to him, need further precise formulation as they suffer from an intrinsic ambiguity and thus, remain open to certain objections which could easily be avoided if the ambiguity were removed. In fact, he explicitly mentions certain earlier Naiyāyikas such as Vāsudeva Sārvabhauma whose objections arise from a misunderstanding of these positions. The problems in the definition of *vyāpti*, primarily arise from the fact that concomitance between the ground, that is the *hetu*, and the consequent, that is, *sādhya*, should be of such a nature that wherever and whenever the former is present, the latter should be present and if the former is absent, the latter should be absent. As the latter states a relationship between two 'absences' or *abhāvas* it creates all the problems that a universalized statement of a necessary relation between two absences generates. In the western tradition, 'P implies Q' is always taken to imply 'not Q implies not P'. However, in a strict implication not only 'P implies', but 'not P implies not Q' also, that is, to put it in Nyāya terminology if the *hetu* is not present, the *sādhya* is also not present.

The correct definition of *vyāpti* which is the basis of all inference meets a basic objection from the possibility of those instances where what is inferred is always present and hence, can never be absent. The issue may be better understood in the context of, say, the definition of causality or even implication. The notion of strict causality is understood through what has come to be called the joint method of agreement and difference, that is, the effect is present where the cause is present and the effect is absent where the cause is absent. The definition however assumes that something can be absent for, in case it is of such a nature that it can never be absent, the definition will be inapplicable. A similar case is presented by something which is always absent and never present for, here the first part of the definition will not be applicable.

Gaṅgeśa seems to have been troubled only by the former possibility, that is, how is a *vyāpti* possible in case of those *sādhyas* which are always present. He did not seem to have taken into consideration the reverse possibility, that is, those case where the *hetu* is always absent. Perhaps he did not do so because he was only interested in the inference from the *hetu* to the *sādhya* and not conversely, from the presence of the so-called *sādhya* to the *hetu* where the relation between the two is formulated in such a manner that the *sādhya* is there, if and only if, the *hetu* is there. It would be interesting to find if the Nyāya thinkers have made a distinction between what is called strict implication and implication only.

Another problem raised by Gaṅgeśa is that can everything knowable be nameable. He does not however distinguish between statements which are true by definition or only analytically true and those whose truth depends upon experience. He assumes, for example, that the absence of nameability is impossible, but he does not give any reasons to show why it should be so. It is an unquestioned assumption of the system that everything knowable should be nameable but what if something is not knowable? Also, it has not been made clear as to what exactly is meant by knowability.

In any case, it appears that in order to avoid this difficulty he postulated the notion of *vyādhikaraṇa dharmāvacchinnābhāva* which means that, in case there is a property which, for some reason is always present, then one may make a compound joint property which consists of it along with some other property which is sometimes present and sometimes absent. Thus, for purely theoretical purposes, 'absence' can be 'inducted' into the property which is always present by treating it as an element or part of a compound property the other element or part of which can be absent. This is reminiscent of the conjunction in modern logic where, if one of the sentences is false, then the whole compound sentence is considered to be false even if the other sentence is true. The conjunction, of course, may have more than two sentences as its members and, if so, the compound sentence so formed will be false if one of its constituent sentences is false even though all the other sentences may be true. It is not, however, clear what advantage is gained by this purely formal device and at least some Naiyāyikas seem to have rejected this way of solving the problem. It is not known, however, whether they offered any other solution to the problem concerned.

The idea of a property which jointly belongs to a number of objects in their togetherness and yet cannot be said to belong to any of them separately is developed by the Naiyāyika in his notion of *vyāsajyavṛtti.* The simplest example of this is that of number, where 'twoness' or 'threeness', for example, can be meaningfully said to belong to any two or three objects, but it would be meaningless to assert that property of any single object by itself. The Naiyāyika has raised the question here as to how the twoness or threeness can be said to belong as a property to the objects concerned when, taken individually, it can not be predicated of them.

The simultaneous presence and absence of the property is explained by saying that while such a property is present by *samavāya saṁbandha,* it is absent by a relation called the *paryāpti* in the Nyāya system. It is not however known whether the *vyāsajyavṛtti* is only postulated to account for numerical properties alone or there are other instances of its application. The example given by Professor Prahlada Char is not clear (see Appendix) as the conjoint absence of *ghaṭa* and *paṭa* will be true even if *ghaṭa* alone is present and *paṭa* is absent or, conversely, if *paṭa* alone is present and *ghaṭa* is absent. Also, if the example is to be made congruent to the example of twoness and threeness, then one would have to treat the quality of being both *ghaṭa* and *paṭa* as being jointly predicated of something which individually cannot be characterized as either *ghaṭa* or *paṭa.* But this would reveal the absurdity of the reduction of the non-numerical qualities which are essentially qualitative in characer to those which are numerical and hence essentially quantitative in nature. There is no such thing which is both a *ghaṭa* and a *paṭa,* simultaneously, though there may be two objects such as a *ghaṭa* and a *paṭa* on the floor, but then we are treating them as 'two' objects and not as *ghaṭa* and *paṭa* in their specificity. The point is that there is no difference in the ascription of twoness whether there be two *ghaṭas* or two *paṭas,* or one *ghaṭa* and one *paṭa.* The example given by Professor Prahlada Char, therefore, needs further elucidation.

The idea of *vyāsajyavṝtti* is clear at least when applied to numbers, but it seems quite unclear when applied to such a notion as *pratiyogitā.* For while it is true that *pratiyogitā* is a relational term, though it applies by *samavāya saṁbandha* to the terms it relates, it does not apply to the terms it relates by *paryāpti saṁbandha* as is the case with twoness and threeness. In other words, the idea of its simultaneous application and non-application or presence and absence as is the case with twoness and threeness does not apply at all, for it will obviously not apply to the *anuyogī*, at least in that formulation in which it is a *pratiyogī*, as the moment one tries to do this, the *pratiyogī* will become an *anuyogī* and the *anuyogī* a *pratiyogī*. The contention that *ghaṭatvena ghaṭapaṭobhayābhāva*—universal absence cannot be understood without understanding it as *vyāsajya vṛtti* is not clear for firstly, the same would be true of *ghaṭatvena paṭābhāva* and, secondly, if it is held to be a *vyāsajyavṝtti* here, then it will have to be accepted as a *vyāsajyavṛtti* everywhere for one cannot say that *pratiyogitā* in one context is a *vyāsajyavṛtti* while in another context it is not. Perhaps, the problem arises because the nature of conjoint absence which is being asserted has not been analysed fully. Nor perhaps has the notion of the assertion of a meaningful absence for, unless the presence of the object concerned was expected, there is no point in saying that something is absent. One does not say, for example, that there is the absence of an elephant in the room or there is an absence of a whale in the forest or there is an absence of *vandhyāputra* in the world. The last case is interesting for the reason that it is not clear what exactly would be the *pratiyogī* of the *abhāva* in such an assertion. One can manufacture innumerable, meaningless absences as, for example, the absence of *tritva* in *ghaṭapaṭobhayābhāva*, etc. but the multiplication of these meaningless absences leads to no gain. Moreover if, following Gaṅgeśa, one brings in the notion of the absence of a relation into the picture as he seems to do, then one can juggle with such absences also and say that there is *pitṛtvābhāva* in the *putratva* relation of Rāma to Daśaratha. Ultimately, one will have to develop some criteria to distinguish meaningful absences from those which are vacuously asserted perhaps in the same manner as Udayana had tried to do with respect to universals.

There seems to have been an attempt in the Navya Nyāya tradition to distinguish between the genuine experience of absence and the vaccuous absences formulated in the notions of *āpatti* and the related property of *āpādyatā* which meant that something is apprehended to be absent even though it is *imagined* to be there. Here the absence is positively apprehended as that which is absent was either expected to be there and for some reason, is not there or it is apprehended in imagination only and the perceived situation is found to differ from it. Harirama Tarkalankara in *Viṣayatāvāda* has discussed whether such an apprehension of an imaginary object will have to be granted a specific *viṣayatā* of its own. There is an added complexity in the situation as it is suggested by someone that the apprehension of an absence is always seen as a negation of something that is apprehended as an object in the imagination and thus the perceived situation is a *pratibandhaka* of that which is imagined. According to Professor V.N. Jha who has edited and translated this text, there seem to be a discrepancy in the text regarding the exact position which Harirama Tarkalankara adopts on the issue. His own solution is that while Harirama Taralankara rejects the idea of granting a special *viṣayatā* to the imagined object of knowledge, Raghudeva, who perhaps added the last seven–eight lines objected to this view of Harirama and treated it as a *pūrvapakṣa* concluding that a special kind of *viṣayatā* has to be accepted in this situation. But, whatever be the specific position of Harirama on this issue, was pursued later in the Navya Nyāya tradition? The generalized problem, in the Nyāya context, is known as *ādhāryajñāna* but it is not clear what is the relationship of the general discussion to the specific issue which has been discussed by Harirama Tarkalankara.

In the apprehension of *abhāva*, the imagined object whose absence is perceived, is itself the result of 'desire' on the part of the mind as, otherwise, it would be difficult to understand why one would imagine it and hence perceive the absence if it is not there. There is an added discussion whether desire need be postulated as a cause or *uttejaka* of the occurrence of the imagined object.[11] The larger question is raised by the whole realm of objects created for imaginative apprehension alone. In art and literature, for example, the actual absence of that which is imaginatively apprehended is not only accepted as a necessary condition for their enjoyment but any possible reception into actuality would immediately destroy the whole wealth all together. No one, for instance, would like to see the situations associated with *vibhatsa, raudra, bhayānaka, karuṇā* and even *śṛṅgāra* to actually occur and be perceived as such. This, however, does not seem to have occupied the attention of the Nyāya theorists of *abhāva* whom we have been dealing with here. Nor is it clear whether the discussion relating to these aspects of the issue was carried further and, if so, how.

The relations of formal or 'material' implications and strict implications find a parallel in the distinction between the notions of causality and strict causality in the empirical domain. By 'causality' we generally mean that if the cause is present, the effect is present also, while in the assertion of strict causality it is implied that if the cause is absent the effect is absent as well. But, as Nyāya does not make a distinction between purely logical and empirical relations, it generally asserts the relation of *vyāpti* in terms of both strict causality and strict implication without making any distinction between the two. In the western tradition the distinction is drawn on the basis of a hidden assumption that in the case of causality there has to be an empirical, actual relation between the cause and the effect whereby the cause 'results' or 'produces' the effect. This assumption regarding the nature of the causal relation is given up in the case of purely formal implications giving rise to what have been called the paradoxes of 'material' implications. As Nyāya does not make this distinction some of its counter examples seem to arise because of the fact that it has not made this distinction.

However, they have expanded in almost six-hundred-year-long period. From Gaṅgeśa in the middle of the 'fourteenth century to Bachcha Jha at the beginning of the twentieth (A.D. 1853–1918), deficiencies were revealed in the successive definitions offered of the *vyāpti* relation by some of the most acute minds in the Indian tradition. The relevance of this for the wastern formulations has been seen, particularly as the latter also postulates two absences, that is, 'not P and not Q' as the ground of inference whether causal or implicational.

Yet, inspite of the great reputation that Bachcha Jha enjoys amongst the traditional scholars of Navya Nyāya, he does not seem to have made any new innovations or departures in the traditional mode of thinking on the subject laid down by earlier thinkers.

What seems to have dominated the minds of the majority of Naiyāikas in this period were issues relating to the epistemological on the one hand, and linguistic meaning on the other. The discussion of course was not confined to epistemological issues or those concerned with language and meaning but also related to such issues as cosmic dissolution (*pralaya*) God (*Īśvara*) or the causes of liberation (*mokṣa*) (see appendix). But the interest in these seemed to be only marginal.

However, if the *Vādagranthas* primarily dealt with a particular issue as pointed out above and thus evidenced a radical departure from the earlier mode of writing which primarily included *bhāṣya, vārttika, vṛtti, ṭīkā,* etc., the beginning of the writing of the *Kroḍapatras* reveals an even more radical departure in the history of Indian philosophy as it is concerned not with specific issues as the *Vādagranthas* were, but with a specific point raised in the definition or arguments in the *Vādagrnthas* or even other *granthas* which, in the opinion of the writer of the *Kroḍapatras* were thus a new genre of philosophical writing, perhaps never seen in the history of Indian philosophy before. Seen retrospectively, they seem to be a logical development of a type of philosophical mentality that is revealed in the *Vādagranthas.* Philosophers increasingly see themselves as specialists and do not write like, say, Vātsyāyana, Udyotkara, Vācaspati Miśra or Udayana, who tend to include whatever they like whether it has anything to do with the matter under discussion or not.

At the very beginning of the eighteenth century, in A.D. 1700 we find, for example, a *Kroḍapatra* on Gadādhara's *Sāmānya Nirukti* written by Hanumada Bhaṭṭa. In fact, Gadādhara seems to be the favourite choice for persons writing on Nyāya. Veṇīmādhava in A.D. 1750 appears to have written a commentary entitled *Prabhā* on Gadādhara's *Gādādharī.* Saṅgameśvara in A.D. 1800 wrote a *Kroḍapatra* on Jagdīśa and in A.D. 1810 Kālīśaṅkara had written *Kroḍapatras* on Gadādhara, Jagdīśa and Mathurānātha. He seems to have been the most prolific writer of *Kroḍapatras* as he wrote on all the major thinkers who had occurred in the seventeenth century. This new style of writing in philosophy continued into the twentieth century; A.D. 1820. Pattabhirama Shastri had written a *Kroḍapatra* on Gadādhara and in A.D. 1925 Vamacharana Bhattacharya I wrote a *Kroḍapatra* on Jagdīśa. Thus, it appears that beginning from A.D. 1700 a new style of philosophical writing which flourished till A.D. 1820 during which there were five eminent practitioners of the new genre. After A.D. 1820, the practice of writing *Kroḍapatra* seems to have declined till Vamacharana Bhattacharya revived it in A.D. 1925, though it does not appear to have caught the practicing Naiyāyika's imagination. Recently, Paṇḍit Gauda Subramaniam Shastri has brought out a collection of *Kroḍapatras* entitled, *Dākṣiṇātya Kroḍapatrasaṁgraha* but as it has not yet been studied and commented on by scholars, little can be said about it. It, however, clearly shows that this style of philosophical writing has not only continued to attract the attention of Naiyāyikas but also that the fashion has spread deep into the south, far outside Bengal where it had first arisen.

Of the nature of the discussion in the *Kroḍapatras* a typical example, is provided by Kalisamkara Bhattacharya and Candranarayana Bhattacharya in a discussion of the modifications introduced by Gadādhara and Raghunātha in the definition of *hetvābhāsa* by Gaṅgeśa. According to Kalisankara Bhattacharya the modifications introduced by Raghunātha and Gadādhara whereby they had added the terms *viśiṣṭa* and *yadrūpa* to the definition given by Gaṅgeśa do not remove the essential ambiguity in the definition as those examples to which the definition would not be applicable because of the nature of the object concerned are not clearly demarcated.

If, for example, one says that the inferential cognition that the "lake has fire because there is smoke" is not generally made because of the fact that it is the very nature of the lake not to have fire. This is supposed to follow from the fact that water, by its very nature, can never have fire in it, and the lake is generally full of water. What obstructs the inference in this case, therefore, is the fact that the apprehension of something having water entails the fact that it cannot have fire in it. Kalisankara Bhattacharya, in his *Kroḍapatra,* raises the issue regarding the specificity of the relation between the absence of 'fireness' in the 'lakeness' and suggests that it cannot be the same type of relation which obtains between the absence of a pot and the ground on which it is absent which is generally characterized as a *svarūpa saṁbandha.* The point seems to be that while both are 'absences', the nature of the absence in the two cases is radically different in character, for if the former were to be the same as the latter, it could not obstruct the fallacious inference. The point made by Kalisankara perhaps is that the relation between absence of 'fireness' in 'lakeness' has to be of a more positive character in order to obstruct fallacious inference in this regard.

There is a necessary connection between the 'lakeness' and the 'absence of fireness' which is the ground for obstructing the fallacious inference, and not just the accidental absence which characterized the absence of 'potness' on the ground from which it is absent. In the case of the latter, the ground could have had the pot on it, or may have it at some future time; but in the case of the lake, it can never have fire because it is the very nature of the lake not to have fire at any time whatsoever.

Kalisankara's suggestion that this positive character of the relation should be conceived as *sāmānādhikaraṇya,* that is, as 'copresent' in the same locus and not as *svarūpa.* But the solution suggested seems to indicate that he himself has not clearly understood the point of the objection as the basic question is whether the co-presence of absence is accidental or necessary.

To say that two or more properties belong to the same locus or have *sāmānādhikaraṇya* does not help us in discovering the criteria on the basis of which some properties or certain kinds of properties cannot in principle have the same locus or *sāmānādhikaraṇya* unless one wants to hold that any group of properties may occupy the same locus without any restriction whatsoever. Kalisankara's discussion of *sāmānādhikaraṇya*, however, seems to move in a different direction as it is primarily concerned with the absence of precise formulation of the relation between the lake and the absence of fire in the Nyāya perspective. As for a Naiyāyika lake is characterized by 'lakeness' which in turn is characterized by the 'absenceness' and 'fireness' which together are further characterized by the 'absenceness of fireness'. This 'absenceness' characterized by 'fireness' itself characterizes 'lakeness' which characterizes the lake.

But Kalisankara is not satisfied even with this formulation and appears to suggest that the formulation would also prohibit the inference of the presence of fire in the mountain if for some reason someone were to think that the absence of fire was as much a characteristic of a mountain as it is of a lake. This objection is strange as the crux of the matter was that there is a radical distinction between lake and mountain and while the first can never be characterized by the presence of fire the other could possibly do so.

What Kalisankara seems to be groping for is the distinction between formal grounds for inference on the one hand and essential and inessential properties or necessary and contingent relations on the other. As the Nyāya framework of analysis does not normally permit these distinctions he is unable to formulate the objections clearly in the *kroḍapatra.*

The discussion regarding the *sāmānādhikaraṇya* is carried forward by Chandranarayana Bhattacharya. The issue that he is raising may perhaps be better understood if it is reformulated in the following manner: Can universals in their universality have *sāmānādhikaraṇya* which only particular properties are supposed to have when they characterize the same object? Candranarayana also raises the issue as to why the term, *yadrūpa* cannot be understood as lake characterized by absence of fire.

The writers of the *kroḍapatras* also seem to be concerned with the problem of uniqueness of reference and how language, particularly the Sanskrit language, tries to attain this and the difficulties that are involved in the attempt. Here again the discussion in the *kroḍapatras* does not tackle the general problem but instead confines itself too narrowly to particular examples which are treated as paradigmatic and the particular specificities of the Sanskrit language from which the examples are chosen. For example, one of the sentences chosen is *Atra ghaṭaḥ asti* where the uniqueness of reference is supposed to be conveyed by the declension or the *vibhakti* which is attached to the word *ghaṭa* by the suffix. The objection raised to such an understanding is that one can use the sentence even when there are two or more pots on the ground and, in that case, the unique singularity of reference would not be conveyed by the suffix as it would be mistaken.

If as suggested the condition is added that no other object of the same kind should be present there, even this modification meets with certain difficulties. The Naiyāyika's ingenious imagination can think of situations which would render the definition inadequate for the purpose of conveying the uniqueness of reference which it was intended to ensure. The ambiguity is caused by the word of the same kind as one can imagine a situation where there are two jars of different colours where even though there are more than one objects of the 'same kind' one can easily convey the singularity of reference by the suffix in case one qualifies the jar with the particular colour that it has such as, say, a yellow or a blue jar. In the Sanskrit language, the sentence conveying this singularity will be '*atra nīlaḥ ghaṭaḥ asti*' or '*atra pītaḥ ghaṭaḥ asti*', where the singularity of *ghaṭa* is conveyed by the suffix even though there are two objects occupying that space. The discussion, it is obvious, does not distinguish between '*ekatva*' and '*viśiṣṭa*', that is numerical oneness of the object conveyed by the suffix and the uniqueness of the object.

The Naiyāyika continues to complicate the situation by imagining another situation where there are not two pots on the ground but two brahmanas where one gives a cow to the other. Here there are two persons belonging to the same caste and not distinguished in any other way and yet the suffix conveying numerical singularity will be used in the situation. The objection does not take into account the fact that though both persons belong to the same caste, they are still distinguished by the fact that while one is giving, the other is receiving a cow. But, the *kroḍapatra* writer is not deterred as he suggests another sentence permitted by the rules of the Sanskrit language where a term like '*dārā*' is always used in the plural even if it refers to only one person as in the sentence '*Rāma dārā Jānakī*'. As the oneness here cannot be conveyed by the suffix because of grammatical reasons, it is supposed to be conveyed by the term '*Jānakī*' which, in turn, is supposed to qualify the term '*dārā*' which though plural in character conveys the singularity of reference because it is modified by the term '*Jānakī*'. The specificity of this relation is termed in Navya Nyāya as *svābhinnamukhyaprakāratāvat.*

In fact, the proliferation of diverse relations made necessary by the requirement of accounting for these different kinds of situations is further complicated in that every relation generates a universal to which it has again to be related by some relation or other. A brief discussion of this has already been undertaken earlier in connection with the notions of *anuyogitā, pratiyogitā* and *avacchedakatā.* Some philosophical interesting relations which have to be postulated in this process are *svābhinnatva, svavṛttitva, svāśrayatva, svasamānādhikarṇatva, svaviśiṣṭatva, svatādātmya, svāvacchedyatva, svanirūpitāvacchedakatva, svanirūpitāviśeṣyatātva, svanirūpitātva,* etc.

Though all these seem to be examples of what is called reflexivity in modern logic, which has not explored this type of relation in such diversity and complexity as Navya Nyāya appears to have done.

The *vāda* as well as the *kroḍapatras* hardly discuss the issues that had engaged the attention of the author of the *Nyāya Sūtras* or the older Naiyāyikas, as for example: the non-eternity of sound, the radical difference between hearing and vision as sources of perceptual knowledge, the specific problems relating to visual perception, the problems relating to eternity or the transience of knowledge or the issue as to whose property knowledge should be considered to be when it arises. Similarly, the problem of the whole and the part and the exact nature of the *śabda pramāṇa* seem to have receded from the attention of the philosophical world. What sort of philosophical problems engaged the attention of Nyāya philosophers in the successive stages of its development from Gautama onwards?

The *Kroḍapatras* seem to have ceased being written roughly sometime at the beginning of the twentieth century, with the exception of Paṇḍit Gauda Subramaniam Shastri's work on the *Kroḍapatras* referred to above. Perhaps the last *Kroḍapatra* was written by Ramsastri Mysore giving rise later both to a refutation and defence entitled respectively, *Śatkoṭikhaṇḍanam* and *Śatkoṭimaṇḍanam*. The reason for the sudden cessation of writing of the *Kroḍapatras* is not known, but their influence on some of the later writers such as Bachcha Jha, is clearly evident.

The *Vādagranthas* and the *Kroḍapatras* are an evidence of increasing specialization in the writing of philosophical literature in India, a trend which may be regarded as distinctly 'modern' in the contemporary sense of the word even though many of these writers lived in the pre-modern times and did not know anything of what goes by the name of modern tradition in the west.

However, the Navya-Naiyāyikas appear to have been living in a 'closed' world of their own where only the adequate formulation of a definition seemed to matter, and remained little affected by the realms to which the definition was supposed to apply, or by the changing social and political environment in which they lived. The autonomy of a cognitive realm could hardly have been carried any further. The case of Navya Nyāya in India should be a cause for reflection as to whether such a situation obtains in many areas of contemporary philosophical thought in the West. If an acquaintance with Navya Nyāya occasions such a reflection, comparative philosophy would have achieved one of its purposes, that is 'freeing' one from the limitations and prejudices of one's own intellectual traditions. On the other hand, an acquaintance with Navya Nyāya may also reveal the unexplored possibilities and directions of contemporary logical and epistemological thought in the western tradition. Either way, it would make a real contribution deriving from a confrontation between two powerful intellectual traditions which developed independently in complete ignorance of each other.

But in the tradition of Navya Nyāya thinking in twentieth century, India ultimately found a new radical innovator in the personality of Paṇḍit Badrinath Shukla who was regarded as one of the most outstanding Naiyāyikas of his time and whose recent death has robbed India of one of its greatest traditional practitioners. His two works entitled, *Śatślokī* and *Dehātmavāda* provide a striking example of the possibility of creative original thinking even within the older settled classical modes of philosophical thought in India. These are short works, the former consisting of only a hundred *ślokas*, as its title indicates, and the latter, a lecture given on the occasion of a gathering of eminent Nyāya scholars from all over India at Sarnath in Varanasi in A.D. 1985. The gathering itself was unique as it, for the first time, brought together the foremost Naiyāyikas from different parts of India to discuss issues raised in the context of Nyāya by modern philosophers trained in the western tradition in India. The meeting lasted for four days and the lecture was delivered in the evening of the third day to the Paṇḍits gathered there along with many others from Varanasi.

The *Śatślokī* starts with a discussion regarding the notion of *mokṣa* or *apavarga* in Nyāya and argues against the traditional view held by almost all Naiyāyikas that in the state of liberation, the *ātman* is not conscious of anything and hence its having any positively felt state of consciousness such as pleasure or bliss does not arise. In the course of his discussion on the subject, Paṇḍit Badrinath Shukla raises new questions about the notions of *apavarga* and *niḥśreyasa* on the one hand and *mithyājñāna* and *tattvajñāna* on the other. He points out that nowhere in his discussion of the subject, has Gautama in his *Nyāyasūtras* identified *apavarga* and *niḥśreyasa* or defined the latter as that where the possibility of all suffering ceases. Surprisingly, he does not refer to Uddyotkara's discussion of the subject wherein he clearly states that every realm of knowledge has its own *niḥśreyasa* and that it is only the *ātmavidyā* which may be said to have *mokṣa* or *apavarga* as its *niḥśreyasa.* Thus, if Uddyotkara's contention had been taken seriously, a clear distinction would have been drawn between the two in the Nyāya tradition which, for some reason, did not take place.

In his discussion of the notion of *mithyājñāna,* Badrinath Shukla makes an even more fundamental point which, if seriously taken, would cut at the very root of one of the most firmly-held, axiomatic tenets in the Indian tradition. This relates to the identification of the self with the not-self such as body, mind, *buddhi,* etc., which has been regarded as the paradigmatic example of false knowledge or *mithyājñāna* or *adhyāsa* in the Indian tradition. Surprisingly again, though Shukla points out that such an interpretation of *mithyājñāna* is nowhere to be found in Gautama's *Nyāyasūtras,* but is, so to say, imposed on it by Vātsyāyana in his *Bhāṣya* on the *Sūtras.* Shukla, however does not see that such an understanding of *mithyājñāna* is not peculiar to Vātsyāyana's Nyāya alone, but is common to Śāṁkhya and, later, to what came to be called Advaita Vedānta in the Indian tradition. Badrinathji's questioning of this interpretation of *mithyājñāna,* thus, not only subverts Vātsyāyana's interpretation of the subject in the Nyāya tradition but also the Śāṁkhyan and the Advaitic interpretations which are closely similar to it. In fact, Vātsyāyana's interpretation itself might have been influenced by the Śāṁkhyan thought prevalent in his times. In any case, Shukla's contention that one may clearly differentiate between two entities such as, say, the body and the self, and yet attribute or 'impose' the qualities of the one on the other without necessarily giving rise to 'false' knowledge raises a fundamental objection to the widely-held argument regarding the identification of the self with the 'not-self' and the ascription of those properties to it which primarily belong one to the 'not-self' at its various levels. Such a situation had generally been known and discussed in the tradition, but only in the context of the *alaṁkāra śāstra* where *lakṣaṇā* and *vyañjanā* were always accepted as legitimate dimensions of meaning without which no literary creation could be conceived. There was the related problem of understanding *sādṛśya* and *rūpaka* in the context of understanding artistic creations. The former, in fact, plays a significant role in the acceptance of *upamāna* as a separate *pramāṇa* even in Nyāya, where it is similarity between 'cow' with which one is familiar and the 'gavaya' which one has not seen but which in many respects, is similar to the cow and hence this similarity or *sādṛśya* is the ground of inference regarding it. There is also the problem of *āhāryajñāna* which is generally accepted by everybody. But, inspite of all these similarities, affinities and earlier intimations on the subject, no one seems to have as clearly and focally formulated the issue, particularly in the context of the basic *adhyāsa* on which a large part of the super structure of Indian philosophy has been built, as has been done by Paṇḍit Badrinath Shukla in his *Śatślokī*.

In *Śatślokī*, Shuklaji, suggests that the term 'desirable' and 'undesirable' should be understood as that which leads to the upward growth or development (*utkarṣa*) of the self or to its degradation and downward movement (*apakarṣa*), respectively. This is to link *preyasa* to the *śreyasa*, though he uses the term *anukūla* and *pratikūla* and suggests that this is how the terms '*sukham anukūlam*' and '*duḥkham pratikūlam*' should be understood. Such an understanding however would require an independent criterion of what is to be regarded as *utkarṣa* or *apakarṣa*, a direction that Shuklaji does not explore. Instead, he reverts back to the traditional Nyāya understanding of self as omnipresent, eternal and blemishless forgetting his own contention made later on in his lecture on *Dehātmavāda* that one need not postulate any independent self for understanding experience but also that such spatio-temporal characteristics as omnipresence and externality can hardly be ascribed to the self which is essentially non-spatio temporal in nature.

Shuklaji's *mithyājñāna* or foundational ignorance appears to lie in the belief that anything can possibly affect the self or lead to its *utkarṣa* or *apakarṣa*. But this will tend to undermine the whole realm of *dharma* or moral action, and not only the possible linkage of *utkarṣa* and *apakarṣa* with pleasure and pain, as Shuklaji seems to think. Also how will the removal of this *mithyājñāna* have any effect? If by its very nature the self cannot be affected by anything then how can it be affected by *mithyājñāna* as Shuklaji seems to contend. Though he has neglected this problem he has considered in detail the usual Nyāya objection that if any positive effect is produced by such a knowledge, then like all effects, it can only be transient in nature. Shuklaji's answer to this age-old objection is that, firstly, it would lead to the Buddhist theory of momentariness which is not acceptable to the Naiyāyika and secondly, that, a positive effect is destroyed only if it is the result of some previous *adṛṣṭa karma* and as the occurrence of bliss is not produced because of any *adṛṣṭa karma* since they all have been destroyed by the removal of *mithyājñāna*, the so-called positive effect need not be destroyed, at least in the framework of Nyāya analysis. It is not clear, however, as to how the removal of *mithyājñāna* produces its effect only on the self and not on anything else including the *karma* of the person concerned. This, of course, is a general problem with all those schools of Indian philosophy which believe in the notion of a foundational ignorance and that its removal will result in final liberation which itself is unending in character. There is, however, another problem with regard to Shuklaji's analysis and that relates to the question, whether 'blissfulness' or *ānanda* was a intrinsic character of the self or whether it occurs just as a result of the removal of foundational ignorance. In case he believes in the former, then the question would arise as to how his position is different from that of Advaita Vedānta which also believe that *ānanda* is a natural 'property' of the self.

In the course of his treatment of the subject, Shuklaji discusses some of the specifically Nyāya doctrines regarding the destruction of a special quality by *saṁyoga* and the necessary destructibility of any perceivable quality by another. However, there seems to be some apparent inconsistency in his arguments in this regard, particularly as in the case of the latter he seems to deny the perceivability of blissfulness in the ordinary sense of the term and in his discussion on the subject he brings in the notion of *adṛṣṭa*, merit or demerit which is supposed to permanently belong to the self because it is not perceivable in the usual sense of the term. But, according to Shukla himself, *adṛṣṭa*, even though a permanent property of the self, does get destroyed when *mithyājñāna* is destroyed; but if so, the question is how can he maintain in principle the non-destructibility of *ānanda* resulting from the destruction of *mithyājñāna*. However, there can be little doubt that Shuklaji is struggling to get rid of the notoriously inconvenient heritage of Nyāya regarding the absence of any feeling in the state of liberation and that in the course of his attempt, he has said many interesting things in the *Śatślokī*.

But, far more radical is his denial of the necessity for postulating any separate *ātman* or self. He suggests that the body itself may be considered as the self for all practical purposes. The establishment of *dehātma-vāda* in the Nyāya framework was such a radical step that only the Cārvākas in the Indian tradition are supposed to have upheld it and no one could believe that such a great Naiyāyika, who was also a deeply religious person, could possibly have argued for it. But, Shuklaji did, and that too in a public lecture delivered at the Conference of Nyāya scholars from all over India who had gathered at Kashi, one of the holiest places for them. It was a shocking experience for all and they must have tried to forget it as soon as they could. Yet, the arguments he had given invite the philosophical attention of all those who are not committed to any particular metaphysical belief and challenge the practicing Naiyāyika and even the non-Naiyāyika in the Indian tradition not only to refute the arguments he had given but also to creatively develop them in new directions.

The main contention of Paṇḍit Badrinath Shukla seems to be that there is no necessity of postulating the separate ontological reality of a third entity such as *ātman* when the two entities which Nyāya postulates and accepts, that is, the body and the mind, can by themselves satisfactorily account for all the phenomena for which the *ātman* has been postulated in the system. This ultimately would be an argument from Okkam's razor which states that one need not unnecessarily postulate the existence of entities if one can avoid doing so. The Buddhists have been the standing example of such a position in the Indian tradition. But, then the Buddhists do not postulate the existence of any substances, whether spiritual or material. The very notion of *dravya* or substance is denied by them to have any 'reality', except for heuristic purposes.

Shuklaji however tries to deny the necessity of postulating the reality of *ātman* only in the limited context of Nyāya metaphysics. He does not deny the notion of substance or that body and mind are actual substantive realities. Most of his arguments are basically concerned with accommodating the accepted Nyāya positions and in replying to the objections which are urged against ascribing qualities such as knowledge, pleasure, pain, desire, hatred, effort to the body and qualities such as merit, demerit, *saṁskāra* to the mind. According to him, most of these objections are untenable and he argues that the said properties can easily be considered as the properties of the body or the mind. Shuklaji's analysis comes close to the western position which generally has not made a distinction between the mind and the self, though surprisingly he considered knowledge as a property of the body and not the mind as most western philosophers have thought. Ultimately, Shuklaji ascribes externality to the mind and thus invests it with all those properties which are generally ascribed to the *ātman*. He also seems to have forgotten his own views in the *Śatślokī* and does not attempt to reconcile them with the one's he argues for in his lecture on *dehātmavāda*. Both the *Śatślokī* and lecture on *dehātmavāda* show a great original mind steeped in the philosophical traditions of India yet, struggling to get out of the settled modes of classical Indian thought. But, it is equally clear that he is not able to throw out the metaphysical baggage which every traditional Indian thinker carries with him so as to address himself to the pure philosophical problem that he is dealing with. The creative possibilities that lie within the domains of the classical tradition of Indian philosophical thought are exhibited here as also how if those who are steeped in that tradition when challenged to think anew can do so. It may be remembered in this context that Paṇḍit Badrinath Shukla had not only participated in the Rege experiment which has been documented and published as *Samavāya*, but was also the guiding spirit therein. He also had provided the leadership in the convening of the conferences on Nyāya, Mīmāṁsā and Kashmir Śaivism in which an attempt was made to give a new direction to traditional thought in these systems. It is difficult to say how his continuous interaction with persons steeped in the western philosophical tradition contributed to the innovative experiments he made in the *Śatślokī* and the *dehātmavāda* lecture but there can be little doubt that the philosophical atmosphere he breathed in must have had something to do with it. His sudden departure from the philosophical scene of India was a great loss as he provided a bridge between the two philosophical traditions in India, something no one else has been able to provide since his passing away.

I
DEVELOPMENT OF THE NYĀYA SCHOOL OF PHILOSOPHY DURING THE EIGHTEENTH CENTURY AND ONWARDS

To trace the development of the Nyāya School of philosophy during the period of the Eighteenth century, is indeed a very tough job. This does not imply that the writing done in this field, is very scanty. As a matter of fact, the impetus given by Gadādhara and other stalwarts of the Nyāya System during the second half of the seventeenth century, through their excellent commentaries on the *Dīdhiti* of Raghunātha Śiromaṇi as also some of their independent works, inspired, many a thinker during the eighteenth and nineteenth centuries to contribute to the continuity and development of this philosophical system. From the bibliography prepared under the editorship of Dr. Karl H. Potter, we come to know that during this period more than a hundred works, that enriched the Nyāya tradition, were written. Some of them, are widely known and studied seriously even today. But, it is equally true that many other works are still in the form of manuscripts awaiting publication. As the number of students and researchers interested in a serious study of the works of this school, is diminishing fast it is unlikely that these will be published in the near future. In these circumstances, an assessment of the development of this School based mainly on a superficial study of some of the published works, may not be as authentic and accurate as required. Yet, on the basis of the printed material available, a sincere attempt has been made here to trace the development of the Nyāya school of philosophy during the eighteenth and nineteenth centuries.

As a preliminary to this task one must examine the influence that the seventeenth century wielded on later developments. In the entire history of the Nyāya school, particularly that of the Navya Nyāya school, the seventeenth century has to be considered as the golden age of the Navya tradition. It was during this period that the Navya Nyāya tradition developed as a major branch of the philosophical system of this country, through the excellent commentaries on the *Dīdhiti* of Raghunātha Śiromaṇi which itself was a superb commentary on Gaṅgeśopādhyāya's *Tattavacintāmaṇi.* Though there are some other commentaries on the *Tattvacintāmaṇi* and *Dīdhiti*, the three written during this century, namely *Gādādharī, Jagadīśī* and *Māthurī*, which are thus widely known being associated with the names of the authors, stand apart from the other commentaries by their critical approach as well by their use of a perfect Nyāya terminology with the help of which they could analyse issues with a subtlety that was hither to unknown in the philosophical world. Further, being elaborative in nature, these commentaries actually rendered yeoman service to carry further discussions on the topics dealt with by *Tattvacintāmaṇi* and *Dīdhiti* where they are typically brief. Little wonder then that these commentaries dominated the later period to such an extent that Nyāya students engrossed in the study of some of the portions of these texts neglected the study of the *Tattvacintāmaṇi* and *Dīdhiti* in their entirety. Thus the domination of these commentaries though it contributed in its own way to the continuity and development of the Nyāya tradition, in the later period, should also be held responsible for the decline of interest in discussing and evaluating many significant philosophical issues that the *Tattvacintāmaṇi* and *Dīdhiti* raise. This attitude of the *Naiyāyikas*, in the eighteenth and nineteenth centuries, which was due to the enormous influence of the commentaries of Gadādhar and others, did cost the system dearly, for it unfortunately checked the growth of the Nyāya tradition as a philosophical movement. Whatever may be the adverse effects of these texts, their invaluable contribution to the Nyāya system as a whole and the tremendous influence that they wielded on the later period can never be minimized.

Another interesting and equally significant development in the seventeenth century, was that it is during this period that the two works of Nyāya, the study of which later came to be regarded as a must for any beginner in the Nyāya studies, were written. They are *Tarkasaṁgraha* and the commentary-*Dīpikā* by Annaṁbhaṭṭa and *Kārikāvalī* with the commentary - *Nyāya Siddhānta Muktāvalī* by Viśvanātha Pañcānana Bhaṭṭācārya. These two works, though very brief, brought out in the simplest possible, terms, the latest position of the *Naiyāyikas*, comprehensively covering the Nyāya school in its entirety. It is also significant that the usefulness of these works, was soon recognised and commentaries were written almost immediately. The famous *Muktāvalī Prakāśa*, well known as *Dinakarī* by Dinakara Bhaṭṭa (A.D. 1660) and the commentary thereon called *Taraṅgiṇī* also known as *Rāmarudrīya* by Rāmarudra (A.D. 1680) were written very soon after and students and scholars alike received them with appreciation. Thus in the seventeenth century, the achievement in the Nyāya school was indeed spectacular. During this period, not only were the principal commentaries on the *Maṇi* and *Dīdhiti*, of a very high standard, but the texts that could make the Nyāya school familiar to all the students of *Darśana*, irrespective of the fact that actually they were the ardent pursuants of the other *Darśanas*, were also written. The implications of this development were far reaching. The commentaries on the *Maṇi* and *Dīdhiti* were so impressive not only from the point of view of their contents but also from their style that most of the Nyāya works written during the eighteenth century and onwards, were directly or indirectly commentaries on those commentaries. Meanwhile, a tradition of solely studying one particular out of these three commentaries on the *Dīdhiti*, also developed. Thus in the southern parts of the country the study of *Gādādharī* mostly became popular while the study of the *Māthurī* and the *Jagadīśī* became popular in the other parts of the country. The study of *Nyāya Śāstra* came to be regarded as a necessary prerequisite for the students of all the other *śāstras*. The influence was so perceptible that the scholars of the *Vyākaraṇa* and even *Alaṅkāra Śāstra* adopted the Navya Nyāya technical language to expound their respective theories. These are some of the implications of the development in the field of Nyāya, that took place during the seventeenth century.

The term 'development', in any other context, is used to denote a further step in expounding a theory or a concept revealing a new idea higher or unknown, or sometimes, entirely rejecting what has been stated on the topic so far. Such a development had taken place in the other areas of Indian philosophy such as the Pūrva Mīmāṁsā, the Uttara Mīmāṁsā, grammar and poetics. In the Pūrva Mīmāṁsā School, Prabhākara rejected many concepts evolved by Kumārila Bhaṭṭa and expounded many theories which were altogether novel. In the Uttara Mīmāṁsā, each succeeding ācārya rejected the earlier *Siddhānta* in its entirely and propounded new theories interpreting the *śrutis, smṛtis* and the *sūtras,* in a totally different manner. In Grammar many new theories were floated by the Navyas. In poetics, new *Prasthānas* such as *alaṅkāra, rīti, dhvani, vakrokti,* etc. were discovered by the poeticians who found fault with the earlier theories and with great vehemence attempted to establish their new findings. Thus in almost every school, a lot of changes had taken place.

Whether such a meaningful change or development, did really take place in the entire history of the Nyāya school at any stage need to be explored. It is in Udyotakara, Vācaspati Miśra, Jayanta and Udayana that we see an attitude which, if it could be said, led to the development of the school. On several occasions, they reject the earlier interpretation of the *Sūtras* and offer a new interpretation. But, interestingly they never seem to question the very concepts and theories of the earlier thinkers. Their contribution lies in clarifying the Nyāya concepts more convincingly and putting forward new arguments to counter the arguments of the other philosophical schools, particularly those of the Buddhists and also in defending their *Siddhāntas* from the onslaughts of the other philosophical schools. Perhaps, Bhāsarvajña among the Prācīna Naiyāyikas and Raghunātha Śiromaṇi among the Navyas, were the only two prominent figures among the Naiyāyikas who not only criticized the earlier concepts but also suggested their own modifications. But, the later Naiyāyikas never took theories seriously. Some occasional academic interest might have lead to a study of their works in which earlier theories are rejected, but they are generally ignored. Raghunātha Śiromaṇi himself does not seem to be very serious about his own criticism of the Nyāya-Vaiśeṣika theories in his *Padārthatattva Nirūpaṇa.* For, in his commentaries on *Tattvacintāmaṇi* for which he is held in high esteem, he explains *Tattvacintāmaṇi* in a splendid manner faithfully following the Nyāya-Vaiśeṣika tradition which he severally criticises in his small independent work—*Pdārthadharma Nirūpaṇa.*

Gokulanātha Upādhyāya (1710)

If the development of the Nyāya School is seen in terms of a gradual evolution of the concepts that took place, from time to time, such an evolution during the eighteenth century and onwards, does not exist. By the eighteenth century in fact all the concepts that the Nyāya School evolved, had taken a definite shape and the later Naiyāyikas had little scope to enforce any modification in those concepts. In other words, all the possible alternatives of a problem were thought of and the investigation of the issues reached such saturation that no new modification that could be named as development occurred. Actually, the contribution of the later Naiyāyikas lies in their taking a particular view of a problem of which several views are held and substantiating it with the arguments consisting of new points which were not discussed earlier. Thus the later Naiyāyikas by their fresh look and also definiteness of the issues already known, infused fresh breath and vigour to the School hence this activity cannot be termed as worthless. Here, I shall select a few authors whose creative intelligence succeeded in advancing some new points against the views believed to be final. Such an instance is provided by the *Padavākyaratnākara* of Gokulanātha Upādhyāya.

This Nyaya thinker who flourished during the first half of the eighteenth century A.D, was a native of Mithila.[12] Some hold the view that he belonged to the second half of the sixteenth century. But, the presence of critical analysis of many views of Gadādhara Bhaṭṭācārya in the works of Gokulanātha Upādhyāya indicates that the latter belonged to a period succeeding that of Gadādhara Bhaṭṭācārya. Since Gadādhara belongs to the second half of the seventeenth century, Gokulanātha is rightly assigned the date of the first half of the A.D. eighteenth century. Through his works we learn that he studied all the *śāstras* under his father Digambara Upādhyāya.

Gokulanātha Upādhyāya[13], credited with the authorship of more than twentyfive works, was a Naiyāyika of a very high order. Most of his works are on Nyāya, but he also wrote on the Vedānta and Alaṁkāra Śāstra. He has also written some literary works which include a drama called *Amṛtodaya Nāṭakam.* It is noteworthy that the reputed Naiyāyika, Giridhara Upādhyāya, the author of *Vibhaktyarthanirṇaya* (published 1902) was one of his disciples.

Among his many works the *Padavākyaratnākara* is held in high esteem by scholars. P.B. Anantacharya who published *Padavākyaratnākara* for the first time in 1904, stated that it excelled even *Vyutpattivāda* and *Śabda Śaktiprakāśikā* of Gadādhar Bhaṭṭācārya and Jagadīśa Tarkālaṅkāra, respectively. As the very title indicates *Padavākyaratnākara* discusses the important subtle issues connected with *pada* and *vākya,* in twenty three chapters. In this work he not only clarifies the Nyāya position, but also presents both the grammarians' and the poeticians' views, with a critical, comparative outlook. While clarifying the Nyāya views, he refers to both the Prācīnas and the Navyas. Thus, on many occasions he criticizes Gadādhar Bhaṭṭācārya also. An instance where Gokulanātha Upādhyāya criticizes the stand taken by Gadādhar Bhaṭṭācārya is outlined below.

There are two views regarding the manner in which *abheda,* i.e. identity is presented by the statements which are known as identical statements such as *Nīlaḥ Ghaṭaḥ.* According to one view, identity is presented in verbal cognition as a qualifier (*prakāra*), while the other view holds that it is presented as just a relation (*saṁsarga*). In case it is considered as a qualifier, it is said to be the meaning of the singular case affix *su* which is added to the word *nīla.* Gadādhara Bhaṭṭācārya has discussed the point in his *Vyutpattivāda* at length and finally concluded in favour of the view that *abheda* is presented in verbal cognition as relation only as there is simplicity. Gokulanātha, in his *Padavākyaratnākara,* reopens the issue and opposes the stand taken by Gadādhara Bhaṭṭācārya. He points out that if *abheda* is presented as a relation in a verbal cognition, for instance in the cognition produced by the sentence *'Nīlaḥ ghaṭaḥ'*, then the *anupūrvī* (sequence of letters) in the form of being the term '*ghaṭa*' which ends with the case affix '*su*' and is uttered along with the term '*nīla*' ending with the case affix '*su*' (*svāntanīlapada sambhāvyāhṛta svānta ghaṭapadatva*) will have to be admitted as the *ākāṅkṣā* that leads to the verbal cognition. Since this *anupūrvī* consists of many letters it will entail the defect of *gaurava.* If *abheda* is considered as the meaning of the case affix and hence as a qualifier then the simplicity is obvious. In the given instance, i.e. '*nīlaḥ ghaṭaḥ*' the meaning of the term '*nīla*' now becomes the qualifier and the meaning of the case affix, i.e. *abheda* becomes the qualificandum. And again the same *abheda* becomes the qualifier and the meaning of '*ghaṭa*' becomes the qualificandum. Thus, the cognition arising from the sentence, '*Nīlah ghaṭaḥ*' has *abheda* as the qualificandum in respect of the *nīla* and has the same *abheda* as the qualifier in respect of the *ghaṭa.* Now, we can say that for the verbal cognition in which *abheda* is the qualificandum and the *nīla* is the qualifier, the *ākāṅkṣā,* i.e. the sequence of the words '*nīla*' and '*su*' is essential. Similarly, for the cognition where *abheda* is the qualifier and *ghaṭa* is the qualificandum, the *ākāṅkṣā* of the words '*ghaṭa*' and '*su*' is needed. When the two *ākāṅkṣās* are thus accepted as the cause of the cognition produced by the said sentence, Gokulanātha argues that there is simplicity, because none of them contains so many letters as does the *ākāṅkṣā* involving both the words '*nīla*' and '*ghaṭa*ḥ'.

Here, one may contend that the above argument is not satisfactory, for the simplicity explained, is just apparent. It is true that the *ākāṅkṣā* suggested by the *saṁsargatāvādin,* as the cause of the verbal cognition, consists of more letters than the *ākāṅkṣā* suggested by the *prakāratāvādin.* But, the *prakāratāvādin* has to admit, as shown by himself two *ākāṅkṣās* as the cause of the verbal cognitions in which all the letters of that single *ākāṅkṣā,* are distributed. Thus the simplicity shown by the *prakāratāvādin* actually does not exist.

Rejecting the contention, Gokulanātha clarifies his point as follows:

The *ākāṅkṣā* held as the cause of the verbal cognition by the *prakāratāvādin* consist of the words '*nīla*' and '*su*', and '*ghaṭa*' and '*su*'. While the *ākāṅkṣā* admitted as the cause of the same cognition by the *saṁsargatāvādin,* is inclusive of both the words—'*Nīlaḥ*' and '*ghaṭah*'. Now, it is clear that due to the possibility of changing the position of the words '*Nīlaḥ*' and '*ghaṭah*' as '*ghaṭo Nīlaḥ*' and '*nilo ghaṭah*', the *saṁsargatāvādin* has to accept the causality in the two *ākāṅkṣās* namely being the word '*ghaṭa*' ending with '*su*' and followed by the word '*nīla*' ending with '*su*' followed by the word '*ghaṭa*' ending with '*su*'. Thus the *saṁsargatāvādin* has to put up with two *gauravas*—firstly inclusion of a large number of syllables in the *ākāṅkṣā* and secondly acceptance of causality in the two *ākāṅkṣās.* But, though the *prakāratāvādin* also has to accept two *ākāṅkṣās* as the causes of the verbal cognition as shown earlier, they do not contain as many letters as the *ākāṅkṣā* suggested by the *saṁsargatāvādin*. This shows that the *prakāratāvādin*'s stand is less defective.

But, the *saṁsargatāvādin* would not admit his defeat at this stage. He continues to argue that the same *ākāṅkṣā* which he accepts as the cause of the verbal cognition, will have to be accepted as the cause, by the *prakāratāvādin* also. To prove his point he chooses the sentence '*Nīlaḥ ghaṭaḥ paṭaḥ śuklaḥ*'. It is clear that the above sentence does not convey the identity of *nīla* in *paṭa*. But, the *Saṁsargatāvādin* contends that if the two *ākāṅkṣās* suggested by the *Prakāratāvādin* are sufficient to produce the verbal cognition of the identity of *nīla* in *ghaṭa*, then the above sentence also should produce such a cognition, since the two *ākāṅkṣās*, namely: (i) Being the word '*nīla*' ending with '*su*', and (ii) Being the word '*ghaṭa*' ending in '*su*' are present here. The only way left to avoid such a situation is to accept an *ākāṅkṣā* in which both the word '*nīla*' and the word 'paṭa' are included as the cause of the cognition comprehending the identity of *nīla* in *paṭa*. Such an *ākāṅkṣā* is obviously the *ākāṅkṣā* suggested by the *Saṁsargatāvādin*. Thus, the *Saṁsargatāvādin* successfully shows that the *Prakāratāvādin*'s view can not claim any simplicity in it.

Gokulanātha Upādhyāya admits the above contention of the *Saṁsargatāvadin*, but still sticks to his claim that *Prakāratāvāda* is preferable to *Saṁsargatāvāda*.

He supports his claim with the following argument:
If *abheda* is considered as a relation then it would be difficult to justify the usages such as '*Śikhi dhvastaḥ*'. In this sentence, the term '*dhvasta*' denotes the counterpositive of destruction (*nāśapratiyogī*). Whenever the identity plays the role of a relation then, provided that the two words end with the same case affix, the meaning of one word will have to relate with the meaning of another word. In the given example, as per the above rule, it is necessary that the meaning of the word '*Naṣṭa*', i.e. counterpositive of destruction, be related by the relation of identity with the meaning of the other word '*Śikhī*' (a person with tuft). Since such sentences are used when the person is still alive with his tuft gone, the sentence is a valid one. If the meaning of the word '*naṣṭa*' is related with the tuft meaning '*Śikhā*' in the part of the word '*Śikhī*', then the meaning conveyed by the sentence would be correct. But, the formation of the sentence would be incorrect, for the use of the same case affix after the two words—'*naṣṭa*' and '*śikhī*' is wrong as they are not conveying the same thing. Thus, the usage of the sentences like '*Śikhī naṣṭaḥ*' can not be justified if the cognition produced by them comprehends identity as a relation. On the other hand, Gokulanātha Upādhyāya contends that if identity is regarded as the meaning of the '*su*' case affix added to the word '*naṣṭa*' then there would not be any difficulty in explaining the meaning of the sentence. For, now, the *abheda* of the *naṣṭa*, the meaning of the case affix added to the word '*naṣṭa*' can be said as related to the meaning of the word '*Śikhī*' by the relation of *svāśrayaviśiṣṭatva*, i.e. being possessed of something which is the locus of '*sva*' the *abheda*. In the above case, the locus of *sva*, is *Śikhā* the tuft. Now, the question may be asked that since it is *śikhā* which actually has the direct relation of the *abheda*, how can the words '*naṣṭa*' and '*śikhī*' be regarded

as *samānādhikaraṇa* - conveying the same thing. Gokulanātha Upādhyāya asserts that to become *samānādhikaraṇa* a word need not convey something which has the identity directly. Instead, if it denotes something which is related with *abheda,* with whatsoever relation, even then it is considered as having *sāmānādhikaraṇya* by virtue of which the word can have the same case affix as the other word.

While here Gokulanātha Upādhyāya finds fault with the views of Gadādhara Bhaṭṭācārya on many other occasions he differs with Gadādhara. The nature of *abheda* is one such example. Gadādhara thoroughly discusses the nature of *abheda* and explains it as *tādātmya.* He further explains it as *tadvyaktitva*—the individuality of the thing or the person, or the absence of difference, the counterpositiveness of which is limited with *tadvyaktitva.* If this explanation is accepted, how can the cognition grasping the *tadvyaktitva* of a thing which is hitherto unknown, be explained. Since this *tadvyaktitva* is unknown, the denotative power of the '*su*' case affix, regarding the so far unknown *tadvyaktitva,* also is unknown. Hence, the case affix can not convey this novel *tadvyaktitva*—is the objection here. Gadādhara tries to answer this objection by suggesting that all the *tadvyaktitvas* are universally known through *sāmānyapratyāsatti.* Just as all the smokes and fires that can not be seen by us directly, can be denoted as being perceived through *sāmānyapratyāsatti,* all individualities can thus be known to us by way of *Sāmānyapratyāsatti,* the *sāmyadharma* being—*Ekamātravṛttitva.* In other words, we may not know all individualities existent individually but it is possible for us to know them generally—as the attributes residing in only one thing. Thus Gadādhara suggests that it is possible to know the denotative power of a case affix even in such individualities that are actually unknown to us, individually. Gokulanātha Upādhyāya solves the same problem in a different way. He suggests that even unknown things can be conveyed through an *Upalakṣaṇa*—an indicator. For instance, pronouns such as '*tvam*' or '*tat*' that are used with regard to things and their properties which are unfamiliar to us, face the same problem, that is the impossibility of knowing the denotative power of those words in such unknown things and properties. Naiyāyikas solve the problem by making use of an *Upalakṣaṇa*—an indicator. The point is that when a pronoun '*Saḥ*' is used to convey a person, say Chaitra who is unknown to us, it is possible for us to explain that we know the denotative power of the word '*saḥ*' with regard to Chaitra. For, the denotative power of such words in things that are possessed of an attribute indicated by 'being a limitor of the contentness determined by our cognition' - *buddhiviṣayatāvaccedakatva* is accepted. It means that when the speaker uses the word '*saḥ*' in a particular context it is obvious that he has somebody in mind. Thus, when we come to know of the intention of the speaker through the context, we also come to know of the person and his attributes as intended to be conveyed by the speaker and instantly we come to know of the denotative power of the word even in such hitherto unknown individuals. Gokulanātha Upādhyāya suggests that the same explanation is possible in the case of affixes having their denotative power in respect of *abheda*—i.e., *tādātmya* or the individuality which is unfamiliar to us. Here, Gokulanātha states that '*Ubhayāvṛttidharma*'—'being a property which does not exist in two' can be taken as *upalakṣaṇa*. Through this, he holds that it is possible now to even know the so far unknown properties and individuals.

Now, it may be argued that there is not much difference between the views of Gadādhara and Gokulanātha in solving the stated problem. But, if we carefully examine the two views, Gokulanātha's views appear to carry more weight. For, according to Gadādhara, the *tadvyaktitvas* are known to us in a general manner and hence when we grasp the denotative power of a case affix in these *tadvyaktitvas*, it is grasped in them only generally. Therefore, when these *tadvyaktitvas* appear in a verbal cognition the denotative power may appear only in a general manner. But, the view of Gokulanātha Upādhyāya on the other hand is that, even those *tadvyaktitvas* which are so far unknown to us, can then appear in a verbal cognition, in the individual forms. This according to him is possible, because the case affixes have their denotative power in all the *tadvyaktitvas* in their individual form only. It is true that such *tadvyaktitvas* are innumerable and most of them are unknown to us. Yet, it is possible because '*Ubhayāvṛttitva*' is considered here as the *upalakṣaṇa*. As an *upalakṣaṇa* it enables us to know all those *tadvyaktitvas* by helping us to grasp the denotative power of the case affixes in all the *tadvyaktitvas* and consequently to be comprehended by the verbal cognitions. At the same time, the *upalakṣaṇa dharma* can remain neutral as not being comprehended by the verbal cognition. This advantage makes the stand taken by Gokulanātha Upādhyāya, more acceptable.

Apart from Gokulanātha Upādhyāyas critique of Gadādhara Bhaṭṭācārya, his contribution to the development of the Nyāya school, during the eighteenth century is indisputable. In fact, any assessment of the contribution of an author is incomplete unless all his works are reviewed. But, since all his works are not available, an attempt is made to evaluate his contribution by reviewing only one of his works, *Padavākyaratnākara*.

Dharmadatta Jha (Bachcha Jha) (1853–1918)

The contribution of Dharmadatta Jha, to the development of Navya Nyāya, is indeed enormous. He was a multifaceted genius an original thinker and a philosopher. He had a mastery over the Vedānta, the Dharmaśāstra, Jyotiṣa and the Sāhitya also. It is said that he had written a commentary called *Tattvāloka* on Madhusūdana Sarasvatī's commentary on the *Gītā*. He is also said to have written a *Campū* called '*Sulocana Mādhava Campū*', apart from several commentaries on Prācīna Nyāya works such as a commentary on *Nyāyakusumāñjali* and a commentary on *Nyāyabhāṣya*. Among his several works it is the Navya Nyāya works that earned him accolades from all sections of traditional scholars in India. His commentaries generally called *Gūḍārtha Tattvāloka* or *Vivecana*, are of a very high order. They are very terse and do not follow the pattern of the other commentaries. Bachcha Jha takes it for granted that the reader is well acquainted with the original text and hence he generally does not bother to explain this, as the other commentators would normally do. He generally picks out certain subtle philosophical points that surface from the discussions found in the original text or the conclusions arrived at. Even seemingly innocent remarks made by the original author, which other commentators would conveniently ignore, attract the attention of this thinker and he uses these to make certain significant points. All his discussions reach a logical end and are never incomplete or wanting, usually ending with a *pariṣkāra*, the mode of solution peculiar to the Navya Nyāya School.

An instance where Dharmadatta Jha draws attention to the significance of the usage of a few words in the original text is provided by the opening sentence in the *Jāgadīśī* on *Siddhānta lakṣaṇa dīdhiti*:

> *Vahnitvāvacchinnasya sarvasyaiva dhūmādiman-niṣṭhābhāva pratiyogitāvacchedakībhūta-tat-tad-vyaktitvāvacchinnatvād avyāptirityanyathā vyācaṣṭe—pratiyogitānavacchedako yo dharma iti.*

> वह्नित्वावच्छिन्नस्य सर्वस्यैव धूमादिमन्निष्ठाभावप्रतियोगितावच्छेदकीभूततत्तद्व्यक्तित्वावच्छिन्नत्वादव्याप्तिरित्यन्यथा व्याचष्टे—प्रतियोगितानवच्छेदको यो धर्म इति।

This introduction to the *Dīdhiti* suggests some modification in the final definition of *Vyāpti* formulated by Gaṅgeśopādhyāya in his *Tattavacintāmaṇi*. The final definition of *Vyāpti*, suggested by Gangeśopādhyāya is:

> *Pratiyogya samānādhikaraṇa-yat-samānādhikaraṇātyantābhāva-pratiyogitāvacchedakāvacchinnaṁ yan-na bhavati tena samaṁ tasya sāmānādhikaraṇyaṁ vyāptiḥ*

> प्रतियोग्यसमानाधिकरणयत्समानाधिकरणात्यन्ताभावप्रतियोगितावच्छेदकावच्छिन्नं यन्न भवति तेन समं तस्य सामानाधिकरण्यं व्याप्तिः।

It means that *Vyāpti* is the co-existence with that which is not possessed of an attribute that is the limitor of the counterpositiveness of an absolute absence, that coexists with the *hetu* and does not co-exist with the counterpositive.

The *Dīdhiti* has modified the above definition as:

> *Pratiyogya-samānādhikaraṇa-yad-rūpa-viśiṣṭa samānādhikaraṇātyantābhāvapratiyogitānavacchedako yo dharmaḥ tad dharmāvacchinnena yena kenāpi samaṁ sāmānādhikaraṇyaṁ tad rūpa viśiṣṭasya tad dharmāvacchinna yāvan nirūpitā vyāptiḥ.*

> प्रतियोग्यसमानाधिकरणयद्रूपविशिष्टसमानाधिकरणात्यन्ताभावप्रतियोगितानवच्छेदको यो धर्मः तद्धर्मावच्छिन्नेन येन केनापि समं सामानाधिकरण्यं तद्रूपविशिष्टस्य तद्धर्मावच्छिन्नयावन्निरूपिता व्याप्तिः।

Among the several modifications made here, in the modification under consideration is the definition by Maṇikāra, *Sādhya*—the meaning of the second '*yat*' should be such that it is different from the one possessing the limitor of the counterpositiveness. The definition modified by Śiromaṇi intends that the limitor of *Sādhyatā* should be different from the limitor of the counter-positiveness.

Jagdīśa explains the reason for this modification as:

Vahnitvāvacchinnasya sarvasyaiva dhūmādiman-niṣṭhābhāva pratiyogitāvacchedakībhūta tat tad vyaktitvāvacchinnatvād avyāptirityanyathā vyācaṣṭe—pratiyogitānavacchedako yo dhrma iti.

वह्नित्वावच्छिन्नस्य सर्वस्यैव धूमादिमन्निष्ठाभावप्रतियोगितावच्छेदकीभूततत्तद्व्यक्तित्वावच्छिन्नत्वा-दव्याप्तिरित्यन्यथा व्याचष्टे—प्रतियोगितानवच्छेदको यो धर्म इति।

This implies that if the definition offered by the Maṇikāra is retained as it is, then the definition would suffer from the fallacy of *Avyāpti*. For, in the instance '*Vanhimān dhūmāt*', the definition is not applicable. Here, the *Sādhya* is not a particular fire, instead it is fire in general. Thus the definition becomes applicable only if all fires (without exception) do not possess the limitor of the counter-positiveness of the absence that co-exists with the *hetu*—smoke. But, when the fires are taken individually, it is quite possible to show that each of them does not exist in some other location where another smoke is present. Thus, all the individualities (*tadvyaktitvas*), without exception, can be shown as being the limitors of the counterpositiveness that belong to all the individual fires. In other words, in the inference, '*Vanhimān dhūmāt*' all the fires which are the *sādhyas*, are possessors of the limitors of the counter-positiveness of those absences that co-exist with the *hetu*—smoke. Thus, the definition is not applicable to the above inference and consequently, is to be considered as fallacious. In order to avoid the above fallacy, Raghunātha Śiromaṇi suggested the modification with which it becomes possible to avoid the fallacy.

This elaboration only serves the background in which Jagadīśa used the phrase '*Vanhitvāvacchinnasya sarvasyaiva*' in the first sentence of his commentary and we are not at present, concerned with the question as to how Raghunātha succeeded in avoiding the above fallacy. The pertinent question being raised here is why is, it that Raghunātha said—'*vanhitvāvacchinnasya sarvasyaiva*'—'all those that are qualified with fireness', when in its place he could simply say—'*vanheḥ sarvasyaiva*'—'all the fires'. The question appears to be very trivial. But, Bachcha Jha does not fail to notice the significance of the use of those words. He remarks :

Atra vanhitvāvacchinnasyetyuktiḥ sārvabhauma vyākhyānaṁ dūṣayitum

अत्र वह्नित्वावच्छिन्नस्येत्युक्तिः सार्वभौमव्याख्यानं दूषयितुम्।

Accordingly, when Jagadīśa said '*vanhitvāvacchinnasya*' instead of '*vanheh sarvasya*', it was to reject the interpretation of the same definition of *Vyāpti* by Sārvabhouma. To avoid the same fallacy of *avyāpti*, Sārvabhouma interprets the definition in a different way. He suggests that the second '*yat*' in the definition offered by Maṇikāra, should be taken as ending with the locative case affix which is elided. Thus, '*yat*' means *yasmin*—'in which'. Again the word '*avacchinna*' in the definition, should be interpreted as meaning '*avacchedakatānirūpita*'. Thus, according to Sārvabhouma, the modified definition of *Vyāpti* would be:

> *Hetusamānādhikaraṇa pratiyogivyadhikaraṇābhāva pratiyogitāvacchedakāvacchinna pratiyogitvātyantābhāva vat sādhyatāvacchedakāvacchinna sāmānādhikaraṇyam.*
>
> हेतुसमानाधिकरणप्रतियोगिव्यधिकरणाभावप्रतियोगितावच्छेदकावच्छिन्नप्रतियोगित्वात्यन्ताभाव वत्साध्यतावच्छेदकावच्छिन्नसामानाधिकरण्यम् ।

According to this modified definition, the *sādhya,* in an inference, should have the absolute absence of the counterpositiveness which is determined by the limitorness which in its turn, is determined by the counterpositiveness determined by an absence that co-exists with the *hetu* and does not co-exist with its counterpositive. The co-existence of such a *sādhya,* is considered here as *vyāpti.* When Sārvabhouma, thus modified the definition, he held the view that 'counterpositiveness' is an *avyāpyavṛtti* attribute. An *avyāpyavṛtti* is that which co-exists along with its absence. Thus, in the inference '*vanhimān dhūmāt*' all the *sādhya* individuals in their individual capacity, may be absent in some locus of the *hetu* and therefore may not be the '*apratiyogins*' of an absence co-existing with the *hetu.* Yet, since '*pratiyogitā* is accepted as *avyāpyavṛtti,* its absence also can be present in the same *vanhi* when it is present in the locus of the *hetu.* Thus, in a valid inference, the absence of the counterpositiveness determined by the limitorness which is determined by the counterpositiveness which in its turn, is determined by the absence co-existing with the *hetu,* can be shown as present in the sādhya.

Bachcha Jha remarks that it is to reject this interpretation offered by Sārvabhouma, that Jagadīśa used the words '*vanhitvāvacchinnasya sarvasyaiva*' where he could simply say '*vanheḥ sarvasyaiva*'. Explaining the view of Jagadīśa here, Bachcha Jha states that the whole of Sārvabhouma's interpretation is based mainly on the notion that *pratiyogitā* could be *avyāpyavṛtti.* But, this idea is wrong, for it is the nature of *pratiyogitā* to be invariably present in all the instances of the limitor of *pratiyogitā.* In the above instance, the limitor of the *pratiyogitā,* viz. the innumerable *tadvyaktitvas* are always present in their respective loci - the innumerable fires. Therefore, it would not be correct to hold that the *pratiyogitā* limited by the *tadvyaktitvas* can be absent in their loci when the *pratiyogitā* is limited by the generic attribute '*vanhitva*'.

Badrinath Shukla

Śataślokī by Sri Badrinath Shukla is a small treatise consisting of, as the title indicates, just hundred, very simple ślokas. Though Sri Badrinath Shukla is well known as an erudite traditional scholar of Nyāya Śāstra, here he has shown that when it comes to philosophical issues, he is an independent thinker.

In this small work he discusses the nature of *niḥśreyasa*, i.e. *mokṣa*. Naiyāyikas believe that this *niḥśreyasa* is the absolute cessation of all sufferings. But the interesting point towards which Sri Shukla draws our attention, is that nowhere in his *sūtra*, has Gautama said anything about the nature of *niḥśreyasa*.[14] Many hold the view that Gautama has clearly stated in the *sūtra* that *apavarga* is the absolute annihilation of sufferings. Since, *apavarga* and *niḥśreyasa* are the same, they contend that according to Gautama *niḥśreyasa* is nothing else, but super annihilation of sufferings. But, again, Sri Shukla reminds us that nowhere has Gautama said that *niḥśreyasa* and *apavarga* are the same.[15] Sri Shukla also draws our attention to Gautama's view that *mithyājñāna* is the root cause of all our sufferings and that it will be uprooted by the *tattvajñāna*. However it has never been disclosed as to what is the exact nature of *mithyājñāna* or *tattvajñāna*.[16] Therefore, Sri Shukla holds that if we are simply guided by the sūtras it is impossible to conclude the nature of *Niḥśreyasa*, i.e. *mokṣa*.

But, the Nyāya School has maintained all along that emancipation is only the super annihilation of sufferings and this stand, as Sri Shukla points out, is based on the *Vātsyāyana Bhāsya*.[17] Vātsyāyana seems to hold the view that the *mithyājñāna* is the identification of body, sense organs, etc. with the self. This identification makes the self to think that whatever is pleasant to the body is pleasant to the self and whatever causes pain to the body, causes pain to the self. Thus, the delusion makes the self love certain things and hate others. Due to this *rāga* and *dveṣa* the self will indulge in performing virtuous, impious or neutral actions. As a result of these, the self will have births and rebirths in which it has to suffer as if endlessly. When the self obtains the *tattvajñāna* and realizes the difference between the self and the body, etc. immediately the false knowledge which was the root cause of this bondage—full of sufferings, will get destroyed. As a result, the self will be free from *rāga* and *dveṣa* which are the causes of all sorts of actions. In the absence of actions the self will not have any merit or demerit that cause the chain of births. Thus, the self will be totally released from all the sufferings.[18] This, in short, is the Nyāya view of emancipation.

Sri Shukla raises a very fundamental question based on common experience, as to how a person of a discerning nature, can aspire for a state in which there is no pleasure. For, no person howsoever frightened of suffering, would like to abandon pleasure. Therefore, Sri Shukla argues, that one can not aspire for complete cessation of the cycle of birth and rebirth, which actually is the state of emancipation according to the Naiyāyikas, since then one will have to lose pleasure also, permanently.[19] The Naiyāyika's argument in defence of their stand as put forth by Vātsyāyana, is that there is no pleasure which is not associated with pain and hence one who is afraid of pain, should not crave for pleasure too.

In order to reject this view, Sri Shukla re-examines the nature of *mithyājñāna* and *tattvajñāna* as described by Vātsyāyana and his commentators.[20] Vātsyāyana says that *mithyājñāna* is a cognition of the identity of body in the self. But, Sri Shukla argues that this does not seem to hold good.

It may be contended that if there is no identification of the body with the self, how is it that the attributes of the body such as thinness are super-imposed in the self. Sri Shukla convincingly argues that it is not necessary to identify the body with the self in order to explain the super-imposition of the attributes of the body in the self. Although two things are known as quite different, the super-imposition of the one on the other is also seen. For instance, the victory gained by an army is attributed to the king, although the king is known as being quite different from the army. Similarly, the self might be known as distinct from the body and yet the super-imposition of the attributes of the body would be possible. Sri Shukla also points out that unless there is an erroneous cognition of the identity of the two things, the super-imposition of the attributes of them on the other is impossible, therefore similarly the super-imposition of the attributes of different sense organs on the self simultaneously would be impossible. A person who is both blind and dumb, super-imposes blindness and dumbness—the attributes of the sense organs on the self. Here, it cannot be said that the person has a false cognition of identity with the two sense organs. For, he knows that eyes and ears are two distinct sense organs. This shows that the self never erroneously cognises the identity of either the body or the sense organs with itself. Therefore, Sri Shukla concludes that it will be wrong to hold the view that *mithyājñāna* is to cognise the identity between the self and the body or sense organs.

If the cognition of identity between the self and its body, etc. is not the *mithyājñāna*, for it can never arise, then what exactly is *mithyājñāna*? Sri Shukla replies that *mithyājñāna* is the cognition that grasps pleasure as desirable and suffering as undesirable. But one may dispute this by pointing out that pleasure is actually desirable and similarly suffering also is actually repulsive and hence how could such cognitions be considered as *mithyājñāna*. Sri Shukla replies that a thing can be considered as *anukūla*, i.e. desirable only when it causes some *samutkarṣa*, and similarly, a thing can be considered as *pratikūla* i.e. repulsive only when it causes some *apakarṣa*, i.e. degrading. When this '*anukūla*' and '*pratikūla*' are found to have quite different connotations, it will be clear as to why the cognitions '*sukham anukūlam*' and '*duḥkham pratikūlam*' are to be regarded as *mithyājñāna*. For, as the cognitions mentioned above, pleasure and pain should be *anukūla* and *pratikūla* to the self. But, the self by nature, is omnipresent, eternal and blemishless. Hence neither pleasure nor pain can affect it in any manner. Therefore, Sri Shukla holds that pleasure or pain cannot be discarded on the ground that they will affect the self.

The point that Sri Shukla's arguments highlight, is that when a person knows about himself, the false view about *sukha* and *duḥkha* will definitely get uprooted. Then just as the erroneous cognition leads to a sense of pleasure which is invariably associated with pain, the realization of the self, since it is a *tattvajñāna*—a true knowledge, should also lead to the experience of bliss. Thus,

Sri Shukla, by admitting the presence of pleasure even during the state of emancipation, challenges the time-old *Siddhānta* view guarded with all vehemence by the Naiyāyikas.

Again, Sri Shukla admirably answers certain objections raised, namely that the pleasure which is produced by *tattvajñāna* during the state of *mokṣa* is a positive effect—*bhāvakārya* and as a result it should get destroyed after some time. If thus the bliss in the *mokṣa* is prone to destruction, there cannot be any difference between *saṁsāra* and *mokṣa*. Sri Shukla ridicules this argument as smacking of the theory of momentariness advocated by the Buddhists. Clarifying the point he argues that if by just happening to be a positive and also an effect, a thing gets destroyed then it should get destroyed soon after its production. In fact, a positive effect gets destruction if and only if it is produced by *karmādṛṣṭa*—the merit produced by the earlier action. Since the state of *mukti* is attained only after all the previous actions are destroyed, the bliss in *mokṣa* cannot be a product of earlier actions. Thus, due to the absence of a destroyer, the bliss in *mokṣa*, though it is a positive effect, can last eternally.

An argument according to which the bliss in the state of *mukti* cannot be eternal, is that a special quality of an all-pervasive substance is destroyed by the ending of a special quality. Therefore, the bliss of a liberated soul being considered as a special quality of the all-pervasive self, will have to be destroyed by a quality, say by a *saṁyoga* that occurs in the self.

Sri Shukla rejects even this argument pointing out the inherent inconsistency in it. As per the argument only such special qualities which are perceivable, are destroyed by a succeeding quality. If a special quality is non-perceivable, it is never destroyed by such qualities. For instance, *adṛṣṭa*—merit or demerit, the special quality of the self is never destroyed by any successive quality. Similarly, the bliss in the state of *mukti*, though a special quality is not perceivable in the normal sense of the term. For, the only sense organ that can perceive bliss is mind. But, *mukti* is such a state in which no sense organ exists. Therefore, the bliss in *mukti* is like the *adṛṣṭa* in self. Hence it is not destructible like the pleasure that we experience during the state of *saṁsāra*.

Another significant point Sri Shukla makes is that if *mukti* means merely the annihilation of pain then it has to be admitted as a state devoid of any consciousness, and in that case nobody would aspire for it.

In addition to these arguments Sri Shukla also employs as per the Nyāya tradition, certain inferences to prove his point.

Sri Shukla's, paper on '*Dehātmavāda*' which he presented at the Seminar on Nyāya held in Saranath in the year of 1985 is another very important and interesting work. Here also Sri Shukla, as in his '*Śata-Ślokī*', treats a new path by questioning a faithfully accepted stand point of the Nyāya School which has been followed by the Nyāya traditionalists. While Raghunātha Śiromaṇi and even earlier, Bhāsarvajña had raised objections against certain doctrines of the Nyāya Vaiśeṣika tradition, the '*Śata-Ślokī*' of Sri Shukla it may be said can only be seen as an extension of the arguments that Bhāsarvajña presented in his work. But the article on *Dehātmavāda* is an absolutely an original thought. Earlier the Cārvākas and other non-believers put forth various theories to reject the separate existence of *ātman*. They argued that either the body or the sense organs, particularly *manas* can be identified with the self and it is not necessary to accept the existence of a separate self. Apparently the '*Dehātmavāda* ' of Sri Shukla also appears to uphold the same theories. But, a closer observation reveals that he modifies the earlier theory of *Dehātmavāda* by holding that it is not merely the body that is identified with the *ātman*; instead the body associated with mind is *ātman*. This modification suggested by Sri Shukla is a very significant one and it helps him to avoid all the flaws that were shown in the earlier theories. The arguments can be summed up as follows:

There is no need for a separate *ātman*. All the functions that an *ātman* is supposed to perform, can be managed by body itself along with the mind. It is held by the Nyāya Vaiśeṣikas that *ātman* is the locus of fourteen qualities such as cognition, pleasure, pain, desire, hatred, effort, merit, demerit, impression, number, dimension, severality, conjunction and disjunction. Sri Shukla maintains that among these qualities those such as cognition, pleasure, pain, desire, hatred and effort which are perceptible, are actually the qualities residing in the body. The imperceptible qualities such as merit, demerit, and impression (*saṁskāra*) belong to mind. Thus there is no need to accept a separate substance called *ātman* as the locus of the above qualities.

The Nyāya Vaiśeṣika School contends that the above qualities cannot be the qualities of body as they belong to the category of special qualities. The special qualities, according to the school, are produced either by the similar qualities of the parts which are the inherent causes of the substance—product, or by heat (*pāka*). Cognition, pleasure, etc. cannot be said to be produced in the body by the similar qualities of its parts. For, the parts of the body being non-sentient, do not possess such qualities. Neither can heat be considered as the cause for the production of such qualities in the body because, the qualities produced by heat, are always preceded by the destruction of the similar qualities in the same locus. For instance, the yellow colour in a mango fruit, produced by heat, is preceded by the destruction of the green colour in the same fruit. But, the first ever cognition produced in a body can not be preceded by the destruction of a similar cognition in it. Thus, the Nyāya Vaiśeṣika School contends that if body is the self it is impossible to explain the occurrence of qualities such as cognition etc. in the body.

Sri Shukla rejecting the above contention states that the above argument of the Nyāya Vaiśeṣika School is mainly based on the assumption that cognition, etc. are special qualities of *ātman*. He points out that this assumption of the Nyāya Vaiśeṣika School is a baseless one as these qualities can also be considered ordinary qualities such as conjunction (*Saṁyoga*) etc. are. The ordinary qualities, as we know them are, sometimes, produced by a cause other than the similar qualities of the parts or heat. The advantage in accepting cognition, etc. as ordinary qualities of body is illustrated by the following. Generally a special quality of a substance continues to exist till the destruction of the substance. But, in case the body itself is not soul and cognition, etc. are special qualities of it how is soul that the qualities are destroyed when the soul continues to exist.

Sri Shukla further argues that the problem does not arise when cognition, etc. are considered as special quality of the earthy body. For, a special quality of any earthy object is either produced by the similar special quality of the parts or by heat. But, Sri Shukla points out that cognition, etc. cannot be considered as special qualities of body, for a special quality is that which resides in only one substance. Smell of earth, sound in space, etc. are such qualities and are considered as special qualities of earth, etc. But, cognitions etc. when regarded as the qualities of the earthy body, cannot be held as special qualities for they reside in the other substances also, such as the bodies made of water, etc. Thus when they are not the special qualities of the earthy body, they question as to why these are not produced by the similar special quality of the body, etc. would not be relevant.

Sri Shukla also refers to other pertinent objections raised against the *Dehātmavāda* and replies, as presented below:

If cognition etc. are the qualities of body, then why are these not perceived by the *Cakṣus*. It may be replied, that there is no such rule that all the qualities of body be grasped by a single sense-organ. In fact, the qualities such as colour, etc. are also not grasped by a single sense-organ. While the colour of a body is grasped by the *Cakṣus*, its smell, touch, etc. are grasped by various other sense organs. Similarly, cognition, etc. and qualities of body, are grasped by the mind. It is true that qualities of body such as colour, etc. are grasped by only the external senses. Hence one may argue that cognition, etc. also must be grasped by the external senses only. To this, Sri Shukla's reply is interesting. He maintains that the name '*Antarindrīya*', i.e. internal sense organ, even though it grasps some qualities that belong to the external thing like body, is quite correct, for, unlike the other sense-organs it is internally situated in the body. As a matter of fact, there is no harm even if we consider the mind as an external sense organ. However the name *antarindrīya* which has been in vogue since a long time, is also justifiable. For, the mind can grasp only such qualities which are inside the body.

It may be argued further that just as the qualities of body can be perceived by a different person, cognition, etc., if they are the qualities of body, must also be grasped by other persons. Sri Shukla rejects the argument and maintains that it would have been possible for the mind to grasp the cognition residing in another body, had it been in contact with it. But, mind which is atomic in size resides always inside the body and cannot have any contact with the cognition residing in the other bodies. Thus, Sri Shukla maintains that it can grasp only those cognitions that reside in the same body in which the mind also is present.

Another strong objection raised by the Nyāya tradition against the *Dehātmavāda* is that since a body is continuously changing, in old age the body is quite different from the body of boyhood. Thus a person in old age cannot remember what he had experienced earlier in his boyhood. For, nobody can remember something experienced by others. Sri Shukla maintains that this objection cannot find place in the *Dehātmavāda* expounded by him. According to his theory, *saṁskāra* which causes recollection later, is not produced in the body itself when the experience took place. As per his theory it is produced in the mind. He maintains that though the experience takes place in the body, due to the peculiar contact with the mind, the experience though is residing in the body which is the locus of the experience, can generate the impression in mind. Since this mind unlike the body, is eternal, it continues to exist in old age also. Impressions residing in it can produce the recollection in the aged body also, as the locus of the *saṁskāra*, the mind has a peculiar contact with the aged body.

Another objection raised against the *Dehātmavāda* by the tradition, is that with the death of body, the actions performed by it will also get destroyed without yielding any result to the performer. Similarly, the body newly born, will have experienced the results of the actions which it did not perform at all. If an *ātman*, separate from the body, is accepted, since it is an eternal thing, it is possible to explain that no action will perish unless it yields the results to the performer and no *ātman* will escape the results of the action performed. Pt. Shukla maintains that his *Dehātmavāda* has an answer to the objection. According to his theory the merits and demerits caused by the actions of the body, do not reside in the body. Instead, they become the properties of the mind which is an eternal substance. After the death of the body the performer of actions, the mind will get associated with a new body which is produced as a result of the previous actions still residing in the mind. Now the new body will experience the fruits of the earlier ācārs. Thus Sri Shukla maintains that no action as per this theory, will get destroyed without producing the results. However, the other question as to how the new body the non-performer of the previous actions could be able to experience the fruits of the actions done by another body, still remains. But, Sri Shukla sets aside the question holding that his theory does not accept the rule that only the doer should experience the fruits of the actions. Instead, he asserts that a body will experience the fruits being controlled and associated by only that mind, being associated with which a body could perform the actions. In short, according to his theory, what is needed for the experience of the results of actions, is just the association of the mind the carrier of the merits and demerits and not the identity of the performer.

Sri Shukla also refers to another objection raised against his theory of *Dehātmavāda*. The objection is that the theory in its enthusiasm in rejecting a separate *ātman*, has unwittingly ended in conferring *ātmatva* to the two things, namely, body and mind. One absurdity of this stand is that the theory will have to admit the co-existence of two contradictory properties such as eternality and non-eternality in the *ātman* which is identified with both body and mind which are non-eternal and eternal, respectively.

Rejecting the objection, Sri Shukla clarifies that his theory identifies the *ātman* only with body and not with both—body and mind. For, he points out, that the marks of *ātman* such as desire, volition, etc. which are enumerated by Gautama in his Nyāya *sūtra*, are admitted by this theory in body only. The mind which just carries the qualities such as merit, demerit and also impressions, is just an aid to the *ātman* and hence the absurdity pointed out earlier, is due to the lack of proper understanding of the *Dehātmavāda* .

The above brief exposition of the contents of *śataślokī* and *Dēhātmavāda* shows that Sri Shukla, inspite of his commitment of the School, was an independent and original thinker. But, the unfortunate thing is that the two treatises did not generate any serious discussion either among his contemporaries or among the young Nyāya-Scholars but has remained as just a symbol of Sri Shukla's sharp intellectual exercise.

Kṛṣṇam Bhaṭṭa Ārde (1800)

Among the several Nyāya writers of the nineteenth century, Kṛṣṇam Bhaṭṭa Arḍe occupies a very prominent place. The Arḍe family, had the reputation of being a family of authors.[1] His commentary on Gādādharī, *Mañjūṣā* generally known as *Kṛṣṇambhaṭṭīya,* is regarded as one of the most scholarly commentaries on Gadādhara's works. We have his commentary on the whole of the *Vyāpti Grantha* of Gadādhara, which includes *Pañcalakṣaṇī, Caturdaśalakṣaṇī* and *Siddhānta lakṣaṇa*. Besides this, his commentaries on *Avayava, Pakṣatā, Satpratipakṣa* and *Savyabhicāra Sāmānyanirukti* of Gadādhara, also are held in high esteem by the Naiyāyikas. He has also written a commentary on *Jāgadīśī* by the same name *Mañjūṣā* or *Toṣiṇī.* It is also learnt that he had commented upon Udayana's *Kiraṇāvalī. Padārtha Candrikā Vilāsa* written in refutation of Mādhava Sarasvatī's *Mityābhāṣiṇī* is also attributed to him.

His commentaries are written in very terse Navya Nyāya style, and not only explains the Gādādharī text wherever it is necessary, but also, on many occasions carry further the discussions where Gadādhar has left. Thus, his commentaries not only render a very valuable assistance in understanding the original text, but also contribute a lot to the development of thought. The following is an instance that reflects his contribution to the development of thought regarding a very subtle Navya Nyāya epistemological concept.

While introducing the definitions of *Vyāpti,* consisting of "absence limited by a property whose loci are different from its counter-positive" (*vyādhikaraṇa dharmāvacchinnābhāva*) Gaṅgeśa cites the absence of *vācyatva (Samavāyitvena Vācyatvābhāva*), with the help of which the definition of *Vyāpti* becomes applicable to even such *hetu-s* whose *sādhyas* are only positive. Here, Gadādhar gives expression to the objections raised by some about the nature of the absence mentioned. It is contended that the absence of *Vācyatva* as limited by *Samavāyitva,* can not be considered as an absence limited by a property whose loci are different from its counterpositive. In support of this view, they point out that *vācyatva* which actually is *padaśakti,* is, according to the Naiyāyikas, the will of God. Hence, they argue that *vācyatva* being a quality, has *samavāyitva*—the limitor of the counter-positiveness, in it and consequently the absence cannot be regarded as *vyādhikaraṇa-dharmāvaccinnābhāva.*

Admitting the contention that *vācyatva* is the will of God, an attempt is made to explain that the absence is still *vyādhikaraṇadharmāvaccinnābhāva.* The point made here is that *vācyatva* the counterpositive is not mere will, but is a qualified will—*tatpadabodhyatvaprakārakatvaviśiṣṭā icchā.* Thus, the *pratiyogitā* of the absence resides by *paryāpti* relation here both in the qualifier and the qualificandum namely, *icchā* and *tatpadabodhyatvaprakārakatva.* Between the two, the will—the qualificandum has *samavāyitva,* while the qualifier which is none of the five—*dravya, guṇa, karman, sāmānya* or *viśeṣa* has not. Since thus the locus of the *pratiyogitāparyāpti,* does not have the limitor of counterpositiveness, the absence has to be regarded as *vyādhikaraṇadharmāvaccinnābhāva.*

The above contention that the absence under consideration, is *vyādhikaraṇa-dharmāvaccinnābhāva,* is based on the notion that *pratiyogitā* is a *vyāsajyavṛttidharma* (property of pair). But, it is held that the very notion is wrong, for the *pratiyogitā* of an absence of a qualified thing, resides only in the qualificandum, being limited by the qualifier and it never resides in the qualifier also. In short, *pratiyogitā* is not at all a property of pair. Therefore, *samavāyitva* the limitor of the *pratiyogitā* of the absence under discussion, can not be considered as a *vyādhikaraṇadharma,* as it is present in the will of God wherein the *pratiyogitā* also resides by *paryāpti* relation.

As against the above view, it is also strongly contended that it is necessary to consider *pratiyogitā* as a property of pair. Otherwise, it is pointed out that the absence '*ghaṭatvena ghaṭa-paṭobhayam nāsti*'—'*ghaṭa* and *paṭa* both do not exist, as limited by *ghaṭatva*' would not be a universally present absence. It is obvious here that this absence is universally present. But this characteristic of the absence, cannot be explained if *pratiyogitā* is not *vyāsajyavṛtti.* For, an absence, as is known, does not exist where the *pratiyogin* possessed with the limitor, is present. In the present case, if *pratiyogitā* is not *vyāsajyavṛtti,* it means that different *pratiyogitās* reside in *ghaṭa* and *paṭa* separately. As a result, the instances where *ghaṭa* is present, can be said as the instances of the *pratiyogin* qualified with *ghaṭatva*—the limitor of *pratiyogitā,* in the present case and in such instances the presence of the *abhāva*—'*ghaṭatvena ghaṭapaṭobhayam nāsti*' can not be satisfactorily explained. In case, *pratiyogitā* is accepted as *vyāsajyavṛtti,* the *pratiyogitā* of the present absence, will have to be admitted as residing by *paryāpti* in both - *ghaṭa* and *paṭa.* Since this pair cannot be the possessor of the limitor namely *ghaṭatva,* there is not a single instance where the locus of *pratiyogitā paryāpti* possessing the limitor, is present. Hence, only by accepting *pratiyogitā* as *vyāsajya-vṛtti,* the universal presence of the above *abhāva,* can be satisfactorily explained.

But, Gadādhar has a different solution to the problem. He contends that the universal presence of the *abhāva*—'*ghaṭatvena ghaṭapaṭobhayam nāsti*', can be explained by holding *pratiyogitāvaccedakatā*—limitorness determined by *pratiyogitā,* as *vyāsajyavṛtti.* In the present case, the *pratiyogitāvaccedakatā* is residing by the *paryāpti* relation, not only in *ghaṭatva* but also *ghaṭapaṭobhayatva.* Since an absence is opposed to the *pratiyogin* possessing an attribute that has the *paryāpti* of *pratiyogitāvacchedakatā*, the *abhāva* under consideration, can now be explained on its universal presence. The point is that we cannot find a single instance where a thing possessing both *ghaṭatva* and *ghaṭapaṭobhayatva*, the locus of the *paryāpti* of *pratiyogitāvaccedakatā*, is present and hence the *abhāva* '*ghaṭatvena ghaṭa-paṭobhayam nāsti*' being unopposed, can be present universally.

Though Gadādhar could thus satisfactorily explain the universal presence of the *abhāva* under discussion, without accepting *pratiyogitā* as a property of pair, as he himself points out, another problem will surface. The problem is the difficulty in explaining the non-universality of the absence '*ghaṭa-paṭau na staḥ*'—'*ghaṭa* and *paṭa* both do not exist'. It is obvious that this absence not being a *vyādhikaraṇa-dharmāvaccinnābhāva*, is not universally present. But, if an absence is held as being opposed to the *pratiyogin* possessing an attribute that has the *paryāpti* of *pratiyogitāvacchedakatva*, then the *abhāva* mentioned above, will have to be universally present. For, the *pratiyogitāvacchedakatā*, of this *abhāva* has *paryāpti* in the three properties namely *ghaṭatva*, *paṭatva* and *ghaṭapaṭadvitva* and the *pratiyogin* possessing all the three is nowhere present.

Having thus presented the problem, Gadādhar himself suggests a solution by the following single statement:

Tathā ca tatra dvitvadharmitāvacchedakatāpannasyaiva ghaṭatvādeḥ avacchedakatā pratīyate, atra svātantrayeṇāpīti bhedaḥ

तथा च तत्र द्वित्वधर्मितावच्छेदकतापन्नस्यैव घटत्वादेः अवच्छेदकता प्रतीयते, अत्र स्वातन्त्र्येणापीति भेदः ।

Apparently, the above statement seems to be rather very simple. But, the superb explanation offered by Kṛṣṇam Bhaṭṭa, garbed in exquisite Navya Nyāya terminology, would reveal the subtleties which otherwise a student would fail to notice. At the outset, he pinpoints the property with which an absence has the opposition:

Yadyat sambandhāvacchinnā yadyaddharmaniṣṭhā pratiyogitāvacchedakatā tat tat sambandhāvacchinna tat tat dharmāniṣṭhāvacchedakatā nirūpita pratiyoginiṣṭhādheyatā nirūpitādhikaraṇatayā sākamabhāvasva virodhaḥ.

यद्यत्सम्बन्धावच्छिन्ना यद्यद्धर्मनिष्ठा प्रतियोगितावच्छेदकता तत्तत्सम्बन्धावच्छिन्नतत्तद्धर्म-निष्ठावच्छेदकतानिरूपितप्रतियोगिनिष्ठाधेयतानिरूपिताधिकरणतया साकमभावस्य विरोधः

The above can be explained by means of an example. The cognition 'ghaṭapaṭau na staḥ (घटपटौ न स्तः)' which comprehends the absence of *ghaṭa* and *paṭa*, also grasps the *pratiyogitāvacchedakatā*—limitorness determined by the *pratiyogitā*, in the attributes namely—*ghaṭatva*, *paṭatva* and *ghaṭapaṭobhayatva*. The *avacchedakatās* that are thus comprehended, are further limited by different relations. The *avacchedakatā* residing in '*ghaṭa-paṭobhayatva*' being a property of pair, resides there by the relation of *paryāpti* qualified with *ghaṭatva-vyāpakatva* and *paṭatva-vyāpakatva.* On the other hand, the *avacchedakatās* residing in *ghaṭatva* and *paṭatva,* are limited by the relation of *samavāya* which is qualified with *dvitva-vyāpyatva.*

Now, when there are both *ghaṭa* and *paṭa* on the ground, it is possible to have a right cognition—'*bhūtalam ghaṭa-paṭobhayavat*'. This cognition comprehends the *bhūtala* as the *adhikaraṇa* and also the *adhikaraṇatā* in it. Similarly, it also comprehends both *ghaṭa* and *paṭa* as *ādheya* and the *ādheyatā* in them. The *avcchedakatā* determined by this *ādheyatā* lies in the three properties namely, *ghaṭatva, paṭatva* and the *ubhayatva.* The *avacchedakatā* determined by the *ādheyatā,* in the above case, is limited by the same relations with which the *avacchedakatās* determined by the *pratiyogitā* of the absence '*bhūtale ghaṭapaṭau na staḥ*'—'*ghaṭa* and *paṭa* are not on the ground'. Thus, it can be said that an absence is opposed to such an *adhikaraṇatā,* the *ādheyatā* determined by which, is residing in a *pratiyogin,* the *pratiyogitā* residing in which, determines an *avacchedakatā* which is limited by a relation and a property which are the same as the relation and property that limit the *avacchedakatā* determined by the *pratiyogitā* of the absence. And as earlier explained, where there are both *ghaṭa* and *paṭa* on the ground, it has the *adhikaraṇatā* described above. Hence, there will not be the absence. When both of them are not on the ground, it does not have the said *adhikaraṇatā* and hence the *abhāva* can exist. Thus, the above *abhāva* is not universally present.

Though thus, the non-universality of the absence comprehended by the cognition '*bhutale ghaṭapaṭau na staḥ*' can be satisfactorily explained, the question as to how to explain the universal presence of the absence cognised by the cognition '*ghaṭatvena ghaṭapaṭau na staḥ*', may still persist. Since the *pratiyogitāvacchedaka* properties such as *ghaṭatva, paṭatva* and *ghaṭa-paṭobhayatva* are the same for the absence discussed earlier and the absence mentioned now, the question becomes very important.

As stated earlier Kṛṣṇambhaṭṭa very convincingly explains Gadādhar's reply against the background of his explanation of the property with which an absence has the opposition. First, he brings out the main difference that exists between the cognition '*bhūtale ghaṭapaṭau na staḥ*' and '*ghaṭatvena ghaṭapaṭau na staḥ*'. Accordingly, just as the cognition '*bhūtale ghaṭapaṭau na staḥ*' grasps limitorness in the three properties such as *ghaṭatva, paṭatva* and *ghaṭa-paṭobhayatva,* the cognition '*ghaṭatvena ghaṭapaṭau na staḥ*' also grasps the *pratiyogitāvacchedakatā* in all the same three properties. Similarly, the relation—the *paryāpti* qualified with *ghaṭatvavyāpakatva* and *paṭatvavyāpakatva* that limits the *avacchedakatā* in *ghaṭa-paṭobhayatva,* and also the relation—the inherence qualified with *dvitva-vyāpyatā* that limits the *avcchedakatā* in *ghaṭatva* and *paṭatva,* are also grasped by the cognition '*ghaṭatvena ghaṭapaṭau na staḥ*'. Yet, it is distinct from the cognition '*ghaṭapaṭau na staḥ*', for this reason that it also grasps *avacchedakatā* in *ghaṭatva* separately, as limited by the relation of pure inherence. When we thus notice the distinction, it is easy to see why the absence '*ghaṭatvena ghaṭapaṭau na staḥ*' is universally present. Here the *pratiyogin* of the absence is *ghaṭapaṭobhaya.* The *ādheyatā*—the occurrence that it has, can never be limited by mere *ghaṭatva* which is not a property of *paṭa*. Hence, it is obvious that *ghaṭatva* which by the relation of pure inherence is the limitor of the *pratiyogitā*, cannot be the limitor of the *ādheyatā* residing in the both *ghaṭa* and *paṭa*, by the relation of pure inherence. This means that the *adhikaraṇatā* determined by the *ādheyatā* limited by mere *ghaṭatva* and pure inherence does not exist at all. When thus the opposition to the absence—*ghaṭatvena ghaṭapaṭobhayābhāva*, is a non-entity, it is but quite natural for the absence '*ghaṭatvena ghaṭa-paṭobhayābhāva*' to be a universally present absence.

The above explanation offered by Kṛṣṇambhaṭṭa appears to be quite satisfactory. But, he himself, is not willing to accept the explanation. The reason is not that it is logically incorrect. Instead, he is afraid of the possibility of inconsistency in the views expressed by Gadādhar in this context. Earlier Gadādhar, having rejected *pratiyogitā* as a *vyāsajyavṛtti* held that the universal presence of the absence '*ghaṭatvena ghaṭapaṭobhayābhāva*', can be managed by admitting *avacchedakatā* as *vyāsajyavṛtti.* Suppose, the explanation offered by Kṛṣṇambhaṭṭa is accepted, there will not be any necessity in admitting the *avacchedakatā* also as *vyāsajyavṛtti.* This is stated by Kṛṣṇambhaṭṭa as the view of others:

Atra vadanti—evaṁ sati prakadharmāvacchinnāparyāptitvarūpavirodhaṁ niṣkṛya avacchedakatāyā vyāsajyavṛttitva svīkāravaiyarthya parasaṁgaḥ.

अत्र वदन्ति—एवं सति प्राकधर्मावच्छिन्नापर्याप्तित्वरूपविरोधं निष्कृष्य अवच्छेदकताया व्यासज्यवृत्तित्वस्वीकारवैयर्थ्यप्रसंग: ।

In order to avoid such an inconsistency in Gadādhar's views, Kṛṣṇambhaṭṭa gives another explanation which clarifies Gadādhar's stand without leading to any inconsistency. Accordingly :

The cognition '*ghaṭapaṭobhayam nāsti*' comprehends the absence, of which *ghaṭa* and *paṭa* are the *pratiyogins*. The *pratiyogitā* residing in them has '*dvitva*' as its limitor. The limitorness of this '*dvitva*' is, in turn, is limited by the relation of *paryāpti* qualified with '*ghaṭatvavyāpakatva*' and '*paṭatvavyāpakatva*'. When *ghaṭa* and *paṭa* are on the ground, it means that the *pratiyogin* namely, both *ghaṭa* and *paṭa* are there on the ground being qualified with '*dvita*', the limitor of *pratiyogitā*, with the relation of *paryāpti* mentioned above. In such a situation the above absence cannot exist and, thus, it is not universally present. The following words of Kṛṣṇambhaṭṭa convey the above idea:

Vastutas tu ghṭapatobhyaṁ nāstītyādau ghatatvavyāpakatvaviśiṣṭa paṭatva-vyāpakatvaviśiṣṭaparyāptisambandhāvacchinnadvitvaniṣṭhāvacchedakatāka evābhāvaḥ pratīyate/Ghaṭapaṭobhayavati ca tadṛśabhavasya sarvatrikatvam/ pratiyogitāvacchedakatāparyāptyadhikaraṇadharmaviśiṣṭapratiyogyadhikaraṇatayā sādharmabhāvasya virodhāt.

वस्तुतस्तु, घटपटोभयं नास्तीत्यादौ घटत्वव्यापकत्वविशिष्टपटत्वव्यापकत्वविशिष्टपर्याप्ति-सम्बन्धावच्छिन्नद्वित्वनिष्ठा-वच्छेदकताक एवाभाव:प्रतीयते । घटपटोभयवति च तादृशसम्बन्धेनो-

भयत्वविशिष्टस्य सत्त्वात् न तादृशाभावस्य सार्वत्रिकत्वम्। प्रतियोगितावच्छेदकतापर्याप्त्यधिकरण-धर्मविशिष्टप्रतियोग्यधिकरणतया सार्धमभावस्य विरोधात्।

But, unlike the above *abhāva*, the absence '*ghaṭatvena ghaṭa-paṭobhayam nāsti*', is universally present. Kṛṣṇambhaṭṭa's explanation is as follows:

Although, as in the case of *ghaṭapaṭobhayābhāva*, the *pratiyogitā* of the absence '*ghaṭatvena ghaṭapaṭobhayam nāsti*', resides both in *ghaṭa* and *paṭa*, unlike in the earlier case, the *avacchedakatā* resides by the relation of *paryāpti* not merely in the *dvitva* but also in *ghaṭatva*. Thus, the locus of the *avacchedakatā* by *paryāpti* relation or the locus of the *avacchedakatā-paryāpti* are both '*ghaṭatva* and *ghaṭa-paṭa-dvitva*'. Since these two attributes have the opposition of 'non-co-existence', nowhere can we find a thing possessing them. Therefore, the absence - '*ghaṭatvena ghaṭa-paṭobhayābhāva*' has to be accepted as universally present absence. Kṛṣṇambhaṭṭa puts these views in the following words:

Ghaṭatvena ghaṭapaṭobhayṁ nāstīti pratītisiddhābhāva-pratiyogitāvacchedakatāyāḥ ghaṭatvatādṛśobhayatvaitad ubhayaparyāptatayā pūrvokta-rītyā tayordharmayorviruddhatayā tathāvidhāvacchedakatāparyāptyadhikaraṇoktadharmadvayaviśiṣṭa-pratiyogyaprasiddhyā sārvatrikatvam ityeva bhaṭṭacāryeṇa mahgsayaḥ iti.

घटत्वेन घटपटोभयं नास्तीति प्रतीतिसिद्धाभावप्रतियोगितावच्छेदकतायाः घटत्वतादृशोभयत्वैतदुभयपर्याप्ततया पूर्वोक्तरीत्या तयोर्धर्मयोर्विरुद्धतया तथाविधावच्छेदकतापर्याप्त्यधिकरणोक्तधर्मद्वयविशिष्टप्रतियोग्यप्रसिद्ध्या सार्वत्रिकत्वमित्येव भट्टाचार्याणामाशयःइति।

The above explanation is an example of the manner in which the commentary runs. The main intention of the commentator is to bring out the logical or philosophical points that the original text contains. During this exercise, he substantiates the point being discussed with his own ideas. But, if the original text cannot be supported due to its own weak points, the commentator strives hard to explain the consistency that the text might possess. The student may not find any development of thoughts here, but the benefits of the logical, epistemological or philosophical insights that are presented, is the purpose served by the commentary of Kṛṣṇambhaṭṭa Arḍe.

Raghunatha Parvate Shastri (1853)

As the name indicates Raghunatha Parvate Shastri was of Maharastrian origin with versatility in Advaita Vedānta as well as Nyāya. His well-known Advaita work, *Śaṅkarapadabhūṣaṇam* was written in refutation of the famous Dvaita Vedānta work of Śrī Vyāsa Tīrtha—*Tātparya Candrikā.* He also wrote a commentary called *Nyāyaratna* on some portions of Gadādharī. His *Nyāyaratna* on the *pañcalakṣaṇī* portion of Gadādharī was published by Nirnaya Sagar Press, Bombay. The *Nyāyartna* on the *caturdaśalakṣaṇī* portion of Gadādharī was published by the Adyar Library, Madras, in 1986.

Raghunatha Shastri's *Nyāyaratna* is one of the superb commentaries on the *Gādādharī* and it excels in bringing out the subtle points that Gadādhar makes in his text. In fact, Raghunātha Śāstrin's explanation are more valuable for highlighting such subtleties that carry more information with clarity. It would be interesting to compare *Nyāyaratna* with the *Mañjūṣā* of Kṛṣṇambhaṭṭa Arḍe and the explanation of *Nyāyaratna* on the distinction between the absences - '*ghaṭapaṭobhayābhāva*' and '*ghaṭatvena ghaṭapaṭobhayābhāva*' in the *Gādādharī* dealt with by Arde earlier, affords this opportunity.

Raghunatha Shastri, at the outset, clarifies the problem in very clear terms. Accordingly, the cognition '*ghaṭapaṭau na staḥ*' cannot be regarded as grasping the *pratiyogitāvacchedakatā* in the '*ubhayatva*' alone. For, in that case, the *abhāva* would not be comprehended even in such instances where some *ubhaya* (some two things) are present. Hence, it is necessary to hold that the cognition grasps *avacchedakatā* in such an '*ubhayatva*' which co-exists with *ghaṭatva* and *paṭatva.* Now, the dilemma arises as to whether '*ubhayatva*' co-existing with *ghaṭatva* and *paṭatva,* is to be considered as the limitor, or whether the *ghaṭatva* and *paṭatva* co-existing with the '*ubhayatva*' be considered as the limitor. Since there is nothing which can make the second alternative unacceptable, we have to agree to the suggestion that the cognition comprehends limitorness in *ghaṭatva* and *paṭatva* also. Further, it is generally known that a property grasped in the *pratiyogin* is the limitor of *pratiyogitā.* Thus, in the present case, *ghaṭatva* and *paṭatva* which are grasped in the '*ubhaya*'—the *pratiyogin* must be regarded as the limitors. The result is that since the three limitors namely *ghaṭatva, paṭatva* and *ubhayatva* have the opposition of not having the co-existence, we cannot find a thing anywhere, possessing the *avacchedakas*. Therefore, just as the absence '*ghaṭatvena ghaṭa-paṭobhayābhāva*', the absence '*ghaṭa-paṭobhayābhāva*' also will have to be regarded as universally present.

In the words of Raghunatha Shastri,

> *Nanu ghaṭapatau na staḥ iti pratītiḥ kevalam ubhayatve nāvacchedakatvam avagāhate, tathā sati yatkiñcid ubhayavatī tādṛśapratītyanudayāpatteḥ/Ato ghaṭatva-samānādhikaraṇa-paṭatva samānādhikaraṇ dvitve'vacchedakatvam avagāhata iti vaktavyam/tatra ca dvitvasamānādhikaraṇaṁ ghatatvaṁ paṭatvaṁ veti vinigamanāvirahāt pratiyogyaṁśe bhāsamānatvād vā ghaṭatvapaṭatvayor-apyavacchedakatvāvagāhan aucityāt trayāṇāmevāvacchedakatva prasaktau teṣāṁ caikadharmāvacchinnāparyāptikatva-rūpavirodhāśrayatvāt viruddhobhaya-dharmāvacchinnābhāvavat ghaṭapaṭobhayatvāvacchinnābhāvasyāpi kevalānvayitvaṁ syād iti śaṁkate-yadyapīti.*

ननु 'घटपटौ न स्तः' इति प्रतीतिः केवलमुभयत्वे नावच्छेदकत्वमवगाहते, तथा सति यत्किञ्चिदुभयवति तादृशप्रतीत्यनुदयापत्तेः। अतो घटत्वसमानाधिकरण-पटत्वसमानाधिकरणद्वित्वेऽवच्छेदकत्वमवगाहत इति वक्तव्यम्: तत्र च द्वित्वसमानाधिकरणं घटत्वं पटत्वं वेति विनिगमनाविरहात् प्रतियोग्यंशे भासमानत्वाद्वा घटत्वपटत्वयो- रप्यवच्छेदकत्वावगाहनौचित्यात् त्रयाणामेवावच्छेदकत्वप्रसक्तौ तेषां

चैकधर्मावच्छिन्ना-पर्याप्तिकत्वरूपविरोधाश्रयत्वात् विरुद्धोभयधर्मावच्छिन्नाभाववत् घटपटोभयत्वावच्छिन्ना-भावस्यापि केवलान्वयित्वं स्यादिति शंकते - यद्यपीति।

In the elucidation of the very brief statement made by Gadādhar as the reply to the above objection, Raghunatha Shastri is remarkably clear. His views may be summed up as follows:

When we closely analyse the cognition '*ghaṭatvena ghaṭa-paṭobhayam nāsti*' we may find that *ghaṭatva* is grasped here, twice. Once as a property of *ghaṭa* wherein *dvitva* also is grasped, and again independently. Thus, we can say that two kinds of *pratiyogitāvacchedakatās* are grasped here in *ghaṭatva.* One is that *avacchedakatā* which co-exists with *dvitva* and naturally, *ghaṭatva* has *dvitvadharmatāvacchedakatā* also. Another *pratiyogitāvacchedakatā* grasped in *ghaṭatva* is independent. The independence, as Raghunatha Shastri puts it is—'*pratiyoginiṣṭha-viśeṣyatānirūpitā-prakāratvaprayojyatvam*', i.e. its presence is not due to the *ghaṭatva* being a qualifier of the qualificandum, which in the present case is the *pratiyogin.* This *avacchedaka* is also *vyādhikaraṇa,* i.e. it does not exist where the *pratiyogitā* exists. In the present case, *ghaṭa* and *paṭa* are the *pratiyogins* and *ghaṭatva* does not exist in *paṭa* which has *pratiyogitā.* Between the two *avacchedakatās* mentioned above the first one resides in three properties namely, *ghaṭatva, paṭa*tva and *dvitva*—which are the qualifiers of the *pratiyogin—ghaṭapaṭobhaya.* This *avacchedakatā* actually resides in them by the relation of *paryāpti*—the number '*tritva*' being its limitor. The other *avacchedakatā* resides in *ghaṭatva* alone by *paryāpti* relation and its limitor, is the *tadvyaktitva*—the individuality of *ghaṭatva.*

Now, Raghunatha Shastri points out that we can satisfactorily explain why '*ghaṭa-paṭobhayābhāva*' is not universally present while '*ghaṭatvena ghaṭa-paṭobhayābhāva*' is. In case of the *ghaṭapaṭobhayābhāva,* the *pratiyogitāvacchedakatā* resides in the three properties namely *ghaṭatva, paṭatva* and the *dvitva,* by the relation of *paryāpti.* The limitor of this *paryāpti* is the number *tritva.* Similarly, since we have a valid cognition like '*ghaṭapaṭobhayavad bhūtalam*', in the same '*tritva*' the limitorness is determined by the *paryāpti* of the *avacchedakatā* of *nirūpakatā,* which in its turn, is determined by the *adhikarantā* residing in the *bhūtalam.* It is this *adhikaraṇatā* with which the *abhāva* is opposed. Therefore, in those instances where the above *adhikaraṇatā,* is present, in other words, wherever *ghaṭa* and *paṭa* are present, the *abhāva* cannot exist. On the other hand, the absence, '*ghaṭatvena ghaṭa-paṭobhayam nāsti*' can be a universally present *abhāva,* for the *pratiyogitāvacchedakatā* of the absence, by the relation of *paryāpti,* lies not only in *ghaṭatva, paṭatva* and *dvitva,* but also in *ghaṭatva* again, independently. Thus the limitorness of this *paryāpti* resides in the *tritva* residing in '*ghaṭatva-paṭatva* and *dvitva*', and also in the '*tadvyaktitva*' residing in *ghaṭatva.* But, since nobody has a valid cognition like '*ghaṭatvena ghaṭa-paṭobhayvad*', the *adhikaraṇatā*—the *nirūpakatāvacchedakatāparyāpti* of which could be in the above three properties and also in *ghaṭatva* and consequently the limitorness of this *paryāpti* could be in the '*tritva*' and '*tadvyaktitva*' is a non-entity. As a result, the absence—

'*ghaṭatvena ghaṭa-paṭobhayābhāva*', being un-opposed, can have the universal presence. This is the sum and substance of the following passage in the *Nyāyaratna*:

> *ayaṁbhāvaḥ—ghṭatvena ghaṭapaṭobhyaṁ nāstiītyatra ghṭatve dvividham avacchedakatvam, ekaṁ dvitvadharmitāvacchedakatvena, aparaṁ ca vyadhikaraṇatvena* ı *tatra prathamāvacchedakatāyāḥ tad abhāvīyapratiyogiviśeṣaṇatāpannatvāvacchinnāvacchedakatātvarūpeṇa ghaṭatvapaṭatva-dvitvaitattritayaparyāptatā/tad-avacchedakaṁ tat tritvaṁ/dvitīyāvacchedakatvasya ghaṭatva-mātra-paryāptatayā tad avacchedakaṁ ghaṭatva-niṣṭha-tad-vyaktitvam/tathā ca pratiyogitāvacchedakatā-prayāptyavacchedakatā-vyāpakāvacchedakatāka-paryāptikāvacchedakatāya nirūpakatākādhikaraṇatauaova anjāvasya virodhāt ghaṭapatobhayābhāvīya-pratiyogitāvacchedakatā-paryāptyavacchedakatā-vyāpikā ya ghaṭatvapaṭatvadvitvaitat-tritvaniṣṭhā ghaṭapaṭobhayavat bhūtalamiti pratītisiddhaghaṭapṭobhayatvā-vacchinnādhikaraṇatā-nirūpakatāvacchedakatāparyāptyavacchedakatā tat paryāptikā yā tādṛśa tritayanisṭhā nirūpakatāvacchedakatā tatkā ya tādṛśobhayanṣṭhā dheyatvarūpā nirūpakatā tannirūpitādhikaraṇatā ghaṭapaṭobhyādhi karaṇe vartate iti na tādṛśobhayatvāvacchinnābhāvasya kevalānvayitvam/ghaṭatvena ghaṭapṭobhayaṁ nāstīti pratītiviṣayābhāva-pratiyogitāvacchedakatāparyāptya-vacchedakatāyāḥ tādṛśa-tritva-ghaṭatvaniṣṭha tad vyaktitvayoḥ sattvena ghṭatvena ghaṭapaṭobhayavad iti pratītavirahena tādṛśāvacchedakatā-vyāpakāvacchedakatā-paryāptikavacchedakatāka-nirūpakatāyā aprasiddhatvena virodhino'bhāvāt tādṛśābhāvasya kevalānvayitvam iti.*

> अयंभाव: - घटत्वेन घटपटोभयं नास्तीत्यत्र घटत्वे द्विविधमवच्छेदकत्म्; एकं द्वित्वधर्मितावच्छेदकत्वेन, अपरं च व्यधिकरणत्वेन। तत्र प्रथमावच्छेदकताया: तदभावीयप्रतियोगिविशेषणतापन्नत्वावच्छिन्नावच्छेदकतात्वरूपेण घटत्वपटत्वद्वित्वैतत्त्रितय-पर्याप्तता। तदवच्छेदकं तत्त्रित्वम्। द्वितीयावच्छेदकत्वस्य घटत्वमात्रपर्याप्ततया तदवच्छेदकं घटत्वनिष्ठतद्व्यक्तित्वम्। तथा च प्रतियोगितावच्छेदकतापर्यप्त्यवच्छेदकताव्यापकावच्छेदकताकपर्याप्तिकावच्छेदकता- कनिरूपकताकाधिकरणतयैव अभावस्य विरोधात् घटपटोभयाभावीयप्रतियोगितावच्छेदकतापर्याप्त्यवच्छेदकताव्यापिका या घटत्वपटत्वद्वित्वैतत्त्रित्वनिष्ठा घटपटोभयवत् भूतलमिति प्रतीतिसिद्धघटपटोभयत्वावच्छिन्नाधिकरणता-निरूपकतावच्छेदकतापर्याप्त्यवच्छेदकता तत्पर्याप्तिका या तादृशत्रितयनिष्ठा निरूपकतावच्छेदकता तत्का या तादृशोभयनिष्ठाधेयत्वरूपानिरूपकता तन्निरूपिताधिकरणता घटपटोभयाधिकरणे वर्तते इति न तादृशोभयत्वावच्छिन्नाभावस्य केवलान्वयित्वम्। घटत्वेन घटपटोभयं नास्तीति प्रतीतिविषयाभावप्रतियोगितावच्छेदकतापर्याप्त्यवच्छेदकताया: तादृशत्रित्वघटत्वनिष्ठतद्व्यक्तित्वयो: सत्त्वेन घटत्वेन घटपटोभयवदिति प्रतीतिविरहेण तादृशावच्छेदकताव्यापकावच्छेदकतापर्याप्तिकावच्छेदकताकनिरूपकताया अप्रसिद्धत्वेन विरोधिनोऽभावात् तादृशाभावस्य केवलान्वयित्वमिति।

The above elucidation of Navya Nyāya concepts by Raghunatha Shastri is an example of his clarity and his marvellous presentation of the subtle issues in which he excelled. The critical analyses which we find in abundance in the *Nyāyaratna* have made the commentary a very valuable one.

Giridhara Upādhyāya (1720)

Giridhara Upādhyāya Jhā was one of the disciples of Gokulanātha Upādhyāya. His only available work the *Vibhaktyarthanirṇaya,* is indeed very useful for its presentation of the Nyāya interpretation of the entire *kāraka prakaraṇa.* In this work, Giridhara also refers to other interpretations such as that of the Grammarians and Poeticians. He also refers to the views of his teacher Gokulanātha Upādhyāya. His explanations are very critical and he often makes very novel and interesting points.

To highlight this the following discussion serves as an example:

It is generally admitted by the Naiyāyikas that a relation which is *vṛttyaniyāmaka,* i.e. that which is not an occurrence exacting, is not the limitor of the *pratiyogitā* of an absence. But as to why it should not be admitted to be so, is the question raised. Gadādhar, in his *Vyutpattivāda* discusses the problem briefly. He only says that if such relations are accepted as the limitors of *pratiyogitā* then it leads to *gaurava* as innumerable *pratiyogitas* limited by such relations, will have to be accepted. Though this reply contains some logic yet it does not seem to be convincing. But, Giridhara offers an interesting and more satisfactory answer. He points out that if a relation is not *vṛttiniyāmaka,* it means that the cognition of a thing as residing in a locus, with such relations, can never arise. If even such relations are the limitors of *abhāvapratiyogitā,* then such absences will have to be considered as universally present, since such absences are without any opposition. Therefore, he holds that a non-occurrence—exacting relation cannot be considered as the limitor of an *abhāva-pratiyogitā.*

It is obvious that this explanation is more satisfactory.

This work was published by Chowkhamba Sanskrit Series in the year 1901.

II
ANVITĀBHIDHĀNA VĀDA VS ABHIHITĀNVAYA VĀDA, AND, *PRAKĀRATĀ* VĀDA VS *SAMSARGATĀ* VĀDA

Anvitābhidhāna vāda and Abhihitānvaya vāda

I feel, some clarification is necessary regarding the theories mentioned above, as is stated in the summary, *anvitābhidhāna vāda* and *abhihitānvaya vāda* are generally known as the 'sentence theory of meaning' and the 'word theory of meaning', respectively. But in my view, these English phrases do not convey what the Sanskrit terms intend. *Anvitābhidhāna vāda* is the theory upheld by the Prābhākara Mīmāṁsakas and also supported later, by some Vedānta schools such as Viśiṣṭādvaita and Dvaita. The Bhāṭṭa Mīmāṁsakas took the opposite stand and upheld the *abhihitānvaya vāda.* The Nyāya school and also the Advaita school supported this stand.

The two theories opposed each other on the issue of how *anvaya,* i.e. the relation between word-meaning is conveyed. The *abhihitānvaya vāda* contends that words in a sentence, convey just their meanings and the relation between them is communicated by *samabhivyāhāra,* also called *ākāṅkṣā. Samabhivyāhāra* is the utterance of the word in a sequence. Since, this *samabhivyāhāra* can be described as a property of sentence, the relation of word-meanings, conveyed by a property of sentence such as *samabhivyāhāra,* is called *vākyārtha* i.e. sentence meaning.

The Prābhākaras and their allies, on the other hand, took a different view. They strongly contended that a word in a sentence, cannot convey just an unrelated thing. In other words, the *anvaya* i.e. the relation which the *abhihitānvayavādins* considered as *vākyārtha,* is held by the *anvitābhidhānavādins* as *padārtha*—a meaning conveyed by word itself. This, in short, is the difference between the two theories. This controversy, has existed right from the time of Kumārila Bhaṭṭa, the founder of the Bhaṭṭa Mīmāṁsā school, and Jayanta Bhaṭṭa. The latter celebrated Naiyāyika of *Nyāyamañjarī* fame, vehemently upheld the *abhihitānvayavāda,* and Prabhākara and his followers along with some Vedānta schools mentioned above, equally vehemently supported the *anvitābhidhāna vāda.* It is also noteworthy here that even the Bhāṭṭas and the Naiyāyikas though generally known as abhihitānvayavādins, have many differences in explaining the theory. Similarly, the Prabhākara school and other Vedānta schools also differ in presenting the anvitābhidhāna vāda.

Prakāratā vāda and Saṁsargatā vāda

The Nyāya school holds that the *viṣayas,* i.e. the contents of a cognition can be broadly divided into three, namely-*viśeṣya*—qualificandum, *prakāra*—qualifier, and *saṁsarga*—relation. Accordingly, *viṣayatā*—contentness also is of three kinds: (i) *viśeṣyatā*—qualificandum-ness residing in qualificandum, (ii) *prakāratā*—qualifierness located in qualifier, and (iii) *saṁsargatā*—residing in *saṁsarga*—relation. In a verbal cognition, if anything is presented by a constituent of the sentence, be it a nominal base, suffix, root or an indeclinable—all of which are regarded as words by the Nyāya school, it is either *viśeṣya* or *prakāra* and has either *viśeṣyatā* or *prakāratā* in it. As against this, the relation between the *padārthas,* i.e. *viśeṣya* and *prakāra,* which is also a content of a verbal cognition, is neither *viśeṣya* nor *prakāra,* for according to the Nyāya school, it is conveyed only by *samabhivyāhāra* and not by any word of the sentence. Thus, now it is clear that the contentness called *Prakāratā* resides only in such contents of a verbal cognition, which are conveyed by the words of that sentence, to be precise—in *padārthas.* But, the contentness called *samsargatā* can reside only in that which is presented in a verbal cognition by *samabhivyāhāra* and not by any word. Thus, *prakāratāvāda* is a theory which holds a particular content of a verbal cognition, as presented by a word and similarly, *saṁsargatāvāda* is that theory which holds that the particular content referred to, is not presented by a word, but by *samabhivyāhāra.*

Now, this explanation, I feel, is sufficient to make it clear that neither Gadādhara nor Jagadīśa can exclusively be dubbed as either Prakāratāvādin or Saṁsargātavādin. For, both of them, being *abhihitānvayavādins,* hold the view that in a verbal cognition, there are three types of contents namely *viśeṣya, prakāra* and *saṁsarga,* and whatever, in that cognition, is presented by a word, is *prakāra* or *viśeṣya* and that presented through *samabhivyāhāra* is *saṁsarga.* So, the question as to whether Gadādhara or Jagadīśa is Prakāratāvādin or Saṁsargatāvādin, can be raised only in respect of a particular content of a particular instance. For example, both of them concur that identity statements such as '*nīlaḥ ghaṭaḥ*' convey identity between *nīla* and *ghaṭa* which are presented in the verbal cognition produced by the above statement, by the words '*nīla*' and '*ghaṭa*'. Therefore, in respect of the contents such as '*nīla*' and '*ghaṭa*', in the above instance, both Gadādhara and Jagadīśa, are Prakāratāvādins. But in respect of the identity, Jagadīśa contends that the identity here is conveyed by the suffix added to the word '*nīla*' and therefore, it is a *padārtha* and hence a *prakāra.* Thus, while Gadādhara is Saṁsargatāvādin in respect of identity, and Prakāratāvādin in respect of the other contents such as *nīla* and *ghaṭa* of the verbal cognition, Jagadīśa is Prakāratāvādin in respect of all the three namely—*nīla, ghaṭa* and identity. But, the point which deserves our attention is that Jagadīśa also has to admit that some other relation, if not identity, ought to be conveyed by *samabhivyāhāra,* even in case of the identical statements. The following explanation will make the point more clear:

Nīlaḥ ghaṭaḥ ('नील: घट:') - this identical statement consists of four words *nīla* + *su* - (नील + सु) and *ghaṭa* + *su* (घट + सु). (सु is a nominative case affix which is indicated by the symbol ':'). According to Gadādhara, both the case affixes added to the two words are meaningless and yet are necessary for the sake of grammatical correctness. Since, here, the identity is not conveyed by any word, but only by *samabhivyāhāra,* Gadādhara is a Saṁsargātavādin in his approach. On the other hand, Jagadīśa holds that only the 'su (सु)' after 'ghaṭa (घट)' is just for the sake of grammatical purity, while the 'su (सु)' after 'nīla (नील)' conveys identity. The following may explain Jagadīśa's position, more clearly:

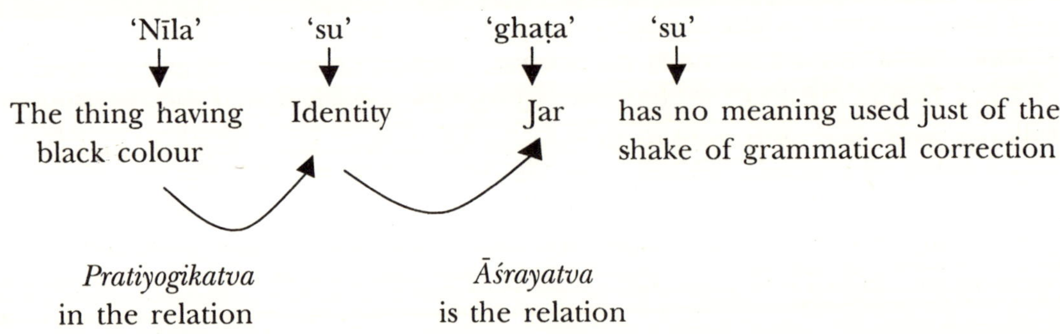

So, as per Jagadīśa *pratiyogikatva* (प्रतियोगिकत्व) and *Āśrayatva* (आश्रयत्व) are the two relations that are conveyed by *samabhivyāhāra*, in the cognition produced by the sentence *nīlaḥ ghaṭaḥ* (नील: घट:). Thus, he has a *Saṁsargatāvādin* approach if these two relations are taken into account.

I hope that the above explanation is clear enough to convey the fact that no Naiyāyika is either Prakāratāvādin or Saṁsargatāvādin exclusively.

The next question as to what difference is made philosophically if one accepts one or the other of these two theories, is a bit difficult to answer. I shall only point out one difference, among a few made by these two theories. If that can be called a philosophical difference, it can also be regarded as the philosophical significance of these theories.

If *prakāratā vāda* is accepted, as already explained, it means that a particular thing is conveyed by a word in the sentence. This particular thing, being a *prakāra*—a qualifier, is to be related with another meaning conveyed by another word of the sentence. Thus, the relation of these two things also will have to be a content of the cognition. For instance, in the sentence '*nīlaḥ ghaṭaḥ* (नील: घट:)', if the identity between *nīla* (नील) and *ghaṭa* (घट) is considered as something conveyed by the term '*su* (सु)' added to the word *nīla* (नील), then it becomes a *prakāra*. Then this identity is to be related with *ghaṭa* (घट) conveyed by the other word *ghaṭa* (घट). Here, the relation is *āśrayatva* (आश्रयत्व), for the *ghaṭa* (घट) is the *āśraya* (आश्रय)—the locus of the identity. On the other hand, if this identity is not considered as a thing conveyed by the '*su* (सु)' then it ceases to be a *prakāra*, for it is conveyed by *samabhivyāhāra* and hence is a *saṁsarga*. It is admitted by all the Naiyāyikas that a relation conveyed by *samabhivyāhāra* does not need another relation to be related. As a consequence, if a particular thing is regarded as *saṁsarga* then the contents of the cognition are less in number. If the same thing is a *prakāra*, the contents of the cognition will be more, for the relation of the *prakāra* will be an additional content. This is one of the significant difference made by these two theories. Thus, Gadādhara and Jagadīśa are both Prakāratāvādins and Saṁsargatāvādins. But, regarding a particular content of a particular verbal cognition, they may take opposite stand and then, accordingly may be called Prakāratāvādin or Saṁsargatāvādin as per the stand taken.

Definition of Vyāpti and Vyādhikaraṇadharmāvacchinnābhāva

Concomitance, is one of the most seriously discussed topics in the Nyāya School. Prior to Gaṅgeśopādhyāya, several Naiyāyikas had attempted to offer a satisfactory definition of *Vyāpti*. Gaṅgeśa, in his *Tattvacintāmaṇi*, has criticised all those definitions, as they contain in their body the absence of *sādhyabhāvā* (साध्याभाव). For example, *sādhyābhāvavadavṛtititvam* (साध्याभाववद्वृत्तित्वम्) is one of these definitions.

It means—concomitance which is the essential characteristic of a reason, is "the absence of the relation of the reason in the instances of *sādhyābhāva*". Gaṅgeśa points out that this definition and also such other definitions which contain *sādhyābhāva* in their body, can be applied only to such inferences where *sādhyābhāva* is a possibility. But, there are some inferences, the *sādhyas* of which, are universally present. For example, in the inference "this is nameable as it is knowable" (idaṁ vācyaṁ jñeyatvāt [इदं वाच्यं ज्ञेयत्वात्]) the *sādhya,* i.e. nameability (vācyatva), is a universally present attribute and hence its absence is an impossibility. Therefore, the definitions of *vyāpti* consisting of *sādhyābhāva* are not applicable to the inferences as the above.

In order to avoid such a defect in the definition of *vyāpti,* several Naiyāyikas brought in the concept of *vyādhikaraṇadharmāvacchinnābhāva.* According to them, there are two types of *abhāvas*: (i) *samānādhikaraṇadharmāvacchinnābhāva* (S.A.), and (ii) *vyādhikaraṇadharmāvacchinnābhāva* (V.A.). S.A. is that absence of a thing which is characterised by an attribute that actually exists in it. For instance, the absence of a jar characterised by jar-ness *ghaṭatven ghaṭābhāvaḥ.* This absence does not exist there where a jar characterised by jar-ness, is present. Hence, it is not universal. As against this, V.A. is such an absence of a thing which is characterised by an attribute which does not exist in it. For example, the absence of jar, as characterised by *paṭatva.* It is obvious that *paṭatva* is not an attribute of a *ghaṭa* and *ghaṭa* does not exist anywhere being characterised by *paṭatva.* Therefore, such an absence is universal. Thus, the main difference between S.A. and V.A. is that while an S.A. can not be universally present, a V.A. can be universally present. Some Naiyāyikas suggested that though in some inference, the S.A. of the *sādhya* (e.g. nameability), is not found anywhere since, the *sādhya* itself is present everywhere, it is possible to show the application of the definition of *vyāpti* in such inferences also by making use of V.A. of the *sādhya,* which is universally present. Raghunātha Śiromaṇi, in his commentary on *Tattvacintāmaṇi* of Gaṅgeśa presents some such fourteen definitions which include two of his own while the others were formulated by the earlier Naiyāyikas. This portion of the text is called '*Caturdaśa lakṣaṇī*'. Later Gaṅgeṣa rejects even these definitions on the ground that there cannot be an absence called V.A. According to him, '*ghaṭa* does not exist being characterised by *paṭatva* (*paṭatvena ghaṭo nāsti*) means that there is no *paṭatva* in *ghaṭa.* Thus, it is only the absence of *paṭatva* in *ghaṭa,* and this absence is S.A. only.

In my article on Kṛṣṇam Bhaṭṭa Arḍe, I have chosen a context in which Kṛṣṇam Bhaṭṭa and Raghunatha Shastri both of whom, are though commentators of the same Gādādharī text yet, while answering an objection raised against Gādādharī, have shown originality in their approach by offering different solutions.

Vyāsajyavṛtti dharma and Paryāpti relation

Among the innumerable attributes that we come across, some are *Vyāsajyavṛtti* while the others are not so. *Vyāsajyavṛtti* is such an attribute which can exist sufficiently or fully in more than one locus. For instance, numbers such as *dvitva, tritva,* etc. or other. When there are two jars, it is obvious that they have the number 'two'—*dvitva.* That means each one of them possesses the attribute *dvitva.* But what is significant is that none of them can be said to possess the *dvitva* sufficiently or fully. If that were the case, then even when there is only one jar on the ground, we should have been able to grasp it and say—'there are two jars on the ground'. Since we do not have such a cognition, it is obvious that a single jar does not have the *dvitva, fully.* At the same time, we can neither say that there is no *dvitva* in a single jar. For, as already said, *dvitva* being a number and hence a quality, should be residing in each of the group of two jars. Therefore, the Naiyāyikas hold the view that *dvitva,* etc., numbers are both present and not present in each member of the group. They are present in each by mere *samavāya* relation and at the same time, are not present in them by the *relation of sufficiency* which is named as the relation *paryāpti.* Since, each of the members does not possess *dvitva, tritva,* etc., by the relation of *paryāpti,* we do not, pointing out to a single jar, say—'this is two or three'. But, since each member has the number *dvitva,* etc., by the relation of mere *samavāya* we can only say that each member of the group, has the number *dvitva* or *tritva.*

Just as the numbers reside in their locus, by the relation of *paryāpti,* there are some other properties which also reside in their locus by the relation of *paryāpti. Pratiyogitā, avacchedakatā,* etc., are such properties. In the case of the absence of both *ghaṭa* and *paṭa,* both of them are the *pratiyogins* of the absence and hence have *pratiyogitā* in them. Then, the question arises as to what is the difference between the absence of mere *ghaṭa* and the absence of both *ghaṭa* and *paṭa,* for both the absences have *ghaṭa* as their *pratiyogin.* The answer given by the Naiyāyikas is that though both the absences have *ghaṭa* as their *pratiyogin* the former one is that absence the *pratiyogitā* of which is related to mere *ghaṭa* by the relation of *paryāpti,* while the latter one has its *pratiyogitā* related to both *ghaṭa* and *paṭa* by the relation of *paryāpti.*

Regarding the exposition of relation of *paryapti* and *Vyasajyavṛttitva* may be said that as these two concepts are of significance in the discussion on the nature of certain *abhāvas,* familiarity with them is essential. Further, regarding the issues discussed while commenting on the work of Kṛṣṇam Bhaṭṭa and Raghunatha Shastri, I have to make it clear that those are not the central issues discussed either by Gadādhara or by his commentators. Their main concern, in the text called *Caturdaśa lakṣaṇī,* is the definition of *vyāpti* containing *vyādhikaraṇa-dharmāvacchinnābhāva* in its body. Since the understanding of the nature of such an absence is required to formulate a definition of *vyāpti,* these also are incidentally discussed. Though these issues are thus not of primary concern, I have chosen them as they involve many interesting epistemological and philosophical points and the commentators have demonstrated their originality in solving a certain problem.

The distinctive nature of the several absences that are discussed in my article may be summed up in conclusion. Accordingly, *ghaṭatvena ghaṭo nāsti* (घटत्वेन घटो नास्ति) is a *samānādhikaraṇadharmāvacchinnābhāva* (S.A.), and is not universally present, for it cannot exist wherever a ghaṭa (घट) being qualified with *ghaṭatva* (घटत्व) is present. But, the absence *ghaṭatvena ghaṭo nāsti* (घटत्वेन घटो नास्ति) which is a *vyādhikaraṇadharmāvacchinnābhāva* (V.A.) is universally present, for a piece of cloth can nowhere exist being qualified with *ghaṭatva.* Similarly, *ghatapaṭobhayaṁ nāsti* (घटपटोभयं नास्ति) which is S.A. is not universal, for it cannot exist in the instances where both *ghaṭa* and *paṭa*—the *pratiyogin* exist. But, the absence *ghaṭatvena ghaṭapatau na staḥ* (घटत्वेन घटपटो न स्तः) or *ghaṭatvena ghaṭapaṭobhayaṁ nāsti* (घटत्वेन घटपटोभयं नास्ति) which is a V.A. is universally present. For though one of the *pratiyogin* namely *ghaṭa* can exist being qualified with *ghaṭatva* the other namely, *pratiyogin* can no where exist being qualified with *ghaṭatva.* In other words, both *ghaṭa* and *paṭa,* together have no existence anywhere in the universe, being qualified with *ghaṭatva* and hence the absence of the both being characterised by *ghaṭatva,* is universally present. Since the distinctive nature of these absences can be clearly brought out by introducing the concepts of *vyāsajyavṛttitva* of *pratiyogitā* or *pratiyogitāvacchedakatā,* they are discussed here.

Due to the ambiguity of the Nyāya technical terms which are profusely made use of here, the persistence of further questions is quite natural. However, the points discussed here regarding *ghaṭa-paṭobhayābhāva,* etc., are purely epistemological, even ontological. The references that are made to some metaphysical view points of the Nyāya school, are just incidental and are assumed as universally admitted. For instance, the reference to the nature of *vācyatā* as the will of God; the later Naiyāyikas as a matter of fact, explained *vācyatva* as mere 'will' in the form 'let this thing be conveyed by this word'. Thus, they tried to include even the modern conventions created by all, including laymen. Therefore, though some metaphysical points may have been mentioned they may be ignored as they do not have any bearing on the present discussion. Hence, the logical and epistemological points discussed here can be disengaged from both—the Nyāya metaphysics and the Sanskrit language, and their logical worth can be seriously examined.

III
KROḌAPATRAS

Among the voluminous works of Nyāya, written during the eighteenth and nineteenth centuries, we come across two types of works which have made a unique contribution in the development of the Nyāya School. These are the *Vādas* and

Kroḍapatras. Between the two, the *Vādas* are generally small treatises which aim at upholding a Nyāya view of a concept by means of a thorough discussion of the same. In fact, the genesis of these *Vāda* works can be traced to the eighteenth century itself. It seems that Raghunātha Śiromaṇi started writing such *Vādagranthas* as *Ākhyātavāda, Nañavāda, Kṛtisādhyatānumānavāda, Vājapeyavāda*, etc. As the very titles indicate, these were written to thoroughly discuss certain specific topics. Later, Harirāma Tarkavāgīśa, Gadādhara Bhaṭṭācārya and others continued to write such treaties. Gadādhara Bhaṭṭācārya's *Vyutpattivāda, Viṣayatāvāda, Prāmāṇyavāda* etc. are works of the same type. During the eighteenth and nineteenth centuries such innumerable *Vādas* were written.

The *Kroḍapatras* are slightly different from the *Vādas*. They are not as lengthy as the *Vādas*. Though these *Kroḍapatras* were written to explain certain sentences that occur in the original text they cannot be considered as commentaries because they do not continue to explain each and every sentence within the text but treat only selective points made in the original text while discussing them thoroughly. Thus, they may be considered as independent works of the author, because except at the beginning, nowhere does the author explain or comment on any part of the text neither summarising the points which a commentator generally does. Disregarding the text as an entity he concentrates on a particular point by raising an objection on it. He proceeds by rejecting any modification or clarification, pointing out the loopholes in it. When this exercise reaches a stage beyond which no further justification is possible, he presents his own solution, normally by suggesting an *anugama*, a technical device discovered by the Navya Naiyāyikas, by which the point under discussion is ultimately vindicated by plugging all the loopholes. The ingenuity with which the author of a *Kroḍapatra* imagines peculiar instances which nobody can ever think of and points out the untenability of the arguments defending the point under discussion, is indeed something remarkable. He can be compared to a very shrewd chess player who while practising the game, plays the role of two players, one strongly defending a position and the other savagely attacking the same.

The very title '*Kroḍapatra*' suggests the purpose and scope of the small treatises that are called *Kroḍapatras*. '*Kroḍa*' means '*madhya*'—middle. The term '*patra*' which in common parlance means a letter, also means an article, analytical in nature. Thus, a *Kroḍapatra* is an article or a collection of articles with a critical perspective that aim at discussing a point which occurs midway in the content being discussed in the original text. Another explanation given for the term is that *Kroḍapatra* is a paper kept in between the pages. While copying the manuscripts, sometimes some sentences may be missed and in such cases, it becomes necessary to offer some explanation for that portion. At times some scholar may write something to express his own views on a certain point discussed in the text. *Kroḍapatra*, by this explanation, is an article written with either of the intentions mentioned above and kept in the middle of the pages. But in the *Kroḍapatras*, it is seldom so, that the author is trying to fill in the gaps that were created by the person who copied the manuscript. As a matter of fact, the authors of the

Kroḍapatras generally commence their discussion with a point which the original writer has stated as final.

The contribution of the *Kroḍapatras* to the development of the Navya Nyāya tradition is illustrated by two *Kroḍapatras—Kālīśaṅkarīya* and *Candranārāyaṇīya* named after the authors Kalisankara Bhattacharya and Chandranarayana Bhattacharya who flourished during the A.D. eighteenth century. These two *Kroḍapatras* are held in high esteem in the Nyāya circle and even today they are studied as a part of the advanced study of Nyāya. These two *Kroḍapatras* are on the *Hetvābhāsasāmānya-nirukti* of Gadādhara Bhaṭṭācārya, which in turn is a commentary on Raghunātha Śiromaṇi's *Dīdhiti* on the *Hetvābhāsa* portion of Gaṅgeśa's *Tattvacintāmaṇi.*

Gaṅgeśa in the *Hetvābhāsaprakaraṇa* of his *Tattvacintāmaṇi,* suggests one after the other, three definitions of the fallacies of reason. The second definition is:

yadviṣayakatvena jñānasyānumiti-pratibandhakatvam tattvam

यद्विषयकत्वेन ज्ञानस्यानुमितिप्रतिबन्धकत्वं तत्त्वम् ।

This means that a fallacy of reason is that by comprehending which a cognition prevents an inferential cognition. *Vanhyābhāvavadhrada* is an instance of this definition. It is called the fallacy of *bādha,* while the inference is '*hrado vanhimān dhūmāt*'. The definition is applicable here because the cognition of this fallacy, which arises in the form '*hrado Vanhyābhāvavān*' prevents the inferential cognition.

Commenting on the definition, Raghunātha Śiromaṇi suggests a slight modification by replacing *yadviṣayakatvena* into *yādṛśaviśiṣṭa-viṣayakatvena.* Suppose this modification is not made, the definition would not be applicable to any fallacy. For, since mere '*hrada*' is identical with the '*hrada* qualified by *vanhyabhāva*' the cognition of mere '*hrada*' also is the cognition *vanhyabhāvavadhrada.* But, the cognition of mere '*hrada*' does not prevent the inferential cognition '*hrado vanhimān*'. Therefore, the cognition of *Vanhyabhāvavadhrada* cannot be said as preventive of the inferential cognition. Thus, the definition suffers from the defect of *asaṁbhava.* If the term '*yadviṣayakatvena*', is replaced by the term '*yādṛśaviśiṣṭaviṣayakatvena*', this defect can be avoided. Apparently, this modification suggested by Śiromaṇi, is meaningless. For, since a qualified object is identical with the 'mere object', the *hrada* qualified with '*vanhybhāva*' is the same as the mere '*hrada*' and hence the cognition of mere '*hrada*' is also the cognition of the *viśiṣṭa*—the *hrada* qualified with *vanhyabhāva.* But, as Gadādhara suggests here the term '*Yādṛśaviśiṣṭaviṣayakatvena*' should be taken in the sense of '*Yadrūpāvacchinnaviṣayakatvena*'. Now the definition is –

yadrūpāvacchinnaviṣayakatvena jñānasya anumitipratibandhakatvaṁ tadrūpāvacchinnatvam

यद्रूपावच्छिन्नविषयकत्वेन ज्ञानस्य अनुमितिप्रतिबन्धकत्वं तद्रूपावच्छिन्नत्वम् ।

It means—'A fallacy of reason is the possessing of that property, by comprehending the thing possessed of which property, the cognition prevents the inferential cognition'.

In case of the instance, '*hrado vanhimān dhūmāt*', Gadādhara seems to hold the view that the property by possessing of which the reason in the above inference is considered as fallacious, is '*vanhyabhāvavadhrdatva*'—'Lakeness qualified with the absence of fire'. However, he does not specifically spell it out and moves to the next topic. From this point, the *Kroḍapatras* commence their analysis.

Kalisankara Bhattacharya raises the question—'*atha yadrūpapadena kim dhartavyam*?—What is signified by the term '*yadrūpa*' (which property) in the definition? The ready answer would be '*vanhyabhāvavadhradatvam*' in case of the fallacious inferences—'*hrado vanhimān dhūmāt*'. But, Kālīśaṅkara continues to question—*vanhyabhāvavadhradatva* means the property called lakeness qualified with *vanhyabhāva* and what is this relation with which *hradatva* is said to be qualified with *vanhyabhāva*? Of course, the relation cannot be the relation of *svarūpa* by which an absence is normally expected to be present wherever its counterpositive does not exist. For, since, fire the counterpositive in the above case, can never be imagined to exist in '*hradatva*', its absence naturally always exists in it and the cognition 'the lake has lake-ness that has no fire' cannot prevent the inferential cognition '*hrado vanhimān*'. Therefore, the possible relation with *vanhyabhāva* here, should be the relation of *sāmānādhikaraṇya* or co-existence. It may be held that one who knows *hradatva* and *vanhyabhāva* existing together, cannot have the cognition '*hrado vanhimān*' and hence the cognition that 'the lake has the property of lakeness which is qualified with *vanhyabhāva* by the relation of *sāmānādhikaraṇya* will definitely prevent the inferential cognition—'*hrado vanhimān*'. Kālīśaṅkara points out that this view is not tenable, because there are some such cognitions which cannot prevent the inferential cognition but comprehend a thing which is possessed of the said property. For instance, the cognition—'*sāmānādhikaraṇyasambandhena vanhyabhāvavad hradatvavān*'. The peculiarity of this cognition is that it has *hrada* as its qualificandum and *hradatva* qualified with *vanhyabhāva* by the relation of *sāmānādhikaraṇya* as its qualifier. But it does not comprehend any limitor of the qualificandumness. For the same reason it cannot prevent the inferential cognition '*hrado vanhimān*', which has a limitor of qualificandumness, namely, *hradatva*. Since these two cognitions mentioned above do not have the same limitor of qualificandumness, they cannot be held as *pratibadhya* and *pratibandhaka*. But, this cognition also comprehends *hradatva* as qualified with *vanhyabhāva* by the relation of *sāmānādhikaraṇya*. Therefore, '*sāmānādhikaraṇya sambandhena vanhyabhāvavadhradatva*' cannot be the property signified by the term '*yadrūpa*' in the definition.

The other alternative is to hold that *vanhyabhāva* and *hradatva*—the two properties as denoted by the term '*yadrūpa*'. But as in the case of the first alternative, here also it can be shown that even a cognition which is a non-preventor of the inferential cognition '*hrado vanhimān*', has as its content the thing possessed of the two properties—*vanhyabhāva* and *hradatva.* For instance, the cognition '*vanhyabhāvahradatvavān*' which comprehends both *vanhyabhāva* and *hradatva* together in *hrada.* As in the earlier case, even this cognition does not have *hradatva* as the limitor of the qualificandumness, and hence cannot be the preventor of the inferential cognition '*hrado vanhimān*' which has *hradatva* as the limitor of the qualificandumness. Thus, Kalisankara points out that it is not possible to specifically state as to what could be the denotation of the term '*yadrūpa*'.

Kalisankara Bhattacharya then, refers to several attempts made to solve the problem, including that of the 'Navyas' who could be his contemporary Naiyāyikas. He finds fault with some of them. He also refers to the other views without criticising them, thereby indicating that they are acceptable. Only in the case of one view, first, he finds fault with it and thereafter suggests an amendment and accepts it. I shall try to explain here only that view which he concedes as admissible with an amendment. The following are his words -

kecit tu-vanhidharmitāvacchedakatāpannābhāvatvāvacchinnadharmitāvacchedakatāpannahrdatvameva yadrūpapadena dhartavyamityapi vadanti/tanna/tathāsati vanhidharmitāvacchedakatāpannābhāvatvāvacchinna-dharmitāvacchedakatāpanna-parvatatvamādāya bhramaviṣaye'tivyāpteḥ/yadi ca tādṛśadharmitāvacchedakatāpanna yad vanhyabhāvahradatvādikaṁ tad eva yad rūpa padenocyate tadā na doṣa iti dhyeyam/

केचित्तु - वह्निधर्मितावच्छेदकतापन्नाभावत्वावच्छिन्नधर्मितावच्छेदकतापन्नह्रदत्वमेव यद्रूपपदेन धर्तव्यमित्यपि वदन्ति। तन्न। तथासति वह्निधर्मितावच्छेदकतापन्नाभावत्वावच्छिन्न-धर्मितावच्छेदकतापन्नपर्वतत्वमादाय भ्रमविषयेऽतिव्याप्तेः। यदि च तादृशधर्मितावच्छेदकतापन्नं यद् वह्न्यभावह्रदत्वादिकं तदेव यद्रूपपदनोच्यते तदा न दोष इति ध्येयम्।

The solution suggested by *kecit* (some)—in case of the fallacious inference—'*hrado vanhimān dhūmāt*', the term *yadrūpa* denotes the property which has the limitorness in respect of the qualificandumness determined by an *abhāva,* the property—*abhāvatva* of which, has the limitorness in respect of the qualificandumness determined by *vanhi.* The above solution will be easy to understand if we analyse the structure of the cognition—'*hrado vanhyabhāvavān*'. Here *abhāva* is comprehended as qualified with *vanhi.* Thus with reference to *vanhi, abhāva* is the qualificandum and the *abhāvatva* residing in it, is the limitor of the qualificandumness that resides in the *abhāva.* Hence, it can be said that *abhāvatva* has the limitorness in respect of the qualificandumness residing in the *abhāva* and this qualificandumness is determined by the *vanhi.* Similarly, with reference to the *abhāva, hrada* has the qualificandumness and *hradatva* is its limitor.

In short, the term '*yadrūpa*' in the definition, refers to that *hradatva* which has the limitorness in respect of the qualificandumness determined by the *abhāva*; *abhāvatva*, the property of which also has the limitorness in respect of the qualificandumness determined by *vanhi.* Only by comprehending a thing possessed of such a *hradatva*, the cognition could prevent the inferential cognition '*hrado vanhimān*'. Since the other cognitions such as '*sāmānādhikaraṇya-sambandhena vanhyabhāvaviśiṣṭahradatvavān*', '*vanhyabhāvahrada-tvobhayavān*', etc. do not comprehend such a *hradatva*, they cannot prevent the inferential cognition *hrado vanhimān.*

The fault in this second explanation, according to Kalisankara Bhattacharya, is that if such a property as shown above is denoted by the term '*yadrūpa*', then the definition of *hetvābhāsa* will become too wide. For, the inference '*parvato vanhimān dhūmāt*', which is a valid inference, can also be shown as having a fallacy. The point that is being made by him is this—just as the cognition '*hrado vanhyabhāvavān*' prevents the inferential cognition '*hrado vanhimān*', the cognition '*parvato vanhyabhāvavān*' also, actually prevents the inferential cognition '*parvato vanhyābhāvavān*'. The only difference is that while the cognition '*hrado vanhyabhāvavān*' is a valid cognition, the cognition '*parvato vanhyabhāvavān*' is an erroneous one. Anyway, when it occurs, it prevents the inferential cognition '*parvato vanhimān*'. Now, just as the cognition '*hrado vanhyabhāvavān*' comprehends that which is possessed of *hradatva* which has *dharmitā-vacchhedakatā* determined by the *abhāva, abhāvatva* the property of which also has *dharmitā-vacchhedakatā* determined by *vanhi*, the cognition '*parvato vanhyabhāvavān*' also comprehends that which is possessed of *parvatatva* which has *dharmitā-vacchedakatā* determined by the *abhāva, abhāvatva* the property of which has *dharmitā-vacchhedakatā* determined by *vanhi.* Therefore, if the inference '*hrado vanhimān dhūmāt*' is fallacious, similarly, the inference, '*parvato vanhimān dhūmāt*' also will have to be considered as fallacious.

Kalisankara himself shows the way to overcome the above problem. He suggests that in addition to all that is said, it must also be said that the *hradatva* qualified with *vanhyabhāva*, is denoted by the term '*yadrūpa*'. Since *hradatva* is naturally qualified with *vanhyabhāva* by the relation of *sāmānādhikaraṇya* such a *hradatva* which also has *dharmitāvacchedakatā* as explained earlier, can be taken as the meaning of the term '*yadrūpa*'. But in case of *parvatatva* it is not so. *Parvatatva* might be having *dharmitāvacchedakatā* as shown earlier. But it is not qualified with *vanhyabhāva* as the smoky hill has no *vanhyabhāva.* In other words, since such a *parvatatva* does not exist it cannot be the meaning of the term '*yadrūpa*' and it is also not possible to claim that the inference '*parvato vanhimān dhūmāt*' will have to be considered as fallacious.

This is the amendment that Kālīśaṅkara suggests here and he is of the view that with this modification the explanation of the meaning of the term '*yadrūpa*' given by '*kecit*' is acceptable. We do not know who are these '*kecit*' Naiyāyikas. There is also a custom among the *śāstric* writers to float their own views by the names of others. Kālīśaṅkara too might have followed that custom here.

Candranārāyaṇa *Bhaṭṭacārya*'s work, which is a *Kroḍapatra* dealing with the same text of Gadādhara, discusses more elaborately than the *Kālīśaṅkarīya*, the meaning of the term '*yadrūpa*'. In addition to the two possible alternatives that Kālīśaṅkara referred to at the beginning of his analysis, Candranārāyaṇa refers to one more possible meaning of the term '*yadrūpa*' and thoroughly explains all the three alternatives. It is interesting to note that Candranārāyaṇa too, without offering any solution to the problems, just criticises the explanations offered by the others. While examining the third explanation of the term '*yadrūpa*' and also the explanation offered by some, what he ultimately points out is that if these explanations along with the amendments suggested are accepted, then certain *viśeṣaṇas* later included in the definition by Gadādhara would become redundant. Thus he is candid enough to show the inadequacies in the process of analysing the things connected with the definition of *hetvābhāsa* by Gadādhara who first, blindly, introduced the term '*yadrūpa*' in the definition, without bothering to analyse its significance and later included some more *viśeṣaṇas* which would become redundant if the connotation of the term is properly analysed.

Here I shall try to highlight briefly some of the interesting observations that Candranārāyaṇa makes while discussing the significance of the term '*yadrūpa*'.

The first possible explanation of the term '*yadrūpa*' that Candranārāyaṇa refers to is '*sāmānādhikaraṇyasambandhena vanhyabhāvaviśiṣṭa-hradatva*'. Kālīśaṅkara also refers to this explanation. The fault that Candranārāyaṇa finds here is this that if this is the '*yadrūpa*' then it should have been comprehended by the cognition *hrado vanhyabhāvavān* which actually prevents the inferential cognition '*hrado vanhimān*'. But it is obvious that the cognition '*hrado vanhyabhāvavān*' does not comprehend *vanhyabhāva* in *hradatva* by the relation of *sāmānādhikaraṇya.* It may be argued that since, in the said cognition, *hradatva* is the limitor of the qualificandumness through the qualificandum that is *hrada, vanhyabhāva* is comprehended by the relation of *sāmānādhikaraṇya* in *hradatva.* But, Candranārāyaṇa draws our attention to the subtle but significant point that though the cognition thus comprehends *vanhyabhāva* in *hradatva* by the *sāmānādhikaraṇya* relation, it cannot be said that the cognition comprehends *yadrūpāvacchinna.* To be more precise, what is meant by the comprehension of the *yadrūpāvacchinna,* is that the cognition must be the determinant of the qualificandumness which has the *yadrūpa* as its limitor (*yadrūpāvacchinna-viśeṣyatākatva*). But, while *vanhyabhāva* is by an indirect relation *sāmānādhikaraṇya* grasped in *hradatva,* the objecthood that is the *viṣayatā* in *hradatva,* is not the limitorness determined by the qualificandumness (*viśeṣyatāvacchedakatā*). Hence, the cognition *hrado vahnyabhāvavān* cannot be *yadrūpāvacchhinna-viṣayaka* in the sense of '*yadrūpaniṣṭhāvacchedakatākaviśeṣyatāka*'.

Candranārāyaṇa also rejects the second explanation according to which *vanhyabhāva* and *hradatva*—are denoted by the term *yadrūpa.* In that case, the cognition '*hrado vanhyabhāvavān*' which prevents the inferential cognition '*hrado vahnimān*', will have to be regarded as *yadrūpāvacchhinnaviṣayaka* which means *yadrūpa* has the limitorness *(avacchedakatā)* determined by the objecthood of the cognition. It further indicates that *yadrūpa*, that is, *vanhyabhāva-hradatva* together have a limitorness determined by the objecthood of the cognition. But, if we analyse the structure of the cognition '*hrado vanhyabhāvavān*' it becomes clear that it is not so. In this cognition, *vanhyabhāva* is the mode and its modeness is limited by the property *vanhyabhāvatva* and also by the relation called *viśeṣaṇatāviśeṣa*. But, though *hradatva* also is a content of this cognition, it is not a mode. It is the limitor of the qualificandumness residing in the *hrada*. Thus the *hradatva* has the limitorness, which though is limited by the relation of *samavāya*, is not limited by any property. Hence, it is clear that the objecthood residing in the *vahnnyabhāva* is of the nature of modeness, whereas the objecthood residing in *hradatva* is of the nature of the limitorness and thus are absolutely different. This being the case, it is not correct to say that *vanhyavbhāva* and *hradatva* are the *yadrūpa* and that both have the same limitorness determined by qualificandumness of the cognition '*hrado vahynabhāvavān*'. Thus, the second explanation also does not hold good.

As per the third explanation, mere '*vahnyabhāva*' with the relation of *viśeṣaṇatā* qualified with *hradatvāvacchinnānuyogitākatva* is the *yadrūpa*. This explanation and also the explanation offered by some, according to which *hradatva-vahnyabhāva*—these two are the *yadrūpa*, are rejected by Candranārāyaṇa, pointing out that if these explanations with all the amendments that will be suggested, are admitted, then the *viśeṣaṇas* which Gadādhara will include later in the definition would become redundant. I do not propose here to discuss these two explanations and Candranārāyaṇa's criticism thereon. I would only like to point out the frankness and the unbiased attitude of the authors of the *Kroḍapatras*, who after a thorough examination of a problem, are prepared even to reject the stand considered as final by the earlier Naiyāyikas.

Among the large number of *Kroḍapatras* that are known to us, only a few are published while being rarely studied. Some of them were secretly guarded by some scholars. *Tritalāvacchedakatāvāda* published by the Mithila Institute of Darbhanga is an example. It is said that for generations, this *Kroḍapatra* was secretly guarded by a tradition which would make use of the arguments and *pariṣkāras* contained in the *Kroḍapatra*, in debates to baffle their opponents. During the last century, as also in the earlier part of this century, Naiyāyika's studies the *Krodapatras* with much enthusiasm and consequently criticism and justification of the *Kroḍapatras* also emerged on. Mysore Rama Śāstri's *Śatakoṭi Kroḍapatras* on the *Satpratipakṣa* of Gadādhara is an example. This contains one hundred arguments that thoroughly examine the definition of the fallacy—*Satpratipakṣa*, offered by Gadādhara. Two Naiyāyikas, namely Anantalvar and Krisnatatacharya wrote *Kroḍapatras* called *Śatakoṭikhaṇḍana* and attacked the arguments contained in the *Śatakoṭi*. Later, another Naiyāyika authored a *Kroḍapatra* called *Śatakoṭikhaṇḍanamaṇḍana* to justify Rama Shastri's *Kroḍapatra*. Thus, till the early part of this century, the *Kroḍapatra* tradition was a living force but today the tradition flourishes no more.

This article on the *Kroḍapatras*, will be incomplete if the structure of *anugamas* which are frequently made use of in the *Kroḍapatras* is not explained. Hence, an attempt is made here to explain the technique of *anugama*.

The *anugamas* that are suggested as a final solution to a problem are of a wonderful structure. In the beginning they appear to be of a very simple nature. But, soon they will develop into a complex and complicated structure with the peculiar and the multiple relations involved. The structure of an *anugama* thus created is so complex that an ordinary student will find it impossible to penetrate into this fort containing innumerable inner circles.

Here an attempt is made to illustrate an *anugama* with its background.

Anugama

While discussing the meaning of singular case suffix, *(ekavacana-pratyaya)* the Naiyāyikas reject the contention that the number—being one, is the meaning of the suffix. For, such a number is universally present and hence even when there are several jars on the ground, the sentence '*atra ghaṭosti*'—'there is one jar on the ground'—will have to be considered as valid. Therefore, they define *ekatva*—the meaning of the singular suffix in a different manner. Accordingly, *ekatva* means '*sajātīyadvitīyarahitatva*' that is, being devoid of a second which is similar. Now, when several jars are on the ground, the sentence '*atra ghaṭo'sti*' becomes incorrect, because there is another jar similar to it. Here the similarity consists in possessing the attribute:

svasamabhivyāhṛta-padārtha-saṁsargitāviśiṣṭa-prakṛtyarthatāvacchedaka-dharma.

स्वसमभिव्याहृतपदार्थसंसार्गितावििशिष्टप्रकृत्यर्थतावच्छेदकधर्म

that is the limitor of being the meaning of the nominal base *(prakṛtyarthatāvacchedaka)* that co-exists with the relation of the locus conveyed by a word used in the same sentence. In the sentence—'*atra ghaṭosti*' the nominal base of the singular number is the word—'*ghaṭa*'. The limitor of being the meaning of this word, is jarness. This jarness, co-existing with the relation of the locus conveyed by the word '*atra*' used in the same sentence, is to be regarded here as the similarity and it is the absence of a similar object of that kind that is the *ekatva*—the meaning of a singular case suffix. When there are several jars on the ground, each jar has a jar similar to it. For, the other jar has not only the *prakṛtyartha-tāvacchedaka* or jarness, but also 'the relation of the locus conveyed by the word *atra* of the sentence. That is why in a situation when there are several jars on the ground, the sentence—'*atra ghaṭo'sti*' becomes invalid.

Now an objection is raised against this explanation. Suppose there are two jars on the ground, one is black and the other is yellow - the sentence '*atra nīlaghaṭo'sti*' cannot be said to be incorrect, because actually there is only one black jar on the ground. But, as per the above explanation of the meaning of the singular case suffix, even such sentences will have to be rejected as incorrect as in the given situation, the black jar has a similar jar with it. In other words, the yellow jar is similar to the black jar, because it has both the *prakṛtyarthatāvacchedaka*—jarness and also the 'relation of the locus' conveyed by the term '*atra*'. Thus, as the black jar has another similar jar with it, and, if the singular case suffix conveys the meaning as is described above, then the sentence when there is a *pītaghaṭa* also, will have to be rejected as incorrect.

The untenability of the explanation of the meaning of the singular case suffix, is shown by another instance also.

The sentence '*brāhmano brāhmaṇāya dhenuḥ dadāti*'—'one Brahman gives away a cow to another Brahman', conveys the *ekatva* of two Brāhmans, of whom one is the giver and other is the receiver. The singular case suffix added to the two 'Brāhmana' words here, conveys the *ekatva* of both of them. But, if the meaning of the singular case suffix is as above then that cannot be explained in either case. For, as per the explanation, each of them, should be *svasajātīyadvitīyārhahita*, that is, must have possessed the absence of the second similar to it. And the similarity as explained earlier consists in possesing the *prakṛtyarthatāvacchedaka* and also *samabhivyāhrtasaṁsarga*. Here the nominal base for the *ekavacana* is the word '*brāhmaṇa*' and hence 'Brahmanhood' is the *prakṛtyarthatāvacche-daka*. This is present in both the giver and the receiver here. Again both of them possess *samabhivyāhrtasaṁsarga*—the relation of the object conveyed by a word used in the sentence. Here, such an object is the action 'giving away' or '*sampradānakriyā*' that is conveyed by the word '*dadāti*'. It is obvious that the relation of this object is present in both the giver and the receiver. Thus, both the Brāhmanas denoted by the two '*Brāhmana*' terms of the sentence have the *samabhivyāhrtasaṁsarga*. Therefore, each of the two Brāhmanas here, has a *sajātīya*, a second person similar to him. Hence, none of them can be said to possess the *ekatva* denoted by the singular case suffix here.

In order to avoid the above objections the following *anugama* is suggested:

ekavacana viśiṣṭam ekatvam ekavacanārthaḥ

एकवचनविशिष्टम् एकत्वम् एकवचनार्थः ।

This simply means that a singular case suffix means the *ekatva*, that is, 'being one' which is related with an *ekavacana*—singular case suffix. Thus, in the instance '*atra ghaṭo'sti*' the singular suffix that is added to the term '*ghaṭa*', means the *ekatva* that is related with the *ekavacana* (the singular case suffix).

Now, naturally, the question arises as to what is the relation of *ekavacana* in *ekatva*. In reply, the following relation is suggested :

sva prakṛtyarthatāvacchedakatva-svaviśiṣṭa-saṁsargatānirūpakatvobhaya-sambandhena yat svādhikaraṇaṁ tanniṣṭhabheda-pratiyogitānavacchedakatvam.

स्वप्रकृत्यर्थतावच्छेकवत्त्व-स्वविशिष्टसंसर्गतानिरूपकत्वोभयसंबन्धेन यत्स्वाधिकरणं तन्निष्ठभेदप्रतियोगितानवच्छेदकत्वम् ।

In the second relation mentioned above, certain *saṁsargatā* is to be related with the *ekavacana* which is referred to by the term '*sva*'. The following is the relation of '*sva*' in the *saṁsargatā*:

sva-prayojya-śābdabodha-viṣayatvasāmānādhikaraṇya-svasamānādhikaraṇa-prayojya-śābdabodhaviṣayatā/sāmānādhikaraṇyānyatara-sambandhena.

स्वप्रयोज्यशाब्दबोधविषयत्वसामानाधिकरण्य-स्वसमानाधिकरणप्रयोज्यशाब्दबोधविषयता सामानाधिकरण्यान्यतरसंबन्धेन ।

The understanding of the above relations demands a familiarity with various technicalities, used by the Navya Nyāya school. I shall take it for granted that the reader is sufficiently familiar with those technicalities and will try to explain the above relations as simply as possible.

Let us suppose that there is only one jar on the ground. Only in such a situation the *ekatva*—'oneness' the number residing in the *ghaṭa* becomes related with the *ekavacana* that is added to the nominal base '*ghaṭa*'. This *ekatva* which is in the *ghaṭa* is related with the *ekavacana* by a relation which involves in it two relations such as *svaprakṛtyarthatāvacchedakatva* and *svaviśiṣṭa-saṁsargatānirūpakatva.* Since this is the relation of *ekavacana*, here '*sva*' refers to the *ekavacana.* Its *prakṛti* (the nominal base), is the word '*ghaṭa*'. The *prakṛtyarthatāvacchedaka*, that is the limitor of 'being the meaning' of the *prakṛti* is *ghaṭatva.* As a matter of fact, this *ghaṭatva* is present even in a jar kept somewhere else. But, that jar does not have the second relation of the *ekavacana,* namely, *svaviśiṣṭasaṁsargatānirūpakatva.* Here the term *saṁsargatā* refers only to that *saṁsargatā* which resides in the *saṁsarga*—the relation between the ground and the jar that are before us. That relation is the *ādheyatā* residing in the jar before and is determined by the ground. At present, we have to assume that only this *saṁsargatā* is related with the *sva* and not any other *saṁsargatā.* This point will become clear when we try to analyse the relation of *sva* in the *saṁsargatā.* The relation is:

sva-prayojya-śābdabodha-viṣayatva-sāmānādhikaraṇya-svasamānādhikaraṇa-pratyaya-prayojyatādṛś-viṣayatā-sāmānādhikaraṇya etad anyatarasambandha.

स्वप्रयोज्यशाब्दबोधविषयत्वसामानाधिकरण्य-स्वसमानाधिकरणप्रत्ययप्रयोज्यातादृशविषयतासामाना-धिकरण्यएतदन्यतरसंबन्ध ।

The above relation, actually, contains two relations and the *saṁsargatā* is intended to be related with *sva* by either of the two relations. The two relations are:

i. svaprayojya-śābdabodha-viṣayatva-sāmānādhikaraṇya (स्वप्रयोज्यशाब्दबोधविषयत्वसामानाधिकरण्य), and

ii. svasamānādhikaraṇa-pratyaya-prayojyādṛśa-viṣayatā-sāmānādhikaraṇya. (स्वसमानाधिकरणप्रत्ययप्रयोज्यादृशविषयतासामानाधिकरण्य ।)

In the case of the instance '*atra ghaṭaḥ asti*', '*sva*' as already said, refers to the *ekavacana* suffix added to the word '*ghaṭa*'. The '*ghaṭa*' mentioned here in this sentence, is the *ghaṭa* which is on the ground before us (*atra*). That *ghaṭa* has the *saṁsarga*, namely *ekadeśa-nirūpitā ādheyatā*. This *ādheyatā* being a *saṁsarga* has a *saṁsargatā*. This *saṁsargatā* is *svaviśiṣṭā* which is related with the *ekavacana* by the second of the two relations mentioned above. This can be explained as follows. The relation is:

svasamānādhikaraṇapratyayaprayojyaśābdabodhaviṣayatva
(स्वसमानाधिकरणप्रत्ययप्रयोज्यशाब्दबोधविषयत्व)

sva is the *ekavacana* that we hear after the word '*ghaṭa*'. *Sva-samānādhikaraṇapratyaya* means the suffix that co-exists with the *ekavacana*. In the sentence '*atra ghaṭaḥ asti*' both the *ekavacana* and the suffix *trala* which is a part of the word *atra*, are present. Here the *trala* suffix can be said as *svasamānādhikaraṇapratyaya*. The meaning of the *trala* is *ādheyatā*. By conveying that meaning the *trala* makes it possible for this *ādheyatva* to become an object of the verbal cognition produced by the sentence '*atra ghaṭaḥ asti*'. Therefore, the *ādheyatā* has the objectness. This objectness, that is, *viṣayatā* resides here as *svasamānādhikaraṇa-pratyayaprayojyaśābdabodha-viṣayatā*. Since this *viṣayatā* resides in the *saṁsarga—ekadeśanirūpitādheyatā*, it is now clear that *saṁsargatā* of this *saṁsarga*, has the coexistence of the above *viṣayatā*. Thus the *saṁsargatā* which is in the *ādheyatā*, has *svasamānādhikaraṇa-pratyayaprayojya-śābdabodha-viṣayatā—sāmānādhikaraṇya*. In other words, the *saṁsargatā* is related with the *sva*, that is, *svaviśiṣṭa* by the above relation. Since this *saṁsargatā* is determined by the *ghaṭa* which actually has the *saṁsarga*, that is, *ādheyatā*, it is now clear that *ghaṭa* is *svaviśiṣṭa-saṁsargatānirūpaka*. Thus, by the two relations, namely, *svaprakṛtyartha-tāvacchedakatva* and *svaviśiṣṭasaṁsargatānirūpakatva*, *sva* is related to the *ghaṭa* or, in other words by these two relations, the locus of the *sva* is the *ghaṭa* before us. The *ekatva* with which we are concerned now and which has to be shown by us as being related with the *ekavacana* of the word '*ghaṭaḥ*', also belongs to the same *ghaṭa*. The difference which may be said to be present in the *svādhikaraṇa ghaṭa*, is the difference of some other *ghaṭa*, and is never that of the same *ghaṭa*. Hence, the counterpositive (*pratiyogī*) of the difference is another jar and the *ekatva* residing in that *ghaṭa* can be said to be the limitor of the counterpositiveness. But the *ekatva* residing in the same *ghaṭa* cannot be the limitor of the counterpositiveness. Hence, when there is only one jar on the ground then only the sentence '*atra ghaṭaḥ asti*' becomes valid. For, as already explained above, the jar which is there alone on the ground, can be the possessor of the meaning of the singular case suffix, the meaning being '*ekavacanaviśiṣṭam ekatvam*'.

Suppose there are two jars on the ground, then the sentence '*atra ghaṭaḥ asti*' becomes incorrect, because none of the two jars, has the meaning of the singular case suffix. This can be briefly explained as follows:

The meaning of the singular case suffix is '*ekavacanaviśiṣṭam ekatvam*'. The *vaiśiṣṭya* or the relation of *ekavacana* in the *ekatva* is:

Svaprakṛtyarthatāvacchedakatva—svaviśiṣṭa-saṁsargatānirūpakatvobhaya saṁbandhena yat svādhikaraṇam tanniṣṭhabhedapratiyogitānavacchedakatva. Since both the jars are present on the same ground, both of them become *svādhikaraṇa,* that is the locus of *ekavacana* by the two relations, namely—*svaprakṛtyarthatāvacchedakatva* and *svaviśiṣṭasaṁsargatānirūpakatva.* Since the *ekatva* that is oneness of each jar can be the *pratiyogitāvacchedaka* of the *bheda* residing in the other, none of the jars does possess the *ekatva* which is not the limitor of the counter-positiveness of the difference.

Similarly, when there are two jars on the ground—one being *nīla* and the other *pīta*—the sentence '*atra nīlaghaṭaḥ asti*' can be justified.

Here the singular case suffix, added to the word *ghaṭa,* can be said to be related with only the *nīla*-jar and not with the *pīta*-jar for the following reasons. Between the two relations, namely, *svaprakṛtyarthatāvacchedakatva* and *svaviśiṣṭasaṁsargatānirūpakatva,* the *pītaghaṭa,* as a matter of fact, is related with the *ekavacana* in the word '*ghaṭaḥ*' by the first relation, because the *prakṛtyarthatāvacchedaka*—the limitor of being the meaning of the nominal base '*ghaṭaḥ*', that is, '*ghaṭatva*' is very much present in the *pītaghaṭa* also. But, the *pītaghaṭa* is not related with the singular case suffix, by the relation—*svaviśiṣṭasaṁsargatānirūpakatva,* for, the *saṁsargatā* which is *svaviśiṣṭa,* that is, related with the *ekavacana* here, is the *saṁsargatā* residing in the *ādheyatā* that belongs to *nīlaghaṭa* alone. This is because that *saṁsargatā* alone has the relation of *sva,* namely *svasāmānādhikaraṇa-pratyayaprayojya-śābdabodhaviṣayatā-sāmānādhikaraṇya.* A brief explanation of this is as follows: *Sva* is the singular case suffix. The *pratyaya* co-existing with *sva,* is the *trala* in the word '*atra*'. The *viṣayatā,* that is, objectness determined by the verbal cognition, resides in the *ādheyatā* of *nīlaghaṭa* only. Since the *pītaghaṭa* is not an object of the verbal cognition produced by the sentence '*atra nīlaghaṭah asti*', the question of its *ādheyatā* having the objectness belonging to *pītaghaṭa* and that too being caused by the *tral,* does not arise. In short, the *pītaghaṭa* though it exists on the same ground on which the *nīlaghata* exists, is not related with the *ekavacana* by the second of the two relations. What actually is thus related with the *ekavacana* here, is *nīlaghata.* Since *nīlaghaṭa* has the *bheda* with *pītaghaṭa,* the *ekatva* of *pītaghaṭa* becomes the *bhedapratiyogitāvacchedaka.* On the other hand, since *nīlaghaṭa,* cannot have the *bheda* of itself, the *ekatva* of it, becomes the *bhedapratiyogitāvacchedaka.* The meaning of the *ekavacana* suffix, as pointed out earlier, is the *ekavacanaviśiṣṭaikatva.* Such an *ekatva* is actually present in the *nīlaghaṭa,* in spite of the fact that *pītaghaṭa* also is present on the same ground. Thus, the sentence '*atra nīlaghaṭaḥ asti*'—when there are *nīlaghaṭa* and *pītaghaṭa* on the ground, can be justified.

The origin of this complicated structure of *ekatva* can be traced to the simple statement '*sajātīyadvitīyārthahitatvam ekatvam*' made by Gadādhara in his *Vyutpattivāda,* while discussing the meaning of *ekavacana.* To make the concept more clear, Gadādhara himself elaborated it as *svasajātīyaniṣṭhabhedapratiyogin-avacchedakaikatva* and further clarified by stating the *sajātyam,* that is, similarity, contained in it, as—*sajātyam* ca *svasamabhivyāhārapadārthasaṁsargitvaviśiṣṭaprakṛtyar-*

thatāvacchedakatvarūpeṇa. The above *anugamana* suggested by Pt. Bachcha Jha, is clear now that it is based only on these certain statements made by Gadādhara.

As a matter of fact, the *anugama* now shown is a simple one compared to the still complicated structure which Pt. Bachcha Jha, suggested later in order to avoid certain objections raised against the above *anugama.* I do not propose here either to discuss or elaborately explain the objections raised and the structure of *anugama* suggested to avoid the objections. But, just to show the mind-boggling complications, which are the result of the various relations that are involved, I shall merely demonstrate the *anugama* with all the relations contained in it.

ekavacanaviśiṣṭam ekatvam ekavacanārthaḥ

(एकवचनविशिष्टं एकत्वम् एकवचनार्थः)

This just means that the meaning of a singular case suffix is the *ekatva* which is related with the singular case suffix. Thus, in the sentence '*atra nīlaghaṭaḥ asti*', the singular case suffix added to the word '*nīlaghaṭa*' means the *ekatva* of *nīlaghaṭa*, denoted by the term '*nīlaghaṭa*'. The following is the relation of the singular case suffix in the *ekatva*:

svaprakṛti-prayojya-viṣayatā-viśiṣṭa-nirūpakatādhikaraṇatātvāvacchinnānuyogitāka-paryāptikasambandhāvacchinnavadvṛttibheda-pratiyogitānavacchedakatvam.

(स्वप्रकृतिप्रयोज्यविषयताविशिष्टनिरूपकताधिकरणतात्वावच्छिन्नानुयोगिताकपर्याप्तिक-संबन्धावच्छिन्नवद्वृत्तिभेदप्रतियोगितानवच्छेदकत्वम्। [Here, '*sva*' refers to the *ekavacana*])

In the above relation, '*nirūpakatā*' is stated as related with '*svaprakṛti-prayojyaviṣayatā*'. The relation of the *viṣayatā* in the *nirūpakatā* is one of the following four relations:

Nirūpaktāyāṁ vaiśiṣṭyaṁ ca (निरूपकतायां वैशिष्ट्यं च)

1. *svabhinnamukhyaviśeṣyatāvattva* (स्वाभिन्नमुख्यविशेष्यतावत्त्व)
2. *svabhinnamukhyaprakāratāvacchedakatāvattva* (स्वाभिन्नमुख्यप्रकारतावच्छेदकतावत्त्व)
3. *svabhinnamukhyaprahāratāvattva* (स्वाभिन्नमुख्यप्रकारतावत्त्व)
4. *svābhinnatādṛśa viśeṣyatāvacchedakatāvattva-anyatamasaṁbandhena* (स्वाभिन्नतादृशविशेष्यतावच्छेदकतावत्त्व-अन्यतमसंबन्धेन।)

There are four possible, different instances in which a singular case suffix can be found. They are:

1. Where the singular case suffix is added to a word that denotes the main qualificandum (*mukhyaviśeṣya*) for example, '*atra ghaṭaḥ asti*'. Here the word '*ghaṭa*' denotes the main qualificandum. The singular case suffix added to this is taken care of by the first of the above four relations.

2. The second type of singular case suffix is that which is added to the word that denotes the 'limitor of the qualifierness' (*prakāratā-vacchedaka*). For example,

'*puruṣoyam rājñaḥ*'—'This is a king's servant'. Here the *ṣaṣṭhī—ekavacana* added to the word '*rājan*' is being covered. In the cognition produced by this sentence, 'servant' is the qualifier and the king is the limitor of the qualifierness. To explain the meaning of this *ekavacana* the second of the above four relations, is mentioned.

3. Among the above four relations, the third one, namely '*svabhinnamukhya-prakāratāvattva*' is included to cover the instance—'*Rāmadārāḥ Jānakī*'. Here the word '*Rāmadārā*' denotes the qualificandum and the word '*Jānakī*' refers to the qualifier. Since the word *Rāmadārā* is in plural number, that suffix cannot convey the *ekatva* of '*Rāmadārā*'—consort of *Rāma*. As a matter of fact, the suffix is considered here as meaningless, but added just for the sake of grammatical correctness of the word. Here the *ekatva* of *Rāmadārā*, will have to be conveyed by the singular case suffix which we hear after the word '*Jānakī*'. As told above, this instance is covered by the third relation.

4. The fourth of the four relations being explained now, is *svabhinna-mukhyaviśeṣyatāvacchedakatāvattva*. This is included here to cover the instance '*rājñaḥ puruṣaḥ atrāsti*'. Here there are two terms ending with a singular case suffix. One is the term '*rājñaḥ*' which is in *ṣaṣṭhī - ekavacana*. Again, the main qualificandum of the cognition produced by this sentence is '*puruṣa*'. The *ekatva* of him is conveyed by the singular case affix added to the word '*puruṣa*'. But, if the *ekatva* of the '*rājan*' also is intended in the given sentence, to cover it, this fourth relation becomes necessary.

Before we continue further with this *anugama*, it will be helpful, if we briefly repeat what we have explained so far:

The meaning of a singular case affix is:

svaprakṛtiprayojya viṣayatā (स्वप्रकृतिप्रयोज्यविषयता)
viśiṣṭta (विशिष्ट)

|

nirūpakatādhikaraṇatātvāvacchinnānuyogitākaparyāptika-
sambandhāvacchinnavadvṛttibhedapratiyogitānavacchedakatvam.
(निरूपकताधिकरणतात्वावच्छिन्नानुयोगिताकपर्याप्तिक-
संबन्धाावच्छिन्नवद्वृत्तिभेदप्रतियागितानवच्छेदकत्वम् ।)

The *nirūpakatā* underlined above is related with one of the four relations, mentioned below:

1. *svabhinna-mukhya-viśeṣyatāvattva* (स्वाभिन्नमुख्यविशेष्यतावत्त्व)
2. *svābhinna-mukhya-prakāratāvacchedakatāvattva* (स्वाभिन्नमुख्यप्रकारतावच्छेदकतावत्त्व)
3. *svabhinna-mukhya-prakāratāvattvam* (स्वाभिन्नमुख्यप्रकारतावत्त्वं)
4. *svābhinna-tādṛśaviśeṣyatāvacchedakatāvattva* (स्वाभिन्नतादृशविशेष्यतावच्छेदकतावत्त्व)

In all the above four relations, '*sva*' refers to '*svaprakṛtiprayojyaviṣayatā*' in which '*sva*' refers to the singular case suffix, the meaning of which is being discussed now. It may be noticed here that each of the above involves relations. Thus, the first relation involves relations of *svabhinnamukhyaviśeṣyatā* in the *nirūpakatā*. The relations of the *mukhyaviśeṣyatā* in the *nirūpakatā* is either of the following two relations:

1. *svasākṣānnirūpakatāvacchedakatāttva* (स्वसाक्षान्निरूपकतावच्छेदकतात्त्व),
2. *svanirūpita mukhya prakāratāttva* (स्वनिरूपितमुख्यप्रकारतात्त्व ।)

It is obvious that both the above relations which are the relations of *svabhinnamukhya-viśeṣyatā* in *nirūpakatā*, involve relations. The relations of *sva-sākṣānnirūpakatāvacchedakatāvattva* in the *nirūpakatā*, are four. They are:

1. *svasāmānādhikaraṇya* (स्वसामानाधिकरण्य)
2. *svāvacchedaka sambandhāvacchinnatva* (स्वावच्छेदकसंबन्धावच्छिन्नत्व)
3. *svāvacchedakānavacchinnatva* (स्वावच्छेदकानवच्छिन्नत्व)
4. *svavṛttitva* (स्ववृत्तित्व)

So far, we have explained the first relation of *svābhinnamukhyaviśeṣyatā*. The second relation of *svābhinnamukhyaviśeṣyatā* in the *nirūpakatā* is *svanirūpita-mukhyaprakāratāvattva*. *Mukhyaprākaratāvattva* means 'being replaced with the *mukhyaprakāratā*'. The relations of the *mukhyaprakāratā* in the *nirūpakatā*, are two. They are:

1. *svāvacchedakatātvāvacchinnapratiyogitākaprayāptyanuyogitāvacchedaka rūpavṛttitva* (स्वावच्छेदकतात्वावच्छिन्नप्रतियोगिताकपर्याप्त्यनुयोगितावच्छेदकरूपवृत्तित्व)
2. *svāvacchedakasambandhāvacchinnatva* (स्वावच्छेदकसंबन्धावच्छिन्नत्व)

Here is a chain of the relations with which *svaprakṛtiprayojyaviṣayatā* is connected with the first of the four relations, namely *svābhinna-mukhyaviśeṣyatāvattva*.

The second relation of *svaprakṛtiprayojya-viṣayatā* in the *nirūpakatā*, is *svābhinnamukhya-prakāratāvacchedakatāvattva*. Since this is a relation of *svaprakṛtiprayojyaviṣayatā*, as before, here also '*sva*' refers to *svaprakṛtiprayojya-viṣayatā*.

The relation *svābhinnamukhyaprakāratāvacchedakatāvattva* means 'being related with *svābhinna-mukhyaprakāratāvacchedakatā*. Now, we have to show as to how this *mukhyaprakāratāvacchedakatā* has the relation in *nirūpakatā*. Either of the following, is the relation of *mukhyaprakāratāvacchedakatā* in the *nirūpakatā*,

1. *svaviśiṣṭāvacchedakatāvattva* (स्वविशिष्टावच्छेदकतावत्त्व)
2. *svāśrayatva* (स्वाश्रयत्व ।)

The first of the above two relations, namely, *svaviśiṣṭāvacchedakatāvattva* involves two relations. One is the relation of '*sva*', that is, *svābhinnamukhya-*

prakāratāvacchedakatā, in a certain *avacchedakatā*. We call this as 'certain *avacchedakatā*' as we are not, at this stage, familiar with this *avacchedakatā* which is briefly stated as '*svaviśiṣṭāvacchedakatā*'. The other is the relation of this *avacchedakatā* in the *nirūpakatā*. The following two are the relations of *mukhyaprakāratāvacchedakatā* in the particular *avacchedakatā*:

1. *svasākṣānnirūpakatā* (स्वसाक्षान्निरूपकता)
2. *svāvacchedyaprakāratānirūpitaviśeṣyatvānavacchinnatva* (स्वावच्छेद्यप्रकारतानिरूपितविशेष्यत्वानवच्छिन्नत्व)

The relations of the particular *avacchedakatā* in the *nirūpakatā* are the following four:

1. *svasāmānādhikaraṇya* (स्वसामानाधिकरण्य)
2. *svāvacchedakasaṁbandhāvacchinnatva* (स्वावच्छेदकसंबन्धावच्छिन्नत्व)
3. *svānavacchedakānavacchinnatva* (स्वानवच्छेदकानवच्छिन्नत्व)
4. *svavṛttitva* (स्ववृत्तित्व)

So far, we have explained the first chain of the relations of *mukhyaprakāratāvacchedakatā* with the *nirūpakatā*. Now, we have to explain the second relation, namely *svāśrayatva*. Here '*sva*' is *mukhyaprakāratāvacchedakatā*. The *nirūpakatā* is said to be the locus of *mukhyaprakāratā-vacchedakatā* with the three relations. They are:

1. *svāvacchedakasmbandhāvacchinnasaṁbandhitvasaṁbandhāvacchinnatva* (स्वावच्छेदकसंबन्धावच्छिन्नयंबन्धित्वसंबन्धावच्छिन्नत्व)
2. *svāvacchedyaprakāratā-nirūpitaviśeṣyatvāvacchedakāvacchinnatva* (स्वावच्छेद्यप्रकारतानिरूपितविशेष्यत्वावच्छेदकावच्छिन्नत्व)
3. *svaviśiṣṭa-viṣayatātva-vyāpakatva* (स्वविशिष्टविषयतात्वव्यापकत्व)

The last of the above relations again involves two more relations. One is the relation of '*sva*' in the *viṣayatā* and the other is the relation with which *vyāpakatva*, that is pervasiveness of the *nirūpakatā*, is limited. The relations of the '*sva*' in the *viṣayatā*, are the following:

1. *svāvacchedya-viṣayatā-nirūpitaviṣayatvāvacchinnatva* (स्वावच्छेद्यविषयतानिरूपितविषयत्वावच्छिन्नत्व)
2. *svanirūpitatva* (स्वनिरूपितत्व)

The *vyāpakatāvacchedakasambandha*, that is, the relation which is the limitor of *vyāpakatā* is:

svanirūpitāvacchedakatāvṛttitva (स्वनिरूपितावच्छेदकतावृत्तित्व)

As per the above relation, the *nirūpakatā* is pervasive of *viṣayatātva* as it resides in all the instances of *viṣayatātva* by the relation of *svanirūpitāvacchedakatāvṛttitva*.

This relation holds good when the *nirūpakatā* resides in the *svanirūpitāvacchedakatā*. The relation with which the *nirūpakatā* is required to be present in the *svanirūpitāvacchedakatā*, is actually not one, but two. They are:

1. *svāvacchedakāvacchinnatva* (स्वावच्छेदकावच्छिन्नत्व)
2. *svaviśiṣṭaviśeṣyatā-nirūpitaprakāratāvachhedasaṁbandhāvacchinnatva* (स्वविशिष्टविशेष्यतानिरूपितप्रकारतावच्छेदसंबन्धावच्छिन्नत्व)

In the second of the above relations, certain *viśeṣyatā* is required to be *svaviśiṣṭa*—related with *sva*. The relations of *sva* in the *viśeṣyatā*, are three. They are:

1. *svāśrayatva* (स्वाश्रयत्व)
2. *svānavacchedakānavacchinnatva* (स्वानवच्छेदकानवच्छिन्नत्व)
3. *svavṛttitva* (स्ववृत्तित्व)

Of the above three, as per the first, *viśeṣyatā* is supposed to be the locus of *sva*. Here the relation is either of the following two:

1. *svatādātmya* (स्वतादात्म्य)
2. *svāvacchedyatva* (स्वावच्छेद्यत्व)

So far, of the two relations with which *nirūpakatā* is required to be present in the *nirūpakatāvacchedakatva*, the second, namely *svaviśiṣṭaviśeṣyatānirūpita*, etc. is explained. The other, that is, the first relation is *svāvacchedakāvacchinnatva*. This is described as *svābhāvavadavacchedakatvānirūpitatva*. Here, *svābhāva* means the absence of *sva*. The *pratiyogitāvacchedakasambandha* of this absence, that is the relation with which the *sva* is negated, is either of the following two:

1. *svanirūpitāvacchedakatāvatva* (स्वनिरूपितावच्छेदकतावत्व)
2. *svāvachedya-prakāratā-nirūpitaviśeṣyatvāvatva* (स्वावच्छेद्यप्रकारतानिरूपितविशेष्यत्वावत्व)

Of the above two relations, the first one refers to the possession of *avacchedakatā* and the second one to the possession of *viśeṣyatā*. The following are the relations with which the possession of *avacchedakatā* and *viśeṣyatā*, is intended.

1. *svasāmānādhikaraṇya* (स्वसामानाधिकरण्य)
2. *svāvacchedakasaṁbandhāvacchinnatva* (स्वावच्छेदकसंबन्धावच्छिन्नत्व)
3. *svanavacchedakanavacchinnatva* (स्वानवच्छेदकानवच्छिन्नत्व)
4. *svavṛttitva* (स्ववृत्तित्व)

Here ends the chain of relations connected with the second relation referred to in the original definition of *ekatva*, that is, *svaprakṛtiprayojyaviṣayatāviśiṣṭa-nirūpakatākādhikaraṇatātvāvacchinna*, etc. The third relation with which *svaprakṛti-prayojyaviṣayatā* is related with the *nirūpakatā*, is—*svābhinnamukhyaprakāratāvattva*. The relation of *mukhyaprakāratā* in the *nirūpakatā*, is either of the following two:

1. *svanirūpitāvacchedakatāvatva* (स्वनिरूपितावच्छेदकतावत्व)
2. *svāśrayatva* (स्वाश्रयत्व)

The second relation *svāśrayatva* means being the locus of *sva*, namely, the *mukhyaprakāratā*. The following two are the relations with which *nirūpakatā* is intended to be the locus of *mukhyaprakāratā*:

1. *svāvacchedakasaṁbandhāvacchinnasaṁbandhitvasaṁbandhāvacchinnatva* (स्वावच्छेदकसंबन्धावच्छिन्नसंबन्धित्वसंबन्धावच्छिन्नत्व)
2. *svanirūpitāviśeṣyatāvatva* (स्वनिरूपितावशेष्यतावत्व)

Viśeṣyatāvattva in the second relation here means 'possessing *viśeṣyatā*'. Similarly, in the first relation of the two mentioned a bit earlier as the relations of *mukhyaprakāratā* in the *nirūpakatā*, *avacchedakatāvattva* is included. *Avvacchedakatāvattva* means 'possessing of *avacchedakatā*'. The relations with which *nirūpakatā* is intended to be possessed of this *avacchedakatā* and also the relations of *viśeṣyatā* which is mentioned above, are:

1. *svasāmānādhikaraṇya* (स्वसामानाधिकरण्य)
2. *svāvacchedakasaṁbandhāvacchinnatva* (स्वावच्छेदकसंबन्धावच्छिन्नत्व)
3. *svānavacchedakānavachinnatvam* (स्वानवच्छेदकानवच्छिन्नत्वं)
4. *svavṛttitva* (स्ववृत्तित्व)

Here ends the chain of the relations of *mukhyaprakāratā* in the *nirūpakatā*. The fourth and the final relation of *svaprakṛtiprayojyaviṣayatā* in the *nirūpakatā* of the original definition of *ekatva*, is *svābhinnamukhyaviśeṣyatāvacchedakatāvattva*. Either of the following can be called the relation of *mukhyaviśeṣyatāvacchedakatā* in *nirūpakatā*:

1. *svaviśiṣṭāvacchedakatāvattva* (स्वविशिष्टावच्छेदकतावत्त्व)
2. *svāśrayatva* (स्वाश्रयत्व।)

The first of the above two relations, involves the relation of *sva* in the *avacchedakatā* and also the relation of *avacchedakatā* in the *nirūpakatā*. Those relations are the following:

1. *svasāmānādhikaraṇya* (स्वसामानाधिकरण्य)
2. *svāvacchedakasaṁbandhāvacchinnatva* (स्वावच्छेदकसंबन्धावच्छिन्नत्व)
3. *svānavacchedakānavacchinnatva* (स्वानवच्छेदकानवच्छिन्नत्व)

The second relation, *svāśrayatva*, means that the *nirūpakatā* is the locus of *viśeṣyatāvacche-dakatā*. The following are the relations with which the *nirūpakatā* is intended to be the locus:

1. *svāvacchedakasaṁbandhāvacchinnasaṁbandhitvasaṁbandhāvacchinnatva* (स्वावच्छेदकसंबन्धावच्छिन्नसंबन्धित्वसंबन्धावच्छिन्नत्व)

2. *svanirūpitāvacchedyaprakāratānirūpitāviśeṣyatvāvacchedyaviṣayatāvacchedakāv_ acchinnatva* (स्वनिरूपितावच्छेद्यप्रकारतानिरूपिताविशेष्यत्वावच्छेद्यविषयतावच्छेदकावच्छन्नत्व)
3. *svanirūpitamukhya-prakāratāvad-avacchedakatāvatva* (स्वनिरूपितमुख्यप्रकारतावदवच्छेदकतावत्व)
4. *svaviśiṣṭaviṣayatātvavyāpakatva* (स्वविशिष्टविषयतात्वव्यापकत्त्व)

The last relation here involves the relations of *sva* in a *viṣayatā* and also *vyāpakatva*, that is, pervasiveness. The relations of *sva* in the *viṣayatā* are the following:

1. *svanirūpitatva* (स्वनिरूपितत्व)
2. *svāvacchedya-viṣayatā-nirūpitaviṣayatābhinnatva* (स्वावच्छेद्यविषयतानिरूपितविषयताभिन्नत्व)
3. *svanirūpita-mukhya-prakāratāvad-anyatva* (स्वनिरूपितमुख्यप्रकारतावदन्यत्व)

The *vyāpakatā* mentioned earlier, is intended with either of the following relations:

1. *svavṛttitva* (स्ववृत्तित्व)
2. *svanirūpitāvacchedakatāvṛttitva* (रवनिरूपितावच्छेदकतावृत्तित्व)

Though this chain of relations can be developed further, we may stop here and can say that this explanation of *ekatva*, can cover all the instances of *ekatva*. For a layman, why, even for a scholar who is able to follow the Navya Nyāya terminology only up to an extent, all this exercise may seem to be absolutely meaningless. It is also impossible to convince a layman of the necessity of conceiving innumerable relations, each of which involves many other relations and are mostly unintelligible. But when one notices the use of the singular case in different contexts, it becomes clear that a simple explanation cannot cover all the cases. For instance, take the sentence '*puruṣoyam rājñaḥ*'. Here the singular case suffix is used more than once. The singular case that we hear after the term '*puruṣa*' denotes the *ekatva* that belongs to the qualificandum, whereas the singular case suffix heard after the word 'rajñaḥ' denotes the *ekatva* that is related to the qualifier, because as per the Sanskrit linguistic rules—*puruṣa* is the qualificandum and *rājan* is the qualifier here. Any explanation of *ekatva* will have to cover all these instances. There are also some peculiar instances wherein the use of singular case affix poses a problem. Bachcha Jha refers to many such instances. When a servant is carrying some money which actually belongs to two kings, the use of a sentence—*rājñaḥ dhanam gṛhītvā jigamiṣati rājño dāsaḥ*—"The servant of the king desires to go, taking the money of the king" is not valid if the *ekatva* of the *rājan* is intended in both cases - '*rājñaḥ dhanam*' and '*rājñaḥ dāsaḥ*'. In one case, that is, '*rājñaḥ dāsaḥ*' the use of *ekavacana* is quite valid because the person is a servant of only one king, but the same cannot be said in the case of '*rājñaḥ dhanam*', because the money actually does not belong to only one king.

The various relations involved in this *anugama* takes care of this instance also, the validity of which, otherwise cannot be established.

Similarly, there are sentences like 'Rāmadārā Jānakī'. Here, as per the desire of the speaker, either the term 'Rāmadārā' can be taken as the term denoting the qualificandum (*viśeṣya*) or the term 'Jānakī'. In either case, the plural number used after the word Rāmadāra is not intended. Since the word *dārā*, as per the Sanskrit linguistic rules, for the sake of grammatical correctness has to be used in plural number, it is so used. But, the singular number after the word Jānakī, denotes the *ekatva*. Certain relations introduced in the *anugama* are intended to cover instances such as these also. Therefore, though it is very difficult even to make an attempt to explain the utility of the seemingly meaningless relations included in an *anugama*, it can only be said that an *anugama* is employed as a last weapon by the Naiyāyikas through which they can avoid many inconvenient questions and achieve precision to a maximum extent. The *anugama* mentioned above, which satisfactorily explains the *ekatva* that the singular case suffixes used in different situations denote, was designed by the great Naiyāyikas of this century, Bachcha Jha, in his *Gūḍhārthatattvāloka*, a commentary on the *Vyutpattivāda* of Gadādhara. Though Gadādhara discusses the meaning of the singular case suffix in his *Vyutpattivāda* and offers an explanation of *ekatva* which is, by and large, accepted to all, Bachcha Jha continues the discussion further, pointing out the problems that cannot be solved by the explanation of *ekatva* offered by Gadādhara. The objections that he raises and the solutions, including the above *anugama*, are entirely his own. This is only a small instance of the amazing ingenuity for which Bachcha Jha is recognised as a legendary Naiyāyika of this century.

NOTES AND REFERENCES

1. Tarkālaṁkāra, Harirāma, *Viṣayatāvāda*, p. xxix.
2. Tarkālaṁkāra, Harirāma, *Viṣayatāvāda*, p. xxx.
3. Some doubts have been raised regarding the *sūtra* 1.1.4 which enumerates the six original *padārthas* accepted by Kaṇāda.
4. See the Appendix No. 1.
5. Jagdīśa. *Śabdaśakti Prakāśikā.*
6. Jagdīśa. *Tattvacintāmaṇi*, IV. II: 781.
7. Mohanty, *Gaṅgeśa's Theory of Truth*, p. 35.
8. Tarkālaṁkāra, Harirāma. *Viṣayatāvāda*. ed. V.N. Jha. Pune: University of Poona.
9. *Ibid.* p. xxxii, Text 48.
10. Interestingly Professor Badrinath Shukla has pointed out during the discussion later published as *Saṁvāda* that there is a radical distiction in *abhāva* when it comes to first-level sentences and second-level analytical sentences. The denial of second-level analytical sentence does not necessarily mean the denial of the association made in first-level sentences.
11. Tarkālaṁkāra, Harirāma. op. cit. pp. xxviii–xl.
12. Anantācārya, P.B. 1904. *Padavākyaratnākara.*
13. The following are the works ascribed to Gokulanātha Upādhyāya :
    (i) *Dikkāla Nirūpaṇa*—(Nyāya)
    (ii) *Lāghava gaurva rahasya*—(Nyāya)

(iii) *Muktivāda*—(Nyāya)
(iv) *Ṭippaṇa* on Udayana's *Kusumāñjali*—(Nyāya)
(v) *Nyāya lakṣaṇa vicāra*—(Nyāya)
(vi) *Nyāya Siddhāntatattva* or *Siddhāntaviveka*—(Nyāya)
(vii) *Padavākyaratnākara*—(Nyāya)
(viii) *Prabodha Kādambarī of Pramāṇa lakṣaṇa*—(Nyāya)
(ix) *Pramāṇabodha or moda*—(Nyāya)
(x) *Śaktivāda*—(Nyāya)
(xi) *Yogarūddhi vicāra*—(Nyāya)
(xii) *Viṣayatā vicāra*—(Nyāya)
(xiii) Svatra vāda—(Nyāya)
(xiv) Tarkatattva nirūpaṇa—(Nyāya)
(xv) Vivaraṇa or Vidyota on Pakṣadhara's Tattva cintāmaṇyāloka—(Nyāya)
(xvi) Cakraraśmi on Tattavacintāmaṇi—(Nyāya)
(xvii) Vidyota on Raghunātha śiromaṇia's *Tattavacintāmaṇi* Dīdhiti—(Nyāya)
(xviii) Mithyātvanirukti—(Vedānta)

P.B. Anantācārya ascribes the following also to Gokulanātha:
(i) Kāvyaprakāśa Ṭīkā (Poetics)
(ii) Dvaitanirṇaya Ṭīkā
(iii) Kunda Kādambarī
(iv) Kādambarī praśnottaraṇī
(v) Ekāvalī
(vi) Kādambarīkīrti Ślokaḥ
(vii) Śivastutiḥ
(viii) Amṛtodaya Niketan

Introduction to Padavākyaratnākara by P.B. Anantācārya.

14. Shukla, Badrinath. *Śataślokī*. Śloka No.82
15. *Ibid.*, Śloka No. 83.
16. *Ibid.*, Śloka No. 11.
17. *Ibid.*, Śloka No. 12.
18. *Ibid.*, Śloka Nos. 13–24.
19. *Ibid.*, Śloka Nos. 26–28.
20. *Ibid.*, Śloka No. 35.

CHAPTER 7

The Controversy Between the Advaitins and the Non-Advaitins from Madhusūdana Sarasvatī Onwards

A Reconstruction Based on the Construction by Kutumbashastri Entitled "The Advaita vs. non-Advaita: Anantakrishna Shastri's Reply to Vedānta Deśika"

I

Apart from the developments in Mīmāṁsā, the Nyāya, the Vaiśeṣika, Śāṁkhya and the Yoga which have been highlighted in the earlier chapters, devel opments in the Vedānta can only be understood in the context of the great debate between the Advaitins and the non-Advaitins culminating in the well-known work of Madhusūdana Sarasvatī entitled *Advaita-siddhi.* As the Advaitins first appeared on the scene with Śaṁkara as their *ācārya* at the beginning of the eighth century, all other schools of Vedānta had to define and defend their position against Śaṁkara who had formulated his own position as the correct understanding of *tīrtha* propounded in the so-called *prasthānatrayī,* that is the *Upaniṣad,* the *Brahma Sūtra* and the *Gītā.* As Śaṁkara had given his reasons for his own understanding of these texts, it became incumbent on all later Vedāntins who differed from him to justify their own interpretation by questioning his understanding of these texts and also to provide ground for an alternative interpretation. The myth of the *prasthānatrayī* may be said to have arisen in this way. An impression was created that these three texts were the main sources of all philosophical developments in India, and, if any philosophical position claimed to be "orthodox", it had to be in accordance with what was maintained in these texts. However, this was never the position in reality as the other *ācāryas* did not write independent commentaries on all these three texts and, as pointed out elsewhere, new texts such as the *Śrīmad Bhāgvat* were accepted as authoritative by the Vedāntin *ācāryas* in the tradition.

It was inevitable, that the debate between the Advaitin and the non-Advaitin schools of Vedānta should centre around Śaṁkara's central premise namely, the denial of the reality of all difference in order to establish his radical Advaitic position as being a true interpretation of the texts deemed by him to be the basic authoritative texts of the tradition. The debate in the discussion initiated by him took two forms: One was related to certain basic statements in the texts mentioned above regarding the reality or non-reality of the difference at the ultimate ontological level. The second was with regard to the reality of difference at the epistemological, ontological and axio-logical levels independently of what was said in any particular statement in the texts chosen by Śaṁkara for his authoritative statement on the subject. And, though the Naiyāyikas were the prime protagonist, in the second type of debate with the Advaitins, many of the non-Advaitic Vedāntin thinkers were also seen as arguing at this level, though inevitably, they had to defend their own interpretation of the texts chosen by Śaṁkara to establish the *tīrtha* of his interpretation.

The beginnings of the debate between the Advaitins and the non-Advaitins can be tentatively dated to early second millennium. Thus, Rāmānuja in the twelfth century in his famous *Śrī Bhāṣya* on the *Brahma Sūtras* had not only exhaustively articulated Śaṁkara's position in his *pūrva pakṣa* but also refuted it to establish his own counter-interpretation of the Vedāntic position. The position he espoused has been called *Viśiṣṭādvaita* in the tradition. Yet, though Rāmānuja's work has an authoritative position in the *Viśiṣṭādvaita* tradition, it was Vedāntadeśika in 1330 whose criticism of the Advaita position in his work entitled, *Śatdūṣaṇī* became the paradigmatic anti-Advaitin work from this school. However, with the appearance in the non-Advaitic tradition of Vedānta of Madhva who was the most uncompromising dualist in his interpretation of the foundational texts of Vedānta, it appears that the criticisms given by Rāmānuja and Vedāntadeśika took a secondary place in the debate, the focus having shifted to the more outspoken and trenchant criticism of the Madhva school which needed to be replied to by the Advaitins. Madhva himself was followed by such outstanding thinkers as Jayatīrtha (A.D. 1370) and Vyāsatīrtha II (A.D. 1535) who in their works entitled, *Nyāyasudhā* and *Nyāyāmṛta,* continued the criticism of the Advaitic position and developed it further. The work of Jayatīrtha, however, seems to have been overshadowed by Vyāsatīrtha II as the latter became the real focus of the controversy for the Advaitins. The frames of this controversy were fed further by Madhusūdana Sarasvatī's outstanding point by point refutation in his *Advaitasiddhi* of Vyāsatīrtha's *Nyāyāmṛta.* As Madhusūdana Sarasvatī lived in the seventeenth century, the stage was thus already set for the controversy to be carried further into the subsequent centuries.

The controversy took an interesting turn when one of the Advaitins, that is, Āgneya Paṇḍit (A.D. 1750) in his Vyāsatātparyanirṇaya argued that Vyāsatīrtha II rather than refuting the Advaitic position intended to support it. This contention not popularly acceptable was rejected in detail by Kapisthala Desikacharya (A.D. 1911) in his work entitled *Vyāsasiddhāntamaṅthana.*

One of the most important defenders of the Advaita position, in the twentieth century was Anantakrishna Shastri who, it appears, took upon himself the responsibility of replying those anti-Advaitic thinkers who had not been answered satisfactorily by the earlier Advaitins. Choosing Vedāntadeśika's *Śatdūṣaṇī* from the Viśiṣṭādvaita school he replied the arguments in his work entitled *Śatbhūṣaṇī.*

He also answered the questions raised in Jayatīrtha's *Nyāyasudhā* from the Madhva school and in his work entitled *Advaitatattvasudhā*. So far, no refutation had been attempted perhaps as Vyāsatīrtha II in his *Nyāyāmṛta* appears to have taken all the previous anti-Advaitic and Advaitic arguments and summarized them in such a masterly manner that Madhusūdana Sarasvatī thought that in refuting him he was refuting all the anti-Advaitic arguments that had been given until then. Anantakrishna Shastri, however, presented a detailed discussion and refutation of the arguments given by Jayatīrtha and Vedāntadeśika despite the existence of those that had been given by Vyāsatīrtha II in his *Nyāyāmṛta*.

Anantakrishna Shastri perhaps felt that it was necessary to reply to Jayatīrtha's work, as it had not been replied to adequately earlier and hence wrote *Advaitatattvasudhā*, completing the exercise on the Advaitic side. The work summarizes the points of agreement and difference between the Advaitins and non-Advaitins, even though Vidyāmanyatīrtha from the Madhva school who wrote a reply to his work, did not agree with all the so-called points of agreement between the Advaitins and the non-Advaitins as indicated by Anantakrishna Shastri in his own presentation of the subject. Vidyāmanyatīrtha's work is explicitly entitled *Advaitatattvasudha Samikṣā*. In fact, it is surprising that Anantakrishna Shastri could have ever seriously meant that the Advaitins regarded the *Vedas* as 'eternal' and all its parts as equally authoritative, particularly those which dealt with various sacrifices and other sundry matters. To claim this in the face of Śaṁkara's explicit statement that if even a hundred *śrutis* were to declare that fire is cold, no one would believe it, is to ignore the essential limitation imposed on the statements of the *Veda* (though specifically and differently) by both the Advaitins and the Mīmāṁsakas even though the limitations they impose pertain to different types of statements in it. The Advaitin's criticism of the Mīmāṁsaka makes no sense in the context of Anantakrishna Shastri's listing of the points on which the Advaitins and non-Advaitins agree. One important difference in the controversy between the Advaitins and non-Advaitin Vedāntins on the one hand and between the Advaitins and the Naiyāyikas on the other that emerges in that there is a hermeneutical dimension in the controversy, which is completely lacking in the other long controversy, which the Advaitins had with the Naiyāyikas. But then, the 'hermeneutical' enterprise is central to Mīmāṁsā also and the difference between the Mīmāṁsakas and the Vedāntins in this regard does not seem to have been explored. In any case, the long hermeneutical debate with respect to the interpretation of the Vedic texts reveals that this kind of debate remains inconclusive, as all the sides adhere steadfastly to their own interpretation, a result which might have some lessons for those who expect much from the hermeneutical studies these days.

Perhaps for the first time, a detailed examination of the works of Vedāntadeśika was made by Shastri who classifies the objections into basic topics or issues with which the discussion is concerned. He divides these issues under nine heads which deal with the interpretation of the words in some of the key *sūtras* of the *Brahmasūtra*, such as the first word of the first *sūtra*, that is, "*atha*" and the words '*tat*' and '*tvam*' in the well-known Upaniṣadic *mahāvākya* '*tat tvam asi*', the meaning of which he propounds in non-Advaitic terms. Besides these are discussed the meanings of the words in the sentence, "*tat tvam asi*" which are crucial both for the Advaitins and the non-Advaitins as they accept the unquestionable authority of the texts in which they occur. The other topics that he mentions are *avidyā, māyā* (falsity of the world), and *jīvanamukti* of which obviously only the first two are of philosophical significance. He also mentions Bhartrprapañca's doctrine of *niṣprapañcīkaraṇa* and Niranjana Sanyasin's, doctrine of *alepakamata.* It may be interesting to note that Vedāntadeśika in his work written in the fourteenth century had considered the views of Bhartrprapañca and Niranjana Sanyasin important enough to discuss them in detail apart from the other issues mentioned earlier. The detailed subdivision of the topics under each of these heading makes interesting reading as it maps the areas of philosophical concerns which seemed pertinent to Vedāntadeśika in the context of the debate between the Advaitins and the non-Advaitins.

ISSUES IN THE DEBATE—VEDĀNTADEŚIKA

One of the fundamental philosophical issues relates to the actuality of illusion and error that infects our knowledge and renders, many a time, what one had considered to be as true. This, as is well known, raises a generalised doubt regarding everything held as knowledge and considered to be true, leading to the suspicion that it may not really be so. The problem has recurred in western philosophy and both Descartes and Husserl are recent examples of the attempt to ground philosophy in a radical certitude after everything has been doubted or 'bracketed'. Russell's attempt to ground philosophy on the two separate certitudes of sense data, on the one hand, and logical relations, on the other, is another example of this.

What are the consequences of this false knowledge when it is regarded as true of what status are these consequences is an issue that has not been tackled so far. Because of the fact that one acts on the belief that the knowledge one entertains is "true", these consequences are apparent in the objective world as also in oneself as one has actually entertained this false knowledge in one's consciousness. In fact, a "false" knowledge may be as much about oneself as about something in the world and as the knowledge was believed to be true, one had acted on this belief and brought certain consequences into being, both for oneself and the world.

Another dimension to this issue of false knowledge is provided by the world of art and imagintion. Something is entertained as true, even though one knows that it is not really so. This has profound consequences apparent in the creations of man which stimulate people to participate by an act of imaginative empathy. The observor "lives" out all the emotions which are normally experienced in connection with the actual world which alone is considered to be the object of true knowledge and true judgements.

There is yet another level where what might be meant by "true" knowledge about this world is created and posited and lived through by a willed acceptance of it as being "true" even though the assumption is "known" to be false. The Naiyāyika has tried to deal with this in the notion of *āhāryajñāna*, but it is not clear whether he has succeeded in dealing with the epistemological and ontological problem associated with this issue.

The ontological status of the object of erroneous cognition, which has been treated extensively in Indian philosophy, surprisingly, does not find any significant place in the western tradition of philosophising. However, even in the Indian tradition, the discussion relating to the problem has not been extended to the erroneous cognition of the self and the ontological status that such an object might possibly possess. The term "*jīva*" usually connotes such an erroneous cognition of the self which, in its true nature, is supposed to be the *ātman* or the *puruṣa* in Vedānta and Śāṁkhya respectively. But whom does this erroneous cognition of the self belong to as it cannot belong to the *jīva* which is constituted by the erroneous cognition itself and it cannot belong to the *ātman* also, as the *ātman* or the *puruṣa* cannot be the locus of an erroneous cognition since, by definition, it cannot have anything erroneous or false in it.

This issue is raised in the debate between the Advaitin and the non-Advaitin with respect to the locus of *avidyā*. The question asked is whether Brahman can be its locus, or in other words, whether *avidyā* can even be considered to be a property of this locus. If it cannot be so considered, then whose property is it?[1]

A related problem which again has not been in the centre of philosophical discussion in the Western tradition is in regard to what exactly does the erroneous cognition do to the true nature of the object which it conceals or distorts or modifies? The Advaitin/non-Advaitin discussion focusses attention on this issue but raises it primarily to highlight how *avidyā* conceals the nature of the Brahman. It is not necessary that the question be posed only in these terms, for *avidyā* in general can conceal the nature of the object as much as that of the pure subject of experience. It is the Advaitin's presupposition that the object is there because of *avidyā* and that even the so-called relation between the subject and object occurs because of it. But, philosophically, this is not necessary as the notion of erroneous cognition is not necessarily tied to any specific view regarding what is to be considered as true.

The "positive" character of error and falsity and its difference from ignorance is similarly relevant to all thinking about knowledge. Ignorance is that of which one does not know anything at all, while when one is in error or when one entertains a belief that is false, one is aware of the object, but conceives of it incorrectly. There is, in this situation, a two-fold problem and it would be interesting to find if the Advaitin/non-Advaitin controversy has taken note of it. The problem relates to the fact that when one entertains a false belief about something, it can seldom be the case that one is wholly in error or that the belief that one entertains is false in all respects. What is more likely is that only some aspects or features of the belief are mistaken while some others are true and, if so, the erroneous cognition of the object will have to be considered as partially true and partially false. This then raises the paradoxical nature of the erroneous cognition as being not entirely erroneous in nature.

This "positive nature" of the erroneous cognition is in contrast to the sheer state of ignorance from which it has to be radically distinguished. In case it is positive, it must have a being of its own as it cannot be pure non-being or something like pure ignorance of which one cannot even be aware, for to be aware that one is ignorant is already a step away from it and a movement towards knowledge. But if it has a being, it must be effective and hence must produce consequences, thus raising the question as to how such causal effectivity is different from that which one ascribes to true being or existence in general. In other words, *avidyā*, if it is positive, has an *arthakriyākāritva* of its own. And if so, how would one distinguish it from *vidyā* except perhaps in terms of the nature of the consequences which follow from them? Normally, the distinction in the Indian tradition has been made in terms of bondage and freedom, while in the western tradition, it has been made in terms of the success and failure of action. But both the criteria are ambiguous as it is not easy to define what is bondage or freedom or the success or failure of action. Further, it is only after the consequences occur that one knows whether one was in a state of *vidyā* or *avidyā*. On the other hand, both notions of ignorance and error involve the possibility of their removal and thus raise the question as to how this removal occurs and how one can be sure that it has really been removed. There seems to be a radical difference in this respect between ignorance and error as one can be sure that one is not ignorant if one has even some sort of knowledge about anything; while in error it is easy to fall into the illusion that one is rid of it when, in fact, one may have fallen into another error having rid oneself of the earlier one. But, if knowledge is a unified whole, then error with respect to any part of it will in fact affect the whole in some sense or the other. On the other hand, if knowledge is considered atomistically or item-wise, then one will have to find some criteria of demarcation and distinction between one knowledge and another. In any case, as the Advaitin/non-Advaitin debate is concerned not only with *avidyā* but also with its removal, the arguments given in this regard will be of wider relevance to this epistemological issue of truth and error in general.

While there can be grounds for believing that some particular objects of apparent cognition are unreal, that the Advaitin considers the whole world to be ultimately "unreal", appears meaningless for how can we say everything is unreal, as unless we know something as real, how can we call something else unreal? The Advaitin appears to have argued that an analysis of the notion of difference shows it to be self-contradictory and that distinction or difference is the constitutive condition of the world and hence the world is bound to be unreal. The debate between the Advaitin and the non-Advaitin, thus, ultimately hinges on the analysis of the notion of difference but, at another level, it could equally concern the axiomatically presupposed idea that if something is self-contradictory in its nature, then it cannot be real. The notion of self-contradiction itself could be the subject of philosophical analysis and it could be inquired as to whether it can be relevantly applied to empirically experienced reality.

The discussion of the word "*atha*" at the beginning of the first *sūtra* in the text of the *Brahmasūtra* is totally irrelevant as the same word occurs in many other basic texts including the *Mīmāṁsā Sūtras* so that the discussion is not confined to the context of the *Brahmasūtras*, but somehow this has not been noticed in the Advaitin/non-Advaitin debate, which only shows how preconceptions can blind one to the existence of obvious objections.

The Advaitin/non-Advaitin debate raises some interesting issues: whether the function of knowing and knowership is an accidental property of the self; whether the so-called *jñātṛtva* and *bhoktṛtva* are properties imposed on it by false identificatory consciousness; whether the "witness-consciousness" should be treated as an adventitious property or not. In fact, can self-consciousness be said to have any property at all which may be regarded as its intrinsic or essential property? Similarly, can consciousness or the self be considered as a unity if there is nothing for it to unify, as all multiplicity in it is unreal. If multiplicity is unreal, then unity will also have to be unreal.

There is an interesting relationship between the well-known controversy in the Indian tradition regarding the primacy of meaning in the sentence over word meaning or the converse contention that meaning belongs primarily to the individual word and that sentential meaning is a construct. The controversy between the Advaitin and the non-Advaitin regarding the meaning of the statements of the *śruti* appears to be related to the controversy regarding the primacy of the sentential meaning over the word meaning. The non-Advaitin insists that knowledge of the meaning of Brahman precedes its meaning being established as knowledge in the sentences in which it occurs. He also seems to suggest that no secondary meaning can ever be established without first knowing the primary meaning of a word. In such a theory, therefore, *lakṣaṇā* and *vyañjanā* are always secondary to *abhidhā*. On the other hand, the Advaitin seems to argue that the sentential meaning occurs not only over and above the meanings of the individual words which are supposed to give rise to it, but even that their individual meaning can only be understood in the context of the meaning of the whole sentence of which they form a part, since at least in spoken language, the words cease to exist by the time the totality of the sentence is comprehended and its meaning grasped by the listener. In a fundamental sense, therefore, the meaning of a sentence is always primary. Also, if the context of the occurrence as well as the intention of the speaker is taken to be relevant to the understanding of the meaning, then the sentential meaning cannot but have a secondary or tertiary character to which the words in their combination only contribute in an indirect way. In other words, they can only function in a *taṭastha* manner. But if this is accepted, what exactly would be meant by the notion of primary meaning? And what exactly would be meant by the meaning of the word outside the context of the sentence in which it occurs? Moreover, if the meaning of the sentence itself gets modified by the sentences which have preceded it or those which follow it, then would not the meaning of an individual sentence be like that of a word and function as primary meaning in relation to other sentences? Yet, even then there would remain an essential difference between the primary meaning of a word and the primary meaning of a sentence, for the latter in relation to the words which constitute it will always have a secondary character, while the meaning of a word, in case there is any such thing, will always be primary as the letters or sounds that constitute it are not considered by anybody to have any meaning at all. But, then the relation between the primary and the secondary meaning of a sentence would become relative and that which is secondary in one context will become primary in another.

Other issues in the Advaitin/non-Advaitin controversy relate to the knowledge of an object which is devoid of all qualities whatsoever. As the first *sūtra* of the *Brahmasūtras* relates to the desire for the knowledge of the Brahman, it assumes that Brahman is knowable in principle and that one cannot only have the desire to know it, but that the desire is attainable in principle. Yet, the Advaitin holds that the Brahman is devoid of all qualities whatsoever and is still knowable, implying thereby that something that is absolutely without qualities can be known, although it is not quite clear whether this knownness or being known affects the Brahman in any way or makes it possess a property which it did not possess before. On the other hand, if the absence of a property is itself treated as a property, it will then be impossible in principle for Brahman not to possess a property. It is not quite clear whether the absence of a property as a property has been the subject of the debate between the Advaitin and the non-Advaitin, on what has been, the Advaitin's reply to it? It may be said that knowledge of the Brahman is not like the knowledge of any object as it is beyond the subject-object distinction.

Yet, the *ātman* is supposed to be both devoid of this knowledge through beginningless *avidyā* and desirous of having it. Not only this, in the state of liberation, it is supposed to attain this knowledge which, in fact, is identical with "liberation" itself. In other words, 'liberation' and 'bondage' are the same as the presence or absence of this knowledge in the *ātman*. In fact, one may distinguish the three stages in the process: First, when one is completely ignorant about Brahman and does not know anything about it and hence no desire to know it would possibly arise. The second stage is when one has heard that there is such a thing as Brahman and one has the desire to know it. What is meant here by this desire of 'knowing' and how is this desire different from other desires for knowledge? This leads one to explore the phenomenology of the desire for knowledge and the different kinds of knowledge that there can be and the differences in the desire for them. Such a phenomenological epistemological analysis has perhaps not yet been undertaken. Nor has the analogous problem regarding an analysis of the desire for the knowledge of the Self been undertaken.

In fact, what difference would it have made if the *Brahmasūtras* were called the "*Ātmasūtras*" instead and the first *sūtra* been written as "*Athāto ātma jijñāsā*"?

The third stage is supposed to arise when this desire for knowledge has been fulfilled. Here, two questions arise: (i) whether any desire can ever be fulfilled, and (ii) whether the desire for knowledge can ever be completely fulfilled. Normally, the fulfillment of a desire gives rise to another desire which may be of the same kind or of a different kind. As for the desire for knowledge, it seems to be of a very peculiar nature as the criterion for its fulfillment itself means that some new questions have arisen which demand further answers. It is true that one may feel a state of satiation after the fulfillment of a desire, just as one may feel that the question that one had raised has been answered and that there are no more questions to be asked. But such a state is only temporary, because if one is physically alive, the desire will arise once again and, similarly, if one is intellectually alive, new questions will arise to challenge one's desire for knowing once more. It is true that it has been suggested that the final and absolute cessation of this process is itself the goal of seeking which is variously named as the *mokṣa* or *nirvāṇa* of brahman-realisation or *kaivalya* or *Śiva-śakti sāmarasya*, implying that the dichotomy between the seeking and the sought, the desiring and the desired, the subject and the object has finally been overcome. But then, non-existence of such a dichotomy exists almost by definition in the state supposed to characterize non-living, material objects which are devoid of all consciousness. If so, how does one distinguish between this state and the state in which all dichotomies have been finally overcome absolutely and forever. And, if one makes a distinction between the two states how will the Advaitin deal with this final distinction which still haunts and affects the so-called state where no distinctions whatsoever can be ascribed or conceived.

The problem of the knowledge of that which is completely without any attributes whatsoever has arisen in the western tradition in the philosophies of Locke and Kant. Locke had called a substance a 'know-not-what' while Kant had called a thing-in-itself an object of thought, but not of knowledge. The problem was never directly tackled even though both Berkeley and Hegel tried to get rid of such a postulated entity in different ways, and argued that the distinction between thought and knowledge was untenable. It would be interesting to find whether the Advaitin/non-Advaitin controversy has dealt with this problem.

Are there any entities which can be known only through the secondary significance of the words, as no primary meanings can ever indicate them or apply to them? Many points of discussion are raised while examining the concept of secondary meanings from the Advaitin and non-Advaitin perspectives. The world created by secondary and tertiary meanings and its autonomy and independence from the world of primary meanings needs to be investigated. In the contemporary epistemological discussion relating to the philosophy of science the ontological status of theoretic entities are postulated to understand primary sense experience. However, it is not quite clear whether the two are the same or if there is any relation between them. Further, what exactly is meant by primary meaning? Does it apply to primary objects alone, or to that which can be grasped by the senses, or to that which can be known by reason and inference but never by perception, or does it apply to possible percepts, which can be imagined but which are never the objects of perception? Anantakrishna Shastri contends that the Viśiṣṭādvaitin had to take as much recourse to the primacy of secondary meaning in his own description of ontic reality as the Advaitin does. The deeper problem however, which this observation of Pt. Anantakrishna Shastri raises, is whether any thinking about reality can avoid positing entities whose meaning primarily arises from their secondary significance and which are not only known by their primary meaning but are also incapable of being so known in principle. But if such is the case, as Pt. Anantakrishna Shastri seems to contend, then how does one choose between the different entities so posited if they themselves are opposed to one another. The problem in the context of the Advaitin/non-Advaitin debate may be put in the following way: if both of them are forced to posit such entities, then what is the ground for preferring one to the other?

Regarding the consequences of false knowledge, Śaṁkara himself had argued that a false knowledge can have "real" consequences. But it is doubtful if he would have accepted that a knowledge that is false can lead to liberation or *mokṣa* or freedom. It is not clear why such a limitation on the nature of consequences following from the falsity of knowledge should be imposed and on what grounds. There would be no problem if the falsity of knowledge resulted in no consequence whatsoever, but in case it does, it is not clear why the consequence should be only evil and not good. One may, for example, meaningfully achieve a very significant state of consciousness by means of a great imaginative creation which in itself is not real or which may even represent something that is totally false, just as by meditating on an image of a deity, one may achieve a state of consciousness which is of profound significance and which itself may later have desirable observable effects on one's behaviour. The relation between the "falsity" of knowledge and the specific nature of the consequences that alone may follow from it is an ontological supposition in Advaita and non-Advaita Vedānta which needs justification and further exploration. (The Advaitin seems to posit a third state between something which is not characterised by any property whatsoever and something which is characterised by properties which are generally called *upādhi* and this he calls *Saupādhika Brahman* which is not supposed to have any *upādhi* but which is not completely devoid of all attributes or properties either as it is related to *jīva*. This distinction is made by Vacaspati Miśra I in his *Bhamati* and needs to be clarified further.)

The discussions in Advaita Vedānta regarding the destruction of ignorance or false knowledge have to be seen not only in the specific context of the relationship between Brahman, *jīva* and *avidyā*, etc., but also in the ordinary instance of erroneous cognition and its removal in day to day life. However, as pointed out earlier, a distinction has to be drawn between the removal of ignorance and the removal of erroneous cognition. Further can an erroneous cognition be said to remove ignorance, for ignorance is the total absence of any awareness regarding a thing that exists or is real, while an erroneous cognition is aware of it, but is supposed to misapprehend it in some way or other. Should one therefore regard the state of ignorance as being better than a state in which one has an erroneous cognition about the object of which one was ignorant or should one regard an erroneous cognition as a better state, as it is at least aware that something is there about the existence of which one was previously ignorant. Another aspect to be examined is that of the relation between the erroneous cognition and the same cognition when it is corrected by subsequent knowledge because a memory of the erroneous cognition still haunts or infects the corrected cognition in some sense or the other. This may be considered as analogous to the Advaita Vedānta context in which the notion of the *Śatapatha Brahman* is postulated which itself gives way to a pure *Śuddha Brahman*. The difference between the two is said to be that while in the former there is still a reference to the *avidyā* that has been corrected, in the latter even such a reference does not exist. This, of course, happens in the case of all erroneous cognitions and is not peculiar to the knowledge of Brahman alone, even though the discussion between the Advaitins and the non-Advaitins do not see it in this way.

The distinction between knowledge as an essential property of consciousness or as an accidental and adventitious property is usually formulated in the classical discussion of the subject as *svarūpa jñāna* and *vṛtti jñāna* or between *dharmī jñāna* or *dharma jñāna*. The former is treated as the natural property of the self and the latter as its accidental property. The distinction, however, is linked to what exactly is meant by *svarūpa jñāna* or *dharmī jñāna*, for in both cases, the self or consciousness will have to bifurcate itself into the subject and object of cognition, unless one can think of a state of consciousness in which such a distinction does not exist. The Advaitin, however, cannot in principle, admit any distinction at the ultimate level and hence cannot legitimately employ the notion of *svarūpa jñāna*.

Eternality of Knowledge

The eternality or non-eternality of knowledge adds another dimension to the discussion for, if the self has knowledge as a property then obviously, this would be the essential property ascribed to it as long as the self is there. But, if knowledge is something relational, that is, if it is knowledge of "something", then the self will always have to be at least aware of itself in relation to something else of which it has the knowledge. On the other hand, even in such a situation in respect of that of which the self is supposed to have knowledge there can be no "necessity" regarding the supposed knowledge. As, in case it is knowledge of anything other than itself then generally such a knowledge is supposed to be accidental or adventitious as there can be no necessity about having knowledge of one thing rather than another. What will be necessary in such a situation is only that one is aware of "something", but there is no necessity regarding what that something is or ought to be.

However, the question will remain as to what happens to the specificity of the knowledge when it ceases to be. Does it, for example, leave any trace of itself, any *saṁskāra*, anything which becomes the ground for remembering what one had known and which makes memory possible? In case it does, the so-called *vṛtti jñāna* or *dharma jñāna*, even though adventitious and accidental, would make a difference to the consciousness itself as the consciousness will not only be aware of itself but also of itself as having had those *vṛtti jñānas* which have ceased to be. The memory, of course, need not always be present in consciousness, but it certainly can occur at any time and when it does, it certainly becomes not only an object to consciousness, but it also affects it in some way or the other. In distinguishing between the *vṛtti jñāna* of memory as different from the *vṛtti jñāna* of that of which it is supposed to be a memory, one generally says that the difference lies in that in memory the object or event of which one is aware, is attended by the consciousness that it had happened in the past. It would be interesting to ask about the temporal dimension of the *vṛtti jñāna* in perception, in memory, in dreams, in respect to imagined objects and in self-consciousness. The *Viśiṣṭādvaitins* seemed to hold the peculiar doctrine that *vṛtti jñāna* and *dharma jñāna* are eternal in nature and come into being and are destroyed because of expansion and contraction which, according to this school, is the peculiar nature of all such knowledge. How do they explain the awareness of an object that had never been known before?

The issue of the eternity of knowledge in the controversy between the Advaitin and the non-Advaitin, in fact, raises the wider question as to how anything can even be regarded as eternal, particularly when it arises and ceases to be in the context of human experience. The problem arises, for example, in relation to sound, the eternity of which is accepted by the Mīmāṁsakas and disputed by Gautama in his *Nyāya Sūtras.* One would then have to distinguish between eternity and non-eternity, between the object of awareness and the awareness itself, for knowledge generally appears and disappears whatever be the nature of the object concerned. The Vedāntins have argued for the eternity of awareness and the non-eternity of the object of awareness on the basis of the *anvayavyatireka* as the one always seems to change while the other remains constant.

The predication of eternality itself to anything whatsoever is matter for discussion, and, in case it is predicated, how can one determine its validity. In the western philosophical tradition, a distinction is made between two meanings of eternality, one relating to the fact that temporal predicates are irrelevant to the object concerned, while in the second meaning, it merely refers to indefinite endurance in time. The usual example given of the former kind of objects relates to mathematical entities and the relationships between them. As for the second, it is obviously difficult to give an example of this unless time itself were to be given as an example as it would be difficult to prove that something which has endured in time would continue to do so for ever. However, this is explored in the Nyāya tradition in respect of their concepts of *prāgabhāva* and *dhvaṁśābhāva* and *atyantābhāva.* The external character of the predicates "true" and/or "false" in respect to tautological and self-contradictory statements in the western tradition are also discussed. There is a similar problem in respect of the so-called *tīrtha* or falsity of those expressions whose suitable spatio-temporal co-ordinates are clearly provided.

The Advaitin/non-Advaitin controversy does not seem to have taken note of these issues even tangentially. Nor does it seem to have asked the central question as to what is the relation of Brahman and *ātman* to time. In case, time is an illusion, what would it mean to call Brahman or *ātman* eternal? There is also postulated the non-destructibility of that which has no parts, such as the Vaiśeṣikā atom and the consequent eternality derived from its non-destructibility. But ontological destructibility does not imply that the thing will not get new properties because of its relation with other entities or even because of the fact that it becomes an object of knowledge and awareness.

How eternality can be ascribed to any entity which undergoes actual or possible changes is a particularly interesting issue, especially, in the context of the Śāṁkhya system where the eternality of *prakṛti* is accepted in spite of the fact that it undergoes constant transformation and modification. Similarly, the Jainas believe that the *ātman*, though eternal, expands and contracts and in fact has a spatial dimension to it. The Advaitin does not accept any change or modification in Brahman, but it does accept a distinction in the *ātman* between the state of knowledge and the state of ignorance and the transition from one to the other. He then would have to accept a radical difference between the Brahman and the *ātman*, unless māyā is supposed to play the same role with respect to Brahman as *avidyā* does in the case of the *ātman*.

Whether an eternal object can have possible changes or modifications in it is an issue that leads further to an exploration of whether the property that such an eternal object possesses must also be eternal as is maintained by the Naiyāyikas. The Viśiṣṭādvaitins hold that knowledge is a substance and not a property of the *ātman* as is held by the Naiyāyikas. What could possibly be meant by understanding knowledge as a substance and not as a property? On the other hand, the distinction between the Naiyāyika and the Advaitin would be that for the Naiyāyika, knowledge is an emergent property which when it occurs belongs to the self which, however, does not have it as its essential property. For the Advaitin, on the other hand, knowledge would be an essential property of the self, though it is not quite clear what could possibly be meant by this as the Advaitin does not accept either the self or anything else as an object of this knowledge.

The problem of identity and difference, however formulated, cannot be made intelligible in the context of the Advaitin's assertion of the identity between the self and the Brahman as all examples would be those of identity and difference, that is, *tādātmya*, as it is understood in Nyāya, where the identity between the pot and the clay is supposed to be because of the causal relation or the identity of the body and the self which though non-causal still maintains the difference between the two even while asserting identity. The crucial point of the debate seems to be how to conceive of the identity relation in an intelligible fashion and how to understand, epistemologically and ontologically, ignorance and erroneous consciousness and its removal.

To comprehensively sum up, Vedāntadeśika's discussion of Advaita, it may thus be considered as focussing mainly on two fundamental and interrelated issues: one, relating to foundational ignorance, and the other relating to the unreality of the world. All the other issues appear to be related either to questions of textual interpretation about which one can disagree or an empirical possibility such as that relating to the realization of complete liberation during one's lifetime. The doctrines of *Bhartṛprapañca* and *Nirañjana Sanyāsin* seem too specific in character and most probably were of importance at the time when he was writing on the subject. Ultimately, the philosophical issues of dispute between the Advaitin and the non-Advaitin relate to the ontological reality of the world and the argument for the rootedness of its unreality in some foundational constitutive ignorance inherent in the very structure of human consciousness which, however, permits its own awareness and the annihilation of that ignorance.

The Advaitic position may be, in fact, reformulated in more trenchant philosophical terms as that of the meaning of an identity statement of the form "A is B" along with what can possibly be meant by a statement which ascribes "unreality" to anything in a statement such as "X is unreal". Similarly, the third issue relating to the idea of "*jīvan mukti*" may be reformulated as to whether it is possible to conceive of the realization of the ideal of freedom within the limitations, restrictions and necessities imposed by the requirements of living, both at the biological, the psychological and the socio-cultural levels.

Formulated in this way, the issues assume a contemporary relevance and profound significance for philosophical thought, and the discussion in the tradition of these assumes a significance far beyond the specific context of the Upaniṣadic *mahāvākyas* or the statements in the *Brahmasūtra* in the context of which they had usually been carried on. Does the statement of identity deny the difference between A and B in the sentence 'A is B' and, if so, how is it different from the statement 'A is A'? It may be recalled in this connection that Aristotle is supposed to have formulated the law of identity as 'A is A'; while the Nyāya tradition in India is supposed to have rejected the statement 'A is A' as altogether meaningless for it contains no information at all. Abstract identity is also attacked in the western tradition by Hegel and many others on the ground that it is not identity at all.[2] On the other hand, if difference is admitted between A and B, then what is the point in calling them identical? In other words, what exactly is the difference between the notions of 'identity' and 'similarity'? However, even in the statement "A is similar to B", it may be asked 'similar in what respect?' and whether the aspects in which they are similar, are not to be regarded as identical. For, if they are not treated as identical, then again we will expect some difference between them. Then further there is numerical difference or spatio-temporal difference, but as there are objects with respect to which spatio-temporal predicates are irrelevant, the problem of identity with respect to them will remain.

Similarly, the identity between a substance and its attribute and between the universal and the particular instances in which it is supposed to be exemplified, need to be explored. The problem of identity and difference, then, is central to philosophical thought and the Advaitin and the non-Advaitin debate on it needs a closer analysis.

The issue of unreality and that of whether what we consider as real may actually be so or does not hold the same central place in philosophy. What exactly is meant by the terms 'real' and 'unreal' and what is the status of that which is declared to be unreal? In recent philosophy, Quine has raised this issue in his well-known paper entitled 'On What There Is' and has suggested how one may significantly assert a negation of something without postulating any 'possible' being for it. But then, all significant negations will become equivalent as there will remain no way to distinguish between 'X does not exist' and 'Y does not exist'. Further, one may meaningfully attempt to distinguish between the notions of 'reality' and 'existence' and examine whether 'existence' is a predicate like other predicates which may be supposed to be present or absent as the case may be. The notion of "possibility" is closely related to these issues and though recent developments in modal logic have added new dimensions to this, the ontological significance of this is not quite clear.

The 'real-unreal' dichotomy was brought into the western philosophical discussion by Kant in his new notion of what may be called a 'transcendental illusion'. This means that something that was presupposed as a condition for objectivity was itself apprehended as an "object" and treated self-evidently as such, giving rise to fundamental insoluble problems for thought and that it was only a transcendental critique which exposed the illusoriness of such an illusion.

These are trans-cultural and trans-civilizational issues that occupy the centre stage in philosophical debate in all traditions of philosophy and go beyond the Advaitin/non-Advaitin debate. Similarly, the values that all cultures have postulated for man's realization are linked to man's biological, psychological and social necessities within which inevitably and only may one actualize the values and ideals of human life including the ideal of freedom or liberation.

NON-ADVAITIC SCHOOLS

The Advaita/non-Advaita controversy has primarily centered between the followers of Rāmānuja or Madhva and those of Śaṁkara. However, non-Advaitic schools of Vedānta continued to be formed after Madhva, the most well-known being of the school of Vallabhācārya, who flourished in the last part of the fifteenth century and the early part of the sixteenth century (1479–1531). He stayed near Banaras and is supposed to have become a focal point of controversy in both the Mīmāṁsaka and the Advaitin camps. He is said to have clarified his position in a paper which he put on the doors of the Vishwanath temple. As this paper outlined Vallabhācārya's position as different from both the Mīmāṁsakas and the Advaitins, it assumed central importance as a position in the non-Advaitic Vedānta which differed from that of Rāmānuja and Madhva in that it attempted to come to terms with both the Mīmāṁsaka and the Śaṁkarite interpretations of the *śruti.* It is interesting to note that hardly any representatives of Rāmānuja and the Madhva School existed in Banaras as one does not hear of any objections to his position from these schools of non-Advaitic Vedānta. Perhaps, the situation continues to be the same as the Rāmānuja and the Madhva *saṁpradāyas* are not well-known outside the southern peninsula where these schools had appeared and still continue to flourish.

Vallabhācārya's position, as presented in his paper, has been commented upon by Giridharjī, Śrī Harirāyajī and Sri Puruṣottamajī. Recently, Shri Shyam Manoharji Gosvami brought out all these commentaries, along with the original text, and published them together in a volume entitled *Patrāvalambana.* It is interesting to note that according to Sri Shyam Manoharji, Sri Vallabhācārya does not accept that the *Karmakāṇḍa* of the *Mīmāṁsāsūtras* and the *Jñānakāṇḍa* of the *Brahmasūtras* form a unified whole as has been argued by many people including Rāmānuja. Rather, according to him, they relate to totally different subjects, the only relation between them perhaps being that they belong to the same life of man. He also draws attention to the fact that Śrī Vallabhācārya bases his interpretation of the *Upaniṣads* on the statement, "All this is Brahman".

But, though there is a *prima facie* attempt to delink the two *Mīmāṁsās* at a deeper level, there seems to be an attempt to place them in some sort of a unified perspective where Brahman is equated with Īśvara and Īśvara with the Kṛṣṇa of the *Bhagvadgītā* and the *Bhāgavat.* Also, there seems to have been some adaptation of Rāmānuja's idea that the world is a body of the Supreme Spirit, that is, God. This was attempted specifically with respect to the various *yajñas,* such as the Agnihotra, the Darśapūrvamāsa, the Soma, and so forth dealt with in the *Mīmāṁsāsūtras* which are regarded as parts of the body of the Supreme Being whose head is the *Jñānakāṇḍa* as treated in the *Brahmasūtras.* The so-called *karma* dealt with in the *Mīmāṁsasūtras* and the *jñāna* dealt with in the *Brahmasūtras* are also related to the different *āśramas* in a man's life as are usually accepted in the Indian tradition. Vallabhācārya also makes a distinction between *yajñas* which are done with knowledge and those which are not done with knowledge and he makes an interesting distinction between the *sāttvika,* the *rājasika* and the *tāmasika yajña.* This distinction helps him to explain how the performance of the Vedic *yajñas* may lead to liberation in case they are done with the knowledge propounded in the *Brahmasūtras* as everything is Brahman. On the other hand, if performed without this knowledge, one only gets to heaven. However, in both the cases, he brings in the grace of God and disrupts the mechanical relation between the Vedic *yajña* and its results propounded in the *Mīmāṁsā* or the immediate, spontaneous attainment of liberation on the realization of the meaning of the *mahāvākyas* as is maintained by the Advaitins. He also tries to reconcile *karma, jñāna* and *bhakti* by equating the Brahman with Īśvara and Īśvara with the Kṛṣṇa of the *Bhagvadgītā* and the *Śrīmad Bhāgvat,* forgetting that the *karma* which

Kṛṣṇa is asking Arjuna to engage in is not the performance of a Vedic *yajña* but that of a righteous battle for the sake of maintaining *dharma* in which one has to kill one's near and dear ones. It is strange to find that even in the sixteenth century the problem of reconciling the *Pūrva* and the *Uttara Mīmāṁsā* continues to haunt the orthodox Indian mind and that a person of the stature of Vallabhācārya felt the necessity for writing a fresh commentary not only on the *Brahmasūtras* but also on the *Mīmāṁsāsūtras* while questioning, at important points, Śabara's interpretation of the later *Sūtras*, just as he had questioned Śaṁkara's interpretation of the *Brahmasūtras.*

In the *Patrāvalambana* by Sri Shyam Manohar Gosvami the following topics are discussed:

1. The doctrine of Brahman.
2. The creation of the world according to the doctrine of Brahman.
3. The relation of the world of form and action with the world of names.
4. A comparison between the experience generated by words and the one generated by perception.
5. That the doctrine of Brahman is the same as the identity relation between word and its meaning and a sentence and its meaning.
6. The Veda as being equivalent to sentences which are both *sādhya* and *siddha,* while God is the essential meaning of those sentences.
7. The *Pūrvakāṇḍa* determines or tells what is to be attained (*sādhya*) while the *Uttarakāṇḍa* names that which is attained (*siddha*).
8. The conflict between two parts of the Mīmāṁsā and Vedānta is similar to the conflict between Rahu and Kabandha and the resolution of this conflict.
9. The unity of a *śāstra.*
10. The difference or non-difference or identity of Veda and Vedānta.
11. Injunctive meaning and Mīmāṁsā.
12. The meaning of injunctive sentences according to Vallabha Vedānta.
13. Actions differentiated on the basis of the fact as to whether they are performed in fulfillment of an injunction or for sheer joy or play or for their own sake.
14. Forms of teaching or learning.
15. Reflection and analysis of Śaṁkara's view-point.
16. The analysis of teaching, learning and knowing according to Vallabhācārya.
17. A comparative study of the attempts at a unified interpretation of the whole Vedic corpus.
18. A summary of the doctrines of the Vallabha Vedānta.
19. A comparative analysis of the different schools of Vedānta.
20. The determination of the meaning of the *śruti* according to one's own reasoning faculty and doubts that one may raise regarding it versus the determination of the meaning of the *śruti* according to the sentences.

21. The problem of the validity of the *śruti* sentences and ordinary sentences.
22. The presentation of the four *puruṣārthas* in the *Pūrva* and the *Uttarakāṇḍa* of the Veda.

Shri Shyam Manohar Gosvami's extended discussion of various issues in the *Patrāvalambana* of Śrī Vallabhācārya focus attention upon the central concerns in the Vedāntic tradition of philosophising in India. The discussion relates to: one, the relation between Brahman and the world; two, to the problem of the interpretation of the Vedic sentences and the unity of meaning of the Vedic text itself, and three, to the relation between the concept of Brahman and the idea of a personal God or Īśvara. In the interpretation of the Vedic corpus, a divergence emerges between the *yajña*-centric interpretation of the *Mīmāṁsā* and the Brahman-centric interpretation of the *Brahmasūtras.* This creates the problem of the reconciliation between *karma* and *jñāna* or between the injunctive sentences of the Veda which enjoined one to perform sacrifices and those which asserted the unity of the self and everything else with the Brahman.

In his exegetics of Vallabha Vedānta, Shri Shyam Manohar Gosvami does not delink the hard core philosophical issues which arise in this connection from the specificity of the context in which those issues had arisen. The very first distinction between a Vedic sentence and a non-Vedic sentence is, from the linguistic point of view, untenable as all language *qua* language is one and hence the problem of meaning of word and sentences cannot in principle be divided into the meaning of words and sentences of the Veda, on the one hand, and the words and sentences of non-Vedic language, on the other. The attempt to derive the distinction from the fact that non-Vedic linguistic sentences are human productions and hence liable to be infected with falsity and other kinds of defects, while the Vedic sentences are intrinsically free from these as they are not the utterances of anybody, rests on the questionable assumption that the Vedic sentences have no source other than themselves. This obviously could not be the position of those who believe in a personal God or Īśvara as, according to them, the source of Vedic sentences must be God himself and hence their authority can be derived only from the fact that God is their author. However, then they cannot establish the reality of God or Brahman from the Vedic sentences themselves as this will not only involve the fallacy of circular reasoning but also make God dependent on the interpretation of the Vedic sentences themselves. This would also apply to those who deny Īśvara and believe in Brahman, for it is not quite clear as to what for them would be the relation between Brahman and the Vedic sentences on the grounds of which they believe in its reality. Moreover, in this entire discussion, the exact nature and content of the Vedic corpus is completely ignored and only generalised statements are made about this. To say that each *vākya* of the Veda and the totality of the Vedic sentences only refer to Īśvara who is identical with Hari or Kṛṣṇa, is as arbitrary as to say that it refers to Brahman or to *yajña.* One cannot avoid the introduction of the notion of *arthavāda* as Shri Shyam Manohar Gosvami seems to do, as one would have to take individual sentences and show how they refer to Śrī Hari or Brahman or an injunction to do *yajña*, as the case may be.

In fact, the strategy adopted by Bhartṛhari seems better, as he discards the distinction between ordinary and Vedic language and formulates the distinction between manifest and unmanifest language, the latter having three levels of its own called *madhyamā, paśyantī* and *parā*, the last being identical with unitary, undifferentiated reality called *śabda-Brahman*. In his discussion of action Vallabhācārya's identification of the Upaniṣadic Brahman with the Īśvara as the creator of the world and his further identification of this Īśvara with the Kṛṣṇa of the *Bhagvad Gītā* and the *Bhāgvat* had a long history in continuty with the other *ācāryas* of the Vedānta tradition. Though Śaṁkara himself had initiated such an enterprise by writing a commentary on the *Gītā* and composing beautiful hymns in praise of various Gods and Goddesses, he had resisted the temptation of identifying Brahman with Īśvara or Īśvara with Kṛṣṇa as the later *ācāryas* seem to have done. In fact, in Śaṁkara's strict philosophical formulations, Īśvara belonged to the realm of ignorance and *avidyā* while the idea of the world being a creation of God was a part of the general illusion. He also seems to have resisted the identification of Īśvara with Kṛṣṇa as he is supposed to have said in his commentary on the *Gītā* that Kṛṣṇa was a *māyika* creation of Īśvara himself. In any case, it appears that Śaṁkara as a philosopher was not overwhelmed by the emotions of devotion to a personal God, in an exclusive form as seems to have occurred later. This fact has to be viewed in the context of the eighth century when Islam was non-existent in India and the main antagonists were the Buddhists who themselves had developed the concept of *śūnya* which was beyond all rational description and determination. Yet, there must have been some compulsion for Śaṁkara to take the *Gītā* seriously and to give it an Advaitic interpretation which obviously did violence to it.

In the eleventh century when Yāmunācārya appeared in the south, the situation in the North had changed dramatically. Mahmud of Ghazni had attacked India repeatedly and won some decisive victories symbolically destroying the temple of Somnath. This perhaps resulted in the shifting of the intellectual activity from the North to the South. It is not quite clear whether Yāmunācārya wrote a commentary on the *Brahmasūtras* and whether he identified Brahman with Īśvara. But that he explicitly wanted to establish the authority of both the *Gītā* and the *Śrīmad Bhāgvat* as coordinate with that of the *Upaniṣad* and the Veda is clear, for he wrote his *Āgama Prāmāṇya* to establish just this point. However, whether he wanted to restrict the term "*āgama*" only to those two texts or whether he was using it in a wider sense to include the Jaina, Buddha and Tantra *āgamas* as well is not certain. In case the latter texts were included, the differences between these, if held as equally authoritative, would need to be reconciled. Moreover, when Yāmunācārya is not supposed to deny the authority of the *śruti* according to tradition, how would he have reconciled the differences between the *śruti* and all these āgamic traditions?

With the appearance of Rāmānuja in the twelfth century, the identification of Brahman not only with Īśvara but with Viṣṇu or Śrīhari seems to have been complete and the world itself was treated as his body. The path of real devotion to a personal God was thus philosophically founded in the orthodox Vedic tradition itself. But it is not quite clear whether the identification of Viṣṇu with Kṛṣṇa took place explicitly in the thought of Rāmānuja, even though the authority of the *Gītā* and the *Śrīmad Bhāgvat* seems to have been more firmly established with him. The reality of both the world and a personal God along with the identification of the latter with a well-known mythic personality of the *Purāṇas*, however, was slowly taking shape among the so-called Vedāntic *ācāryas* whose primary interest seems to have been to move away from the world inhabited by both the Vedic thinkers belonging to the *yajña* and the *jñāna* traditions and the one occupied by the *āgamic* tradition of the Buddhist and the Jainas. The latter had, obviously, no place for a personal God as a creator of the world and hence no question could arise of his identification with any mythic personality of the epics of the tradition, that is the *Rāmāyaṇa* and the *Mahābhārata*.

Madhva, in the fourteenth century carried the movement further by radically developing the notions of difference, thus granting an independent reality both of the world and the individual selves, even though both were seen as creations of a personal God, that is, Īśvara equated with Brahman. It is not clear how far he identified this personal God or Īśvara with Viṣṇu or with Kṛṣṇa as seems to have clearly been the case with Rāmānuja. These identifications are complete with Śrī Vallabhācārya at the end of the fifteenth and early sixteenth century, and the assertions of a personal God and his identity with Viṣṇu, on the one hand, and Kṛṣṇa, on the other, are carried to the extreme and the life in the world was completely vindicated if it was lived in the consciousness of and service to the Lord Himself.

The period from the eleventh to the sixteenth century is characterized by two factors which have to be taken into account in understanding this movement of philosophical thought in India. The first is the complete disappearance of the Buddhists as the antagonists with the destruction of Nālandā in the A.D. 120. The second is the gradual intrusion of the Muslims in different parts of India and the establishment of political control by them. This should be seen as a socio-political and cultural situation where the political power centre was in the hands of those who believed in a different religious tradition which had nothing to do with the tradition of India and which, in its ideological orientation, was completely hostile to the religious and cultural ethos of India as it had developed over two millennia of its history. At the same time, there was an intense assertion of a personal God who had created the world and who had sent his personal messenger to reveal the truth to mankind. The development of Indian theism from the eleventh century onwards, then, has to be seen in the political context of those times and the challenge that it had presented to thinkers of that period.

In fact Udayana, who stands at the transition from A.D. first millennium to the second millennium, is a classic example of a person who tried to combine these diverse trends in his personality. As Buddhism had not yet disappeared from the scene, his main antagonists were the Buddhists. He also argued against the Mīmāṁsā tradition, perhaps the most uncompromising example of philosophical thought in any tradition in its propounding the notion of an authoritative text independent of any God, personal or impersonal. He was also influenced by the Advaitic tradition of Śaṁkara and tried to reconcile the Nyāya position with regard to the self with the Advaitic notion as developed by Śaṁkara. The establishment of the reality of a personal God by Udayana indicated the direction of the developments, but there still did not exist any dominance of devotion in Udayana or the identification of this personal God with Viṣṇu or Kṛṣṇa as was to happen later.

It should not be forgotten that from the eighth century onwards is also a period of great temple building in India, culminating somewhere around the thirteenth century with the great temple complexes of South, East and Central India. The simultaneous development of the literature in regional languages from the eleventh century onwards and the dominance of the devotional tradition in it should therefore be seen as a reflection of the activity of the *ācāryas* in the Sanskritic tradition.

This is also the period when the South continued to be ruled by Hindu kingdoms for a substantially longer period of time than the North. Yet, gradually, Bijapur, Golkunda and Ahmadnagara came under Islamic rule, while the Hindu Vijaynagar empire in the deep South lasted till the latter half of the sixteenth century. However, the Vijaynagar Empire was surrounded by Islamic rulers on all sides and some of its intellectual activities may be understood only in this context. If, the *ācāryas* had turned to the *Brahmasūtras*, the *Gītā* and the *Śrīmad Bhāgvata,* Sāyaṇa Mādhava of the Vijaynagar Empire turned to the Vedas and wrote his famous commentaries on them during this period. The work of the Vijaynagar scholars is similar to the impulse that made Dayanand Saraswati go back to the Vedas and write his commentary on them. One could compare Sāyaṇa's introduction to the *Ṛgveda Bhāṣya* with Dayanand's, written four hundred years later when a new political power and a new religion had appeared on the scene. However, the impact of Islam appears only tangentially in the devotional literature in the regional languages where its uncompromising stand against idol worship or any form of representation of God seems to have had some influence on the development of the *Nirguṇa saṁpradāyas* which emphasised the worship of a formless god with no attributes whatsoever, the greatest representatives of whom were Kabir and Nanak. It is interesting, however, to learn that the impulse to worship something had become so strong in the Indian tradition that many of the sects worshipped the book or the sayings of the master rather than the image of God. Both in Sikkhism and in the followers of Dadu, it is the *Vānī* which is kept in the temple and worshipped and not the image of any God. Dadu went even further and adopted a practice from the Zorastrians who give up their dead bodies to be eaten by birds or animals so that at least they were of some use to someone.

Vallabhācārya's was perhaps the last attempt to take the claims of the *śruti* seriously and to try to reconcile not only *Pūrva* and the *Uttara Mīmāṁsā* but also, as we have said earlier, to equate Brahman with Īśvara and the latter with the Kṛṣṇa of the *Gītā* and the *Śrīmad Bhāgvat.* Caitanya, who appeared immediately after Vallabha, gave up the whole attempt and treated *bhakti* as an independent, autonomous enterprise, having no relation with *śruti* whether of the *Mīmāṁsā* or the *Brahmasūtra* tradition. Nor does he try to find an equation between Īśvara and Kṛṣṇa. He simply assumes it and considers Kṛṣṇa to be the real Īśvara. He did not write any book but created Vrindavan where nothing existed and indicated the places where Kṛṣṇa had performed his various *līlās.* Also, he distances the Kṛṣṇa of the *Mahābhārata* and the *Gītā* completely just as Jaideva had done in his *Gīta Govinda.* His immediate disciples, Rūpa Gosvāmī and Jīva Gosvāmī did not reveal even a trace of the tensions and arguments which had plagued the great *ācāryas* from Rāmānuja onwards. In his *Bhaktirasāmṛtasindhu,* Rūpa Gosvāmī explicitly states that there is no place for one who has no faith to enter the realm of *bhakti.* The standpoint taken by Jīva Gosvāmī in his work entitled, *Nīlamaṇidarpaṇa* is similar. It is quite clear, then, that by the middle of the sixteenth century, the tradition had radically changed and the philosophical concerns of the first half of the A.D. second millennium, particularly of the non-Advaitic *ācāryas,* had completely receded into the background.

The polemical debate between the Advaitins and the non-Advaitins had, of course, taken a new turn with Vyāsatīrtha II who was almost a contemporary of Caitanya and Rūpa Gosvāmī. In his *Nyāyāmṛta,* he took over all the concepts and arguments of the Advaitins from Śaṁkara onwards, formulated them topic wise and refuted them both on argumentative and scriptural grounds. Vyāsatīrtha hailed from Karnataka and his work seems to have created an immediate challenge for the Advaitin camp. This was met by Madhusūdana Sarasvatī from Bengal who belonged to the latter half of the sixteenth century. In his *Advaitasiddhi,* he tried to reformulate the crucial key concept of Advaita in such a way so as to escape the criticism of Vyāsatīrtha. The subsequent debate between the Advaitins and the non-Advaitins is of interest only to hard-core philosophers as *bhakti* needed no more defence from anyone, nor did the cult of Kṛṣṇa which had assumed an autonomous validity and reality in the Indian tradition, both at the Sanskritic and non-Sanskritic levels.

In this connection the role played by Jayadeva's *Gīta Govinda* is extremely interesting. In fact, the phenomenal success of Jayadeva's *Gīta Govinda* which is supposed to have been composed sometime at the end of the twelfth century suggests that Kṛṣṇa *bhakti* had already taken hold of the minds and hearts of people in large parts of India, even before Caitanya appeared on the scene. Perhaps this development occurred because the great *ācāryas* from Yāmuna to Rāmānuja onwards argued for it on sophisticated philosophical grounds and the Alvaras and the Nayanars had lived and practiced it for even a longer time. Perhaps the *ācāryas* were only formulating this cult in intellectual terms and arguing for what had already become a fact at the grass roots level. Even the

Advaitins could not escape its large scale influence. Thus, Madhusūdana Sarasvatī who chose, on intellectual grounds, to oppose the arguments of Vyāsatīrtha II in his *Advaitasiddhi,* ultimately became a *bhakta* and explicitly wrote that he did not know of any reality other than Kṛṣṇa (*Kṛṣṇāt paraṁ kimapi tattvamahaṁ na jāne*). The dichotomy between the intellectual and emotional, reason and the heart could not have been exemplified better than in the personality of this great philosopher who is supposed to have been first a Naiyāyika, then an Advaitin and then a devotee of Kṛṣṇa.

Madhusūdana Sarasvatī's example seems to confirm that the intellectual ratiocinative life of philosophy gradually assumed a relatively autonomous form, unrelated to the emotional or spiritual concerns of those very people who simultaneously engaged in both kinds of pursuits. This, of course, has happened in other cultures and civilisations as well, but the close relationship between spiritual pursuits and the intellectual life which is supposed to be such a characteristic feature of the philosophical enterprise in India, appears to be so completely disrupted so as to question the truth of this contention so often asserted by most writers on Indian philosophy.

However, the intimate association of almost all the Vedāntic schools of philosophy with the particular *saṁpradāyas* founded by their respective masters, resulted in a peculiar situation where philosophical speculation and controversy developed specifically within the context of these division between the *saṁpradāyas,* where each defended the position of his school against all the others, particularly if they happened to dispute or attack one's position. This tendency is confirmed even in the twentieth century, as for example when Vasudeva Shastri Abhyankara or Paṇḍit Anantkrishna Shastri defended the position of Advaita Vedānta against the non-Advaitins, the scholars belonging to those *saṁpradāyas* felt it was their specific responsibility to defend the position of their school.

However, philosophers like Professor Govind Chandra Pande are exceptions to this, as is evidenced by his first Badrinath Shukla Memorial Lecture at the Sampurnanand Sanskrit Vishvavidyalaya, Varanasi, entitled *Bhaktidarśana Vimarśaḥ.* Diverse issues relating to *bhakti* were examined in this lecture independently of any particular affiliation to one *sampradāya* or another.

Professor Pande highlights the difficulty of defining a term like *bhakti* where *lakṣya* and *lakṣaṇa* appear to show dialectical interdependence. Originally meaning 'sharing', 'serving', it came to mean 'attachment', 'belonging to', 'loyalty', 'devotion'; and further, 'self-surrender', 'resignation', 'communion', 'love'. As the consciousness aspiring for the Transcendent, *bhakti* is concomitantly characterised by its willingness to give up all egoistic and empirical attachments so as to receive the grace of the uplifting power of the Transcendent through which alone *bhakti* can realize itself.

The focus of *bhakti* is shifted from an intense emotional relationship with the Lord conceived in some form or another to the surrender of the self to some higher possibility of itself which may be called by the generic term *lokottara* or *puruṣottama* which also occurs in the tradition. However, as this surrender of the self to a higher potentiality of itself is a characteristic of the pursuit of all values, Professor Pande has to distinguish the pursuit of the value of *bhakti* from the pursuit of not only all other values but also from other forms of spiritual realization where man seeks the realization of some higher self without its taking the form which, at least until now, has been associated with the *bhakti* tradition in India and elsewhere. He seeks to highlight the role of *bhakti* as *śaraṇāgati* within the pursuit of spiritual values in general. According to him, *bhakti* is really the quest for the Transcendent through self-surrender and is as such the essential mark of all modes of spiritual life, whether belonging to "primitive" culture or to materially advanced civilisations; whether expressed in the feelings of love and compassion; or the heroism of the struggle of right against wrong; or in the tranquility of meditation; or in the dispassionate passion of the quest for truth.

But this is obviously too wide a definition as it would make *bhakti* co-terminus with the pursuit of any value whatsoever. Not only this, it would take away the specific emphasis on the development of the "feeling" mode of being and the different forms that it may take in relation to the ultimate reality where a possible "reciprocity" is the heart of the matter. Also, all "self-surrender" cannot be regarded as *bhakti*, except in a metaphorical sense, for the self-sacrifice of millions in the cause of the glorification of the national state or even in the service of a cause such as the establishment of a "liberal" or "classless" society can scarcely be regarded as "*bhakti*" in any specific sense of the term. Further, it may be difficult to treat "self-surrender" as the essence of even what has traditionally been accepted as paradigmatic forms of *bhakti* such as are typified in the well-known, five-fold possible relationships with the Lord. It will be difficult, for example, to treat "self-surrender" as the essence of the devotional mode of relationship which is known as friendship or as the *sakhābhāva*. Similarly, in *vātsalya*, the notion of self-surrender will be radically different as also in the case of "*mādhūrya*", unless this is taken totally in the traditional sense of what the ideal man-woman love relationships ought to be. Today, when the relationship is seen more in terms of "equality", the "self-surrender" will have to be mutual rather than one-sided as it has generally been traditionally conceived. The objection that this is too wide a definition as it would make *bhakti* co-terminus with the pursuit of any value whatsoever is answered by Professor Pande stating that as the end of *bhakti* is the relationship with the Transcendent, this distinguishes it from the pursuit of secular values. As for different religious and spiritual paths, all these initially require devotion as self-surrender, but the further expressions, interpretation, and formulations of *bhakti* reveal this as a divergent tradition with a multilinear dialectic—spiritual, cultural and conceptual *sādhana* and discourse of its own. He seeks to trace this dialectic of *bhakti* from its initial expression as the aspiring self-surrender of the empirical ego through dedicated work and illumination to its culmination in the ecstasy of love. He argues against the one-sidedness of those who absolutize the distinctions of *karma, jñāna* and *bhakti* as also of the spiritualities of different religions and paths. This argument is elaborated in his more recent publication entitled *Ekaṁ sad viprā bahudhā vadanti** where he examines the different approaches current in the *History of religion* and seeks to correlate religious attitudes to spiritual experiences of different levels.

Professor Pande appears to make a radical distinction between what he calls *āgama, śāstra* and *darśana. Āgama* is a record of spiritual experiences by human beings, while the *śāstra* attempts a theological interpretation of the same and *darśana*, a free ratiocinative reflection on it. Interestingly, for him all of these are human enterprises. Pande's work is based on the Advaitic postulate of the unity of spiritual experience graded into many levels and culturally diversified (*upādhibheda* and *adhikārabheda*). At the *āgamic* level, the articulation of the spiritual experience is called, following Shelley, a "multi-coloured dome".

Professor Pande examines the role of emotion and imagination as having an important constitutive place in *bhakti* and suggests that the search for reality should start not by dogmatically accepting the reality of the perceptual world but rather, to apprehend "the questionable reality of the world and to move from it to the ultimate nature of reality". Similarly, he argues that

> "the obvious role of imagination and emotion in *bhakti* is not a reason for devaluing *bhakti* but for revaluing imagination and emotion by discovering the true nature as a possible means towards the revelation of subjective or spiritual truth".

In fact, if there were no feelings and emotions the world would not be the same. *Bhakti* then may be seen as assigning feelings and emotions their rightful place for the cognition of what is ultimately real and to establish a meaningful living relationship with it.

The sequencing of Professor Pande's thought regarding *bhakti* seems to have an inner tension with an attempt at resolution that may be summarised as follows. He begins by defining *bhakti* as self-surrender to the Transcendent in consciousness itself. After he finds that this definition is what may be called *ativyāpta*, he makes a distinction between the secular and spiritual Transcendents placing *bhakti* in the latter. This however appears to give no role to feelings which in the *bhakti* tradition, as we know it today, are central to this specific spiritual path. Next he seems to integrate emotion into *bhakti* and also adds imagination in his final formulation. He says that there can be no human life or life of consciousness without emotion and imagination and that thus these are bound to have a cognitive role in any human understanding of reality. *Bhakti* is unimaginable without them. Thus, through these different stages of arguments Pandeji's thought tries to grasp the specificity of *bhakti* comprehending the life of feelings as integral to it. However, what is the distinction between emotions and imagination and what are their relations has not been outlined by Pandeji. Further, what is the specific role of emotion and imagination in *bhakti* for if they are common to

---

*Sanskrit University, Varanasi, as the Griffith Memorial Lectures, 1970.

all human understanding what is it that makes them *Vyāvartaka* in *bhakti* is a question that remains.

Professor Pande argues for a coordinate co-relationship between the object and the subject in man's search for the ideal which may be oriented towards the realization of any value whatsoever. For him, the realization of any value is, simultaneously, the realization of an ideal self also and hence all values ultimately are only different forms through which the self realises itself and which therefore may themselves be considered as forming the ideal of that higher self which man wants to realize. This, according to him, is the essence of *bhakti*:

> "Value thus may be defined as self-realization where the ideal 'self' of man is the higher or universal self of the seeker. Its highest grade would be the communion of the individual with the universal self, which is *bhakti*. *Bhakti*, thus, would be the ultimate value to which all other values seek to approximate".[3]

But unfortunately, in the realisation of this best of all possible worlds what is forgotten is that there are not only deeper, inner conflicts between values but that the realisation of some values not only stand in the way of other values being realised but also impede the realization of the self. The cultivation of logical and analytical rigour many a time hampers the development of emotional sensitivity and the conflict between active and contemplative values is well known in all traditions. The realms of polity and economy have always posed a challenge to the pursuit not only of spiritual values but also to those of the cognitive and artistic life. Ultimately, the realm of values is neither as coherent nor as harmonious as presented, nor is their relationship to the value of self-realization so simple.

Ultimately, Professor Pande's discussion leads him to the denial of some well-known oppositions including *dharma* and *mokṣa* and *pravṛtti* and *nivṛtti*. This follows the classical conception of *dharma* as in the *Gītā* or the *Bhāgavat* or the *Manu smṛti* which outline such a synthesis. It should not be forgotten that regarding this a long debate existed in the Indian tradition and also that both the Buḍḍha and the Mahāvīra renounced the world in order to seek the ultimate truth.

An interesting distinction between *rasa* and *bhava* is made by Professor Pande and he suggests that while the latter may be indefinitely many, the former is a unitary whole expressed through them. He also suggests that the uniqueness of the self lies in the fact that it is grasped through feeling, though this feeling may not be adequate to the nature of the self, just as knowledge may not be adequate to the nature of the object. Also, the communication of feeling is generally through an image or, better still, through an act of imaginative apprehension just as the communication of knowledge is through a concept and the image through which the feeling is communicated may not be adequate and thus fail in its purpose. This is an interesting idea, but here again, Professor Pande's treatment of the aesthetic domain is opposed to the view that feelings have to be adequate, not to the subject experiencing them, but to the object that is to be aesthetically appreciated. His views regarding this have been elaborated elsewhere.*

This analysis of *bhakti*, thus, seems to be thoroughly influenced by the neo-Vedāntic formulations so popular since the latter part of the nineteenth century which totally exclude classical discussions of the subject as given in the standard texts. Also, he does not seem to take into account the radical rethinking on the subject found in the thought of K.C. Bhattacharya who formulated the notion of "alternative absolutes" and the further development of that idea by Kalidas Bhattacharya in his thought on the subject.

Paṇḍit Ramavtar Sarma

One of the most radical departures from the traditional philosophical thought of India was made by Paṇḍit Ramavatar Sarma, a Sanskritic scholar, trained and steeped in the tradition in the early years of the twentieth century in his work entitled *Paramārtha Darśana.* The work was published around A.D. 1913 and the author himself wrote a commentary on it as had been the tradition in earlier Sanskrit philosophic writing. The work does not exactly belong to any particular school of traditional Indian philosophy though it shows an awareness of most of the major systems of philosophical thought in India and, in fact, criticises them as he propounds his own views on the subject.

The Vaiśeṣika system, for example, is subjected to a detailed critique in the sixth chapter of his work where the categories proposed by the Vaiśeṣika thinkers are shown to be untenable. The author certainly shows the influence of Vedānta, particularly in its notion of the witness consciousness or *sākṣī caitanya* which underlies and accompanies all changing states of consciousness and hence is the only constant factor among all that varies in experience. Yet, the conclusion that the author draws from this is different from the one that most of the Advaitic thinkers have drawn as he distinctly denies the reality of any substantive self or *ātman* on the basis of this. Instead, he treats it as pointing to an impersonal consciousness lying at the basis of all reality, a statement which is reminiscent of the reality of the impersonal Brahman in Advaitic thought. But as against the Advaitin, he denies the transcendent character of this impersonal consciousness and treats it as completely immanent in the universe. The immanence thus seems to give a reality to everything which again seems to be in line with the general assertion of the reality of the world in all streams of Indian thought which occur after the British impact at the beginning of nineteenth century. But, though Paṇḍit Ramavatar Sarma's thought suggests that he is rehabilitating the Upaniṣadic statements which asserted that 'All this is Brahman' (*sarvaṁ khalvidam Brahman*),

**Saundarya-darśanavimarśaḥ* (Varanasi Sanskrit University).

yet he departs from the tradition in that he rejects rebirth and the law of *karma* along with the ideal of *mokṣa* which had been accepted by almost all the traditions of Indian thought except the Cāravāka. Not only this, he also rejects the idea of both *śruti* and *āgama* which were the corner-stones of all Indian thinking except again for the Cārvāka. He accepts the notion of *śabda pramāṇa*, but interprets it to mean the advice of a person who is both trustworthy and benevolent in disposition and rational in his outlook. This is practically the same definition as given by Gautama of an *āpta* person in the *Nyāyasūtras.* It may be noted here that the validity of any statements by such a person is confined, as in Mīmāṁsā and Nyāya, to prescriptive statements only. It does not extend to statements that give information as their validity has to be established either by perception or inference or both. Ramavatar Sarma, however, does not discuss what one should do when the prescriptive statements emanating from the so-called *āpta* persons conflict with each other or how to identify who is an *āpta* person, particularly when one does not happen to be one oneself. He also does not seem to have discussed the notion of *ātma-tuṣṭi* in the context of the knowledge of *dharma* as mentioned by Manu and its relation to other sources of the knowledge of *dharma.*

Though Ramavatar Sarma seems to be radically different in his rejection of almost all the basic contentions of both the Vedic and the non-Vedic traditions in the country, he yet seems to be deeply influenced by the Advaitic idea of a universal, impersonal consciousness pervading all reality and thus finding the root cause of all evil in the foundational ignorance caused by the biological fact of one's having a body which makes one inevitably feel not only distinct but different from all others. It is in the rectification of this foundational ignorance that one's liberation may be said to occur. Yet, one should remember that such a liberation has to be achieved in this very life, as he does not accept the idea of liberation after death.

N.V. Banerjee like Ramavatar Sarma denies most of traditional concepts and, like him, finds the root cause of ignorance in the idea of separation which the biological condition of man inevitably imposes on his self-consciousness. However, unlike him, he presents some principles to guide life after an awareness occurs of the foundational ignorance in which self-consciousness is enveloped. The remarkable novelty of Banerjee's principles and his essential difference in this respect from Ramavatar Sarma lies in his acceptance of the fact of suffering and of death which no other thinker, has yet argued for in the Indian tradition. The invitation to "bear the cross" and to beware of the desire for immortality in any form whatsoever are the two radically innovative prescriptions for the guidance of man in his this-worldly life, given by Banerjee, which seems to have no parallel in the thought of Ramavatar Sarma. But, while Ramavatar Sarma's thinking shows radical departures from the field of Advaitic thought which somehow has not evoked the interest either of the Advaitin or the non-Advaitin until now, the work of Nischaladasa has evoked great interest. He wrote an Advaitic work in Hindi that was considered of such great merit that it was translated into Sanskrit arousing interest amongst scholars for both its exposition of the Advaita point of view and the innovations that he makes in its presentation. Normally, a philosophical work in a language other than Sanskrit is seldom paid much attention to by scholars who still continue to be mainly Sanskrit-oriented. Nischaladasa, however, appears to have been an exception. He gives an interesting definition of perception in a sense that totally disengaged the notion of perceptual knowledge from that of the senses with which it is invariably associated. He has probably done so for two reasons: to emphasize the direct immediacy of apprehension which seems to be such a characteristic of consciousness and of all the knowledge that it has. Secondly, he argues that if senses are considered to be essential for the definition of perceptual knowledge, then one cannot be said to have any 'perception' of pain which, perhaps is the most palpable piece of knowledge that one has. In fact, the whole field of introspective awareness becomes excluded from perceptual knowledge if one confines it to the five bodily senses alone, unless one postulates an internal sense organ as some seem to have done. In fact, he suggests that the usual inclusion of perception among the *pramāṇas* is not correct, as *pratyakṣa* or immediate apprehension by consciousness does not require validation by any *pramāṇa* whatsoever. This, according to him, is because of the almost total identity between consciousness and what it apprehends. Such an approach to perceptual knowledge opens the way to the ultimate Advaitic truth which asserts the complete identity of consciousness with whatever it apprehends and treats the apprehended 'difference' as a result of a misunderstanding of the knowledge involved in perception due to the fact that we mistakenly confine it to sense perception alone. The identity in most direct, immediate apprehension which occurs at all levels of experience is, however, limited by the fact that both the 'consciousness' that apprehends and the 'object' that is apprehended are themselves conditioned or delimited by a *vṛtti* or specific formation that does not allow the identity to be absolutely complete. Remove the *vṛttis* and you get the absolute identity which the Advaitin talks about. The two *vṛttis* by which the consciousness and the object are limited in this immediate, direct apprehension have been named as "*vṛttyāvacchinna caitanya*" and "*viṣayāvacchinna caitanya*", respectively by Nischaladasa. What is special in this formulation is that the object is also supposed by Nischaladasa to be essentially of the nature of consciousness as he holds that 'consciousness' cannot relate to anything which is completely alien to itself. However, neither the diversity of the *vṛttis* which delimit consciousness nor the diversity of the *viṣayas* which delimit the object seems to have been explained in detail by Nischaladasa. Nor does he seem to have squarely faced the problem of the 'veridicality' of such knowledge as many of the *vṛttis* which delimit consciousness and cloud and distort it sometimes, stand in the way of the correct apprehension of the specific *viṣayatva* of the *viṣaya* which is apprehended. Not only this, as the psychic formations themselves become 'objects' to consciousness, the distinction between the *vṛtti* and the *viṣaya* would, at least in their case, become relative. The problem has been specifically formulated in Śāṁkhya which treats even the *buddhi* and the sense of 'I-ness' as 'object' to consciousness.

Similarly, many of the so-called 'objects' are themselves delimited by psychic factors akin to those which are supposed to delimit the apprehending consciousness. Other human beings are the classic instance of such objects and it is not easy to treat them only as 'objects' as one's apprehending consciousness itself is an 'object' to them. Perhaps, Nischaladasa has examined these issues in detail in his work entitled *Vṛtti-prabhākara* which is said to have been written on Vidyāraṇya's *Pañcadaśī.*

The work of Nischaladasa also seems to show an obsessive concern with a dimension of classical Vedānta which has been underplayed in most of the modern writings on Vedānta. This relates to the two dogmas which all the *ācāryas* in the Vedānta tradition were specially anxious to uphold. The first concerns the contention that the truths of Vedānta can only be available through the *Upaniṣads* and the *Brahmasūtras,* while the second concerns the interpretation of the so-called *Mahāvākyas,* the 'understanding' of which alone reveals the Vedāntic truth directly and immediately to the one who understands them. In fact, Anantakrishna Shastri in his polemical controversy with the contentions of Jayatīrtha in enumerating the common points of acceptance between the Advaitic and non-Advaitic Vedāntins, examines only these issues to a large extent. Nischaladasa also discusses in detail how the *Mahāvākyas* are to be interpreted and suggests that, in their case, one would have to postulate a special kind of *lakṣaṇa* which is called the *bhagatyāga* or the *jahadājahad lakṣaṇa.*

However, it is not clear that such a *lakṣaṇa* applies only to the *Mahāvākyas* and to nothing else which is linguistically formulated either actually or possibly. In case there is, it is a purely *ad hoc* solution to save the Advaitic interpretation. On the other hand, if this kind of *lakṣaṇa* is found in those linguistic occurrences which are not considered to be *Mahāvākyas,* then the Advaitic relation of identity will be found not only between the self and the Brahman but amongst other things also. It is not clear whether Nischaladasa or any other Advaitin has taken note of this objection and dealt with it. In any case, Nischaladasa's work provides evidence of the vitality of the Advaitic tradition in philosophical thought in India and needs to be examined further.[4]

Interestingly, the debate between the Advaitin and the non-Advaitin seems to show the signs of lessening, as our attention has been drawn to a recent work entitled *Madhva Kudūṣaṇapeṣṇam.* The work is written by Bommkanti Sitaramshastri and published by Pt. Gauda Subramaniam Shastri.

II
THE ADVAITA VS. NON-ADVAITA
ANANTAKRISHNA SHASTRI'S REPLY TO VEDĀNTA DEŚIKA

Within Indian philosophy the task of identifying the contribution to the advancement of knowledge of an author or a group of authors, belonging to a particular historic period, poses some difficulties. Certain peculiarities of Indian philosophy make this evaluation difficult.

First, most books written on Indian philosophy are in the form of commentaries on the original texts and commentators comment not only on the texts but also to show their ingeniousness so that all that they discuss is apperently told in the original text itself. The method of commenting, consisting of an *avatārikā*, a word-to-word explanation and an exposition, enables them to depict the new ideas also as existing in the text itself.

The development of thought moreover seems to possess a backward motion, as every author of a commentary or an independent text strives hard to establish that everything he discussed is indeed, reflected in the *bhāṣya* or some other source book (*ākāragranthas*). Often a theory or a concept after being developed well by an author is simply put aside or dropped if it is found contradicting the *bhāṣya* or other *ākāragranthas*. Sometimes, such a theory is discarded simply on account of its being not mentioned in those books (*sūtra-bhāṣyādi-viruddhatvāt/ anuktatvāt*). The reader of the original text in Indian philosophy gathers an impression that the *sūtra, bhāṣya* and one or two other *ākāragranthas* constitute everything in that system.

Second, the origin of Indian philosophical systems is also very peculiar. Most of the systems have originated with the writing of the *sūtras*. We see in the case of the sciences and other subjects that are in the developing stage, that a *sūtra* or equation of some such thing happens, always, to be the culmination of research of an individual or a line of generations of individuals. The same should hold good with regard to the *sūtra* of the schools of Indian philosophies too. Seen from this point of view, the concerned *sūtras* of every system in Indian philosophy should not be held at the point of origination of the system, but, on the other hand, should be held at the culmination of the thought-process in that particular system. This fact is further substantiated by the references made by the writers of *sūtras* to their predecessors. Therefore, whatever be the philosophy of any system which is recorded in the *sūtras* of that particular system, it was speculated, discussed, examined and finalised before the *sūtras* were written. The main purpose of writing the *sūtras* was to pass on the conclusions to the posterity through the oral tradition, as there was no other way to record or transmit the same. We do not see any other explanation for the significance of the *sūtra* literature, as in any other branch of knowledge anywhere in the world, *sūtra*-like-literature is not seen to be the point of origination of a system of thought. Therefore, the job of the *bhāṣyakāras* and the writers thereafter, was to recall and retell the philosophy through the medium of *sūtra*-literature on the strength of the oral tradition which was alive until very recent times. This can be the lone explanation to solve the problem of experience of "backward motion" in the development of Indian philosophical thought.

Third, the *Vedānta* is mainly in the form of interpretation and explanation of the *śruti* texts. This fact has had the effect of being a limitation to the intellectual exercise of the thinkers.

Fourth, the Vedāntic literature down the line of *bhāṣyakāras*, is more interpretative and explanatory in its character than an independent and speculative exercise.

In the western system of philosophy by contrast we find almost every thinker rebelled against or significantly modified the thought of his predecessor. Indeed, on this account western philosophy has developed as a thinker-based philosophy, where the thinkers play a greater role than the school of thought they uphold. Whereas in Indian philosophy, the role played by the individual thinkers is insignificant with regard to the role played by the school of thought they uphold.

'Turning our attention towards the Advaita Vedāntic literature of the last two centuries, we can divide it into three to four groups: (1) polemical works; (2) commentaries on important original works mainly intended to elucidate the concepts and theories in a simple way of writing; (3) introductory works; (4) critical expositions.

1. Polemical Works

With regard to the polemics of Advaita, in the last four to five centuries, the celebrated critic of Advaita, namely, Śrī Vyāsatīrtha deserves to be mentioned foremost of all others. His magnum opus, the *Nyāyāmṛta*, set the ball of criticism in motion and this has continued till today. In this regard the works written are as follows:

Nyāyāmṛta by Vyāsatīrtha—critique of Advaita.
Advaitasiddhi by Madhusūdana Sarasvati—critique of the *Nyāyāmṛta*.
Taraṅgiṇī by Rāmatīrtha—critique of the *Advaitasiddhi*.
Laghucandrikā and *Gurucandrikā* by Gauḍa Brahmānanda—critique of *Taraṅgiṇī* Sārasvatī.
Nyāyāmṛtasaugandhya by Vanamālimiśra—critique of the *Laghucandrikā*.
Advaitasiddhānta Vaijayantī by Bhaṭṭa Trayambaka Śāstrī—critique of the *Saugandhya*.
Saugandhyavimarśaḥ by Anantakrishna Shastri—critique of *Saugandhya*.
(Both *Saugandhya* and its criticisms are found incomplete).
Nyāyabhāskara by Anantācārya—critique of *Laghucandrikā* and its commentary the *Viṭṭhaleśīya*.

Four books were written by the Advaitins to counter the criticism made by Anantācārya.

Nyāyenduśekhara I by Kuṇigal Lakṣmīnṛsimha Śāstri
Nyāyenduśekhara II by Mahāmahopādhyāya Tyāgarājā-dhvarin.
Nyāyendusekharapariśiṣṭam by M.M. Harihara Śāstrī.
Nyāyabhāskarakhaṇḍanam by Ramasubrahmanya Śhastry.
Brahmānandīyabhāvaprakāśaḥ by M.M. Panchapangesha Shastry.

There is yet another line of polemical works in the Advaita Vedānta. Vedānta Deśika, the writer of Viśiṣṭādvaita, has written a polemical work by name *Śatadūṣaṇī*. Śrī Anantakrishna Shastry in his *Śatabhūṣaṇī* has offered his criticism and clarifications with regard to the charges of Śrī Vedānta Deśika.

2. Commentaries

Coming to the second variety of works, namely, lucid expository commentaries on well-known classical works, the contribution of these lies mainly in their clarity and the facility and ease they provide in an understanding of the difficult classical works. They are explanatory in nature and no serious effort is usually made in these works for the advancement of thought. They are very useful to those scholars who want to understand the original. Clarity of thought is their main contribution.

Under this category, is the lucid, and explanatory commentary on the *Advaitasiddhi*, namely, the *Bālabodhinī* written by Sri Yogendranath Bagchi which is most useful to the students of Advaita Vedānta in understanding the thought of Madhusūdana Sarasvatī. It is free from the Nyāya style and is very simple. The other celebrated commentaries, namely, *Laghucandrikā* and *Viṭṭhaleśīya*, etc. are meant only for those scholars who are Naiyāyikas rather than Advaitins. Similarly, the commentaries, *Prakāśa* and *Vikāsa* on the *Bhāmatī* by Shree Lakshminath Jha deserve special mention as they contribute significantly in understanding the *Bhāṣya* and *Bhāmatī*. The author takes care to discuss the subjects which have a direct bearing on the text in the *Prakāśa*, leaving any further elaboration on the same subject to the *Vikāsa*. This helps the reader in a significant way.

The commentary of Sri Vasudeva Abhyankar Shastry on the *Siddhāntabindu* of Śrī Madhusūdana Sarasvatī is yet another masterpiece in this category. Sri Shastry is known for his simplicity and clarity in writing. Again, this commentary helps to understand the original more than the commentary written on it by Śrī Gauḍā Brahmānanda. Sri Bellamkonda Ramaraya kavi wrote a commentary on the *Gitābhāṣya* of Śrī Śaṅkara. It is one of the major works of Sri Ramaraya kavi. On several points critical expositions are made upholding the position of the Advaitins. His style is admirably lucid and free from the Naiyāyika's jargon. I understand that there is a commentary on the *Siddhāntaleśasaṅgraha* of Appayya Dīkṣita written by a Bengali scholar. Udasina Swami Amaradasa has made an elaborate commentary on the *Śikhāmaṇi* of Ramakrishnadhwarin, the celebrated son of Sri Dharmarajadhwarin, the writer of the *Vedāntaparibhāṣā*.

3. Introductory Works

With regard to the third category of works, namely, the introductory works, these are called *prakaraṇa granthas* and these are written in large numbers throughout the history of any school of philosophy. The main purpose of these works is to introduce the student to the thought of the particular school, their method being to record the conclusions arrived at by their predecessors after long discussions. To cite a classic work belonging to this category, the *Tarkasaṁgraha* of Annaṁbhaṭṭa summarises the entire thought of *Nyāya-vaiśeṣika* into a few pages in an admirable way. Its utility in remembering and mastering the position of the Nyāya-vaiśeṣika system is well known. A thorough knowledge of such texts only can enable one to undertake a strenuous journey into the jungles of the *Bhāṣyas* and their commentaries.

With regard to the Advaita Vedānta, the paucity of work on the lines of the *Tarkasaṁgraha* is often felt. The *Vedāntaparibhāṣā* is too tough for a beginner especially with regard to its chapters dealing with the problems of epistemology. The *Vedāntasāra* is good but incomplete regarding most of the aspects of the Advaita Vedānta as is the case with the *Laghuvāsudevamananam*. Seen against this background, Sri Bellamkonda Ramaraya kavi's excellent work, *Vedāntasaṁgraha* can be praised for being just on the lines of the *Tarkasaṁgraha*. Divided into fifteen chapter it runs into only forty pages and covers all the areas of the Advaita Vedānta. More attention is paid to the ontological and metaphysical aspect of the Advaita Vedānta. He shows several ontological divisions. Indeed, he starts his work with a sentence, classifying the entire universe into two categories, namely, *dṛk* and *dṛśya*. The significance of this small work is that in the form of short statements he clarifies the position of the Advaitins *vis-à-vis* other schools. For example, Swami Nischaladasa of the *udāsīna saṁpradāya* wrote his *Vicārasāgara* in Hindi, in which he discussed all the concepts of the Advaita Vedānta in a detailed manner, using very simple language. This work has been translated into Sanskrit by Sri Vasudeva Brahmendra Saraswati. Written in a very simple Sanskrit this book throws light on several problems of the Advaita Vedānta.

The commentary by M.M. Vasudeva Shastri Abhyankar in the *Siddhāntabindu* is yet another masterpiece. It is very lucid and discusses several fundamental aspects of the Advaita Vedānta.

4. *Critical Expositions*

With regard to the fourth category of works, there are good number of books written as critical expositions of the Advaita Vedānta. Sri Bachcha Jha has written the *Gūḍhārtha Tattvāloka*, which according to him, is a commentary on Madhusūdana Sarasvatī's commentary on the *Bhagavdgītā*. We purposefully omitted this work under the list of commentaries because this work can be considered as an independent one. Sri Bachcha Jha has defended the position of the Advaitins against all others on most of the topics where they differ mutually. This book is very valuable for Advaitins because it is an attestation given by a great *dārśanika* of recent times.

M.M. Anantakrishna Shastry is an illustrious writer who wrote several polemical as well as expository works on the Advaita Vedānta, mainly, to answer the criticism against this school made by the Dvaitins and the Viśiṣṭādvaitins. We have already made a reference to his major work, namely, *Śatabhūṣaṇi*. His *Advaitatattvasudhā* is an illustrious work worth mentioning here. Apart from these, two major works, several of the lengthy introductions to the works he edited also throw light on the concepts of Advaita. Further, they are useful to resolve the contentions of the Dvaitins and the Viśiṣṭādvaitins.

M.M. Gauda Subrahmanya Shastri made an excellent attempt to show the *anumāna prayoga* of each *adhikaraṇa* of the *Śaṅkarabhāṣya*, in his *Brahmasūtrabhāṣya-pradīpikā*. This is similar to the attempt made by Pujyashri Satyapramodatirtha Swamin, in his work, *Brahma-sūtrādhikaraṇa Sasrirasaṁgrahaḥ*.

Another Advaita writer who deserves to be mentioned here is Sri Sachchidanandendra Saraswati Swamin of Holenarasipur who has written several works. His magnum opus is the *Vedānta-prakriyā-pratyabhijñā*. From a preliminary reading of his works it appears that he wants to establish that the main and lengthy succession of the *vivaraṇa* school of interpretation of Śrī Śaṁkara has misrepresented him. He also raised the controversy that *mūlāvidyā* is not acceptable for both the *Bhāṣyakāra* Śrī Śaṁkara and *vārttikakāra*. His works are interesting and significant, on account of being a critical standpoint from within the camp. Apparently, he could not establish his ideas well because very few people among Advaitins took him seriously.

Advaitāmoda by M.M. Vasudeva Shastri is yet another important work belonging to this category.

Śatabhūṣaṇī of M.M. Anantakrishna Shastri's is a reply to Vedānta Deśika

Śatabhūṣaṇī is a polemical work pertaining to the Advaita Vedānta. It mainly intendeds to provide answers to the numerous criticisms made by Śrī Vedānta Deśika, the fourteenth century illustrious and prolific writer held in high esteem. While, Śrī Deśika raised a total of sixty six objections against various aspects of Advaita and titled his work as *Śatadūṣaṇī*, Shri Shastri considered the sixty sixth objection as, indeed, all-comprehensive in its nature, as it tries to establish that the *Brahmasūtras* are not in favour of an Advaitic interpretation of the *Upaniṣads* (*paramate sūtrasārasya-bhaṅgavāda*). He groups the rest of sixty five objections under nine heads, namely, the objections related to: A. *avidyā*, B. the falsity of the world, C. and D. the meaning of the word *atha* in the first *sūtra*, namely *athāto brahmajijñāsā* as it is explained in the two systems, E. the analysis of the meaning of the word *tvam*, F. the analysis of the meaning of the word *tat*, G. the sentential meaning of the *mahāvākya*, namely, *tat tvam asi*, H. the concept of *jīvanamukti*, and I. the concept of *niṣprapañcīkaraṇa* of Bhartṛprapañca and the theory of *alepakamata* of Nirañjana Sanyāsin. This attempt to group these objections which are found scattered in the *Śatadūṣaṇī* text on the basis of a theme speaks well of Shri Shastri's scholarship and clarity of thought.

The following list of topics is discussed under each group. The numbers within bracket indicate the number of objections according to the *Śatadūṣaṇī.*

A. Under *Avidyā* the following seven topics are discussed:
  1. Brahman as the locus of *avidyā* (29)
  2. Brahman as subject to concealment by *avidyā* (34)
  3. That *avidyā* is a positive entity i.e:, not-*abhāva* (39)
  4. *Jīva* as the locus of *avidyā* (40)
  5. The nature of *avidyā* (41)
  6. The remover of *avidyā* (43)
  7. The removal of *avidyā* (44)

B. Under the subject of the falsity of the world, the following are considered:
  1. The impossibility of discussion if the world is false (9)
  2. Criticisms of the concept of difference (13)
  3. Falsity of the world and inference (14)
  4. The establishment of falsity of objects on account of their mutual distinctness (16)
  5. That relation between *dṛk* and *dṛśya* is possible only on the basis of falsity of the world (17)
  6. Whether the false can arise from the true (30)
  7. Whether coordination can arise on the basis of super-imposition (32)
  8. The distinction between *māyā* and *avidyā* (31)
  9. That *jñāna* is the aspect of the world is illusory (47)
  10. That Brahman can be the *upādāna kāraṇa* only on the basis of the falsity of the world (53)
  11. That *māyā* too can be *upādāna kāraṇa* only on the same basis (54)
  12. That all effects are only appearances (55)
  13. That *vivartavāda* alone can explain the *sadasad-vilakṣaṇatva* of the *prapañca* (60)

C. The next group relates to the meaning of *atha,* and discusses the question whether *Brahmavicāra* comes only after *karmavicāra* or after *sādhanacatuṣṭaya sampatti:*
  1. Whether *Pūrva* and *Uttaramīmāṁsās* constitute one whole or not (3)
  2. Whether knowledge is *upāsanā* or intuition (4)
  3. Whether *karma* is meant to desire for knowledge (*vividiśā*). (6)
  4. The possibility of desire for release on the basis of Advaita (63)

D. Next are grouped the following:
  1. The possibility of *sādhanacatuṣṭaya* preceding *śāstravicāra* (8)
  2. The possibility of qualification of *Śāstravicāra* (49)
  3. That the unqualified Brahman cannot be *nitya.*
  4. The *śāstric* character of *saṁnyāsa* according to Advaita.

E. The discussion of *tvaṁ padārtha* relates to the following topics :
1. The knowability of the *ātman* (20)
2. The contention that the *cidrūpa* of *ātman* is subject to origination (21)
3. The criticism of the inference relating to the *nānātva* of the *ātman* (23)
4. The criticism of the Advaitic view that *ātman* is *cidrūpa* (25)
5. The contention that the ego and the *ātman* are one (26)
6. The criticism of the Advaitic view that *jñatṛtva* is super-imposed on the *ātman* (27)
7. The criticism of the witness-consciousness (28)
8. The criticism of the unity of *ātman* (33)
9. The criticism that in *mukti* the *ātman* is not *nirviṣaya* (52)
10. The criticism of the unity of *Jīva* (61)

F. The following criticisms relate to *Tat-padārtha*:
1. That Brahman cannot be subject of expression (1)
2. That there cannot be inquiry into Brahman (2)
3. That what is *nirviśeṣa* cannot be self-effulgent (10)
4. That the qualityless Brahman cannot be the object of indeterminate knowledge (11)
5. That the *Sat* alone is not the cause of valid knowledge (12)
6. That on the basis of Advaita, the Vedas will loose their validity (14)
7. That differentiated knowledge of external objects is impossible (18)
8. That the *cit* cannot be inferred (24)
9. That qualitylessness cannot be inferred (24)
10. That Advaita creates conflict between *pratyakṣa* and *śāstra* rendering *śāstra* invalid (29)
11. That qualitylessness of Brahman cannot be spoken of by Vedānta (45)
12. The consequent invalidity of the *purāṇas* (48)
13. The distinction of *saguṇa* and *nirguṇa śrutis* (52)
14. The meaning of the *anantatva* of Brahman (56)
15. That *nirviśeṣa* Brahman cannot be of the nature of *ānanda* (57)
16. That the *śruti "ekamevādvitīyaṁ"* will be meaningless in Advaita (59)
17. The a*pasūdrādhikaraṇa* will not have meaning according to Advaita (62)

G. Relating to the *mahāvākya "tattvamasi"* as a whole, the criticisms of Śrī Vedānta Deśika are grouped as follows:
1. That *śabda* cannot produce perception (7)
2. That there can be no teaching of Advaita (34)
3. That the Advaita of *ātman* cannot be established (36)
4. That there is no identity of *Jīva* and *Īśvara* (37)
5. Criticism of the possibility of expression of what is unitary and impartible (38)
6. The contention that it is impossible to affirm identity (49)

H. The criticisms relating to *Jīvanamukti* are listed hereunder:-

1. That there cannot be residual *vāsanās* after *Jīvanamukti* (5)
2. The *Jīvanamukti* itself is impossible (31)

It would appear from this analysis that many of the criticisms advanced by Śrī Vedānta Deśika overlap and are repeated in different places.

Whether the word "Brahman" signifies the Ultimate Reality according to Advaita

In order to fully appreciate the value of Shri Shastri's contribution to the Advaita the essence of one or two chapters from the Śatabhūṣaṇī are presented here.

Vedānta Deśika contends that the word "Brahman" cannot signify the attributeless-Brahman (*nirguṇa-brahman*), (hereinafter referred to as "*śuddhabrahman*") even on the basis of secondary signification as maintained by the Advaitins; as in all the cases of secondary signification (*lakṣaṇa*) the words should be well known to have their primary meaning (*mukhyārtha*) too. For example, in the case of secondary usage, *gaṅgāyām ghoṣaḥ* (village in the Ganges), the word "Gaṅgā" is well known as signifying the meaning of water-currents by its primary function (*abhidhā* or *mukhyavṛtti*). Similarly, in the case of secondary usage, *kākebhyo dadhirakṣyatām*, the word "*kāka*" which signifies all the animals which spoil the curds by its secondary function, is also well known with regard to its primary meaning, i.e. the crow. Therefore, a word, which does not have its primary meaning, cannot signify the secondary meaning. So, unless the word "Brahman" signifies something as its primary sense, it cannot signify the *śuddhabrahman* as its secondary sense. Now, what could be such primary sense of the word "Brahman" according to the Advaita? Is it *śuddhabrahman* or the Brahman which is delimited with some or the other adjunct? It cannot be the *śuddhabrahman* as the etymological description of the word "Brahman" as a thing that grows or nourishes or the great etc., cannot apply with regard to the *śuddhabrahman*, as it is devoid of any attribute whatsoever. Then it remains to be accepted as that the term "Brahman" refers to the Brahman which is delimited by one or the other adjunct/adjuncts. Advaitins cannot accept such an adjunct as being real. Their theory that such an adjunct of the Brahman is non-real (*mithyā*) cannot be maintained as it is against all the possible authoritative sources of knowledge such as, perception, inference, verbal cognition (of Vedic texts as well as *smṛti* texts), and the *sūtras*.

Also, the Advaitins are required to clarify whether the knowable Brahman, whose knowledge dispels the *ajñāna*, is *śuddha* or delimited by some adjunct. In the second alternative, the Advaitins fall into the camp of the Viśiṣṭādvaitins, who maintain that the Brahman, who professed with several auspicious attributes is enjoined as knowable in the first *sūtra* on the basis of two types of definitions of the Brahman, *taṭastha* as well as *svarūpa*. Also, since delimited by an adjunct is non-real (*mithyā*), according to the Advaitins, it follows that the liberation (*mokṣa*) becomes attainable through a non-real means. If, on the other hand, the first alternative is accepted, it becomes difficult to maintain as the word "Brahman" does not have etymological applicability (*vyutpatti*) in the *śuddhabrahman*. Therefore, Vedānta Deśika concludes that since the word "Brahman" is not known to have any object as its primary meaning, it cannot signify the *śuddhabrahman* by its secondary function too.

From the above discussion two issues are made clear: (1) The word "Brahman" cannot signify the *śuddhabrahman* on the basis of secondary signification, (2) If the Brahman which is enjoined as knowable in the first *sūtra* is accepted as one which is delimited by some adjunct or adjuncts, then liberation as accepted by the Advaitins becomes impossible. On the other hand, the *śuddhabrahman* cannot be accepted as knowable even according to the standpoint of the Advaitins.

Sri Shastri tries to resolve the first problem as follows. Advaitins follow the *abhihitānvayavāda* of Bhāṭṭas with regard to the sentential meaning. According to this theory, the words stop functioning after giving rise to the independent word-meanings. Thereafter, such word-meanings give rise to the sentential meaning on the basis of secondary signification located in the word-meanings. Therefore, according to this theory all the sentential meanings are uniformally secondary in their nature. Since, the meaning arising out of the statements "*tat tvam asi*" etc., is also a kind of sentential meaning it can arise out of the secondary significatory function of the word-meaning and there is no necessity that *śuddhabrahman* must have been well known to be the primary meaning of any word. Therefore, even though the *śuddhabrahman* is not the primary meaning of either of the two words, namely, "*tat*" and "*tvam*" yet to maintain the validity of the sentence (*vākyaprāmāṇyanirvāhārtham*), on the basis of the power of the word-meanings, named *lakṣaṇa,* which is the nature of power to convey the sentential meaning, and on the basis of purport (*tātparya*) of the words "*tat*" and "*tvam*", the word "*tat*" and "*tvam*" convey the *śuddhacaitanya* by their secondary signification. This is the answer in nutshell.

Shastri then proceeds to show that such a position is not exclusively maintained by the Advaitins alone, but is maintained by others also in one or the other case. For example, Vaiśeṣikas define earth as a thing possessing smell. According to them, the *paramāṇu* is not perceivable. Yet, the quality namely, smell is accepted as to be existing in them even though they themselves are not known. Similarly, *Īśvara* is accepted as the possessor of eternal knowledge though He himself is not given to our knowledge. Similarly, the *saguṇa brahman,* namely, Viṣṇu or the residence of Lord Viṣṇu, namely, *Vaikuṇṭha,* etc. are all not given to our knowledge by any other means than by such words. Hence, they have to agree that on the basis of context, etc. principal words give rise to the meaning of a thing which is not otherwise given to us by any other valid means of knowledge. In such a case, the words "*tat*" and "*tvam*" etc., can also give rise to the meaning of the *śuddhacaitanya,* even though it is not given to our understanding by any other means of knowledge.

Also, the Viśiṣṭādvaitins accept that Lord Viṣṇu who possesses both sentient and insentient objects as his body, who is devoid of any kind of blemish whatsoever, and who is the possessor of an infinite number of auspicious qualities, is the meaning of the word "Brahman". The word "Brahman" does not signify such a person on the basis of its primary signification as it is known to mean: (1) a person belonging to a class of people called brāhmaṇas, (2) primordial cause, (3) the Vedas, (4) the *Jīvātman*, etc., only by its primary signification. Therefore, even the Viśiṣṭādvaitin should accept the meaning of the word "Brahman" as described above, only on the basis of the purport (*tātparya*) of the entire context of the *Upaniṣad* or the *Upaniṣads.* In this way, non-applicability of primary function (*mukhyavṛtti*) in case of both the *saguṇa* and *nirguṇa* Brahman is common for both the parties, i.e. the Viśiṣṭadvaitins and the Advaitins. Hence, it should not be pointed out by anyone against any other. Also, texts such as "*yato vāco nivartante*" etc., declare categorically that Brahman cannot be spoken of in terms of words. Therefore, all the words which are supposed to be signifying the Brahman do so only on the basis of secondary signification only.

Having thus countered the arguments of the opponents, Sri Shastri cites the *Siddhāntabindu* which says that an attributeless self is very much part of our experience during our deep sleep and in a yogic state called *asamprajñātasamādhi.* He cites the *Bhāmatī* which says that the differentiation in the taste of sweet between the cane, milk, jaegery etc., cannot be spoken of even by Goddess Sarasvatī. So, there is no difficulty in accepting that the word "Brahman" conveys the *śuddhabrahman* by its secondary signification.

On the basis of the *Tattvacintāmaṇi* of Gaṅgeśopādhyāya, Sri Shastri, then, proceeds to state that no secondary signification is necessary with regard to conveying the *śuddhabrahman* by the word "Brahman". According to this theory, a word which signifies a qualified thing (*viśiṣṭa*) by its primary signification is also fit to signify the qualification part (*viśeṣaṇa*) or qualificand (*viśeṣya*) along independently; if such a meaning enjoys the support of the purport (*tātparya*) in it. Since the meaning of the word "*tat*" and "*tvam*" in favour of the meaning of *śuddhabrahman* enjoys the support of purport of the entire passage, the word "*tat*" and "*tvam*" signify the pure consciousness by primary signification itself, even though they are otherwise known to have their primary signification in the qualified consciousness.

To elucidate the above point we may cite one or two examples as follows. The expressions *ghaṭaḥ anityaḥ* (pot is non-eternal), or *ghaṭam ānaya* (bring the pot) are valid expressions according to all the schools. According to the position of the Nyāya-Vaiśeṣikas the word "pot" signifies a qualified pot, i.e. the individual "pot" as qualified by its universal "pot-ness". In the said expressions the non-eternality and the objectivity of the action of bringing do not apply in the case of the qualification "pot-ness" for obvious reasons. Therefore, the word "pot" in the said expressions signifies only the substantive part, i.e. the individual pot alone but not pot as qualified with pot-ness, even though the latter is the meaning of the word "pot" according to the Nyāya-Vaiśeṣikas. In this case no one concedes the above expressions as secondary expressions. Similarly, the words "*tat*" and "*tvam*" signify the pure consciousness alone even though their meaning is a qualified one, by the very primary function (*mukhyavṛtti*) without resorting to the secondary signification. Therefore, all the difficulties pointed out in case of adopting secondary signification are thus warded off as no secondary signification is resorted to in the case of deriving the meaning of identity from the *mahāvākyas.*

Now, the second issue, namely, whether the Brahman enjoined as knowable in the first aphorism is the *śuddhabrahman* or the Brahman delimited by one or the other adjunct (*upahita brahman*) is to be examined. Viśiṣṭādvaitin is of the opinion that it cannot be the *śuddhabrahman* because the word "Brahman" cannot signify the *śuddhabrahman* either by primary signification or by secondary signification. This point is well discussed and suitably answered in the above pages. If, on the other hand, the knowable Brahman is the *upahita brahman,* the Viśiṣṭādvaitin criticises this by asking how liberation (*mukti*) is possible by knowing the *upahita brahman* which is also non-real (*mithyā*) like any other object; since knowledge of truth alone can dispel ignorance, but not knowledge of non-real objects.

Advaitins answer this question in various ways. Vivaraṇācārya's position is that the knowable Brahman is the *śuddhabrahman* only but not the *upahita brahman.* Yet, the application of the word "Brahman" in the *śuddhabrahman* is possible as discussed above in detail. According to the Bhāmatī School, however, the knowable Brahman is the *upahita brahman* but not the *śuddhabrahman.* But, when they say *upahita brahman* they mean Brahman which is delimited by that adjunct *vṛtti* which is the form of identity of *Jīva* and Brahman, but not delimited by any other adjunct such as *avidyā,* etc. They also contend that the knowledge of an *upahita* object need not necessarily be the knowledge of *upādhi* (adjunct) too. So the knowledge of the *upahita* is not non-real knowledge according to them but a real one. Therefore, it can dispel the *ajñāna* which is its counter-co-relative.

To put Vācaspati's position in clear terms, he accepts that Brahman, when associated with *avidyā,* becomes the universal cause. When the Brahman is associated with *vṛtti* or *vidyā* (the verbal knowledge of the identity of *Jīva* and Brahman) it becomes the object of Vedāntic inquiry. When verbal knowledge of Vedāntic statements, such as "*tat tvam asi*", etc. arises the *avidyā* along with its effect gets dispelled. But, at this stage, just for a moment, there remains the *śuddhabrahman* along with the delimiting factor *vṛtti* or *vidyā.* Since this *vṛtti* or *vidyā* is also an effect of *avidyā,* it cannot remain for long after its cause *avidyā* is destroyed. Such *vṛtti* or *avidyā* also ceases to exist on its own account as fire ceases to exist after fuel is totally consumed. After such self-destruction of *vidyā* or *vṛtti,* the *śuddhabrahman* alone remains. Therefore, in the said process, the knowledge of the *upahita brahman* causes liberation indirectly through destroying the *avidyā.*

In this way, Shri Shastri clarifies the position of both the Bhāmatī and the Vivaraṇa schools and counters the arguments of Śrī Deśika.*

---

*On the basis of Chapter, namely, "*Brahmāṇī—śabdavṛttyānupattivādaparikṣā*", pp.45–58.

Inconsistencies in the Viśiṣṭādvaita

Mahamahopadhyaya Anantakrishna Shastri highlights the inconsistency in maintaining the eternality and naturality (*svābhāvikatva*) of *dharmabhūtajñāna* in the system of the Viśiṣṭādvaita as attempted by Purisai Śrīrangācārya in his work* by Kudṛṣṭi-*siddhāntamārtaṇḍa.* The Viśiṣṭādvaitins accept that the *dharmabhūtajñāna* is eternal and yet undergoes contradiction and expansion. By the term *dharmabhūtajñāna* they refer to the *jñāna* of the Nyāya-Vaiśeṣikas and the *vṛttijñāna* of the Advaitins. Indeed, *jñāna*[5] is accepted as one of the characteristics of the *ātman* by most of the schools, such as the Vaiśeṣikas, the Naiyāyikas, the Mīmāṁsakas, the Sāṅkhyas, the Pātañjalas, and the Advaitins, etc. But all of them accept it as non-eternal and adventitious (*āgantuka*) to the *ātman.* It is only the Viśiṣṭādvaitins who maintain that it is eternal and natural (*svābhāvika*) to the *ātman.* There also, the eternality is based on the naturality (*svābhāvikatva*) of it as all the *dārśanikas* are unanimous in conceding that any characteristic which is natural to an object (*dharmin*) cannot get destroyed until and unless the object which possesses such characteristics gets destroyed. For example, the heat of the fire cannot get extinct without the extinction of the fire. Since the *dharmabhūtajñāna* is considered as a natural characteristic of *ātman,* which is eternal, it is also considered to be eternal by the Viśiṣṭādvaitins. In this way, the aspect of naturality of *dharmabhūtajñāna* is the basis depending on which they argue in favour of its eternality. Therefore, the question of the naturality of the *dharmabhūtajñāna* deserves to be examined according to Shri Shastri.

The Viśiṣṭādvaitins and all other opponents of this theory base their mutually opposed contentions on the same *śruti* text, namely, *na vijñātur vijñāteḥ viparilopo vidyate advināśitvāt.* The Viśiṣṭādvaitins and the Nyāya Vaiśeṣikas understand the case *ṣaṣṭhī* in "*vijñātuḥ vijñāteḥ*" as non-colocative (*vyādhikaraṇa*) whereas all others understand it as colocative (*sāmānadhikaraṇya*). The result of such a differential interpretation is that the Viśiṣṭādvaitins establish the eternality of the *jñāna* of *ātman,* whereas others establish the eternality of *ātman,* which is of the nature of *jñāna.*[6] The interpretation adopted by the non-Viśiṣṭādvaitins is supported further by the common man's experience of the origination and destruction of *jñāna* (*jñānam utpannam; jnanam naṣṭam*). Now to account for the above said common man's experience, Viśiṣṭādvaitins accept that the *jñāna,* which is eternal, undergoes contraction and expansion, which is mistaken as origination and destruction by the common man.

Shri Shastri contends that where thing is universally experienced and has a usage by the common man in terms of being originated and destructed, it is not wise on the part of any one to accept the eternality of such an object. For example, the light of a lamp is experienced as originated and destructed. Therefore, even though there is, in fact, only contraction and expansion of light, the origination and destruction of light is accepted on the basis of the said experience

*Potter—TAP Śrīrangācārya 1850 *Karyādhikaraṇavāda.*

and usage. As against this, where there is contraction and expansion but no experience or usage of origination and destruction as in the case of a lotus, if anyone uses "lotus is originated" or "lotus is destructed", it should be treated as secondary usage only. Following this principle, since there is unilateral experience and usage of origination and destruction of *dharmabhūtajñāna*, it should be accepted as non-eternal only.

Also, if eternality is accepted in an object which undergoes modification (*pariṇāma*), then the distinction of the Viśiṣṭādvaita becomes untenable with regard to: the *Sāṅkhya*, who accepts *prakṛti* as eternal, even though it undergoes modification, the Jainas, who accept the eternal Brahman as modifying into the world (*brahmapariṇāmavāda*); and those who accept that the eternal *ātman* undergoes contraction and expansion. Therefore, Shri Shastri adds, that the position of the Advaitins is flawless as they accept non-eternality in all objects which undergo modification. Therefore, only the Advaitins can criticize the Jainas, the Sāṅkhyas and the Bhāskarīyas, etc. concludes Shri Shastri.

The basic philosophical issue involved in this discussion is whether an object can be accepted as eternal even though it undergoes modification. The Sāṅkhyas, the Jainas, the Bhāskarīyas and the Viśiṣṭādvaitins say "yes", whereas the Avaitins say "no". Shri Shastri asks how can the Viśiṣṭādvaitins criticize the Jainas and others, when they themselves maintain such a position with regard to the *dharmabhūtajñāna*?

He also points out that in the case of the interpretation of the said *śruti*, the explanation based on non-colocation (*vidyādhikaraṇya*) is not proper as long as there exists a possibility of explaining the text based on colocation (*sāmānādhikaraṇya*). He cites the authority of *Niṣadasthāpatyādhikaraṇa* of *Pūrva Mīmāṁsā* in his favour.

Shri Shastri finds yet another inconsistency with regard to this theory. The Viśiṣṭādvaitins accept eternality on the basis of a theory of the Naiyāyikas who say that the characteristics that exist in an eternal object also are eternal. To cite an example, the singularity that exists in the substance such as *ākāśa*, etc. is eternal whereas the same is non-eternal when it exists in such objects as the pot, etc. But, following the Naiyāyikas, the Viśiṣṭādvaitins do not accept *jñāna* as a quality of the *ātman*, but regard it as substance.

Another central theory of the Viśiṣṭādvaitins, namely, that the Brahman is *nitya-sūkṣma-cidacid-viśiṣṭa* is also untenable for the similar reasons. Shri Shastri says that if the subtle *prakṛti* the nature of which undergoes modification into the gross world is accepted as eternal, how then does the Viśiṣṭādvaitin differentiate his theory from that of the Jainas who accept that the eternal *ātman* can modify into the world. For the Advaitins, there is no inconsistency as they accept that all modificables are non-eternal including *prakṛti*.

Shri Shastri also criticises the theory of the contraction and expansion of the *dharmabhūtajñāna*. The Viśiṣṭādvaitins offer the definition for contraction and expansion as a distinct contact with nearer and farther places, respectively. Shri Shastri examines the process further and asks how is such contact with the object attained by the *jñāna*? Is it on account of the capacity of *jñāna* to pull the objects nearer without itself moving as per the example of the magnet or is it due to such power on the part of the objects? In either case does that Viśiṣṭādvaitin accept increase and decrease in number of the parts of either *dharmabhūtajñāna* or the object or not? If not, he is contradicting the experience of all in the world, both scholars as well as laymen. Likewise, the theory that the upward moving *dharmabhūtajñāna* pulls the objects to its proximity, is also a contradiction of universal experience. That the unmoving objects pull the *dharmabhūtajñāna* to a distance of proximity, thus, causing an increase in the numbers of parts so that such *jñāna* results are yet to be accepted. But, such an acceptance will prove to be suicidal to the Viśiṣṭādvaitin as it contradicts their fundamental position of maintaining the *apṛthak-siddhi* relation between the *jñāna* and the *ātman*, and the naturality of *jñāna* as well. In this way, while explaining the contraction and expansion, there is no way to escape from accepting the increase and decrease in the number of parts of the *dharmabhūtajñāna* and once they are accepted it becomes impossible to maintain the eternality of the *dharmabhūtajñāna*.

Even with regard to the concept of *apṛthak-siddhatva*, there is inconsistency. *Apṛthak-siddhatva* is nothing but *ayutasiddhatva*. It is the identity in difference (*tādātmya*) between two objects according to the Viśisṭādvaita. In the case of the identity in difference (*tādātmya*) between the clay and pot, the causal relation (*kāryakāraṇabhāva*) between them is responsible for it. Whereas in the case of the identity in difference (*tādātmya*) between the body and the self *śarīraśarīrī-bhāva* is responsible for it, but not the causal relation, according to the Viśiṣṭādvaitins. Now, Shri Shastri poses the question as to what would be responsible for the identity in difference between *svarūpajñāna*, i.e. the Brahman and the *dharmabhūtajñāna*, since neither of those above two relations hold good in this case?[7]

NOTES AND REFERENCES

1. It may be recalled in this connection that Gautama in his *Nyāya Sūtras* discusses the question as to whose property knowledge is, that is, of the body, or the mind or the *buddhi* or the *ātman*, but he does not discuss the question as to whom the erroneous cognition belongs.
2. See the discussion on Identity Statement in Nyāya in *JICPR*.
3. Bhakti Darśana Vimarśaḥ, Badrinath Sukla Memorial Lecture, Published in Sanskrit by Sampurnanand Sanskrit Visvavidyalaya Varanasi.
4. A more detailed exposition of the views of Nischaladasa is contained in the Project volume entitled "*Systems of Vedānta*" edited by R. Balasubramaniam. However, the article by Surendra Kumar Srivastava is primarily expository in nature and does not raise critical issues with respect to his work.
5. *Jñāna* is of two types according to the Advaitins as well as the Viśiṣṭādvaitins. To make a distinction between them, the Advaitins describe the first as *śvarūpajñāna*, i.e. *jñāna* which is a very essential nature of *ātman* or Brahman, while the other one is *vṛttijñāna*, i.e. the *jñāna* of the pot, cloth, etc. Viśiṣṭādvaitins refer to the first by the term *dharmībhūtajñāna*,

and to the second one by the term *dharmabhūtajnāna.* In this section, the term *jñāna* is used only to refer to the *Vṛttijñāna* and *dharmabhūtajñāna.* However, where reference is to be made to the first type of *jñāna,* the term *svarūpajñāna* is used.

6. Here the *jñāna* should be understood as *svarūpajñāna.*
7. *Śatbhūṣaṇī,* Introduction, pp.xxxvii–xliii.

CHAPTER 8

Dharmaśāstra Literature from Eighteenth Century Onwards

The roots of India's social, political and legal thought can be traced to the literature known as the *Dharmasūtras*, the *Smṛtis*, the *Nītiśāstras* and the *Arthaśāstras*. The *Dharmasūtras* are perhaps the earliest literature dealing with the subject though they are said to form an integral part of that literature which consists of the *Śrautasūtras*, the *Gṛhyasūtra* and what is collectively known as the *Kalpasūtras*. These seem to deal respectively with the life of the householder centered in the performance of the Vedic ritual and the fulfilling of familial and social obligations. The earliest *Dharmasūtras* are supposed to be those of Gautama, Baudhāyana, Āpastambha and Hiraṇyakeśin. Of these Āpastambha is perhaps the oldest, as it is generally assigned to 300 B.C. Āpastambha belonged to the south and hence it is clear that as early as 300 B.C., outstanding Vedic scholars belonged not only to the North but also to the South and that they exercised as much authority as the former. The Vedic civilization thus already had a pan-Indian character and attracted scholars who attained eminence and authority from different parts of the country.

The *Dharmasūtras* ascribed to Gautama and Baudhāyana are apparently fairly old as they belong to approximately the same period. The date assigned to Hiraṇyakeśin is not exactly known, but if surmised approximately, the dates of these works would appear to be post-Pāṇini, which is very unlikely. Also, as they seem to have been written by the same family of scholars who have also compiled the *Śrauta sūtras* and as these relate to the performance of the Vedic ritual, it is unlikely that they would have been written so late. Perhaps, all these texts were composed much earlier and have been given a final shape in the period to which they have been assigned being thereby the final edition of texts which had gone into successive editions earlier.

The *Dharmasūtra* literature gave rise to what has been called the *Smṛti* literature later, the most important example of which is perhaps the *Manu smṛti* which is also known as the *Mānavadharmaśāstra* or *Mānavadharma Saṁhitā*. The earliest example is supposed to be the *Hārita smṛti* which however has not exercised the same influence and authority as some of the later ones such as *Manusmṛti* and *Yājñavalkyasmṛti.* Besides the *Smṛti granthas* which deal with man both as a social and political being, the emphasis being on his moral obligations in both the contexts, we have a different kind of texts which are primarily concerned with *nīti* of which the first example is perhaps the *Cāṇakyanīti Darpaṇa.* It is not quite clear whether this is the same Cāṇakya who was the author of the *Arthaśāstra,* the first known systematic work on political thought and administration in India. His date is again sometime around 300–200 B.C.

The period during which independent *smṛtis* appear ends sometime around A.D. eighth century with fourteen well-known *smṛti* texts having been written up to this period. Thereafter begin the period of the commentaries which are generally called *ṭīkās* and not *bhāṣyas* or *vārttikas* as for the other foundational texts of the tradition. The first *ṭīkā* is supposed to have been written on the *Nāradasmṛti* perhaps around A.D. eighth century by Asahāya. The second most important *ṭīkā* is by Medhātithi on the *Manusmṛti* written in ninth century even though in the same century a *ṭīkā* by Viśvarūpācārya on the *Yājñavalkyasmṛti* existed. It appears that from ninth century onwards, the *Yājñavalkyasmṛti* enjoyed the same authority as the *Manusmṛti* as we find the same number of commentaries on it. In the eleventh century, for example, we have Govindarāja's *ṭīkā* on the *Manu smṛti* and Vijñāneśvara's *ṭīkā* on the *Yājñavalkyasmṛti.* Thereafter in the twelfth century we have Aparāditya's *ṭīkā* on the *Yājñavalkyasmṛti* and Sarvajñanārāyaṇa's *ṭīkā* on the *Manusmṛti.* In the twelfth century, an increased interest in the earlier *Dharmasūtra* literature occurs as we have not only the two *ṭīkās* mentioned above but also two *ṭīkās* by Maskarī and by Haradatta on the *Gautama Dharmasūtra* and one on the *Āpastamba Dharmasūtra* by Haradatta. In the thirteenth century, a continued interest in the *Manusmṛti* is evident from the writing of one of the most important commentators after Medhātithi, namely, Kullūkabhaṭṭa. The traditional *ṭīkās* continue in the fourteenth century with a *ṭīkā* on the *Parāśarasmṛti* by Madhavācārya, as evidence of the rise of interest in *smṛtis* other than the *Manusmṛti* and the *Yājñavalkyasmṛti.* However, the interest in these two major *smṛtis* continues as we have a new *ṭīkā* on *Yājñavalkyasmṛti* by Śulapāṇi in this century and on the *Manusmṛti* by Rāghavānanda in the next. In the fifteenth century, we also have a *ṭīkā* on *Nāradīya Manusaṁhitā* by Bhavasvāmī, thus, giving an indication that there were different recensions and editions of the *Manusaṁhitā.* However, exact differences between these different versions have perhaps not been studied in detail up till now.

The seventeenth century sees a revival of interest in *smṛtis* other than those of Manu and Yājñavalkya as we have a *ṭīkā* on the *Viṣṇusmṛti* by Nandapaṅḍita which is one of the earliest *smṛtis* written by a Vaiṣṇava and ascribed to Viṣṇu. However, there seems to be no detailed study indicating how this differs from the others. Also, it had not been the subject of any special attention until this late period when perhaps it was the rise of Caitanya, etc. in the sixteenth century that might possibly have triggered an interest in this *smṛti.* However, the *Yājñavalkyasmṛti* continues to hold its own against the *Manusmṛti*, as we have a commentary written on it in this period by Mitramiśra. An increased interest continues in the eighteenth century in the *smṛti* and *Dharmasūtra* literature with two commentaries on the *Manusmṛti* by Nandanācārya and Rāmacandra, respectively and one on *Yājñavalkyasmṛti* called *Mitākṣara* by Bālabhaṭṭa Pāyagunḍe which is very famous. Besides, we have a new commentary on *Baudhāyana dharmasūtra* which is perhaps the first commentary on this work.

Besides, the *ṭīkā* literature which starts from eighth century onwards, we have a new genre of writing called the *nibandha* which being in the twelfth century and continues up to the eighteenth or nineteenth century. The first *nibandha* is entitled *Rājadharmakalpataru* by Lakṣmīdhara and appears to deal with the duties of a king. The *nibandha* form of writing from twelfth century onwards is exclusively concerned with matters of polity and deals either with *rājadharma* or *rājanīti*. There is a distinction between *rājadharma* and *rājanīti* and the difference is clearly reflected in a separate branch of literature called the *Nītigranthas*. While the first *nibandha* was on *rājadharma*, the second on *rājanīti* is entitled, *Rājnītiratnākara* written by Canḍeśvara in the fourteenth century who wrote another *nibandha* called *Vivādaratnākara*. In the sixteenth century we have a *nibandha* entitled *Nītimayūkha* by Nīlakaṇṭhabhaṭṭa followed by Mitramiśra's *nibandha* entitled *Rājanītiprakāśa* in the seventeenth and Anantadeva's *nibandha* entitled *Rājadharmakaustubha* in the eighteenth century.

This development denotes the rise of a very specialised kind of writing and an increasing concern with the political realm in the traditional political thought of India due to the emergence of Islamic rule in this country. What exactly are the concerns of these thinkers and how do they depart from earlier thinkers in this field appears to be reflected in the increase in commentaries on *Nītigranthas* from eighteenth century onwards such as the two commentaries on the *Kāmaṇḍakīya Nītisāra* by Śaṅkurāya and *Nītivākyāmṛtaṭīkā* by the same author and another commentary on *Śukranīti* by Jīvānandavidyāsāgara.

Thus, to tentatively outline a comprehensive picture of classical literature on society and polity in India the following divisions are suggested: *Dharmasūtra* from the sixth to the third century B.C.; *Smṛti Granthas* from the third century B.C. to eight century; and the commentaries on the *Smṛtis* from the A.D. eighth century onwards.

These texts dealing with society, polity and law thus naturally divide along the subject matter of primary concern, even though there may be some overlapping between them. The text relating to polity, for example, may deal simultaneously with the maintenance of the social order which is the primary concern of texts relating to *dharma* in general, as of the ruler has to mediate between the conflicting claims that inevitably arise between the interests of the different *varṇas* that constitute a society, this issue is of relevance here. The changing character of these texts and the interrelationships between them mirror the changes occurring in the socio-political scene of those times. The legal texts of necessity are even more specific as they have to "decide" in favour of one or the other party and hence vague generalities about what is *dharma* or *adharma* cannot serve the purpose.

The primary issues with which a *rājadharma* or *rājanīti* work deals with, were bound to be different from works of thinkers who were primarily concerned with society and its functioning. However, some overlap was present as one of the rulers' duties, of course, was to maintain the smooth functioning of the social order. This could only be ensured by seeing that all the members of a society performed their functions with reasonable honesty and public spirit. Generally, this is a subject of what has been called the *varṇāśrama dharma* or norms governing the behaviour of four distinct sections of society necessary for the maintenance of a functioning social order. These, of course, are the well-known classes designated as the intellectual class, the mercantile or the trading class, the warrior class and those who are primarily engaged in physical labour of any sort in the process of production or services. The ruler's function, however, was also concerned with securing the safety of the state from other neighbouring kingdoms and to guard himself from possible aspirants to power within the polity itself. Thus, the political thinker was keenly aware of the dilemma posed by the ambivalent functions of the ruler who, on the one hand, was supposed to espouse the welfare of his people and to ensure the observance by them of the moral norms laid down by the *Dharmaśāstras.* On the other, by the dictates of statecraft the king was meant to use all fair and foul means both against the possible aspirants to power in his own realm and the kingdoms outside who could turn inimical at any time and wage war on his territory. Also, as offense is the best means of defence, the ruler himself was supposed to take the initiative by conquering the other kingdoms at an opportune time and to weaken them, by all means at his command. The ruler's primary duty, at least to his own people was to ensure justice and welfare for everyone concerned, even though the members of the polity were always prone to deceive the state and get all sorts of advantages out of it by every underhand means they could think of. Thus, even in the internal realm, the problem of the ruler was how to ensure honesty amongst the citizens, particularly amongst the trading classes which were primarily responsible for the creation of wealth and prosperity in the state. Kauṭilya's *Arthaśāstra* is a classic example of a text which is not only aware of all these ambivalences and dilemmas but also gives detailed instructions regarding how to deal with such situations which are bound to arise for any one who exercises the ruling function. The ruler, or rather the ruling class, is itself exposed to all the temptations which power provides and the author of the *Arthaśāstra* and the subsequent texts on the polity are clearly aware of this also.

Thus the texts dealing with the realm of the political class had a different focus from those concerned with norms for the conduct of human beings in different situations and roles. The thinker who is primarily concerned with law, or *vyavahāra* as it is called in the Indian tradition, has to provide concrete guidelines for the punishments to be awarded to those who have committed offences of various kinds and provide clear, unambiguous, specific instructions regarding what was to be considered an offence and the degree to which it required to be punished. The same is true of civil disputes where also a decision has to be arrived at in favour of one party at the expense of the other.

The problems that the writers on *dharma, rājanīti* and *vyavahāra* faced, have seldom been discussed or highlighted because of the undue emphasis by scholars on the ideal of *mokṣa* in the Indian tradition. It has seldom been realised that the acceptance of the ideal of *mokṣa* as the *param puruṣārtha* itself created a problem for these thinkers as they were dealing with the concrete problems of society, polity and law.

The most comprehensive survey of Indian thought on these issues from the Vedas to the most recent times has been attempted by Paṇḍit Laxman Shastri Joshi whose work, apart from that of P.V. Kane, is the most exhaustive on the subject. Joshi's work is primarily a reference work and is aptly entitled *Dharmakośa*, but it is not the usual kind of *Kośa* and not even similar to most Encyclopedia's. Instead, it divides the realms of *dharma* into 11 *kāṇḍas* comprising of *dharma* in the *Upaniṣads, saṁskāras, vyavahāra, rājanīti, varṇāśrama dharma, śuddha-śrāddha, prāyaścitta, śānti, Purāṇa-Āgama dharma, samaya* and *mokṣa.* Of these volumes only four of the *kāṇḍas (Vyavahāra, Upaniṣad, Saṁskāra and Rājnīti*), have been published along with the first volume of the *varṇāśrama dharma.*

Within these major divisions the discussion has been further classified into various important topics and is arranged chronologically from the Vedas down to the latest works available on these subjects. Original quotations from the text in support of the views on these issues have been given, mentioning the exact reference to the original which may be seen for greater detail. Brief introductions in Sanskrit to the issues that are discussed highlighting some of the important points are made therein.

The first published volume of the *Dharmakośa* was the *Saṁskāra kāṇḍa* in A.D. 1937 and though many years have passed since, this rich source material on all its aspects of *dharma* has remained unutilised by the social, political and legal thinkers of India. Even if we ignore, for the moment, the *Upaniṣad kāṇḍa* which deals primarily with the trans-social, trans-political and trans-legal dimensions of *dharma,* the remaining volumes deal with the totality of what is today called the 'secular' domain of life. A brief survey of the topics discussed in the volumes, dealing with *vyavahara, samskara* and *rājanīti* reveal the variety in issues that engaged the attention of the political, legal and social thinkers of India and their changing attitudes to the same. There is, thus, a historical dimension to the discussions on these topics which is documented in these pages. But neither the structural nor the conceptual, nor the historical aspect has caught the attention of those who are interested in these subjects. Nor, for that matter, has their problematic thought been grasped so that the discussion, and the changing perspectives in respect of it, could make sense to the modern student of the subject.

By way of example, the safeguarding of the intellectual from the coercive power of the State, seems to have been dealt with through the legal formulation that the Brahmins, the intellectual class *par excellence* should never be punished. The term used for this was *adaṇḍya* (one who cannot be punished). However, as this offended the sense of justice, the later thinkers argued for a differential theory of punishment. In other words, they said that as society expected different functions from different classes, and as these required different standards and norms of behaviours, the punishment meted out to them should also be in accordance with what was expected from them. Thus, it was argued that for many of the actions for which a *śūdra* need not be punished at all, such as, say, drinking or gambling, the Brahmin guilty of this offence should be severely punished. On the other hand, for some other offences for which the *śūdra* was to be punished severely, the Brahmin would not be punished at all or punished very lightly. Later thinkers argued that the Brahmin in no case should be given capital punishment. This, however, was also felt to discriminate in favour of the Brahmaṇs and the *Śukranīti*, which is supposed to be a later work ascribed by many scholars to as late as the eighteenth century, argued that not only the Brahmaṇs but no one else should ever be given capital punishment. Thus from *adaṇḍya* to *avādhya* we have a long debate in thinking pertaining to legal matters where the demand for equality and justice forced thinkers to change positions.

Similarly, the discussion regarding who shall be entitled to be a ruler or even, what exactly is the distinctive characteristic by which someone becomes a ruler and is recognised as such continued over a long period. Starting from the contention that only a *Kṣatriya* can be a ruler, the discussion leads ultimately to the position that whoever can rule efficiently and justly ought to be a ruler, no matter if he is even a *Śūdra*. An interesting formulation, for example, regarding the "collective" nature of the social and the political order took the form that whoever was a ruler shared in the merit or demerit, that is, *puṇya* and *pāpa* of his subjects as he was, at least partly, responsible for the fact that they engaged in actions which were virtuous or non-evil in character.

There is, however, an important distinction between the texts which are primarily devoted to *dharma* in the general sense and those which are specifically devoted to law or polity, as while the former deal with the subjects of law and polity in a peripheral or marginal manner, seeing them primarily from the point of view of the ideal, or what they should or ought to be, the texts mainly dealing with law and polity present them in terms of the dilemmas they present for the moral consciousness on the one hand, and the almost insoluble problems they pose for the value consciousness because of the very nature of the issues they deal with. Thus, a political thinker is intensely aware of the fact that a polity is always surrounded by other polities which can, and many a time do turn hostile to it. Also, that any one who is exercising the ruling function is always threatened by those within the polity who want to usurp power, by legitimate or illegitimate means. The problems of external and internal security are thus involved in the very nature of the realm with which the political theorist is concerned. Similarly, the legal thinker cannot avoid the problems of crime and the dispute about property, or the nature of the evidence on the basis of which someone's statement is to be believed.

Another distinction that emerges from these structural differences in various works is that while the texts dealing with issues of law, etc. in the broadest possible sense tend to be unchanging in their concerns, the political and legal thinker shows a historical awareness of the changes in the times in which, and for which he is writing. Thus, while the texts on the *Dharma Śāstras* occur primarily in the form of commentaries on the few texts which are regarded as foundational in the tradition, new and independent works on *vyavahāra* and *rājanīti* continued to be written as these spheres demanded new thought to deal with the continuously emerging problems. For example, the basic texts of the *Dharma Śāstra* continue to be the two major *smṛtis,* that is the *Manu* and the *Yājñavalkasmṛti* which have been the subject of continuous commentary since the ninth century. There has been no such tradition however either in respect of the texts dealing primarily with matters relating to politics or law. Thus, the first independent legal text itself seems to belong to late eleventh or early twelfth century and its author is Jīmutvāhana. After him, we find that there are about 35 independent works from the fifteenth to the eighteenth century.

As for political science, the situation seems to be different as the *Arthaśāstra* ascribed to Kauṭilya is accepted by everybody as one of the earliest texts dealing with the subject and its authority, though not as recognized as that of the two major *smṛtis* mentioned above is fairly well recognised. The commentaries on it continue to be written right up to the twentieth century, the last one being that of Ganapati Shastri (1923) while the other, the work of Rajesvara Shastri Dravida was written later. Apart from these exist the independent texts of the *Nītiśāstra* and *Nibandha granthas* dealing with political thought. The earliest known *nibandha* seems to have been written by Lakṣmīdhara around A.D. 1100–1150 and is entitled *Rājadharma Kalpataru.* The tradition of *nibandha* continues in the later period. We have, for example, a *nibandh* entitled *Rājnīti Ratnākara* around A.D. 1314–1324 by Caṇḍeśvara after which we have *Nītimayūkha* by Nīlakaṅṭha Bhaṭṭa ascribed to the fifteenth or sixteenth century. Mitra Miśra's *Rājanītiprakāśa* around A.D. 1623 and Anantadeva's *nibandha* entitled *Rājadharma Kaustubha* around A.D. 1650–1675. After the seventeenth century, the *Dharmakośa* does not mention any independent *nibandh* or *nītigranthu* dealing with the realm of politics. Instead, we have works in the *ṭīkā* tradition only on the *nīti* and the *Arthaśāstra granthas* such as *Kāmaṇdakīya nītisāraṭīkā, Nītivākyāmṛtaṭīkā, Śukranītiṭīkā* (A.D. 1882), Kauṭilya *Arthaśāstraṭīkā* (A.D. 1923).

However, the texts mentioned in the *Dharmakośa* cover only some aspects of *dharma,* presumably because other texts dealing with the remaining aspects of *dharma* were to be the subject of later volumes. The volumes published so far deal primarily with *vyavahāra, rājanīti* and *saṁskāra* and hence mention only those texts which deal with them in one way or another. But some interesting texts dealing even with these subjects seem to have escaped the notice of the editor of the *Dharmakośa,* as for example, an interesting documents called the *Ājñāpatra* is not mentioned in it. Perhaps, the most probable reason for this was that the text is not in Sanskrit but in Marathi and was written for the Peshwas by an explicit order from the ruler. This suggests that the works dealing with *rājanīti* were used for the education of the princes to make them aware of the nature and complexity of the problems in the polity. The original manuscript issued by Sambhājī of Kolhapur in A.D. 1716 sheds interesting light on the new problems that were being faced in the political life of those times. This consisted of the intrusion of a new class of trader-politicians from the West who, though ostensibly engaged in trading activities and requested facilities for the same, actually had the political interest also. That this did not escape the eyes of the Maratha rulers of those times is evidenced by the following passages in the *Ājñāpatras* which have not been paid attention to up till now:

> Among the merchants, the Portuguese and the English and the Dutch and the French and the Danes and other hat-wearing merchants also do carry on trade and commerce. But they are not like other merchants. Their masters, every one of them, are ruling kings. By their orders and under their control these people come to trade in these provinces. How can it happen that rulers have no greed for territories? These hat-wearers have full ambition to enter into these provinces to increase their territories, and to establish their own opinions (religion). Accordingly, at various places, they have already succeeded in their ambitious undertakings. Moreover, this race of people is obstinate. Where a place has fallen into their hands they will not give it up even at the cost of their lives.

Policy Towards Them: Their intercourse should therefore be restricted to the extent of only their coming and going (for trade). They should strictly never be given places to settle. They should not at all be allowed to visit sea-forts. If some place is sometimes to be given for a factory, it should not be given at the mouth of an inlet or on the shores of the sea. If land is given in such places, it may be that they remain obedient as long as they like; they would, however, establish new forts at these ports at some time or with the help of their navy to protect them. Their strength lies in their navy, in guns and ammunition. As a consequence so much territory would be lost to the kingdom. Therefore, if any place is at all to be given to them it should be given in the midst of two or four famous great towns about eight to sixteen miles away from the mouth of the sea, just as the French were given lands at Rajapur.[1] The place must be such that it must be low-lying and within the range and control of the neighbouring town so as to avoid trouble to the town. Thus by fixing their place of habitation, the factory should be permitted to be built. They should not be allowed to build (strong) permanent houses. If they live in this way by accepting the above conditions it is well; if not, there is no need of them. It is enough if they occasionally come and go, and do not trouble us; nor need we trouble them.

NOTES

1. A market town and inland post (not in the open sea) in the Southern Konkan where the pepper and cardamom trade flourished in 1649. The English had opened a factory there. It was closed in 1682–83.

CHAPTER 9

Developments in the *Alaṁkāraśāstra* from Eighteenth Century Onwards

Thinking that is centered on the arts is as old in India as the Vedas them selves. Right from the beginning the *mantras* which were to be chanted or sung were treated separately and in fact provided the ground for the collection of that part of the *Ṛgveda Saṁhitā* which is now called the *Sāma Veda.* The *mantras* included in the *Sāma Veda,* perhaps on the ground that they were specifically amenable to being sung, were further divided into those that were to be sung in the forests and those to be sung in towns or villages, that is, where settled human habitation occurred. These are called *Araṇya-gāna* and the *Grāmageya-gāna* respectively.

There seems to have also been an early controversy regarding the necessity of the exact order and enunciation of the words of the Ṛgvedic *mantras* in the context of singing, as the exigencies and requirements of singing necessitated a different emphasis on the way the words of the Ṛgvedic *mantra* were to be pronounced and the sequence in which they were to be uttered. It may be remembered in this connection that the utterance of a Ṛgvedic *mantra* had to conform completely to the rules laid down for this purpose and that there had to be a strict *varṇānupūrvī, śabdānupūrvī,* and *svarānupūrvī* to ensure this. The requirements of singing, however, led in a different direction and there is an interesting story in the *Jaiminīya Brāhmaṇa Upaniṣad* which narrates how the singers of the *Sāma Veda* ultimately decided to get rid of the Ṛgvedic words from the *mantras* in order to achieve purity of singing.

Reflections on the singing of the *Sāma,* thus, appears to have provided the first occasion, at the very beginning of the tradition, for thinking about music as a pure art in which the involvement with words was seen to be as essentially secondary in character.

There is some reflection on art as representation in Yāska's *Nirukta* which is perhaps the earliest text to theoretically articulate the problems arising from an attempt to understand the Vedas and the Vedic ritual. The *Nirukta* discusses the idea of *upamā* or simile in the context of the Veda and shows perhaps the earliest reflection on this essential element of poetic composition. The *Nighaṇṭus*, though accepted to be earlier than the *Nirukta*, are concerned only with pointing out the important homonyms and synonyms that occur in the Vedic lexicon so that it could be understood better. The Vedic altar and the ritual ceremony associated with the various Vedic sacrifices is of course supposed to be 'representative' of the cosmic processes and, in fact, believed not only to integrate man with the cosmic reality through the medium of the ritual but also to help in the restoration of the cosmic equilibrium itself.

The Vedic seer at places appears to be self-conscious of his power and role as a creative artist who fashions a poem out of the vision of the 'meaning' that he apprehends. This simultaneous fusion of vision and craftsmanship marks all art, but in the Indian tradition it was the seer-poet who first seems to have felt it self-consciously, as Poetry. Music and representation of the structure and processes of the cosmic reality seem to have directly emanated from a reflection on the Vedas themselves. On the other hand, it was perhaps the parallel *Āgamic* tradition associated with the name and form of Śiva, deriving perhaps from an even earlier pre-Vedic tradition stretching back to the Harappan civilization. Śiva himself is supposed to have danced at the very beginning of Creation, the world itself being a continuance of his cosmic dance. There appears to be, however, little evidence in the Vedas themselves with respect to dance as an original art form which required independent reflection. In fact, there is little evidence to show that dance forms an integral part of Vedic ritual.

The earliest reflection on dance as an art form is by Tāṇḍu who is supposed to have composed the first work on dance, analysing it into its component elements. The story regarding this occurs in the *Nāṭya Śāstra* of Bharata which self-consciously tried to combine all the different arts of music, dance and poetry into a dramatic form which was 'representative' not so much of the cosmic forces as in the Vedic ritual but of the human world with all its emotions and passions. However, besides this, it also theoretically reflected on what it was trying to do and developed in this connection a number of concepts which specifically related to the world of art. It also tried to 'understand' what this world consisted in and what its creators were trying to do.

The *Nāṭya Śāstra* of Bharata gave rise to a systematic thinking about the arts in general and the dramatic and literary arts in particular. This became the source of all subsequent reflection which depended heavily on the conceptual apparatus that it evolved for the understanding of the arts and it replaced, to a large extent, the earlier formulation which had developed in the context of *Sāma* and the art of representation in the Vedic tradition and of dance in the Agamic tradition represented by the work of Tāṇḍu.

Bharata's thinking on the *nāṭya* revolves mainly around the central concept of *rasa* which, according to him, distinguishes the field of arts in general from all other realms. However, in his analysis of the notion of *rasa* he makes it heavily, and even exclusively dependent on notions and ideas which can be applied meaningfully only in the case of drama. This has resulted in an essential limitation on all subsequent thinking about the arts in the Indian tradition as the concepts that it uses primarily seem to apply to one art alone. Thus drama in particular, and the literary arts in general began to assume a central place in India, ignoring or marginalising all other arts, including music and dance which had been the object of the earliest reflection in the tradition on this subject.

Bharata's *Nāṭya Śāstra* however did not employ only the concept of *rasa* for understanding the reality created by the world of drama. It also used *alaṁkāra, vṛttis, guṇa, doṣa, lakṣaṇa* as well as concepts such as *arthaprakṛtis, kāryāvasthā* and *sandhi* and *sandhyaṅgas* for understanding the aesthetic reality of drama.

After the *Nāṭya Śāstra,* a work by Kohala played an important role in developing the thought of Bharata further. But the most important thinker after Bharata seems to have been Bhāmaha (middle of the A.D. sixth century), who seems to have appeared after Bhartṛhari and Dignāga (as he refers both to *apoha* and *sphoṭa*) but before Dharmakīrti with whose views he is not familiar. He is also mentioned as an authoritative writer by Ānandavardhana (A.D. 850) and is supposed to have been responsible for the separation of the *Alaṁkāraśāstra* from the *Nāṭya Śāstra* so that the primary emphasis was no longer on dramatic presentation but on the literary production. Bharata had emphasised a combination of the different art forms where each was subordinated to the aesthetic values involved in the total dramatic representation. Bhāmaha's separation of the Alaṁkāraśāstra from Natya śāstra thus represents a continuity with the pre-Bharata period where each of the art forms was the subject of independent reflection. However, it is difficult to say whether such a tradition of reflection as exists on music and dance is also present in respect of the poetic compositions in the *Ṛgveda.* The self-consciousness in the poet, as we have already noted, was present as also the awareness of the direct metrical forms in which poetical compositions were to be created. But, there is little evidence of a second order critical reflection on the art of poetry itself. Bhāmaha thus seems to initiate a second order reflection on literary composition and, interestingly, he criticises in this enterprise, concepts from both Bhartṛhari and Dignāga. This is evidence of both a lively interaction between the philosophers and the aestheticians of that period as well as the carving of an independent discourse for aesthetics, especially poetry.

The concepts of *sphoṭa* and *apoha* are criticized by Bhāmaha who also elucidates the distinct nature of the poetic realm. He uses the interesting notion of *sauśabdya* where words themselves become the objects of 'seeking' as their exact, apt and purified form alone would give rise to a poetic meaning which arouses both wonder and delight at the same time. He also uses the idea of *Kāvyānvaya*—the logic of poetry—to distinguish the methodology and norms relevant to the aesthetic domain proper, thus marking its autonomy from those fields where Nyāya is used as *anumāna* with its own syllogism in what may be called the *pramāṇa vyāpāra.* He elaborates the concept of *doṣa* in literary compositions as analogous to what is regarded as *hetvābhāsa* in the *Nyāya sūtra.* He also made an attempt to distinguish between *pratibhā* (natural in-born creative impulse), and *vyutpatti* (learned, nurtured understanding) as the sources of poetic composition.

After Bhāmaha the most important work is supposed to have been that of Daṇḍin who not only wrote the well-known *Daśakumāracarita* and *Avantīsundarīkathā* but also a work on poetics entitled, *Kāvyalakṣaṇa.* There has been a lot of controversy about the relative dates of Daṇḍin and Bhāmaha but some scholars feel that after the discovery of *Avantīsundarīkathā* by Daṇḍin, it may be safely concluded that Daṇḍin occurred after Bhāmaha. Both of them presumably lived in the South. At least Daṇḍin definitely belonged to that region after he had migrated from Gujarat.

After Bhāmaha and Daṇḍin the scene dramatically shifts to the extreme north in Kashmir where, from the eighth century onwards, we have a galaxy of great aestheticians such as Udbhaṭṭa, Rudraṭa, Ānandavardhana and Abhinavagupta, the last two being justly famous in the history of Indian aesthetics as they started new trends in literary criticism and also propounded alternative theories to those which were dominant at that time.

With Ānandavardhana begins the famous new school of *dhvani* which attempts to replace the *alaṁkāra* theorists with a new alternative way of understanding poetic meaning. Its relation to the school which emphasises *rasa* does not seem to be very clear though it may perhaps be reasonably surmised that it laid more emphasis on poetic meaning rather than aesthetic emotion or delight. The emphasis perhaps was primarily on the unexpectedness of the new meaning generated by the poetic use of word and the consequent wonder that was the inevitable accompaniment of such an apprehension. Abhinavagupta, Mammaṭa, Ruyyaka Viśvanātha, Rājaśekhara, Jayadeva, Kṣemendra, Śarada-tanaya, Bhānudatta, Rūpa Gosvāmī, Appaya Dikṣita and Paṇḍitarāja Jagannātha were all well known as exponents of *dhvani.*

Thus there is an extraordinary presence of eight outstanding theoreticians who reflected on the problems of poetics and literary creation from the eighth to twelfth century.

After Ruyyaka, developments in this field seem to have shifted once again from the North to the South, perhaps due to political reasons. Among these a significant contribution was made by Appaya Dīkṣita at the beginning of the sixteenth century who developed the new notion of *arthālaṁkāra* and wrote three works on poetics, namely, *Kuvalayānanda, Citra Mīmāṁsā* and *Vṛtti Vārttika.* Of these, the *Citra Mīmāṁsā* is perhaps the most important as it started a controversy when it became the subject of criticism by Paṇḍitarāja Jagannātha who lived during the reign of Shahjahan in the seventeenth century and wrote a work entitled, *Citra Mīmāṁsā Khanḍana.* Appaya Dikṣita III seems to have replied to Paṇḍitarāja Jagannātha in his *Citra Mimāṁsā-doṣadhikkāra.* There appears to have been one Pradhāna Venkamatya who, in his "Alaṁkāra Maṇidarpaṇa" (unpublished) defended the views of Appaya Dikṣita I against Jagannātha. The controversy seems to have continued as Lakṣmaṇasūri came to the rescue of Jagannātha in his work entitled, "Sābhūpālaṁkāra" (unpublished).

The works on *Alaṁkāraśāstra* from eighteenth century onwards take off principally from where Appaya Dikṣita I and Paṇḍitarāja Jagannātha had left the thinking on the subject in the seventeenth century.

A work which seems to have exercised a great influence both in style and content was written by Vidyānātha in the subsequent period. Entitled, *Pratāparudrīyayaśobhūṣaṇa* it was used as a model to such an extent that many of the writers of this period called their work *Yaśobhūṣaṇa* of one patron or another. One of the main characteristics of this type of writing was that it was written in praise of the patron of the poet-writer concerned and that he composed poetic creations of his own to illustrate the points made in the course of the discussion. There is thus a historical dimension to these works, along with the literary and rhetorical, where the one is so finely blended with the other that it is difficult to separate the two.

An increasing tendency to write expository pieces without going into the traditional method of anticipating objections and refuting the counter positions to the ones held by the author also becomes apparent. Besides this, an interesting amalgamation occurred of the two streams in Indian poetics—the first deriving from the *Nāṭya Śāstra* of Bharata while the other concentrated more on poetry and literature, deriving from Daṇḍin and Bhāmaha. Also, there seems to be a great influence of Candrāloka and Kuvalayānanda on their writings.

Another dimension to writing on the *Alaṁkāraśāstra* during the post-Jagannātha period relates to the increasing influence of the Navya Nyāya mode of analysis and its technical terms. But, while such a mode of analysis apparent in all cognitive enterprises in India, helps in achieving precision in the statements that are made, it also renders them unintelligible at least to those who are uninitiated in the vocabulary of the techniques of Navya Nyāya analysis. Many of these works deal with all the issues that were traditionally discussed in the *Alaṁkāraśāstra*, but there are many others which deal only with specific subjects or topics. In this, they show a distinct influence of the new trend in the intellectual life of India, as scholars begin to concentrate more and more on specialised problems, issues and often on only one or two important aspects of an issue.

The most important of these thinkers seem to be Nṛsimha Kavi, Venkaṭāmātya, Rāmasudhī, Acyutarāya and Viśveśvara Paṇḍita. Among these, Nṛsimha Kavi was an outstanding thinker in the south during the eighteenth century, and is reported to have been associated with the pre-Hyder Ali kingdom of Mummadi Krishnaraja Odeyar of Mysore, whose minister named Kalale Nanjaraja was his patron. His work is entitled, *Nanjarāja Yaśobhūṣaṇa.* His model was the well known work of Vidyānātha who had included the name of his patron in the very title of his work, the *Pratāparudrīya-yaśobhūṣaṇa.* Nṛsimha Kavi discussed exhaustively all the issues relating to both poetics and dramaturgy and even illustrated all these points through the composition of a drama which he himself wrote. His discussion of *Alaṁkāra* takes into account all the developments that had taken place since the time of Vidyānātha while introducing new points of his own. The notion of *Alaṁkāra*, like most other concepts, shows the dual tendency of being narrowed down to some very specific characteristics alone with a possibility of being widened to include almost every characteristic which other thinkers had ascribed to some other concept. This, as we shall see later, has also been attempted with some interesting results in respect to the notion of *rasa* particularly in the work of Acyutarāya Modaka whose work is entitled, *Sāhityasāra.*

Venkaṭāmātya, a younger contemporary of Nṛsimha Kavi, was associated with Hyder Ali, and wrote a work entitled, *Alaṁkāramaṇi-darpaṇa.* He shows an awareness of the work of his senior contemporary, Nṛsimha Kavi, whose definition of *Kāvya* he criticises. Nṛsimha Kavi had emphasised the necessity of expression and thought being in conformity with prevalent poetic conventions (*Kavi Samaya*) already established with regard to the usage of *Vyañjanā Vyāpāra* while utilising the poetic devices of *guṇa, Alaṁkāra,* etc. Venkatāmātya did not accept this conformity to *Kavi Samaya* as essential as it could not become an exclusive characteristic of poetic creation. Instead, he emphasised *Sarasatva* as the distinct feature of poetry.

Evidence of the new tendency amongst writers of *Alaṁkāraśāstra* to use the phraseology, techniques and modes of analysis of hard-core philosophical disciplines such as those of Nyāya and Mīmāṁsā is also present in the work of Nṛsimha Kavi. In fact, this tendency reaches its climax in the work of Viśveśvara Paṇḍita whose work, entitled *Alaṁkāra-kaustubha,* is famous for its extensive use of the Navya Nyāya techniques to achieve precision in the definition of *alaṁkāras.* It is not clear, however, how this attempted precision in the various definitions achieves anything significantly new in our understanding of them.

Other prominent names in the *Alaṁkaraśāstra* tradition are those of Vidyārāma, Aśadhara Bhaṭṭa and Bhaṭṭa Deva Śaṅkara Purohit, who belong respectively to Mysore, Rajasthan and Gujarat. Little is known about Vidyārāma and Aśadhar Bhaṭṭa but there is important information about Bhaṭṭa Deva Śaṅkara Purohit who not only lived in the period of the Peshvas but has also explicitly written about some of them such as Raghunātha Rāo, Mādhava Rāo, Nārāyaṇa Rāo etc. He has also described the death of Viśvāsa Rāo in the third battle of Panipat. Thus, the work of Purohit is of interest not only to students of the Alaṁkāraśāstra in this period but also as it provides literary evidence for the history of this period.

Besides the historical dimension of Bhatta Deva Śaṅkara Purohita's work on the Peshvas, who were perhaps his patrons, he also explores the different dimensions of *arthālaṁkāra* in detail and discusses the views of his predecessor Rāja Cūḍāmaṇi Dikṣita in respect of *Kuvalyānanada,* differing from him on many points.

The work of Vidyārāma is interesting as he separately mentions *bhakti* as a distinct *rasa* and devotes the fourth part of his *Rasadīrghikā* to it. However, the work of Aśadhar Bhaṭṭa reveals thinking about language seen primarily as a commingling of *abhidā, vyañjanā* and *lakṣaṇā* together, like the meeting of Gaṅgā, Yamunā and Sarasvatī at Prayag where it is called Triveṇī. His work after this analogy is named *Triveṇikā,* explicitly stating therein that though *abhidā* appears to be the primary meaning of language, the bluish thing to it is given by the *lakṣaṇā* and the hidden secret dimension is provided by *vyañjanā*. The third, though visible only to few, is the real heart of the language. This is what opens the language to the unmanifest transcendent and brings it to the region where it becomes accessible to man through its power.

Thus his thinking about language is essentially *vyañjanā*-centric which alone provides a key to the poetic use of language. Interestingly, among the grammarians, it is only Nāgeśa Bhaṭṭa who has paid any thought to *vyañjanā* in his reflection about language.

It is, perhaps, in the work of Acyutarāya Modak that we find a new way of thinking. He, not only, classifies the notion of *rasa* into *laukika* and *alaukika*, but also divides the latter into those which arise in the context of day-dreaming, dreaming and imagining such as is evidenced in the activity of seeing figures in the clouds, etc. However, he does not seem to have applied the distinction of *sāttvika, rājasika and tāmasika* to *rasas* that are supposed to arise in the *laukika* and the *alaukika* realm. Nor is it clear whether the active imagination that results in the creation of a work of art is given a separate place in the context of those types of objects which give rise to the *alaukika rasa*. In any case, the whole discussion does not seem to distinguish between the emotion which arises in the context of a work of art and that which arises in respect of other kinds of objects. Nor does there seem to be any attempt to distinguish between different kinds of aesthetic objects with respect to which the aesthetic emotion is said to be engendered. Bharata's formulation of the theory of *rasa* in the context of dramatic representations seems to have been a stumbling block for the aestheticians of India though the increasing centrality of poetry as an art form in the discipline of aesthetics tried to free this from some of the limitations that Bharata's discussion had imposed on it. Still, since many forms of poetry are close to drama, and contain dramatic elements in them, the separation never seems to have been completely achieved.

Acyutarāya's acceptance of the notion of *laukika rasa* sounds strange as it would be difficult to accept the idea that the *rasa* which one feels in respect of an art object, can be transposed into an ordinary situation where any natural object is enjoyed by the senses. It is true that Bharata himself had initiated the conclusion by talking of *rasa* on the analogy of taste, thus, giving an impression that taste was something like *rasa* and as one could mix different tastes one could blend different kinds of emotions to get a more complex *rasa*.

The problem was further compounded by the controversies regarding the inclusion of *śānta* and *bhakti* amongst the *rasas* already mentioned by Bharata. The acceptance of these two in the category of *rasa* could mean that *rasa* need not be something which arises specifically and exclusively in the context of a dramatic representation of the human situations where emotions are first experienced in their raw form. *Śānta rasa* is obviously something that may be said to be directly and immediately experienced in the meditative consciousness, while the *bhakti rasa* may be said to be directly experienced when one worships the

Lord or engages in *bhajana* or *kīrtana*. In this context, the work of Vidyārāma who mentions *bhakti* as a distinct *rasa* and devotes the fourth part of his *Rasadīrghikā* to it, is significant. These, two *rasas* thus, are closer to the day-to-day experiences of *rasa* which arise through the contact of the various senses with their objects. One may, of course, treat the *bhakti rasa* as arising through the contemplation of the imagined life of the Lord as is done in *bhakti* or *śānta* as evoked by the stories of the great renouncers such as the Buddha and the Mahāvīra. After accepting this inclusion, it will be difficult to withhold the applications of the idea of *rasa* to all other realms which imagination creates. This, perhaps, is the reason why Acyutarāya Modak has included day-dreaming and imaginative fantasy in the category of *alaukika rasa* along with the creations of art which are generally included in it.

The problem of accounting for an almost total absence of *rasas* such as *vibhatsa, bhayānaka, raudra,* etc., will occur in this case as it is only in the realm of art that these can be experienced as *rasa.* In the *laukika* realm of experience these can never be experienced as *rasa,* and even in the realms which Acyutarāya Modak includes under the category of the *aluakika,* it would be difficult to say if *vibhatsa,* etc. can be experienced as *rasa* in the situations corresponding to them. It is true that the element of "virtuality" which informs works of art is also present in imaginary creations which are the result of day-dreaming referred to by Acyutarāya, yet, normally the "distancing" that marks an artistic creation is absent in them.

One may, possibly, treat *śānta rasa* in a way different from now as it has been treated in the Indian tradition. It may be understood as *catharsis* is understood in the western tradition, that is, as the ultimate culminating *rasa* to which all of the *rasas* contribute in a really great work of art. Therefore, according to this interpretation, there would be only one *rasa,* the *rasa* to which all other so called *rasa's* contribute, that is, the *rasa* of *rasas,* the *rasa par excellence* or the pure aesthetic emotion, unalloyed by any other element. The term *catharsis* has been used in the western tradition only to signify the effect that a great tragedy culminates in, but there is no reason why it cannot be extended to cover the essence of all aesthetic emotion—an essence which is more adequately conveyed by the term *śānta,* which has been used in the Indian tradition. It may perhaps be understood in the sense which is conveyed by the Shakespearean phrase "Rightness is All", or what the *Upaniṣad* suggests when it says "*śānto'yam ātmā*'.

But if this is accepted, then *śānta rasa* will be the only *rasa* and all the other *rasas* would be seen as contributing to it or culminating in it as the different *bhāvas* are supposed to give rise to *rasa* which is seen as an emergent quality arising out of them. This, however, would leave the problem of *bhakti rasa* unsolved unless *bhakti,* in the aesthetic context is seen as emotion aroused by the inexhaustible realms of beauty revealed in and through the works of art in their myriad forms arousing an unsatiable longing for being with it and immersed in it eternally. This, obviously, is not what has been generally understood by *bhakti* in the Indian tradition.

But a reflection on what the *gopīs* have come to symbolize in the Indian tradition might reveal that our reformulation of the idea of *bhakti* is not too far away from it. Kṛṣṇa symbolises eternal, inexhaustible, unfathomable charm and beauty inherent in reality which ever attracts and enchants us and draws us towards itself again and again and we feel desolate and dry and foresaken when we are unrelated to it. The relation of the *gopīs* to Kṛṣṇa may thus be said to symbolize man's relation to Art which reveals in a transparent manner a living embodiment of that hidden dimension of reality which is conveyed by the well-known Upaniṣadic statement "*Raso vai saḥ*".

The *śānta* and the *bhakti* may thus be seen as the two poles of consciousness as it encounters the world of art and apprehends its reality through these two alternating modes of consciousness. Yet, the world of art is not the whole world, just as the Kṛṣṇa of the *Gītagovinda* or even *Śrīmad Bhāgavat* is not the whole of Kṛṣṇa.

But can the idea of *rasa* which was developed by Bharata in the context of *nāṭya* and later elaborated in the context of *kāvya*, be extended not only to the other arts and get modified by a reflection on them, but to the whole of life which man lives and which he tries to transform, so that it may be more meaningful and beautiful? The attempt to introduce the idea of *māyā* as a *rasa* by Bhānudatta in the later part of the fifteenth century seems to have been a step in this direction. The world of *nāṭya* and, in fact, the whole world created by man has something of the character of *māyā* as understood in the Advaitic tradition. *Māyā* is said to be *sadasad vilakṣaṇa* i.e., neither *sat* nor *asat* and hence *anirvacanīya*, i.e., indescribable as either true or false. A work of art shares both these characteristics in a pre-eminent sense. In fact, Abhinavagupta is said to have discussed the question regarding the ontological status of a work of art and has concluded that it has a reality which is *sui generis* as it cannot be subsumed under any other category.

But, if the world itself has the character of *māyā* from an ontological point of view and man's artistic creations have that very character from the point of view of the world in which man normally lives, then he would have two levels of *māyā*, one created by man and the other created by Īśvara. In that case, however, we will have to distinguish between the *rasa* produced by the world of art created by man, and the *rasa* produced by the world in which man normally lives. Perhaps, the attempt to distinguish between *laukika* and *alaukika rasa* was an attempt in this direction. But, if the analogy has to be carried further then one will have to treat the *rasa* enjoyed by human beings at the *laukika* level of *vyavahāra*, as something akin to that which is enjoyed by the actual participants in a dramatic performance and the experience of *rasa* as it is, as it occurs in the mind of the beholder, that is, the *sahṛdaya* will have to be treated as more akin to that which presumably is enjoyed by Īśvara. But then what would be the distinction between *māyā* and *līlā*? Perhaps what is *līlā* for Īśvara is *māyā* for man, just as what is 'play' for the beholder is something different from that which is 'work' for the actors who have to sweat for it. Shakespeare has said, "all the world is a stage", but he forgot to ask that if this was so, who was the "beholder" of this play.

Though in a different context, Bhaṭṭanāyaka, a thinker referred to by Abhinavagupta in his famous commentary entitled, *Abhinavabhāratī* expresses a similar view. According to Abhinavagupta, Bhaṭṭanāyaka is supposed to have said that the purpose of the creation of *Nāṭya* as an art form by Brahmā, the Creator of the world was to make men aware of the similarity between the apparently real, though essentially illusory world of *nāṭya* and the world in which he actually lives. Thus man may realize that this too is finally devoid of reality just as the world of dramatic representation which the spectator sees on the stage, participating in its joys and sorrows as if it were the real world. Bhaṭṭanāyaka uses the word *prapañca* which recalls the later use of it in Advaita Vedānta to convey the character of the world as *māyā*. But like Shakespeare, Bhaṭṭanāyaka also does not ask the question as to who is the spectator of this world play and, in case it is Brahma himself, then it is a sad reflection to think that the world he has created is so full of unnecessary pain, suffering, misery and ugliness when it could certainly be made better, unless, of course, one thinks with Leibnitz that this is the best of all possible worlds as any other world would have been worse than this.

If the different theories of *rasa* are applied to the non-representational forms of art what consequences would emerge? Would one, for example, be able to apply the concept of *māyā* to a non-representational work of art such as, say, the Chinese Jar which "moves perpetually in its stillness" or the *śuddha*, pure *ālāpa* of a *dhrupada* sung by a great vocalist. Some recent attempts at the extension of the concept of *rasa* in these fields especially music, will be examined later but it is surprising that most writers on *Alaṁkāra Śāstra* have rejected Bhānudatta's suggestion that the *rasa* of *māyā* be treated as a distinct kind of *rasa* different from all others. Their objections do not seem very convincing as they completely ignore the *māyā* character of *nāṭya* itself. The main objections relate to the beginninglessness of *māyā*, its *mithyātva* and its total difference from Brahman. For example, Cirañjīva Bhaṭṭacārya, Viśveśvara Paṇḍita and Ghāsīrām Paṇḍita appear to raise these objections. But, as far as the beginninglessness of *māyā* is concerned the Brahman also is as beginningless as *māyā* and as for *mithyātva* nothing at least in Advaita Vedanta can be regarded as "real" as Brahman. Also, as everything is different from Brahman the objection that *māyā* is different and hence cannot be regarded as something which can have *rasa* in it, is blatantly absurd, for in that case, neither *nāṭya* nor *kāvya* could be said to have *rasa* in them or produce it in the beholder. An interesting suggestion of Bhānudatta is that just as *nivṛtti* can be said to give rise to *śānta rasa*, so *pravṛtti* may be considered to give rise to *rasa* of *māyā*. But then *māyā* would have to be conceived as the only *rasa* excluding *śānta* and all the other *rasas* would have to be subsumed under it. It would be difficult to decide whether *bhakti*, if it is accepted as *rasa*, could be included under this classification. The suggestion of Ghāsirāma Paṇḍita that the *rasa* of *māyā* may itself be subsumed under the *rasa* known as *adbhūta* which is already accepted by the tradition, has not been taken seriously by those who have considered the issue in detail. All in all, the important innovations suggested by Bhānudatta do not seem to have received the attention they deserve.

Two other issues which appear to dominate the thinking on *Alaṁkāraśāstra* during this period relate to first, the controversy between Appayadīkṣita I and Paṇḍitarāja Jagannātha, and second, the increasing importation of not only the *Mīmāṁsā* and the Navya Nyāya terminology in the formulation of the issues relating to *Alaṁkāraśāstra,* but also the use of concepts pertaining to these domains for the understanding and illumination of some of the key problems in it. The controversy seems to relate to the definition of *alaṁkāra,* that is, the diverse linguistic, rhetorical devices to enhance the beauty of a poem and its relationship to *rasa* or the aesthetic delight which is supposed to be the essence of any poetic or dramatic creation. The linguistic and rhetorical devices are themselves divided into those which pertain exclusively to language and others which arise primarily because of the play on the diverse meanings of the words used. Appayadīkṣita is supposed to have contended that the use of *alaṁkāra* plays an important role in the production of aesthetic delight or *rasa* as it intensifies it in certain ways. This was denied by Paṇḍitarāja Jagannātha who appears to have held that basically *alaṁkāras* have little to do with *rasa* and many a time stand in the way of its emergence, apprehension and appreciation.

The controversy was epitomized, long ago by Kālidāsa in the apprehension of the beauty of Śakuntalā by Duṣyanta when he sees her for the first time. The king was accustomed to seeing beautiful women in the palace adorned with all the ornaments which they had and therefore came to regard these embellishments as the inevitable accompaniment of anything that was to be considered as beautiful. His new response in the presence of the beauty of Śakuntalā is described by Kālidāsa in a marvellous sequence of lines. At first, he thinks of a lotus which is surrounded by the muddy water of the pond, and yet beautiful. Then he thinks of the moon whose beauty is enhanced by the spots it has. Finally, he moves on to the realization that basically Śakuntalā is prettier *because of* the ordinary rustic clothes she is wearing proving that there is no relation between real beauty and the myriad efforts at its enhancement through ornamentation. Kālidāsa, of course, is not involved in the controversy, but it has been perennial in the reflection on the beauty of a work of art even though it is associated, at least for this period, with the names of Appayadikṣita I and Paṇḍitarāja Jagannātha.

The controversy over the *śleṣa* or double and multiple meanings has the same character. Ultimately the words and the meanings and whatever is suggested by them are so intimately fused with one another in a great poetic creation that it is difficult to separate one from the other. The Indian thinking on poetics seems to have been so enmeshed in the counting of numbers of different *alaṁkāras,* both *śabdālaṁkāras* and *arthālaṁkāras* that it seems to have lost the wood for the trees. When Mammaṭa enumerated the total number of *alaṁkāras,* he raised the inevitable question: whether there could be more *alaṁkāras* than the ones he had described and classified or could their number be reduced by treating some as instances of others. This happens with all classifications. Many thinkers on poetics after him tried to increase the number of *alaṁkāras* by pointing out that there were other *alaṁkāras* which could not be possibly accommodated in his scheme. Inevitably others attempted to deny the necessity of this and Viśveśvara Paṇḍita is the most eminent name amongst the rhetoricians of the period to argue in favour of Mammaṭa and against his successors.

As for the use of the Mīmāṁsā and Navya Nyāya modes of achieving precision and distinguishing one concept from another, the writers of this period seem to be influenced by the general intellectual climate which prevailed in all branches of learning during this period. The Navya Nyāya concepts in respect of which the technique of *pariṣkāra* were used most are *sādṛśya āropa, adhyavasāya* and *sambhāvanā*. The thinkers who have attempted the method of *pariṣkāra* for analysing *alaṁkāras* such as *upamā, rūpaka, atiśayokti,* etc., are Jayarāma Nyāyapañcānana, Vidyānātha Tatsat and Viśveśvara Paṇḍita. The Mīmāṁsā concepts which are used effectively, seem to be those of *aṅga* and *aṅgī, mukhya* and *gauṇa* and *phalabheda* and *āśrayabheda.* Thus the distinction between *vṛtti* and *rīti* is explained by the analogy of *phalabheda* and *āśrayabheda.* For example, the difference between *vṛtti* and *rīti* is said to be that, *vṛttis* suggest *rasas,* while *rītis* bring forth *guṇas.*

However, the thinkers in the tradition of *Alaṁkāraśāstra* do not always blindly accept the Nyāya or Mīmāṁsā doctrines in the context of their own thinking. The Nyāya doctrine, for example, that the *guṇas* cannot have *guṇas* of their own, is explicitly rejected by Acyutarāya even though the doctrine was supported by such an authority as Paṇḍitarāja Jagannātha himself. His reason for rejecting the relevance of the Nyāya doctrine for *Alaṁkāraśāstra* was that the *guṇas* that one talks about in the context of *Alaṁkāraśāstra* are not the same as the natural *guṇas* such as *rūpa, rasa, gandha, sparśa,* etc. which the *naiyāyika* is talking about. But, Acyutarāya does not seem to realise the radical implications of such an assertion. If the *guṇas* which the *Alaṁkāraśāstra* deals with are totally different in nature from those which are dealt with in the *Nyāya Śāstra,* then what is their ontological status and how is knowledge about them validated. It is not surprising that the notion of *Āhārya Jñāna* has been used by thinkers of this period dealing with *Alaṁkāraśāstra* to provide a basis for discussing such problems. Yet, the larger problem of the epistemological validation of judgements relating to *kāvya* and *nāṭya* does not seem to have been discussed, even though the notion of *aucitya* seems to have played some role in their thinking. The idea of '*rasābhāsa*' which could have provided an important entry point for the discussion of this issue somehow got entangled in moral considerations which were totally irrelevant to the aesthetic domain.

The traditional concern with the question as to wherein the essential nature of poetry resides, or consists in, has continued to engage the attention of many persons in the older Sanskritic tradition continuing even into the twentieth century. Some of those who deserve mention are Professor Rewaprasada Dvivedi and the well-known scholar of Kālidāsa, Professor Brahmanand Sharma.

The former, Professor Dvivedi has extended the meaning of the term *alaṁkāra* to include other aspects of poetry such as *dhvani*, etc. in his book, *Kāvyālaṁkārakārikā*. However, he appears to consider *rasa* as the effect produced by poetry in the mind of the *sahṛdaya*, or one who critically and appreciatively apprehends its meaning in its various dimensions and depths.

Also, interestingly, he appears to consider the poetic meaning itself as symbolising something else which is the real essence of poetry and to which all the elements, that is, *alaṁkāra* in the usual sense of the term, *dhvani, guṇa* and *rīti*, etc. contribute and which produces *rasa* in the person who has developed the capacity and the sensibility over a long period of cultivating it through a continuous acquaintance with the great poetic works with which he has 'lived' almost the whole of his life.

Paṇḍit Brahmanand Sharma, on the other hand-disputes this symbolisation of poetic meaning as, ultimately what poetry conveys cannot be separated from the specificity of the words and the particular sequence in which they occur. Not only this, according to him, if the meaning of the term *alaṁkāra* can be extended as Professor Rewaprasad Dvivedi has done, the same can be done also with the other terms in the tradition such as *dhvani, guṇa* or *rīti* and they may then also be treated as symbolising something beyond them which introduces *rasa* as a consequent emergent quality in the consciousness of one who apprehends this symbolised meaning. Furthermore, the notion of symbolisation, which, according to him, Professor Dvivedi has used, would necessitate some further operation in the conveying of poetic meaning besides the one that is usually conveyed by the term '*vyañjanā*' in traditional vocabulary employed to understand the realm of poetic meaning. His own view on the contrary, is presented in his work entitled, *Kāvyasatyāloka*. He states that poetic meaning consists in a deeper apprehension of truth which ordinary declarative discourse cannot do, as it misses many of the most significant dimensions of the human personality which apprehends reality through them also. Poetry, for him, fuses these diverse dimensions of meaning into a unified, integrated whole which then is apprehended in its totality as true in the real sense of the term.

The central, yet hitherto unasked question, whether the theory of *rasa* can really be extended and applied to arts other than those of *nāṭya, kāvya* and *abhinaya*-centered *nṛtya* was raised and dealt with by Paṇḍit Omkaranatha Thakur. He delivered his lectures at the Baroda University in the days when it was a lively academic centre under the Vice-Chancellorship of Dr. Hansa Mehta. A well-known vocalist of north Indian music and a Professor of Music at the Banaras Hindu University, his lectures in Gujarati were later published under the title '*Rāganīrasa*'.

Paṇḍit Omkarnath Thakur in his lectures explores this idea in detail and suggests that the whole theory of *rasa* developed by Bharata in connection with human situations as depicted in dramatic representation could easily be transposed to music as it has developed in India from the time of the *Sāmaveda* onwards.

In fact, he finds a clue to his attempt in the *Āśvalāyana Gṛhyasūtra* wherein the word "*sāma*" is itself understood to mean the unity of *Sa* and *am*, that is 'you' the feminine principle and 'I' the masculine. This strategy permits him to understand music in terms of a combination of masculine and feminine principles, a move that helps him bring in the theory of *rasa* in terms of what has come to be called the *nāyaka-nāyikā bheda* in the later Indian aesthetic tradition. The fact that Indian music is itself classified under *rāga* and *rāginīs* and that many of these have been represented in painting as if they were embodiments of masculine and feminine characters, helps him to easily make the required transition. However, the deeper point that he makes in this connection is that no emotional meaning can ever be conveyed without the help of the modulation of voice involved in the utterance of the word, which brings in music as providing that element which *alone* generates that central core of meaning without which utterance will become totally inert and dead. This suggests that musical modulations of the notes is an integral part of the communication of meaning at the human level as without it, it would relapse into the type of communication that may be supposed to occur between inert particles of matter. Perhaps, the whole world of living beings communicate in this manner and as life becomes more evolved, the more subtle and dominant becomes this aspect of communication.

Paṇḍit Omkarnath Thakur's subtle analysis of the different ways in which such emotive meaning is conveyed through different *rāgas* and *rāginīs* deserves special attention. So also, does his attempt at establishing correlations between the musical *rāgas* and *rāginīs* and the different types of *nāyakas* and *nāyikās* described so minutely in the Indian tradition. However, the overwhelming and unwarranted influence of the *nāyaka-nāyikā* mode of analysis in the traditional understanding of *rasa* and the inability of the learned Paṇḍit to expand the perspective is a limitation. Instead of treating music as an autonomous realm to be understood on its own terms, he seems to have made it subservient to a mode of analysis which was primarily developed in the context of different art forms, i.e. poetry and drama.

Similarly, according to this appreciation the emotions generated by music are too dependent on the words of the song which are sung, forgetting that in the *śuddha ālāpa* no words are needed at all and that deep and profound effects in the realm of feeling are still generated by the pure sounds which has no verbal accompaniments to them. The *ālāpa* of Dhrupad is well known in this context and in the hands of a great master it will produce effects which transcend all the so-called emotions generated by the *nāyaka-nāyikā* mode of analysis of the *Rāga* and *Rāginī*. Also, whether his theory can apply to all types of music, Indian or non-Indian, and whether even the trained listener will feel the same emotion if ever he/she were not to know the words of the song which is being sung, is not explored by him. Further, if this is accepted then the whole realm of instrumental music is completely neglected as there are no words to help one in understanding the emotion or the mood or the *rasa* that is being generated there.

Yet, in spite of all these limitations there can be little doubt that Paṇḍit Omkarnath Thakur questioned the application and relevance of the theory of *rasa* to other arts, besides those of drama and poetry in the context of which it was developed. Perhaps, the best way would be to explore the concept of *rasa* as immanently pursued in each of the arts without being constrained by the way it has been thought about up till now. One may, later on build a generalized theory of *rasa* which might take specific forms in different arts taking into account the relevant differences among them.

Paṇḍit Omkarnath Thakur's attempt seems to have been carried on further by one of his students, namely, Sri Pradip Dikshit who has written a book entitled, *Rāga Rāginī Vargīkaraṇa aur Nāyaka Nāyikā Bheda.* But the most radical and innovative move in this context has been made by Dr. Mukund Lath in his *Vatsal Nidhi* lectures entitled, *Saṅgīta aur Cintana.* He had made music the central reference point of his thinking and tried to understand the whole realm of creativity including that of thought in this perspective. He concentrates on the notion of *ālāpa* and distinguishes it from *dhuna* a distinction which may be found not only in all musical traditions, but also, in all realms of culture, which ultimately are nothing but a result of human creativity. Dr. Lath draws our attention to the fact that while in the case of *dhuna,* we are expected to *repeat* it without any alteration and to play or sing the same thing in the same tune over and over again, in *rāga* we are expected to innovate continuously within the broad structures provided by the *rāga,* and that this continuous creativity is exhibited in what is called as *ālāpa* in the musical tradition of India. Thus, while in the former any departure from what is treated as the norm or the standard is frowned upon and looked at as a "deviation" requiring correction, in the latter innovation, change, deviation is the heart of the matter. No one expects even a master to "repeat" himself and if he does so, it is treated as a sign of decline in creativity.

Dr. Lath has treated this distinction as a clue to understand the creative element in the process of thinking where, according to him, there is an element of what he has called *ālāpa* in the realm of music. In fact, the point relates to the question as to how a thought develops, and how thinking itself may be seen as a creative act demanding continuous variation and innovations as in *rāga* music.

This may be seen not only as an attempt in distinguishing different cultures and civilisations but also different realms within the same culture or civilization and the way it has varied over time. The recitation of the Vedic *mantras* with their fixed *svarānupūrvī, varṇanupūrvī* and *śabdānūpurvī,* for example provide an instance of what he has called a *dhuna* in the Indian culture. On the other hand, the evolution of *Gandharva* from *Sāma* might provide an example of the *rāga* in the Indian tradition.

In a bold attempt, he has tried to correlate the concepts of *śabda* and *svara* on the one hand, and *satya* and *rasa* on the other. One may question these corelations as they blur the essential differences between the enterprises of thought and the enterprise which is embodied in the different arts. But there can be little doubt that he has pointed to an essential similarity which belongs to all domains where creativity is the essence of the matter. In any case, it gives evidence of continuity and change on the concerns which have been evinced in thinking about the arts since the earliest times and it has continued right up to the present.

Dr. Lath's attempt, though interesting in itself, does not utilize the repertoire of concepts elaborated over millennia in thinking about *nāṭya* and *kāvya* which could have easily been done if he, like all the others, had not felt tied to the *specificity* of the meaning of these concepts in the Indian tradition, determined as they were by the *accidental* circumstances of their origin. The extension, modification, widening and deepening of the meaning of these concepts can easily be achieved if one were to search for the meaning of such terms as *vṛtti, rīti, alaṁkāra, rasa, dhvani, guṇa, doṣa,* etc. in arts other than those to which they were usually applied, that is, *kāvya* and *nāṭya.* Such an attempt would reveal the 'functionality' of the concept in the process of thinking and its intimate, interactive inter-relationship with the other concepts in association with which it forms the conceptual net with the help of which the thinkers in the tradition had tried to take hold of the reality of the aesthetic domain.

The focal concern is neither the work of art that is created, whether it be *kāvya, nāṭya,* etc., nor the *sahṛdaya* or the appreciator who enjoys the work of art, nor the critic who tries to 'analyse' its beauties and critically evaluate its qualities and defects, but rather the creator, or the creative consciousness which brings the original work into being and which has been seen in terms of *pratibhā* in the Indian tradition. If the definition of *pratibhā* as *nava navonmeṣa śālinī buddhi* were taken seriously, then wherever this consciousness is present and whatever its result, it would be analysable, in principle, in terms of the various concepts which the tradition has employed in its long history, modified to suit the specific particularities of each domain of creation. *Alaṁkāra,* for example, would not mean the same in music or architecture as it does in *kāvya* for the simple reason that there is neither *śabda* nor *artha* in the usual senses of these words. Similarly, *dhvani* would be very different and perhaps would be better understood if taken out of the context in which Ānandavardhana first employed it. It should be kept in mind that the concepts elaborated belong to entirely different dimensions of creativity and unless we are clear about the aspect to which it has to be applied, we would not be able to take hold of the complexity of the exercise in question. The concepts of *alaṁkāra, vṛtti, rīti* and *dhvani,* for example, apply primarily to the object that is created. The concept of *rasa,* on the other hand, applies primarily to the *sahṛdaya,* the audience or person who appreciates the work created. The concepts, *guṇa* and *doṣa* arise primarily in the context of the critic even though they are concerned with the work that is the object of their critical reflection.

The issue is complex and needs careful exploration and further elaboration but unless this is done the rich resources of India's thinking in the aesthetic domain will remain confined to the context of *nāṭya* and *kāvya* in which they arose and in the discussion of which they are usually presented. Paṇḍit Omkarnath

Thakur and others have in their diverse ways tried to open up the tradition for further thinking on this matter. So have the works of Paṇḍit Rewaprasad Dvivedi and Paṇḍit Brahma Dutta Sharma. The insights of these and of others like Acyutarāya Modaka have to be taken note of and utilised in the challenging task of carrying the Indian thought in the realm of aesthetic further.

CHAPTER 10

Some Developments in Jaina Thought from Yaśovijaya Onwards

Jaina philosophical thought has hardly been paid the attention that it deserves, perhaps because it is generally supposed to hold that every statement is true from some point of view or other. Its doctrine of *anekāntavāda, syādavāda* and *saptabhaṅgī naya* are well known, but the way they have been really presented has probably stood in the way of their being taken seriously by others. Anyone who says that everything is "true", rules himself out of court from serious discussion on any subject, as he is not contending that what his opponent is saying is false or mistaken. Surprisingly, the same fate should have befallen the other extreme position which holds that no statement or position is "true". Yet, both the Mādhyamika Buddhist and the Advaitin have held some such position and still been the subject of continued discussion and debate amongst the philosophical traditions of India. Both of them have dismissed the Jaina position perfunctorily without much discussion, as if it did not deserve to be seriously considered. In fact, the term "*anekāntika*" is usually used in the sense of a fallacy in the *Nyāya Sūtras* and enjoys this usage in other traditions of philosophising also. The reason for this lies obviously in the fact that thinking normally moves in terms of a two-valued logic where "truth" and "falsity" are opposed to each other in such a way that the same statement cannot be true and false together and has to have at least one of them as its value, that is, be it true or false. The law of contradiction and the law of excluded middle provide the basic structure on which all thinking proceeds and if one seriously denies them, it is difficult to see how one can argue with such a person or proceed in the activity of thinking any further.

Recent advances in logic have questioned the necessity of the law of excluded middle and of the two-valued logic which it presupposes. There have also been attempts to further differentiate the notion of negation on which the usual statement of the law of contradiction is based. But in spite of all the multifarious developments in logic, the foundational problem of "exclusion" remains as thought cannot move without "excluding" or "denying" something, a point that was firmly grasped by the Buddhist in the doctrine of *apoha.* Furthermore, if this is the very character of the thinking process and if it is held to be unacceptable for some reason, then one would be driven to the conclusion that thought cannot, in principle, grasp the nature of that which is supposed to be "real" or "true". Both the Buddhist and Advaitin accepted this conclusion in different ways. The modern logicians, on the other hand, do not seem to accept this as an inevitable conclusion of what he seems to be essentially trying to contact for. He, in essence appears to be, at least *prima facie,* in the good company of the Jaina, who tried to do so long ago in the Indian tradition. Or, perhaps, he does not worry about the metaphysical consequences of what he is trying to do, for he sees himself as a pure "technician" who is only concerned with seeing what are the consequences of the various assumptions which one is "free" to make in respect of both the so-called "axioms" and rules or derivations.

Jaina philosophical thought has hardly been seen in a historical perspective, a neglect which all the so-called schools of Indian philosophies suffer from. It is treated as if all the distinctive doctrines which are ascribed to the Jainas were formulated all at once and that subsequent Jaina thinkers made no additions or modifications in them. Besides this, the treatment of Jaina thinking on philosophical issues has always been presented in such a way as to give the impression that it was not effected in any way by the other schools of Indian philosophy, even though this is not the case either with the presentation of the long debate between the Buddhists and the Nyāya logicians on the one hand and the Buddhist and the Advaitic thinkers on the other. The influence of Buddhist on Gauḍpāda is well known and Śaṅkara has been called, with some justification, a *Pracchanna Bauddha.* It is also well known that the Nyāya positions were greatly modified in the light of the Buddhist criticism of them. This, of course, occurred only in A.D. first millennium as the Buddhists had disappeared from the theatre of Indian philosophy after the destruction of Nālandā in A.D. 1200. The long debate between the Advaitic and Non-Advaitic Vedāntins on the one hand and between the Advaitins and the Naiyāyikas in A.D. second millennium on the other, does not seem to have the same effect as all the sides in the dispute appear to have stuck to their positions.

The Jainas, in contrast, to the Buddhist, the Vedāntins and to the Naiyāyikas, do not seem as apparent from a study of philosophic thought, to have entered in India into a long continuous debate with others on any of the philosophical issues that they held. Yet, even a brief acquaintance with some of the original Jaina arguments will be sufficient to make one doubt the truth of this impression. Sāmantabhadra, for example, is said to have given arguments against the Advaitin's denial of the reality of difference.

In fact, right from the time of Kuṅda king and Umā Svātī, the Jaina philosophical thinking may be seen not only as dealing with the same problems from its own point of view, but also "mirroring" the various conflicting doctrines of other systems in an attempt to reconstruct and reconcile them in as harmonious a way as possible. Thus, the changing philosophical scene in India may be reconstructed from the writings of successive outstanding Jaina thinkers who tried to come to terms with it in their own way. In this attempt, many a time, the differences and conflicts become a part of the Jaina position itself, as elaborated by Jaina thinkers holding different positions on them. Thus, for example, a dispute seems to have risen whether the *jñāna* of the *kevalin* was simultaneous or successive in character. Or in other words, whether the Omniscience ascribed to the *Kevalin* consisted of a simultaneous knowledge of everything, past, present and future or it consisted of successive acts of such knowledge. Siddhasena Divākara (A.D. 700) and Jinabhadra Sūri (A.D. 1140) are supposed to have taken opposed positions on this issue. In fact, the developments in Jaina logic and epistemology can only be understood if they are seen in the context of the developments that were taking place in these fields amongst the other schools of Indian philosophy. The Jaina thinkers had to develop a *Pramāṇa Śāstra* of their own, just as they had to develop a whole complex theory of Nyāya in order to accommodate their own theory of knowledge. Surprisingly, they also took a lot from the *Yoga Sūtras* of Patañjali and modified this to suit their own tradition of meditative practices.

Thus, the philosophical developments among the Jainas were not a purely self-contained, immanent and internal affair of the Jainas alone. It is true that there are supposed to be deep differences between the Digambaras and the Śvetāmbaras on many crucial issues and that independent developments in the Digambara philosophical thought seem to have ceased very early. But, at least among the Śvetāmbaras, philosophical thinking seems to have continued vigorously and Yaśovijaya who appears at the close of the seventeenth century shows clearly in his writings the influence not only of Navya Nyāya, but also of *Advaita Vedānta*, the *Yoga Sūtra* and the *Bhagvad Gītā*. He takes into account the developments that had occurred in India's *Pramāṇa Śāstra* from Siddhasena Divākara onwards. In his well-known work entitled, "*Sanmati Tarka*" Divākara is supposed to have initiated new developments in Jaina thinking about the subject. So also, he is supposed to have integrated the later developments introduced by Haribhadra Sūri and Prabhācandra in the elaboration of the subject. But, his main innovative contribution seems to have been to make use of the Navya Nyāya modes of analysis to explain and strengthen some of the well-known contentions of *anekāntavāda* along with the doctrine of "Nyāya" that is entailed. Yaśovijaya made a clever use of the Navya Nyāya analysis of *abhāva* to establish the Jaina position that the *abhāva* of an object may still be said meaningfully to characterize it even when it exist. Similarly, Yaśovijaya also tried to assimilate or at least show the similarities between the notion of "nyāya" in the Jaina tradition and the notion of *avacchedaka* in the Navya Nyāya tradition, particularly as both tried to achieve absolute precision of statement without any ambiguity whatsoever. However, Yaśovijaya did not use only Navya Nyāya to establish and strengthen the well-known Jaina position against critics, but also took recourse to the discussions in Advaita Vedānta to emphasize the tenability and viability of some Jaina doctrines, which were not accepted by non-Jaina philosophers including the Advaita Vedāntins.

But, perhaps, the most interesting aspect of Yaśovijaya's work in this context is his use of the *Gītā* which at least *prima facie* seems surprising as it is not only supposed to be the word of the Lord himself, but deals with *karma* which, according to Jainism, is the primary cause of bondage. The *Gītā*, may be remembered, deals, amongst other things, with this problem itself and advises of *karma* done in a certain way so that it may not produce bondage at all. It argues that it is not action, *per se*, which is the cause of the bondage but the desire which prompts us to engage in action and which seeks its fulfillment through it. Thus, it suggest that there is a way of doing actions so that they may not result in bondage, as had been argued almost by everybody else, except perhaps the Mīmāṁsaka, in the Indian tradition. This type of action is well known as '*niṣkāma karma*', and it is surprising to find Yaśovijaya accepting or adopting it in the Jaina context.

The discussion on *karma* in the *Gītā* should be understood against the backdrop of the controversy between *jñāna* and *karma* in the Indian tradition, the arguments deriving from the Buddha Śramaṇik and the Upaniṣadic tradition on the one hand and those deriving from the Vedic and the Dharmaśāstra traditions on the other. Surprisingly, Yaśovijaya raises the issue once again in his writings and following the usual advaitic line, treats *karma* as only a means to achieving the state of *jñāna* which alone can lead to the highest state of consciousness which is held to be identical with liberation. Yaśovijaya accepts the notion of *niṣkāma karma* as propounded in the *Gītā* but still considers action of any type and at any level inferior to *jñāna*. In this, he follows Śaṅkara's interpretation of the *Gītā* forgetting like him, that the whole discourse of the *Gītā* was meant to inspire in Arjuna once again the will to fight the war which involved the killing of hundreds of thousands of people. Yaśovijaya also does not seem to take into account the dimension of *bhakti* which is not only propounded in the *Gītā* but with which it closes, recommending complete surrender to God and to none else.

Yaśovijaya seems to be heavily influenced by the *Upaniṣads* also and describes the reality of the *ātman* in terms of its famous formula of *sat-cit-ānand*. But, as he is also a committed Jaina thinker, he tries to reconcile the diverse conflict of thought with easy recourse to *anekāntavāda* and the doctrine of Nyāya forgetting that neither the Buddhists, nor the Advaitin or any other school of philosophy in Indian tradition permit such a reconciliation. In fact, the term "*anekāntic*" is generally used in other systems of philosophy to indicate a fallacy in thought. The ultimate Advaitic position relegates the realm of *anekāntavāda* and Nyāya to *Māyā* in the context of which alone it may be held to be true. Still his valiant attempt to incorporate the insights of Nyāya, Advait Vedānta, the *Gītā* and Yoga tradition shows that the Jaina thinkers were open to influences from other schools of Indian philosophy and that they were not as "isolated" or monadic in the development of their philosophical thought, as has generally been implied in the presentation of their thought by historians of Indian philosophy. In fact, all the so-called "schools" of Indian philosophy have continuously interacted with one another modifying their positions accordingly. Perhaps, the Jainas were more "open" to outside influences in this respect because of their initial acceptance and espousal of *anekāntavāda.* The non-Jaina thinkers on the other hand seem to have interacted mainly amongst themselves as they excluded the Jainas from the philosophical arena because of the position that they held. One cannot argue with a person who holds that every statement is true, and as the Jainas held this position, nobody seems to have taken them "seriously". Thus, while sufficient evidence exists of the influence of other schools on Jaina thinkers, there is hardly any evidence apparent of the counter-influence of the Jainas on them.

Yaśovijaya appeared at the end of the seventeenth century and it is extremely unlikely that subsequent Jaina thinkers from the eighteenth century onwards were not heavily influenced by him or developed his thought further in various respects. In fact, there seem to have been a number of persons who wrote commentaries on some of his works, particularly on the *Jñānasāra* and the *Ādhyātmasāra.* Thus we have Deva Candra Yatipati in A.D. 1738 writing a commentary on his *Jñānasāra* and Lavanyasuri writing as late as A.D. 1946 on a number of his logico-epistemological works such as the *Navarahasya.* In between, we have Gambhīravijaygaṇi and Vijayanemisūri whose dates are not known. The former wrote in Gujrati, thus, giving evidence of his profound influence on a large number of people who did not know Sanskrit. The differences amongst various commentaries, as far as we know, have not yet been studied.

Yaśovijaya was however, not the only thinker during this period. There are many others whose works are mentioned in Potter's bibliography. A list of them has been given in the appendix but for some reason they have not attracted the attention of those who have concerned themselves with developments in Jaina thought during this period. Most of them have assumed that nothing of philosophical significance was produced after Yaśovijaya, and have concentrated mainly on the various sects that arose during this period and the reforming tendencies in them. The impression, though widespread may be as mistaken as we have found it to be in the case of other traditions of philosophising in India during this period. A considered judgement, however, is only possible after a serious study of at least some of these works. Till then, we can only say that it would be extremely surprising if the Jainas were to prove an exception to what we have found to be the case with all the other "schools" of Indian philosophy during this period.

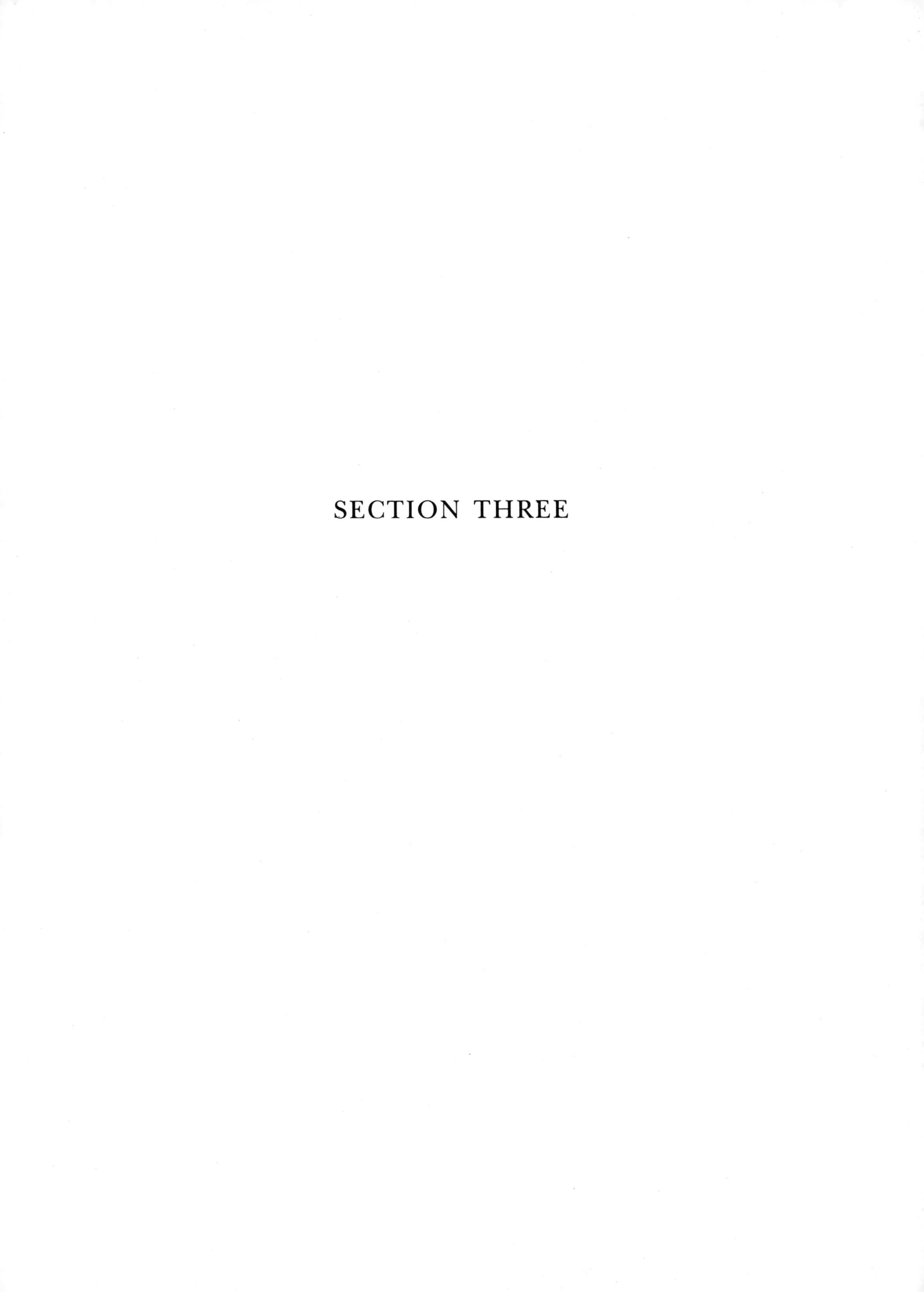

SECTION THREE

CHAPTER 11

Developments in Indian Philosophy Since the Coming of the British

The history of India's philosophical traditions in various fields underwent a radical transformation with the coming of the British and the spread of their political and administrative domination in India between 1757 and 1857, a period during which the whole of India came under their effective control. However, it is between 1857 and 1947 when the British educational system was firmly implanted on the Indian soil thereby creating a totally new system of education that the actual impact became evident.

The long period of Islamic rule in different parts of India had hardly left any impression on traditional modes of indigenous learning as there seems to have been a strict segregation of Arabic and Persian institutions of learning from those that carried on the maintenance, transmission and development of the classical knowledge of India. Also, the system of patronage of traditional learning was not affected in any way by the new political climate that occurred in different parts of the country. There was some interaction in such fields as medicine, astronomy and mathematics, between Arabic and Persian learning and traditional Sanskrit learning while there appears to have been none in the field of philosophy as there is no reference whatsoever in any of the Sanskritic works to Arabic or Greek philosophy. This is extremely surprising as the borrowing in the field of mathematics from Greek and Roman sources has been not only known from earliest times but was also explicitly acknowledged in Indian texts.

The long history of interaction between Greek, Chinese and Indian centres of learning prior to the coming of Islam is still to be investigated. And, though there are ample references to the achievements of Indian medicine, astronomy and mathematics and the borrowing from them in Arabic and Persian sources, there does not seem to be similar evidence in the Sanskritic sources in India of borrowing from Arabic, Persian, Greek and Chinese achievements in various fields of knowledge of the same order as are found elsewhere. Professor Rahman's extensive bibliography on Arabic, Persian and Sanskrit works in Science from the eighth to eighteenth century lists 94 translations. However, as Rahman has not taken philosophy into consideration, it is difficult to say whether any philosophical works were translated into Sanskrit from Arabic and Persian or vice versa.

Al-Biruni is supposed to have come to India with Mahmud of Ghazni in A.D. 1000 in search of knowledge in various domains. However, he mainly talked about the *Bhagvadgītā*, the theory of *avatāra* and some of the *Śmṛti* texts which were known at that time. It is not quite clear whether he had any deep acquaintance with the diverse schools of Indian philosophy which had shown a remarkable development and consolidation of their positions by the time Al-Biruni arrived on the scene. Even his references to Buddhism do not take note of the radical philosophical positions which it had espoused or the central position it held in the philosophical discussions of these times. Recent investigations show that Buddhism was a dominant philosophical force in A.D. first millennium and had spread far beyond the confines of what was then known as India. It is also not clear if Al-Biruni had any acquaintance with the remnants of Buddhism which still might have marginally survived in parts of West and Central Asia during his times. In any case, there is little evidence of any substantive influence of Arabic philosophy on the various schools of Indian philosophy during the long period of Muslim rule in various parts of the country.

In the case of the Europeans, the situation, however, was different, particularly in the case of the British presence in this country. Right from A.D. 1800 when institutions of British learning had begun to be established in Calcutta, there was an intense interest in European thought along with a learning of the English language which helped in opening doors not only to a new civilization but also to a different kind of cognitive enterprise in almost all fields of knowledge. In fact, that a society existed for the acquisition of General Knowledge in 1838 in Hindu College is evidence of the desire for a deeper acquaintance with western knowledge. The role that Derozio (1817–1823) and Ram Mohan Roy (1772–1833), amongst others, played in the transformation of the attitude of the younger generation of the students towards western knowledge and the enthusiastic acquisition of the same in India is well known.

It is not that the acquisition of Persian learning was not regarded very highly during the earlier period when Islamic rule had prevailed over many parts of India, but it was more in the context of literature and law that it was cultivated and not so much for the knowledge of science or philosophy which still appeared to be the preserve of those who knew Sanskrit well. In fact, Persian was the language of the ruling class and thus had all the prestige which is associated with such a language, particularly as it happened to be the language of administration as well. The English language, too had all these advantages associated with it, but it was also primarily seen as providing access to a particular kind of knowledge and a system of values which gave a radically different foundation to both society and polity in this country. Bengal became the centre of this new enthusiasm as also of the attempt to find some sort of a new creative civilizational response to this western impact so that its own civilizational and cultural identity was not completely lost.

The movement of neo-Vedāntism has to be seen in this light and the writings from Ram Mohan Roy onwards, who was proficient both in Sanskrit and Persian, should be seen as an attempt to come to terms with this fascination with the West which simultaneously aroused ambivalent feelings amongst those who came in deep contact with it. It is interesting to note that while most of the thinkers in Bengal and elsewhere turned to the *Upaniṣads* for their inspiration, and bypassing the long controversy regarding their interpretation as embodied in the debate between the Advaitins and the non-Advaitins, found in the doctrine of the formless absolute the ground for a new reconciliation between one of the oldest philosophical traditions of India and the challenge from the West which emphasized the knowledge of the world in all its multiplicity and the use of this knowledge for the intellectual, material and cultural prosperity of man. The ideals of equality and fraternity which the French Revolution had bequeathed to mankind and which the liberal British thought brought to India were seen as expressions of the fundamental Vedāntic truth embodied in such Upaniṣadic statements as "*Sarvam Khalvidam-brahman*", underlying the long tradition of Upaniṣadic interpretation right from the *Brahma Sūtras* which had denied access to the *śruti* of a large part of mankind including both women and *śūdras*. Neo-vedāntism also ignored the distinction between *vyavahāra* and *paramārtha*, that is, the ordinary world of everyday life and the spiritual truth which was supposed to be radically different from it and hence was literally of no relevance to the actual empirical concerns in which man was mainly involved. Not only this, it showed little awareness of the conflict between *jñāna* and *karma*, or the life of contemplation and the life of action which had continuously plagued the Indian tradition right from its beginning. Thus, ignoring the whole tradition of more than two thousand years of India's philosophical concerns, the neo-Vedāntins bypassed the different and tricky problems raised by the earlier discussions and debate and gave a radically new interpretation which reconciled everything by vague references to the ultimate unity of everything in the indescribable, formless reality of Brahman that permeated everything and thus was the essence of all that is.

As against this, it was Dayanand Saraswati (1824–1883) in the north who went back not to the *Upaniṣads* but to the Vedas to meet not only the challenge from the West but also the challenge of Islam which had dominated India for such a long time. The presence of Islam was still something of a socio-cultural problem, particularly in the regions to which he belonged even though its political power had been eclipsed by that of the British who had gained almost complete and effective control over most of India. But Saraswati too, bypassed the whole development that had occurred from the time of the Vedas onwards though he did not ignore it so completely as the neo-Vedāntins from Ram Mohan Roy onwards had done as he did controvert Śaṁkara and many others in his *Satyārtha Prakāśā*. But, though there is great difference between the two, there is also a radical similarity between them as both Dayanand and the neo-Vedāntins used the Vedic-Upaniṣadic heritage for purposes of social reforms which almost no one in the past had done. The social realm was always treated as a preserve of the *Dharma Śāstras* and what was right and what was wrong was always supposed to be determined by the texts relating to *dharma* and *vyavahāra* or the customs prevalent in a particular group or region which was always recognised as authoritative unless it violated some of the basic norms accepted in the *Dharma Śāstras.* In fact, many of the practices which seemed to have been prevalent in ancient times were prohibited on the grounds that they were not permitted in the *kaliyuga.* Sanction for social reform sought in the Vedas and the *Upaniṣads* spilled over, as we will see later, into a desire for political liberation from the British. This was a characteristic feature of many of the neo-Vedāntic spiritual personalities such as Vivekananda and Swami Rama Tirtha amongst others. While there is evidence for some of the saints having taken interest in political matters primarily on account of Islamic rulers, there seems to have been hardly any notion of political bondage or liberation which was clearly evident in the writings and utterances of many of these persons. The demand for political independence was most probably a result of the contact with European thought which occurred at least from A.D. 1800 onwards. One interesting aspect of this phenomenon was the fact that even though there were great differences between the Hindus and the Muslims, they somehow felt closer to each other against the British who were seen as outsiders. This fact became evident in the rebellion of 1857 where both Hindu and Muslim rulers seem to have united to some extent, to fight the British to throw them out of India.

Besides the use of the Vedic-Upaniṣadic heritage for social and political purposes, there was in addition the creation of new institutions to achieve these purposes such as the Brahmo Samaj (1828), the Arya Samaj (1867) and the Prarthana Samaj (1764). These institutions were not based primarily on doctrinal differences or concerned only with spiritual and religious matters. They also had a self-conscious social and political purpose which they sought to realize through the creation of new educational institutions where Vedic-Upaniṣadic traditions were as much a part of the teaching tradition as the new western knowledge. The latter was seen both as a liberating influence from the innumerable superstitions which the post-Upaniṣadic Paurāṇic tradition had encouraged and also as providing an access to modern scientific knowledge which led to power both in the military and the economic spheres. Some of these institutions which in the north, under the inspiration of the Arya Samaj, were called "Anglo-Vedic" schools and colleges and were examples of this dual influence.

It is of course true that the use of spirituality for purposes of social reform was not unknown in the Indian tradition. Most of the saints in the *bhakti* tradition had always had a social dimension as an integral part of their spiritual teachings. The tāntric tradition was even more self-consciously radical in this respect. However, the present movement was interesting and led not from below but from the top and it was the newly educated in English elite with some knowledge of Sanskrit who were responsible for initiating movements against what was seen as social evils. In some cases, they demanded legislative action by the British to stop those practices. This was totally new. In India, the Brahmanical or the Islamic elite had earlier not been known to have initiated movements for social reform, nor were social changes through legislation ever attempted except perhaps indirectly by the authors of the new *dharma* and the *Vyavahāra Śāstras.*

The intellectuals of both the neo-Vedāntic and the neo-Vedic movement viewed at the philosophical development that had taken place in India for at least two thousand five hundred years with a critical attitude and some of them were openly contemptuous of what was practised as Navya Nyāya in Bengal. Isvarchandra Vidyasagara is the classic example of this attitude, though he is supposed to have been a great Sanskritist himself. He denounced Sanskrit learning as practised in his time and advocated teaching in the English medium as it would provide the younger generation with more relevant knowledge.

The use of the Vedic/Upaniṣadic tradition for the purposes of social reform and political action was facilitated by the fact that the *Dharma Śāstras,* the *Vyavahāra Śāstras* and the *Artha Śāstra* never formed an integral part of what was considered as *śruti* in the Vedic tradition. This resulted in a strange paradoxical situation where the protagonists of the neo-Vedāntic and what may be called neo-Vedic formulations were in direct conflict with the votaries of the orthodox Sanskritist tradition in India as the latter upheld the authority of the *smṛti* texts in the field of social and legal behaviour as much as they did the *śruti* texts in the realm relating to *adṛṣṭa* or the transcendent. On almost all matters of social reform, the orthodox opinion stood firmly against the reformists who derived their information from the Vedas and the *Upaniṣads* interpreted in a certain way and hence did not care for the classical, social, political and legal texts of India.

This was in strange contrast to the persons in Islamic faith for whom the *Shairiat* or the legal rules relating to family and society were as much an integral part of the Quranic revelation as the other parts relating to matters of faith. For a Muslim to be orthodox meant not only to believe in Allah and Muhammad but to believe also in all the detailed variegated rules relating to personal, social and legal behaviour. This entailed that one could not be orthodox in one's religious inspiration and radical in one's thought relating to social, legal and political matters. This fact has been an obstacle in the way of any real innovation or reform in societies, polities and communities where Islam is taken seriously by the people.

Besides the two sources accepted as *śruti* in the Vedic tradition, the *Gītā* had also acquired a standard authoritative position, particularly after the early A.D. eighth century when Śaṁkara had commented upon it along with the *Upaniṣads* and the *Brahma Sūtras* to establish the orthodoxy of his interpretation of the philosophical tradition of India. This had important implications as, besides the *Vedas* and the *Upaniṣads,* the *Gītā* came to play an important part in legitimizing the new interpretation regarding the role of *karma* or action in the social and political transformation that seemed to inform all those trying to come to terms with the western, primarily Christian, critique of Indian society and culture. In fact, the Kṛṣṇa of the Mahābhārata became more important than the Kṛṣṇa of the *Śrīmad Bhāgvat*, a fact highlighted not merely in the work of Bankim Chandra who wrote an independent work on Śrī Kṛṣṇa but also in the work of Tilak who wrote a full-length independent commentary on the *Gītā* entitled the *Gītā Bhāṣya* or the *Karma Yoga Śāstra.* Even Gandhi wrote a commentary on the *Gītā* to prove that his doctrine of *ahiṁsā* was in accordance with it.

Apart from the plurality of authoritative texts even within the Vedic tradition and that the rules relating to personal and civic law did not form an integral part of what was known as the *śruti* in the tradition, there was also the *āgamic* tradition which included not only the Buddhists and the Jainas but many other schools such as the Pāñcarātras, the Śaiva, the Śāktas and the Taṅtra. These enjoyed an almost equal authority for most of the non-Islāmic and non-Christian people of India and had a fairly close interaction with the so-called orthodox Vedic tradition deriving from the *Vedas*, the *Upaniṣads* and the *Gītā*, even though the last was never given the status of *śruti* in the tradition. This provided a basic plurality for what has come to be vaguely called, "the Hindu tradition".

The differential response to the impact of the West among the Hindus and the Muslims in this country from 1800 onwards may be understood in the following context: the Hindus who comprised all this heterogeneous mass had not only a plurality of traditions but also that the laws governing their personal, social and political behaviour did not form an integral part of what they themselves regarded as authoritative in their tradition. Further, *taṅtra* which had begun to assume such a dominant force in late medieval times had already questioned the usual norms of personal and social behaviour deriving from the orthodox *smṛti* texts which provided some sort of a basic ground for what was to be regarded as normally acceptable in society. Thus, even prior to the coming of the British in India there already existed a challenge to norms of social behaviour from within as well as from a long tradition deriving from the unorthodoxy of such well-known sects as those of the Buddhists and the Jainas.

The neo-Vedāntic, the neo-Vedic and the new interpretations of the *Gītā* which had become such prominent features of the non-Islamic Indian response to the western impact in this country led to a continuous debate with the orthodox, traditional, Sanskritic scholars who still believed in the authority of the *Dharma Śāstras* with regard to issues of social reform and political action. This provided them the background for all those intellectual enterprises which arose out of the institutional set-up created by the British after 1857 with the founding of Universities at Calcutta, Bombay and Madras. One can hardly understand the thought of, say, K.C. Bhattacharya, the most outstanding philosopher that India has produced in the twentieth century without an awareness of all the intellectual ferment around him. In fact, he is perhaps the first Indian thinker who was self-consciously aware of the problem that was created for India's intellectual traditions by a transplantation of completely alien modes of thought in this country. His well-known address entitled, "*Swaraja in Ideas*" is evidence of this and the fact that two of India's leading modern philosophers, Professors Ramchanda Gandhi and

K.J. Shah thought it necessary to initiate and invite a debate on it in the pages of the *Indian Philosophical Quarterly* is sufficient evidence of its continuing relevance even today. In fact, *swaraja* in ideas was, as important for him as *swaraja* in the field of politics.

K.C. Bhattacharya is the most eminent figure to have emerged on the Indian philosophical scene in the early quarter of the twentieth century and is easily one of the most original thinkers that India has produced. His radical innovations in thought have hardly been noticed or critically accessed and evaluated by his successors until now. And yet, hardly anyone seems to have seriously grappled with the radical innovations that he brought to bear not only on the age-long tradition of India but also on western thought, particularly that of Kant and Hegel with whom Indian philosophers of his generation were deeply familiar.

K.C. Bhattacharya introduced the notion of "alternative absolutes" which is almost a contradiction in terms. For, if something is absolute then, by definition, it cannot have alternatives to itself. The term 'absolute' was introduced in the western philosophical tradition by Hegel and since then it has generally been used in the sense in which he used it. Yet, K.C. Bhattacharya introduced this notion self-consciously to show that the postulation of an absolute was a necessity of thought to resolve a fundamental problematic question or paradox which was found in self-consciousness itself. It was the self-conscious reflection on "self-consciousness" which gave rise to philosophy and the philosophical enterprise consisted first in becoming aware of the paradox involved in self-consciousness and then, secondly, in the attempt to resolve it. As this resolution, according to him, could be attempted in different ways, the idea of alternative absolutes was entailed by the possibility of alternative ways of resolving the problematic question posed by self-consciousness to the philosophical reflection on it. The paradoxicality of self-consciousness consisted that while self-consciousness necessarily involved a relation between consciousness and object, this relationship seemed to be extremely puzzling in character. For as far as the "object" was concerned, its relationship to consciousness was a purely contingent fact and, it did not seem to be affected in any way by its relationship to consciousness as and when it occurred. This, it may be noted, was involved in the very notion of the 'object', as the 'object' was that which claimed an ontic independence for itself and whose nature, if correctly known, was to be that which it would have been even when it was related to no consciousness at all. Consciousness, on the other hand, felt its relationship with the object as something opposed to its very being, for it not only made it dependent on something that was not itself but also as making it enter into a relationship which alienated it from itself. It was not only that the consciousness of the object in its diversity affected it in many ways but that the objectivity of the object itself seemed to challenge it in the sense that it negated it in some sense or the other. The subject, thus, wanted to be rid of the object to remain in its subjectivity, undisturbed by anything alien to itself. The term 'subject' here should be taken as being almost identical with consciousness.

The relation of the subject and the object as revealed in self-consciousness was thus seen as a relationship between two entities, one of which, that is, the 'object' was 'indifferent' to the other, while the subject, that is, consciousness actively rejected the other, that is, the object. However, besides the subject and the object, there was a third term in the relationship, and that was the 'relationship' itself. This, in the context of consciousness was perhaps the most important of all as it 'felt' its 'dependence' on both the subject and the object to be unnecessary and hence wanted to be independent of both the 'subject' and the 'object' with which it felt itself to be unnecessarily entangled. Such an analysis of the notion of 'relation' may seem fantastic but it makes some existential sense when seen in relation to the quality of feeling which pervades consciousness all the time. In fact, the independence of relation from both the terms between which it holds may be appreciated a little better if we reflect that relations themselves have logical properties of their own and that the same relation may hold between different kinds of objects. It may of course be said that however true this may be, a relation in order to obtain must entail the existence of entities between which it obtains. But, in case a relation can engender a relational quality, and if the relational quality were to be of an existential character such as 'feelings' are supposed to be in the context of a consciously 'lived' experience, one may then perhaps begin to see how such a relational quality engendered by the relation of the subject to the object may demand an independence from both to achieve an absolute autonomy for itself where it becomes sufficient unto itself. In fact, both the subject and the object which are revealed to be related in self-consciousness in a paradoxical and problematic fashion feel themselves to be essentially self-sufficient and only 'accidentally' involved in a relationship from which they want to be freed, but somehow find it impossible to do so.

There seems, however, a distinction between the subject and the object not pointed out by K.C. Bhattacharya. For while the object is certainly revealed in consciousness, the subject seems only a shadowy substantive projection of consciousness buttressed by the belief that as consciousness is a quality, it must belong to something, and that something is what is known as the 'subject'. The Buddhists saw through the spurious necessity of this backward projection and proclaimed its illusoriness in their doctrine of "*anattā*" or what is known in Sanskrit as "*anātmavāda*". But, they failed to see the transcendental 'necessity' of the illusory projection, as consciousness seemed to be essentially different from whatever appeared as 'object' to it. The Sāṁkhyan thinkers had grasped this point and were thus led to distinguish the ultimate subject of experience from everything that appeared, or could appear, as 'object' to it. It was this insight which led them to treat not only the body but also the mind, the intellect and even the sense of "I-ness" as belonging not to the self, but to *prakṛti*, that is, that which is totally opposed to consciousness.

K.C. Bhattacharya's thought develops this Śāṁkhyan insight in a remarkable dialectic which almost parallels the Hegelian dialectic and complements it in a way not commented upon until now. Hegel's dialectic moves through negation, towards a synthesis resulting in an ultimate synthesis where all earlier negations are preserved or transformed into a positivity that is his notion of the absolute idea. K.C. Bhattacharya's dialectic, on the other hand, moves through what may be called a process of identification and de-identification where each step in de-identification reveals the earlier 'identification' to have been both voluntarily mistaken. The dialectic, of course, is that of Sāṁkhya. But it has been given a new turn by K.C. Bhattacharya which again has hardly been noticed even by those who have paid attention to his thought. First, according to him, the very act of de-identification, reveals not only that one is not 'really' that which one thought oneself to be, but that this wrong identification must have been in some sense a 'free' act of one's own, since one can negate or withdraw from it. The second important innovation that K.C. Bhattacharya makes in his employment of the Sāṁkhyan dialectic is that each level of subjectivity which results from the identification of the subject with the object creates its own correlate world of objectivity which alone is 'real' to it at that level. Thus, to the extent that one identifies oneself with the body, the world of sense perception which is the correlate object revealed by it, cannot but be held not only as real but also as the paradigmatic example of what 'real' is or can be. But the moment one identifies oneself as intellect or reason, it is the world of concepts and ideas which begins to assume an overwhelming reality of its own and the world of perception, which alone was earlier held to be 'real', and now is seen as a fleeting instance, a mere shadow, an incomplete and imperfect exemplification of the universal which alone is now considered to be paradigmatically real.

The identification with the intellect or reason is however as arbitrary as the identification with the body. One may, for example, identify oneself with 'will' and, if one does so then only the world of ideals and values is seen as real, for it is that which one wants to realize through action and which alone impels one not only to action but also to find significance and meaningfulness in one's life and the world one lives in. But, for K.C. Bhattacharya, the identification with 'willing' is as arbitrary as it was with the body or the intellect and reason; for. one may as well identify oneself with feeling and, if one does so, it is only the world of emotions and passions with its nuances and shades of joy and sorrow, delight and despair which begins to assume such an overwhelming reality that one can not even imagine how anything else can be 'real' at all. In the realm of feeling, the object merely becomes the occasion and loses completely its reality whether perceptual or ideational and the subject is only a shadowy projection, for what matters is the feeling and not the one who 'feels' it.

The subtle delineation of the levels of identification and the correlate worlds which alone are regarded as real at those levels has to be carefully seen in K.C. Bhattacharya's writings in order that full justice may be done to it. However, one need not believe that he has exhausted the levels of identification or the correlate worlds that become 'real' at that level of identification. In fact, K.C. Bhattacharya seems more interested in moving from one level to another rather than dwelling in detail at the levels themselves or in attempting a phenomenological study of the correlate worlds that each level of identification creates and requires for the subjective correlate to be the 'subject' in relation to it. He is in a hurry to reach the subject as freedom, forgetting the lesson from Hegel that the real life of the subject as freedom is in the phenomenology of identification and de-identification along with the creation and dissolution of worlds and not only in the complete withdrawal of the spirit into itself without any correlate world at all with which to relate or to withdraw from. It is of course true that without postulating this foundational withdrawal, freedom would perhaps have no ultimate ontological foundation, but K.C. Bhattacharya seems to forget his own insight that the identification was as much an act of freedom as the de-identification, even though it was only retrospectively realised to be so. He has also not thought of the possibility of a freer re-identification after the de-identification where the former would almost have the same element of 'freedom' in it as the de-identification is supposed to have.

The rich and varied thought of K.C. Bhattacharya demands to be developed in different directions. It is not clear, for example, as to why the problematic paradoxicality of self-consciousness should be articulated only in the way that he has done. Nor is it clear as to why the paradoxicality needs to be resolved only in the manner that he has delineated. The idea of alternatives has to be explored further and the pursuit of the objectivity of the object as an ideal has to be seen almost in the same way as the pursuit of the ideal subject which is freed from reference to any objectivity, actual or possible.

Strangely enough, K.C. Bhattacharya's thought, though leaning heavily on Sāṁkhya with Vedānta and even some strands of Jainism in it, does not seem to have taken into account the possibility of alternative Vedāntic constructions of Rāmānuja, Madhva, Vallabha, Nimbārka and Caitanya which had been at the centre of the controversy in the long debate between the Advaitic and the non-Advaitic interpretations of the Upaniṣadic texts. The construction of the alternative absolute grounded in the ideal of feeling becoming independent of both the terms to which it is related, though interesting in itself, neglects the demand for the relationship with a personal god which has been explored in diverse forms in the Indian tradition. Similarly, he does not seem to have seen the epistemological and ontological difficulties in the Jaina theory of alternative standpoints, even though he has creatively developed the Jaina idea in a new direction. The same seems to be true of the Kantian and Hegelian influences which he has so beautifully interwoven into his system. There seems to be nothing of the transcendental *a priori* in the development of the three alternative absolutes postulated to resolve the paradoxicality encountered in self-consciousness in three different directions. It would have been interesting to work out the transcendental suppositions involved in the three different movements so tantalisingly suggested by K.C. Bhattacharya in his thought. But, regardless of these undeveloped aspects of his thought, there can be little doubt that his mind was one of the most powerful and seminally philosophical one that brought into a unitary philosophical reflection, diverse strands of Indian and western philosophical thought combining them into a powerful system which continuously challenges the reader to plunge into its profound depths and develop it in new directions.

One of the most original thinkers of modern India who succeeded K.C. Bhattacharya, Kalidasa Bhattacharya (1911–1984) happened to be his son. His *Alternative Standpoints in Philosophy* which though published in 1953, was written as a doctoral dissertation at an unbelievably young age. He tried to provide a logical underpinning to K.C. Bhattacarya's thought and not only developed it in a new direction but also tried to see the whole history of western philosophy from its perspective. Kalidasa Bhattacharya sees the whole history of western philosophy as built around the three alternative absolutes of K.C. Bhattacharya moving in three different directions which he called "philosophy of the object, philosophy of the subject and philosophy of the absolute". Not only this, he developed the logic of alternation as providing the logical and epistemological foundation for K.C. Bhattacharya's theory of alternative absolutes. To do this, he turned to the disjunctive judgement in modern logic and suggested that it is logically more fundamental than the conjunctive judgement which generally is held to be more foundational in the context of logic as it derives from the law of contradiction which is universally conceded as basic to all rational thought about reality.

The disjunctive judgement, as everyone knows, takes two forms. The one treats the disjunction as exclusive while the other treats the disjunction as non-exclusive. Once this distinction is upheld on logical grounds, the non-exclusive disjunctive judgement becomes as fundamental as the exclusive disjunctive judgement which basically articulates the law of contradiction according to which rational thought generally moves. In the non-exclusive disjunctive judgement, the alternatives are related in such a way that while both of them can be true, both cannot be false together. This, it should be noted, is different from the relation of contrariety where the alternatives cannot all be true together, though all of them can be false in the situation as there may be another alternative which has not been mentioned in the judgement. Thus, the non-exclusive disjunctive judgement is supposed to deny *only* the falsity of both the alternatives and hence is 'true' in all the other three situations where either both of them are true, or one is true and the other is false, or the other is true and the remaining alternative is false.

Kalidasa Bhattacharya articulates this relationship in the non-exclusive disjunctive judgement in a novel way and says that in such a judgement the assertion of one of the alternatives may either be 'indifferent' to the truth or falsity of the other, or 'actively reject' the truth of the other. He applies this interpretation to the paradoxical situation in the relationship between the subject and the object as revealed in self-consciousness by K.C. Bhattacharya. According to him, the subject and the object in self-consciousness are united in a disjunctive way so that if the object is asserted as true, it is indifferent to the truth of the other term in the relationship, that is, the subject, as its relationship to the subject is completely contingent to it. This is the well-known realist contention that the fact of being known is totally contingent to the object known and does not affect it in any way whatsoever. On the other hand, in the case that the other term in the relationship, that is, the 'subject's' truth is asserted, it actively rejects the object in order to be existentially itself. This too is in accord with the well-known idealist position where the ultimate subjectivity of the subject has no relation to the object whatsoever and in fact denies the so-called independence of the object from all reference to any subjectivity.

Kalidasa Bhattacharya's phenomenological reconstruction of the non-exclusive disjunctive judgement overlooks that logically the notion of 'active rejection' cannot be applied in some situations. In case the non-exclusive disjunctive judgement is considered to be in its logicality, it only denies the falsity of both the alternatives and asserts that at least one of the alternatives must be true in order that the non-exclusive disjunctive judgement may be true. It, of course, allows the situation where both the alternatives are true without affecting the truth of the non-exclusive judgement. In fact, the non-exclusive disjunctive judgement is merely one of the sixteen possible logical operators in a two-valued logic with a dyadic logical operator, and has no special privileged position *vis-à-vis* the other possible dyadic logical operators in a two-valued logic which allows all the permutational possibilities involved in the situation.

Despite this qualification, there can be little doubt that the 'phenomenological' existential interpretation of the non-exclusive disjunctive judgement given by Kalidasa Bhattacharya to serve as the logical grounding of K.C. Bhattacharya's theory of alternative absolutes is both extremely original and challenging to philosophical thought, particularly if the logic itself is seen philosophically rather than mathematically.

The significance of Kalidasa Bhattacharya's thrust in this direction becomes evident with the last alternation that he propounds in his book which carries K.C. Bhattacharya's insight perhaps to the farthest point possible. But it is necessary to note here that Kalidasa Bhattacharya reinterprets the notion of alternative absolutes as formulated by K.C. Bhattacharya as ideals immanent in the paradoxical situation revealed to self-consciousness by reflection on itself for resolving the paradoxicality that is revealed in this situation. K.C. Bhattacharya himself had formulated the notion of 'demand' to suggest this direction but had not developed the idea to the fullest extent and further it was not related to the three fundamental paths for man's ultimate realization in the Indian traditions, namely the paths of knowledge, of action and of devotion. Kalidasa Bhattacharya in developing this further suggests that the apprehension of alternative absolutes involved in the paradoxical situation of self-consciousness 'demanding' its resolution in these three alternative directions is also pursued through different paths which have been characterised in the Indian traditions as paths of knowledge, action and feeling, or *jñāna, karma* and *bhakti.*

He not only links these three, well-known paths for the realization of the ultimate in the Indian traditions to the alternative absolutes formulated by K.C. Bhattacharya, but also grounds them phenomenologically in his logic of alternation. According to him, in action the object is given only a negative reality as its positivity is negated in the context of its transformation by action into something different which it 'ought' to be rather than the way it already is. Thus, it is seen in terms of what it should be rather than in terms of what it already 'is'. On the other hand, in knowledge one seeks to understand whatever appears as object not in terms of itself, but rather in terms of the concept of the universal which it exemplifies not only accidentally but also as intermingled with other irrelevancies from which they have to be separated for its truer understanding. Not only this, but at a deeper level, it has to be seen in relation to the forces which have brought it into being and those which will ultimately lead to its decay, dissolution and non-being, that is, in terms of those universal forces which bring it temporarily into being and make it pass away. Thus, for Kalidasa Bhattacharya, the movement of knowledge is a movement away from the specificity of the 'object' and in fact a rejection of it in the interest of something other than itself. According to him, it is 'feeling' that tries to grasp the specificity of the object in its unique individuality, a fact that becomes evident in relation to aesthetic objects which themselves try to grasp the particular objectivity of the objection a way which is not only totally different but completely opposed to the direction that knowledge takes.

Kalidasa Bhattacharya's grounding of these three dimensions of self-consciousness and their relationship to the immanent alternative absolutes formulated by K.C. Bhattacharya is fascinating, but it is not clear whether the way he has understood knowledge, feeling and action is the same as that of K.C. Bhattacharya; at least *prima facie*, there seem to be important differences between the two and, if so, it will be interesting to explore and highlight them further.

Kalidasa Bhattacharya's development of K.C. Bhattacharya's thought in all these different directions deserves serious study as perhaps it is singular in recent Indian philosophical thought that not only a predecessor's thought sould be taken seriously but also that it should be developed further in new directions. Kalidasa Bhattacharya moreover, formulates even an ultimate alternation of which K.C. Bhattacharya had not even thought of. His last and final alternation is related to the question whether the alternative formulations that we are forced to make are merely due to the limitations not only of our intellect but also on account of our way of experiencing the world along with the manner in which we are constituted or whether it is an intrinsic and inalienable nature of reality itself. As this is an unanswerable question, we are, according to him, ultimately left with an alternation where we might choose any of the alternatives but where we can never assert on any substantive ground that any one of them *alone* is true.

This is similar to situation that the enterprise of knowledge, in respect to physical reality seems to have reached in its search regarding the real nature of matter that surrounds us everywhere. Present day physics, as is well known, encountered the dilemma with the rise of the study of quantum phenomena resulting in the famous formulation of Heisenberg's principle of indeterminacy and the controversy that it gave rise to. The fact that Einstein never reconciled himself to this is well known and though most physicists have opted for the alternatives which Einstein was not happy with, the choice is as arbitrary as the faith or the belief of others who insist that such could not be the case and that we cannot impose on reality what is merely a consequence of the limitations inherent in the process of 'measurment' itself.

Physicists have only talked of the inherent and immanent limitations involved in any process of measurement, ignoring the question of the intrinsic limitations involved in the structure of the knowing consciousness or in the structure of rationality through which usually one tries to cognize what is real and to distinguish it from that which is unreal. Kant had talked long ago of such a structural limitation involved in all knowledge, but much attention does not seem to have been paid to this aspect of the problem by the physicists. Kant's specific formulation might be questioned, but the generalised issue that he raised is not substantially affected by any questioning of the particularity of his specification. The rise of non-Euclidean geometries does not, in any way, affect the substance of Kant's contentions as has generally been thought by many of his critics. Yet, even Kant's analysis does not seem to have been formulated in terms of an ultimate alternation, as Kalidasa Bhattacharya has suggested, for, Kant chooses one of the alternatives and does not see that the other alternatives are equally possible. Hegel chose the other alternative, as for him, the real was rational and the rational was real. But the choice between Kant and Hegel is itself ultimately the assertion of an alternative and not that only one of them was justified as against the other as they both believed.

The challenging reformulation of K.C. Bhattacharya's theory of alternative absolutes is one of the most remarkable events in the history of Indian philosophy even though it has not yet been seen as such. In fact, the Jainas who are supposed to be the great formulators of the theory of alternatives in the Indian traditions have not seen that even they have to accept an ultimately undecidable alternation between the *srvajñatā* of Mahāvira and the *syādvāda* of the knowledge of ordinary people. Is the knowledge of the *sarvajnatā* itself infected by *syādvāda* or does it, in principle, have to be free of it, is the final dilemma that Jaina empistemology faces, a dilemma which can only be answered by asserting an ultimately irresolvable alteration, thus once again, justifying Kalidasa Bhattacharya's reformation of K.C. Bhattacharya's thought?

Contemporaries of K.C. Bhattacharya were enormously influenced by him as evidenced by the fact that most of them have acknowledged it. G.R. Malkani, Rasbehari Das, D.M. Datta, T.R.V. Murti and many others have mentioned this in their writings, but hardly anyone has systematically carried forward his ideas or developed them in new directions as did his son, Kalidasa Bhattacharya. Dr. N.V. Banerjee who was also his student and who delivered the first K.C. Bhattacharya memorial lecture, on his well-known essay entitled "The Concept of Philosophy" shows little direct influence, though some trace of it might be found.

Another independent thinker produced by India in recent times is N.V. Banerjee as he has self-consciously repudiated the most widely accepted presuppositions of Indian thought and philosophised independently of both the Indian and the western traditions. In an extremely bold and radical manner, he looks at almost all the human enterprises in the field of knowledge, art and action as being primarily an 'escape' from the foundational problem which human beings face, which for some inexplicable reason, they are involved in from the very moment of their birth. According to him, man always feels separated and distinct from others while basically his reality demands that he conceive of himself as essentially and inalienably in relation to them. Thus, though for some reason he always conceives of himself as an 'I', his reality consists in the 'We', that is, 'I with others' which he somehow always forgets and so treats others as apart from him. N.V. Banerjee steers clear, thus, of both solipsism and skepticism which, according to him, have plagued philosophical thinking right from its inception as it has concentrated on self-consciousness considering this in abstracted isolation from the 'others' with whom one is in essential relationship. His thought is thus essentially anthropocentric and he argues that human thinking cannot, in principle, but be rooted in the human condition in which it arises and of which it remains an essential part, however, much one may delude oneself to believe in the contrary. But, once the human situation is accepted and human thought seen as an integral part of it, many philosophical problems, particularly those relating to epistemology and metaphysics, become redundant. Philosophical reflection reveals them to be rooted in a foundational fallacy which treats the 'ego-centric predicament' as unavoidable and intrinsically incapable of being overcome even though the fact of human communication, not only with other human beings, but also with the animal world in general, always negates this.

Thus, the very starting point of N.V. Banerjee's thought negates almost the whole tradition of western and Indian philosophy which primarily takes as its starting point, the isolated self-consciousness of the human mind and not an embodied person which is with others and in constant communication with them. His is not the isolated Cartesian 'cogito' or the Husserlian 'transcendental ego' which has ''bracketed' the world or the pure *puruṣa* of Sāṁkhya who is the eternal subject which can never be an object to itself or know that there are other *puruṣas* in the world besides itself, or the Advaitic *ātman* which has no 'others' of the non-Advaitic *ātmans* which have an essential relationship only with the Lord and which either have no knowledge of other selves or knows them only as fellow devotees who are totally immersed in some form or other of *bhakti* or the divine. Rather, it is man in the plural, man not as 'I', but as 'we', the 'we-s' who alone may communicate and have a dialogue or rather a 'multilogue between themselves'.

The denial of transcendence could not be greater and the ultimate acceptance of what had been earlier rejected in tradition as the world of *vyavahāra* has perhaps never been argued as thoroughly at the philosophical level as has been done in Banerjee's thought. It is true that the identity of *paramārtha* and *vyavahāra* or the *saṁvṛtti-sat* and *nivṛtti-sat* had been maintained by Nāgārjuna earlier, but Banerjee does not accept the notion of a *paramārtha-sat* at all and the reality of the *vyāvahārika* realm, for him is infected by a foundational ignorance which treats the 'I' as independent of others. Not only this, Banerjee's thought is an even more radical departure from almost all traditional Indian thought as it accepts suffering as an essential part of the human condition rather than seeing the abolition of its very possibility as the ultimate goal of all human endeavour. Banerjee goes even beyond this and not only denies immortality but regards the seeking for immortality as one of the greatest obstacles in the realization of one's essentiality to others and an expression of 'egoistic' centrality which itself is the result of that foundational ignorance which has to be overcome. The acceptance of suffering, the denial of transcendence, whether in the form of *mokṣa* or immortality, along with the rejection of the 'SELF'-centric thought of India are the hallmark of Banerjee's thought which has hardly been given any attention until now by anyone in this country or abroad.

But despite this radical departure from tradition, Banerjee's thought yet shows a deep continuity which perhaps he himself did not recognize. This lies in the notion of a primordial, beginningless *avidyā* which infects the human condition. Through a philosophical reflection on the human situation awareness of what ought not to be actually obtains and thus demands to be overcome and abolished so that the *avidyā* may disappear and truth shine once more. The departure from tradition lies in his analysis of the nature of *avidyā* and the context in which it is supposed to arise and in the nature of the 'demand' to be overcome. It is not in the paradoxical nature of self-consciousness, as argued for by K.C. Bhattacharya, but in the fact that one inevitably considers himself as essentially apart from others which however is not the case. But, as in K.C. Bhattacharya, the notion of 'demand' is accepted. However, the idea of alternatives is totally given up and, in fact, all the enterprises of man including which belong to the realm of morality also are seen as 'escapes' from the basic task of getting rid of the foundational *avidyā* in which man somehow is involved in by the very nature of his psychophysical being.

Banerjee's prescription for the overcoming of this foundational *avidyā* does not consist in suggesting any new system of *yoga* or *sādhanā*. Rather, he takes recourse to formulating three new maxims for human living similar to Kant's three famous maxims of morality. These maxims by which the basic *avidyā* can be overcome or mitigated basically derive from the fact that man continuously behaves through a consciousness that is essentially 'ego-centric' while in reality it is not so. The continuous self-conscious denial of ego-centricity is thus central to the solution and the three principles that he formulates follow from it either directly or indirectly. However, Professor N.V. Banerjee's formulation of the universal principle involved in all morality derives from the ontological rejection of ego-centricity and not from some universalistic requirement which most formulations assume. In fact, Kant's own formulation of the principle generally presented as "Act as if thy will were to become a law universal" presupposes the idea of the universality of law and that the individual will, in case it is to be moral, should be in accordance with it. This formulation by Banerjee, however, does not 'deny' the individuality of the will on moral grounds but on the ground of its being rooted in a foundational ignorance of the fact that the human reality is the 'we' and not the isolated, unrelated 'I' which Kant accepts along with almost all other thinkers in the western tradition.

Banerjee's radical departure from Kant in his formulation of the other two principles follows from this basic difference in understanding the universality which is implied in all morality. Banerjee formulates his second and third principles as:

1. So behave in any given circumstance that your behaviour is not circumscribed by ego-consciousness but is such as to present itself to be, as it were, any one's behaviour in that circumstance.
2. So behave that your behaviour is in no circumstance governed either directly or remotely by the dread of death and the desire for personal immortality.
3. So behave that your behaviour is on no occasion governed, either directly or remotely by aversion to bear the Cross.

Banerjee's thought bears a striking resemblance to that of Ramavatar Sharma discussed earlier, who not only wrote in Sanskrit but was completely within the old Sanskrit tradition of philosophising even though he lived in the twentieth century. It is extremely unlikely that N.V. Banerjee was aware of the thought of Ramavatar Sharma as this thought was not much in vogue even amongst Sanskritic scholars there having hardly any reference to him or any attempt at a refutation of his views by thinkers belonging to other *sampradāyas.* However, as Sharma was invited to give a Sri Gopal Basu Malik Lecture in 1907–08 in Calcutta on Vedāntism, his reputation must have travelled wide. And, as his lectures were given in English, it is very likely that what he said there was not so unknown amongst English-knowing philosophers in the country. Even then, there is little evidence of his influence as neither K.C. Bhattacharya nor any other well-known writer on Vedānta, either from Bengal or elsewhere seem to have referred to him.

These three original thinkers namely, K.C. Bhattacharya, Kalidasa Bhattacharya or N.V. Banerjee, produced by the western system of philosophical education in this country were, however, far less known as compared to S. Radhakrishnan who came to epitomize and symbolize philosophy in India and dominated the Indian philosophical scene as almost its sole representative abroad. This was due to, among other things, his great rhetorical ability to sway intellectual audiences in India and abroad, his occupation of the Spalding Chair at Oxford and the political positions that he occupied after India became independent in 1947. His two volumes on Indian philosophy almost became the standard work along with S.N. Dasgupta's *History of Indian Philosophy* on the subject. Similarly, his *Idealist View of Life, Western Thought and Eastern Religions* and the *Hindu View of Life* provided to many of his contemporaries the support for the generally accepted view about the dichotomy between the West and the East and the idea that most of Indian philosophy was essentially 'spiritual' and 'idealistic' in character. The publication of a volume on his philosophy in the well-known series edited by Paul Arthur Schilik confirmed the general impression that he was the foremost philosopher from India. However, subsequently his place in the philosophical world of India was seen as more historical rather than philosophical. He seems to have defined religion in such a way that its essence lay in the mystic consciousness which again was interpreted primarily in Advaitic terms. Along with this, is present the usual idea of the formless and unspeakable truth which was articulated in diverse ways and embodied in different forms but none of which could ever, in principle, be adequate or embody it fully. Yet, in all these contentions, he does not seem to have taken seriously the long debate regarding these issues in India's philosophical traditions even though he must have been well aware of them, especially as he himself had written a survey of the field in his two volumes on Indian philosophy. The close relation between philosophy and religion, and religion and mysticism which is supposed to be the hallmark of Indian thought was strongly advocated by him both in his numerous speeches and writings and this helped to strengthen the mystical image of Indian philosophy and culture which has been built right from Ram Mohan Roy onwards and had become almost an axiomatic truth about India.

One of the strange legacies of this presentation of Indian thought and culture was the debate regarding the place of reason in philosophy and whether Indian philosophy could even be regarded as philosophy in the proper sense of the term. Most Indians trained in educational institutions modelled on the western pattern where predominantly western philosophy was taught, had internalised the notion of 'philosophy' as it was usually presented in that tradition. For them, it was a serious question as to whether Indian philosophy could be strictly regarded as an enterprise of reason, as it always seemed subservient to the transrational goal of seeking *mokṣa.* Also, it appeared to be tied down to the acceptance of the authority of some classical text or other and seemed mainly engaged in an exegetical dispute regarding what the authoritative text exactly meant. Many Indian thinkers asserted a radical distinction between what they called *darśana* and philosophy and generally opted for the superiority of the former over the latter, except for a few lone voices.

Radhakrishnan, along with many others, played a decisive part in presenting this deep dichotomy between the philosophical tradition of India and the West, forgetting the long linkage of philosophy with the ideology of the "good life" in the West as well as the long tradition of hard-core ratiocinative thinking in India where debate and discussion was the life-blood of philosophical thinking and where skeptics and agnostics were as frequently found as those who believed in something transcendent. Yet, even the latter were never unquestioning believers, for if they were so, they were never regarded as philosophers.

The assertion of truth and the reality of the empirical life and of the social and political realm was, however, as much a part of Radhakrishnan's thought as it had been with every thinker from Ram Mohan Roy onwards. The combination of the idealistic position in metaphysics, generally of the Advaitic variety with an assertion of the reality of the empirical world including its social and political dimensions, seems to have been a prominent feature of most of the thinkers who belong to this period. In fact, if we take the articles written in the volume on *Contemporary Indian Philosophy* (edited by Radhakrishnan and Muirhead and published in the Muirhead Library of Philosophy) as a fair representation of the philosophical scene in India during that period, it is striking that most of these thinkers included, subscribed to some form of idealism. Amongst the twenty-five persons who have written on their own philosophy, most of them seem to be inclined towards some form of idealism. The only exception, G.C. Chatterjee has entitled his essay "Common Sense Empiricism". There also seems to be an explicit concern with the nature of the philosophical enterprise and an attempt to demarcate for it a special area as distinct from science and also, as different from a purely ratiocinative exercise. K.C. Bhattacharya's explicit distinction between empirical thought and all other levels of thought attempts to demarcate this as clearly as possible. He considers empirical thought as characterised by the fact that it always refers to that which is perceived by the senses or is perceivable in principle in terms of it. This obviously is a straight positivistic position where all cognitive meaningfulness is defined by translatability in terms of possible sense experience which then would determine its truth or falsity.

K.C. Bhattacharya, however, adopts the strategic move of excluding all such thought from the domain of philosophical consideration and considers philosophy as dealing only with the other three levels or types of theoretic consciousness. These, according to him are pure objective thought which is concerned only with 'meanings' irrespective of whether such 'meanings' have any relation to what is perceived or perceivable, as is necessary in the case of empirical thought. This is the first level of theoretic consciousness where thought frees itself from sensory experience and deals with a 'reality' which is independent of it. The other two levels of theoretic consciousness are designated by him as spiritual thought and transcendental thought. Both of these are concerned not with the object as was the case in the earlier types of thought. At these levels, thought is concerned with itself or rather with the subjectivity that is embodied in the word "I", and in self-consciousness continuously "negates" all that is presented to it or even spoken of as the subject. These two levels he calls spiritual and transcendental thought, the former referring to the self or the subject as self-aware in consciousness, and the other as a negation of even this self-awareness as it objectifies the self to some extent and makes it "appear" as if it were an "object" to awareness. The interesting point about K.C. Bhattacharya's attempt lies in his separate demarcation of the area of philosophy as a cognitive enterprise from science which by his time had become the paradigmatic example of knowledge.

The attempt, however, does not seem confined to K.C. Bhattacharya alone as a number of other articles deal with the same problem in this volume. Ananda Coomaraswamy, T.R.V. Moorthy, V. Subramaniam and Swami Abhedanand have written on the same theme, but none of them seems to have dealt with the problem as focally and as clearly as K.C. Bhattacharya has done. The concern with philosophy and the concern with the self as the focus of philosophical attention seemed to go together in the thought of most of the Indian thinkers of that period as at least three other articles, by Bhagwan Das, Radhakrishnan and P.T. Raju are devoted to this theme. In fact, the title of the article by Bhagwan Das "*Ātma Vidyā* or the Science of the Self" almost suggests that philosophy and *ātma vidyā* or science of the self are the same.

The self with which the philosophical thought of India had been concerned, both in traditional and modern times, gradually takes a fuller content and becomes more "this worldly" as philosophical thinking moves into the latter half of the twentieth century. N.V. Banerjee had already cut off its moorings from the quest for immortality and relationships with the transcendent, seeing it essentially in relationship to other beings with whom one was, or could be, in possible communication. Even earlier, a moral dimension seems to have been added to it right from Vivekanand onwards, by-passing the deep conflict between *dharma* and *mokṣa* which had characterised Indian thinking in this regard from the beginning. A new kind of anthropocentrism and humanism appears to have taken hold of Indian thinkers and we have the interesting spectacle of a development of man-centred thought in different directions. Thus, we have the radical humanism of M.N. Roy, the value-centred thought of N.K. Devaraj and the anthropocentric and history-centred thought of Professor D.P. Chattopadhyaya who, by contrast, is more seriously concerned with the universalistic and impersonal claims of scientific knowledge in his book, *Anthropology and Historiography of Science* (Ohio, 1990). He has argued vigorously not only for science being a human enterprise like other enterprises but also that it has an essentially historical dimension in its development, thus making it as much subservient to the processes of historical change as any other human enterprise. The impersonal and universal presentations of scientific knowledge were thus questioned at its foundations and it became, like everything else, a creature of time and historical circumstance limited by the humanity of human beings who undertook this enterprise.

However, it is not clear whether Professor D.P. Chattopadhyaya subscribes to the cumulative and evolutionary base of human knowledge generally claimed for most of scientific knowledge in modern times. Sri Aurobindo had earlier been profoundly affected by the idea of evolution which had swept through almost all areas of human endeavour, and had tried to integrate it in a creative manner with India's traditional thought of which the centre had been the spiritual quest of man. He argued that the central fact of evolution can only be understood in terms of the emergence of mind and the gradual control and transformation of material and vital processes by it in the service of some end which went beyond them, and consisted in the achievement of a state of consciousness which he named as super-mind, and of which it was only very vaguely aware. Mind itself was seen as having different levels with both continuity and radical breaks which can be seen in his ideas of higher mind, intuitive mind, over-mind, culminating ultimately in the perfect stage of super mind. The radical novelty of Sri Aurobindo's thought lies in his insistence on the transformation of matter, life and mind through forces that are superior to them in status, quality and value along with a rejection of the renunciatory ideal which involved a denial of the reality of this world and the claim that the ultimate truth could only be realised through a rejection of the life of man in family, society and polity. The human being, in this perspective, was himself seen in super-human terms whose mission was to actualize this imminent divine reality which was hidden within him.

Most of these thinkers, however, were the product primarily of British system of education introduced at the beginning of the nineteenth century spreading gradually all over India as British rule penetrated into different regions consolidating its political and administrative control over them. Bengal the key centre in this enterprise was followed by Maharashtra, Madras and U.P. where British educational institutions provided knowledge of western learning in all fields and created a new class of learned men in India with a greater knowledge of western tradition in most fields of knowledge and naturally considered it not only as superior to all previous forms of knowledge but also as the only form of knowledge which deserved that title. This class as it gradually emerged and enlarged itself, dominated the field of knowledge in India by occuping visible seas of power but also as they manned institutions of learning and thus represented what came to be seen as the 'educated' class within this country.

But as the traditional forms of learning also continued during this period and were segregated by self-conscious British educational policy, they provided a subterranean counterpoint to the new dominant educational class in India with hardly any inter-relationship between them. Thus, three different streams of education existed in the British period from the beginning of the nineteenth century. The first, and most visible consisted of those who were the direct products of the British system of education in the country. The second, consisted of those who were the products of the new institutions of traditional learning created by the British to maintain and foster traditional forms of learning and Sanskritic studies on the one hand and Arabic-Persian on the other. The third, consisted of those who were the products of traditional institutions which survived the British institutional innovations and were primarily maintained and fostered by non-governmental patronage in British India and by a princely patronage in princely India. There was a certain overlap between the last two as they taught the same kind of texts and courses, though there was a distinct difference in the method of teaching and the way in which examinations were conducted. There was also, a difference in the status of the persons belonging to these two streams, at least in British India, as those working in the British-sponsored institutions had better financial support than the ones patronised by non-governmental agencies. In fact, there was great discrimination in even the salary scales between the institutions of traditional learning fostered by the British and those which gave a western type of education in the newly-created seats of learning. This deliberate policy of segregation and financial discrimination in the salaries given to the teachers belonging to these two different types of institutions had a deep and lasting influence on the intellectual scene in India during the one and a half century of British influence in the field of education. The whole world of classical knowledge and those who pursued and practised it became gradually invisible to those who came out of the new institutions modelled on the British pattern and thus produced an intellectual environment which was only aware of the western traditions in knowledge as its reference point and treated India's traditional intellectual enterprises either as having had no value at all or as having been completely superseded by the developments of knowledge that had taken place in the West and were, therefore, completely irrelevant to the contemporary quest for knowledge. The two worlds thus developed in almost complete ignorance of each other and had hardly any awareness of the other or interaction. There were occasionally a few persons who were aware of both, but one either belonged to the one tradition or the other and even when one was aware of the other tradition, it was too marginal in character to have any substantial effect on one's thought or one's standing in the tradition to which one belonged.

There was yet another stream which primarily related itself to the institutions of Sanskritic learning created by the British and which made use of those traditional scholars who were completely outside the modern stream for its own purposes. This stream derived from the work initiated by the Royal Asiatic Society which was founded by Sir William Jones in 1784 and which primarily engaged in the work of collecting, editing, publishing and translating classical Sanskrit texts all over the country. The great interest in Indological studies outside the country, particularly in Germany and England, provided an inspiration for the establishment of these types of research institutes all over India, many of which prided themselves on adopting the latest philological and historical methods in Indological research and in publishing texts through a critical comparison of all the available manuscripts, thus resulting in the search for the original texts which had become gradually distorted by later additions.

The establishment of the Royal Asiatic Society in Bengal, the Adyar Library and Research Centre in Madras, the Bhandarkar Oriental Research Institute in Poona, along with the creation of such well-known centres of Sanskrit learning as the Sanskrit College, Calcutta and the Sanskrit College, Benaras were important steps in this direction. So also was the launching of a number of publication series such as the one associated with the Saraswati Mahal Library in Travancore, the Gaekwad Oriental Series at Baroda, the Vijainagaram Sanskrit Series and many others resulted in an amazing resurgence of the awareness regarding the unbelievably rich and varied heritage of the intellectual and literary enterprises of India in various fields over at least three million years of its recorded history.

The story of what was achieved during this period of about 150 years since, say, 1800 to 1950, is truly amazing and has yet to be written in detail to discover what actually happened during this period in various parts of the country. However, slowly, the effects of the apartheid introduced by the British in the educational system began to manifest themselves and negated the aim of this whole exercise undertaken by some of the best minds in the country. The dawn of Independence and the imperatives of modernisation along with the massive training programmes of Indian students abroad under the various programmes launched by the U.S., British, Soviet and European governments had resulted in a situation where a new class of educated Indians came into being who did not know any Sanskrit. This class was totally unaware of the Indian heritage in all fields of knowledge being firmly convinced that there nothing of that kind existed and hence became totally uninterested in it. A situation obtained where most educated people in the country were hardly aware of the living traditions of their own country, as the traditional scholars led a totally different kind of life, segregated in institutions with which they had no contact whatsoever. There was, however, a growing feeling amongst some persons aware of this dichotomous development, that something was wrong and that bridges had to be built between the two traditions and a dialogue established between them.

The most significant step in this direction was taken by Professor M.P. Rege in Poona who organised a dialogue between traditional, well-versed in the philosophical traditions of classical India with modern scholars trained in western institutions of learning in the country who had some knowledge of Indian philosophy and a passing acquaintance with Sanskrit. The innovation of Professor Rege lay in that he not only provided the facility of a bilingual dialogue between traditional and modern scholars, but prepared the ground for it by meeting individually the scholars concerned and explaining to them the purpose of the dialogue. Also, he chose a subject which lay on the borderlands of contemporary and traditional philosophy and formulated the issues which were to be discussed in the dialogue in as precise a manner as possible and in a language which was well known to traditional *paṇḍits,* that is, Sanskrit. He thus created an atmosphere where traditional scholars could feel free to express their ideas in their own language on issues of relevant contemporary philosophical concerns which engaged the minds of those who were trained in that subject in institutions modelled on the western pattern in India. The first dialogue of this kind was organised at Poona in July 1983 and an edited transcript of it was published in 1991 under the title *Saṁvāda: A Dialogue Between two Philosophical Traditions* by the I.C.P.R., Delhi. The work has been hailed as "the First Exercise in doing comparative philosophy, rather than in 'talking' about it".

The experiment was followed by a number of other activities such as a meeting of the most eminent scholars in the field of Nyāya, Mīmāṁsā and Kashmira Śaivism to discuss pertinent questions relating to their own school of Indian philosophy and to think of ways and means of carrying traditional thought further in the contemporary philosophical context.

The Rege experiment also led to the organisation of Summer and Winter schools in the field of modern logic and Navya Nyāya where modern logic was taught to traditional *paṇḍits* and Navya Nyāya to modern logicians who were interested in it. This experiment was again organised and conducted by Professors M.P. Rege and D. Prahladachar, the latter being one of the most outstanding young Naiyāyikas in the country. The idea of having a dialogue with traditional scholars on contemporary intellectual issues was later extended to the field of linguistics and a dialogue was organised on current issues in linguistics under the leadership of Professor Rege and Professor Patnaik, the then Director of the Indian Institute of Languages, Mysore. Also, as a consequence of all this activity, it was felt that along with this the dialogue experiment should be expanded beyond the field of classical Sanskrit scholarship to cover Arabic and Persian scholars in the field of philosophy and at least two dialogues were organised, one at Lucknow and the other at Hyderabad where issues in contemporary philosophy were formulated and discussed with scholars in the field of West Asian philosophy with the same facilities for bilingual translations which were such a novel feature of the Rege experiment earlier held at Poona.

This attempt to build bridges and foster a dialogue with the living representatives of traditional knowledge in India was not confined only to the activities that have been mentioned above. In fact, the need for such an interaction was independently felt by many other groups and scholars, chief among whom was the organisation known as PPST that is Patriotic and People-Oriented Science and Technology under the leadership of M.D. Srinivas. This group regularly published a bulletin wherein an attempt was made to revive traditional scientific and technical knowledge and establish creative links with it. Later still, Dr. Navjyoti Singh of the National Institute of Science and Technology for Development launched a similar project entitled in cooperation with the PPST group at Madras. At the level of individual scholarship, Veena Das in the introduction to her well-known work entitled, *Structure and Cognition* argued for "the articulation of both the manifest and the implicit conceptual structures embedded in the texts and the use of them for the understanding of Indian social reality". While Sudhir Kakkar explored the world of indigenous psychiatry and psychoanalysis and established an interactive relationship with it as reported in his well-known work entitled, *Shamans, Mystics and Doctors.*

As a result of all this ongoing activity, a need was felt for a Who's Who of the traditional Sanskrit scholars of India listing many of the living practitioners in each field of classical knowledge that were there in the country with whom a dialogue on contemporary intellectual issues relating to those fields could be meaningfully attempted. As a result of the combined efforts of the ICPR, the Rashtriya Sanskrit Sansthan and the Sahitya Academy a *Who's Who of Sanskrit Scholars* was prepared and published in 1991.

The search for a reconciliation of the transcendental and the ordinary 'lived in' life of the world continues amongst thinkers of the younger generation of whom perhaps J.N. Mohanty and Sundara Rajan have made the most serious and sustained attempt in this direction. Mohanty has been at home both in the Sanskritic tradition of Indian philosophy, particularly pertaining to the one known as Nyāya as well as with the western philosophical tradition, particularly the phenomenological existentialism that centered in Europe and beginning from Husserl onwards. He is one of the few Indian philosophers who has an equal command both of Sanskrit and German, not to speak of English, which almost everyone knows well as they have studied in that language. His work on Gaṅgeśa and Husserl is respected both by Sanskrit-knowing Nyāya specialists and German-knowing Husserlian specialists. His authority is recognised in both the traditions and he is perhaps one of the best persons to interpret one philosophical tradition to the other.

However, while his work on Nyāya is basically explanatory, his work in phenomenology is creatively original and departs from traditional formulations of Husserl without suggesting that he is betraying the tradition of the master. In fact, his distinction between what he has called 'philosophy of suspicion' and 'philosophy of respect' is relevant not only to western traditions of philosophizing in the context of which he has made this distinction but to all modes of philosophising whether western or non-western. "Philosophy of suspicion", according to him, privileges a particular mode of consciousness at the expense of all other modes which it treats as inferior, while the "philosophy of respect" treats all modes of consciousness as almost equally valid, at least at their own level and from their own point of view. This is almost a Jaina position, even though Mohanty has not explicitly said that it is so. There is of course the problem of the relation between these different modes of consciousness and the way they view each other along with the question of the immanent criteria of the "real" and the "unreal", the "meaningful" and the "meaningless" and the "significant" and the "insignificant" within each of them. Besides this, there is the deeper question regarding the compatibility or conflict in the courses of action or *puruṣārtha*, which each of these modes of consciousness may entail. Ultimately, the question is not just one of a recounting of the modes of consciousness and seeking of clarification of each of them within its own perspective, but of the sort of "living" that it demands and the "life-world" that it requires both to sustain it and also to fulfill the ideal immanent in it. This is even more necessary, as for Mohanty, the "life-world" is an integral part of the transcendental consciousness with all its diverse modalities. The relation of the whole of consciousness to the specific life-world and the tension that diverse "life-worlds" pose for different modes of consciousness does not, however, seem to have been intensively explored in Mohanty's work. Not only this, the relation between transcendental consciousness and the modes of consciousness and the relations of both to the life-world has not been given the attention that it deserves. Nor is there perhaps any attempt to explore the relation of the so-called "life-world" to culture and history on the one hand and to biology and ecology on the other, in which it is necessarily embedded.

Mohanty appears to adopt the idea of "originary experience" from Husserl and thinks that the clarification of meaning in each mode of consciousness through a search for the "originary experience" which brought it into being might be seen as the real task of phenomenology without, however, seeing that the notion of "originary" experience is a myth, a convenient construction to help in the search for something that may function as a suitable substitute for the notion of *eidos* or "essence" that was said to have been given up.

Mohanty's thought struggled with the incorporation of the notions of "corporeality", "historicity", "intersubjectivity" and "communicability" in the idea of the transcendental subjectivity itself. This, of course, is a heroic attempt, but it not only presupposes that these notions have an unambiguous clarity about them but also that their incorporation into the notion of transcendental subjectivity would not affect it in such a radical manner as to involve an abdication of all that has until now been associated with it. The retention of the term 'transcendental subjectivity' in such a situation would only be systematically misleading and it might be better if some other term which has no misleading past association is substituted for it. What exactly, for example, would the term "subjectivity" still mean in such a situation where subjectivity itself is inter-subjective, and what would "transcendentness" mean if temporality, corporeality and historicity are essentially involved in it? These are questions that need to be attended to as their relation to what is transcendental is the heart of the matter.

Regarding the notion of abstract universal reason and the notions of rationality associated with it, Mohanty suggests the idea of a relationality towards which one strives through some sort of a communicative dialogue between what may be called cultural rationalities or rationalities embedded in concrete, particular, specific cultures. He has developed, the interesting notion of "overlapping *neomata*" which provides some sort of a continuity without involving the essential commonality, a point earlier articulated by Wittgenstein in his notion of "family resemblance" developed in a different context. However, here too, Mohanty does not appear to have seen that cultural rationalities which are themselves not fixed or all of a piece, as the cognitive enterprises in a culture undergo vast changes over a period of time where even paradigm shifts occur, to use a phrase from Kuhn. Not only this, within the same culture, norms of rationality embodied in different realms of culture need not be the same or even cohere amongst themselves as many a time it is the tension between these which gives rise to the dynamics of change in the culture.

There seems to be little or no relationship between what Mohanty has said in the context of rationality and what he has considered to be the proper task of philosophy, as consisting in the activity of what he has called philosophical description. Is this activity "inter subjective", "historical", "temporal", "linguistic" or is it the activity of a pure transcendental subjectivity enclosed within its own intuitions, unwilling to go in any direction whatsoever? He has explicitly distinguished it from deduction or the framing of a hypothesis or the construction of interpretative frameworks or theoretical models, or a rational reconstruction of experience. But if it does not do any of these and only engages in "philosophical description" in his sense of the term, then the question arises as to what is the relation of this "activity" to all other activities which one can probably undertake if one so wishes. This, may not then be "philosophising" in Mohanty's sense of the term but then what is that which makes one undertake one activity rather than another? And at a deeper level what is this freedom which makes one choose between these undertakings amongst which, on Mohanty's argument, there can be no grounds for choosing? In fact, Mohanty does not seem to have conceived of the possibility of even alternative phenomenological descriptions of what he calls "philosophical facts", for presumably he will grant that there are different philosophers employing the phenomenological method and perhaps differing amongst themselves with regard to the phenomenological description of a philosophical fact. The phenomenologist, it seems, does not develop a decision theory for what to do in a situation where different phenomenologists differ amongst themselves with regard to a philosophical description of the same fact or when the same phenomenologist gives two conflicting philosophical descriptions of the same philosophical fact at different moments of time.

The same situation obtains to a certain extent regarding Mohanty's plea for an ontological non-commitment in respect to the phenomenological description of a philosophical fact and his suggestion that it may be seen either as: (i) linguistic or a meaning structure; (ii) an ontological structure; (iii) a structure of subjectivity or consciousness. This reminds one of K.C. Bhattacharya's theory of alternative absolutes and Kalidasa Bhattacharya's further elaboration of it in terms of a series of ultimate alternations based on the logic of alternatives. However, he seems to have forgotten K.C. Bhattacharya's warning that the conjunction of the alternative is only a vacuous conjunction, for if one is asserted the others are automatically excluded. Further, there is nothing like the notion of "demand" which occurs so prominently in K.C. Bhattacharya's thought where each of the alternative absolutes "demands" its actualization and realization in one's consciousness. Furthermore, neither the two Bhattacharyas nor Mohanty seem to have raised the question as to what "determines" the choice between these alternatives. If there can be any ground for choice between these in principle, then the choice cannot be arbitrary and the notion of 'alteration' will collapse at its foundations. On the other hand, if it is an exercise of pure freedom, then it is a purely arbitrary act "*un acte libre*" as the existentialists call it.

Mohanty's radical distinction between speculative and descriptive philosophy is interesting and has far reaching implications for both the practice of philosophy and the theorizing about it. However, here he seems to fall prey to a false dichotomy against which he had professed so powerfully in other domains. The speculative construction does not remain merely speculative, but has a deep influence on the consciously-lived life of experience which provides a profound backing of "intuitive givenness" on which Mohanty builds his notion of philosophical description. Śaṁkara's Advaita and Plato's pure realm of ideas are not just speculations but have given rise to long processes aiming at existential realization known as *sādhanā* in the Indian tradition. Perhaps K.C. Bhattacharya's notion of "demand" might have helped him to bridge the gap which he considers unbridgeable in principle. Also, a recent contention of Professor D.P. Chattopadhyaya may help to bridge the gap in another way. He has contended that the distinction between "mediate" and "immediate" is not as clear-cut as most philosophers tend to assume. What appears to be immediate to consciousness in the present may itself be the result of a long process of mediation when we see it in the context of the historical past of which it happens to be a resultant. This, according to him, becomes clear when we encounter cultural products of a different civilization and feel baffled by them as we cannot find in our "responsive immediacy" that could make them meaningful to us, just as we find in the presence of those which we encounter in our own culture. The reason for this, according to him, lies in the fact that the "immediacy" of our response to things in our own culture is mediated by a long historical past which we have incorporated into our own consciousness by a process of assimilation and acculturation since the time of our birth.

The concerns of Mohanty seem to be shared by one of the most seminal thinkers in the field of transcendental philosophy, Sundara Rajan. He also appears to have devoted his major works to a reworking of transcendental philosophy, but in such a way that the Kantian enterprise does not result in a loss of what has later come to be called the "life-world". He reformulates the famous Kantian formulation of the problem, "How is knowledge possible" in a deeper and more fundamental manner in the form, "how is life possible", for unless human living itself were not there, there would be neither knowledge nor action. This attempt to relocate self-consciousness with all the transcendental elements involved in it back into the concrete world is evidenced by the very titles of Sundara Rajan's work: *The Humanization of Transcendental Philosophy* and *Transformations of Transcendental Philosophy*. His work entitled, *Towards a Critique of Cultural Reason* marks a significant step in answering the question, "How is life possible", or rather "How is human living possible", as one cannot conceive of human living without its being embedded and constituted by culture. The understanding of culture, thus, and the immanent reason involved in it, is for him, a precondition for understanding the human situation as without it one would only "understand" a certain truncated part of the human individual giving it an illusory, self-enclosed, monadic identity which, in the Kantian perspective, may be supposed to be considered as open to some extent by the consciousness of the categorical imperative. Taking a cue from Ricoeur's work, Sundara Rajan makes a distinction between signification and symbolization, the former where the meaning is relatively "context free" and the latter where it is more context-bound. It is this basic distinction which helps him to move away from the categories of understanding that primarily pertain to the world of nature, understood basically in a context-free manner, to the socio-cultural world where understanding is not only context-bound, but is in principle not possible without it. Sundara Rajan makes another interesting move and distinguishes between objects which can primarily be understood in terms of their "essence", that is, class characteristics or "species" characteristics and those which have such an individual, organic unity of their own, that they have to be understood in terms of their own specific, unique, individual identity and not in terms of any class membership to which they may also belong. This obviously is a characteristic of art objects where individuality is the heart of the matter. Sundara Rajan goes further and makes an even more interesting distinction amongst the latter type of objects. This is based on those that are relatively far more context-free and others which are context-bound. The latter are the "cultural objects" *par excellence* as they find their meaning in the cultural matrix in which they are situated and to which they belong. This is Sundara Rajan's return from the transcendental retreat of Kant to the individual self-consciousness, locating it without losing the insights of the transcendental withdrawal, into the cultural world where man truly lives and outside which he will feel like fish out of water, and, dies.

Sundara Rajan uses this occasion of the transcendental self-consciousness within a cultural matrix embodying itself in "objects" which derive their whole meaning and significance from the cultural context in which they are embedded to understand and explore once again the meaning of "science" and reformulate the current philosophy of science in the context of this understanding in his work *Beyond The Crisis of the European Sciences.* He examines in it the relevance and significance of the three major issues that have recently emerged in western thought, the linguistic, the feminist and the ecological for the understanding of the activity of "science" as a cultural product of society. He examines in this context, Husserl's Eurocentrism and discusses "science" as a fact, a problem, a possibility and a hope.

Interestingly, Professor Sundara Rajan's concern with the notion of the transcendental is used by him for the understanding of *puruṣārtha* in the Indian tradition and he has made some remarkably new formulations in connection with the understanding of this age-old concept. He has explored the possibility of treating the idea of *puruṣārtha* in terms of the transcendental forms of "willing". He has also applied the hermeneutical method to understand the realm of the political and the phenomenological perspective in order to explore the relation between innovative competence and social change.

The return to the temporal, historical, living world of the embodied being who is a member of society and polity and actively participates in the building up of a common inter-subjective world in cooperation with other human beings seems to be a common concern of most Indian philosophers who have written in the English language after their contact with the western world. But yet, while the emphasis in K.C. Bhattacharya's thought was primarily on a return from the identifications of the self with each succeeding level of objectivity, seeing thereby the essential freedom of man as consisting in this de-identification, it is only in later thinkers starting from N.V. Banerjee that the isolated, de-identified self is understood not in terms of 'freedom' but as deprived and cut off from its relationship with the 'others' which constitute, according to him, the essential reality for the self, and in the fulfillment of this relational obligation lies its real freedom. Kalidasa Bhattacharya stands somewhere in between but basically he has not yet given up the understanding of the self in its "aloneness" and isolation from everything else. In Mohanty and Sundara Rajan, we find the impulse to "return" more self-consciously and concretely formulated; a 'return' which becomes even more emphatically visible in the concern with historicity so explicitly manifest in the writings of D.P. Chattopadhyaya.

The bringing together of Marx and Sri Aurobindo into one common perspective, points to D.P. Chattopadhyaya's concern with the historical and evolutional dimensions of their thought which, starting from radically-opposed presuppositions, tend to converge in the idea of a future state of man where the empirical contradictions with which he has struggled and lived in up till now will get resolved. The difference in the methodological praxis prescribed by these two thinkers for reaching this ideal state of affairs was perhaps not sufficiently noticed by Professor Chattopadhyaya though it was indirectly reflected in his epistemological concern with what has generally been called, methodological individualism Vs. methodological collectivism. However, as both of these are only methodological tools for the understanding of human reality, they may be easily combined. On the other hand, the difference between Marx and Sri Aurobindo lies in the field of action and the praxis they prescribe for the achievement of transcending the present stage of human society and polity which, because of its structural constraints can never achieve the ideal state of affairs which men desire, without overcoming those structures themselves. Sri Aurobindo's prescription for transcending the present state of affairs is ultimately an individual one and is concerned with the psychological transformation of the individual self-consciousness, geared of course towards the ultimate transformation, of what he has called, the physical, the vital and the mental life of the human individual. It is of course true that Sri Aurobindo does conceive of this great effort of transformation as being collectively made by a fairly large number of individuals in order that such a transformation may be meaningfully achieved at the social level. But, it should not be forgotten that the effort has to be made by each individual at his or her own personal level, even though one may surmise that the success achieved by one will help others to realise their own transformation to some extent.

Marx, on the other hand, prescribes a collective effort by a large number of persons belonging to one class who have been brought together by a historical process labelled as "capitalism" by him. Such a collective, joint effort according to him is the necessary pre-condition of the transcendence of the present structures which alone will ensure a transition to a more desirable state of society and polity in the future.

Professor Chattopadhyaya's concern with historicity, temporality and the concreteness of man in society leads him to examine the claim of science to overcome these limitations and give us a trans-temporal, trans-historical and trans-human truth. 'Science' appears to him to have usurped the claim of religious and spiritual truth to be essentially a-historical, a-temporal and trans-human. And, perhaps it is this aspect of the claim of "science" that led him to question the widely held pre-suppositions about the nature of scientific truth in the "*Anthropology and Historiography of Science*'.

The dialectics between immediacy and mediacy, structures that appear to give stability and permanence to human thought and action and the evolutionary and historical perspective that sees them as being the products of long-term processes which have vanished from one's consciousness appears to be the central theme of his thought. If there are laws of evolutionary change and/or of the unfoldness of history, then there would be some laws, some structure, however hidden, behind the temporal process itself. Also, the transformation of temporality on the plane of history and society on the one hand and human consciousness on the other needs perhaps to be explored a little more closely, even though a concern with both ideology and utopia have played an increasingly significant role in his later work. All these diverse interests of one of the most versatile thinkers of present-day India seem to have finally converged in the inter-disciplinary project which he has launched relating to the history of science, technology, philosophy and culture of India, two volumes of which have already appeared (*Science, Philosophy and Culture: Multi-disciplinary Explorations*, 2 vols. 1996, 1997).

One of the most neglected thinkers of the recent past has been Basant Kumar Malik whose work was published in the West. He has hardly been paid any attention by thinkers in India or abroad. Malik has emphasised in his thought the reality of the "negative" element along with that of the positive. Hegel, had similarly emphasised the equal relevance and reality of the element of non-being in his dialectics. However, Malik does not seem to have developed any special dialectical logic of his own. The triadic form of his dialectic, however, seems to appear in his thinking in the form of a universe with three stages, the first where only non-being exists, the second where both being and non-being are supposed to be there and the third, where perhaps only the being remains. The first is supposed to be monadic, unrelated and beginningless but has an end as it is followed by the world which has both being and non-being in it and thus has both a beginning and an end. The second is not monadic as it is plural and related and is discontinuous in character. The third stage is supposed to have a beginning and no end and has the same characteristics as the first, that is, it is monadic, unrelated and continuous. It is not quite clear however what is the relation between these three universes or whether they are three stages in a series where the first and the third are postulated as logical necessities, for what we actually 'know' is only the second stage as it is the one in which we 'live'.

The notion of non-being (as exemplified, for example, in such instances as shame, guilt, indignation, anger, etc.) taken from the second universe in which we live can however, in no case, apply to the first stage of the universe where only non-being is supposed to exist. The equation of 'non-being' with the purely negative aspect in experience is strange if it is considered to be equally necessary for the positive element to be there in experience. As for the preponderance of the one over the other, it is not quite clear how such a notion will ensure harmony between them. On the other hand, if both the elements are supposed to be equally necessary, then it is difficult to see how one can preponderate over the other for long, as he seems to contend. Not only this, he seems to ascribe the notion of an immanent purpose to the second universe which perhaps lies in the complete overcoming of the negative element and achieving of a harmony whose perfect exemplification is perhaps to be found only in the third phase of his triadic universe.

Ultimately, the same problem faced by all those who have tried to give the element of the negative an ontological position in their thought confronts Malik. Even Hegel or Marx who in spite of their postulation of the negative as an ultimate constituent of what they consider to be 'real', are forced to postulate a final stage where the really negative element in 'negativity' would be eliminated or transcended in such a way that its negativity is completely nullified.

There also remains the problem of making a relevant distinction between contrariety and contradiction and if, as Malik seems to do, one opts for the former as being more fundamental, then one has to find the basis on which the exclusion of one contrary predicate from the other is made. Mere difference is not 'opposition' and much of the 'opposition' between predicates is based on ordinary empirical experience which is open to revision in the light of further experience.

Malik's thought has another interesting dimension consisting in the distinction between percept, image and concept on the basis of which he postulates the notion of perceptual and categorical experience. Perceptual experience, according to him, is only referred to but does not itself refer to anything else. On the other hand, the image refers to the percept along with a temporal dimension such as past and future. The categorical stage perhaps consists of concepts which may refer to the percept if they are empirical but need not do so if they achieve an independence from them. This perhaps is described by him as pure categorical experience which is supposed to be a stage of realization. But, though Malik seems to talk of perceptual and categorical experience, he does not appear to talk of any distinct stage of experience consisting of 'images' occurring at their level.

Malik's thought culminates in his work entitled, *Possibility and Mythology* where he emphasises the reality of the negative element without however clarifying what exactly is meant by the 'negative'. Malik's thought, as it has developed over a period of time, has changed but little attention has been paid to his work or to evaluate his contribution. But at least on a *prima facie* reading, it is clear that his thought deserves more serious consideration that it has received up till now.

J.L. Mehta, whose work on Heidegger is well-known, lived long in the West and faced the challenge of the 'other', the western civilisation at all levels of his being. He responded to it, perhaps, more creatively than either Malik, Mohanty and Matilal who also happened to live in the West for most of the creative period of their life. None of these thinkers seemed to have undergone the encounter with the contemporary West as Mehta seems to have done, even though traces of it may be found in their works. Also, in the case of both Mohanty and Matilal, the response seems to have been primarily 'defensive' in the sense that they tried on behalf of Indian philosophy to articulate and substantiate the claim of 'rationality'. This claim had been disputed by most western thinkers, and in challenging it Mehta seems to have been led to a deeper discovery of his own 'self' and the tradition in which it was rooted by this encounter and dialogue with the western thought and culture. Perhaps, as he was located in the West at the *Centre for the Study of World Religions* at Harvard, for him, the encounter was primarily at the 'existential' and not at the 'intellectual' level. Mehta's last lecture, in fact, was given there only a month before he died. The lecture entitled, 'Problems of Understanding'[1] appeared as almost an obituary note along with his photograph, a rare tribute to an Indian thinker by a western publication.

The very title of the lecture summarises in a deep sense Mehta's own reflection on the encounter between civilisations and the phenomenon of understanding the 'other' which, according to him, leads inevitably to a deeper and renewed 'understanding' of the self. This 'understanding' is, for him, not a one-time affair but a life-long process in which one goes back to one's primordial roots which are always found in those scriptures from which not only one's civilisation itself seems to have taken birth but these have also provided a perennial source of inspiration, challenging all subsequent generations to their 'understanding'. Thus, for him, life was a pilgrimage to a sacred text, and the civilisation and self were 'way farers' on this unending journey which resulted simultaneously in an illumination of both the text and the self.

Strangely, Mehta appears to have followed Gadamer more in this understanding of the enterprise of 'understanding' than Heidegger, his first love and about whose thought he had written with such lucidity and depth of understanding. In fact, he has transposed the problem of 'understanding' from the usual contexts in which it has generally been discussed to the understanding of civilizations by each other, especially relating this to the possibility of an 'understanding' between the different religions which are predominantly associated with them. This identifies civilizations with religions and underplays not only other dimensions of a civilisation, but also the deep cleavages within the religion itself which is supposed to be associated with a particular civilisation and identified with it. Mehta, in a subtle and clever move thus identifies not only civilizations with a religion but with the foundational scriptural texts in which these religions are rooted and thus the usual hermeneutical exercise in respect of 'text' is brought in the understanding of civilizations. The enterprise of "understanding", thus becomes the enterprise of returning to the sacred scriptural texts of one's own tradition in the light of the sacred scriptural texts of another religion which is the foundation of the other civilisation.

But, Mehta had earlier held that "these texts are the products of a way of life adopted by an entire people and in turn have inspired and nourished their faith, that the texts here play a crucial role within the context of a whole way of being living and thinking".[2] But, if this is so then how can the texts be "understood" if that whole way of living, of which they were the product, has itself substantially changed. Further, Mehta seems to assume that the way of living of a people has not changed substantially over millennia for, if he were to accept this, then the so-called foundational scriptural texts would have lost their intelligibility long ago. On the other hand, if changes in forms of living do not substantially affect the 'understanding' of these texts then they must be supposed to address themselves to a feature of life which remains constant in spite of all the changes in the forms of living. But if the 'scriptures' of different religions and thus, of different civilizations are different then one would have to argue for 'constants' in life which themselves are different. On the other hand, if the 'constants' are supposed to be the same for all human living irrespective of space and time in which that life is lived then one would have to suppose some super, over-arching scriptural text which is manifested and articulated in different texts. This is the idea of perennial philosophy which, however, is rejected by the devout followers of most religions except perhaps the neo-Vedāntins.

Mehta's metaphor of pilgrimage and 'way farer' are both illuminating and seductive but here, as elsewhere, is the reality overlooked of actual pilgrimages where so-called holy places are full of those who exploit the unwary pilgrim in various ways. Further, the places of pilgrimage themselves are different for the votaries of different religions and thus there seems to be no common place for pilgrimage for all mankind just as there seems to be no overarching text to which all may return, to search for that primordial source of their identity from which everything seems to have originally gushed forth like the eternal spring of life itself.

Mehta tries to overcome this difficulty by suggesting that it is the encounter with the 'other' that makes us understand the 'self' better. But this is to underwrite the primacy of the other in an understanding of one's own self and would go against the long experience of the seekers of 'self'-knowledge who have pursued their own *Sādhanā* without caring much for the other paths to the realization of the self, or even the 'no-self' (*anattā*) as in Buddhism.

Mehta appears to have ignored not only the history of the spiritual pursuit of mankind but also the history of organised religions which are full of schisms and persecution and crusades both against the heretics within and unbelievers outside. The realms of polity, economy and law with which organised religion has been enmeshed always also seems to have escaped the attention of Mehta. Perhaps the 'rule of metaphor', to borrow the title of a well-known book by Ricouer, has blinded Mehta to these facts and indirectly reveals the essential weakness of this style of thought which has been made fashionable by philosophical hermeneutics following Gadamer and Ricouer recently.

A little dose of the analytical tradition in philosophy so fashionable in the Anglo-Saxon world of England and America might have helped to balance the perspective of this deep and profound thinker whose work requires to be 'lived' with and pondered over in order to grasp its insights into the human situation.

Like Mehta and Mohanty, Matilal too had chosen the West as his second home and like them, he too encountered the western philosophical tradition on its own ground and responded to it in his own way. He was, however, primarily a scholar of classical Indian philosophy and felt that what needed to be rebutted was the western philosopher's impression that Indian philosophy was not philosophy in their sense of the term as it primarily believed not in reason but in the authority of some primary foundational text. Such texts were known as *śruti* and *āgama*, the former referring to the texts belonging to the Vedic corpus and the latter consisting of those non-Vedic texts which were regarded as 'authoritative' by the philosophical traditions which claimed derivation from them.

The āgamic texts included not only the well-known Buddhist and Jaina traditions of philosophy, but also the *Vaiṣṇava*, the *Śaiva*, the *Śākta* and other schools in traditions that were allied to these, but slightly differed from them. The rejection of the appellation, 'philosophy' in the case of Indian thinking on this ground may be said to have started from Hegel and has continued to be accepted as an almost axiomatic truth by others following him, including such great names as Husserl and Heidegger. The acceptance of *Śabda Pramāṇa* as an independent *pramāṇa* by most of the schools of Indian philosophy seems to support this view held by most western thinkers during the last two centuries. Matilal, amongst others, tried to rebut this evaluation by establishing the credentials of Indian philosophy in terms of what has been regarded as philosophy in the western tradition.

In fact, Matilal's major work perceptions was written after he was appointed the Spalding Professor of Eastern Religions and Ethics at the University of Oxford[3] with quotations from Hume, Locke and Flew to this effect. He also admits to the charge against him which some western critics had made of showing a tendency of "leaning over backwards in my writings to show the analytic nature of Indian philosophy"[4] as he considers it necessary "to correct persisting misconceptions and sometimes even to remove ignorance". Surprisingly, he does not refer to the great European masters who were primarily responsible for this widespread misimpression about Indian philosophy.

The central theme of the book, *Perceptions* is that Indian philosophy may be understood more correctly as an attempt to refute skepticism regarding the possibility of acquiring a knowledge of the nature of what is ultimately real and possibly also of realising it in a more intimate and deeper sense than theoretic cognition is capable of giving. Russell had made a distinction between "knowledge by acquaintance" and "knowledge by description" as two radically different kinds of knowledge. The Indian tradition was perhaps arguing for a deeper truth which is known both by description and by acquaintance which, in a sense, may also be regarded as a characteristic of all empirical science as ultimately, the theoretical truth which can always be in terms of description alone has to be correlated with what is directly experienced by 'acquaintance'.

This aspect of the Indian philosophical enterprise or at least of that part of it which goes under the name of Sāṁkhya and Vedanta was emphasized by Matilal at the inaugural lecture that he gave in the University of Oxford after his appointment as Spalding Professor entitled, "Logical Illumination of Mysticism". Thinkers like Nāgārjuna and Śrī Harṣa may be said to illustrate vividly this aspect of a particular tradition of Indian philosophy. But it is not so much the verification of what is theoretically understood to be the nature of reality that is exemplified in the thought of these thinkers, but rather the intrinsic impossibility for reason to apprehend because of its very nature, what is ultimately real. This, perhaps, is closer to the position of Kant, even though the latter did not pronounce anything definite on the possibility of what he called 'intellectual intuition' and held that what we call 'knowledge' can never know what is 'real' in itself, because the very structure of reason, makes it impossible to know what is independent of that structure. Bradley, perhaps, would be a more appropriate example in order to understand the position of Nāgārjuna and Śrī Harṣa than Kant.

The analogy with the empirical sciences is appropriately exemplified by K.C. Bhattacharya's way of understanding Indian philosophy. This may be understood as the 'discovery' of certain possibilities by a pure theoretical reflection which may be called strictly philosophical possibilities, which are then realised by a process of *sādhanā* or spiritual praxis. The relation between philosophical reflection which is mainly of a theoretical, ratiocinative and argumentative kind is thus shown as intimately and integrally related to spiritual realization which is supposed to be the distinctive hall-mark of Indian philosophy by many scholars.

The challenge of the western philosophical tradition and its rejection of Indian philosophy as being truly 'philosophical' is felt by many other Indian thinkers besides the one's mentioned above. Thus Professor K. Satchidananda Murty's, book, *Reason and Revelation in Advaita Vedanta* shows his concern for the establishment of reason in its due place in Indian philosophy. Mohanty's recent work on Indian philosophy, *Reason and Tradition in Indian Thought* displays the same anxiety. It may be noted that Mohanty has substituted the word 'tradition' for revelation as the later is grossly inadequate in the Indian context where it carries with it all the implications and presuppositions it has in the western theological tradition. Neither the texts designated as *śruti* or *āgama* were never considered as revelations given to man in the sense in which both the Christian and the Islamic traditions have understood it.

Perhaps the most interesting and a radically different response may be found in the work of Sivajiban Bhattacharya who instead of rebutting the claim made by so many western thinkers has juxtaposed with remarkable lucidity and clarity the two modes of analytical reason in dealing with philosophical problems of a cognate type. He has chosen the most abstract and complex Navya-Nyāya analysis of such key philosophical concepts as *viṣayatāvāda* or the theory of objectivity and *nirvikalpakavāda* or the theory of indeterminate perception in the text of Gaṅgeśa. He has discussed these in his two introductions which form part 1 of each of these two separate volumes. The unwary reader will hardly be aware of the fact that Sivajiban Bhattacharya has contrasted the most recent western discussion of these subjects as handled by such thinkers as Frege, Russell, Geach, Dummett, Carnap, Tarski, Church and others. Unfortunately, few are aware of this fact as the only persons who are likely to consult this work are those who are specialists in Navya-Nyāya and there are not many such persons in the English-speaking world, even in India.

Sivajiban Bhattacharya has a rare mastery of both the western and the Indian traditions of philosophy with a grasp of the specific details of each. This enables him to see the discussion of the problems in the context of their own discourse and the way it has been developed over millennia by successive thinkers. He has written extensively on various topics relating both to the western and Indian philosophical traditions including the one relating to developments in modern logic in recent times. But, though it is widely respected and admired for learning and scholarship, his work has hardly been the subject of intensive discussion on the part of his contemporaries either in India or abroad.

Professor K. Satchidananda Murty has worked on the Vedānta but is nevertheless neither a committed Vedāntin like Malkani or Mahadevan nor just a profound scholar of one school of Indian philosophy, like T.R.V. Murty whose main work dealt with the central philosophy of Buddhism for which he became justly famous. K. Satchidananda Murty's interests have been wide ranging, and he has written not only on philosophical subjects but also on such topics as *Indian Foreign Policy* (Calcutta, 1964) and *Problems of Peace* (Bombay, 1960). He is, in fact, the only contemporary philosopher in India who has shown an interest in non-Indian and non-western philosophical traditions, particularly those of China and Japan, which are totally neglected by almost all Indian scholars who write as if there were no philosophical traditions outside India and the West. In fact, he has published a book entitled, *Far Eastern Philosophies* (Mysore, 1975) trying to bring to the attention of his colleagues these living philosophical traditions, but in vain as hardly any Indian philosopher has become interested in the subject after the lectures he had delivered at the University of Mysore which were later published in a book form by the same University.

Besides these wide-ranging interests, Professor Murty is perhaps the only contemporary philosopher in India, who is not over-awed by the aura of authority which most western philosophers enjoy in the Indian mind. Like the proverbial child in Anderson's story who could see the Emperor as he was uninfluenced by all the adulation and adoration of the so-called adults about him, he is able to see the follies and foibles of the greatest western thinkers and points them out in his downright, no-nonsense manner. He has commented, for example, that Socrates, the so-called father of western rationality did not only believe in the temple oracle of Delphi but had also vowed to sacrifice a cock to some god of medicine like all other non-rational or irrational mortals. In fact, this is one of the last things he asks one of his friends to do for him as he had not been able to fulfill the vow till then in his life. And, as for Descartes, the father of modern philosophy and the initiator of the method of radial doubt, Professor Murty points out his totally irrational pilgrimage to some sacred holy place in France. It is not that facts such as these are not known to scholars of the subject, but that they are usually underplayed or brushed aside as irrelevant. Professor Murty, on the other hand, not only takes note but openly states what he feels about the views of the eminent writer or thinker who has a great reputation. His lectures at the Indian Institute of Advanced Studies, Shimla, entitled "The Realm of Between" are replete with such judgements.

Another person belonging to the generation of Professor Sivajiban Bhattacharya and Professor K. Satchidananda Murty who has symbolized the very spirit of linguistic analysis as embodying the essence of philosophy is Professor Rajendra Prasad who has pursued this method with relentless vigour for the elucidation and clarification of diverse philosophical problems and concepts, both Indian and western. Two works containing his numerous articles on various subjects are entitled, *Karma, Causation and Retributive Morality and Regularity; Normativity and Rules of Language and other Philosophical Analysis.* His main work has been on ethics and metaphysics in which, among other things, he has questioned the generally-accepted belief in Naturalistic fallacy in the field of contemporary Anglo-Saxon ethics. He has also subjected many of the Indian concepts such as those of *puruṣārtha, mokṣa,* the idea of *jīvana mukti* and *karma* to a searching analysis which raises many new questions about these. His latest work is entitled, *Niṣkāma Karma.*

Most of the writers mentioned here have written either in the English or Sanskrit language, or sometimes in both, as is the case with Professor G.C. Pande whose contributions we have primarily included in the part devoted to developments in classical Indian thought in this period. However, much has also been written in the Indian languages though little attention and no critical evaluation has been made of the work produced in those languages. The work of Nischaldasa, to which we have referred to in the chapter on Vedānta, is an example of this. The work was written in Hindi but later translated into Sanskrit as it was considered to be an important contribution by many scholars who had the occasion to read it in the original language.

The work of Shri Yashdev Shalya, however, falls in a completely different category. He has only written in Hindi and has, over the past four decades, established himself as an original thinker who has combined the Indian and western traditions of thought in a unique manner. His contribution to the cause of philosophy is not however restricted to these writings alone, as he has founded the premier institution, *Akhila Bhārtīya Darśana Pariṣad* for the propagation of philosophy in Hindi. He has also edited a number of philosophical journals of a very high quality in Hindi.

Shalya's main contention is that it is only in self-consciousness and in a reflection on it that one may 'understand' the philosophical quest which consists primarily in 'understanding' both the world and the self and their diverse relations to each other. In fact, it is in self-consciousness alone that the world finds itself 'illuminated' as it gets not only 'known' but also 'felt' in all its beauty and splendour. In self-consciousness, the 'object' occurs at two levels, the first is concerned with what may be called 'object' in general or the 'world' at all its various levels; while the second is the self as 'object' which however also functions as subject to the object in the first sense, that is the world in general. It is this self which is simultaneously both subject and object which seeks a meaningful relationship with the world, that is the pure object *par excellence,* in the modes of knowing, feeling and willing and thus endows it with a meaning, significance and value which it could hardly have on its own without this relationship. But there appears to be a radical difference between the 'object' at these two levels as the 'object' at the first level, that is, the world in general can be subjected to the various processes of validation and thus be determined as to its veridicality. Whereas the object at the second level, that is, self as object appears as 'self-validating and beyond the process of validation outside itself'. But as the self itself is an 'object' to self-consciousness, this along with that, is the relationship with the pure subject, the self itself becomes a subject of a second order reflection which questions it in its very foundation and begins to see both the object at the first level and the egoity or the sense of I-ness which relates to it as the subject in a new manner.

In this second order reflection, it seems to discover that the essential nature of consciousness consists in its seeking of value, meaning and significance and that it seeks these both in respect of all that appears as object at the first level and also that which appears as 'object' at the second level, that is the empirical self or the ego constituted by the I-consciousness. The two directions of the seeking, however, are inter-related even though one may not be aware of it and the seeking in the external world is indirectly related to the seeking in what may be called the inner realm which itself is constituted or brought into being by the fact of self-consciousness which gives rise to 'egoity' or sense of 'I-ness' and thus provides the foundation for that basic split which characterizes self-consciousness at the human level.

There is an infinity in the pursuit of meaning, value and significance in both the directions, particularly as it seems to be the inherent character of self-consciousness to endow or apprehend an infinite depth in whatever it apprehends as 'object' whether this object be anything in the world or its own self seen as object.

In this sense then, the search for meaning, values and significance in the world of 'objects' at the first level may be seen as an attempt to know the self itself or to get rid of the 'false' knowledge that one may have regarding it. But the seeking for the self is only indirectly present in all such seekings which are primarily directed towards the object. On the other hand, when the self is directly sought, these diverse seekings in respect of the object themselves become the object of reflection and an attempt is made to find as to what exactly their meaning and significance consist in. The feeling of the 'falsity' or 'unreality' of the world may arise in the context of this direct concern with the realization of the true nature of the self and sometimes the seeking for meaning, significance and value in respect of objects at the first level may begin to appear as a hindrance in that process. In the language of the *puruṣārthas,* we may say that the pursuit of *dharma, artha* and *kāma* are indirectly pursuits of the ideal values involved in the self-itself, though it is only the pursuit of *mokṣa* that is directly concerned with it.

Thus, the fact that the world is a correlate of consciousness is revealed to self-consciousness through a critical reflection on what is given to it as an 'object'. It is also simultaneously revealed that the world, though a correlate of consciousness, is essentially to be understood as 'not-self' in relation to it.

However, this means that consciousness in its ordinary or natural state is either incompletely or partially apprehended as self as it is overwhelmed by that which is not-self and hence has to regain itself by a process which may be called *sādhanā* which essentially consists in overcoming this dominance of the 'not-self' and the achievement of its own primacy and its establishment within itself. This may be called the self as Brahman in traditional language or the self in its complete ideality. However, this is not something which is to be understood as already achieved or established or as something eternally present but rather as something which is achievable through an effort made for its realization. The 'not-self' can thus not be considered to be completely real, even though its existence cannot be denied. Its reality consists in the form of something that is to be overcome and hence it has the same type of reality which defects or imperfections have in the sense that it has an essential negativity about it, a negativity which has a positive effect and which itself has to be negated in order that an absolute positivity may be both asserted and achieved.

Shalyaji's thought shows a continuity with the dominant trends in Indian philosophizing, specially those associated with Sāṁkhya and Advaita Vedānta in the tradition, and it has both the virtues and the deficiencies of that style of thinking. The basic question that has remained unasked is that, if consciousness is conceived of as essentially seeking meaning, significance and value, then how can that which it 'creates' through this activity of 'seeking' be treated as essentially defective and hence something to be overcome. In fact, the term not-self in such a perspective is essentially misleading, for it is that which gives meaning to the self and functions as a 'mirror' in which it recognises itself.

Another problem with this way of thinking is that it only talks of the 'object' at two levels and totally ignores the essential plurality of self-conscious beings where each is an 'object' to all the others. There is, thus, not just self-consciousness but 'self-consciousness', each of them essentially involved in a psycho-physiological matrix, which has a development curve from birth to death, a process in relation to which 'self-consciousness' seems to be a creature as it can do nothing about it. In fact, 'self-consciousness', at least as involved in the psycho-physiological matrix seems to have a 'history' as it is normally only achieved at a certain level of biological growth and does not seem to be there since childhood or the moment of one's birth. The demographic explosion of 'self-conscious' beings poses another problem so far unaddressed by anyone philosophizing in this vein. So is the anomalous fact that not only self-consciousness but even consciousness or life as we know it does not seem to exist anywhere in the universe except on this little planet, earth. The millions of galaxies which astronomical observation has brought to our notice seem to be totally bereft of any evidence of life and, though it is impossible to say, with any certainty, that there is no life in any of the planets circling around the myriad of suns about which astronomers write, there is little doubt that at least in our planetary system there is no evidence of there being life on any planet other than on our own. The challenge that this poses to any consciousness-centric philosophizing is almost impossible to meet and yet, it is difficult to see how else can man think except in the context of the fact that he finds himself 'thinking'. The foundational paradox of philosophising perhaps lies in this fact that man is essentially caught in what may be called a consciousness-centric 'predicament' which he cannot get out of, but there is no necessity why this 'predicament' should become 'ego-centric' or 'self-centric' when it is obvious that there is a plurality of self-conscious beings and that one achieves whatever self-consciousness one has in the context of a society of such beings who share a common culture consisting of a commonality both of language and a self-remembered, half-imagined past.

However, there are many thinkers who have made, in their own way, significant contributions to the activity of such philosophising under the western impact during the last seventy years or so. A fair representation of these may be found in the various collections on *Contemporary Indian Philosophy* published by various editors. A well-known work under this title in the Murhead Library of Philosophy was edited by Murhead and Radhakrishnan in 1936 and was revised in the form of an enlarged edition in 1952. A volume with the same title was later published under the editorship of Margaret Chatterjee and called the second series containing contributions by philosophers of the next generation. A rough comparison of the volumes in the two series provides some interesting data regarding both the region-wise concentration of philosophical activity in India, as well as the major subjects of interest that preoccupied the thinkers. One may also notice the shifting emphasis with regard to both these if one makes a comparative study of the volumes. One must however allow for the surprisingly large presence of philosophers from Delhi University perhaps because the editor herself happened to be from there.

Even a more representative source of information about the contribution of eminent philosophers may be found in the Presidential Addresses delivered at the Indian Philosophical Congress from 1926 onwards as it may be assumed that the persons so invited were regarded as eminent in their field by their colleagues and that they utilized the occasion to articulate the best of what they had to say on the subject. As all of these addresses have now been collected and published by the Indian Council of Philosophical Research under the editorship of S.C. Dube, they have become easily accessible to anyone who would like to study the development of philosophy in India in the last 75 years of the twentieth century. Many of these thinkers had also been represented in the two series published in the Murhead Library of Philosophy and it would be interesting to compare what they had written there with what they have said in their Presidential addresses. The Presidential Addresses, in fact, have fortunately been organised thematically by the editor in four volumes under the titles.

The recently published, "Subject and Author Index" of the *Philosophical Quarterly*, the first philosophical journal to be published in India, provides additional information regarding the writers who contributed to this journal as also the subjects which they wrote on. However, no analytical study has yet been made of the data provided in it nor any comparative study undertaken with the author indexes of the following: *Journal of the Indian Academy of Philosophy* founded by Ras Behari Das; The *Philosophical Annual* published by the Department of Philosophy, Madras University; and the *Journal of Indian Council of Philosophical Research* whose Subject and Author Indexes have also been prepared by Professor R.S. Bhatnagar and published by Indian Council of Philosophical Research.

Besides the general field of philosophy, in which Indian thinkers, both in India and abroad, have played a significant role and made important contributions, there is also some work which has recently been done in such technical fields as those in modern logic and philosophy of science. Most of the important work in logic has been done by those working in computer science such as the work of Anand Pillay at the University of Notre Dame and Rohit Parikh in New York. The former has contributed to a branch of model theory known as the 'stability theory' while the latter has contributed to the 'recursion theory'. Besides these, is the important seminal work of Anil Gupta, the former editor of the *Journal of Philosophical Logic*, who along with Nuel Belnap has tried to show that circularity is not necessarily a defect in definition, as has generally been supposed since the dawn of logic. He has shown that circular definitions and systems of mutually interdependent definitions are "logically legitimate". This, they call, the "Revision Theory of definitions" which, if accepted, would lead to a basic revolution in the very notion of fallacious thinking. The other important work is that of Amartya Sen, the well-known economist who was recently awarded the Noble Prize for Economics. He has worked on the social choice theory, particularly in the context of Arrow's theorem and also written in the field of social philosophy and ethics.

The work of Amartya Kumar Sen is primarily in the field of economics even though he has made an important contribution in the context of Arrow's theorem as noted above and some other topics in philosophy, particularly those relating to public policy. The contribution symbolizes, in a sense, the astounding success of the implantation of modern traditions of western knowledge in India by the British. Both in the natural sciences and the social sciences, Indian work has been remarkable by world standards and compares favourably not only with most other countries in Asia, Africa and Latin America but also with many other western countries such as, say Spain or Portugal or Italy. In fact, the unbelievably remarkable work at the very frontiers of knowledge done in India starting from the first quarter of the twentieth century is even more astonishing as there were hardly any facilities available then. The works of S.N. Bose, Meghanath Saha, C.V. Raman, P.C. Ray, J.C. Bose, Ramanujan and many others are included in this category. After independence, the centre of research in India has shifted, as everywhere else, to more applied fields and the work done in the field of space research and nuclear technology is evidence of this.

The foundations for the development of skills in these fields were laid down by the British in the various institutes they had set up in the country, particularly the ones relating to agricultural research by setting up the *Indian Council of Agricultural Research* and the various surveys of India such as the Archaeological

Survey, the Geological Survey, etc. After independence, under the leadership of Nehru and Sir S.S. Bhatnagar, various National Laboratories were set up in different parts of the country which gradually trained manpower for massive research work in all branches of natural sciences. The same work was done in the field of social sciences and the humanities by such institutions as ICSSR, ICHR, the various academics and the Indian Council of Philosophical Research.

However, though there have undoubtedly been outstanding personalities in almost all fields of modern knowledge in India during this period, it would be difficult to say that they have had any significant impact on the philosophical thinking.

As for developments in the older, Sanskritic tradition of philosophizing it is surprising to note the almost total absence of any influence of the modern ways of philosophizing on it. The two seem to have seem to run almost parallel to each other except in some very recent deliberate and self-conscious efforts to foster some sort of dialogue so that something new may emerge.

NOTES AND REFERENCES

1. *Philosophy East and West,* Jan. 1989, p.xxxix, I, p. 372.
2. *Ibid.,* p. 5.
3. A Chair earlier occupied by S. Radhakrishnan
4. *Perceptions,* p. 4.

SECTION FOUR

CHAPTER 12

Problems and Issues still remaining to be explored in Intellectual History from Eighteenth Century upto the Present Time

The success of a research project of this kind consists not only in what it actually achieves in the context of the task it had set for itself, but also the new questions it raises and the problems it discloses for further investigation, beckoning towards horizons which had not been suspected before. This chapter therefore, tries to highlight and focus attention upon the tasks which are yet to be done and which we have not attempted because of the constraints of time and the limitation of our capacities and resources.

Even a cursory look at the bibliography of the basic texts we have compiled from different sources would reveal the utter inadequacy of the basis on which we have constructed our picture of the developments in classical and modern Indian thought from eighteenth century onwards. We have only been able to use the two works of Pt. Anantakrishna Shastri for the important arguments in the debate between the Advaitins and the non-Advaitins while the extant material on this issue in the period we have dealt with consists of so many texts and thinkers that it is impossible for anyone, including ourselves, to think of it as meaningfully representative in any sense of the term. Perhaps, the only satisfaction that we have is that, in the field of philosophy, one important argument is worth a dozen books and if we have been able to highlight even a few of the important arguments in the debate, it has not been a complete waste of effort on our part. The list of the works in this debate, which itself may not be complete, thus provides an immediate indication of the work that is still to be attempted in respect of this long-standing controversy in the Indian philosophical tradition.

Similarly, as far as developments in Nyāya are concerned, Professor Prahlada Char has covered the following thinkers only: Gokulanātha Upādhyāya (1710), Kṛṣṇa Bhaṭṭa Ārde (1800), Raghunatha Parvate Shastrin (1853), Dharmadatta (Bachcha) Jha (1853–1918), Badrinatha Shukla. Besides these, there are many others whose work needs to be looked into and critically evaluated so that in case there is anything interesting in them, it may be highlighted and brought to the notice of contemporary Naiyāyikas. The same is true of the *Kroḍapatras* which have been studied even less, both because they are more difficult to understand and also because they are not as easily available as the other texts are.

Of course, this requires that most of these works should be made available at one place so that they may become easily available to scholars who want to work on them. This itself is not an easy task and unless some institution deliberately adopts a long-term policy of acquiring these on a planned basis, it can hardly be done. To find scholars who are really competent to understand this material and critically evaluate it, is an even more difficult task as the competence level in respect of these texts is sharply declining and unless a concerted effort is made in this direction, many of these texts may very soon become completely unintelligible because of the highly terse, condensed and technical vocabulary employed by them. Also, most of these texts, specially the *Kroḍapatras,* discuss issues at the micro-level which can be understood only if one is aware of the long history of thinking about them that has gone before in the tradition, a requirement that is fulfilled by very few living scholars these days. All in all, the task seems so immense and the awareness and the competence so little that it is doubtful if anything really significant can be expected to be achieved in the near future. But the awareness of the task is the first condition and this is what we are attempting to create in this chapter.

Normally, the Nyāya and the Vaiśeṣika are so linked together in the minds of people that they do not feel the necessity of distinguishing between them even though the centre of their interest is totally different. Thus, while there are at least a substantial number of Naiyāyikas who are both interested and knowledgeable in many of the Nyāya works written in this period, there are hardly any who are interested in works concerned primarily with issues which have interested Vaiśeṣika thinkers in the past. The general impression is that no significant Vaiśeṣika work has been done for a long time. This may be true but as a number of works specifically designated as Vaiśeṣika have been written during this period, it would not be fair to pass a judgement unless someone has critically examined them to find what exactly they are saying. A list of such works is given in the appendix.

The same is true to a certain extent of Mīmāṁsā also. Here the works of Khaṇḍadeva, Āpadeva II and Kṛṣṇa Yajvan seem to be the most important as a number of works have been written on them. A more intensive work on these texts and their commentaries is required than has been attempted up till now. Besides these, the enormous discussion on *Phalsāṁkarya* occasioned by the work of Appayadikṣita I needs to be closely examined for the issues raised and the arguments given both in support of his position and against it in the large number of works that have been mentioned in the chapter on the subject in this volume.

As for Sāṁkhya, the material in the Larson volume is fairly exhaustive and perhaps the only thing that needs to be done is to go once more to the original texts which we have discussed and see the works once again from the point of view that we have articulated in the chapter concerned.

Amongst the thinkers we have discussed, the work of Hariharānanda Āraṇya seems to deserve special attention.

As for the material on *Alaṁkāra Śāstra*, a lot seems to have been written during this period and, in fact, continues to be written perhaps because the majority of those who take to Sanskrit studies specialize in *Sāhitya* or Literature. The works of Pt. Rewa Prasad Dwivedi and Pt. Brahmadutt Sharma may be specially mentioned in this connection. There may be many others like them about whose works we do not know but whose writings deserve serious attention. But, till such time, at least the work of those who are known should be studied and critically evaluated for the contribution they are said to have made to the subject.

As for the work on the developments relating to the material on the *Dharma Śāstras*, one can only say that in spite of the monumental work of P.V. Kane on the subject and of Laxman Shastri Joshi on the *Dharmakoṣa*, most of the earlier work remains unanalysed, both in terms of the historical changes that are evidenced in it and the diversity of the points of view in the different *Dharmaśāstra* texts in the tradition. Moreover, the difference between what may be called the strictly *Dharmaśāstra* texts and those relating to *Arthaśāstra* and *Vyavahāra*, that is, polity and law have seldom been articulated and emphasised. Within the former, there is the important difference between *rājadharma* and *rājanīti* pointing to the important difference between *dharma* and *nīti* which relates to the theoretical and practical aspects of *dharma* and has hardly been attended to in most discussions on the subject. The development of the *Nibandha* literature from twelfth century onwards also merits analysis of the topics that were dealt in it and the changes that occurred in it over a period of time.

Perhaps the most important work that has been written during the period that we have been dealing with, is the work of Paṇḍit Rajesvara Shastri Dravida on the *Arthaśāstra* of Kauṭilya. Paṇḍit Rajesvara Shastri Dravida was, by common consent, one of the outstanding Naiyāyikas of his time. Yet during the last years of his life he felt that the roots of everything lay in the exercise of political power and hence chose to write a commentary on the *Arthaśāstra* of Kauṭilya which is regarded as the foundational work on politics in the tradition. However, only parts of the text have been published and the complete text still awaits editing and publishing by the authorities of the *Sampurnananda Sanskrit Vishvavidyalaya* which perhaps has the complete manuscript with it. Earlier, Paṇḍit Ganapati Shastri, the well-known scholar from the South, had written a commentary on the *Arthaśāstra*. The two volumes published by the *Sampurnananda Sanskrit Vishvavidyalaya* and edited by Visvanath Shastri Datara, not only contain the commentaries of the two *paṇḍits* but also those of Sri Yogghamacharya. Since the full texts with all the *adhikaraṇas* has not been published, it is difficult to assess what is new in the contribution of these thinkers or what are the differences in their understanding of the *Arthaśāstra* in the contemporary context. This must await the publication of the full text as only then something can be said regarding it.

The works on Jaina philosophy have hardly attracted the attention they deserve and this remains true even for the period that we have been dealing with. Most Jaina scholars feel that nothing significant has been written after Yaśovijaya's appearance sometime in the seventeenth century. But it is extremely unlikely that out of forty odd Jaina thinkers whose names are mentioned in Potter's Bibliography not event one has said something of significant. But unless someone looks into the extant material, no final judgement can be passed as it seems to have been done by the Jaina scholars whom we had approached for helping us in this regard.

The work on philosophy that has been written in English during the modern period is not only available in plenty but has been covered in a number of anthologies devoted to the subject. Along with these, the recent publication of the Presidential Address edited by S.C. Dube of Jabalpur University and published by Indian Council of Philosophical Research provides ample source material for intensive exploration concerning contributions of those who have written on philosophy in English during this period. But, in spite of this easy availability, hardly any attention has been paid to the work of most of these thinkers. K.C. Bhattacharya and Shri Aurobindo are perhaps the only exceptions but even their thought has not received the critical attention it deserves for providing a take-off point for subsequent thinkers to develop their ideas further. Some preliminary work has been done in respect of the thought of Kalidas Bhattacharya, N.V. Banerjee, Radhakrishnan, J.N. Mohanty, but it is not sufficient to provide even a comprehensive insight into their achievements. A summary survey of the Presidential Addresses made by Professor R.S. Bhatnagar for this volume suggests that there are important insights including, for example, the one's given by H.D. Bhattacharya, M.M. Sharif, S.S. Barlinghe, Hari Mohan Jha, T.R.V. Murty, to name only some of them.

As for the material in the Indian languages, unless intensive work is undertaken for each of the languages, nothing can be said regarding contributions made in them.

A sustained and long-term programme is on the required part of institutions that are concerned not only with fostering the intellectual activity in its various dimensions in the present but also forging a living link between that which was achieved in the past and that which is being done in the present so that it all may become an active ingredient in the building of future. Ultimately, it is a question of 'active awareness' of the achievements of those who have gone before us so that they may provide the inspiration, the incentive and the material to build upon what they had achieved. In this way alone, intellectual cultures are built over a period of time and a continuity with the past is maintained without which no enduring substantial achievement is attained as otherwise amnesia and forgetfulness seems to be the fate of all as each generation tries to achieve in the present with total ignorance of what has gone before. Such seems to be the situation in India at present as little is really known of what had been done in various fields during the last three hundred years or even earlier. If our work contributes even a little in lessening this ignorance and inspires others to unearth the intellectual riches of the past a little further we would feel compensated for the work we have done.

CHAPTER 13

Conclusion

The picture of the past is ultimately a creation of the historian. And that picture becomes the 'truth' in the minds of those who read it, especially the young who are 'educated' in the schools and colleges to 'see' it that way. Once the picture becomes a part of the settled heritage of the mind, then anything that comes to one's attention is itself seen and interpreted in terms of this picture. This is as true of the period with which we have dealt with in these pages as with any other period in the past of this civilisation or that of any other.

The eighteenth century is usually presented as the beginning of a period of decline and decay. The coming of the British is seen as bringing some order and improvement, particularly with the injection and grafting of the European, or rather the British consciousness into it. The period of decay and decline is placed by many scholars even earlier but, then, they do not know what to do with the coming of the Muslim rule in India or the glories of the Mughal Empire whose decline and decay is supposed to have started at the beginning of the eighteenth century with the death of Aurangzeb in A.D. 1707.

We are not concerned here, however, with the dilemmas of the historians but with the fact that whatever the picture he or they create becomes a factor in the 'seeing' and 'interpretation' of that which lies all around. In fact, all that is incompatible with the picture is generally not seen or, if seen, is ignored, underplayed or treated as unimportant. Not only this, the interpretation which is put on the facts is generally done in such a way as not to disturb the picture.

This is borne out by the study that we have done of the developments in classical Indian thought from eighteenth century onwards and is substantiated by almost every chapter we have written. We ourselves had started with this supposition in our mind and were very reluctant to undertake this task as it did not promise to be rewarding if what had been written during this period was only a repetition or a refinement of what had been said earlier. As we did not have a first-hand acquaintance with the original texts written during the period, we naturally approached those who knew better and requested them to help us in this regard. To our surprise, however, they expressed the same judgement regarding the writings of this period even though when we ourselves saw the material they had written for us carefully. The generalised picture of the period appeared to have been so deeply internalized that almost all the scholars did not seem to 'see' what was lying before them in the texts and about which they themselves were writing. This was strange indeed and could make sense only in the light of the fact that their own perception was being deeply affected by the generalised presuppositions they already had in their mind, for if they accepted the importance and the novelty in the thinking of writers during this period, then they would have to give up what they had accepted axiomatically to be 'true' about this period.

One may, of course, say that our own perception has been deeply affected by our desire to see novelty everywhere. But, firstly, such a desire, even if it is there, is not wrong as one ought to be intellectually open and receptive and appreciative of anything that is significantly new in what is said by anybody and ultimately, it is intellectually obligatory on one's part to point it out and bring it to the attention of others so that they may judge for themselves and use it for thinking further about the issue or the problem concerned. This is what we have done. And it is for the readers to judge whether they too find 'significance' and 'novelty' in what we have highlighted in the writings of this period.

Surprisingly, the attitude which we found so pervasive in respect of the writings which are generally called 'traditional' or in other words those which are written in the Sanskrit language and deal with subjects that show a continuity with those written in the past, was also found to be present in the case of works written in English and dealing with subjects that may be regarded as 'western' both in their origin and inspiration. No one, as far as we know, thinks that anything of great significance has been written by any Indian during, say, the last hundred or hundred and fifty years. Yet, our own study has revealed a different picture, a picture that we have tried to delineate in Part III of the volume.

Personally, I am convinced that there is substantive novelty in the writings of Indian philosophers from K.C. Bhattacharya onwards and that there are innumerable insights which need to be recognised and developed further. Yet, here again, something stands in the way of this recognition, and it is difficult and almost impossible to remove it, as deep down, there seems to be an unconscious attitude that the 'source' of all knowledge lies in the West and that nothing new, meaningful or significant can be found in any non-western source, here or elsewhere.

The contemporary Indian mind usually makes a distinction between knowledge and spirituality and is prepared to accept that as far as the latter is concerned, India has not to learn anything from any where. But, as far as the former is concerned, it seems to have no doubt that all the so-called knowledge of the past is already superseded and that this is true even in such realms as philosophy which are not so empirically grounded as the natural sciences are.

Besides the internalisation of the picture deliberately fostered by the historians of developments from eighteenth century onwards and the equally deliberately cultivated belief emanating from almost all western writings on any subject that the sources of all knowledge lie among the Greeks and it is modern, western Europe alone which has developed it further, there seems to be another factor determining the general attitude of the educated Indian to the intellectual achievements of his own countrymen during the last century and a half when he has been in contact with the western intellectual traditions and thinks of himself as integrally belonging to it. This is the unconscious feeling that seems to demand that almost every decade should produce an outstanding thinker of genius whose contributions should be recognised the world over. A few outstanding persons do not seem to satisfy their unconscious thirst for achievement and recognition by the West. It is conveniently forgotten that even in the West, 'genius' is a rare commodity and outstanding thinkers who really make novel contributions are not easy to find. As most ordinary, day-to-day work in the intellectual domain is only competent and carries out the previously achieved knowledge further by small contributions here and there. And that is how knowledge grows. The same was the case in India and still continues to be so. In the history of thought, a century is not a long thing. But most Indians would like a K.C. Bhattacharya or an S.N. Bose, or a Meghanath Saha or a Sri Aurobindo, or to take examples from different fields, a Gandhi or a Tagore everyday in order to feel that something really worthwhile is taking place in their country. This is, of course, "childish". But the expectation of most Indians from their own contemporaries is such in character and there can be little surprise if they are disappointed all the time.

There is another dimension to the problem that we have posed regarding the redrawing of the picture of a period which was seen so differently in the past. We have ascribed the past picture to many factors, but the picture was based on certain facts. No historian ever builds a picture without some evidence, as without it she or he cannot claim to be a historian. What then is the relationship between the evidence on the basis of which the past picture was built and the one on which we have based a counter-picture of the same period. How do the two sets of evidence relate to each other? This problem does not seem to have been squarely faced, as far as I know, by any historian, for the simple reason that it poses an almost insuperable task of reconciling conflicting evidence, which leads to different, and sometimes even opposed conclusions. In case the earlier evidence were really an 'evidence', that is, not spurious in character, then the 'new' evidence has to come to terms with it and show why it does not lead to the construction of the picture that was built by the earlier historians in face of the new evidence that has come to light. The deeper problem, however, relates to the principles of interpretation adopted in the 'construction' itself and the importance and the weightage given to different factors in the evidence itself. The justification of the principles of interpretation that are adopted by historians can, by the very nature of the case, not itself be a part of history-writing itself even though it is necessarily presupposed by it. The practising historian is seldom conscious of it and the so-called philosophers of history have also, for some reason, not concerned themselves with it. The recent engagement with the notion of a 'text' and 'evidence' in what are generally characterised as "post-modernism" and hermeneutical traditions of thought have rendered the ideas as essentially ambiguous and intrinsically incapable of decision as, according to them, every 'decision' is bound to be arbitrary.

The historians have, perhaps, not woken up to the devastating implications of these recent trends but luckily, for us, there has been no previous 'construction' of the intellectual history of the period we have been concerned with and thus, there is hardly any problem of reconciling the new construction based on fresh evidence with the older one based on the previous evidence. There is, of course, the general impression regarding the intellectual achievements of the period about which we have written earlier but, this was not really based on any specific evidence or a serious historical construction based upon it. As for the principles of interpretation we have not adopted any 'new' ones except that we have been 'open' to any and every sign which even faintly suggested that something new and significant was being said by the thinker concerned, or that the extant text contained in it the possibility of a new direction of thought which was only half-explicit in it. This, of course, meant that we not only kept our own intellectual preferences aside but 'suspended' even our own considered judgements regarding what was right or wrong in the matter and let the 'text' take hold of us as if we ourselves were 'recreating' it from within or being led by it in directions which we had not thought of before. This is what Keats perhaps meant by 'negative capability' though we are extending this term to the cognitive context whereas he was primarily concerned with the creations of literary imagination.

A 'real' encounter with texts, is thus, not just a reconstruction of past thought but rather stepping into a living stream where the thought currents of the past, both visible and invisible, carry one into the future as they gently 'force' one to move in directions one had not dreamt of before. The encounter with "history" is, thus, not a movement into the past as has generally been thought but rather a movement into the future because one has stepped into the living currents that flow from the past and have sufficient vitality and force in the present to carry one onwards into the future. At least, this is what we have 'experienced' and the sensitive reader will find on every page the marks of this living encounter, leaving an exciting challenge to carry on the dimly-seen possibility and develop it into directions which are only faintly indicated there.

That there could be so much in a period that has been written off by scholars as sterile and decadent, seems unbelievable, specially if we remember the towering authority of the names that have sustained and strengthened this reputation. But, however unbelievable it may be, it is true. At least, we believe it to be so and the evidence for our belief lies scattered on every page of this volume.

APPENDIX I

List of Important Authors in Various Fields of Philosophy from Eighteenth Century Onwards

Covered in Part II of the Volume Prepared on the Basis of Karl H. Potter's *Encyclopedia of Indian Philosophies* Vol. I and Thangaswami Sarma's *Darśana Mañjarī*, 3 Vols. (1. Nyāya Vaiśeṣika, 2. Advaita Vedānta, 3. Mīmāṁsā)

GENERAL

1.	Nārāyaṇa Tīrtha	A.D. 1700
2.	Jadunātha Sārvabhaum	
	Bauddhadhikkāravivṛtiṭippaṇi	A.D. 1700
3.	Bhāskara Rāya Dikṣita	A.D. 1710
4.	(Abhinava) Nārāyaṇa Sarasvatī	A.D. 1710
5.	Tayumanava Cuvani	A.D. 1710
6.	Nāgeśa or Nāgojī Bhaṭṭa	A.D. 1714
7.	Rāmaśaṁkara Nyāyavāgīśa	
	Tarkasāra (Nyāya?)	A.D. 1730
8.	Cirañjīva Bhaṭṭa Rāmadeva	A.D. 1731
9.	Raghunātha Dāsa	A.D. 1735
10.	Ānandanātha	A.D. 1750
11.	Anantaśaktipāda	A.D. 1750
12.	Śivopādhyāya	
	Vivṛti on *Vijñāna Bhairava*	A.D. 1750
13.	Svāminārāyaṇa	A.D. 1750
14.	Baladeva Vidyābhūṣaṇa	A.D. 1780
15.	Savāi Jaisiṁha	A.D. 1795
16.	Bhavadeva	A.D. 1800
17.	Pādukāsevaka Rāmānuja Yāti	A.D. 1800
18.	Amṛteśvara	A.D. 1800
19.	Nanjuda Śāstrī	A.D. 1800
20.	Lāsaka	A.D. 1800
21.	Divākara	
	Arthadīpa on Narahari's *Bodhasāra*	A.D. 1816
22.	(Svāmī) Nityānanda *Aśārāma*	A.D. 1845

23. Pragyanasarama
    Svātmānandaprakāśikā on Bodhendra's *Bodhārya* A.D. 1850
24. Venkateshvara Suri
    Adhikaraṇa Saṁgrahavyākhyā A.D. 1850
25. G.S. Pathak A.D. 1850
26. Raghunathacharya
    Lakṣmyupāyatattvasamarthanam A.D. 1855
27. Nanda Kumara Datta A.D. 1857
28. Devendranatha Thakkura
    Vṛtti on Īśa *Upaniṣad* A.D. 1862
29. Krishna Jadya A.D. 1865
30. Jagannatha Diksita A.D. 1870
31. Tartavachana Sarman
    Khaṇḍanapariśiṣṭa A.D. 1872
32. Ananadachandra Vedantavagisha
    Bhāṣya on Various Upaniṣads A.D. 1872
33. Mudumba Narasimhacharya A.D. 1880
34. Gaurisvara Udayasamkara Ojha A.D. 1884
35. Anantarama Mishra A.D. 1885
36. Saradacharana Mitra A.D. 1887
37. Taracharana Tarkaratna A.D. 1890
38. Vyankatau Ramachandra A.D. 1900
39. Srinivasa Dikshita A.D. 1901
40. Sudarsanacharya Panjabi A.D. 1901
41. Damodara Devasarman A.D. 1905
42. Nathu Rama Sarman A.D. 1906
43. Syamalala Gosvamin A.D. 1906
44. Krishna Vallabhacharya A.D. 1908
45. Hari Prasada Svami A.D. 1909
46. A.Chinnasvami Sastrin
    Ṭippaṇi on Appaya Dikṣita's *Madhvataṅtramukhamardana* A.D. 1910
47. Radhagovinda Gosvamin A.D. 1910
48. Vidhushekhara Bhattacharya A.D. 1910
49. Balachandra Sastrin
    Kṣepaṇī Kṣemaṇa on a Tattvasaṁgraha Khaṅḍana A.D. 1910
50. Deviprasada Sarma A.D. 1913
51. Ramadayala Majumdar A.D. 1915
52. Rudra Bhatta Sarman
    Parihārakhaṇḍana (Vs. Vedānta Deśika's *Virodhaparihāra)* A.D. 1916
53. Vitamananda Brahmacharin A.D. 1916
54. Sri Narayana Guru A.D. 1917
55. G. Bala Krishna Nayar
    Narayana Guru's *Darśanamālā* A.D. 1917
56. Alaga Singaracharya A.D. 1918

57. Gopanatha Sena Kaviraja
Pratyakṣasarīra Siddhāntanidāna A.D. 1920
58. Viresvara Tarkatirtha
Lakārārthanirṇayadīpanī A.D. 1920
59. Mangala Natha
Śrīvicārabindu A.D. 1920
60. Ramanujacharya
Vidvānamanohara A.D. 1920
61. Parmananda Sarasvati
Śrutisadliṅgasaṁgraha A.D. 1920
62. S.T. Pathaka
Bālabodhinī on Gurunārāyaṇa's *Īśopaniṣadprakāśikā* A.D. 1921
63. Narendra Natha Siddhanta Sastrin
Vyākhyā on Kṣurikā Upaniṣad A.D. 1921
64. Krishna Mohana Sarman
Anvayabodhinī on the *Bhagvadgītā* A.D. 1924
65. Bhaktivinoda Thakkura A.D. 1924
66. Sastri Sarma
Na Ca ratnamālikā A.D. 1925
67. Ramavrata Sarman
Paramārthadarśana A.D. 1925
68. Vishnu Mitra
Vacanāmṛta on *Bhagvadgītā* A.D. 1925
69. Svayasarma
Svayamvimarśa A.D. 1926
70. Gayaprasada
Śrībālabodhinīgītārthacandrikā A.D. 1926
71. Narada Yadav A.D. 1927
72. Krishnalala A.D. 1928
73. Vasudeva Sastri Abhyankar A.D. 1929
74. Padmanandin A.D. 1930
75. (Uttamur) T. Virraghvacharya A.D. 1934
76. Satyadhyana Tirtha A.D. 1935
77. Amritavagbhava A.D. 1937
78. Putankotam Srinivasacharya
Nyāsanirṇaya—pramāṇaniṣkarṣa A.D. 1950
79. Vijaya Laksmana Suri Isvarji A.D. 1950
80. T.G. Siddaparadhya A.D. 1962
81. Srikrishna Vallabhacharya A.D. 1965
82. Jagadisa Chitracharya
Paramaṇudaraśana A.D. 1966
83. D.V. Subbacharya
Vedasvarūpavicāra A.D. 1970
84. Srirupa Siddhantin A.D. 1972

85. Jayachandra Chavana Jaina A.D. 1974
86. Muktinatha Kamala A.D. 1974
87. Pannalala Jaina
Sajjanacandrikā A.D. 1985

MĪMĀṀSĀ

1. Lakṣmaṇa Paṇḍita A.D. 1710
2. (Tatsat) Vidyānātha (Bhaṭṭa) A.D. 1735
3. Dāmodara A.D. 1750
4. Kṛṣṇa Vajvan A.D. 1750
5. Raghavānanda Sarasvatī A.D. 1750
6. Caṇḍeśvara Vācaspati A.D. 1750
7. Rāmānujācārya A.D. 1750
8. Vāsudeva Dikṣita A.D. 1750
9. Gopāla (Bhaṭṭa) Śāstrin A.D. 1750
10. Murārī Miśra A.D. 1750
11. Vedāntācārya A.D. 1800
12. Ramanuja Dasa A.D. 1870
13. Vañcakeśvara Yajvan A.D. 1830
14. Rāmeśvara (Śivayogin) A.D. 1841
15. Govindamrita A.D. 1850
16. Garuradhvaja A.D. 1860
17. Madan Mohana Pathaka A.D. 1875
18. Krishnanath Nyayapanchanana Bhattacharya A.D. 1906
19. Arya Muni A.D. 1906
20. Nityananda A.D. 1915
21. Harihara kripalu Dvivedi A.D. 1921
22. Girindranatha Vedantaratna A.D. 1922
23. Ganganatha Jha A.D. 1930
24. Narayana Krishna Acharya A.D. 1940
25. D.T. Tatacharya A.D. 1950
26. Peri Suryanarayana Shastri A.D. 1950
27. A. Chaterjee A.D. 1956
28. Satyavrata Samasramin A.D. 1970
29. Vachaspati Upadhyaya A.D. 1970
30. Navalpakam Devanathacharya A.D. 1978
31. Suryanarayana Shastri A.D. 1985
32. E.S. Varadacharya A.D. 1991

SĀṀKHYA

1.	Vaṁśīdhara Miśra	A.D. 1700
2.	Kāśirāma (See Advaita) Commentary on Nadraina Tarkavāgīśa's *Ātmaprakāśikā* Commentary on Nadraina Tarkavāgīśa's *Sāṅkhyaprakāśikā*	A.D. 1710
3.	Hari Bhaṭṭa	A.D. 1800
4.	Kavirāja Yāti	A.D. 1800
5.	Kulamaṇi	A.D. 1800
6.	Śrīnivāsa	A.D. 1800
7.	Yogānanda	A.D. 1800
8.	Balarama Udasina	A.D. 1867
9.	Narendra Nath Tattvanidhi	A.D. 1869
10.	Pyarelala Atmaja	A.D. 1886
11.	Mahadevarama	A.D. 1887
12.	Bharati Yati	A.D. 1889
13.	Pramathanatha Tarkabhusana	A.D. 1899
14.	Panchanana Tarkaratna Bhattacharya	A.D. 1906
15.	Arya Muni	A.D. 1906
16.	Kesava Bhatta	A.D. 1910
17.	Kisori Lala Gosvami	A.D. 1915
18.	Hariharananda Aranya	A.D. 1925
19.	Rajesvara Sastri Dravida	A.D. 1932
20.	Guru Prasada Sastrin	A.D. 1933
21.	Kunjavihari Tarkasiddhanta	
22.	Sitaram Sastrin	A.D. 1953
23.	Brahmalina Muni	A.D. 1959
24.	Damodara Mahapatra	A.D. 1971

YOGA

1.	Sadāśiva Brahmendra *Yogasudhakara* on *Patañjali's Yogasūtras*	A.D. 1720
2.	Ānanda Bodhendra Sarasvatī	A.D. 1780
3.	Laxminarayana	A.D. 1886
4.	Udayamkara Nanapathaka	A.D. 1890
5.	Girija Saṃkara Sarman	A.D. 1911
6.	Brahmarsi Sayadeva	A.D. 1932
7.	A.K.K. Kolhatkar	A.D. 1972

NYĀYA

1. Hanumad Bhaṭṭa — A.D. 1700
   (i) *Kroḍapatra* on Gadādhara's *Sāmānyanirukti*
2. Avadhāna Yajvan — A.D. 1700
3. Ṭippā Bhaṭṭa Vipaścit — A.D. 1700
4. (Śrī) Kṛṣṇa Nyāyavāgiśa Bhaṭṭacārya — A.D. 1710
5. Viśvanātha — A.D. 1710
6. Nāgeśa or Nāgojī Bhaṭṭa — A.D. 1714
7. Giridhara Upādhyāya Jhā — A.D. 1725
   Nyaya-Grammar (Vibhaktyarthanirṇaya)
8. Anantārya — A.D. 1730
9. Citradhara — A.D. 1740
10. Veṇīdatta — A.D. 1740
11. Gangārāma Jaṭin — A.D. 1740
12. Tarkṣya Nārāyaṇa — A.D. 1745
13. Acala Upādhyāya — A.D. 1750
14. Ananta Nārāyaṇa — A.D. 1750
15. Asvatthabuddha — A.D. 1750
16. Kṛṣṇa Datta — A.D. 1750
17. Nārāyaṇa Sārvabhauma Bhaṭṭācarya — A.D. 1750
18. Śivādatta Miśra — A.D. 1750
19. Trilocanadeva Nyāyapañcānan — A.D. 1750
20. Veṇīmādhava
    Prabhā on Gadadhar's *Gādādharī* — A.D. 1750
21. Vīreśvara — A.D. 1750
22. Vaṁśadhara Sarman — A.D. 1750
23. Kṛṣṇa Bhaṭṭa — A.D. 1750
24. Jagannātha Tarkapañcānan — A.D. 1754
25. Rāma Nārāyaṇa Tarkapañcānan — A.D. 1770
26. Kṣamākalyānāgni — A.D. 1772
27. Kṛṣṇa Dhurjaṭi Dikṣita — A.D. 1774
28. Kāśīpati Kavirāja — A.D. 1775
29. Kṛṣṇa Jīvan — A.D. 1775
30. Dāmodara — A.D. 1780
31. Kaviratna — A.D. 1780
32. Candranārāyaṇa Bhaṭṭa
    Kroḍapatra on Gadādhara — A.D. 1790
33. Dulāra Bhaṭṭācārya — A.D. 1790
34. Girīśa Candra — A.D. 1790
35. Haranārāyaṇa — A.D. 1790
36. Devabhadra — A.D. 1795
37. Kṛṣṇa Bhaṭṭa Ārde — A.D. 1800
38. Gopikaṇṭha — A.D. 1800

39.	Kṛṣṇāmṛtācārya	A.D. 1800
40.	Kṛṣṇa Rāma	A.D. 1800
41.	Kṛṣṇakānta Vidyāvāgīśa	A.D. 1800
42.	(Rāya) Narasiṁha (Yatīndra) Śāstrin	A.D. 1800
	Prabhā on Viśvanātha's *Siddhāntamuktāvalī*	
43.	Saṁgameśvara	
	Kroḍa on Jagdīśa's *Jāgadīśī*	A.D. 1800
	Pañcalakṣaṇyādi Jagadīśasya *Kroḍapatram*	
44.	Ramānātha Bhaṭṭācārya	A.D. 1800
45.	Śaṁkara Bhaṭṭa Miśra	A.D. 1800
46.	Kālī Śaṁkara	
	Kroḍa on *Gādādharī*, *Māthurī*,	A.D. 1810
47.	Rūpanātha Ṭhakkura Tarkaratna	A.D. 1810
48.	Paṭṭābhirāma	
	Kroda on *Gādādharī*	A.D. 1820
49.	Mukunda Bhaṭṭa	A.D. 1830
50.	Nīlakaṅṭha	A.D. 1830
51.	Golokanatha Nyayaratna	A.D. 1850
52.	Godavarman (Kotilina) Nripati	A.D. 1850
53.	Ramachandra Siddhantavagisa	A.D. 1850
54.	Kirita Venkatacharya	A.D. 1850
55.	Jaya Krishna Tarkacharya	A.D. 1850
56.	Raghuttama	A.D. 1850
57.	Rambhadra Bhatta	A.D. 1850
58.	Mysore Rama Sastrin	
	Śatkoṭi (Satpratipakṣakroḍapatram)	A.D. 1850
59.	Chandrakanta Tarkalamkara	A.D. 1850
60.	Umakantha Bhattacharya	A.D. 1850
61.	Raghunatha Parvate Sastrin	A.D. 1853
62.	Madhavachandra Tarkasiddhanta	A.D. 1855
63.	Krishnananda Bhattacharya	A.D. 1855
64.	Meru Sastrin Godbole	A.D. 1859
65.	Mahesha Chandra Nyayaratna	A.D. 1860
66.	Taranatha Tarkavachaspati	A.D. 1865
67.	Krishna Tatacharya	A.D. 1871
	Pañcalakṣaṇyādīnām Kroḍapatram	
	Sāmānyanirukti Kroḍapatrāṇi	
	Śātakoṭikhaṇḍanama	
	Avacchedakatāsāra	
68.	Jivanananda Vidyasagara	A.D. 1874
69.	Sivachandra	A.D. 1875
70.	Harinatha Tarkasiddhanta Bhattacharya	A.D. 1876
71.	Srinivasa	A.D. 1880
72.	Kasinatha Vidyanivasa	A.D. 1885

73. Uddhavasimha A.D. 1885
74. Chandraja Simha A.D. 1889
75. Radhamohana Vidyavachaspati Gosvamin A.D. 1890
76. Sokattur Vijayaraghavacharya
Śatkoṭikhaṇḍanamaṇḍanam A.D. 1890
77. Rakhaladasa Nyayaratna Bhattacharya A.D. 1890
78. Visvanatha Jha A.D. 1891
79. Kasturi Rangacharya A.D. 1891
80. Asutosa Tarkabhusana A.D. 1894
81. Anandachandra Sarvabhauma A.D. 1896
82. Krishna Sastrin A.D. 1900
83. Babuji Jha A.D. 1900
84. Gandasimha or Govindasimha A.D. 1900
85. Kuruchchi Rangacharya A.D. 1900
86. Rama Bhatta A.D. 1900
87. Durgadatta Sastri A.D. 1902
88. Kamakhyanatha Bhattacharya Tarkavagisha A.D. 1906
89. Gangasahaya Sarman A.D. 1907
90. Dharmadatta (Bachcha) Jha A.D. 1910
91. Khuddi Jha Sarma A.D. 1910
92. Ambadasa Sastrin A.D. 1910
93. Madhava Pada Abhirama
On Annambhaṭṭa's *Tarkasamgraha* A.D. 1911
94. Mukunda Jha Sarman A.D. 1911
95. J. Lallu Rama A.D. 1912
96. G.C. Tarkadarsana Tirtha A.D. 1914
97. Vindhyesvari Prasada Dvivedin A.D. 1916
98. B. Ottangadkar A.D. 1919
99. Balakrishna Mishra A.D. 1919
100. Ambika Prasada A.D. 1921
101. C. Samkara Rama Sastrin A.D. 1923
102. Jadunatha Mishra A.D. 1925
103. Narayana Chandra Gosvamin Tarkatirtha A.D. 1925
104. Vamacharana Bhattacharya
Kroda on *Jāgadīśī* A.D. 1925
105. Dhundhiraja Sastrin A.D. 1925
106. Kalipada Tarkacharya A.D. 1925
107. Gosvamin Damodara Sastrin A.D. 1927
108. Haridatta Sarman Trivedin A.D. 1928
109. Kuruganti Sri Rama Sastrin A.D. 1930
110. Kasinatha Sastrin A.D. 1930
111. Lokanatha Sarman A.D. 1930
112. J.S. Bhattacharya A.D. 1934
113. Harirama Sukla A.D. 1937

114. Kolluru Somashekhara Sastrin A.D. 1939
115. Phanibhusana Tarkavagisha A.D. 1940
116. Srinivasa Paramanu Misra A.D. 1940
117. Siva Narayana Sastrin A.D. 1940
118. Sashinatha Jha A.D. 1940
119. Vamacharana Bhattacharya A.D. 1940
120. V. Subrahmanya Sastrin A.D. 1948
121. Keshava Vadhvedin (Dvivedin) A.D. 1949
122. Giridhara Sarman Chaturvedi A.D. 1950
123. Rudradhara Jha A.D. 1952
124. Raja Narayana Shukla A.D. 1954
125. Rupanatha Jha A.D. 1955
126. Madhusudana Bhattacharya A.D. 1956
127. S.S. Jha A.D. 1957
128. Ananta Kumara Bhattacharya A.D. 1958
129. Ratnanatha Shukla A.D. 1958
130. K.S. Varadacharya A.D. 1959
131. Jaiminikantha Tarkatirtha A.D. 1960
132. Ramachandra Jha A.D. 1960
133. Devanatha Tarkacharya A.D. 1960
134. Jalihala Srinivasacharya A.D. 1961
135. Satyapramoda Tirtha A.D. 1961
136. Bandharyupahva Madhava Sastri A.D. 1962
137. Visvabandhu Bhattacharya A.D. 1964
138. Kasikananda Svami A.D. 1967
139. Yogindrananda A.D. 1968
140. Divyananda S. Ojha A.D. 1970
141. Narayana Mishra A.D. 1970
142. S.B. Raghunathacharya A.D. 1972
143. Mahaprabhulala Gosvamin A.D. 1972
144. Yadavendranatha Raya A.D. 1973
145. Jivan Krishna Tarkatirtha A.D. 1974
146. Jvala Prasada Gaur A.D. 1974
147. N.S. Ramanuja Tatacharya A.D. 1979
148. Ayya Devanatha Tatacharya A.D. 1979
149. Gaurinatha Sastri A.D. 1981
150. Dipaka Ghosa A.D. 1984
151. N. Sanatana Aiyar A.D. 1986

VEDĀNTA

1. Govardhana Āśukarī A.D. 1764
   Vedānta Cintāmaṇi

2. Bhairava Tilaka A.D. 1768
   Tatparyavivaraṇa on *Bādarāyaṇa's Brahmasūtra*
3. Pītāmbarajī A.D. 1846
4. Devakinandana A.D. 1850
5. Krishna Giri A.D. 1854
6. Gangadhara Kavi A.D. 1855
7. Ramadasa Svami A.D. 1860
8. Daksinamurti
   Vrtti on *Bādarāyaṇa's Brahmasūtra* A.D. 1865
9. Vasudeva A.D. 1866
10. Upendra Datta Pandeya A.D. 1895
11. R. Halasyanatha Sastrin A.D. 1904
12. R. Raghavendracharya A.D. 1911
13. Vidyananda Giri A.D. 1928
14. Mukunda Rama A.D. 1928
15. Kalikesha Vandopadhyaya A.D. 1929
16. Raghavendra Svamiracharya Panchamukhi A.D. 1930
17. Simhadasa A.D. 1980
18. Kasikananda Giri A.D. 1986

ADVAITA

1. Gauḍa Brahmānanda Sarasvatī A.D. 1700
2. *Nirvāṇavicāra* (Unknown Author) A.D. 1700
3. Vāśudeva Rāma A.D. 1700
4. Kāśī Rāma A.D. 1710
5. Vāśudevendra Yogin A.D. 1710
6. (Abhinava) Nārāyaṇa Sarasvatī A.D. 1710
7. Śaṅkukavi A.D. 1710
8. Sadāśiva Brahmendra A.D. 1720
9. Ekojīrāja
10. Svaprakāśa Yāti A.D. 1740
11. Vallabhendra Sarasvatī A.D. 1740
12. Mādhava Rāma A.D. 1740
13. Jñānendra Muni A.D. 1740
14. Sāsvatānanda Tīrtha A.D. 1740
15. Upaniṣadbrahmayogin A.D. 1740
16. Anneya Paṇḍita A.D. 1750
17. Hari Yaśo Miśra A.D. 1750
18. Narasiṁha Muni A.D. 1750
19. Umāmāheśvara A.D. 1750
20. Bodhendra A.D. 1755
21. Ghanaśyāma A.D. 1756

22.	Advaitānanda Tīrtha	A.D. 1762
23.	Nalla Dikṣita	A.D. 1770
24.	Abhinava Sītā Rāma Brahmendra	A.D. 1770
25.	Gaṅgādhara Mahadakara	A.D. 1770
26.	Raṅgarāja	A.D. 1770
27.	(Ādi) Veṅkaṭayogin	A.D. 1770
28.	Rāmacandra (Ānanda) Sarasvatī	A.D. 1770
29.	Appā Dikṣita	A.D. 1775
30.	Asadhara	A.D. 1775
31.	Bhiṣma Miśra	A.D. 1775
32.	Ayodhyā Prasāda	A.D. 1778
33.	Sadānanda Vyāsa	A.D. 1780
34.	Rāma Nārāyaṇa	A.D. 1780
35.	Sadāśivendra Sarasvatī	A.D. 1780
36.	Jñānāmṛta	A.D. 1800
37.	Keśavānanda Yāti	A.D. 1800
38.	Kavirāja Yāti	A.D. 1800
39.	(Vellinki) Sītā Rāma Śāstrī	A.D. 1800
40.	Jagannātha Miśra	A.D. 1800
41.	Ānanda Rāma	A.D. 1810
42.	Śivādatta Paṇḍita	A.D. 1810
43.	Dhanapati Sūri	A.D. 1811
44.	Trayambaka Bhaṭṭa Śāstrin	A.D. 1825
45.	Ācārya Rāya Modaka	A.D. 1825
46.	Govindarākṣasa	A.D. 1826
47.	Pāṇduraṅga	A.D. 1827
48.	Viśveśvara Paṇḍita	A.D. 1830
49.	Dayāsaṁkara	A.D. 1830
50.	Anantendra Yāti	A.D. 1840
51.	Rāmacandra Yajvan	A.D. 1844
52.	Adinarayana Sastrin	A.D. 1850
53.	Amareshvara Sastrin	A.D. 1850
54.	Rama Suri	A.D. 1855
55.	Jagajjiva	A.D. 1855
56.	Achyuta Rama Bhikshu	A.D. 1855
57.	Sundaresha	A.D. 1860
58.	Balasastri Garde	A.D. 1860
59.	Sadananda Svamin	A.D. 1865
60.	K.A. Govindavishnu	A.D. 1867
61.	Somanatha Vyasa	A.D. 1869
62.	Tyagaraja Makhin	A.D. 1870
63.	Samkara Rama Yati	A.D. 1874
64.	Krishnadeva Pandita	A.D. 1875
65.	Vaduthe Narayana	A.D. 1875

66.	Govindananda Sarasvati	A.D. 1885
67.	Mohana Lala	A.D. 1887
68.	Kesvananda Svami	A.D. 1887
69.	(Bellankonda) Rama (Raya) Kavi	A.D. 1889
70.	Harihara Paramahamsa	A.D. 1890
71.	Kamakshin	A.D. 1890
72.	Brahmananda Tirtha	A.D. 1892
73.	Sundaramurti	A.D. 1893
74.	Rama Sinha	A.D. 1895
75.	Krishnananda Sarasvati	A.D. 1895
76.	Govinda Parivrajaka Paramahamsa	A.D. 1899
77.	Amaradasa	A.D. 1900
78.	Anantanandagiri	A.D. 1900
79.	Gangadhara Sastrin	A.D. 1900
80.	Haridatta Mishra	A.D. 1901
81.	Sudarsanacharya	A.D. 1901
82.	Vasudeva Brahmendra Sarasvati	A.D. 1902
83.	Nilakantha Yamin	A.D. 1907
84.	Imguva Viraraghava Yajvan	A.D. 1907
85.	T.K. Balasubrahmanyam	A.D. 1910
86.	Sitanatha Gosvami Tattvabhusana	A.D. 1910
87.	Atmananda Sarasvati	A.D. 1910
88.	Vanikantha Sarman	A.D. 1912
89.	Vedantavagisha Bhattacharya	A.D. 1912
90.	Nishchala Dasa Svamin	A.D. 1913
91.	Kali Kumara Mishra	A.D. 1915
92.	Ramasakala Mishra	A.D. 1915
93.	Raghunatha Suri	A.D. 1916
94.	R.S. Senday	A.D. 1917
95.	Samkara Brahmanya Devatirtha	A.D. 1917
96.	G.T. Srinivasacharya	A.D. 1919
97.	Advaitendra Sarasvati	A.D. 1920
98.	Visnu Vamana Bapat	A.D. 1921
99.	Devakinanda Sastrin	A.D. 1922
100.	Raghavendra Rayapala	A.D. 1922
101.	Rameshvara Datta	A.D. 1923
102.	Linganna Simayaji	A.D. 1925
103.	Malladi Ramkrishna	A.D. 1925
104.	Satyanarayana Sarman	A.D. 1925
105.	Vidula Sastrin	A.D. 1925
106.	Suryanarayana Sarma	A.D. 1925
107.	Rama Subrahmanya	A.D. 1927
108.	Natesarya	A.D. 1927
109.	Gangavishnu Shri Krishnadasa	A.D. 1928

111. Jogedranatha Ghosa A.D. 1929
112. Vasudeva Sastri Abhyankar A.D. 1929
113. Ganapati Sastrin A.D. 1930
114. Svami Sastrin A.D. 1930
115. R.S. Sarma A.D. 1931
116. Y. Subrahmanya Sarma A.D. 1934
117. Hariharananda Sarasvati A.D. 1935
118. Samkara Chaitanya Bharati A.D. 1938
119. Subramanya Sastri A.D. 1938
120. Krishna Sastri Karungalam A.D. 1939
121. N.S. Anantakrishna Sastrin A.D. 1946
122. Viramani Prasada Upadhyaya A.D. 1950
123. D.C. Sastri A.D. 1959
124. Sachchidanandendra Sarasvati A.D. 1959
125. Yogindrananda Sarasvati A.D. 1960
126. Chinmayananda A.D. 1967
127. Yogendranatha Bagchi A.D. 1971
128. Rama Samkara Tripathi A.D. 1972
129. Ramananda Pithadhisha A.D. 1973
130. Ramaprapannacharya A.D. 1973
131. Kevalananda Sarasvati A.D. 1976
132. Venkatanatha A.D. 1982
134. Ramadasa Nirankari A.D. 1986
135. Pattabhirama Shastri A.D. 1991

VIŚIṢṬĀDVAITA

1. Govīnda Guru A.D. 1720
2. Nṛsiṁhadeva A.D. 1740
3. (Surapuram) Veṅkaṭācārya A.D. 1745
4. Annaya Ācārya A.D. 1750
5. Gopāla Deśika (Ācarya) A.D. 1750
6. Śrīnivāsa Parikala Yati A.D. 1750
7. Rāghavācārya A.D. 1750
8. Śākṣātsvāmin A.D. 1750
9. Vīrarāghavācārya Bālasarasvatī A.D. 1750
10. Śrīnivāsa Śrīśailayogin A.D. 1750
11. Śrīśaila Śrīnivāsasūri A.D. 1750
12. Śrīnivāsa Saṁghrīdāsa A.D. 1755
13. (Śrībhāṣyam) Śrīnivāsa A.D. 1755
14. (Sathamarśa) or Śrīśaila A.D. 1755
15. (Mahābhāṣyam) Appalācārya A.D. 1770
16. Dharmapuruṣa A.D. 1770

17. Narahari A.D. 1780
18. Appāgoṇḍācārya A.D. 1800
19. Devarāja A.D. 1800
21. Buccī Venkaṭācārya A.D. 1820
22. Raghunatha Varman A.D. 1850
23. (T.A.P.) Srirangacharya A.D. 1850
24. Aniruddha A.D. 1852
25. Srinivasa Shuddhi A.D. 1853
26. Srinivasa Vipaschit A.D. 1855
27. Srinivasa Vedantadeshikavijaya A.D. 1855
28. (Mysore) Anantacharya A.D. 1860
29. T.C.N.R. Tatacharya A.D. 1870
30. Krishna Tatacharya (Also Nyāya) A.D. 1871
31. (Sathakopa) Ramanuja Yatindra A.D. 1880
32. Rama Mishra A.D. 1885
33. T.E.S. Kuppan Aiyangar A.D. 1885
34. Govardhana Rangacharya A.D. 1890
35. Krishnamacharya (Gargya) A.D. 1892
36. Gopalacharya A.D. 1899
37. Parankusacharya A.D. 1900
38. Srinivasa Pattacharya A.D. 1900
39. Raghupati Bhattacharya A.D. 1905
40. Parakalasamgamindra A.D. 1903
41. Annayacharya A.D. 1903
42. Srinivasacharya Lakshmipuram A.D. 1905
43. Van Sathakopa A.D. 1905
44. T. Nilamegha Sastrin A.D. 1906
45. Srinivasa (Bharadvaja) Suri A.D. 1907
46. Srinivasacharya Tatacharya A.D. 1909
47. Kapisthalam Desikachariar A.D. 1911
48. Sri Krishna Brahmatantra Mahadesika A.D. 1914
49. Prativadibhyankar Anantacharya also worked on Śuddhādvaita A.D. 1915
50. Harirama Sarman A.D. 1918
51. Sridharacharya A.D. 1918
52. Varadacharya A.D. 1918
53. Narayana Aiyangar A.D. 1919
54. Jayadeva Mishra A.D. 1920
55. Koti Lingapuragoda Varmaraja A.D. 1920
56. T. Laksmanacharya A.D. 1924
57. Bhagavadacharya A.D. 1930
58. Ramachandra Pansikar A.D. 1938
59. Navalpakkam Tattacharyasvami A.D. 1950
60. D.T. Tatacharya A.D. 1950
61. Abhinava Ranganatha Parakalayati A.D. 1960

62. Vedantadesika Yatindra Mahadesika A.D. 1965

DVAITA

1. Chalari Śeṣācārya A.D. 1700
2. Kṛṣṇacandra Gosvāmin A.D. 1700
3. Vanamālī Miśra A.D. 1700
4. Ananta (Ācārya) A.D. 1700
5. Sumatīndranātha Tīrtha A.D. 1720
6. Śrīnivāsa A.D. 1730
7. Raghunātha Tīrtha A.D. 1740
8. Satyapriya Tīrtha A.D. 1740
9. Veṇīdatta A.D. 1740
10. Jagannātha Tīrtha A.D. 1745
11. Varkhedī Timmanācārya A.D. 1750
12. Padmanābhācārya A.D. 1750
13. Viṭṭhaleśa Upādhyāya A.D. 1755
14. Narasimha Yāti A.D. 1780
15. Jayatīrthācārya A.D. 1810
16. Hulugi Śrīpatyācārya A.D. 1830
17. Satyadharma Tīrtha A.D. 1830
18. (Kāśī) Timmana A.D. 1840
19. Vijayindra Tirtha A.D. 1850
20. Anneyacharya A.D. 1850
21. Krishnacharya (Umarji) Suri A.D. 1860
22. Cochi Rangappacharya A.D. 1870
23. Krishnavadhuta Pandita or Ananda Rama A.D. 1895
24. T.R. Krishnacharya A.D. 1903
25. (Gaudagiri) Venkata Ramanacharya A.D. 1924
26. Setumadhavacharya Kulisa V/s Bhattoji Dikshita A.D. 1931
27. A. Vidyamanya Tirtha A.D. 1961
28. Vidyaranya Tirtha A.D. 1978
29. K.T. Pandurangi A.D. 1990

ŚŪDDHĀDVAITA

1. Śrī Kṛṣṇa Candra A.D. 1700
2. Satyābhinava Tīrtha A.D. 1700
3. Bālakṛṣṇa or Lallu Bhaṭṭa A.D. 1720
4. Vrajarāja (Gosvāmin) A.D. 1720
5. Nirbhayarāma A.D. 1755
6. Icchārāma Bhaṭṭa A.D. 1815

7.	(Yogī) Gopeśvara	A.D. 1830
8.	Giridhara Prapanna (Gosvāmin)	A.D. 1830
9.	Gopalananda Svamin	A.D. 1851
10.	Gokula or Gopal Krishna Bhatta	A.D. 1855
11.	Rama Krishna Bhatta	A.D. 1860
12.	Mathuranath	A.D. 1865
13.	Lallu Bhatta	A.D. 1875
14.	Gattulala	A.D. 1890
15.	Raghunatha Gopala Kokaja	A.D. 1910
16.	Tribhuvanadasa Pitambardasa Saha	A.D. 1910
17.	Giridhara Dasa	A.D. 1919
18.	Sridhara (Trayambaka) Sastri Pathaka	A.D. 1919
19.	Balabhadra Sarman	A.D. 1922
20.	Kaka Vallabha	A.D. 1924
21.	Aniruddhacharya	A.D. 1925
22.	Mohana Lala Kasirama	A.D. 1935
23.	Govindalala Haragovinda Bhatta	A.D. 1943
24.	Balakrishna Sastri	A.D. 1950
25.	Rama Natha Bhatta	A.D. 1950
26.	Arunachandra D. Sastrin	A.D. 1963

ACINTYABHEDĀBHEDA

1.	Viśvanātha Cakravartī	A.D. 1720
2.	Rādhā Dāmodara	A.D. 1760
3.	Rūpa Kavirāja	A.D. 1770
4.	Baladeva Vidyābhūṣaṇa	A.D. 1780
5.	Bhavānīcarṇa Tarkabhūṣaṇa	A.D. 1828
6.	Krishnadeva Vedantavagisha	A.D. 1850
7.	Virachandra Gosvamin	A.D. 1878
8.	Kedaranatha Datta Nhaktivioda Thakkura	A.D. 1920
9.	Aksaya Kumara Diksita Sastrin	A.D. 1927
10.	Gauda Kisora Gosvami	A.D. 1930
11.	Anupanarayana Tarkasiromani	A.D. 1930
12.	Vrindavana Tarkalamkara	A.D. 1930
13.	Bhaktisiddhanta Sarasvati	A.D. 1932

JAINA

1.	Daddha	A.D. 1700
2.	Devacandra Yatipati	A.D. 1738
3.	Matiratna Sūri	A.D. 1747
4.	Devendrakīrti	A.D. 1750

5.	Hamsarāja	A.D. 1750
6.	Harṣavardhana	A.D. 1768
7.	Ramcandra	A.D. 1750
8.	Māyācandra	A.D. 1754
9.	Rāmavijaya Gaṇi	A.D. 1760
10.	Jinlābha Sūri	A.D. 1780
11.	Vijayalakṣmī Sūri	A.D. 1787
12.	Bhoja Kavi	A.D. 1820
13.	Devacandra	A.D. 1833
14.	Abhinava Cārukīrti	A.D. 1845
15.	Hulugi Narasimhacharya A	A.D. 1850
16.	Rajachandra	A.D. 1895
17.	Dharmasuri	A.D. 1905
18.	Radha Govinda Gosvami	A.D. 1906
19.	Gopaladasa Barija	A.D. 1910
20.	Virachandra Dipachandra	A.D. 1910
21.	Hemahamsa Gani	A.D. 1911
22.	Ratnamandira Gani	A.D. 1911
23.	Author Unknown	A.D. 1912
24.	*Nyāyavijaya*	A.D. 1913
25.	Ratnakara Pathaka	A.D. 1917
26.	Mangala Vijay Maharaja	A.D. 1918
27.	Rama Gopalacharya	A.D. 1918
28.	Vijaya Darsa Suri	A.D. 1918
29.	Buddhisagara	A.D. 1924
30.	Labdhasuri	A.D. 1925
31.	Phulachandra Sastri	A.D. 1927
32.	Anandasagara Suri	A.D. 1930
33.	Nemisuri	A.D. 1940
34.	Lavanya Suri	A.D. 1946
35.	Mahendra Kumara	A.D. 1950
36.	Hiralala Jain	A.D. 1964
37.	Munichandra Suri	A.D. 1969
38.	Uday Chandra	A.D. 1970
39.	Acharya Tulasi	A.D. 1989
40.	Ratnakirti Deva	A.D. 1984

KRODAPATRA

1. Sarasvatī Vigrah Deśikācārya
   Vyutpattivāda Kroḍapatram
2. Maṇḍayam Anantācārya
   Vyutpattivāda Kroḍapatram

APPENDIX—I-A

List of Mīmāṁsā Thinkers from Eighteenth Century Onwards

Prepared by K.T. Pandurangi

1. Vañceśvara Dikṣita (1798–1832)
   Bhaṭṭa Dīpikā Vyākhyā on *Bhaṭṭa Cintāmaṇi.*
2. Vaidyanatha Sastri (1850–1950)
   Śābara Bhāṣya Vyākhyā.
3. Abhayankar Vasudeva Sastri (1880–1950)
   Mīmāṁsā Nyāya Prakāśa Vyākhyā.
4. Madanamohan Sharma
   Mīmāṁsā Nyāya Prakāśa Ṭīkā.
5. Chinnaswami Sharma
   Mīmāṁsa Nyāya Prakāśa Vyākhyāsatvivecanī.
6. Uttamur Viraraghavacharya
   Mīmāṁsā Nyāya Prakāśa Vyākhyā—Śuddha Svāda.
7. Rameṣvara Sivabhogi
   Arthasaṁgraha Vyākhyā.
8. Krishnanatha Panchanana
   Arthasaṁgraha Vyākhyā.
9. Tatacharya (1890–1950)
   Arthasaṁgraha Vyākhyā—Tantraprakāśikā.
10. Jivananda Vidyasagara (1900)
    Arthasaṁgraha Vyākhyā—Arthadīpikā.
11. Pattabhirama Sastri (1900–2000)
    Arthasaṁgraha Vyākhyā—Arthadīpikā.
12. Pramathanatha Tarkabhusana (1900–2000)
    Arthasaṁgraha Vyākhyā—Amalā.
13. Sudarsanacharya (1907)
    Śāstradīpikā Vyākhyā.
14. Peri-Suryanarayana Sastri (1900–1992)
    Bhaṭṭa Rahasya Vyākhyā—Bhāvaprakāśikā.

15. Subramanya Sastri (1900–1920)
    Bhaṭṭa Rahasya Vyākhyā—Viṣamagranthībhedinī.
16. Tatacharya
    Mīmāṁsā Paribhāṣā Vyākhyā—Pariṣkāra.
17. Chinnaswami Sastri (1870–1950)
    Taṅtrasiddhānta Ratnāvalī.
18. Krishna Tatacharya (1875)
    Bhaṭṭasāra.
19. Karavira Pithadhipati (1937)
    Bhāvabodhinī.
20. Srinivasacharya (1900–2000)
    Mānmeyodaya Śloka.
21. Pattabhirama Sastri
    Mīmāṁsāmañjarī.

APPENDIX—1-B

List of Some Important Naiyāyikas from Eighteenth Century Onwards

Prepared by D. Prahladachar on the Basis of
Karl H. Potter's *Encyclopedia of Indian Philosophies,* Vol. 1

1. Gokulanātha Upādhyāya (fl. 1810)
   1. *Dikkāla Nirūpaṇa*—(N. Cat. VI, 113; IX, 33)
   2. *Lāghava gaurava rahasya*—(N. Cat. VI, 114)
   3. *Muktivāda*—(N. Cat, VI, 114)
   4. *Ṭippaṇa* on Udayana's *Kusumāñjali*—(N. Cat. VI, 113)
   5. *Nyāya lakṣaṇa vicāra*—(N Cat, VI, 113)
   6. *Nyāya Siddhānta tattva* or *Siddhānta viveka*—(N. Cat. VI, 113)
   7. *Pramāṇollāsa*—(N. Cat. VI, 113)
   8. *Pramāṇa prabodha*—(N. Cat. VI, 113)
   9. *Śaktivāda*—(N. Cat. VI, 114)
   10. *Yogarūḍhivicāra*—(N. Cat. VI, 114)
   11. *Viṣayatāvicāra*—(N. Cat. VI, 114)
   12. *Svatva vāda*—(N. Cat. VI, 114)
   13. *Tarka tattva nirūpaṇa*—(N. Cat. VI, 113; VIII, 113)
   14. *Vivaraṇa or Vidyota* on Pakṣadhara's *Tattva cintāmaṇyāloka*—(N. Cat. VI, 112; VIII, 40)
   15. *Cakraraśmi* on *Tattva cintāmaṇi*—(N. Cat. VI, 112; VII, 22)
   16. *Vidyota* on Raghunātha Śiromaṇi's *Tattva cintāmaṇi Dīdhiti*—(N. Cat. 112; VII, 31; IX, 58)
2. Giridhara Upādhyāya (fl. 1720)
   1. *Vibhaktyartha Nirṇaya*
3. Rāma Śaṅkara Nyāya Vāgīśa (fl. 1730)
   1. *Tarkasāra* (N. Cat. VIII, 132)
4. Anantārya (fl. 1730)
   1. *Nyāyaviveka* on Gopinātha Thakkura's *Tarka-bhāṣānyāyavilāsa* (N. Cat. I, 189l; VIII, 119)

5. Citradhara (fl. 1740)
    1. *Pramāṇa pramoda* or *Īśvaravāda* (N. Cat. II, 227; VII, 39) Ed. with Dukhamochana Jha's commentary by Ujjvala Śharma—Delhi 1968.
    2. *Pratiyogyāropa Vicāra* (N. Cat. VII, 39)
    3. *Samskārasiddhi (Dīpikā)* (N. Cat. VII, 39)
    4. *Vibhaktyartha Nirṇaya* (N. Cat. VII, 39)
6. Gangārāma Jatin or Jadin (fl. 1740)
    1. *Ṭippaṇa* or *Khaṇḍana* on Dinakara's *Dinakarī* (N. Cat. V, 213; IX, 40)
    2. *Nyāyakautūhala* (cf. Opper I, 173 forms ...)
    3. *(Svarṇa) Caskā* on Jagadīśa's *Tarkāmṛta* and *Tātparya Ṭīkā* thereon (N. Cat. V, 213; VIII, 134)
7. Acala Upādhyāya or Śarman (fl. 1750)
    1. *Śabda vicāra* or *Dhātvarthavāda* (N. Cat. I, 70)
    2. *Vādārtha* (N. Cat. I, 71)
    3. *Vākyavāda* (N. Cat. I, 70)
8. Ananta Nārāyaṇa (fl. 1750)
    1. Commentary on Viśvanātha's *Bhāṣā paricceheda* (N. Cat. I, 171)
    2. Commentary on Annaṁbhaṭṭa's *Tarka Saṁgraḥ*
9. Aśvatthabuddha (fl. 1750)
    1. *Prakaśa* or *Bhāvasaṁgraha* on Gadādhara's *Gādādharī* (N. Cat. I, 438, V.347; VIII, 30).
    2. *Vyākhyāna* on Gadādhara's *Vyutpattivāda* (N. Cat. I, 348)
10. Gopīnātha Maunih (fl. 1750)
    1. *Vikāsa* on Udayana's *Nyāya Kusumāñjali* (N. Cat. VI, 165)
11. Kṛṣṇa Datta (fl. 1740)
    1. *Nyāyamanoramā* on Viśvanātha's *Siddhānta-muktāvalī* (N. Cat. IV, 315)
12. Nārāyaṇa Sārvabhauma (fl. 1750)
    1. *Jñānakāraṇatāvāda* (N. Cat. VII, 220)
13. Śivadatta Miśra (fl. 1750)
    1. *Gaṅgā* on *Gādādharī*
    2. Gaṅgā on *Jagadīśī*
    3. *Dīpikā* on Gadādhara's *Vyutpattivāda*
14. Trilocanadeva Nyāyapañcanana (fl. 1750)
    1. *Vyākhyāna* on *Kusumāñjali* (N. Cat. VIII, 262)
    2. *Nyāyasaṁketa*
    3. *Locanī* on Viśvanātha's *Siddhānta Muktāvalī* (N. Cat. VIII, 262)
15. Veṇīmādhava (fl. 1750)
    1. *Prabhā* on *Gādādharī*
16. Vīreśvara (fl. 1750)
    1. *Nyāya Siddhānta Jyotsnā* on Bhavānanda's *Bhavānandī* (N. Cat. VIII, 34)
    2. *Ṭīkā* on *Jāgadiśī* (N. Cat. VII, 209)
17. Viśvanātha (fl. 1750 ?)
    1. *Vivṛti* on *Gādādharī*

Sādṛśyavāda and *Jyeṣṭhatāvāda* sections edited with Viśvanātha's *Vivṛti* on *Śaktivāda* and on the *Lakārārtha vāda.*
   2. *Vivṛti* on Gadādhara's *Muktivāda*
   3. *Vivṛti* on Gadādhara's *Śaktivāda*
   4. *Ṭīkā* on *Tarkasaṁgraha*
   5. *Vivṛti* on *Vyutpattivāda*

18. Jagannātha Tarkapañcānana or Nyāya Pañcānana (fl. 1754)
   1. *Viveka* on Raghunātha Śiromaṇi's *Nañavāda* (N. Cat. IX, 323)
   2. *Tarka Kroḍapatra* (N. Cat. VII, 135; VIII, 22)
19. Rāma Nārāyaṇa Tarkapañcānana (fl. 1770)
   1. *Bālabodhinī* on Annaṁbhaṭṭa's *Tarkasṁgraha* (N. Cat. VIII, 132)
20. Kṣamākalyāṇagaṇi (fl. 1720)
   1. *Subodhinī* on Śāntisūri II's *Jīvavicāra-prakaraṇa*
   2. *Phakkikā* on Annaṁbhaṭṭa's *Tarkasṁgraha* (N. Cat. V, 147; VIII, 116, 128)
21. Kṛṣṇa Dhurjatī Dikṣita (fl. 1774)
   1. *Siddhāntacandrodaya* on Annaṁbhaṭṭa's *Tarkasṁgraha* (N. Cat. See e6739; e6398)
22. Kviratna Khageśa (fl. 1780)
   1. Commentary on Gaṅgeśa's *Tattvacintāmaṇi* (N. Cat. III, 280; VIII, 21)
23. Candranārāyaṇa Bhaṭṭa (fl. 1790)
   1. *Candranārāyaṇī* on Gadādhara's *Gādādharī* (N. Cat. VIII, 312; V, 347)
   2. *Kroḍa* on Jagadīśa's *Jagadīśī* (N. Cat. VI, 387; VII, 209)
   3. *Ṭīkā* on Udayana's *Nyāyakusumāñjali* (N. Cat. VI, 387)
   4. *Vṛtti* on Gautama's *Nyāyasūtras* (N. Cat. VI, 357)
   5. *Ṭippaṇi* on Gaṅgeśa's *Tattvacintāmaṇi* (N. Cat. VIII, 22)
   6. *Kālakhaṇḍanavicāra* (Nyāya) (N. Cat. IV, 15)
   7. *Tarkagranthaṭīkā* (Nyāya) (N. Cat. VI, 387)
   8. *Kroḍapatras* (Nyāya) (N Cat, V, 142; VI, 356–358)
24. Dulāra Bhaṭṭācārya (Fl. 1790)
   1. *Ṭīkā* on Gadādhara's *Gādādharī* (N. Cat. V, 303; IX, 92–930)
   2. Anugama on Gaṅgeśa's *Tattvacintāmaṇi* (N. Cat. II ff. under names of sections)
25. Girīśa Candra (fl. 1790)
   1. *Ṭīkā* on Viśvanātha's *Siddhāntamuktāvalī* (N. Cat. VI, 24)
26. Haranārāyaṇa (Fl. 1790)
   1. Commentary on Gadādhara's *Gādādharī* (N. Cat. V, 348)
   2. Commentary on Jagadīśa's *Jagadīśī* (MS at Ayodhya Prasada, Banaras).
   3. Commentary on *Tarkasṁgraha* (Nyāya) of NO II, 18 for MS citation.
   4. Commentary on Gaṅgeśa's *Tattvacintāmaṇi* (N. Cat. entries under names of sections)
27. Devabhadra (fl. 1792)
   1. *Pauṣavāda Kathā* or *Pauṣavādavyākhyā* (Nyāya) (N. Cat. IX, 115–116)

28, Veṇīdatta (Vāgīśa Bhaṭṭa, fl. 1800)
1. *Bhedajayaśrī*
Ed. by T.P. Upādhyāya POWSBT 49, 1933
Padārthamaṇḍana (Nyāya)
Ed. by G.S. Nene POWSBT 30, 1933
Satkāryakhaṇḍana (Nyāya) (Cf. HDV 784 for MS citation)
Tarkasamayakhaṇdna (N. Cat. VII, 132)

29. (Parvatīya Śrī) Viśveśvara (Pāṇḍeya) (fl. 1800)
1. *Tarkakautūhala* (Nyāya) (N. Cat. VIII, 111)
Ed. by Janardana Shastri Pandeya Banaras 1971
Praveśa on Raghunātha Śiromaṇi's *Dīdhiti* (N. Cat. VIII, 35)

30. Gopīkānta (fl. 1800)
1. *Nyāyapradīpa* (Nyāya) (ms. at Paṇḍit Syamalal Duve's Ajiganj)

31. Kṛṣṇamitra Ācārya or Durbalācārya (fl. 1800)
1. *Bhāṭṭataraṅgiṇī* (Nyāya) (cf. Oudh VI, 12 for ms. citation)
2. *Pradīpa* on Bhavānanda's *Bhavānandī* (N. Cat IV, 343)
3. *Ṭīkā* on Gadādhara's *Gādādharī* (N. Cat. IV, 343)
4. *Laghunyāyasudhā* (Nyāya) (cf. Oudh X, 16 for ms citation)
5. *Laghusāmagrīvyāpti* (Nyāya) (Cf. Oudh X, 16 for ms citation)
6. *Laghutarkasudhā* (Nyāya) (cf. Oudh X 16 for ms citation)
7. *Ṭīkā* on Raghunātha Śiromaṇi's *Nañavāda* (cf. Oudh X 14 for ms citation)
8. *Vyākhyā* on Rāmabhadra Sārvabhauma's *Padārthatattvanirūpaṇaṭippaṇa* (N. Cat. IV, 343)
9. *Padārthapārijāta* (Nyāya) (N. Cat. IV, 343)
10. *Ratnāvalīvādasudhāṭīkā* (Nyāya) (Cf. Oudh X 18 for ms citation)
11. *Sāmagrīvādārtha* (Nyāya) (cf. Oudh Xm 18 for ms citation)
12. *Sāmagrīvyāpti* (Nyāya) (cf. Oudh X 18 ms citation)
13. Commentary on Īśvarakṛṣṇa's *Sāṁkhyakārikās* (Cf. NW 390; Oudh XIX, 108 for mss citations)
14. *Ṭīkā* on Gadādhara's *Śaktivāda* (cf. Oudh 1877, 36; X, 16 for mss citations)
15. *Siddhāntarahasya* (Nyāya) (cf. Oudh X 14 for ms citation)
16. *Tarkapratibandharahasya* (Nyāya) (cf. Oudh X, 14 for ms citation)
17. *Tarkasudhāprakāśa* (Nyāya) (N. Cat. VIII, 133)
18. *Prakāśa* on Raghunātha Śiromaṇi's *Tattvacintāmaṇidīdhiti* (N. Cat. IV, 343; VIII, 29)
19. *Tattvamīmāṁsā*
20. *Vādasaṁgraha* or *Vedacūḍāmaṇi* (N. Cat. II, 9)
21. *Vādasudhākara* (Nyāya) (cf. L. 2353; Oudh IV, 11; VI, 12 for mss citations)
22. *Kuñcikā* on Nāgeśa Bhaṭṭa's *Vaiyākaraṇasiddhānta.*

32. Kṛṣṇakānta Vidyāvāgiśa or Siddhāntavāgīśa (fl. 1800)
    1. *Prakāśikā* on Brahmānanda Sarasvatī's *Nyāyaratnāvalī* (cf. L. 603 for ms citation)
    2. Commentary on Raghunātha Śiromaṇi's *Padārthatattvanirūpaṇa* (N. Cat. IV, 302)
    3. *Sandīpinī* on Gautama's *Nyāyasūtras* (N. Cat. IV, 302)
    4. *Śaktisandīpinī* on Jagadīśa's *Śabdaśakti-prakāśikā* (N. Cat. IV, 302) See e5287
    5. *Taraṅgiṇī* on Rāmakṛṣṇa Bhaṭṭācārya's *Tarkāmṛta* (N. Cat. V, 9, VIII, 134)
    6. *Nyāyaratnaprakāśikā* (Nyāya) (N. Cat. IV, 302)
    7. *Dipti* on Gaṅgeśa's *Tattvacintāmaṇi* (N. Cat. IV, 302; VIII, 22) See e5287
33. Saṁgameśvara (fl. 1800)
    1. *Kroḍa* on Jagadīśa's *Jāgadīśī* See e6336
34. Ramānātha Bhaṭṭācārya (fl. 1800)
    1. *Ṭippaṇī* on Jagadīśa's *Jāgadīśī* (N. Cat. VII, 209)
    2. Commentary on Raghunātha Śiromaṇi's Nañavāda (N. Cat. IX, 324)
    3. Commentary on Viśvanātha's *Siddhāntamuktāvalī* (ms. at Veni Datta's, Varanasi)
    4. *Ṭīkā* on Annaṁbhaṭṭa's *Tarkasaṁgraha* (N. Cat. VIII, 132)
35. Śaṁkara (Bhaṭṭa) Miśra II (fl. 1800)
    1. *Sarvopakāriṇī* (N. Cat.V, 348; VIII, 31)
    2. Commentary on Jagadīśa's *Jāgadīśī* (N. Cat. VII, 209)
36. Śaṁkara Miśra (fl. 1800)
    1. *Kroḍapatra* on Gadādhara's *Gādādharī* (N. Cat IV, 79)
       Ed. with Kālī Śaṁkara's *Kroḍapatras* on Mathurānātha's *Māthurī*, Gadādhara's *Vyutpattivāda*, *Śaktivāda* and *Muktivāda*, Jagadīśa's *Śabdaśaktiprakāśikā* and Udayana's *Nyāyakusumāñjali*, by V.P. Dvivedin, Dundhiraja Sastri and Vamacharana Bhattacharya II, 2 Vol. ChSS 25, 19191, 1924. see e5315; e5319.
    2. *Kroḍa* on Jagadīśa's Jāgadīśī (N. Cat. VII, 209)
    3. *Kroḍa* on Mathurānātha's *Māthurī* (N. Cat. IV, 79). Ed. Banaras 1874.
    4. *Kroḍa* on Gadādhara's *Muktivāda.* See e6982.
    5. *Kroḍa* on Jagadīśa's *Śabdaprakāśikā* (N. Cat. VII, 209). See e6982.
    6. *Vyākhyā* on Upamāna section of Gaṅgeśa's *Tattvacintāmaṇi* (N. Cat. IV, 79)
    7. *Kroḍa* on Gadādhara's *Śaktivāda.* See e6982.
    8. *Ṭīkā* on *Tarkasṁgraha* (Nyāya) (N. Cat. IV, 79)
    9. *Kroḍa* on Gadādhara'a *Vyutpattivāda.* See e6982.
37. Kirti Veṅkaṭācārya (fl. 1810)
    1. *Khaṇḍanajhañjhāmāruta* on Gadādhara's *Gādādharī* (N. Cat. V, 303; VIII, 31).

38. Paṭṭābhirāma (fl. 1820)
 1. *Kroḍa* or *Ṭippaṇi* on Gadādhara's *Gādādharī* (N. Cat. V, 203, 347; VIII, 31)
 2. Viveka on Raghunātha Śiromaṇi's *Nañavāda* (N. Cat. IX, 323)
 3. *Mañjūṣā* on Viśvanātha's *Siddhāntamuktāvalī*
 Part One, up to abhāva section, ed. in Telugu characters by Kapisthalam Desikacharya, Tirupati 1912.
 4. *Vākyārthabodhinī* or *Nirukti* on Annaṁbhaṭṭa's *Tarkasaṁgraha* (N. Cat. VIII, 130–31). See 6414.
 5. *Prakāśikā* on Annaṁbhaṭṭa's *Tarkasaṁgrahadīpikā* (N. Cat. VIII, 129).
 6. *Ṭīkā* on *Triṃślokī* (Nyāya)
 Ed. by P.R. Pishoroti and V.S. Sastri, AUSS 5, 1937.
 7. Patra on Gadādhara's *Vyutpattivāda* (cf. Rice 11 for ms citation)
39. Mukunda Bhaṭṭa or Gaḍagila (fl. 1830)
 1. *Īśvaravāda* (Nyāya) (cf. K.142 for ms citatin)
 2. *Taraṅgiṇī* on Jagadīśa's *Tarkāmṛta* (N. Cat. VIII, 134). See 3.6389.
 3. Candrikā or Mukundabhāṭṭīya on Annaṁbhaṭṭa's *Tarkasaṁgraha.* ed. Bombay 1912.
 4. Commentary on Gaṅgeśa's *Tattvacintāmaṇi* (N. Cat. VIII, 24)
40. Nīlakaṇṭha (Bhaṭṭa) (Śāstrin) (fl. 1830)
 1. Commentary on Gadādhara's *Gādādharī* (N. Cat. V, 347) see 6414.
 2. *Ṭīkā* on Jagadīśa's *Jāgadīśī* (N. Cat. VII, 209; VIII, 32).
 3. *Prakāśikā* on Annaṁbhaṭṭa's *Tarkasaṁgrahadīpikā* (N. Cat. VIII, 1128–29).
 See e6382, e6385, e6393, e6414.
 4. Commentary on Raghunātha Śiromaṇi's *Tattvacintāmaṇi* (N. Cat. VIII, 32)
41. Golokanyāyaratna (fl. 1850)
 1. *Muktamālā* or *Golokanyāyaratnīya* on Gadādhara's *Gādādharī* (N. Cat. VI, 181; VIII, 31)
 2. *Nyāyaratna* on Mathurānātha's *Māthurī* (N. Cat. VI, 181)
42. Godavarman (Koṭilīna Nṛpati) or Yuvarāja (fl.1850)
 1. *Hetvābhāsoddharaṇa* (Nyāya)
 Ed. in *Kāvyetihāsasaṁgraha* IV–V (Poona 1888)
 Ed. and tr. by V. Varadachari in Dhruva III, 206ff.
43. Rāmacandra Siddhānata Vāgīśa (Śarman) (fl. 1850)
 1. *Ṭippaṇi* on Raghunātha Śiromaṇi's *Ākhyātavāda.* See e5937.
 2. *Vivecanā* on Raghunātha Śiromaṇi's *Tattvacintāmaṇi* (N. Cat. VIII, 35)
44. Jayakṛṣṇa Tarkācārya (fl. 1850)
 1. *Nyāyavādartnamañjarī* (cf. UM, p.449)
45. Rāmabhadra Bhaṭṭa (fl. 1850)
 1. *Prakāśikā* on *Divākarī* (or *Dinakarī?*) (ms at Ayodhya Prasad, Jaunpore).
 2. *Prabodhinī* on Jagadīśa's *Śabdaśaktiprakāśikā* (cf. L.194, 1844; NW 342; Oudh X, 16 for mss citations)

46. Rāma Śāstrin (fl. 1850)
   1. *Śatkoṭi* on Gadādhara's *Gādādharī* (N Cat. I, 411; VIII, 31). See e6620.
47. Candrakānta Tarkālaṁkāra (fl. 1850)
   1. *Ṭīkā* on Udayana's *Nyāyakusumāñjali* (N Cat. VI, 346). See 33945
   2. Interpretation of Haridāsa's *Nyāya-kusumāñjalivyākhyā* ed. 1865.
48. Raghunātha Parvate Śāstrin (fl. 1853)
   1. *Nyāyaratna* on Gadādhara's *Gādādharī* (N Cat. V, 347; VIII, 31). Published Poona 1853. See e5289.
   2. *Pañcalakṣaṇī* section edited Bombay 12919. See e5320.
49. Maheśa Candra Nyāyaratna(fl. 1860)
   1. Notes on Haridāsa's *Nyāyakusumāñjalivyākhyā* Ed. 1864.
   2. *Navyanyāyabhāṣāpradīpa* (known as "Brief Note")
      Edited and translated into Bengali, with editor's Bengali commentary by Kalipada Tarkacharya. Calcutta 1973.
50. Tārānātha Tarkavācaspati (fl. 1865)
   1. *Saralā* on Harirāma Tarkavāgiśa's *Anumitermānasatvavicārarahasya.* See e6483.
   2. *Śabdārtharatna* (Nyāya). Published Calcutta 1851.
   3. *Tarkaratnākara* (Nyāya). Published Banaras 1868.
51. Jayanārāyaṇa Tarkapañcānana(fl. 1867)
   1. *Padārthatattvasāra* (Vaiśeṣika). Published Calcutta 1867.
   2. *Navyanyāyabhāṣāpradīpa* (known as "Brief Notes")
      Vṛtti on Kaṇāda's *Vaiśeṣikasūtras* (N. Cat. VII, 179)
   3. *Vivṛti* on Śaṁkara Miśra I's *Vaiśeṣika-sūtropaskāra,* See e481; e484; e495; 1499.
52. Kṛṣṇa Tātācārya (Tirupputkuzki) (fl. 1871)
   1. *Anupalbdhivivādārtha* (Nyāya) (N. Cat. IV, 313)
   2. *Avacchedakatāsāra* (Nyāya) (N. cat. I, 303)
   3. *Kroḍapatras* on Gadādhara's *Gādādharī* (N. Cat. IV, 313–314)
53. Jīvānanda Vidyāsāgara (fl. 1874)
   1. Commentary on Laugākṣī Bhāskara's *Arthasaṁgraha* See e6650.
   2. *Vādārtha* on Jagadīśa's *Jāgadīśī.* Published Calcutta 1897.
   3. *Phakkikā* on Mathurānātha's *Māthurī.* See e5291.
54. Harinātha Tarkasiddhānta Bhaṭṭācārya or Tarkavāgīśa (fl. 1876).
   1. *Nyāyatattvaprabodhinī* (Nyāya). Published Calcutta 1876.
   2. Commentary on Gadādhara's *Śaktivāda.* See e613; e6616.
55. Ratnanātha Śukla (fl. 1879)
   1. *Prabhā* or *Mayūkha* on Viśvanātha's *Siddhāntamuktāvalī.* See e6532, e6538, e6541.
   2. *Prabhā* on Jagadīśa's *Tarkāmṛta.* See e6331.
56. Śrīnivāsa (fl. 1880)
   1. *Nyāyasiddhāntamañjarī* (Nyāya) (cf. Burnell 122b; Radh 13 for mss citations)

2. *Nyāyasiddhāntatattvāmṛta* (Nyāya)
N. Subrahmanya Sastri, "*Prameya-Tattva-Bodhinī*", JVSRI 9.2, 1948; 101–102. ed. by S. Subrahmanya Shastri, MGOS 19, 1950.
3. *Avayavakroḍapatra* (N. Cat. I, 421).

57. Uddhvasiṁha (fl. 1885)
1. Abayavarahasya (Nyāya) (N. Cat. I, 281).
Ed. Banaras 1885.

58. Candajā Siṁha (fl. 1889)
1. *Padakṛtya* on Annaṁbhaṭṭa's *Tarkasaṁgraha* (N. Cat. VI, 343, 353; VIII, 130).
See e6380, e6394, e6399, e6401, e6408, e6414, e6418, e6419.

59. Rādhāmohana Vidyāvācaspati Gosvāmin Bhaṭṭācārya (fl. 1890)
1. *Vivaraṇa* on Gautama's *Nyāyasūtras*. See e790.

60. Sokttur Vijayarāghavācārya (fl. 1890)
1. *Bādhakroḍapatra* (Nyāya) (cf. MD 4273 for ms citation)
2. Commentary on Gadādhara's *Gādādharī* (N. Cat. VIII, 31)
3. *Śatakoṭikhaṇḍanamaṇḍana* (N. cat. V, 177)
4. *Sāmānyabālavicāra* (Nyāya) (Cf. MD 4313 for ms citation)

61. Viśvanātha Jhā (fl. 1891)
1. *Prakāśa* on Udayana's *Lakṣaṇāvalī*. See e3942.

62. Kāsturi Raṅgācārya II (fl. 1890)
1. Commentary on Gadādhara's *Gādādharī* (N. Cat. VII, 30)

63. Kṛṣṇāvadhūta Paṇḍita or Ānandāśrama (fl. 1895)
1. *Padārthasāgara* (Nyāya) (N. Cat. V, 21)
2. *Vākyārthavivṛti* on Annaṁbhaṭṭa's *Tarkasaṁgraha* (N. Cat. V, 20).

64. Ānandacandra Sārvabhauma (fl. 1896)
1. *Ānandamayīvyākhyā* on Viśvanātha's *Siddhāntamuktāvalī* (N. Cat. II, 102). See e6510.

65. Gandasiṁha or Govindasiṃha or Nirṁala Paṇḍita (fl. 1900)
1. *Viṣamasthalaṭippaṇi* on Annaṁbhaṭṭa's *Tarkasaṁgraha*. Published 1904.

66. Kurucci Raṅgācārya (fl. 1900)
1. *Sāmānyaniruktiṭippaṇi* or *Nakṣtramālikā* on Gadādhara's *Gādādharī* (N. Cat. VIII, 31)

67. Rāma Bhaṭṭa (fl. 1900)
1. *Nyāyabuddhisopānopādāna* (Nyāya) Ed. by T. Chandrasekharan. BGOMKM 3.2, 1950, 1–32.

68. Rāma Bhaṭṭa (fl. 1900)
1. *Nyāyanayāmbuddhisopānopādāna* (Nyāya)
Ed. by T. Chandrasekharan. BGOMKM 3.2, 1950, 1–32.

APPENDIX II

Vāda Granthas

List compiled from Karl H. Potter's
Encyclopedia of Indian Philosophies, Vol. I

Abhāvavāda (Dāmodara)
Advaiteśvaravāda (Raghunātha)
Ākāśādhikaraṇavāda (Anantācārya)
Akhaṇḍasvarūpavāda (Ālaga Singarācārya)
Ākhyātīvāda (Raghunātha Śiromaṇi)
Ānandamayādhikaraṇavādārtha (Anantācārya)
Anantaryavāda (Rāma Subrahmanya)
Andhakāravāda (Puruṣottama Pītāmbara)
Anumitimānasavāda (Gadādhara)
Anupalabdhivādārtha (Kṛṣṇa Tātācārya)
Anyathākhyātivāda (Timmana)
Ātmavāda (Puruṣottama Pītāmbara)
Ātmavāda (Gopeśvara)
Avatāravādāvalī (Puruṣottama Pītāmbara)
Avyāptivāda (Prabhādeva)
Bhaktirasatvavāda (Puruṣottama Pītāmbara)
Bhedābhedavāda (Vaṃśīdāsa)
Bhedavāda (Anantācārya)
Brahmanairguṇyavāda (Vidula Śāstrin)
Brahmaśabdavāda (Anantācārya)
Brahmapadaśaktivāda (Anantācārya), (Śrīnivāsa Śrīśailayogin)
Brahmatvādidevatāvāda (Puruṣottama Pītāmbara)
Brahmavāda (Harirāja) (Puruṣottama Pītāmbara), (Vrajarāja), (Vrajahātha)
Citrarūpavāda (Harirāma Tarkavāgīśa)
Daśalakāravādārtha (Bhāvananda Siddhāntavāgīśa)
Dīdhitikṛnnyunatāvāda (Rākhāldāsa Nyāyaratna Bhaṭṭācārya)
Evakāravādārtha (Harirāma Tarkavāgīśa)
Gurumatānuvāda (Tinmayayajvan)

Guruparāmarśavāda (Harirāma Tarkavāgīśa)
Īśvarvāda (Mahādeva Puṇyātaṁkara)
Īśvaravāda (Citradhara)
Īśvaravāda (Mukunda Bhaṭṭa)
Īśvaravāda (Saśīdhara)
Iśvaravādīmataparikṣā (Jitārī)
Janmādyadhikaraṇavāda (Anantārya)
Jātiśaktivāda (Ananta Bhaṭṭa)
Jñānakāraṇatvavāda (Nārāyaṇa Sārvabhauma Bhattācārya)
Jñānāyathārthyavāda (Anantācārya)
Kārakavāda (Harirāma Tarkavāgīśa)
Kāraṇatvavāda (Harirāma Tarkavāgīśa)
Kāraṇavāda (Anantācārya)
Kartṛvāda (Harirāma Tarkavāgīśa)
Kevalānvayivāda (Harirāma Tarkavāgīśa)
Kevalavyatirekīvāda (Harirāma Tarkavāgīśa)
Khelālāpanavidhvaṃśavāda (Puruṣottama Pītāmbara)
Khyātivāda (Puruṣottama Pītāmbara)
Khyātivāda (Śaṁkara Caitanya Bhāratī)
Maṅgalavāda (Vallabha)
Maṅgalavāda (Harirāma Tarkavāgīśa)
Mokṣakāraṇatāvāda (Anantavāda)
Muktivāda (Gokulnātha Upādhyāya)
Muktivāda (Gadādhara)
Muktivāda (Govinda Yajvana)
Mūrtipūjanavāda (Puruṣottama Pītāmbara)
Nañavāda (Puruṣottama Pītāmbara)
Nañavāda (Raghunātha Śiromaṇi)
Navakoṭibhañjanavāda (Kṛṣṇa Tatācārya)
Nayavāda (Prabhādeva)
Nirvikalpavāda (Tarkavāgīśa)
Nirviśeṣaprāmāṇyudāsavāda (Anantācārya)
Nyāyamatavāda (Gadādhara)
Oṁkāravāda (Anantācārya)
Oṁkārvādārtha (Vidyādhīśa Tīrtha)
Oṁkārvādārtha (Śrīnivāsācārya)
Oṁkārvādārtha (Rama Subrahmaṇya)
Pauṣavādārtha (Devabhadra)
Prahastavāda (Puruṣottama Pītāmbara)
Pramāṇavādārtha (Yaśasvatsāgara)
Prāmaṇyavāda (Harirāma Tarkavāgīśa)
Prapañcavāda (Puruṣottama Pītāmbara)
Pratibandhakatāvāda (Gadādhara)
Pratibimbavāda (Puruṣottama Pītāmbara)

Pratijñāvādārtha (Anantācārya)
Pratikṛtipūjanavāda (Puruṣottama Pītāmbara)
Sādṛśyavāda (Gadādhara)
Sādṛśyavāda (Mahādeva Puṇyātaṁkara)
Śaktivāda (Gokulanātha Upādhyāya)
Śaktivāda (Gadādhara)
Sāmagrīvāda (Gaṅgādhara)
Samānādhikaraṇyavāda (Ananatācārya)
Samāsavāda (Govinda Śarman)
Śaṁkhacakrādidhāraṇavāda (Puruṣottama Pītāmbara)
Sarīravāda (Anantācārya)
Śāstraikyabhaṅgavāda (Rāma Subrahmaṇya)
Śāstraikyavāda (Anantācārya)
Savyabhicāralakṣānuvāda (Appā Śāstrin)
Sṛṣṭibhedavāda (Puruṣottama Pītāmbara)
Suvarṇataijassatvavāda (Rāmabhadra Sārvabhauma)
Svatvavāda (Gokulanātha Upādhyāya)
Svavṛttivāda (Puruṣottama Pītāmbara)
Ūrdhvapuṇḍradhāraṇavāda (Puruṣottama Pītāmbara)
Vākyabhedavāda (Anantadeva)
Vākyavāda (Raghudeva Nyāyālaṁkāra Bhaṭṭācārya)
Vākyavāda (Raghunātha Sārvabhauma Bhaṭṭācārya)
Vākyavāda (Acala Upādhyāya)
Vāyuvāda (Kaṇāda Tarkavāgīśa)
Vāyuvāda (Rāmabhadra Sārvabhauma)

APPENDIX III

Indological Series Published from Nineteenth Century Onwards

Prepared By S.N. Biswas

Achyuta Granthamala (Banaras)
Agamodaya Sanskrit Series
Advaitamanjari Series (Kumbhakonam)
Anecdota Oxoniensa, Aryan Series 1 (1881) – 9 (1909)
Asutosh Sanskrit series (Calcutta)
Anandasrama Sanskrit Series (Poona)
Allahabad University Sanskrit series
H.W. Bailey, Khotanes Buddhist texts, Cambridge Oriental Series 3, London 1951
Buddhadasa P. Kirthisinghe (Ed.), Buddhist Concepts Old and New. Bibliotheca Indo-Buddhica No.9 Delhi 1983
Benaras Sanskrit Series
Bibliotheca Indica (Calcutta)
Bibliotheca Indo-Buddhica Series 1 (1982) – 53 (1988)
Bonner Orientalische Studient (= Studia Indologica)
Bombay Sanskrit and Prakrit Series
Calcutta Sanskrit series
Chowkhamba Sanskrit Series (Banaras)
Chowkhamba Sanskrit Studies
Calcutta Oriental Series
Gaekwad's Oriental Series (Baroda)
Government Oriental Series, Bhandarkar Oriental Research Institute, Classes A to C
Haridas Sanskrit series, Banaras
Harvard Oriental series
Indianisme et Bouddhisme offerts a msgr. Etienne Lamotte, Publications de l'Institut Orientaliste du Louvain 23, Louvain-la-Neuve 1980

Gerhard Oberhammei (Ed.), Inklussivismus, Eine Indische Denkform, Publications of De Nobili Research Library Occasional Papers 2, Wien 1983
Jaina Atmananda Grantharatnamala (Bhavnagar, Bombay)
Jivaraj Jaina Granthamala (Sholapur)
Gyana—Pitha Murtidevi Jaina Granthamala (Banaras)
Seth Devachand Lalbhai Jain Pustakoddhar Fund Series (Bombay)
Kashi Sanskrit Series
Kashmir Series of Texts and Studies
Lalbhai Dalpatbhai series (Ahmedabad)
Library of Jain Literature
Madras University, Department of Indian Philosophy Publication
Manikachandra Digambara Jain Granthamala
Madras Government Oriental Series
Christian Lindther (Ed.), Miscellanea Buddhica Indiske Studien 5, Copenhagen 1985
Mysore Oriental Library Publications
Madras Oriental Series
Mysore University Studies in Philosophy
Madras University Philosophy Series
Madras University Sanskrit Series
Nava-Nālandā-Mahavihara Research Publications (Nālandā) 1 (1957), 2 (1960)
Oriental Research Series (London), 1 (1927) – 6 (1931)
Oxford University Papers on India, 1 (1966) – 2.1 (1988)
Prachyabharati series (Varanasi)
Publications of the Greater India Society (Calcutta)
Poona Oriental Series
Princess of Wales Saraswati Bhavan Texts
Publications de l'Institut de Civilization Indiens, Paris
Pali Text Series
Pali Text Society, translation series
Punjab Oriental series
Royal Asiatic Society Monographs
Rayachandra Jaina Sastra Mala (Bombay)
Rajasthan Puratan Granthamala
Sri Balamanorama Series
Saraswati Bhavana Granthamala
Studies in Comparative East Asian Religion, 1 (1988)
Shri Chunilal Gandhi Vidyabhavan Studies (Surat)
Studies in Comparative Religion (England), 1 (1967) – 2 (1968)
Saddarshanachintanika or Studies in Indian Philosophy (Poona), 1 (1967)
Serie Orientale Roma
Sevartham (Ranchi), 7 (1982) – 16 (1991)
Shri Garib Dass Oriental series (Delhi), 1 (1981) – 78 (1988)

Studies in Indo-Asian Art and Culture, 1 (1972) – 5 (1977)
Studien zur Indologie und Iranistik (Germany), 1 (1975) – 18 (1993)
P.K. Gode, Studies in Indian Literary History, Volume One (= SJS 37), 1853, Volume Two (+SJS 38), 1954, Volume Three, Poona 1956
Sanathana Jaina Granthamala (Banaras)
Sri Bahadur Singh Jaina Series
Sastramuktavali series (Conjeeveram)
Studia Philologica Buddhica Monograph Series (Tokyo)
Studia Philologica Buddhica, Occasional Papers Series (Tokyo), 1 (1977) – 4 (1081)
Sri Samkara Gurukula series
Sanskrit Sahitya Parishad Series (Calcutta)
Sanskrit Savitri Series (Trivandrum)
Studies of the Sri Venkatesvara Oriental Institute (Tirupati)
M.P. Marathe, M.A., Kelkar and P.P. Gokhale (eds.), Studies in Jainism. Indian Philosophical Quarterly Publications, 7, Poona 1984
Sri Venkatesvara Oriental Series (Tirupati)
Sri Vallabha Studies Series (Baroda), 1 (1984) - 11, 17.
Sri Vani Vilas Series
Tanjore Saraswati Mahal Library Series
Trivandrum Sanskrit Series
Tibetan Sanskrit Works Series (Patna)
Gerhard Oberhammer (Ed.), Transzendenzerfahrung Volluzugshorizont des Heils, Das Problem in Indischer und Christlicher Tradition, Publications of the De Nobili Research Library 5, Wien 1978
University of Baroda Research Series
University of Poona Sanskrit and Prakrit Series
Visva-Bharati Studies
Vedanta Desika Granthamala (Ed. P.B. Ananthachariar), Conjeeveram 1941
Vizianagram Sanskrit Series
Vidvana Manoranjini Series (Madras)
The Wheel Publications, 1 (1958) – 374 (1991)
Yasovijaya Jaina Granthamala

APPENDIX IV

Dharmaśāstra Literature from Eighteenth Century Onwards at Prajñā-Pāṭhaśālā Maṇḍala, Wai (Maharashtra)

Sent by M.P. Rage

S. No.	Name of the Book	Author's name	Period
1.	*Akālabhāskara*	Śambhunātha Siddhāntavāgīśa	1794
2.	*Ahalyākāmadhenu*	Keśavadāsa	1770–1790
3.	*Āgamagrantha*	Nāgeśa	1741–1782
4.	*Ācāradīpaka*	Gaṅgāviṣṇu	1750–1752
5.	*Ācaraṇavanitam*	Appā Dikṣita	1684–1711
6.	*Ācārabhūṣaṇam*	Trayambaka Ok	1819
7.	*Ācārendu*	Trayambakamāte	1838
8.	*Ācārenduśekhara*	Nāgojībhaṭṭa	1700–1750
9.	*Ādidharmasārasaṁgraha*	Tulājīrāja	1765–1788
10.	*Apastambāhnikam*	Rudradeva	1710
11.	*Aśaucanirṇaya*	Jīvadeva	1750
12.	*Aśaucanirṇaya*	Trayambakapaṇḍita	1760
13.	*Aśaucanirṇaya*	Nāgojībhaṭṭa	1700–1750
14.	*Aśaucenduśekhara*	Nāgojībhaṭṭa	1700–1750
15.	*Badrīśrāddhanirṇaya*	Marchegana Vithobacharya	1926
16.	*Balaṁbhaṭṭi*	Balambhaṭṭa Payaguṇḍe	1730–1800
17.	*Caṇḍīprayoga*	Nāgojībhaṭṭa	1700–1750
18.	*Chāndogyasandhyā-sūtrabhāṣyam*	Nagojibhatta	1909
19.	*Chandogāsana Sūtrabhāṣyam*	Nagojibhatta	1909
20.	*Dattakacandrikā*	Kuberopādhyāya	1800
21.	*Dattakacandrikā*	Raghumaṇi	1700
22.	*Dattaka*	Dada Karajagi	1769

23.	*Dattaśaucavyavasthā-panavāda*	Rāmasubramaṇya Śāstrī	1700
24.	*Dayādharmasaṁgraha*	Śrīkṛṣṇa Tarkālaṁkāra	1750
25.	*Dayātattvavāṭikā*	Rādhāmohanagosvāmī Bhaṭṭācārya	1700
26.	*Dayāpīḍā* (Dayābhāgaṭīkā)	Śrīkṛṣṇa Tarkālaṃkāra	1750
27.	*Dinabhāskara*	Śambhunātha Siddhāntavāgīśa	1715
28.	*Durgotsava Kṛtyakaumudī*	Śambhunātha Siddhāntavāgiśa	1715
29.	*Devipūjanabhāskara*	Śambhunātha Siddhāntavāgiśa	1715
30.	*Dravyaśuddhidīpikā*	Puruṣottama	1668–1725
31.	*Dharmatattvaprakāśa*	Śiva Caturdhara	1776
32.	*Dharmasindhu*	Kāśīnātha Upādhyāya	1791
33.	*Dīpa (Ekādaśītattvaṭīkā)*	Rādhāmohana Gosvāmi Bhaṭṭacārya	1800
34.	*Gaṅgābhaṭṭprakāśa*	Harinandana	1795–1796
35.	*Gayāśrāddhādipaddhati*	Taranatha Tarka Vachaspati Bhattacharya	1872
36.	*Gāyatripuraścaraṇa paddhati*	Saṁkara Ghare	1753
37.	*Gāyatripuraścaraṇa prayoga*	Kṛṣṇabhaṭṭa	1757–1859
38.	*Gṛhapaddhati*	Vāsudeva Dikṣita	1756
39.	*Gṛhasaṁgrahabhāṣyam*	Sri Chandrakanta Tarkalamkara Bhattacharya	1909
40.	*Gotrapravaranirṇaya*	Nagoji Bhatta	1900–1950
41.	*Gotrapravaranirṇaya*	Āpadeva	1751
42.	*Gotrapravaravatsa (Ahalyākāmadhenu)*	Keśavadāsa	1770–1790
43.	*Godānavidhi Saṁgraha*	Madhusūdana Gosvāmī	1756
44.	*Gobhilīyaśrāddhak alpabhāṣyam*	Sri Chandrakanta Tarkalamkara Bhattacharya	1909
45.	*Gobhilīya śrāddhak alpapariśiṣṭabhāṣyam*		1909
46.	*Ghṛtadānapaddhati*	Premanidhi panta	1753
47.	*Ghṛtapradānaratnam*	Premanidhi panta	1753
48.	*Jayamādhavamānasollāsa*	Jayasiṁhadeva	1771, 1750
49.	*Jayasiṁhakalpadruma*	Ratnākara	1713
50.	*Jīvatipitṛ kartavyanirṇaya*	Bālakṛṣṇa Bhaṭṭa	1725
51.	*Jīvatipitṛ kavibhagavyavastha*	Madhusūdana Gosvāmī	1756
52.	*Jīvatipitṛ havibhāgavyavasthā sāra*	(author) -do-	1756
53.	*Jīvatipitṛ kavibhāgavyavasthā sārasaṁgraha*	(author)	1756
54.	*Kāmadhenu*	Yatīśa	1784
55.	*Kalātattvavivecanā sārasaṁgraha*	Śambhubhaṭṭa Kavimaṇḍana	1708
56.	*Kālyarcanācandrikā*	Nilakamala Lahadi	1879

57.	*Kāśīkhaṇḍaṭīkā*	Chaitanyavanapara ... Ramananda	19th century
58.	*Kuṇḍacamatkṛta*	Vāsudeva Mahājana	1680–1760
59.	*Kuṇḍādikapāla*	Kāśīnātha Upādhyāya	1791
60.	*Kuṇḍapaddhati*	Nāgojībhaṭṭa	1700–1750
61.	*Kuṇḍaprakāśa*	Rudradeva	1710
62.	*Kuṇḍaratnāvali*	Ramachandra Jade	1868
63.	*Kṛtyamañjarī*	Bāpūbhaṭṭa Kelkar	1718
64.	*Kṛtyarāja*	Navadvīparājaputra Kṛṣṇacandra preraṇya	1750
65.	*Kṛtyarāja*	Rādhāmohana Gosvāmī Bhaṭṭacārya	1800
66.	*Kṛtyaśiromaṇi*	Tuphani Sharma	1889
67.	*Kṛṣṇambhaṭṭīya (Nirṇayasindhuṭīkā)*	Kṛṣṇabhatta Ardhe	1786
68.	*Kevalānandī*	Kevalananda Sarasvati	1950
69.	*Mantrakaumudī*	Aniruddhabhaṭṭa Mahāmahopādhyāya	1795
70.	*Malamāsatattvaṭikā*	Rādhāmohana Gosvāmī Bhaṭṭācārya	1800
71.	*Mitākṣaraṭīkā*	Rādhāmohana Gosvāmī Bhaṭṭācārya	1800
72.	*Mahārudrapaddhati*	Anantadikṣita	1575–1750
73.	*Mitākṣarasāra*	Madhusūdana Gosvāmī	1756
74.	*Mridulā*	Mukunda Sarma	1923
75.	*Nirṇayasaṁgraha*	Madhusūdana Gosvāmī	1756
76.	*Nirṇayasāra*	Nandarāma Miśra	1780
77.	*Nirṇayasindhuṭīkā*	Śambhubhaṭṭa Kavimaṇḍana	1708
78.	*Prabhuprakaraṇam*	Govindarāja	1740–1749
79.	*Parabhuprakaraṇam*	Bākdevabhaṭṭa Atle	1740
80.	*Pariśiṣṭa Dīpaka*	Nityananda Parvatiya	1932
81.	*Pākayajñaprakāśa*	Rudradeva	1710
82.	*Pākayajñaprayoga*	Śambhubhaṭṭa Kavimaṇḍana	1708
83.	*Pistapaśukhaṇḍanamīmāṁsā*	Nārāyaṇapaṇḍita	1720
84.	*Puruṣārthacintāmaṇi*	Viṣṇubhaṭṭa Athavale	1780–1784
85.	*Pūjāpaddhati*	Rāmacandrabhaṭṭa Chajavalkara	1810
86.	*Putraprakāśa*	Rudradeva	1710
87.	*Pṛthvīpremodaya*	Prema Nidhi Panta	1737–38
88.	*Pratāpanarasiṁha*	Rudradeva	1710
89.	*Pratāparka*	Viśveśvaramahāśabda	1750
90.	*Pratiṣṭhāsāradīpikā*	Pāṇduraṅga Ṭakale	1780
91.	*Pratiṣṭhendu*	Trayambaka Mate	1838
92.	*Prabhā (Katyāyanasmṛtiṭīkā)*	Sri Chandrakanta Tarkalamkara Bhattacharya	1909

93.	*Prayogaratnam*	Ananta Dikṣita	1575–1750
94.	*Prayogaratnam*	Prema Nidhi Panta	1753
95.	*Prayogaratnamālā*	Vāsudeva	1620–1760
96.	*Prāyaścittatattva ṭīkā*	Rādhāmohan Gosvāmī-Bhaṭṭacārya	1800
97.	*Prāyaścittaprakāśa*	Chaturthilala	1921
98.	*Prāyaścittapradīpa*	Premanidhipanthe	1753
99.	*Prāyaścittamañjarī*	Bāpūbhaṭṭa Kelkar	1814
100.	*Prāyaścittasaṁgraha*	Devarāja	1770–1781
101.	*Prāyaścittenduśekhara*	Nāgojī Bhaṭṭa	1700–1750
102.	*Prāyaścittasārasaṁgraha*	Nāgojī Bhaṭṭa	1700–1750
103.	*Prāyaścittasārasaṁgraha*	Kāśīnātha Upādhyāya	1791
104.	*Pretamuktidā*	Kṣemarāja	1720
105.	*Rāmanibandha*	Kṣemarāja	1720
106.	*Rāmāyaṇabhūṣaṇam*	Govindarāja	18th century
107.	*Rāmārcanaratnākara*	Keśavadāsa	1770–1790
108.	*Rudrānuṣṭhānapaddhati*	Saṁkara Ghāre	1753
109.	*Rājadharmasārasaṁgraha*	Tulājīrāja	1765–1788
110.	*Śaṁkhacakradhāraṇavāda*	Puruṣottama	1668–1725
111.	*Śabdārtha Cintāmaṇi (Śaradaṭīkākaṭīkā)*	Premanidhi Panta	1737
112.	*Śivatoṣiṇī (Lingapurāṇaṭīkā)*	Gaṇeśa Ballāka Nātu	1847
113.	*Śukranītiṭīkā*	Jīvānanda Vidyāsāgara	1882
114.	*Śuddhitattvaṭīkā*	Rādhāmohanagosvāmi Bhaṭṭācārya	1800
115.	*Śrāddhagaṇapati Kimvā Srāddhasaṁgraha*	Ramakṛṣṇa Koṇḍaprayāgabhaṭṭa	1751
116.	*Śrāddhapaddhati*	Kṣemarāma	1720
117.	*Śrāddhapradīpa*	Dhanarāma	1750
118.	*Śrāddhamañjarī*	Bāpūbhaṭṭa Kelakara	1810
119.	*Śrāddhenduśekhara*	Nāgojībhaṭṭa	1700–1750
120.	*Śrīmūla*	T. Ganapatishastri	1923
121.	*Sañjīvanī (Baudhayanagṛhyaṭīkā)*	Shri Ramachandra Shastri Suri	1987
122.	*Sanyāsanirṇayavivaraṇam*	Puruṣottama	1668–1725
123.	*Saṁskāragaṇapati*	Rāmakṛṣṇa	1750
124.	*Saṁskāradīpaka*	Nityanandapantaparvatiya	1932
125.	*Saṁskāranirṇaya*	Ṭippābhaṭṭa	1776
126.	*Saṁskāraprakāśa*	Rudradeva	1710–1711
127.	*Saṁskāraratnamālā*	Gopīnāthabhaṭṭa	1765–1780
128.	*Saṁskāraratnamālā*	Nāgojībhaṭṭa	1700–1750
129.	*Saṁskāravatsa (Ahalyā Kāmadhenu)*	Keśavadāsa	1770–1790
130.	*Śaṅketakaumudī*	Śambhunātha Siddhāntavāgīśa	1715

131.	*Sacchūdrācārasmṛti*	Anvarasaundarya Bhaṭṭa	
132.	*Sadācārahāsyam*	Ananta Bhaṭṭa	1715
133.	*Sapiṇḍīmañjarī-Sapiṇḍyanirṇaya*	Nāgojī Bhaṭṭa	1700–1750
134.	*Saptasaṅsthāprayoga*	Anantadikṣita	1575–1750
135.	*Sahanumaraṇaviveka*	Anantarāma	1810
136.	*Sāpiṇḍyakalpalatā Ṭīkā (Kiṁvālaṭīkā)*	Nārāyaṇadeva	1750–1780
137.	*Sāpiṇḍyapradīpa*	Nāgeśabhaṭṭa	1700–1750
138.	*Siddhāntasaṁgraha (Mitākṣaraṭīkā)*	Rādhāmohana Gosvāmi Bhaṭṭācārya	1800
139.	*Subodhinī (Mīmāṁsāsūtraṭīkā)*	Ramesvarasuri	1909
140.	*Snānasūtrapariśiṣṭabhāṣyam*	Śrīcandra kānta Tarkālaṁkāra Bhaṭṭācārya	1776
141.	*Smṛtiprāyaścittam*	Ṭippābhaṭṭa	1708
142.	*Smṛtikaustubha*	Śambhubhaṭṭa Kavimaṇḍana	1720–1722
143.	*Smṛticandra*	Bhāvadevaśarman Nyāyālaṁkāra	1834
144.	*Smṛtimañjarī*	Kālīcaraṇa Nyāyālaṁkāra	1741–1782
145.	*Smṛtyarthamuktāvalī*	Nāgeśa	1741–1782
146.	*Tadgadapratiṣṭhāvidhi*	(author)	1756
147.	*Tāntrikamuktāvalī*	Nāgeśa	1741–1782
148.	*Tithinirṇaya*	Nāgojī Bhaṭṭa	1700–1750
149.	*Tithenduśekhara*	Nāgojībhaṭṭa	1700–1750
150.	*Tirthakaumudī*	Saṁkara Ghare	1753
151.	*Tirthenduśekhara*	Nāgojī Bhaṭṭa	1700–1750
152.	*Tirthodyāpana Kaumudī*	Saṁkara Ghare	1753
153.	*Trinśak*	Śambhubhaṭṭa Kavimaṇḍana	1708
154.	*Trinślokī vivaraṇa śiroddhāra*	Śambhubhaṭṭa Kavimaṇḍana	1708
155.	*Tirthasthalīsetusāra saṁgraha*	Nāgojī Bhaṭṭa	1700–1750
156.	*Utsarjanopakāraprayoga*	Bāpūbhaṭṭa Kelkar	1814
157.	*Upakṛtitattvam*	Balaṁbhaṭṭa	1792
158.	*Varṣakṛtyadīpaka*	Gopālaśāstrī Nene	
159.	*Varṣabhāskara*	Śambhunātha Siddhāntavāgīśa	1715
160.	*Vasantalakṣmī (Vivāhavṛndāvanaṭīkā)*	Pt. Sitarama Jha	1935
161.	*Vārttikasāra*	Yatīśa	1784
162.	*Viṭṭhalārṇavamantra-sāraṇabhāṣyam*	Kāsīnātha Upādhyāya	1791
163.	*Vināyaka Pūjā*	Rāma Kṛṣṇa	1702
164.	*Vivādabhaṅgārṇava*	Jagannātha Tarkapañcānana	1773
165.	*Vivādasārārṇava*	Sarvoru Trivedi	1789

166.	*Vivādārṇavasetu (Vivādārṇavabhañjana)*	Vīreśvara (Bañceśvara)	1773
167.	*Viṣamapadālambīyavyākhyā (Kātyāyanapariśiṣṭavyākhyā)*	Sridhara Shastri	1959
168.	*Vaiśākhamahātmyaṭīkā*	Harikṛṣṇa Śāstrī	
169.	*Vaiṣṇavākūṭacandrikā*	Ratnagarbha Bhaṭṭācārya	
170.	*Vyavasthāsārasaṁgraha*	Madhusūdana Gosvāmī	1756
171.	*Vyavahāranirṇaya*	Māyārāma Miśra Gauḍa	1700–1750
172.	*Vyavahāraprakāśa*	Śarabhojī	1798–1833
173.	*Vyavahāraśiroddhāra kimvā vyavahārārthsāra*	Mudhusūdana Gosvāmī	1799
174.	*Vyavahārasiddhānta Piyūṣaṁ*	Chatrapati	1803
175.	*Vyavahārārtha Smṛtisāra Samuccaya*	Śarabhojī	1798–1833
176.	*Vratarāja kimvā vrataprakāśa*	Viśvanātha	1736
177.	*Vratodyāpanakaumudī*	Śaṁkara Ghare	1703–1753
178.	*Yajuśakhābheda Tattvanirṇaya*	Pāṇḍuraṅga Ṭakle	1780

APPENDIX V

List of Eminent Paṇḍits who have Contributed in the Field of Philosophy in the Last One Hundred and Fifty Years

Compiled on the Basis of Information Received from R.N. Dandekar, K.T. Pandurangi, S.D. Joshi, Thangaswami Sarma, Srimanarayana Murti, Amir Chandra Shastri and Sri Ram Sharma

A. Subrahmanya Shastri
Anantalal Thakur
Abhyankara Vasudeva Shastry
Ananta Krishna Shastry
Appasastri Rashivadekar
Agnihotram Ramanuja Tatacharya
A.R. Tatachariar
Atmaramashastri Jere
A.M. Ghatage
Arya Prasad Mishra
Baliram Shukla
Baldeva Upadhyaya
B.R. Sharma
Bhargavasastri Joshi
Bhimacharya Jhalkikar
Brahmaleen Muni Yudhishthir Mimamsak
Bhagwan Dev
Bulusu Appanna Sastri
Balai Hardas
Balamukunda Ramaraya Kavi
B.K. Matilal
Bhaskarashastri Abhyankar
Charu Deva Shastri
Chinnaswamy Shastri

C. Kunjan Raja
C.G. Kashikar
Devanayakacharya
Dharmadatta alias Bachcha Jha
Devaswarup Mishra
Devinatha Tatacharya
E.S. Varadachari
Goda Subrahmanyasastri
G. Hayagrivacharya
Ganga Nath Jha
Gaudigere Venkataramanacharya
Golok Bihari Mishra
H. Musalagaonkar
H.S. Ramana Tatacharya
H. Ramakrishna Shastri
H.D. Velankar
Haridasa Siddhanta Vagisa Bhattacharya
Hariram Shukla
Jhalakikar Vamanacharya
Karyakantha Vasistha Ganapati Muni
Kashinatha Sastri Abhyankar
Kevalananda Sarasvati
Krshna Sastri Ghule
Kolluru Somasekhara Sastri
K.V. Sarma
Kashinathashastri Abhyankar
Kuppuswamy Sastri
Kevalananda Sarasvati
Kunjan Raja
K.V. Sharma
K.A. Subrahmanya Iyer
Kulamani Mishra
Kavishvar Sastri
Kailashpati Tripathi
K.D. Tripathy
Laksamana Sastri Joshi
Laxmana Sastri Murgadkar
Lakshmipuram Srinivasacharya
Lanka Venkatrama Sastri
Ladukesvara Satapathy
Manikya Sastry
Mahadeva Sastri Joshi
Mahadeva Sastri Divakar
Mallavajjula Subbarama Sastri

Malledevera
M.C. Dixit Shastri
Maringati Srirangacharya
Madhukar Krishnamurti Shastri
N.S. Anantakrishna Sastri
N.S. Ramanuja Tatacharya
Nagesa Sastri Uppinabetagiri
Narayanashastri Vadikar
Nityananda Pant
N.S.R. Tatacharya
Narayan Mishra
Oruganti Rayalal Shastri
Panduranga Sastri Goswami
Purusottama Sastri Nanal
Pattabhirama Sastry
Peri Suryanarayana Shastry
Peri Venkateswara Sastri
Peri Suryanarayana Shastri
Prativadi Bhayankaram Annagarchariar
P.V. Kane
Phanibhushana Tarkavagisa
Peri Suryanarayanasastri
Purshottam Sastri Nanal
Ramasubha Shastry
Raghunatha Sastri Kokje
Reddy Rangacharya
Renukadasa Rajesvara Ayachit
Remilla Suryaprakasha Sastri
R. Krishnamurti Shastri
R.V. Shukla
Rani Narasimha Sastri
Rewa Prasad Dwivedi
Ram Chandra Pandey
Rewa Prasad Dwivedi
Rajeshwar Shastri Dravid
Rangacharya Reddi
Raghavendracharya Gajendragadkar
Ramavarma Parikshit Thampuran
Sripada Damodar Satawalekar
Sripada Sastri Hasurka
Siddhesvara Sastri Chitrav
Sridhara Sastri Pathak
Sridhara Sastri Ware Lele
Srinivasa Shastri (T.S.S. Sastri)

S.K. Belvalkar
S.N. Mishra
Sadasiva Ratna Sharma
Sadananda Ramanuja Das
Suryanarayan Shastri
S. Shankaranarayan
Sannidhanam Laksmana Narayana Shastri
Surirama Koti Shastri
Sriman Prahladacharya
Satyanarayana Shastri
Shiva Datta Sharma Chaturvedi
Shripadasatyanarayana Shastri
Sudhanshu Sekhara Sastry
Sudhakar Dikshit
Sannidhanam Suryanarayana Sastri
S.M.S. Varadachar
Shivramkrishna Sastri
Shankara Shastri Marulkar
Surendra Nath Dasgupta
S. Suryanarayan Sastri
Tata Subbaraya Sastri
T.K.V.N. Sudarsanacharya
T.G. Mainkar
T.M.P. Mahadevan
T. Ganapati Sastri
Tarlateertja Laksmanashastri Joshi
Trinath Sharma
Uttamuri Veeraraghavacharya
Uttamur T.V. Raghavacharya
Uppinabettigeri Bhalachandrasastri
Varasansi Raghunatha Sarma
Vasudev Sastri Abhyankar
Visi Bapat
Vasudeva Sastri Bagavadikar
Vamana Sastri Bhagawat
Vaidyanatha Sastra Sastry
Vepatturu Subrahmanya Shastry
V.S. Ramachandra Sastri
V.A. Ramaswamy Sastri
V.K. Dongre Shastri
V. Venkatachalam
V.B. Bhagvat
Vasudevshastri Ghushe
Vishvanath Gopalkrishna Sastri

Vishvanath Baman Dev
Vishvanath Datar
Vasudeo Sastri Abhyankar
V. Subrahmanya Shastri
Vamanshastri Jhalkikar
V.S. Sukhtankar
V. Raghavan
Visnusastri Bapat
Vinayak Parmeshwar Bhatta
Yajnesvara Sastri Kasture

APPENDIX VI

Eminent Indian Philosophers of Western Tradition in the Twentieth Century

Abhedanand, Swami
Adhikari, P.V.
Atreya, B.L.
Andrews, C.P.
Bagchi, Kalyan Kumar
Balasubramanian, R.
Banerjee, K.K.
Banerjee, N.V.
Barlingay, S.S.
Bhadra, Mrinalkanti
Bhagwandas
Bhatt, S.R.
Bhattacharya, Chandrodaya
Bhattacharya, H.D.
Bhattacharya, K.C.
Bhattacharya, Kalidas
Bhattacharya, Sibajiban
Chandra, Suresh
Chari, C.T.K.
Chatterjee, G.C.
Chatterjee, S.C.
Chattopadhyaya, D.P.
Chattopadhyaya, S.K.
Choudhary, Prawas Jivan
Chingle, S.M.
Chubb, J.N.
Coomaraswamy, Ananda K.
Damle, P.R.
Das, A.C.
Das, K.C.

Das, Rasvihari
Das, S.K.
Dasgupta, Surendranath
Datta, D.M.
Deshpande, D.Y.
Devasenapathy, V.A.
Devraja, N.K.
Dhruva, A.B.
Gandhi, M.K.
Gregorius, Paulos Mar
Gupta, K.C.
Haldar, Hiralal
Hiriyanna, M.
Hogg, A.H.
Javadekar, A.G.
Jha, Ganganath
Jha, Harimohan
Kabir, Humayun
Kaul, R.N.
Krishna, Daya
Kuppuswami, B.
Langley, G.H.
Mackenzie, J.
Mahadevan, T.M.P.
Maitra, S.K.
Malashekhar, G.P.
Malkani, G.R.
Mathrani, G.N.
Mishra, Guneswara
Mishra, Nityananda
Mohanty, J.N.
Mookerjee, Arun K.
Mukharjee, A.C.
Murty, K.S.
Murti, T.R.V.
Naidu, P.S.
Nayak, G.C.
Nikam, N.A.
Pandeya, R.C.
Prasad, Kali
Prasad, Rajendra
Radhakrishnan, S.
Raja, C. Kunjan
Raju, P.T.
Ramaswamy Aiyer, C.P.
Ranade, R.D.
Rao, Laxman

Ray, B.N.
Saxena, Sushil Kumar
Sengupta, N.N.
Sengupta, Santosh
Sharif, M.M.
Sharma, I.C.
Sinari, Ramakant
Sircar, M.N.
Smet, Richard de
Srinivasachari, P.N.
Srinivasa Ayangar, K.
Srivastava, R.S.
Subramaniam, B.
Thakur, Rabindranath
Tripathi, R.K.
Umaruddin, M.
Urquhart, W.A.
Vadekar, D.D.
Vahiduddin, Syed
Valiuddin, Mir
Wadia, A.R.
Yajnik, J.A.

Index

† Part 5	Development of Modern Indian Thought and the Social Sciences	S. Bhattacharya (ed.)
† Part 6	International Relations of India with South Asian & Some Neighbouring Countries	Jayanta Kumar Ray (ed.)
* Part 7	Political Ideas in Modern India : Thematic Explorations	V.R. Mehta & Thomas Pantham (ed.)
Volume XI Consciousness, Science, Society, Value and Yoga (CONSSAVY)		
* Part 1	Philosophical Consciousness and Scientific Knowledge: Conceptual Linkages and Civilizational Background	D.P. Chattopadhyaya (ed.)
* Part 2	Self, Society and Science: Theoretical and Historical Perspectives	D.P. Chattopadhyaya (ed.)
* Part 3	Consciousness, Indian Psychology and Yoga	Kireet Joshi & Matthijs Cornelissen (ed.)
* Part 4	The Enworlded Subjectivity: Its Three Worlds and Beyond	R. Balasubramanian (ed.)
Volume XII Levels of Reality (CONSSAVY)		
† Part 1	A Conceptual-Analytic Study of Indian Philosophy of Morals	Rajendra Prasad (ed.)
† Part 2	A Historical-Developmental Study of Indian Philosophy of Morals	Rajendra Prasad (ed.)
* Part 3	Vedic Vision of Consciousness and Reality	S. P. Singh
† Part 4	Modern Atomism in Europe and India	J. Pasupathy (ed.)
† Part 5	Materialism and Immaterialism in India and Europe	Partha Ghose (ed.)
† Part 6	Life and Vitalism	N. S. Rangaswamy (ed.)
‡ Part 7	Elements in Indian Systems of Thought	(Under plan)
Volume XIII Theories of Natural and Life Sciences (CONSSAVY)		
† Part 1	Indian Role in Global Physics : Then and Now	A.N. Mitra (ed.)
† Part 2	From Physiology and Chemistry to Biochemistry	D.P. Burma (ed.)
‡ Part 3	Psychology and Psychoanalysis	(Under Plan)
† Part 4	Cognitive Sciences: Brain, Psychology and Computer	Shobini L. Rao (ed.)
† Part 5	On the Foundations of Sciences	B.V. Sreekantan (ed.)
† Part 6	History of Science and Philosophy of Science	P.K. Sengupta (ed.)
† Part 7	Science in India	J.V. Narlikar (ed.)
Volume XIV Natural and Cultural Sciences (CONSSAVY)		
† Part 1	Relations between Nature and Culture	Roddam Narasimha (ed.)
† Part 2	Types of Social Sciences	Yogendra Singh (ed.)
† Part 3	Ethics and Economics	Ashok Guha (ed.)
† Part 4	Different Types of History	Bharati Ray (ed.)
† Part 5	History of India's Polity, Governance and Constitutional Culture	Subhash C. Kashyap (ed.)
Volume XV Science, Technology and Philosophy (CONSSAVY)		
† Part 1	Science, Technology, Imperialism and War	J.B. Dasgupta (ed.)
† Part 2	Science and the Public	Ashok Jain (ed.)
† Part 3	Science, Literature and Aesthetics	Amiya Dev (ed.)
† Part 4	Science, Colonialism and Nationalism, c. 1820 to c. 1940	Uma Das Gupta (ed.)
Volume XVI Yoga (CONSSAVY)		
† Part 1	Psychology, Parapsychology and Yoga	K. Ramakrishna Rao (ed.)
† Part 2	History of Yoga in India	S.P. Singh (ed.)
† Part 3	Varieties of Yogic Experience	Manoj Das (ed.)
† Part 4	Synthesis of Yoga	Kireet Joshi (ed.)
‡ Part 5	Yoga, Evolution and Mutation of Human Species	(Under Plan)

Monographs

1.	Science, Philosophy and Culture in Historical Perspective	D.P. Chattopadhyaya & Ravinder Kumar (ed.)
2.	Some Aspects of India's Philosophical & Scientific Heritage	D.P. Chattopadhyaya & Ravinder Kumar (ed.)
3.	Mathematics, Astronomy and Biology in Indian Tradition: Some Conceptual Preliminaries	D.P. Chattopadhyaya & Ravinder Kumar (ed.)
4.	Language, Logic and Science in India: Some Conceptual and Historical Perspectives	D.P. Chattopadhyaya & Ravinder Kumar (ed.)
5.	Primal Spirituality of the Vedas: Its Renewal and Renaissance	R. Balasubramanian
6.	Interdisciplinary Studies in Science, Technology, Philosophy and Culture	D.P. Chattopadhyaya
7.	Ancient Yoga and Modern Science	T.R. Anantharaman
8.	Prolegomena to Any Future Historiography of Cultures & Civilizations	Daya Krishna
9.	Science and Spirituality: A Quantum Integration	Amit Goswami & Maggie Goswami
10.	On Rational Historiography	V. Shekhawat
11.	*Kauṭilīya Arthaśāstra Revisited*	Surendra Nath Mital
12.	The Ways of Understanding the Human Past	D.P. Chattopadhyaya
13.	The Architecture of Knowledge	Subhash Kak
14.	Karnataka Music as Aesthetic Form	R. Sathyanarayana
15.	Indian Philosophy and Philosophy of Science	Sundar Sarukkai

---

* Already Published
† In the Process of Publication
‡ Under Plan